For Such a Time as This
- The Spiritual Awakening of Israel

REBORN, REDEEMED, RESTORED

BRUCE R. DEBAUN

Son light dispels darkness

"For Such a Time as This – The Spiritual Awakening of Israel"

Reborn, Redeemed, Restored

by Bruce R. DeBaun

Copyright © 2022 Bruce ben Oppenheimer-DeBaun

Copyright on this work and its contents, excluding pictures, photographs and images which were obtained by the author under contracts may be reproduced in full or in part with full acknowledgment to the author and a link to www.GuardPostPublishing.com so long as it is done freely and not sold. Contact Guard Post Publishing, Inc. for permission to reproduce this content in other media formats; https://GuardPostPublishing.com; publisher@guardpost.com

Pictures, photographs and images have been obtained under license with stock image companies; GoodSalt, Alamy, Getty, Istock, Selah Art, Crystal Graphics, and with private artists and third-party owners. Photographs are historical, editorial and used for educational purpose.

Published by Guard Post Publishing, Inc.
P.O.B. 1463, Corning, NY 14830
Corning, New York

Guard Post Publishing, Inc. is a 501(c)(3) ministry & foundation

Printed in the United States of America by Ingram Spark

First Edition 2021

Copyright TXu 2-084-819

Library of Congress Cataloging-in-Publication Data

DeBaun, Bruce

For Such a Time as This – The Spiritual Awakening of Israel / by Bruce DeBaun

Paperback ISBN: 978-0-9998806-0-9
Hardcover ISBN: 978-0-9998806-1-6

1. Apologetics. 2. Bible Prophecy. 3. Typology. 4. Israel—History. 4. Hebraic—Analysis 5. Messianic Judaism. 4. Zionism—History. 5. Rome & Romanism—History

I see no greater call than to be a "watchman upon the wall" and a teacher of truth. So this treatise is dedicated to the "One hundred and forty-four thousand of all the tribes of the children of Israel," and to the tribulation saints; to you the "remnant" who have discovered your Savior during the dreaded Time of Jacob's trouble. Carry on and share these truths with the house of Israel.

> "I have set watchmen upon thy walls, O Jerusalem, which shall never hold their peace day nor night: ye that make mention of the LORD, keep not silence…Go through, go through the gates; prepare ye the way of the people; cast up, cast up the highway; gather out the stones; lift up a standard for the people. Behold, the LORD hath proclaimed unto the end of the world, Say ye to the daughter of Zion, Behold, thy salvation cometh; behold, his reward is with him, and his work before him." Esaias (Isaiah) 62:6, 10, 11

In the entirety of humankind, no one is as difficult to reach for Christ as the religionist; the one who has satisfied their own heart that their religion or membership in their religious organization satisfies the Creator. These are among the disciples of many faiths who have never apprehended the depravity of the human heart or the cost of their sin. There has been no arresting conviction, hence no remorse or the need to delve any further into what is true or what is false. In denying sin they deny any consequence. Refusing to acknowledge their culpability, so do they refuse the only divine remedy for sin; the merciful offer of GOD through the substitutional death of a crucified Christ. They have instead settled for membership into a religious body without membership into the body of Christ whose membership only comes with acknowledgement of sin, the cry for forgiveness, the surrender of self, and the receiving of the regenerative miracle of the new birth.

TABLE OF CONTENTS

The book is written to a diverse audience of those seeking answers, proof and wisdom. Whether one is an inquirer, a pupil or a scholar, they will find a blend of milk and meat in an easy to understand style. Although all the chapters relate to the central theme of the title (Israel's spiritual birth) and teach in a progression, each chapter, subchapter and topic is designed to stand alone (as with an essay) making it possible to read selections whose subjects interest you.

ACKNOWLEDGEMENTS I

FOREWARD 1

PURPOSE 3
    In Pursuit of Truth 4
    The Narrow Gate and the Narrow Path 5

PREFACE 7
    Why Do We Believe What We Believe?? 7
    Knowledge or Revelation? 8

INTRODUCTION 13
    Love and Obedience are of the Heart 13

CHAPTER 1 THE AUTHORITY OF THE HOLY SCRIPTURES 15
    Were GOD to Speak 15
    For Such a Time as This 18
    The Physical and the Spiritual Birth of Israel 19
    Dead Bones, Ye Shall Live! Ezekiel 37 19

CHAPTER 2 JUDAISM: A RELATIONSHIP WITH YAHUAH AND YAHUSHA 23
    GOD Never Made a Single Religion 23
    The Old Paths—Biblical Judaism 25
    Alone Together 25
    The Atonement 28
    We Gods 28
    Why, Lord, Why? 29

    Ebal or Gerizim—Blessings or Curses 30
    We 31
    The Blindness of Israel 33
    Repent and Return 36
    Deliverance is For the Desperate 36
    The King is Coming 37
    Another Chosen People 38
    The Kinsman Redeemer 39
    The Grafting In. 41

CHAPTER 3 THE MYSTERY OF THE SON, MASHIACH BEN DAVID 43
    Isaiah—The Prophet of the Revelation 44
    The Announcement 44
    What is in a Name? 45
    The Conundrum 48
    The Greatest Sin of All 49

CHAPTER 4 יהושע YAHUSHA. THE YAH (GOD) WHO DELIVERS. THE YAH WHO SAVES! 51

CHAPTER 5 THE TIME IN EXILE 59
    The Precursors: The Sacrifice, The Offerings, the Tithe. 59
    Change in the Winds 63
    The WILL and the WORD 64
    The Cornerstone 65
    Why Was He Rejected? 67

CHAPTER 6 HIS ONENESS 69
    Elohim אלהים—GOD of Israel 69
    Our Indivisible—Divisible GOD, the Perfect Amalgamation 71
    One Cluster of Grapes 72
    Names that Speak to Us 73
    The Voice of Scripture. 74
    The Holy Scriptures, Volume 2 76
    Always with Us 78

CHAPTER 7 GOD'S PICTURE BOOK 79
    Yahusha in Manifestations and Types 79
    The Tabernacle in the Wilderness 80
    The Mercy Seat 81
    Redeemer and Priest 82
    Immanuel—GOD With us! 83

CHAPTER 8 PRECIOUS BLOOD 85
    The Sacrificial Lamb 85
    Only by the Blood 87
    Preserved by the Blood 88
    The Sheep Gate 91
    The Aphikomen 91
    The Seder—Remembrance 91
    The Brit Milah—The Circumcision 92
    The Star of Jacob—Our National Emblem! 93
    The Jewish Feasts 94
    Cross the Jordan 97

CHAPTER 9 THE KINGDOM OF DAVID 99
    David Found His Mashiach 99
    The 5 "R's": Realize, Repent, Return, be Restored 100
    The Sacrifice 103
    The Missing Temple 104
    The Living Temple 105

CHAPTER 10 HELL IS FULL OF GOOD PEOPLE 109
    SALVATION—Saved from Sin 109
    Imitators and Imitations 110

CHAPTER 11 WHO? 117
    Who Paid the Price? To Whom do We Owe? 117
    To Know of GOD, or To Know GOD? 118
    Missing GOD 119
    Prevenient Grace 120
    The Apostle Paul Pleads with the Church for Separation 122
    To Believe in His Existence…or Believe in Him! 123

CHAPTER 12 BUT GOD HAS A PLAN! 125
    Covenants and Dispensations 125
    Grace Came Before the Law 126
    A New Assembly and a Greater Covenant 129
    The Sabbath Under the Law, and the Sabbath Under Grace 133

CHAPTER 13 COVENANT PROMISES AND APPLICATION 137
    Protestantism and its Branches 141
    The Last Days and the Latter Rain 142
    Revival GOD's Way 143
    Dependency on GOD's Grace 145

    The Law and Grace. 146
    Seven Dispensations. 147
    The Age of Innocence and Conscience. 148
    The Age of Promise 149
    The Age of Law 149
    The Age of Grace 150

CHAPTER 14 THE NEW COVENANT. 153
    The B'rit HaChadeshah 153
    The Serpent on the Pole—Numbers 21:4–9. 156
    The Jew First. 158

CHAPTER 15 THE RAUCH H'QODESH. 161
    GOD, the Holy Spirit 161
    The Indwelling Holy Spirit. 164
    The New Birth 165
    The Law of Faith 168

CHAPTER 16 ISAIAH RECEIVES THE FIRE!. 169
    A Vision of the King, the Lord of Hosts (Isaiah-Esaias 6:1–13) 169
    The New Birth Experience 170
    The Message of the Cross! 172
    The Baptism of Fire 173
    Then and Now 178
    The Only Hope! 179

CHAPTER 17 GOD PROVES BY PROPHECY. 181
    Foretold and Fulfilled. 182

CHAPTER 18 THE LAW OF PROBABILITY. 193
    One Hundred Thousand Trillion 193
    Behold thy King Cometh! 195
    Lying Spirits, Familiar Spirits, Seducing Spirits. 197

CHAPTER 19 BIBLICAL JUDAISM AND RABBINICAL JUDAISM. 201
    The Jewish Revolt 201
    The Split 202
    Authentic Judaism 204

CHAPTER 20 ENTER THE HOLY SPIRIT 207
    The Comforter 207
    The Church Victorious 209

CHAPTER 21 MINISTERS OF RIGHTEOUSNESS?..........................211
   Truth and Travesty..211
   Versions and Perversions.................................... 212
   Leaven in the Loaf.. 214
   Cults... 215

CHAPTER 22 WINDS OF CHANGE.. 217
   Winds of Change and the Human Propensity.................... 217

CHAPTER 23 BAIT, SWITCH, AND FOOL 221
   Two Masters, but Only One Choice!...........................221

CHAPTER 24 CATHOLICISM VS. CHRISTIANITY 227
   Ghostly Specters.. 228
   Fallacies and Fabrications 231
   Masks and Makeup 233

CHAPTER 25 ROME AND ROMANISM 237
   A History Lesson 237
   Enter the Universal Church 239
   From Emperor to Imposter 241

CHAPTER 26 WHICH BIBLE? 243

CHAPTER 27 PAGANISM 101 249
   Replace and Rename 251
   Apostate Icons 252
   Pious Pirates and Magicians................................. 254

CHAPTER 28 TOLERANCE, PEACE, AND UNITY 257

CHAPTER 29 WHICH CROSS?...261

CHAPTER 30 FROM ASHES TO EMPEROR................................. 263
   Holy Wars 264

CHAPTER 31 LEST WE FORGET!.. 269
   The Master Race and the Master Church.......................271

CHAPTER 32 THE FUTURE COLLABORATION OF THE TWO BEASTS.. 277
   Renewing Old Alliances and Forming New Ones 280
   Current Events and Alliances................................281
   The Deception 281

CHAPTER 33 THE NEW PARADIGM 285
   The Repackaging of Defective Teachings 288

CHAPTER 34 CHEAP GRACE AND COSTLY GRACE 293
   Choices. 294
   The Narrow Gate 295
   Begging the Question. 296

CHAPTER 35 A DIFFERENT CROSS 299
   The Cross has Different Meanings to Different People 299
   In or On ? 300

CHAPTER 36 WHO IS A JEW? WHAT IS A MESSIANIC JEW? WHAT IS A
JEWISH CHRISTIAN? 303
   A Word to Jews who Accept Yahusha-Jesus as their Savior 305
   A Word to Gentile Believers. 306

CHAPTER 37 A RABBI'S TESTIMONY. 307

CHAPTER 38 JUST ONE SIN! 311

CHAPTER 39 THE HUMAN TRINITY—SPIRIT, SOUL, FLESH. 315

CHAPTER 40 THE THREE DEATHS; PHYSICAL, SPIRITUAL, ETERNAL . 319

CHAPTER 41 HELL AND BEYOND 323

CHAPTER 42 THE SUBSTITUTE 329
   The Substitute. 329

CHAPTER 43 THE CONTEST FOR YOUR SOUL 331
   The War We Face 331

CHAPTER 44 THE REAL ENEMY: SATAN 335
   Know Your Enemy 335

CHAPTER 45 KILL THE MESSIAH. 339

CHAPTER 46 DECEIVER, DISTRACTOR, DISSUADER 341

CHAPTER 47 DOUBT, DISTRUST, DISBELIEF. 343

CHAPTER 48 THE PEACE PLOY AND THE NEXT HOLOCAUST! 347
   The Anti-Messiah (Antichrist) 348
   The Time of Trouble 350
   The False Prophet 350
   Even Now. 351

CHAPTER 49 PROPHECY, PROPHET, AND TEACHERS 353

CHAPTER 50 UNFOLDING PROPHECIES. 357
   1. Israel Returns to the Promised Land and Becomes a Nation Once Again 357
   2. The Jews will be Hated of all Nations 357
   3. Who is Gog and What is the Land of Magog? 360
   4. A Global Government and the Migration to Babylon 364
   5. Instituting 666 367
   6. The World Church and the "Falling Away". 368
   7. The Middle East—the "Seething Pot". 369
   8. The Guise of Peace 369
   9. Tolerance, Merging Beliefs, and A One World Religion 370
   10. Society a Sign 371
   11. The Resurrected and the Remnant 374

CHAPTER 51 GOD'S CLOCK 377

CHAPTER 52 THE TWO VISITATIONS; THE LAMB AND THE LION 381
   The Lamb and the Lion 381

CHAPTER 53 THE SUFFERING SERVANT OF YAHOVAH. 383
   Isaiah 52:13–14 and 53:1–12 383
   Isaiah 53: 384

CHAPTER 54 FOR SUCH A TIME AS THIS 391

CHAPTER 55 THE INVITATION. 393
   The Adoption 393
   The End ... No, the Beginning! 395

ABOUT THE AUTHOR AND HIS TESTIMONY. 397

APPENDIX A THE JUDGMENT OF AMERICA 401
   Learning from Israel's Mistakes 403
   Freedom of Religion and Cultural Diversity 404
   America's Last Saving Grace 409
   The Perilous Global Economy 410
   Creating a New Currency. 415
   America's Gold Reserves in Question. 420
   Benefactors and Betrayers. 421
   Time Marches On 425
   The Enemies Within Our Gates 426
   The Caliphate 428
   Executing the Plan 431

The Record 433
A House Divided Will Fall 435
The Herd Mentality, the Millennials, and the Embrace of Socialism 439
Portioning Israel 442
War not Peace—The Sino-Iran-Soviet-N.Korea Alliance 445
The Apostate Protestant Church 446
What is Next? 449
The New World Order 450
The Climate Change Farce 455
The Deep State and the Shadow Government 458

APPENDIX B THE OLIVET DISCOURSE 461
A Study of the Seven Years of "The Time of Jacob's Trouble" 461
Rightly Dividing the Word 465
Disciplines 466
Speaking of Times 468
Harmony of Scripture 470
The Signs and the Times 472
The Deception 473
His Return 476
Misapplication and Dislocation of Scripture 482

APPENDIX C DANIEL'S VISION OF SEVENTY WEEKS 505
A Messianic Prophecy (Daniel 9:20–27) 505
Daniel 9:24–27 506
The Purpose of this Study 506
Interpreting the Scriptures 507
Schools of Thought 510
The Prophetic Dates 512
The *terminus ad quo*, and *terminus ad quem* *513*
Dates, Times, and Events 514
Events Leading Up to Prophecy 514
Seventy Years 517
The Greatest Old Testament Prophecy 517
The Prophecy 519
Meant to Be Understood 520
The Story Begins 520
The Five-fold Promise 521
The Question 524
Seventy Weeks 524
The Partition of the Weeks 529

    Establishing the Actual Dates 532
    Calculating the Time 533
    The Messiah to Die. 534
    Timeline of Daniel's Seventieth Week 536
    Timeline of the Passion Week. 536

APPENDIX D MYSTERY BABYLON—REVELATION CHAPTER 17 539
    Introduction 539
    Mystery Babylon, the Great Mother of Harlots 541
    All Things in Their Appointed Time. 543
    The Mystery 544
    Babel of Genesis and Babylon of Revelation 545
    Babel to Nebuchadnezzar's Babylon. 547
    The Origin and Evolution of Paganism and Romanism 551
    Tricked 555
    The False Prophet 560
    Precept Upon Precept, Line Upon Line 563
    The Seven Headed Beast. 566
    Visions of the Beast of the Eighth Kingdom Expounded. 572
    The Different Beasts 575
    Identifying the Beasts. 576
    Daniel and John's Beastly Visions and the Succession of Empires They Represented . 578
    The Ten Horns, the New World Order, and the Little Horn 578

EPILOGUE 583

ACKNOWLEDGEMENTS

I wish to thank just a few of the people who helped me in my own journey to and up the mountain of discovery which ultimately led to the publishing of this book.

To Ron and Midge Deardoff, who led me to the Lord. To Jimmy Swaggart, who guided me into Pentecost. To Pastors Andy and Jackie Anson who introduced me to the Full Gospel Assembly. To my mentors; Pastors Dr. George and Marie Nuzzolo, Pastors Joseph and Elaine Cedzich, and Pastors Dr. Charles and Dr. AnnaMae Strauser. To my church family, who have placed their trust in me, obligating me to rightly divide the Word. To Elders Richard and Elva Hough, who reviewed numerous chapters. To my technical advisors Andrew and Joanne DonDero, and to J. Michael Garner, whose support launched me in this endeavor; my gratitude to all.

Interior Composition: design, graphic art, and formatting by Tamara Cribley (The Deliberate Page, DeliberatePage.com), a gifted virtuoso in print composition. Given a most challenging manuscript with varied fields of study and writing styles, Tamara has superbly crafted a manuscript into a work of art.

Proofreader: Chris Knight of The Deliberate Page, thanks for your detailed eye and your dedication to creating a polished and professional manuscript.

Book Cover: The magnificent cover by artist Kristine Cotterman (Exodus Design and Graphic Studios, exodusdesign.com) depicts the spiritual birth of the nation of Israel portrayed in Ezekiel, chapter 37. It is the journey of the Jewish people which began when disobedience and indifference toward their Creator compelled HIM to "hedge their way with thorns, that they shall not find their path." (Hosea 2:6). Their journey will continue until that day when in desperation they "seek HIM with all their heart" (Jeremiah 29:13). In that day they shall recognize their true emancipator—their Mashiach (Zechariah 12:10) and be "born again" (Ezekiel 36:24–27; 37:1–14; John 3:1–18). Instantly, the veil that has obscured their understanding (Isaiah 35:5) and prejudiced their beliefs for these many centuries will lift, and they will step into the glorious light. The land of Israel too will be healed from the aftermath of war and cataclysmic events and "become like the garden of Eden" (Isaiah 51:3).

Copyeditor and Forward: Jack A. Minor, Affordablechristianediting.com

Dedication

To my wife Quenda, whose love and support have allowed me the opportunity to write this love letter to you the reader. To my mother Edyth Adel Oppenheimer-DeBaun, who gave me life, love and my birthright. And, to my dad Joseph, who first taught me of Yahusha, and whose love for Him exceeded his religion.

In memory of my grandmother Esther Ehrlich, "Ah Dear," who nurtured me. And especially to my grandfather, Milton C. Oppenheimer, "Gramps," who instilled in me pride for my Jewish heritage and concern for the Jewish people. And, to the memory of Uncle Arnie, Uncle Dick and Bill Mohrmann, my unsung heroes.

Gramps

FOREWARD

As an editor, and previously as a pastor, my concentration has been on theological works. Over my lifetime, I have had the opportunity to read and critique hundreds of books on related subjects. While each has its own story to tell, the majority are little more than a rehashing of material written years, or even decades ago. This is somewhat understandable and even has biblical support, as the wisest man purported to have ever lived wrote, "There is no new thing under the sun."

Since we know it is God's will for all to be saved, I believe that as the world stands on the crossroads of end-time prophesy being fulfilled, this book has the potential to be mightily used of God in the days ahead.

The issue of evangelizing the Jewish people is as old as Calvary. Indeed, the most famous Jewish convert, the Apostle Paul, wrote, "Brethren, my heart's desire and prayer to God for Israel is, that they might be saved." In the ensuing centuries, this has been the prayer of countless Christians as well, yet it often seems like the answer to Paul's prayer remains as elusive as ever.

But God is not static; just as He sent a pair of evangelists to America in the years before the Civil War (Charles Finney in the North and Sam Jones in the South), knowing uncounted numbers of Americans would soon enter eternity, I believe He is likewise preparing to do a similar thing on the eve of the Great Tribulation, an event that will make the Civil War look like a schoolyard brawl.

Having both a Jewish and a Catholic parent, Bruce DeBaun has had broad exposure to both belief systems, which God has used in preparation of his becoming a minister, teacher, and Biblicist. His background and moreover his commission has permitted him to close the gap between two of the world's greatest religions, who despite worshipping the same God and sharing the Old Testament have been adversarial as it concerns the Savior. His insight as to why the Jewish people have an aversion to considering that the one called Jesus is the Jewish Messiah is as startling as it is obvious.

When I was first approached to edit this work, I was pleasantly surprised at both the unique way and the scholarly manner in which it was presented. One example of this is how he illustrates how, by the regression of the Savior's Hebrew name and its having been replaced with the English name (Jesus) the Savior's divine identity has been obscured.

Supporting each supposition with Scripture, the author methodically dismantles one fallacy after another. He reveals the disparity between genuine Christianity and Roman Catholicism with fierce and unapologetic determination that can only come when it is deserved. He points the accusing finger at the Papacy, the Vicars (substitutes) of Christ who have, as a religio-political empire been the instigators of persecution to the Jewish people and non-Catholics, all the while asserting they are the true Christian church. With such a record of malice it is totally understandable why the Jewish people would reject any suggestion that the one they claim to be the Christian Savior could be the Jewish Messiah.

In each case, DeBaun provides historical evidence until that which was never learned or afterward forgotten surfaces from beneath the sands of time where it had been buried since the Reformation.

In a sincere and compelling way, he appeals to Roman Catholics who sincerely love God, but who, like the Jewish people, have also been the victims of deception orchestrated by a satanic composer.

I would do well to suggest that each and every individual who has entered or plans on entering into ministry and that every Bible School serious about anchoring their students to sound teaching include this book in their curriculum. I would further suggest that this book be gifted to those who the Lord has put upon your heart that they may find the Treasure that is hid in the field, and the Pearl of Great Price.

Pastor Jack A. Minor, JM Publications;
Affordablechristianediting.com;
former contributing writer *World Net Daily*.

Chaplain DeBaun when asked about his background often sums it up in a quip.

> "I'm a Jew who was raised Catholic and who became a Protestant minister." When asked what denomination, he replies, "None, I'm a Full Gospel Minister, I minister the unvarnished Word of GOD. I accept and take to heart only and everything from Genesis 1:1 to Revelation 22:21 of the Authorized King James Bible. In so far as denominations are concerned, GOD never made a denomination or a religion. Religion is by and large mans' invention and a substitute for what GOD wants and requires; a deep and personal relationship with HIM."

As the Lord is the author of all knowledge and revelation, should HE graciously share these with an individual, it is not appropriate for that individual to extract wealth from what the Lord communicated to them. They have no legitimate copyright. It was meant to be shared. "Freely ye have received, freely give." (Matthew 10:8) So it is that this work is offered at production costs and overhead. The author has declined any compensation from its revenue.

PURPOSE

I consider myself an ordinary man with few aspirations other than to teach GOD's truths which I see as having been so maligned as to make me quake at the destiny of those whom I know and love, for the Jewish people, and for mankind at large. Love and Truth go hand and hand even if they offend.

"Faithful are the wounds of a friend; but the kisses of an enemy are deceitful." (Proverbs 27:6)

The truths shared in this manuscript have been graciously given by the Teacher of teachers—the Ruach H' Qodesh, the Holy Spirit. It is He who reveals truth to those who are earnestly seeking it when first they seek GOD from the depths of their heart. I can say this with certainty because I have experienced HIS promise firsthand.

"Call unto me, and I will answer thee, and shew thee great and mighty things, which thou knowest not." (Jeremiah 33:3)

What you are about to read in this treatise are not just my suppositions or those of scholars and theologians, but GOD's own words as they appear in the Holy Scriptures.

All HIS authentic teachers have had a common experience. There came a day in each of their lives when they realized that there is a heaven to gain and a hell to shun. Reflecting on their past and recognizing their transgressions they were suddenly confronted with the likelihood that if they were fairly judged they were in grave danger. This conviction was nothing less than mercy; an attempt by GOD to compel the individual to seek HIM from the recesses of their heart and cry out for HIS forgiveness.

What I find most striking is that unless stricken with a terminal illness or recognizing that they are at the end of their days, most people have become passively indifferent to their destiny. Absorbed with the obtainment of temporal things of this world, they go merrily down the stream, unconcerned as to where the stream leads. They purchase life insurance (an oxymoron) and plan for their retirement but at the same time seem indifferent or oblivious as to where they might spend eternity.

Sadly, the majority of those of whom it may be said believe and reverence GOD have been cajoled into believing that there is a limit to how one can relate to HIM; the extent of which is through their religion. Others have become so passive as to believe that if indeed there is an actual heaven or hell, there isn't very much one can do to affect the outcome; therefore, whatever will be, will be. The possibility of having a deep personal relationship with their Creator, as Abram, Moses, and David had is thought to be theoretical at best, even when the Holy Scriptures tell us that we can.

> "And ye shall seek me, and find me, when ye shall search for me with all your heart." (Jeremiah 29:13)

Unbelief has no warrant, and ignorance no excuse, for having made you for HIMSELF and for HIS good pleasure, HE wants you to enter into a deep and personal relationship with HIM; a relationship which culminates with your joining HIM for eternity. So it is that at the moment of your conception HE implanted a seed of faith in your soul and gave you an eternal spirit which is meant to lead you to HIM. Like a seed properly attended, if watered by the Word of Life, that seed will germinate, grow, and afterward bring forth fruit of its own kind. This treatise is meant to water that seed of faith within you.

> "Spinoza wrote of the intellectual love of GOD, and he had a measure of truth there; but the highest love of GOD is not intellectual, it is spiritual. GOD is spirit and only the spirit of man can know HIM really. In the deep spirit of a man the fire must glow or his love is not the true love of GOD." A.W. Tozer, *The Pursuit of God*

> "GOD is a Spirit: and they that worship HIM must worship HIM in spirit and in truth." (John 4:24)

> "And ye shall know the truth, and the truth shall make you free." (John 8:32)

In Pursuit of Truth

(Image Source: Istock)

As in scaling a mountain, one begins on the gentle slopes of the foothills. Gradually, as one ascends, the incline becomes steeper. The elevation that challenges is also that which presents the greater view; such is the progression of this route to the summit of understanding.

It is not easy to conceptualize or describe what it means to "break through an invisible barrier." The invisible barrier to which I refer is the one that separates man and the natural realm from GOD and the spiritual realm. Yet it is this very barrier, thought by the majority to be beyond reach, that can be crossed, yea, that must be crossed if one is to have an encounter with his Creator.

Like a mountain climber scaling the sheer rock face of a cliff, the climber faces a time when he must release his grip from the security of the mountain and trust his life to a thin rope whose width is no thicker than his finger. First, he must make a conscious decision to take the risk. Then he must exercise his faith that the rope will not fail him… And finally, he must let go of the natural rock formation that has offered him security and take what is a leap of faith! So is it with GOD.

The decision to find the truth takes courage, for it may mean discovering that what one has been taught and believed their whole life, and even what has become part of their identity, is flawed. Such a gamble can only be made if we love the Lord our GOD with all of our heart, with all of our soul, and with all of our might. Only by wholly trusting HIM to lead us to the truth can we find the hidden treasure that eludes the proud. It is in the process of discovery that the invisible barrier is crossed, and the searcher has his first spiritual encounter with Melech Hakavod, the King of Glory.

May you be one of the courageous.

The Narrow Gate and the Narrow Path

Over the years, I have attended funerals and listened to the officiating clergy give a sermonette or read a passage from the Bible which gives the listener the impression that just about everyone goes to heaven. But I'm here to tell you this is not the case; not at least according to the Holy Scriptures. According to HIS Word, there is a very narrow gate and a very narrow path that leads to a city which has foundations, whose builder and maker is GOD.[1] Sadly, the Scriptures tell us, few find what is a narrow sheep gate, through which His sheep must pass. Then they must follow this narrow path to reach the summit.

I will show you this gate and even lead you up to it, but ultimately it will be your choice whether to open it and go through or pass by and choose instead to follow the broad glittering path which the majority prefers.

> Who then is bold enough to put their preconceptions on hold and say, "Open thou mine eyes, that I may behold wondrous things out of thy law." (Psalm 119:18)

GOD's eyes are constantly roaming the earth looking for that man or woman who is earnestly looking for HIM. When HE finds such a tender heart, HE opens their eyes and reveals HIMSELF in such a way as to defy human understanding. Instantly that person will sees things that he or she never imagined; things hidden as it were beyond a veil. If one will put aside his or her preconceptions and perhaps even their prejudices, then HIS Spirit will give that person a glimpse of what lies beyond.

---

1   Matthew 7:13, 14

"But God hath revealed them unto us by his Spirit: for the Spirit searcheth all things, yea, the deep things of God. For what man knoweth the things of a man, save the spirit of man which is in him? even so the things of God knoweth no man, but the Spirit of God." (1 Corinthians 2:10-11)

PREFACE

Spoken words are fleeting; they are not suspended in the air, not even for a moment. By the time they reach the hearers' ears, they have evaporated and are gone forever. If the mind of the hearer retains them at all, then perhaps they may be recalled and serve the listener. But if the words are written, engraved in indelible ink and bound in a book, they are retained and may be passed on to others.

In HIS wisdom, GOD dictated to HIS scribes what HE wanted to make available to all mankind. How fortunate we are to have such a book and yet, man appears reluctant to believe that it comes from HIS lips. Few bother to give it more than a cursory look, and fewer still earnestly study it and take it to heart. I dare say, that if one truly believed the Scriptures were from GOD, wouldn't they become the centerpiece of ones' life?

Man is, and always has been consumed with himself, be it his career, sports, leisurely pursuit, the obtainment of wealth, or the pleasures of life. Indeed, how much easier it is to let others study HIS Word, then spoon-feed us what they believe or want us to believe rather than for us to take responsibility for ourselves.

Why Do We Believe What We Believe??

Typically, we are born into an established belief system based on what our parents, their parents, and the generations of parents before them were born into. Essentially, we accept our beliefs based on what we had been taught at an early age from those we love and trust, and from those who teach from a position of spiritual authority.

I believe it would be appropriate to say that what most of us believe has simply been a matter of accepting our religious pedigree. Isn't this why a Muslim is a Muslim, a Buddhist a Buddhist, a Catholic a Catholic, and to some degree, a Jew a Jew?

If my hypothesis is correct, then we should consider the question, am I Jewish because of my ancestry only, or am I Jewish because of what I believe? A second question then might be, is what I believe authentic Judaism?

There is a strong probability that over the course of several thousand years, some rabbi decided to follow a particular stream of Judaism. He may have asked himself, how far and to what extent do I follow the Law? Do I hold to strict Orthodoxy, or Contemporary, or do I take a progressive stance?

The Holy Scriptures however, tell us to follow the "*Old Paths*"—Biblical Judaism.[2] That being said, it then behooves us to find out just what Biblical Judaism is.

I would like to take you back, visit the Hebrew Holy Scriptures, and let you see just where it leads.

In the course of our travels we will see our Judaism from various perspectives. Some of these may challenge you and cause you to ask yourself some provocative questions.

Where, for example, after this brief episode called life, am I going to spend eternity? How can I be certain? What is GOD's criterion for being accepted into HIS holy presence, or what will cause one to be rejected?

To answer these questions, I have taken the path less traveled. I have spent over four decades investigating for myself what GOD said in HIS Word. This required me to suspend what I had been taught for a time in order to be objective. To this end, I have hiked some difficult terrain, challenged some implausible routes, and climbed above clouds of speculation which obscured the promised summit. Now, from a Scriptural vantage point, likened to a climber who has reached the crest, I have a panoramic view and consequently a greater understanding. In the distance, I can make out the skyline of a New Jerusalem and the narrow footpath that leads there.[3]

If you would like to explore the higher regions of Scripture, I would like to guide you. If, after you have seen the view, you choose to return from where you came, that is indeed your choice, but I doubt you will, for ultimately, we all want to know the truth. So, I encourage you to take a chance and come with me on this journey. As GOD said to Isaiah, and Isaiah was to say to the people,

> "Come now, and let us reason together..." Esaias (Isaiah) 1:18

> "And the glory of the LORD shall be revealed, and all flesh shall see it together: for the mouth of the LORD hath spoken it." (Isaiah 40:5)

Knowledge or Revelation?

I want to be clear: I am not a linguist, nor do I consider myself a dedicated philologist. I am simply a teacher of HIS Word and a collator of evidence who strives for truth and accuracy, reminding myself with every supposition that I am a custodian of HIS holy oracles. So it is with fear and trembling I proceed, still aware that as an imperfect human I will err, "For now we see through a glass, darkly, but then face to face: now I know in part..."[4] Nevertheless, it is far better to receive with gratitude what insight GOD chooses to give us and leave the rest for man to quibble over.

---

2   Jeremiah 6:16
3   Isaiah 60:11-20; Ezekiel 48:31-34; Zechariah 2:1; Revelation 21:9-27
4   1 Corinthians 13:2

As a teacher, I owe a great debt to others from whom I've learned. Consequently, what is forthcoming contains little which is truly original. Much of what is presented herein is the fruit and labor of others, many of whom go unnamed.

Works of this kind that put into question deeply held beliefs or expose teachings that run contrary to the Holy Scriptures are certain to be criticized, even denounced. Those who hold lofty positions and have taught error are likely to be the staunchest critics; yet it is my fervent hope that they will recognize truth and courageously amend their teachings.

Teachers only share knowledge, which is information, not revelation. Revelation comes from only one place—GOD.[5] If, when you read what I've shared, and in particular the scriptures themselves and you suddenly find yourself understanding what it is that is being conveyed, then you can be certain that it is GOD who is giving you the revelation. It is HIM speaking and you hearing! As your mind recognizes truth, expect your heart to receive it as well. Then I urge you to follow your heart.

Four appendices (originally written as independent studies) are supplied for the scholarly who wish to study (Hebrew, *doresh*) the Scriptures further and *"Prove all things..."*[6]

In the past one hundred fifty years numerous translations of the Bible have evolved. Translators of these modern versions took the liberty to modify the language—the premise being readability. This has in many instances resulted in corrupting the scriptures significantly. I have taken care, as best I can, to preserve the intended meaning from the original Hebrew and Greek. When warranted I have frequently parenthesized the meaning or the person being referred to.

Regressions (alternative name changes) have over four millennia masked divine names and clouded the identity of who it is that is the centerpiece of the Bible.

In my studies, I have found and elected to use what I believe to be the proper name of GOD, particularly when referring to HIM in HIS capacity as the Father. That pre-exilic name is YAHUAH Elohiym. Primary or Paleo-Hebrew it was written 𐤉𐤄𐤅𐤄.

The name YAHUAH was in common use during the time of the patriarchs, until the Babylonian exile. Afterward, the name Yahweh (from Aramaic derivations) and later Yehovah were adopted and became common vernacular. Masoretes incorporated vowel points which compromised sacred names even further as the emphasis was placed on pronunciation. Similarly, the proper name for our Mashiach (Messiah) is Yahusha. It too underwent regression and became in the common vernacular Yeshua. Awareness, use, and proper transmission of the Messiah's Hebrew name (Yahusha) is crucial, especially for the Jewish people to grasp as it connects Him to His divinity and makes His identity visible. Yah in Hebrew means GOD. Yahusha means the GOD who delivers or the GOD who saves.

> Note: The Father's name YAHUAH is in Hebrew spelled Yohd-hay-wahv-hay. Messiah's name Yahusha is spelled Yohd-hay-wahv-sheen-ahyin. "Sheen" followed by "ahyin" is pronounced "sha."

---

5 John (Yôḥānān) 3:27
6 1 Thessalonians 5:21

To make it easier for the reader to differentiate who is being referred to when applying the pronoun for YAHUAH, capital letters, e.g., HE, HIM, or HIMSELF will be used. Capitals will also be used when referring to YAHUAH as the Father (Elohim – HaAv) or when representing the entire GODhead (Hebrew, Echad). In contrast, He, Him, or Himself (capitalization of the first letter) will be used when referring to Messiah Yahusha (a.k.a. Jesus), or to the Ruach H'Qodesh (a.k.a. Holy Spirit).

The names Hebrews, Israelites and Jews are used randomly and generically, not necessarily as they would be used historically or geographically, as for example during pre-exilic or postexilic periods. This has been done intentionally so as not confuse readers who may not be familiar with the appropriate name used during the divided monarchy when it was important to distinguish between the Israelites and the Judahites as they pertained to the Northern Kingdom of Israel or the Southern Kingdom of Judah. The term Jew will be used extensively throughout to describe or include all the above names. Familiar names like Abraham, Isaac, and Jacob will be used rather than their Hebrew names Avraham, Yitzchak, and Ya'acov; again, so as not to confuse the reader.

In support of my views, I have endeavored to use qualifying scriptures from the Hebrew Holy Scriptures as much as possible. New Testament scriptures have been introduced to reinforce, validate, or illustrate the fulfillment of that which has been presented in the Hebrew Scriptures.

The scriptural references in this manuscript were taken from the Holy Scriptures according to the Masoretic Text [7] and from the Authorized King James Bible.

Like the Masoretic Text, the King James Bible was translated by Hebrew scholars of the highest order. For the sake of accuracy, I have elected to use scriptural selections largely from the Authorized King James (KJB), Open Bible Edition, Thomas Nelson, 1975, unless otherwise cited.

Why the King James? The Hebrew Text used in the King James Bible originated from the Daniel Bomberg edition (1516–1517), which was referred to as the First Rabbinic Bible. In 1524–1525, Bomberg published a second edition edited by Jacob ben Chayyim (or ben Hayyim). This is called the ben Chayyim Masoretic Text and was referred to as the Second Great Rabbinic Bible. This text became the standard for the next four hundred years and was the source of the King James Bible Old Testament. Later, in 1906, Rudolf Kittel edited the Biblia Hebraica based on what is called the Asher Masoretic Text. The Asher Text was based on the Leningrad Codex (preserved in the National Library of Russia, Hebrew manuscript Firkovich B19A) instead of the ben Chayyim Text. This was not the traditional Masoretic Text, and even a footnote in Kittel's Biblia Hebraica suggests that from 20,000 to 30,000 changes were made in the Hebrew Text of the Old Testament.

A common misconception is that older manuscripts such as the Leningrad Codex (1008 AD) are the best. This has been disproven, largely by the sheer number of ancient manuscripts that coincide with one another. Also, heretics began reworking manuscripts in the first century. Today, virtually all modern versions of the Bible apart from the Authorized King James have used the Asher rather than the ben Chayyim Hebrew Text, thus making them untrustworthy. [8]

---

7   A New Translation, published by The Jewish Publication Society of America, 5702-1942
8   D.A. Waite, *Defending the King James Bible*, The Bible for Today Press, Collingwood, NJ., 1992, pp. 27-28

The King James translators adopted a method called verbal or formal equivalence. In this way, words from the Hebrew or Greek were rendered as close as possible into the English; nouns as nouns, adjectives as adjectives, prepositions as prepositions, et cetera.

If the structure in Hebraic was such that it could be brought into English in the same way while maintaining the same form, it was. If a word was presented as a verb, the translators translated it as a verb instead of changing it to a noun or giving it a dynamic equivalence. The end result is a masterful translation. Theological language is important to the degree that it eliminates error and sets us along the path of recognizing GOD's transcendence.

A quotation from the Authorized King James, Open Bible Edition, Thomas Nelson, 1975 presented on page 1224 addresses a crucial point relative to the focus of this manuscript:

> "In 1962, the same organization (the Jewish Publication Society of America) published a new translation of the Pentateuch entitled The Torah, which will be followed by the remaining portions of the Old Testament. This work (The Torah) has been very carefully done, the result of the finest Hebrew scholarship available. But there seems to be a deliberate attempt here to make the Messianic predictions of the Pentateuch void of Messianic meaning, as for example, Genesis 3:15 which (in The Torah translation) reads: 'I will put enmity between you and the woman, and between your offspring and hers; they shall strike at your head and you shalt strike at their heel.' All other modern (Hebraic) translations read 'his heel.'"[9]

"In keeping with proper Hebrew translations, the King James retains the all-important reference to the Messiah and reads, "And I will put enmity between thee and the woman, and between thy seed and her seed; it shall bruise thy head, and thou shalt bruise his heel." In my research and quest for proper transmission of the Sacred Writings, I found the late Dr. I.M. Rubin's translation, *The Holy Bible: Hebrew Text and English Version*; New York: Star Hebrew Book Co., 1928, concurred with the King James Bible and used the appropriate word "his," not "theirs" in the Genesis passage. I commend the late Dr. Rubin on his exegesis.

Caveat: The subject matter of certain chapters and the addendums of this treatise may at times seem irrelevant to the Jewish people, Judaism, or Israel. An example may be the chapter "Bait, Switched and Fooled," or "Catholicism vs. Christianity," which discusses Catholicism as a pretense for Christianity. Later, "Appendix D—Mystery Babylon," (an exposition on Revelation 17) takes the subject to its conclusion. However, all of what is written including geopolitical events unfolding today are relevant to the future of the Jewish people and to you the reader.

---

[9] *King James Bible, Open Edition*, Thomas Nelson, 1975, Publishers Comment, p. 1224

INTRODUCTION

Love and Obedience are of the Heart

The Bible tells us that GOD is love,[10] which means that the single most prominent characteristic and attribute of GOD is for HIM to love. However, love requires an object on which it can be projected, which is why GOD created man.[11] Afterward, and in order for that love to grow, HE would need to tell us, show us, and help us to enter into a close child to parent relationship with HIM.

So it was that HE first spoke to men who inwardly and fervently sought HIM. Later, HE would have HIS prophets speak for HIM and scribes recorded HIS plan on parchment. Still later, HE would continue to speak through select individuals called apostles (sent ones) who HE sent out to tell all who would listen of HIS love and redemptive plan.

HIS plan would be fashioned into a book we call the Bible. Now, in black and white, for all to read is HIS final Will and Testament for man. In it HE bestows on HIS children the promise that HE plans to share HIS eternal Kingdom with them.[12]

> "Arise shine; for the light is come, and the glory of the Lord is risen upon thee. For, behold the darkness shall cover the earth, and gross darkness the people: but the Lord shall arise upon thee, and His glory shall be seen upon thee." Esaias (Isaiah) 60:1, 2

Beginning with their Egyptian bondage, to their Exodus; from their Babylonian captivity, to their emancipation and return to Jerusalem; from the destruction of the Temple and the diaspora, to their repatriation to Palestine in the 20th century, the Israelites have been in a continual state of unrest. Though Moses had warned them that complacency would mean hardship and that their sins would separate them from their GOD, they persisted in going their own way and wandered off the old paths.[13]

Centuries of opportunities to reform and return to HIM came and went. Prophets warned, but their warnings went largely unheeded. So it was that HE allowed their spiritual eyes to

---

10 1 John 4:7
11 John 3:16
12 2 Timothy 2:12; Revelation 20:6
13 Jeremiah 6:16

grow dim, their ears to become dull and their hearts to cool.[14] A curtain descended upon their understanding, even the deep things of GOD. Light was excluded, and darkness (a spiritual darkness) overtook them.

While they retained their identity and continued their religious practices and traditions, HE became a vague impersonal entity. Accepted and acknowledged as the Creator, yes… but marginalized; more a concept than a reality. What was left was a silhouette of the relationship that their ancestors once had. In contrast, what Elohim has always wanted and still wants is a deep personal relationship with each of us as evidenced in the Song of Songs. The litmus test being, who can say with conviction, "I am my beloved's, and my beloved is mine?"[15]

---

14   Isaiah 6:10
15   Song of Solomon 6:3

1

THE AUTHORITY OF THE HOLY SCRIPTURES

"The Bible is the revelation of the Creator and HIS will for HIS creation. It speaks to the hopeless condition that sin imposes on the unregenerated man and the fate of the sinner. It reveals HIS redemptive plan through a sacrificial offering that restores the offender and puts him in right standing with HIM. Its standards are holy, its precepts binding, its decisions irreversible. It is meat for the hungry, light for blind, hope for the lost, and wisdom for the wise. It is assurance for the penitent heart that crumbles and surrenders to the majesty of HIS Savior and of a blissful eternity with one he calls Lord."
-Finis Jennings Dake

Were GOD to Speak

If GOD, the parent of man, chose to speak to HIS child, what would HE say and how would HE say it?

Indeed, HE has a voice for HE spoke with Moses from a burning bush, and afterward on a mountain where HE gave him the dimensions and details of the Tabernacle. HE awoke a sleeping child named Samuel by calling his name. Fifteen hundred years later He would knock a belligerent Sanhedrin scribe named Saul from his horse and declare, "I Am Yahusha, who thou persecutest."[16]

HE has a pen, for HE etched two tables of law in stone, and with HIS finger wrote on a wall the fate of an arrogant Babylonian king and the doom of his empire.[17]

Why then, why indeed wouldn't this GOD who painted the heavens with trillions of stars and formed life from dirt not dictate a letter to HIS most cherished creation? And if HE did, what would this letter say? Would HE not reveal HIMSELF and give insight into who HE is, and how we might know HIM?

---

16   Acts 9:4, 5
17   Daniel 5:24-27

It sounds so logical, so easy, and yet the nature of man is to balk, to doubt, to use his human intellect to the point of denial. Mans' assertions feed his ego; his theories become his prejudices; his very intelligence, an endowment from GOD, may become his nemesis. While the heavens declare GOD's glory, man chooses to dismiss HIS existence, sooner believing he evolved from pond water and slithered his way to his feet.

In the end, men surrender their beliefs to the deductions of lettered men and slide the letter from GOD onto a bookshelf amid their collection of philosophical works.

Spiritual restoration must be accompanied by spiritual awareness, and such awareness may only come from one place—GOD HIMSELF. So, it is to HIS Word we now and repeatedly turn.

> "Let thy mercies come also unto me, O Lord, even thy Salvation, according to thy Word. So shall I have wherewith to answer him that reproacheth me: for I trust in thy Word." (Psalm 119:41, 42)

(Image Source: GoodSalt)

> "Books are the best method of preserving truth in its integrity and transmitting it from generation to generation. Memory and tradition are very untrustworthy. Therefore GOD acted with the greatest wisdom and also in the normal way in giving HIS revelation to men in book form. In no other way, so far as we can see, could HE have imparted to mankind an infallible standard that would be available to all mankind and that would continue intact throughout the ages and from which all people could procure the same standard of faith and practice."[18] Dr. Leander S. Keyser

---

18 Myer Pearlman, *Knowing the Doctrines of the Bible*, Gospel Publishing House, 1937, p. 18, 19

"...but to this man will I look, even to him that is poor and of a contrite spirit, and trembeth at my word." (Isaiah 66:2)

"... For ever, O Lord, thy word is settled in heaven." (Psalm 119:89)

One must believe that the GOD who flung the stars into space and set the universe in motion, the GOD who made order from chaos and brought forth life from the dust of the earth has a plan for HIS most cherished creation.

Would the GOD who made man in HIS own image neglect to tell him the purpose for which he was created? And if this were shared, would it not be written as a binding covenant between Creator and creation? Would not man be free to believe, accept or reject these promises? And finally, could a just GOD hold man accountable if HE didn't tell HIS creation what is required of them and provide a way to meet that requirement?

"The fear of the LORD is the beginning of wisdom: and the knowledge of the holy is understanding." (Proverbs 9:10)

"My people are destroyed for lack of knowledge: because thou hast rejected knowledge, I will also reject thee..." (Hosea 4:6)

Indeed, the Hebrew Scriptures—*Kitvei HaKodesh*—are the Holy Oracles of GOD and were written for the express purpose of redeeming and restoring fallen man back to HIMSELF; that is, "if" that man will come to realize and acknowledge that he needs to be restored![19]

This is the offer the Creator puts before each of us. Do we believe HE has a plan for us? Do we believe HE has authored a book? Do we believe we are in need of being redeemed?

"For there is not a just man upon earth, that doeth good, and sinneth not." (Ecclesiastes 7:20)

"...the soul that sinneth, it shall die." (Ezekiel 18:4)

Where is the man who will admit he has fallen, and has sinned? Where is the man who cries out, I cannot save myself? "... my hope is in thee."[20] I need a Savior! I need a Yahusha!

Haven't we all become too preoccupied, too materialistic, too self-indulgent, too complacent, too proud, or perhaps too trusting in what we have been taught, to consider where we stand in light of GOD's Covenant Word? What then does GOD truly want from HIS creation? Each of these questions shall be addressed and answered scripturally, but first I want to share with you what is in the future for the Jewish people and Israel.

---

19 Luke 1:77-79
20 Psalm 39:7

For Such a Time as This

In the fourteenth book of the Hebrew Holy Scriptures or the twenty-sixth book of the English translation, in the book of Ezekiel, is a prophecy which has become known as "The Valley of Dry Bones."

It describes a time in Israel's future, at the conclusion of a Gentile dispensation, "for such a time as this"[21] when, after centuries of what seemed as if YAHUAH had abandoned HIS people, HE will once again turn HIS full attention to them and reclaim HIS betrothed.

> "O Zion, that bringest good tidings, get thee up into the high mountain; O Jerusalem, that bringest good tidings, lift up thy voice with strength; lift it up, be not afraid; say unto the cities of Judah, Behold your God! Behold, the Lord God will come with strong hand, and HIS arm shall rule for HIM: behold, His reward is with Him, and His work before Him. He shall feed His flock like a shepherd: He shall gather the lambs with His arm, and carry them in His bosom, and shall gently lead those that are with young." (Isaiah 40:9-11)

According to Scripture, before this occurs and in order for this to take place, Israel will experience more war, a false peace, a false Messiah and the dreaded "Time of Jacob's Trouble."[22]

We are now at the threshold of this "time of the end," the *Acharit Hayamim*.[23] At a time of GOD's choosing (the Seventieth Week of Daniel)[24] the Jewish people will enter into a new dispensation; a dispensation of frightful days and perilous times, but also a time of hope and expectation for those who know their GOD. For it is written,

> "...and there shall be a time of trouble, such as never was since there was a nation even to that same time: and at that time thy people (Daniel's people, the Jewish people) shall be delivered, every one that shall be found written in the book." (Daniel 12:1)

"but the people that do know their God shall be strong, and do exploits." (Daniel 11:32)

> Note: Whether or not the false Messiah (the anti-Messiah) will be perceived to be the Messiah, or by Islam as their Mahdi, will depend on what they have been led to believe and are willing to accept.[25] Though some will be deluded, others will not. What is advanced in the Scriptures is that this false Messiah (Antichrist) will be Anti (against) GOD and Anti (against) HIS Anointed.[26]

---

21 Esther 4:14
22 Jeremiah 30:1-11
23 Daniel 12:4
24 Daniel 9:27
25 Matthew 24:23, 24
26 Revelation 13:5, 6

The Physical and the Spiritual Birth of Israel

In 1948 the land of Palestine had its physical rebirth as a nation-state. This was the first time Israel was an autonomous nation since King David had reigned over a united Israel 3,000 years earlier. Still, the Jewish people have yet to experience what the Scriptures refer to as their spiritual birth.[27] We are approaching the season of promise when, as a unified nation, Israel will be afforded the opportunity to appropriate the promised "New Covenant," the *B'rit HaChadeshah*.

> "Behold, the days come, saith the Lord, that I will make a new covenant with the house of Israel and with the house of Judah: Not according to the covenant I made with their fathers, in the day that I took them by the hand to bring them out of the land of Egypt; which my covenant they brake, although I was a husband unto them, saith the Lord: But this is the covenant I shall make with the house of Israel; After those days saith the Lord, I will put my law in their hearts; and will be their GOD, and they shall be My people. And they shall teach no more every man his brother, saying, Know the Lord: for they shall know Me, from the least of them unto the greatest, and I will remember their sins no more. Thus saith the Lord which giveth the sun for light and the ordinances of the moon and the stars for light by night, which divideth the sea when the waves thereof roar; The Lord of Hosts is His name:" (Jeremiah 31:31-35)

At that time, there will be a spiritual restoration where the collective heart, soul, and spirit of the entire nation of Israel will be spiritually restored. Our land, the land of Palestine, has merely been the needed womb in which we would gestate. We are now, by all prophetic indications nearing our full term and the brink of our delivery.

As with the birthing process, there is pain which accompanies the actual birth.[28] Our labor will soon begin…or it may have already begun, depending on when this is being read. However, the pain should not be our focus, but rather the expectation of our restoration as portrayed in Ezekiel's vision as "Dry Bones" coming to life.[29]

Dead Bones, Ye Shall Live! Ezekiel 37

One moment the prophet Ezekiel was a prisoner in a Babylonian city called Telabib; the next moment, he was transported into the midst of a vision.

Straightaway he found himself standing in an open valley strewn with human skeletal remains. As far as his eyes could see lay a canyon filled with bleached bones. As he walked amidst them, he noticed they had apparently been there for a long, long time, for "they were very dry." (v. 2)

It was then the LORD spoke to him, "Son of man, can these bones live?" (v. 3)

---

27 Ezekiel 36:24-26
28 Jeremiah 30:6
29 Ezekiel 37:1-14

(Image Source: GOODSALT)

Instantly, the prophet's human reasoning gave way to his profound abiding faith in his GOD, and the man answered, "O Lord GOD, thou knowest." (v. 3) This priest had become a prophet and intuitively knew that with YAHUAH all things are possible. And so, if GOD wished these lifeless bones to live, they would indeed live.

Then GOD spoke again to HIS servant,

"…Prophesy upon these bones, and say unto them, O ye dry bones, hear the word of the LORD. (v. 4) Thus saith the Lord GOD unto these bones; Behold, I will cause breath to enter in to you, and ye shall live:" (v. 5)

So the prophet obeyed the LORD, and suddenly there was a noise as the bones began to shake. Then, as if drawn by some invisible string the bones came together, reattaching themselves into human forms. Tendons and ligaments appeared, then vessels, muscles, flesh, and finally skin covered the skeletons. As Ezekiel looked across the valley, around him lay a multitude of corpses; but still lifeless.

Then the LORD spoke a third time. "…Prophesy unto the wind… Come from the four winds, O breath (a symbol of the Ruach H'Qodesh—GOD the Holy Spirit), and breathe upon these slain, that they may live." (v. 9). The breath of life, the same breath that gave life and spiritual consciousness to Adam entered into the dead and "…they lived, and stood up upon their feet, an exceeding great army." (v. 10)

GOD then spoke a fourth time. This time HE described what the prophet was seeing. "…these bones are the whole house of Israel: behold, they say, Our bones are dried, and our hope is lost:…" (v. 11)

The scattered bones represent the great and continuous dispersion of the Israelites from the land YAHUAH first bequeathed Abram.[30] After Solomon's death, until the 1900s, they had been scattered across Europe, Asia, Africa, and the Western Hemisphere. Overpowered, overthrown, conquered, and captured, the Israelites were integrated into dozens of pagan nations and cultures.

It didn't take long after their deportation to Babylon where they were made colonists of their Gentile masters that they became contaminated. HIS admonishments to remain separate regardless of where they found themselves were disregarded. Enamored by their new surroundings, their love and passion for YAHUAH waned. Passive is not acceptable to GOD who expects to be loved with all of one's heart, soul, and might.[31] The Israelites had veered off the "old paths" without realizing it.[32]

As with a candle left unattended, the flame which once burned bright inside them for their Creator had slowly burned down to a mere glowing wick. The spiritual relationship that

---

30 Genesis 15:18
31 Deuteronomy 8:11-19
32 Jeremiah 6:16

once sustained them faded. Spiritual death had gradually overtaken them with the subtlety of an anesthetic. Soon idolatry and sacrifice to pagan deities became not only tolerable but even acceptable. There would however, remain "a *remnant*" faithful to the GOD who had made a covenant with Abram.[33]

When in GOD's time (the 20th century) it was ordained that the Jewish people return to Palestine and be restored, they began coming back to the land from all parts of the world as moths drawn to a flame. The shaking and coming together of dry bones symbolize the return of the dispersed Jews to their ancient homeland. Sinew and flesh symbolize Israel's physical restoration, which would have to precede any spiritual restoration. They had returned to Israel, yet still in unbelief; unbelief of who it was that the Scriptures said would redeem them.

It had been the Prophet Isaiah who said that "in one day"[34] those of Israel who have escaped the "fire and the sword"[35] will have their spiritual birth. On that day, Israel will recognize their long-awaited Mashiach ben David.[36]

It is my hope—my *tikvah* and my prayer that in light of the evidence from the Torah and the Tanakh that the truths provided in the Scriptures will cause life to return to the lifeless, and that you will be among the army of Israel which "stood up upon their feet" (v. 10).

> "For thus saith the Lord God; Behold, I, even I, will both search My sheep, and seek them out. As a shepherd seeketh out his flock in the day that He is among His sheep that are scattered; so will I seek out My sheep, and will deliver them out of all places where they have been scattered in the cloudy and dark day." (Ezekiel 34:11-12)

> "Verily, verily, I say unto you, He that heareth my word, and believeth on HIM that sent Me, hath everlasting life, and shall not come into condemnation; but is passed from death unto life. Verily, verily, I say unto you, The hour is coming, and now is, when the dead (the dry bones) shall hear the voice of the Son of God: and they that hear shall live." (John [Yochanan] 5:24-25)

---

33 Isaiah 11:11; Zephaniah 2:9
34 Isaiah 66:8
35 Isaiah 66:15
36 Zechariah 12:10

2

JUDAISM: A RELATIONSHIP WITH YAHUAH AND YAHUSHA

"...I looked this way, and I looked that way, and there was no light. Then I looked towards the king, my lord, and there was light...." Tagi[37]

There is a familiar saying when one is looking for a site to establish a retail business. "There are three things to consider: they are Location, Location, and Location!" Comparably, if one is looking for GOD, there are also three things to be considered: they are Relationship, Relationship, and Relationship!

Nine-tenths of the world has replaced relationship with a belief system we have come to call religion. Man takes pride and comfort in his religion as it provides him with a sense of doing something which he believes honors or pleases his god. At the same time, his religion offers him a sense of security. Should he one day find himself standing before his god and having to give an account, he believes he can, to some extent, rely on his religion to vindicate him should the need arise.

Even as Jews, we share this inclination. We have to a large degree made an idol of our Judaism, our lineage, and our Jewish identity. We have become enamored with our culture, our tradition, our rituals, our customs, and our holy days. In reality we may have lost track of what is the quintessential purpose of being Jewish. Judaism (Biblical Judaism) is not a religion; it is a relationship with the One and Only GOD![38] In the final analysis, all the many laws and observances have but one purpose: they are meant to lead us into a deep and personal relationship with HIM.

Judaism is not a religion; it is a relationship with the One and Only GOD!

GOD Never Made a Single Religion

Religion is the most cherished tool in Satan's toolbox by which he masters the masses. Religion is the golden calf, which man has fabricated, and like the golden calf has replaced GOD. I dare

---

37 The Amarna tablets (14th century BCE); EA 266, Tagi, EA 296, by Yahtiru
38 Deuteronomy 4:39

say that religion has probably been responsible for sending more souls to hell than any single sin, for it keeps people an arm's length away from taking that final crucial step—finding and falling in love with their Mashiach.[39]

We need to recognize that GOD has never made one religion—not even Judaism. The name "Jew" is derived from Judeans who lived in the southern part of Israel circa 930 BCE. Our progenitor Abram was in reality a Gentile, a Semite. Most researchers agree that it was from his ancestor *Eber* that we derive the name *Ebereau* or *Hebrew*.[40] In any case, GOD called this Gentile out of the land of Ur of the Chaldees and then Haran to Canaan.

The Chaldeans worshiped many gods and were steeped in idolatry. YAHUAH couldn't operate on Abram's heart while he was immersed in this pagan culture, but HE apparently observed something special, something different in this man. Abram was apparently a seeker, wanting to know and have a relationship with the GOD of whom his generational great-grandfather Noah had spoken.

It is quite possible that as a child Abram may have sat on Noah's knee and listened to him speak of his amazing GOD. We read that Noah lived for another three hundred and fifty years after the waters receded, which according to the record of Scriptures (which tells how long each of the progenitors lived), we see that Abram was a contemporary of his great-great-great-great-great-grandfather.[41]

Scripture doesn't tell us if Abram might have been meditating or praying on the day GOD first spoke to him. We only know that ELOHIM spoke, instructing Abram to leave his ancestral family and the Chaldean society. YAHUAH didn't tell Abram where he was to go or why; only, "…Get thee out… unto a land that I will shew thee…"[42]

From his very first step, Abram's journey would be a blind walk of faith. Faith can be defined as that which is not entirely known or understood, but yet trusted in. That trust or belief was and still is the key that unlocks the treasure trove for the earnest seeker.

> "And he (Abram) believed in the LORD; and he (GOD) counted it to him for righteousness." (Genesis 15:6)

It is not religion that puts us in right standing with GOD, but our belief and trust (our faith) in Him.

> "Now faith is the substance of things hoped for, the evidence of things not seen." (Hebrews 11:1)

> "But without faith it is impossible to please HIM: for he that cometh to GOD must believe that HE is, and that HE is a rewarder of them that diligently seek HIM." (Hebrews 11:6)

39　Psalm 2; Psalm 16
40　Genesis 11:16-26
41　Genesis 9:28; 11:15, 26
42　Genesis 12:1

Each day, Abram would find himself to be a nomad, wandering from one waypoint to another, until one day GOD would say Stop! You have arrived! Then came GOD's promise to this obedient man who had sought and trusted HIM. "…Unto thy seed will I give this land…"[43] and so, the boundaries were then and there forever established![44]

From the very beginning, YAHUAH had one purpose in mind: HE wanted to make a people for HIMSELF, not a religion! Our Lord knew religion would become a replacement for relationship. HE knew man would embellish it, adding to it and deleting from it at will. And, GOD also knew that religion would be the principal instrument that the "Supplantor," the "Adversary," the "Deceiver," the "Devil" would use to create a substitute for an intimate bond.

YAHUAH has always searched and continues to search for the likes of an Abram, an Enoch, a David, or a Daniel: men and women who have a heart for HIM, and for HIM alone!

The Old Paths—Biblical Judaism

> "Thus saith the LORD, Stand ye in the ways, and see, and ask for the old paths, where is the good way, and walk therein, and ye shall find rest for your souls…" (Jeremiah 6:16)

As forewarned in the Torah, if the Israelites were to leave their first estate (their relationship with YAHUAH), choosing instead to follow the path of the world, they would encounter untold hardship.[45]

Like Lot's wife who was turned into a pillar of salt when she looked back to worldly Sodom, Israel too would be punished if she looked back and craved those things which the heathen seek after.[46] By allowing their minds and particularly their hearts[47] to wander, and by taking on the characteristics of the cultures around them, the Hebrews would drift away from the one and only GOD who simply wanted to be their parent and their Lord.[48]

All GOD ever wanted from HIS children was that parent-to-child relationship and the love, respect, and obedience which comes with it.

Alone Together

During the time of Moses, as the Hebrews made their way through the wilderness of Sinai, not only did Elohim lead them by day, HE would camp with them each night.[49]

As dusk approached, HIS priest would set up HIS Tabernacle (*Mishkan*). As this was taking place, the tribal families would erect their tents at appointed locations surrounding HIS sanctuary.

---

43 Genesis 12:7
44 Genesis 15:18
45 Leviticus 26; Deuteronomy 28
46 Genesis 19:26
47 Jeremiah 3:6-10
48 Deuteronomy 8:11-14
49 Exodus 40:38

Then they could rest, secure under HIS wings, protected in the secret place of the Most High, abiding under the shadow of the Almighty.[50] Because they had made HIM their refuge, no evil could befall them. Physically and spiritually, HE was central and preeminent.

"Moses' Tabernacle in the Wilderness" (Image Source: NORBERT MCNAULTY; © Mark & Jody McNaulty, www.selahart.com)

However, it wasn't long after crossing the Jordan River that their fervency for the GOD who had delivered them from their Egyptian taskmasters and faithfully cared for them for forty years began to wane. Out of HIS love, and in order to keep HIS children from drifting away YAHUAH would send HIS prophets; not to a single generation, but to each generation. From the Prophet Samuel (1070 BCE) to the Prophet Malachi (430 BCE) the message would be the same: return to the "old paths;" return to HIM. Added to the appeal to return was always the admonishment of the consequences if they chose to disregard HIS spokesman.[51]

At the end of Joshua's days, he set a large stone in the city of Shechem as a witness. There the Israelites swore a covenant of faithfulness to YAHUAH; yet after Joshua's death the people returned to their worldly ways in a single generation.[52]

> "...and there arose another generation after them, which knew not the LORD, nor yet the works which he had done for Israel. And the children of Israel did evil in the sight of the LORD, and served Baalim: And they forsook the LORD God of their fathers, which brought them out of the land of Egypt..." (Judges 2:10-12)

---

50   Psalm 91
51   Joshua 24:15-20
52   Joshua 24:26-27

In the Book of 1 Samuel we read the children of Israel broke GOD's heart by wanting a human king of their own just as the heathen nations had. Instead of YAHUAH the Divine King, they would rather have a mortal king. Reluctantly, and with a heavy heart GOD obliged them, and Saul became their human alternative.

> "...I brought up Israel out of Egypt and delivered you out of the hand of the Egyptians, and out of the hand of all kingdoms, and of them that oppressed you: And ye have this day rejected your God, who himself saved you out of all your adversities and your tribulations; and ye have said unto him, Nay, but set a king over us." (1 Samuel 10:18-19)

It wasn't long afterward that the temple offerings, priestly rituals, and repetitious prayers became routine that relationship and intimacy faded. Custom and tradition became the hallmark associated with being an Israelite.

Over time and with learned misguidance, the Israelites began to believe that they were somehow exonerated from the due process of the Law simply because they were the seed of Avraham.[53] Eventually, relationship with YAHUAH became secondary to form and formality and GOD was grieved. The sacrifices and oblations became a stench in HIS nostrils.

> "...Forasmuch as this people draw near me with their mouth, and with their lips do honour me, but have removed their heart far from me, and their fear toward me is taught by the precept of men..." (Isaiah 29:13)

> "To what purpose is the multitude of your sacrifices unto me? saith the LORD: I am full of the burnt offerings of rams, and the fat of fed beasts; and I delight not in the blood of bullocks, or of lambs, or of he goats....Bring no more vain oblations; incense is an abomination unto me;...Your new moons and your appointed feasts my soul hateth:....I will hide mine eyes from you: yea, when ye make many prayers, I will not hear..." (Isaiah 1:11, 12, 14, 15)

> "Cursed be he that confirmeth not all the words of this law to do them." (Deuteronomy 27:26)

As no one is capable of keeping the Law to perfection, where then are we left, if the Law condemns the guilty?

The whole purpose of the sacrificial system had been to show the people that they needed an atonement (Hebrew, רָפַכ *kaphar, capuroth*).[54] The whole Mosaic Law, beginning with the Ten Commandments, was purposely couched in the negative with ten "Thou Shalt Not(s)." The purpose of the ten mandates was to allow us to see that in the final analysis, no one can keep the Law to perfection. This left us with no alternative but to place our faith in an atonement.

---

53 Matthew 3:9; John 8:33, 37
54 *Strong's Exhaustive Concordance*, Thomas Nelson Publishers, 1984, Heb., #3722

The Atonement

The atonement offered through the sacrifice of animals was itself a temporal example and in reality, had no redeeming value. It was instituted to point to the human sacrifice: a life for a life, a human for a human, a Savior for a sinner. Yahusha—GOD our Savior for the man or woman who would accept Him as their personal atonement!

> "Christ hath redeemed us from the curse of the law, being made a curse for us: for it is written, Cursed is every one that hangeth on a tree:...(for he that is hanged is accursed of God..." (Galatians 3:13; Deuteronomy 21:23)

For what purpose was the Law given? "It was added because of transgressions, till the seed (Yahusha) should come to whom the promise was made... But the scripture hath concluded all are under sin, that the promise by faith of Jesus Christ (Yahusha the Messiah) might be given to them that believe....Wherefore the law was our schoolmaster to bring us unto Christ, that we might be justified by faith."[55]

The Apostle Paul would later say, "How shall we escape, if we neglect so great salvation; which at the first began to be spoken by the Lord, and was confirmed unto us by them that heard Him..."[56]

We Gods

The Israelites fashioned a golden calf and made idols of wood, stone, and metal which drew YAHUAH's condemnation. Ten times during the Exodus alone HE drew them back.[57] Ten times they returned to their human folly, but once again they walked away. This time HE allowed them to go and experience what it is like to come out from beneath the shelter of HIS wings.[58]

Today we still construct idols. No, it is not the calf of gold we worship. It is, however, still gold and the attainment of wealth itself. It is not the Tower of Babel whose top will reach the heavens that we look to build, instead it is the tower of success, fame, and independence. We might better call it the freedom to do as we wish without divine constraints.

> "And they said, Go to, let us build us a city and a tower, whose top may reach unto heaven; and let us make a name (for ourselves)..." (Genesis 11:4)

We may have even reached the point of believing we can justify why we should be found worthy to join GOD in HIS eternal paradise when our days have come to an end. How many times have we heard such things as: "I'm a pretty good person, I tithe and take responsibility for my family...What more could GOD expect of anyone?"

---

55 Galatians 3:19, 22, 24
56 Hebrews 2:3
57 Numbers 14:22; Isaiah 54:7
58 Psalm 91

We have become an idol unto ourselves, for we have come to the place where we believe we have the answers and the knowledge to attain whatever we want.

Do we worship another god? Perhaps we are that god. Or perhaps we need to ask ourselves, what is it that we desire the most? Is it something tangible or intangible? Whatever it is that supersedes or supplants HIM in our lives—that has become our god!

In Ezekiel's day, the hearts of the people were full of idols; there was no room left for HIM. The Lord said, "For every one of the house of Israel, or of the stranger that sojourneth in Israel, which separateth himself from me, and setteth up his idols in his heart,… I will set my face against that man,… I will cut him off from the midst of my people…"[59]

Do we trifle or do we tremble at HIS word? Do we even mention HIM by name, or do we simply refer to HIM in a generic sense as God. Or, are we among the reserved that avoid committing ourselves and simply say that we believe in some higher power?

Have we nudged GOD out of HIS rightful place in our hearts and lives and relegated HIM to a subordinate chair next to our throne? If we claim to love HIM "with all our heart and with all our soul, and with all our might,"[60] then how can HE be less than first and foremost in our lives?

> "He that loveth father or mother more than me is not worthy of me: and he that loveth son or daughter more than me is not worthy of me." (Matthew 10:37)

Why, Lord, Why?

One of the most frequent questions which lingers in the Jewish mind is why has YAHUAH allowed the relentless persecution and suffering of HIS "chosen people"?[61] This question needs to be scripturally addressed if we are to ever understand the reason for centuries of affliction, and more importantly HIS plan for our redemption.

The sufferings of the Jewish people came only after repeatedly turning away from GOD and adopting the things which the world offers.[62] The modern word for this is secular and can be defined as earthly, worldly, materialistic, profane, or nonspiritual.

Our history is one of belligerence despite GOD's constant provisions, interventions, and oversight. From the very beginning when Moses brought our forefathers out of bondage we wanted to return to Egypt. The newly emancipated

(Image Source: GOODSALT)

---

59 Ezekiel 14:7-8
60 Deuteronomy 6:5
61 Deuteronomy 14:2
62 Psalm 78:40-41

Hebrews would sooner have the leeks, onions, and garlic they had in Egypt than the promises and assurances YAHUAH had offered them.[63] GOD requires that we learn HIS ways, yet we are notorious for rebelling. HE called us "a stiffnecked people" and threatened to eliminate us and begin all over again with a new people.[64]

Time after time, opportunity after opportunity was afforded us. Reverse course and return to our moorings his prophets would exclaim, but their warnings went unheeded. Finally, the day came when GOD had had enough! HE would not entirely divorce us for HE had made an irrevocable and everlasting covenant, a *Berit Olam*, with Abram,[65] but separate from us HE would. And so it was that HE would avail HIMSELF to another people.

> "I am sought of them that asked not for me; I am found of them that sought me not: I said, Behold me, behold me, unto a nation (Gentiles) that was not called by my name." (Isaiah 65:1)

> "Many who do not understand GOD or HIS Ways consider acts of Judgments cruel, especially when the judgments are severe. What they fail to realize is that there is such wickedness, corruption and evil in the world that, if certain measures were not taken, the wickedness and evil would only be intensified. Even though the surgery would be painful, still, the disease would be far worse. If surgery (judgment) was not performed, the disease (sin) would destroy the patient."[66]

Ebal or Gerizim—Blessings or Curses

Where is our Savior? How was it He allowed millions of us to die in death camps? How is it we are now surrounded by our adversaries which threaten to annihilate us? How can He allow this to continue? When, if ever, is He going to come and vanquish our enemies? When is this all going to end?

Perhaps the answer to these questions, which we might refer to as the Great Whys, is so close and so incriminating that we refuse to acknowledge that we are responsible for our own sufferings! We, according to Leviticus 26 and Deuteronomy 28 and 30 have initiated and perpetuated our own miseries.

> "But if ye will not hearken unto me, and will not do all those commandments; And if ye shall despise my statutes, or if your soul abhor my judgments, so that ye will not do all my commandments, but that ye break my covenant: I also will do this unto you; I will even appoint over you terror, consumption, and the burning ague, that shall consume the eyes, and cause sorrow of heart: and ye shall sow your seed in vain, for your enemies shall eat

---

63   Numbers 11:5
64   Exodus 32:9, 33:3, 5; Deuteronomy 9:13, 10:16
65   Genesis 12:3
66   *Expositor's Study Bible*, Jimmy Swaggart Ministries: Baton Rouge, LA., p. 1611

it. And I will set my face against you, and ye shall be slain before your enemies: they that hate you shall reign over you;…And if ye will not yet for all this hearken unto me, then I will punish you seven times more for your sins. And I will break the pride of your power; and I will make your heaven as iron, and your earth as brass:…" (Leviticus 26:14-19)

I dare say the human tendency is to see oneself as being respectable, and if not respectable, perhaps decent, and if not decent, at least acceptable. It is in measuring ourselves by the human standard or yardstick that we have erred. Subconsciously we are comparing and evaluating ourselves to others. Am I better or worse than that person? How do others perceive me? I dare say no one compares himself to the divine standard, which is absolute perfection. To use a colloquial expression, "we have moved the goalposts." GOD simply says, "Every way of a man is right in his own eyes…"[67]

We

We have become detached from our moorings without realizing it and have drifted away with the tide of humanity. We have chosen not to consider the navigational chart (HIS Word) which HE has provided. We don't believe the divine compass (HIS Spirit) points true North. We float like seaweed and tidal debris, adrift on the currents of human thinking, among a morass of human ideologies. We are surrounded by an oil slick of immorality, godlessness,

Rescue at sea. - A. Morton (1863) (Image Source: ISTOCK)

---

67 Proverbs 21:2

and human ambitions. We are blown in whatever direction the prevailing wind of what is socially acceptable happens to be. We are lost at sea and don't realize it. We are unconcerned. Or are we? Do our eyes search the horizon for that one rescue vessel—our Messiah—in the hope of being saved?

According to GOD's promises,[68] if the Jewish people had harkened unto HIM, their blessings would have been immeasurable. Had they paid attention to Moses' words, that when the Messiah appeared they must hear and receive Him, things would have been entirely different.[69] Israel would have been restored and blessed beyond measure.[70] As a nation, Israel would have advanced to become the leading nation in the world today. They would have been "the head, and not the tail,"[71] but instead, they have led the world in sorrow and heartache.

If GOD was without compassion and grace, the fate of the Jewish people would be forever sealed. They would indeed be a hopeless people, singing the dirges of Lamentations from one generation to the next until the end of time. But GOD has compassion, GOD offers grace, and with grace, opportunity; for there remains HIS irrevocable promise that HE will restore to HIMSELF a remnant who diligently seek HIM with all their heart.

> "And ye shall seek me, and find me, when ye shall search for me with all your heart." (Jeremiah 29:13)

> "...Yea, I have loved thee with an everlasting love: therefore with lovingkindness have I drawn thee. Again I will build thee, and thou shalt be built, O virgin (faithful) of Israel (who awaits her betrothed)..." (Jeremiah 31:3, 4)

We can be assured that when GOD makes a promise, whatever HE has said, whether it is a blessing or a curse, it will indeed come to pass. Unlike man, HE is faithful to keep HIS Word.

> "God is not a man, that he should lie; neither the son of man, that he should repent: hath he said, and shall he not do it? or hath he spoken, and shall he not make it good?" (Numbers 23:19)

The conclusion presented in the B'rit Chadashah is that Redemption and Restoration are available to one and to all. However, the decision rests with each individual to either accept or ignore the New and Greater Covenant.[72]

---

68 Deuteronomy 28:1-14
69 Deuteronomy 18:15
70 Deuteronomy 28: 1-7, 30:16
71 Deuteronomy 28:13
72 Jeremiah 31:31-34; Ezekiel 37:26; Hebrews 8:8-13

The Blindness of Israel

If we are to believe Scripture, we will realize that a spiritual slumber has been divinely imposed on the Jewish nation because they left their first estate (their relationship with HIM) and replaced relationship with religion.

> "For I bear them record that they (the Jewish people) have a zeal of God, but not according to knowledge (what the scriptures are actually saying). For they being ignorant of God's righteousness, (perfection) and going about to establish their own righteousness, have not submitted themselves unto the righteousness of God. For Christ (the Messiah) is the end (the completion) of the law for righteousness to every one that believeth." (Romans 10:2-4)

> "For the Lord hath poured out upon you the spirit of deep sleep and hath closed your eyes: the prophets and your rulers, the seers hath HE covered. And the vision of all hath become unto you as the words of a book that is sealed." (Isaiah 29:10-11)

As inconceivable as it may sound, the Holy Scriptures tell us that spiritual "blindness in part is happened to Israel…" and will continue until "the Salvation of Israel (the Messiah) were come out of (return to) Zion!"[73]

Indeed, it may seem contradictory that YAHUAH would limit the understanding of a book which HE gave the Jewish people so that they would understand; however, this is exactly what HE has done. Even now, and without realizing it, the Jewish people are unable to truly understand "…yea, (even) the deep things of God."[74] Like the person with impaired vision from birth who has never had eyeglasses, they have no idea what it is like to have clear and unfettered vision.

As in Isaiah and Jeremiah's day, the culprit for our divinely induced blindness was, and remains our pride. This is especially true of those who profess to know and teach HIS Word, for pride blurs vision, and one's ability to recognize their own Mashiach.

> "But the natural man receiveth not the things of the Spirit of God: for they are foolishness unto him: neither can he know them, because they are spiritually discerned." (1 Corinthians 2:14)

> "Professing themselves to be wise, they became fools," (Romans 1:22)

Speaking through Moses, the Lord warned we would pay a heavy penalty for our indifference. These words Moses spoke to the Israelites over thirty-four hundred years ago are just as relevant to us today as they were then:

---

[73] Romans 11:25; Psalm 14:7
[74] 1 Corinthians 2:10

"Beware that thou forget not the Lord thy God, in not keeping his commandments, and his judgments, and his statutes, which I command thee this day: Lest when thou hast eaten and art full, and hast built goodly houses, and dwelt therein; And when thy herds and thy flocks multiply, and thy silver and thy gold is multiplied, and all that thou hast is multiplied; Then thine heart be lifted up, and thou forget the Lord thy God, which brought thee forth out of the land of Egypt, from the house of bondage; Who led thee through that great and terrible wilderness, wherein were fiery serpents, and scorpions, and drought, where there was no water; who brought thee forth water out of the rock of flint; Who fed thee in the wilderness with manna, which thy fathers knew not, that he might humble thee, and that he might prove thee, to do thee good at thy latter end; And thou say in thine heart, My power and the might of mine hand hath gotten me this wealth. But thou shalt remember the Lord thy God: for it is he that giveth thee power to get wealth that he may establish his covenant which he sware unto thy fathers, as it is this day. And it shall be, if thou do at all forget the Lord thy God, and walk after other gods, and serve them, and worship them, I testify against you this day that ye shall surely perish. As the nations which the Lord destroyeth before your face, so shall ye perish; because ye would not be obedient unto the voice of the Lord your God." (Deuteronomy 8:11-20)

Scripture goes on to tell us that one day the Jewish people will awake from their slumber and their eyes will suddenly be opened. They will immediately recognize it was Yahusha-Jesus who hung on a Cross on a hill called Calvary two thousand years ago. They will mourn the fact that many rejected Him at His coming, just as many still do.

"And I will pour upon the house of David, and upon the inhabitants of Jerusalem, the spirit of grace and of supplications: and they shall look upon me whom they have pierced, and they shall mourn for Him (the Messiah), as one mourneth for his only son..." (Zechariah 12:10)

How long will this blindness last? Scripture gives us the answer.

"...blindness in part is happened to Israel, until the fullness of the Gentiles be come in." (Romans 11:25)

> Note: "Until the fullness of the Gentiles be come in" means until the end of a dispensation in which Gentiles have been given the same opportunity to receive Yahusha as the Jewish people had. Scripture also gives us a benchmark, telling us this blindness will continue until the dreaded "Time of Jacob's Trouble,"[75] referred to in the New Testament as the time of "Great Tribulation."[76]

---

[75] Jeremiah 30:7; Ezekiel 36:16-27
[76] Matthew 24:21

This then begs the question: Does this mean the Jewish people cannot come to know and understand the Scriptures and recognize who it is that the scriptures speak of until that time?

Indeed no! At the time of this writing, YAHUAH and Yahusha have turned their focus away from redeeming the nation of Israel and concentrate on redeeming the individual! That is, those Jews (part of His remnant) and those Gentiles who have sought Him, believed Him, and received Him as their personal Redeemer, and Savior. These are those who have become His followers and placed their eternal destiny on Him. Irrespective of their ethnicity, they simply go by the name, "the Church."[77]

> Note: It is imperative to make the distinction between the true Church—"Believers," whose love and allegiance is only to the Messiah/Christ—Yahusha/Jesus, and its counterfeit!

This counterfeit is a religious institution of incomprehensible wealth, which wields so much power as to have nation-state status. She is an imposter who touts herself as the embodiment of Christianity when in reality she is the antithesis of what it means to be a disciple of Christ.

Sadly her devotees were captured as infants at a baptismal ceremony. They have been indoctrinated from childhood with religious instruction and have only a smattering of actual Bible teaching because the Bible itself has largely been replaced by a catechism. They have been spoon-fed a steady diet of spurious teaching and without knowing it participate in pagan customs and ceremonies. They truly believe themselves to be followers of Christ when, according to the New Testament,[78] they are not. They are simply and sadly only Roman Catholics.

Yes, there are some Catholics who are saved, but only by believing the same gospel whereby other lost souls are saved. One cannot hold to two contradictory propositions. Either fidelity to an institution, confession, absolution by a man, penance, indulgences, and ritual, secures one's redemption, or by complete and total dependence on what Christ did for them on the Cross!

> Note: There are devout Catholics and Protestants who believe and proudly declare themselves to be Christians when in fact they are coaxed and virtually controlled by religious (demonic) spirits. Though they believe otherwise, most of them do not possess the Holy Spirit. The majority have been led to believe that the Holy Spirit is automatically conveyed at a ceremony called confirmation, presided over by their local bishop. These, who were adolescents at the time, are in serious jeopardy of being eternally lost unless they awaken from their stupor and become biblical Christians. Under the influence of a demonic spirit they are given to say of their priests, "...These men are servants of the most high God, which shew unto us the way of salvation." (Acts 16:26, 17)

From this point forward and to differentiate between genuine Christians and the Church of Rome, (Catholicism), I will refer to the genuine as the Church or Believers.

---

77 Matthew 16:18
78 John 4:23-24; John 14:17

Repent and Return

As a nation (the Jewish people) our passion for YAHUAH has waned and we have rejected the "Holy One of Israel." We rely on our own wit, our own strength, and as a nation—on our military might.[79] Peril, persecution, and the threat of extermination seem to be the only catalyst which makes us return to HIM and beg for HIS intervention. Like the Israelites of old, we need to wail again, "Turn thou us unto thee, O LORD, and we shall be turned; renew our days as of old."[80]

We are told in the book of Joel, which describes the last days when Israel will be confronted by her enemies for the last time, that she will need to cry out for the only one who can save them—their Messiah.

> "Who knoweth if He (Yahusha) will return (come a second time) and repent (have a change of heart), and leave a blessing behind Him; even a meat offering and a drink offering (offer of peace to us) unto the Lord your God (Elohim)? Blow the trumpet in Zion, sanctify a fast, call a solemn assembly; Gather the people, sanctify (separate) the congregation (the people of GOD), assemble the elders, gather the children (the Jewish people), and those that suck the breasts (those unlearned in the Holy Scriptures): let the bridegroom (the Messiah) go forth of his chamber, and the bride (Israel) out of her closet. Let the priests (rabbi), the ministers (teachers) of the Lord, weep (repent and intercede) between the porch (the people) and the altar (GOD), and let them say (plead), Spare thy people, O Lord, and give not thine heritage (HIS name and people) to reproach, that the heathen should rule over them: wherefore should they say among the people, Where is their God?" (Joel 2:14-17)

Deliverance is For the Desperate

Jerusalem will once again come under siege. YAHUAH will again have to "bend us like a reed" and bring us to our knees to make us cry out for HIM.[81] Our renewal will come only after repentance. Repentance, it seems, comes only after anguish.[82]

> "Now therefore, behold, the cry of the children of Israel is come unto me: and I have also seen the oppression wherewith the Egyptians oppress them." (Exodus 3:9)

GOD encourages us in Psalm 50:15, "and call upon me (cry out to ME) in the day of trouble: I will deliver thee, and thou shalt glorify Me."

When suffering in Egypt, the people cried out in desperation to GOD. HE saw and sent a Redeemer... So will HE again!

---

79 Psalm 20:7
80 Lamentations 5:21
81 Isaiah 42:3
82 Isaiah 26:9

> "The Lord redeemeth the soul of his servants: and none of them that trust in him shall be desolate." (Psalm 34:22)

The Great Hebraic Commandment which we recite so often still seems to elude us, yet it is the most crucial verse in Hebrew Scripture. "Hear, O Israel…love the LORD thy God with all thine heart, and with all thy soul, and with all thy might."[83] Only in this way will YAHUAH reveal Yahusha, and our sight be restored!

Spiritual blindness is the result of a heart which has turned away from HIM; subsequently, it can only be restored when a heart turns back to HIM.

The King is Coming

Until now, our vision has been muddied. We challenge, disbelieve, and even defy our own scriptures which are the only means by which we can identify the Messiah with certainty. We recoil at the suggestion of who the Gentiles claim Him to be.

Why indeed would Gentiles recognize our Messiah before we Jews have?[84] However, things are about to change. "Praise be to YAHUAH," (Hebrew, *Halleluyah*) for the scales are beginning to fall, the veil is beginning to lift, and the Valley of Dry Bones are beginning to come to life.[85]

There comes a time when even night must surrender her darkness and twilight her shadows to the rising of the Son.

Yes, while it is true that the majority of Jewish people still wait for their Messiah, some have realized He has already made His first appearance and fulfilled His initial role as the "Suffering Servant of YAHUAH."[86] These same people, whether called Messianic Jews, Jewish Christians, or simply Christians, now look ahead for His promised return (Second Coming).[87]

> "Therefore thus saith the Lord God; Now will I bring again the captivity of Jacob, and have mercy upon the whole house (nation) of Israel, and will be jealous for my holy name; After that they have borne their shame, and all their trespasses whereby they have trespassed against me, when they dwelt safely in their land, and none made them afraid. When I have brought them again from the people, and gathered them out of their enemies' lands, and am sanctified in them in the sight of many nations; then shall they know that I am the Lord their God, which caused them to be led into captivity among the heathen: but I have gathered them unto their own land, and have left none of them any more there. Neither will I hide my face any more from them: for I have (will have) poured out my spirit upon the house of Israel, saith the Lord God." (Ezekiel 39:25-29)

---

83   Deuteronomy 6:4, 5
84   Ezekiel 43:7
85   Ezekiel 37:1-14
86   Isaiah 53:1-12
87   Zechariah 8:3; Isaiah 9:6-7; Luke 1:31-33

The Jews who are fortunate to survive the Great Tribulation (apart from those who rebelled against GOD and take the mark of the beast)[88] will receive and revere Him as Savior and become part of the remnant of Israel.[89]

On that day, Israel will sing praises to GOD and will rejoice throughout eternity.

> "And in that day shall the deaf hear the words of the book (the Entire Bible), and the eyes of the blind shall see out of obscurity, and out of darkness. The meek also shall increase their joy in the Lord, and the poor (humble of spirit) among men shall rejoice in the Holy One (the Messiah) of Israel." (Isaiah 29:18-19)

Another Chosen People

From the time of the Abraham Covenant, Israel was chosen and set apart to show the pagan nations around her the wonders of that nation whose God was Jehovah. However, instead of fulfilling her destiny and commission she ignored the warnings of Moses and the prophets and even murdered some. And, when finally, Immanuel came as prophesied[90] many of His own rejected Him.[91]

So it is that YAHUAH has taken temporary leave of the Jewish people for an unspecified period of time and looked for a people that would recognize Him, respond to Him and accept Him as their atonement. This time it would not be a race, a nation, or a tribe, but a certain remnant of Gentiles. However, not all Gentiles either, for GOD looks at the heart of each man and woman and determines who among them has a heart for HIM. Once that man or woman (Jew or Gentile) fully surrenders to HIM, HE then presents HIS Son.

> "...I will hide my face from them, I will see what their end shall be: for they are a very froward generation, children in whom is no faith. They have moved me to jealousy with that which is not GOD; they have provoked me to anger with their vanities: and I will move them to jealousy with those which are not a people; (not of the Jewish race)..." (Deuteronomy 32:20-21)

> "I am sought of them that asked not for me; I am found of them that sought me not: I said, Behold me, behold me, unto a nation (converted Gentiles) that was not called by my name." (Isaiah 65:1)

> "Behold, the eye of the LORD is upon them that fear him, upon them that hope in his mercy." (Psalm 33:18)

---

88   Ezekiel 20:38
89   Zechariah 13:9; Isaiah 35:10; Zephaniah 3:15-20
90   Deuteronomy 18:15, 18, 19; Isaiah 7:14; 43:3, 10, 11, 14, 15
91   Isaiah 53:3

Scripture tells us that GOD is "no respecter of persons"[92] and just as all parents should, GOD loves each of HIS creations equally.[93] It is however, in HIS offer to adopt, that the child must respond; wanting to love the parent as well. Therefore, any earnest seeker, whether Jew or Gentile, may petition HIM for adoption. Yes, even the Gentile may be grafted into the Covenant Promise and the family of GOD.[94]

> "For I am not ashamed of the gospel of Christ: for it is the power of God unto salvation to every one that believeth; to the Jew first, (was the offer made) and also (afterward) to the Greek (Gentiles)." (Romans 1:16)

The Kinsman Redeemer

Is this really scriptural that a Gentile can become a recipient of the promise? Are we able to see hard evidence in the scriptures? The answer to both questions is yes.

There is a provision in the Law whereby if a person became a debtor and had to sell their land, the nearest "kinsmen" (kin, relative) had the first right to buy back the property which their relative had lost.[95]

If the debtor was sold into slavery the kinsman could pay the ransom and free them from bondage. The word for this redeemer, is in the Hebrew *goel*,[96] which comes from the word *galal*, literally to "roll away," to redeem, buy back, or make good the debt.

Frequently found in Scripture, *goel* is used of GOD when HE redeemed Israel from bondage.[97] It is also used of men who pursued redemption like Job.[98] Job was clearly looking ahead and affirmed his faith that one day his *Goel* would come to the earth and redeem him.

> "For I know that my redeemer liveth, and that he (the Savior—Messiah) shall stand at the latter day upon the earth: and though after my skin worms destroy this body, yet in my (restored) flesh shall I see God:" (Job 19:25-26)

The word *goel* was also used if a husband died leaving a widow. In such a case it was expected that his brother or nearest kinsman would marry her and give his name to the widow.[99] In such an instance, even a Gentile who married a Jew became one with the spouse, and as such was accorded the same covenant promises afforded Israel; that is, so long as they ascribed to the GOD of Israel.

---

92 Acts 10:34
93 Mark 3:31-35
94 Romans 11:17-24
95 Leviticus 25:25
96 Exodus 6:6
97 Exodus 6:6
98 Isaiah 35:9; Isaiah 51:11
99 Deuteronomy 25:5; Genesis 38:8

Perhaps the best example of the redeeming and grafting process is seen in the epic love story of Ruth and Boaz.[100]

Ruth was a Moabite woman (a Gentile) who married into a Jewish family. While still young and in her childbearing years her husband died; so too had the husband of her sister-in-law Orpah, and the husband of her Jewess mother-in-law Naomi.

After Naomi's husband died, she became destitute and decided to return to Judah and to her people. Naomi tried to persuade her two daughters-in-law to return to their respective Gentile families. It was then that both of these young women were faced with making a choice. In the end Orpah would return to her people and follow the god of the Moabites. However, Ruth had become very close to Naomi and made a life-changing decision. She chose to follow her Jewish mother-in-law, return to the land of Judah with her, and make YAHUAH her GOD.

> "And Ruth said, Intreat me not to leave thee, or to return from following after thee: for whither thou goest, I will go; and where thou lodgest, I will lodge: thy people shall be my people, and thy God my God..." (Ruth 1:16)

As the story unfolds, Ruth's nearest willing Kinsman Redeemer would be a "mighty man of wealth...from Bethlehem...whose name was Boaz."[101] Boaz was in type a representation of Israel's Messiah. Even the town from which we are told he came, "Bethlehem," was a divine and deliberate inclusion.

(Image Source: GOODSALT)

This narrative was not provided in the canon of Scripture to simply be read as a Bible story. It was given by the Lord so we might see the kinsman redeeming process. In one act, Boaz became not only Ruth's redeemer but her husband. Such are the ways of GOD whereby a Gentile may become a partaker of the Abrahamic Covenant. It must be emphasized that, as with the marriage proposal, it becomes the decision of the one receiving the proposal to accept it. Who among the proposed will say yes to GOD's Kinsman Redeemer?

I can't help but wonder if Boaz realized just how significant his words were that day when he spoke a messianic promise to Ruth; a promise that applies to any who accept the Bridegroom of bridegrooms. "...a full reward be given to thee of the Lord GOD of Israel, under whose wings thou hath come to trust."[102]

---

100 Book of Ruth
101 Ruth 2:1, 4; Ruth 3:12; Ruth 4:1, 6, 8
102 Ruth 2:12

Another example where it can be seen that a wedding proposal can apply to every human, including a Gentile, can be found in Genesis 24. Abraham sent his servant to go and get his son Isaac (like Boaz, in "type" Christ) a bride. The servant came to Laban the Syrian, who was a relative of Abraham and met Rebekah (a Syrian). He indicated he wanted Rebekah to be a bride for Isaac. When she was asked, "Wilt thou go with this man?" she answered with the answer that determines salvation for every person. She said, "I will go."[103]

> Note: Concerning the Bridegroom—interpretations of the Song of Songs (Hebrew, *Shir Hashirim*) is the literal interpretation of the Song of Solomon. Whereas interpretive views differ widely, the allegorical interpretation has been the most common from ancient times among the Jewish people. It is seen as expressing the love relationship between GOD and HIS Chosen people. The Christian view sees it as a reflection of the love between the Messiah (Yahusha) and His betrothed Church.

The Grafting In

In a letter to the Jewish congregation (Hebrew, *kehilah*) in Rome during the first century, the opportunity for Gentiles (the wild olive branches) to be adopted by YAHUAH is made clear. These wild olive branches could be "grafted in" to the same covenant promise afforded the Jewish people (the natural olive tree) if they accepted YAHUAH's plan of Salvation.[104]

> "For as many as are led by the Spirit of God, they are the sons of God....ye have received the Spirit of adoption, whereby we cry, Abba, Father." (Romans 8:14-15)

Since the time the Kingdom of David disintegrated and the dispersion began, the Jewish people have experienced what it is like for a woman to be separated from her husband.

Not unlike a single woman who has no covering, Israel finds herself alone and in a pagan world which spurns her. Sadly, according to scripture, she will remain in this disparaged state until, at the very brink of her destruction, her betrothed (Messiah) will return and rescue her.[105]

For thousands of years, YAHUAH has without success tried to coax the Jewish people back to HIMSELF. HE desired them to return to Biblical Judaism and the "Book of Life" (Hebrew, *Sefer Chayim*).

HE hoped they would see their transgressions and their need for a savior, but as a nation they have persisted in their unbelief. They have refused to believe their prophets and their own scriptures which so vividly describe and authenticate Him. And, when at last Immanuel—נִמְעָלָאוּ, "El is with us"—came as the Holy One of Israel, (Hebrew, *Kedosh Yisrael*), the Lord of Hosts

---

103 Genesis 24:58
104 Romans 11:11-24
105 Zechariah 14:1-3

(Hebrew, *Adonia Tzva'ot*), Yahusha Ha'Mashiach, they largely rejected Him. So it is written and so it shall come to pass that the final painful chapter is about to begin. Still HIS grace persists and is even now available to those who will turn to HIM with all their heart.

> "Therefore also now, saith the Lord, turn ye even to me with all your heart, and with fasting, and with weeping, and with mourning (repentance): and rend your heart, and not your garments, and turn unto the Lord your God: for he is gracious and merciful, slow to anger, and of great kindness, and repenteth him of the evil (forgives)." (Joel 2:12-13)

For centuries, the Jews would gather every Sabbath in their synagogues (Hebrew, *bet kenesset*) where they spoke His name with reverence. They read aloud of His coming and praised the name of the Father who promised to send Him.

3

THE MYSTERY OF THE SON, MASHIACH BEN DAVID

> "In those days, and at that time, will I cause the Branch of righteousness (Messiah) to grow up unto David; and he shall execute judgment and righteousness in the land." (Jeremiah 33:15)

Before we continue, let us pause and consider just how remiss and negligent GOD would have been if HE had not expounded in great detail about the "Promised One," "the Lord of Hosts," our "Redeemer," our "Savior," the "Deliverer," the "Son," of which David spoke so reverently of in the Psalms.

YAHUAH refers to the Messiah with all of the above titles in order that we may recognize Him in each of His promised roles when He appeared…or appears again.

We are told He would come as a Priest after the order of Melchizedek, and as a High Priest like Aaron who would make the sin offering for the people.[106] He would come as a Redeemer in the way of Moses and would lead His people from bondage (sin) into the Promised Land (ultimately heaven).[107] He would be a favorite Son, as was Joseph;[108] a Prophet, as was Samuel,[109] and most appreciably, as a Suffering Servant—the atoning Pesach Lamb.[110] Soon, Scripture tells us, He will return and fulfill His providential role as the "King of Kings," "the Lord of Lords,"[111] "the Holy One of Israel,"[112] "the Lion of the Tribe of Judah,"[113] and "the GOD of the Whole Earth."[114]

> "For thy Maker is thine husband; the LORD of hosts is his name; and thy Redeemer the Holy One of Israel; The God of the whole earth shall He be called." (Isaiah 54:5)

---

106 Psalm 110:4; Hebrews 5:4-7; Hebrews 7:11-17
107 Isaiah 43:14; Hebrews 3:1-3; Isaiah 59:20
108 Genesis 37:3; Matthew 3:17; Mark 1:11; Luke 3:22
109 Deuteronomy 18:15-19; 1 Samuel 3:20-21
110 Genesis 22:8; John 1:29, 36
111 Revelation 19:16
112 Psalm 71:22; 89:18
113 Revelation 5:5
114 Isaiah 54:5

"I am the LORD, your Holy One, the creator of Israel, your King" (Isaiah 43:15)

Isaiah—The Prophet of the Revelation

Shortly into the first chapter of the book of Isaiah we read these words, "Come now, and let us reason together…"[115]

I ask you today—Will you reason; will you consider; will you allow YAHUAH to speak with you?

Proverbs 30:4 asks these questions, "Who hath ascended up into heaven, or descended? who hath gathered the winds in his fist? who hath bound the waters in a garment? who hath established all the ends of the earth? what is HIS name, and what is HIS son's name, if thou canst tell?"

The prophet Isaiah, indeed, the entire book which bears his name, has as its centerpiece the Jewish Messiah. It is He who has been the figure of expectation as summarized in Isaiah 25:9 and Isaiah 49:26.

> "And it shall be said in that day, Lo, this is our God; we have waited for him, and he will save us: this is the Lord; we have waited for him, we will be glad and rejoice in His (provided) salvation." (Isaiah 25:9)

> "…and all flesh shall know that I the LORD am thy Savior (Yahusha) and thy Redeemer, the mighty One of Jacob (Israel)." (Isaiah 49:26)

> Note: Jacob (supplantor), when he wrestled with Yahusha would not let go of Him until he had received a blessing. He was afterward given a new name, Israel, "a Prince with GOD."[116] So too, must each of us contend for our salvation if we are to become a prince with GOD; that we might afterward reign with Him in His glorious kingdom.[117]

The Announcement

Moses was the first to tell us of the coming of Yahusha in Genesis 3:15, and again in Deuteronomy 18:15. Afterward, YAHUAH sent the prophets (Hebrew, *nevi'im, nebi'im*) to visit each successive generation. Each of them was sequentially given more detail of who it was we were to be looking for.

Here, for example, is a messianic disclosure given to Isaiah. In it we have a depiction of the Messiah as both a Son, "unto us a Son is given," and also as a Father, "His name will be Everlasting Father."

---

115 Isaiah 1:18
116 Genesis 32:28
117 2 Timothy 2:11

"For unto us a child is born, unto us a son is given: And the government shall be upon his shoulder: and his name shall be called Wonderful, Counsellor, The might God, The everlasting Father, The Prince of Peace. (*Pele-joez-el-gibbor-abi-ad-sar-shalom*; that is, Wonderful counselor to the Strong GOD, the Everlasting Father, GOD's Prince /Ruler of peace)." (Isaiah 9:6)[118]

Here is the Hebrew version with the literal word meanings of the above passage.

Ki/Because *Yeled*/a boy *yulad*/born *lanu*/to or for us *ben*/a son *natan*/was given *lanu*/to us *va'tehi*/and shall be *ha'misrah*/the rule or dominion *al Shichmoh*/on his shoulder *va'yikra Shmoh*/and shall call His Name *Pelé*/Wonderful, *Yoh'etz*/Consultant/Counselor, *El Gibor*/God Mighty, *Avi-ad*/Father Eternal, *Sar-Shalom*/Ruler of Peace.

And here it is quoted from the Orthodox Jewish Bible.

"For unto us a *yeled* is born, unto us *ben* is given; and the *misrah* (dominion) shall be upon his shoulder; and *Shmo* shall be called *Peleh* (Wonderful), *Yoetz* (Counsellor), *El Gibbor* (Mighty G-d), *Avi Ad* (Possessor of Eternity), *Sar Shalom* (Prince of Peace).[119]"

The Hebraic words above are literal, and definitely refer to the Meshiach. They tell us that this "son" and "prince" is our "Mighty God." The two beings, father and son are inseparable.

Satan has had success in hiding the personage of Yahusha found in our Scriptures by using a verb "saved or salvation," instead of presenting Him as a person, using the noun "Saviour." The word "salvation," with few exceptions, from Genesis to Habakkuk, is meant as a noun. This becomes exceedingly apparent when preceded by the Hebrew suffix, "my," "thy," or "his."

"Behold, the LORD hath proclaimed unto the end of the world, Say ye to the daughter of Zion. Behold, thy Salvation (Hebrew, Yahusha) cometh; behold His reward is with Him, and His work before Him." (Isaiah 62:11)

What is in a Name?

In the ancient world, knowing someone's name was a special privilege that offered access to that person's life. GOD favored HIS people by revealing HIMSELF with several names which offered special insight into HIS personage and character. YAHUAH (ancient Paleo-Hebrew), Yahweh (Aramaic variation), Yahovah (Hebrew), and Jehovah (English). So it is we have Yahovah-jireh, Yahovah-nissi, Yahovah-shalom, Yahovah-shammah, Yahovah-tsebaoth, and Yahovah-Elohe Yisrael. There are, in fact, over two hundred different names and combinations of names found in Scripture, all descriptive of HIM.

---

118   Quoted from: *Masoretic Text, a New Translation*, Jewish Publication Society of America, 1917 Edition
119   Quoted from: *Orthodox Jewish Bible*, Artist for Israel International, 2002, 2003, 2008, 2010, 2011

It is important to keep in mind that it is YHVH/YHWH; Hebrew, *Ehyeh-Asher-Ehyeh*—"I will be as I will be," English, "I AM who I AM," who defines who HE is, and not mortal man. For each word, each letter, each jot and tittle has divine authority.[120] It is GOD, not man who calls HIMSELF by select names so that HE might reveal to us the complexity and the entirety of who HE is.

It is only after we acknowledge GOD's diversity that light begins to dispel darkness and we begin to understand what previously eluded us. It is each man and each woman's responsibility (not their rabbis) to *doresh* the Scriptures for themselves.[121]

"So then every one of us shall give account of himself to God." (Romans 14:12)

Who but a fool would chance where they will spend eternity on another's suppositions no matter how learned and lettered that person is?

"Thus saith the Lord; Cursed be the man that trusteth in man, and maketh flesh his arm, and whose heart departeth from the Lord." (Jeremiah 17:5)

How serious, even dangerous it is for a person to assume the vocation of a rabbi or the role of a teacher. If those who claim to possess the knowledge to interpret the Word of GOD teach error, whether wittingly or unwittingly, they put themselves in grave danger.

"From which some having swerved have turn aside unto vain jangling; Desiring to be teachers of the law; understanding neither what they say, nor whereof they affirm." (1 Timothy 1:6-7)

"My brethren, be not many masters (teachers or rabbis), knowing that we shall receive the greater condemnation." (James [Ya'aqov] 3:1)

"My people hath been lost sheep: their shepherds have caused them to go astray, they have turned them away on the mountains: they have gone from mountain to hill, they have forgotten their restingplace." (Jeremiah 50:6)

Listen to these scathing words the Lord spoke to Isaiah and Ezekiel concerning the spiritual leaders of their day.

"HIS watchmen are blind: they are all ignorant, they are all dumb dogs, they cannot bark; sleeping, lying down, loving to slumber. Yea, they are greedy dogs which can never have enough, and they are shepherds that cannot understand: they all look to their own way, every one for his gain, from his quarter." (Isaiah 56:10-11)

---

120 Proverbs 30:5
121 2 Timothy 2:15; Proverbs 15:28

> "So will I break down the wall that ye (teachers and false prophets) have daubed with untempered morter (false teachings), and bring it down to the ground, so that the foundation thereof shall be discovered, and it shall fall, and ye shall be consumed in the midst thereof: and ye shall know that I am the Lord." (Ezekiel 13:14)

> "For every one of the house of Israel, or of the stranger that sojourneth in Israel, which separateth himself from me, and setteth up his idols in his heart, and putteth the stumbling block of his iniquity before his face, and cometh to a prophet to enquire of him concerning me; I the LORD will answer him by myself: And I will set my face against that man, and will make him a sign and a proverb, and I will cut him off from the midst of my people; and ye shall know that I am the LORD. And if the prophet (spokesman) be deceived when he hath spoken a thing, I the LORD have deceived that prophet, and I will stretch out my hand upon him, and will destroy him from the midst of my people Israel. And they shall bear the punishment of their iniquity: the punishment of the prophet shall be even as the punishment of him that seeketh (follow) unto him" (Ezekiel 14:7-10)

Those that deceived others, will in the end be found to have deceived themselves. And no fate will be more awful than that of unfaithful ministers of HIS Word.

What is taught today and what was taught before the modern era differ significantly. A study of early rabbinic expositions and the Talmud illustrates that the early masters were passionate about discovering the truth from the scriptures as it pertained to their Meshiach.[122] They believed that scripture was the emphatic Word of GOD and its meanings clear and literal.

Today it appears some rabbis don't even believe in Scriptures divine authorship. Sadly, over the centuries, the Talmud and Midrash have been given parity with the Torah and Tanakh. The emphasis, weight, and solemnity of Scripture have been diluted or diminished. Laureates with impeccable credentials author books swarming with esoteric words lending to the aura that their deductions and defenses are not to be questioned. Regrettably, all too many of those who claim to be teachers have only a cursory understanding of Scripture, and therefore of GOD HIMSELF.

> "But the natural man receiveth not the things of the Spirit of God: for they are foolishness unto him: neither can he know them, because they are spiritually discerned." (1 Corinthians 2:14)

I would have to say that the majority of those in leadership today sermonize rather than teach the Word of GOD as Scripture directs (twenty times in the Torah, and fifty-five times in

---

[122] Alfred Edersheim's monumental work *The Life and Times of Jesus the Messiah* (1883) ends with a lengthy appendix which cites hundreds of passages from the Hebrew Holy Scriptures considered by the writers of the Talmud to concern the person or times of the Messiah in agreement with the Hebrew-Christian position.

the Tanakh). This of course results in the deep meanings and hidden secrets of Scripture being missed. Passages that have Messianic revelations are avoided. Recitations are little more than lectures on morals and ethics. The literal interpretation is replaced with allegories or super spiritualized. Scriptures are taken so far out of context as to have no relationship with what they were meant to convey.

The Conundrum

Rabbinic theology maintains that our Lord concluded HIS Holy Scriptures to the Jewish people about 430 BCE when the last of the Minor Prophets spoke into the sacred record. If that is to be believed, then we are certainly left with a conundrum in that our Lord has remained eerily silent for the last twenty-five hundred years and failed to fulfill HIS prophetic word.

Have we been left alone for two and a half millennia without further word or direction? What of all the unfulfilled promises? Or…has our Lord continued to speak to us? Has HE fulfilled many of these promises? And if HE had more to share with us, would HE not have continued to speak to us in the same manner and form as HE has before? Perhaps through Scripture? Perhaps in another Testament?

If indeed GOD has given us two volumes, but our rabbis will only acknowledge one, who is at fault? Who is responsible? And most importantly, who will suffer the consequence?

> "Woe unto them that are wise in their own eyes, and prudent in their own sight!...because they have cast away the law of the Lord of hosts, and despised the word of the Holy One of Israel. Therefore is the anger of the Lord kindled against his people, and he hath stretched forth his hand against them…" (Isaiah 5:21, 24-25)

The extent of just how far we have strayed from Biblical Judaism can readily be seen in Reform, Liberal, or Progressive Judaism. The Reform Jew today is by and large an entity unto himself. He may no longer believe in the personage of GOD. He may not consider the Holy Scriptures to be the Word of GOD or of divine inspiration (Deism). Instead of a Messiah, he's likely to believe in a messianic age; a day when the world becomes civilized and war ceases.

Some Reform Jews don't necessarily believe in a hereafter. In reality, they have no absolute beliefs, just opinions—subject to change. He or she may be whatever they choose; a Socialist, a Globalist, a Kabbalist, a Humanist, a Deist, an Existentialist, an Ethical Culturist, or an Animist. His beliefs often feed an intellectual ascent to superiority. His discoveries are to him an unearthing of knowledge, even when his conclusions are in direct opposition to the teachings of Scripture. He is indeed a searcher, but one who chooses to challenge the truth of Scripture rather than accept and practice it. Deep inside, he knows his thinking is flawed, yet his pride dominates and enslaves him.

"The question is not resolved in you, and there lies your great grief, for it urgently demands resolution...Even if it cannot be resolved in a positive way, it will never be resolved in the negative way either—you yourself know this property of your heart, and therein lies the whole of its torment. But thank the Creator that he has given you a lofty heart, capable of being tormented by such a torment, 'to set your mind on things that are above, for our true homeland is in heaven.' May God grant that your heart's decision overtake you still on earth, and may God bless your path!" Fyodor Dostoyevsky, *The Brothers Karamazov*

In his book *Betrayed!*, author Stan Telchin reveals a sad admission from his former rabbi; an admission which, in all likelihood, is shared by many others who, despite spending years in study and ministry have never met or known GOD.

In his message to his congregation that Sabbath, this rabbi said, "Some people will come to Temple because they are lonely or because they are looking for business or looking for understanding or looking for a husband or a wife, or for their identity. I don't care why you come but come. And let's pray and let's hope that together we will find God."[123]

How utterly sad that this poor rav was himself only "hoping to find GOD!"

The Greatest Sin of All

Undoubtedly the greatest sin of all is unbelief. For unbelief is the antithesis of faith. Unbelief is not only a sin unto itself but the source of all other sin. Unbelief is more than denial; it is rejection.

It was Eve's unbelief that caused her to ignore what GOD had said concerning the eating of the forbidden fruit.

It was Cain's unbelief in the necessity of a blood sacrifice which prompted him to offer a meager substitute from the fruits of the ground, which GOD had cursed, and so was he also cursed and rejected.

It was unbelief that caused the people of Noah's day to perish because they ignored the preaching of righteousness.

It was unbelief in who they were to worship and glorify that led the people of Babel to have their language confused and become scattered.

It was Abraham's unbelief that GOD would give him a son through Sarah, which led to him father another seed line which went on to become the nemesis of his descendants even to this day.

It was unbelief that caused the Hebrew children to spend forty years in the wilderness rather than believe GOD as Joshua and Caleb did, and take possession of the land of Canaan.

It was unbelief to heed the word of GOD to tear down the heathen altars and reject the heathen gods that caused the Israelites to fall prey to their enemies in Judges.

It was unbelief that caused the Israelites to compromise themselves, fall into idolatry, and be taken into Assyrian and Babylonian captivity.

---

123   *Betrayed!*, Stan Telchin, Chosen Books, 1981, p. 52

Finally, it was Israel's unbelief in their own Scriptures which caused them to disregard all the credentials of their Messiah, and as Moses declared, be scattered, in peril and estranged from their Lord for the past two thousand years.[124]

"But without faith it is impossible to please Him: for he that cometh to God must believe that He is, and that he is a rewarder of them that diligently seek Him." (Hebrews 11:6)

---

[124] Deuteronomy 18:15; 28:62-66

4

עשוהי YAHUSHA. THE YAH (GOD) WHO DELIVERS. THE YAH WHO SAVES!

יהוה
YAHUAH

יהשוע
YAHUSHA

You might ask, why is the Savior's name important? The answer is quite simple. His name identifies who the Messiah is and connects Him to His Divinity!

"Behold, the Lord hath proclaimed unto the end of the world, Say ye to the daughter of Zion, Behold, thy Salvation (Yahusha) cometh; behold, His reward is with Him, and His work before Him." (Isaiah 62:11)

The purpose of this chapter is to show how the Hebrew name Yahusha regressed to the name Jesus. We will learn in the final analysis that although the Messiah's name has been altered, His identity is preserved.
- Whose name is descriptive of GOD's role as our Savior?
- Who is it that the Scriptures tell us will return as GOD to Redeem Israel?

"I, even I, am the LORD; and beside me there is no Saviour (Yahusha)." (Isaiah 43:11)

"...and there is no God else beside me; a just God and a Saviour (Yahusha); there is none beside me." (Isaiah 45:21)

"Who knoweth if He will return and repent, and leave a blessing behind Him..." (Joel 2:14)

"Where is the name Jesus found in the Hebrew Holy Scriptures?" My response is, indeed, it is not, for it is not His Hebrew name.

When our Mashiach left His throne in heaven[125] and came to earth cloaking Himself in human flesh as Immanuel-GOD with us, He came as a Hebrew Jew.[126] As such He was given a Jewish name; a name which His mother Mariam (not Mary) was told to give Him during an angelic visitation.[127]

It is obvious that He was not given a Greek name, *Iaysous*, rendered *Iesous*, or the English name *Jesus* at birth. The closest English translations of the Bible have come to the Savior's actual name is *Joshua*.[128]

His name, in keeping with Jewish tradition, would be descriptive of His function. This is why the angel told Miriam, "for he shall save his people from their sins."[129] His given name would be the same name used by the patriarchs and the prophets before the Babylonian captivity when referring to the Savior. In the ancient Hebrew, He would have been and was called Yahusha.

The name of Moses' successor Joshua, son of Nun, (Hebrew, *Yahowshua*)[130] was actually in Hebrew *Oshe'a*, son of Nun.[131] Moses added the divine prefix *Yah-oshua*, which was afterward written *Jah-oshua*, then *Jeh-oshua*. *Jehoshua* was then contracted to *Jeshua*.[132] Jeshua in late English was pronounced Joshua.[133] Joshua, vwhy or wvwhy, *Yeh-oshua*, (*Strong's Exhaustive Concordance* #3091) is an Aramaic variation and a regression from ancient Hebrew, meaning *Yahu* who delivers, or *Yahu* who saves. The transliteration Yahusha is accepted in the Masoretic Rabbinic Hebrew text; however, the prefix Yah was changed to Yeh or Jeh as in English *Jehovah*. Notice that *Yeshua* and *Jeshua* are identical when the English "J" is restored to a "Y" as in the Hebrew.

Changing names from one language to another generally has to do with finding an equivalent in meaning or pronunciation. About 275 BCE, a Greek translation (the Septuagint) of the Hebrew Tanakh was created, and the Greek equivalent name for Yahu saves or saved was used in reference to the Messiah. The Hebrew name of the Messiah can refer to a man, as in the case of *Joshua*, or it may be found in a shorter form, *Yeshua* (wvy) as seen in Nehemiah 8:17, "…Jeshua the son of Nun…"

Because of the use of language variants, the name Joshua eventually became one of the alternative names for the Messiah.[134] Later in the seventeenth century, the New Testament Greek spelling of the Messiah's name, Greek, *Ihsouß*, pronounced "Yesous" (Strong's, Gk. #2424) was transliterated into English as *Jesus*. Dr. James Strong who began the concordance which bears his name also reasoned that "Yesous" of Hebrew origin is traceable to the Hebrew name Yehoshua (Joshua).

---

125 Ezekiel 1:26, 28; Revelation 4:2-9; Revelation 5:7-9; Revelation 21:5
126 Isaiah 7:14
127 Luke 1:31
128 Hebrews 4:8
129 Matthew (Mattityahu) 1:21
130 *Strong's Exhaustive Concordance*, Heb., #3091
131 Numbers 13:8, 16
132 Nehemiah 8:17
133 Numbers 27:13-23
134 Hebrews 4:8

The unwillingness to acknowledge Jesus as the Jewish messiah may in part be because of the name by which the Gentiles refer to Him! Let us explore this further and resolve the issue. How does one get to the name Jesus when Hebrew was translated into other languages—when there is no letter "J" in Hebrew? I might add, neither is there a "J" in either the Greek or Latin alphabets. The explanation will be forthcoming, but in a sentence, the translation from the name *Yahusha* to *Joshua* to *Jesus* are based largely on phonetics.

Let us begin with some historic facts and work backward in time. The name Jesus first came into general use in England in the late 1600s. This may be observed by the fact that the name Jesus does not appear in the original King James 1611 Bible. Instead, we read the Greek name Iesus. Neither do we find any other names that begin with the letter "J." There is for example, no person named James in the King James 1611 Bible. Instead, we find the Greek name Iames. It was only in the later editions of the King James Bible that the letter "J" was used in place of the Greek letter "I." The letter "J" came into use as an alternative for the "I" for ease in pronunciation by the English-speaking world. The "J" in Jesus created a soft "e" sound; where before the "e" in Iesus had been the dominant sound and had made the "I" unnecessary. We need to remember that when the King James 1611 Bible was written, the English language was still in a state of transformation, with no uniform spelling of words.

In order for one to make the proper correlation between the English name Jesus and the Hebrew name Yahusha, one must go backward through several regressions. The etymology (the origin and development) of the name "Jesus" is the result of no less than five different language revisions from the original Hebrew. The translation of the Messiah's Hebrew name Yahusha to Joshua was largely an effort to retain the original Hebrew sound. These phonetic changes were afterward imposed into written forms. When the scribes translated the ancient Hebrew into other languages (particularly Greek), they substituted a similar sounding letter from a different alphabet for pronunciation purposes.

Today, Jewish people might spell and pronounce the Savior's name Yeshua. This is an Aramaic (Chaldee, Syraic) derivation which evolved when the Israelites were exiled and relocated to Aramaic-speaking Babylonia. Seventy years of Babylonian exile and Chaldean influence (605–535 BCE) produced many changes in Jewish practices as well as alterations to their ancient language.

While the Hebraic language is similar to the Aramaic (keeping in mind that Abram came from Babylon), they are not identical. However, in the course of several generations spent in Babylonian servitude, most Jews became bilingual, picking up Aramaic as a second language. This was needful since Aramaic was the language of trade in Babylon. When the Jews finally returned to what remained of the Holy City of Jerusalem as chronicled in Ezra and Nehemiah, these language variations were imbedded in their culture. As a result, the ancient Hebrew language had undergone noticeable changes.

> Note: The Paleo-Hebrew alphabet is abjad. An abjad is a type of writing system where each symbol usually stands for a consonant, leaving the reader to supply the appropriate vowel. It was an offshoot of the ancient Semitic alphabet and closely related to the alphabet from which it descended. It dates to the 10th century BC or earlier. It was used as the main vehicle for writing the Hebrew language by the Israelites. It began to fall out of use by the Judeans in the 5th century BC when they adopted the Aramaic alphabet. This became the writing system for Hebrew, from which the present Jewish square-script came into use.
>
> Note: Chaldean or Chaldaea is a term for a whole country and took its name after the rise of the Chaldean dynasty. The Babylonians (Babel—sons of Babylon) are among those qualified to be called Chaldeans.[135] The Chaldean language is a Semitic Babylonian dialect.

The influence that the Babylonian exile had on the Hebraic language becomes blatantly obvious when one observes that part of the book of Ezra was written in Aramaic.[136] In addition, we see that the Prophet Daniel, who was captured in the first wave of Jews taken by Nebuchadnezzar, has in the book bearing his name six chapters in Hebrew and the balance in Chaldean. During the Babylonian captivity the early Hebrew name of Yahusha—עושוה—underwent a series of language regressions: Yehoshua, Yeshua, and Y'shua. Later these spellings became established and became the predominant spellings and pronunciations used today.

> Note: The Hebrew name of our Savior Yahusha is presented with six letters, עושהי, but written in English as Joshua, or Jesus. This is evidenced in the Masoretic text.[137] Later, a five-letter spelling, עשוהי was used and is the shorter prevailing form.[138] Both forms are correct. Usually the longer spelling denotes early Hebrew. For example, the Dead Sea Scrolls are older than the Masoretic text and contain the longer spelling.[139] The ancient (long form) Hebrew spelling is more frequent in the Dead Sea Scrolls than in the Masoretic text.

A lexicon is a compendium of words or morphemes in a different language. Morphemes are the small meaningful units or syllables of the language which, when combined, give the word its meaning. Some Hebrew Lexicons, including the *Gesenius Hebrew* (1839), *Chaldee Lexicon* (1846), and some concordances such as *The New Strong's Exhaustive Concordance* (1890) are numerically coded to the King James Bible. Both give the Lord's name and the pronunciation as "Jehoshua/Yehoshua;" however, these are not entirely accurate.

---

135 Genesis 11:28; Ezekiel 23:15, 17, 23
136 Ezra 4:8 through 6:18; 7:12-26
137 Deuteronomy 3:21
138 Judges 2:7
139 4QDeutM (A Qumran cave fragment)

Strong's Concordance was originally completed in 1890 by Dr. James Strong and has since undergone several revisions. It remains a wonderful resource and an excellent place to begin a study of Hebrew and Greek words found in the English King James Bible. However, as with any human undertaking, it is imperfect. On occasion, it has ended its investigation before arriving at the earliest (most ancient) word or name.

For example, Strong's researchers worked backward only one generation from the modern name of "Jesus" to "Jehoshua."[140] Another example in Strong's Concordance is the name Jehovah. If traced backward, we see in Strong's that the regression went from Jehovah to Yehovah and ends there.[141] However, if one continues to trace the origin of the name Jehovah further back, one finds Yahovah. Then, if one goes back further still, one will eventually arrive at the name YAHUAH.

> Note: The regression of a name can distort its association with the person. When the letter "Y" is restored from the "J" as in Jehovah we arrive at "Yeh" as in Yehovah. When Yehovah is properly translated and the vowel sound "e" is removed, we have "Yah" as in Yahovah. The "e" should not have been allowed to become part of the name itself. "Yeh" should have remained "Yah," as in YAHUAH.

Is this important to GOD? To some degree, yes; however, I don't believe our Lord gets terribly upset if His name is pronounced with an "e" sound as opposed to an "ah." Nevertheless, the problem both in spelling and pronunciation lies not so much with the Father's name but with the Son's name, for the prefix "Yah" (Yahusha) links Him to His divinity and His divine relationship with the Father!

> Note: Messiah's name Yahusha is spelled *Yohd-hay-wahv-sheen-ahyin*; The Father's name, YAHUAH, is spelled *Yohd-hay-wahv-hay*.

In Psalm 68, David extols his GOD by focusing on HIS name. The name which predated the Babylonian captivity and the Aramaic derivation was JAH. The "J" was incorporated when translated into late English and should have retained the "Y," leaving the short form of GOD's name YAH. But at least the "A" was retained in Psalm 68:4 and remained *"JAH."*

> "Sing unto God, sing praises to his name: extol him that rideth upon the heavens by his name JAH, and rejoice before him." (Psalm 68:4)

The same grammatical concept applies to the last syllable in the spelling of the Messiah's name. When Yahusha is spelled as Yahushua, the final part—*shua*—of Messiah's Hebrew name is incorrect, referring to the "oo" sound represented by the letter "u." This revised spelling uses the vowel point between the Hebrew letters *sheen* and *ayin*. The vowel points were not part of the

---
140 *Strong's Exhaustive Concordance*, Gk., #2424
141 *Strong's Exhaustive Concordance*, Heb., #3068

original spelling of the Hebrew but were added by the rabbis centuries later. So, if we remove the vowel point and pronounce only the original inspired spelling of the name, we should be pronouncing this last part of His name as *sha*; hence, we have *Yah-u-sha*.

Just how these distortions came about is quite simple. The Masoretes who developed the Masoretic Text were groups of rabbinic scholars working between the 5th and 10th centuries AD. These families of scribes were concerned that Hebrew was becoming a lost language. In order to keep this from occurring and to preserve the pronunciation and sounds of the language, they invented the vowel point system. This became a grammatical guide in the form of diacritical marks placed above and below certain letters, changing the sound of the letter. In this way, the Masoretes would secure the pronunciation of the Holy Scriptures for the universal Jewish community. Because Hebrew, unlike English, is written primarily with consonants, these vowel points were important for pronunciation only. Thus, the speaker would add the vowels when reading the word according to the intended meaning.

> Note: *Matres lectionis*, Latin "Mothers of readings," is the usage of certain consonants to indicate a vowel in the spelling of Hebrew, Aramaic, and Syraic languages. The Hebrew letters that do this are א (*aleph*), ה (*he*), ו (*waw*) and י (*yod*). The י and ו in particular are more often vowels than consonants. The practice of using *matres lectionis* likely originated when (ay) and (aw) diphthongs were written using the י (*yod*) and ו (*waw*) consonant letters respectively. This maintained the vowel sound to simple long vowels (ē) and (ō). In the 9th century, it was decided that the system of *matres lectionis* was not sufficient to imply the vowels precisely enough, so a supplemental vowel pointing systems, *niqqud*, using diacritic symbols joined *matres lectionis* as part of the Hebrew writing system.

There is no lack of evidence that before the rabbinic order came to prominence, Hebrew names were spelled and pronounced as "Yah," not "Yeh," and certainly not "Jeh." It was important to pronounce YAHUAH's name with the prefix "Yah," just as it is written. Prior to the implementation of vowel points, the personal name of GOD was unreservedly referred to as "YAHUAH," not "Jehovah." Similarly, "Yahusha" was not pronounced or spelled "Jehoshua."

This can be seen in cuneiform tablets discovered near the Ishtar Gate built by order of King Nebuchadnezzar II. This particular gate was the main entrance to the capital city of Babylon (circa 575 BCE).

Between 1899 and 1917, archaeological excavations near the gate unearthed nearly three hundred cuneiform tablets dating between the tenth and thirty-fifth years of Nebuchadnezzar's reign. One tablet recorded the distribution of food from the royal storerooms for Israelite nobility and craftsmen. These tablets provide insight into the missing years of Jehoiachin's life while in exile. There are four texts which show monthly provisions for "Ya'u-kīnu, king of Yahudu" *(Jehoiachin, King of Judah)*. These cuneiform tablets coincide with 2 Kings 25:27–30; emphasizing the point that at the beginning of the Israelite captivity, early Hebrew spelling had not yet been distorted.

Other examples of the letter "J" and the phonetically imposed "e" in English Bibles can be seen in other Biblical names that began with the first three letters of YAHUAH's name. In these names, the prefix "Yah" was changed to "Yeho" and then to "Jeho." As a result, "Yehoram" became Jehoram, "Yehoadah" became Jehoadah, "Yehoshphat" became Jehoshaphat, and "YAHUAH" became Jehovah.

One can now see how Yahshua, with an "e" substituted for the "a" and an "o" substituted for a "u" became Yehoshua. This spelling was then further contracted to Yeshua, and then to Joshua.

> Note: In the year 275 BCE, the primary language spoken in the Greco-Roman Empire at that time was *Koine* (common) Greek. This was the language used by Hebrew scribes when they were summoned from Israel by King Ptolemy II Philadelphus of Egypt to translate the Torah and later the Tanakh into Greek. During the translations they used the post-exilic (contemporary) names in lieu of the pre-exilic (ancient) Hebrew names. These variant Aramaic names had been sanctioned by the rabbinic teachers and were widely accepted at that time. Later, when the Masoretes added the vowel points, the modern names were translated phonetically into Greek and other languages.

When the Messiah came to earth His words and deeds were recorded in what became known as the Four Gospels. These accounts and the later Epistles (letters) were written or translated into Koine Greek and shared among the various congregations. As more and more Gentile converts joined the Jewish assemblies it was only reasonable that Greek be spoken and written in these gatherings so that all could understand. Therefore, and thereafter, Greek became the predominate language of the New Testament Church.

We have previously shown how the Messiah's name Yahusha regressed to Yehoshua. We then went on to show how the translators translated Yehoshua to Jehoshua, and from Jehoshua to Joshua. But this still doesn't tell us how Joshua became Jesus. There is one more morpheme (syllable) that needs to be explained. There is no "sh" in Jesus as there is in Joshua, simply because there is no "sh" sound in the Greek language. The "sh" in Joshua and Yeshua regressed and was spelled with an "s." This resulted in the name "Iesous." When the "Y" in Yesous or "I" is exchanged for an English "J" we have Jesous. At this juncture, the Roman equivalent for the Greek spelling *sous* came into the mix. "Sous" is "sus" in Latin, the language of Rome. The Latin spelling of Iesous or Iesus was Isus. The capital letter "I" was eventually replaced with the "J" from the English alphabet, resulting in our Messiah's English name eventually becoming pronounced and then spelled Jesus. Over time, the Messiah's beautiful Hebrew name became obscured and virtually lost to antiquity.

The following is an abridged outline which shows the regression of the Savior's name.

- Old Hebrew: Patriarchal and early Prophets (pre-600 BCE)—Yahusha.
- During and after the Babylonian exile: Yahoshua > Yehoshua, later rendered Yeshua. Eventually it would be pronounced Joshua.

58 • YAHUSHA. THE YAH (GOD) WHO DELIVERS. THE YAH WHO SAVES!

- Contemporary Hebrew to Greek (2 BCE): Yesous > Iesous.
- Greek to Late Latin (300 AD): Iesous > Isus.
- Greek/Latin to Mid-English (late 1600 AD): Iesous > Iesus > Jesus.

By substituting the name Jesus instead of Yahusha in the New Testament writings, Satan has separated the Old Testament references to Yahusha from the New Testament personage of Jesus. This makes it expedient, particularly for the Jewish people, to deny they are one in the same.

Imagine how many Jewish people might be inclined to accept Jesus and the New Testament had His name been left in the Hebrew, Yahusha!

Though the Mashach's name has changed from language to language and culture to culture, His role and who He is has not. He remains the Savior whether called by His correct name Yahusha, or if He is called Yahsha, Yehoshua, Yeshua, Y'shua, Yesous, Iesous, Joshua, or Jesus. Rather than becoming obsessed with His earthly name, we should become obsessed with Him!

To underscore this point, Scripture tells us that one day we will learn His true and heavenly name. "His eyes were as a flame of fire, and on his head were many crowns; and he had a name written, that no man knew, but he himself."[142]

The name Jesus or Yahusha should be used with the same reverence and adoration given to the name of GOD. Both names speak of the one and same Savior. Jewish people should not be stigmatized by a name, for a person is who he is, just as you are who you are even if referred to by another name in another language (Spanish, *Pedro—Peter, Henry—Enrique, John—Juan, Joseph—Jose*, etc.).

> Note: The word Mashiach or Messiah (the anointed one) is an English transliteration from the Hebrew מָשִׁיחַ (*Māšîah*). However, the common language of the ancient Roman Empire (300 BCE to 300 AD) was Koine Greek. The Greek word for the anointed one was Χριστός (*Khristós*) or Christos. Christos became Crist (Old English) and was later standardized to Christ during the 18th century. The word Christian (follower of the anointed one) was the natural progression.
>
> Note: The word "salvation" was derived from the Greek word *sótéria*, which is derived from the word *soter* meaning "savior." It conveys the idea of deliverance, safety, preservation, and restoration. It embodies the objective of GOD whereby HE seeks to rescue man from the fatal power of sin and bestow upon him the wealth of HIS grace. It encompasses a work of GOD on behalf of men, which includes faith, conviction, repentance, forgiveness, justification, redemption, reconciliation, regeneration, sanctification, preservation, and glorification. It also describes the state of a man who has been saved and is vitally renewed and made a partaker of the inheritance of the saints (John 1:12; Colossians 1:12; Ephesians 1:6).

---

142 Revelation 19:12

5

THE TIME IN EXILE

Initially GOD gave HIS Word to the people through numerous prophets. More often than not, their messages were in the form of warnings and if the people were complacent and continued to disregard them, captivity or worse was a certainty.[143] However it is also GOD's practice that after a prescribed time of separation, HE would give a new generation the opportunity to be restored and reconciled to HIMSELF. For example, forty years would be required for the Hebrews to linger in the wilderness until the generation who doubted and murmured had died off. Thereafter, their offspring (the next generation) would be given the opportunity to be restored and receive the blessings that accompany obedience.[144]

Whenever GOD begins again, as HE did in the time of Ezra, HE attempts to bring "the people of the book"[145] back to the Book (now HIS Bible). At the same time, HE restores their cultural identity, charging them to rebuild HIS Temple(s). This begs the question, Why does GOD need a building when heaven is HIS throne and the earth HIS footstool?[146] The simple answer is that HE doesn't, but the Jewish people did, and the religious still do.

The Precursors: The Sacrifice, The Offerings, the Tithe

Originally and until the Exodus, presenting a sacrifice to GOD was more of a giving or gifting to HIM; an expression of gratitude rather than a mandate.[147] Initially there was no law in place nor do we see actual evidence that Adam and his sons Cain and Abel made their offerings as a recompense for their sins. However it is very likely, that after Adam and Eve witnessed the need for GOD to slay animals to cover their sin (disobedience) and the need for a substitutional sacrifice, that the sons were taught the necessity. Able took this to heart and prepared a living sacrifice as GOD had modeled. Cain did not, and instead made a meager offering—the work (good works) of his hands, which are unacceptable to GOD.[148]

---

143 Leviticus 26:17-39
144 Numbers 14:34-37
145 Ezra 8:2-9
146 Isaiah 66:1
147 Exodus 25:2
148 Isaiah 64:5-7; Ephesians 2:9

In Genesis 4:4–5, special attention should be given to the word "offering," not tithing. We shall soon see that offerings preempted tithing and that under the New Covenant we leave the tithe and revert back to offerings.

After the flood and the dispersion of the people of Babel, many pagan cultures, including the Semitic Chaldeans from which Abram had come, customarily gave offerings to their gods.[149] So when Abram gave a tithe (Hebrew, *maaser*)[150] to Melchizedek,[151] he wasn't initiating something new or even something he was directed to do by GOD, but rather something customary to ancient societies. It was also common with the various Semite cultures, that after they were victorious in battle, they would give a tenth of the spoils to the object of their worship.[152]

This custom is spoken of in Scripture where we read, "And blessed be the most high God, which hath delivered thine enemies into thy hand. And he (Abraham) gave tithes (a tenth) of all."[153]

The Law instituted by GOD came some four hundred and sixty-three years later and was, like so many mandates, meant to be a schoolmaster, teaching among other things the principle of giving. So it was that tithing, like many ordinances, was legislated by GOD for the Israelites![154]

However, if one looks closely at the Mosaic Law, they will see something they may have missed. A principle of the tithe was not only to support the Levitical order, but also the needs of the people, and especially the stranger, the widow, and the fatherless. This was GOD's definition of "pure religion."[155]

> "When thou hast made an end of tithing all the tithes of thine increase the third year, which is the year of tithing, and hast given it unto the Levite, the stranger, the fatherless, and the widow, that they may eat within thy gates, and be filled; Then thou shalt say before the Lord thy God, I have brought away the hallowed things out of mine house, and also have given them unto the Levite, and unto the stranger, to the fatherless, and to the widow, according to all thy commandments which thou hast commanded me: I have not transgressed thy commandments, neither have I forgotten them..." (Deuteronomy 26:12-13)

Like many laws, the tithe was meant to teach a principle; in this case, the principle of giving from one's heart.[156] This was recognized by the New Testament Believers. They had been freed

---

149 *New Bible Dictionary*, Second Edition, 1982, Intra-Varsity Press, Tyndal House, p.1205
150 *Strong's Exhaustive Concordance*, Heb., #4643
151 Genesis 14:20
152 *Dake Annotated Reference Bible*, note (r), on Hebrews 7:, p.435
153 Genesis 14:20
154 Leviticus 27:34; Hebrews 7:5
155 James 1:27
156 Exodus 25:2; Acts 2:44, 25

from the Law and with it the need to support the Levitical order and the Temple. Instead of tithing (which is never mentioned in the New Testament as applying to the Church), they "gave" generously to the needs of other Believers.[157] So committed were they in their giving that they took offerings not only for those in their own assembly but for those in other assemblies who were in need.

In the book of 1 Corinthians, the Apostle Paul spoke on this to the Church at Galatia.

> "Upon the first day of the week let every one of you lay by him in store, as God hath prospered him, that there be no gatherings when I come. And when I come, whomsoever ye shall approve by your letters, them will I send to bring your liberality (gift) unto Jerusalem."
> (1 Corinthians 16:2–4)

The word "liberality" (Greek, *charis*) is defined as joy in giving; hence the word charity; especially by the divine influence put upon the heart.[158] It is born of love, of which the citizens of the family of GOD were anxious to participate. This was the way they invested in the Kingdom of God, for the people are living stones,[159] and when offerings are given to His needful children, they are given unto Him.[160]

Even the apostle Paul, who taught more than any other apostle was not tithed to by his disciples but instead received offerings for his own needs and took up collections for those in other assemblies who were in need.[161]

We learn from Scripture[162] that those who are fully engaged in teaching should be compensated;[163] "Thou shall not muzzle the ox that treadeth out the corn. And, The laborer is worth of his reward."[164] Still, it is not a tithe, nor is there a mandate to give ten percent. Rather, it is a fundamental principle which should be recognized (howbeit voluntarily) by the Church in support of their teachers and in appreciation for their labor. GOD continues to bless the cheerful giver. But once again it is not a mandate.

In 2 Corinthians 9:6–7 we read how GOD loves the cheerful giver. In verse 7 we read "Every man according as he purposeth in his heart, so let him give; not grudgingly, or of necessity: for GOD loveth a cheerful giver."

We are encouraged and even expected to give offerings to those ministers and ministries who are engaged in the furtherance of the Great Commission,[165] which is to bring the message of salvation to the lost—that being the message of the Cross.[166] As good stewards of the money

---

157 Acts 2:45
158 *Strong's Exhaustive Concordance*, Gk., #5485
159 1 Peter 2:5
160 Proverbs 19:17
161 2 Corinthians 11:9; 1 Corinthians 16:1–3
162 1 Timothy 5:17–18
163 1 Corinthians 9:13–14
164 1 Timothy 5:18
165 Mark 16:15
166 Romans 5:8

GOD has seen fit to give us, great care should be taken that offerings are not squandered on ministries which fail to educate the people in the basic rudiments of salvation, particularly, that "you must be Born Again!"[167] Too often today ministries collect money to build their own ministries, not the Lords, which is quantified in souls.

In GOD's plan, tithing was the model for giving. In essence it is a form of grace whereby a giver desired to give rather than being required to give. In the New Testament, believers wanted to give, and gave sacrificially out of their abundance from their hearts. In the final analysis, giving is not a commandment (a tithe) unless, that is, if you are a Jew who chooses to remain under the Law.

> "And verily they that are of the sons of Levi, who receive the office of the priesthood, have a commandment to take tithes of the people according to the law, that is, of their brethren, though they came out of the loins of Abraham (the Jew)." (Hebrews 7:5)

> Note: The complex additions made by the rabbinic teachers recorded in the Mishnaic and Talmudic literature turned a beautiful principle into something of burden. This unfortunate tendency may even have contributed to the belief that acceptance with GOD, and subsequently entry into heaven, could be merited through the ritual observance of tithing[168] or philanthropic giving.
>
> Note: Upon examination, one will find that the word "tithe" is mentioned only twice in the New Testament[169] and the word "tithes" six times.[170] In each case the word was applied to the Jew; never to the Gentile or the Church.

The most frequent scripture quoted with regard to tithing is Malachi 3:10; "Bring ye all the tithes into the storehouse, that there may be meat in mine house, and prove me now herewith, saith the Lord of hosts, if I will not open you the windows of heaven, and pour you out a blessing, that there shall not be room enough to receive it." It needs to be pointed out that this Old Testament scripture was for the Jews. The New Testament scriptures—Matthew 23:23; Luke 18:12; 1 Corinthians 9:14–16—often used to support the premise that tithing applies to the Church violates a fundamental rule of expository hermeneutics, which is to recognize who the author is speaking to or referring to. A study of the aforementioned New Testament scriptures will illustrate that even though mentioned in the New Testament, the application is to the Jew. The application of giving from one's heart applies to all.

---

167 John 3:3
168 Luke 11:42; Luke 18:9-12
169 Matthew 23:23; Luke 11:42
170 Luke 18:12; Hebrews 7:5-6, 8, 9, 9

Change in the Winds

During the Legal Dispensation when the Mosaic Law was all there was; bridging the span from the time the Law was handed down at Sinai until Yahusha's death, obedience included relationship, reverence and devotion. In a word, "worship!"

The worship life of Israel centered on the word sacrifice. Four of the five offerings (Burnt, Peace, Sin, and Trespass) required a blood sacrifice for the remission of sin. As such, man needed the Tabernacle and later the Temples to remind him that he was a sinner and needed to continuously come near to GOD through his high priest to make a substitutionary sacrifice. We still must go to the High priest (Yahusha) who not only is the High priest, but who became the substitutionary sacrifice and the antitype of all five offerings as well.

During the years the Israelites spent in Babylonian exile, the absence of the Temple sacrifice and the interruption of the established religious order took its toll. A new rabbinic order began and brought with it some new developments. One of these progressive ideas was that GOD's name—YAHUAH—was too sacred to be spoken by ordinary priests and the general population. The Soferim (scribes) took a passage from the book of Leviticus completely out of context.

In this one particular passage there was a young man who actually blasphemed and cursed YAHUAH. The man's sentence and anyone thereafter who "blasphemeth the name of the LORD, he shall surely be put to death,"[171]

While this Scripture gives no prohibition against speaking GOD's name, the rabbis chose to interpret it to mean that it was forbidden to speak HIS sacred name. The people were thereafter taught to say *"Adonai"* (Lord), or *"HaShem"* (the Name). It likewise became common practice in the English text of sacred writings to use the noun "Lord" in place of "YAHUAH" and, depending upon the degree of orthodoxy, they would omit the "o" writing G_d instead of GOD. This prohibition was also responsible for the use of the tetragrammaton, YHWH (a Latin abbreviation).

Of course this prohibition against using GOD's name is in itself an affront to HIM. HE has given us HIS proper name and not simply a title or the nebulous name "God" to clearly identify HIM and rule out any association with pagan gods. Our GOD, YAHUAH, enjoys hearing HIS rightful name, for it leaves no doubt that it is HE, the GOD of Abraham, the One True and Only GOD whom we recognize, love, and glorify.

> "I am the Lord: that is my name: and my glory will I not give to another, neither my praise to graven images." (Isaiah 42:8).

Properly written it should be, "I am the YAHUAH: that is my name…"

---

[171] Leviticus 24:16

The WILL and the WORD

We would do well to understand that before Yahusha-Jesus took His human name and title Savior, in eons past, while the earth was without form and void, Yahusha's name was "the Word."[172] This has great significance, for the Word of GOD is the Will of GOD for mankind. Therefore, it may be said that GOD's Will and Word are synonymous.

We read in the following passage that GOD manifested HIMSELF in the flesh, as the "Word (Greek, *logos:* expressed thought; word; reason) was with GOD, and (at the same time) the Word was GOD." (John 1:1, confirms His divinity.) "And the Word was made flesh, and dwelt among us …"[173] hence Immanuel, "God with us."[174]

If we believe Scripture, then we accept the fact GOD's prophets and scribes recorded HIS Will and Word in ink into what is now the Bible. So, it is correct to say that the Will of GOD became both the living (human) Word (Yahusha-Jesus) of GOD, and the written Word of GOD.

> "In the beginning was the Word, and the Word was with God, and the Word was God. The same was in the beginning with God. All things were made by him; and without him was not any thing made that was made. In him was life; and the life was the light of men. And the light shineth in darkness; and the darkness comprehended it not. There was a man sent from God, whose name was John. The same came for a witness, to bear witness of the Light (Savior), that all men through him might believe. He (John the Baptist) was not that Light, but was sent to bear witness of that Light (the Savior). That was the true Light, which lighteth every man that cometh into the world. He (Yahusha) was in the world, and the world was made by him, and the world (the masses or majority of people) knew him not. He came unto his own (the Jews), and his own received him not. But as many as received him, to them gave he power to become the sons of God, even to them that believe on his name: which were born (born again), not of blood, nor of the will of the flesh, nor of the will of man, but of God (the Holy Spirit by a spiritual birth). And the Word was made flesh, (Yahusha-Jesus) and dwelt among us, (and we beheld his glory, the glory as of the only begotten of the Father,) full of grace and truth." (John 1:1-14)

In the New Testament at the end of the book of Revelation, we are told four of Yahusha's names and titles: "Faithful and True," "The Word of GOD," "King of Kings" and "Lord of Lords." And then, there is mention of a fifth name; a name which is yet to be revealed, for it is "a name written, that no man knew."[175] So once again, let us not be concerned by whether we refer to Him as Yahusha or as Jesus, for they both refer to the one and only Savior.

---

172 John 1:14
173 (John 1:14
174 Isaiah 7:14
175 Revelation 19:11-14, 16

> Note: Insofar as the title "King of Kings" is concerned, the Jewish people pronounce the following benediction before eating the Paschal lamb to remind the participants of this King. "Blessed be Thou, the Eternal, our God, the King of the world, who hast sanctified us by Thy commands, and hast ordained that we should eat the Passover."
>
> Note: The Jehovah Witnesses' heretical interpretation of John 1:1 degrades and removes Yahusha's divinity. Subsequently, although they use the name Jehovah, this sect should not be confused with Christianity. Christianity refers to a Christian as a follower of Christ and one who recognizes Him as both Savior and the incarnate GOD. The Jehovah Witnesses do not believe He is GOD incarnate (Immanuel),[176] and hence are not His disciples. Their New World Translation, authored by Charles Taze Russell, who had only a cursory knowledge of Greek, wrote, "The Word was a god…" The statement (The Word was a god) is a clear violation of syntactical norm. In Greek syntax, the absence of an article does not imply vagueness; thus, Charles T. Russell's interpretation must be discounted.[177] Furthermore their assertion that Yahusha-Jesus was a created being and not GOD is diametrically opposed to the witness of both Testaments. Another stumbling block for the Jehovah Witnesses is the Scriptures which state that Jesus was the only *"begotten"* Son of GOD. Men will never be begotten (Greek, *monogenes*, which speaks of distinction as having no other sibling).[178] Men and women who are "born again" are not begot or begotten but are adopted into the family of GOD. Scripture is clear that Yahusha-Jesus was the "only" begotten Son,[179] which means that He, as GOD, was the only member of the GODhead to be born in human flesh. The referral to being the "firstborn" (Greek, *prototokos*) in Colossians 1:15 is in harmony with being begotten before all creation. It implies having existed from eternity. The Alpha and Omega, the beginning and the end, the first and the last.[180] This is consistent by the verse, "All things were made by him; and without him was not anything made that was made."[181]

The Cornerstone

Woven into the fabric of the Book of Isaiah with all of its prophetic admonishments are numerous Messianic disclosures. One of these is a revelation of a man; however, not merely a man but one the prophet would refer to as the "Cornerstone"; the stone upon which everything else is built. The correlation should be apparent as we allow these verses to bring the revelation forward.

---

176 Isaiah 7:14
177 *Expository Hermeneutics*, Elliot E. Johnson, 1990, Academie Books, an imprint of Zondervan Publishing House, p. 280
178 *Thayer's Greek-English Lexicon of the New Testament*, Joseph Thayer, 1977, Baker Publishing House, Grand Rapids, Michigan, Gk. #3439
179 John 1:18
180 Revelation 22:13
181 John 1:3

> "Therefore thus saith the Lord God, Behold, I lay in Zion for a foundation a stone, a tried stone, a precious corner stone, a sure foundation: he that believeth (in Him) shall not make haste." (Isaiah 28:16)

The cornerstone of the entire Writ, both the Old and the New Testament, is centered upon this one and same man; a man we are told by our prophets would be the summary of promise. For some He would be a sanctuary, but for others who reject Him, He would be a stone of stumbling and a rock of offense.

> "Sanctify the Lord of hosts himself; and let Him be your fear, and let Him be your dread. And He shall be for a sanctuary (for some who believe); but for a stone of stumbling and for a rock of offence to both the houses of Israel, for a gin and for a snare to the inhabitants of Jerusalem. And many among them (the Jewish people) shall stumble, and fall, and be broken, and be snared, and be taken (because they refuse to believe). Bind up the testimony, seal the law among my disciples. And I will wait upon the Lord, that hideth His face from the house of Jacob, and I will look for him." (Isaiah 8:13-17)

Yes, sadly He would be to many Jews "a stone of stumbling and a rock of offense." From the beginning He was to be Israel's Savior. Not a savior in the sense of a conqueror, crushing Israel's enemies as the Zealots believed, but a savior of their souls. In GOD's divine order, first and foremost is the redeeming of the souls of men from the penalty of sin and eternal separation from Himself. Only afterward, at His second coming, will He physically save those who are alive at the time of His return from their earthly enemies.

Just as Isaiah had told us, Immanuel would come to earth in human flesh and be born of a woman; so too did an angel tell a young Jewess (Miriam) the name of her child was to be Yahusha. (Hebrew vwhy—*Yahu saves.*[182])

> "...and thou shalt call his name JESUS (Yahusha; Savior) for he shall save his people from their sins." (Matthew 1:21)

> "I will praise thee: for thou hast heard me, and art become my salvation. The stone which the builders refused is become the head of the corner." (Psalm 118:21, 22)

We are also told by Isaiah that He would come as a Jew and that "He is (would be) despised and rejected of men…and we hid as it were, our faces from him…"[183]

Think of the irony of it that when our long-awaited Mashiach finally came, not only would many not recognize Him but that some would actually "despise" Him. I ask you; haven't we "hid our face from Him"? Haven't we "rejected" Him?

---

182 Isaiah 7:14; Luke 1:31
183 Isaiah 53:3

Why Was He Rejected?

The New Testament gives us the answer. The Pharisees and the religious hierarchy felt threatened by this commoner whose words pierced the souls of men. A commoner, who was able to explain the hidden and cryptic meanings of Scripture with clarity. An unpretentious man, whose miracles testified that He had GOD's endorsement upon Him.

With their political power threatened by one who pointed out their hypocrisies, these Pharisees and Doctors of Divinity; these pious of the pious, became His accusers, His judges, and His jury.[184]

With His deity denied by the rabbis and His identity obscured by simplicity, He became an enigma, even an anathema to many of His own people. The prophet Jeremiah foretold how men who will be alive at His next Coming will speak of how they were deceived and lead astray by their teachers. "…Surely our fathers have inherited lies, vanity, and things wherein there is no profit."[185]

It is frightening to think how quickly we accept what we are taught by those we love without ever verifying it for ourselves.

> Note: Pharisaic Judaism, which its adherents thought to be the only valid form of Judaism, later became Rabbinic Judaism. Legalism and formality continued to replace relationship. The Torah took precedence over the Tanakh and the messages of the prophets diminish.

I am reminded of a line from the 1960 film, *Inherit the Wind*, which speaks to the Pharisee then and now. It exemplifies the ultra-pious who, with all their piety miss the Savior and the purpose for which He came.

At the conclusion of the trial that pitted creationism v. evolution, a frantic and exasperated Matt Brady (Fredric March) suddenly falls to the floor and dies as he strains to be heard over the din of people leaving the courtroom. Henry Drummond (Spencer Tracy) responds to snide young atheist reporter E.K. Hornbeck (Gene Kelly) and comes to the defense of his now-dead sanctimonious Bible-quoting rival, "A giant once lived in that body. But Matt Brady got lost. Because he was looking for God too high up and too far away."

---

184   Luke 22:66-71
185   Jeremiah 16:19

6

HIS ONENESS

Elohim אלהים—GOD of Israel

Elohim is GOD's title, not HIS actual name. It has great significance not only because it is used over twenty-five hundred times in the Hebrew Scriptures, but also because this is the way GOD first referred to HIMSELF.

> "In the beginning GOD (Elohiym) created..." (Genesis 1:1)

Being spirit, Elohim is not constrained to the physical and natural characteristics of mortal man. HE cannot be comprehended by the human mind or appropriately described in human language. Therefore, we have only one way in which to understand our Creator. We are totally reliant upon HIS Word.

> "Canst thou by searching find out God? canst thou find out the Almighty unto perfection?" (Job 11:7)

Elohim actually speaks of a plurality, meaning "our GODs." The first-person plural possessive of Elohim is Eloheinu. So if we suspend our preconceptions and are bold enough to look beyond rabbinic teaching, we will see that in describing Elohim we are not talking about polytheism (many gods), but in the truest sense of the word monotheism (one GOD), or Oneness.

Elohim may be used in both the singular, when it applies to one GOD as in the GOD of Israel, or it may be used in the plural, referring to more than one god, even gods. "El" is the root name for GOD and refers to GOD in the broadest possible sense. Eloha is the single word for GOD. The Hebrew ending "im" normally indicates a masculine plural, so Elohim is the plural form of "El." The Hebrew word Adonia is the word "Lord," which is a masculine gender plural (literally lords). Adon is the singular word for Lord.

These occurrences are not a random phenomenon of grammatical usage, but words purposed by our Creator with the divine intent of describing HIMSELF.

The concept of a spiritual Tri-unity (Trinity) was not the invention of men, but the revelation of Scripture. Nowhere do the Scriptures infer there are three gods who are independent and self-existing (Tritheism), but three personages who are so inextricably linked as to be co-eternal, co-operative, and co-equal.

So unified are these personages as to be presented as one divine entity. HIS title, Elohim, does not in any way detract from HIS plurality but instead reinforces it. Together this tri-unity is not unlike a rope made of three cords. They can be described as individual strands, or when intertwined as a rope.

Without recognizing the personages of GOD as HE appears in the Scriptures that presents HIM in various forms and capacities, the Scriptures themselves make little sense.[186]

If we look at the very first chapter in the book of Genesis, we are given our first example. There we read, "And God (singular pronoun) said, Let us (plural noun) make man in our (plural pronoun) image, after our (plural pronoun) likeness."[187] We clearly see the single and the plural integrated as GOD refers to HIMSELF as a multiple being. What we have in this verse is GOD speaking of HIS composite unity; the entire Godhead.

Let us look at two other examples recorded in *The Hebrew Holy Scriptures According to the Masoretic Text: A New Translation*, 1943, Jewish Publication Society, which speaks to GOD's plurality.

As LORD GOD (*Yahovah Elohiym*) prepared to expel Adam and Eve from the Garden of Eden, HE said, "Behold the man has become as one of us..."[188]

Then in Genesis 11:7, we are told that the Lord went down to see men build their Tower of Babel and said, "Go to, let us go down, and there confound their language, that they may not understand one another's speech."[189]

A triune being which is at the same time a single being is a very difficult concept for the human mind to "wrap its arms around." On the natural plane, we have nothing to compare it with, nor do we have any idea of what a spirit being may or may not be apart from Scripture.

Still, on the natural plane it might be illustrated in an example such as this: How would you describe this shamrock?

How much more difficulty then does a human have in explaining a God who is both one and three? How does man explain a God who has always been eternal? How does a human explain how a God can be omnipresent (present everywhere); omnipotent (all powerful); and omniscient (all knowing)?

---

186 Isaiah 9:6; Isaiah 49:7
187 Genesis 1:26
188 Genesis 3:22
189 Genesis 11:7

The Holy Scriptures are the only way we have to obtain even a glimpse of our incomprehensible Creator; everything else is pure speculation.

> "Where wast thou when I laid the foundations of the earth? declare, if thou hast understanding. Who hath laid the measures thereof, if thou knowest? or who hath stretched the line upon it? Whereupon are the foundations thereof fastened? or who laid the corner stone thereof; When the morning stars sang together, and all the sons (angels) of God shouted for joy? Or who shut up the sea with doors, when it brake forth, as if it had issued out of the womb? When I made the cloud the garment thereof…" (Job 38:4-9)

> Note: The word Trinity does not appear in Scripture. It is a theological expression which came into use during the second century AD to describe Elohim (the GODhead).

Though the three personages of the GODhead are clearly distinguishable in the Old Testament, they are made infinitely perceptible in the New Testament. For example: The Father testified of the Son.[190] The Son testified of the Father.[191] The Son testified of the Spirit.[192] The Spirit testified of the Son.[193]

Our Indivisible—Divisible GOD, the Perfect Amalgamation

If we were to attempt to tell someone who lived in a remote jungle village and who had no knowledge of the outside world that we came from a faraway place called the United States of America, and then we proceeded to describe our country, we might say something like this.

"The United States of America is one nation, under GOD, indivisible. While we are one nation, we are comprised of fifty individual states. Each state is like a small independent nation. All fifty are separate, but we are one."

The person we are describing this to might then say to us, "How can you say you are one nation if you have fifty individual states which are like independent nations?"

We would then have to explain that we are one nation because we have joined ourselves together in concepts, beliefs, aspirations, laws, and liberties, with one overseeing government and one Constitution. In this way we are indivisible—undivided. We are indivisible in our purpose while at the same time we are divisible in that we are independent states.

The description of this "oneness" of the United States is based on the single word one. But the meaning is subject to the actual word, as well as how it is used and what it was meant to imply. Only by applying the correct word for the word "one" can the meaning be understood.

GOD in HIS wisdom (Hebrew, *chochmah*) did not use a single word for the English word one when describing HIMSELF, but for exactness HE used two words. Each of the Hebrew words

---

[190] Matthew 3:17
[191] John 5:19
[192] John 14:26
[193] John 15:26

for the word one has an entirely different meaning, just as we have three words in the English language with different meanings: two, to, and too. The two Hebrew words which YAHUAH uses to describe HIMSELF are *"Yachidh"* and *"Echad."*

Yachidh describes an absolute unity. *Echad* describes a composite unity or plurality, such as with the title Elohim which refers to the collaborative GODhead.

As evidenced in Scripture, Elohim is an undividable being (*Yachidh*, absolute unity in purpose). At the same time, HE is divisible in personages (*Echad*—a composite).

One Cluster of Grapes

When Moses sent twelve spies to search out the land of Canaan, they returned with "one cluster of grapes." The cluster was so large we are told that it had to be carried on a pole by two individuals.

> "And they came unto the brook of Eshcol, and cut down from thence a branch with one cluster of grapes, and they bare it between two upon a staff; and they brought of the pomegranates, and of the figs." (Numbers 13:23)

The Hebrew word used here in the book of Numbers (*b'midbar*, "in the wilderness") for one is "echad"—a composite unity. With perhaps hundreds of grapes on a central stem it could not be referred to as "yachidh"—an absolute unity.

We also see "echad" used elsewhere, as in Genesis 2:24 where we read, "…and they (husband and wife) shall be one *(bosor echad)* flesh." This passage implies that an external union becomes an internal and spiritual union. This spiritual union is ideally of such closeness and intimacy that there is a galvanization (a oneness) of the mind, heart and will. This is the "echad" oneness which Scripture teaches when describing the personages of Elohim.

Eschol-Echad (Image Source: GOODSALT)

One may also see this usage of the word "echad" in Ezra 3:1: "…the people gathered themselves together as one (*echad*) man to Jerusalem." And in Ezekiel 37:17, "And join them one to another into one stick; and they shall become one (*echad*) in thine hand."

However, it is in the "Shema" that we have the most indisputable evidence. The Shema is a fundamental principle of the Jewish faith. It was Israel's distinct message to a world which worshiped many gods that there was only one GOD.

If we examine the words in the Shema, we see that the Hebrew word for one is also written *echad*. In the Hebrew language we would say, *Sh'ma Yis'ra'eil Adonai Eloheinu Adonai echad*. In the English language we would say, "Hear, O Israel: The LORD our GOD, is one LORD." [194]

> Note: In the Gospel of Mark, a scribe asked Yahusha-Jesus, "Which is the first commandment of all?" Yahusha considered the exhortation of the Shema to be the first and proclaimed it in its entirety, replying, "...The first of all commandments is, Hear, O Israel; The Lord our God is one Lord: And thou shalt love the Lord thy God with all thy heart, and with all thy soul, and with all thy mind, and with all thy strength: this is the first commandment."[195] Later, the Apostle Paul, (Hebrew, *Saul*) a Pharisee, a doctor of divinity, a rabbi and a Sanhedrin scribe who had studied under Gamaliel would also teach of the *echad* oneness. There in his letter to the Church at Corinth, he spoke of the risen Christ. "But to us there is but one God, the Father, of whom are all things, and we in him; and one Lord Jesus Christ, by whom are all things, and we by him."[196]

Names that Speak to Us

The Prophet Isaiah tells us of various names and titles which speak to GOD's oneness and at the same time HIS personages. The earnest seeker who reads Isaiah 9:6 with the intent of arriving at truth can only reach one conclusion. The child born in Bethlehem was Son, Prince, and Mighty GOD. And He is so united with the Father as to be one.

> "For unto us a child is born, unto us a son is given: and the government shall be upon his shoulder: and his name shall be called Wonderful, Counsellor, The mighty God, The everlasting Father, and The Prince of Peace." (Isaiah 9:6)

YAHUAH uses the familiar terms: father, son, and spirit, not because there is a dad, a child, and a spirit being, but because these terms are easily understood. The Torah and Tanakh present all three personages in co-unity; the Father (Creator), the Son (Redeemer), and the Spirit (Facilitator).

As an example, we read,

> "...I will set up thy seed after thee,...and I will establish the throne of his kingdom forever. I will be his father and he shall be my son." (2 Samuel 7:12-14)

Though it is sometimes taught that King David is the one being referred to, this is clearly not the case. It is "unto" David that the Lord of Righteousness (the Son) shall reign at the end of days.

---

194 Deuteronomy 6:4-5
195 Mark 12:29-30
196 1 Corinthians 8:6

> "Behold, the days come, saith the Lord, that I will raise unto David (not David himself but a descendent) a righteous Branch, and a King (Messianic King) shall reign and prosper, and shall execute judgment and justice in the earth. In his days Judah shall be saved, and Israel shall dwell safely: and this is his name whereby he shall be called, The Lord our Righteousness." (Jeremiah 23:5-6)

As described, this Messianic descendent is to be a "King" from the Davidic dynasty, and will go by the name of Yahovah Tsidkenu, (more correctly, Yahusha Sidqenu) "the Lord is our Righteousness." A mere mortal man such as David would never be referred to as Yahovah jireh, nissi, tsidkenu, etc., especially by a Jewish prophet. Only GOD would assume that title!

> Note: Names found in ancient languages had the distinct characteristic of describing or conveying something relative to the person to which it was given. The name Immanuel, for example, means GOD with us, or GOD dwelling with HIS people. In similar fashion GOD's title Elohim and all HIS various compound names give us greater insight into who HE is.

The name YAHUAH is the proper noun and the personal name which GOD gave to HIMSELF. HE used the name YAHUAH in order to bring us into a more personal relationship with Him. YAHUAH was the GOD of the patriarchs, and strictly speaking the only name of GOD. Like Elohim, YAHUAH's plurality is seen when referring to the GODhead (Trinity) as in Isaiah 9:6 and used accordingly over one hundred times in Hebrew Holy Scripture.

The Voice of Scripture

Over the centuries, YAHUAH revealed HIMSELF in increments. Progenitors, patriarchs, and prophets were handpicked and given a vision, a dream, or an audible Word from the Lord.

> "And he said, Hear now my words: If there be a prophet among you, I the Lord will make myself known unto him in a vision, and will speak unto him in a dream. My servant Moses is not so, who is faithful in all mine house. With him will I speak mouth to mouth, even apparently, and not in dark speeches; and the similitude of the Lord shall he behold..." (Numbers 12:6-8)

Each of these appointees (men and women) GOD chose to communicate with had a different role to play in HIS divine program. Each was given what was needful at a particular time and for a particular generation. Adam, Job, Moses, and Abraham were all given great insight into the personage of GOD, whereas later the prophets were largely given revelations about the coming of the Messiah and the future of Israel.

Some of the visions and prophetic words the prophets were given depicted images and events which would have no bearing on the people of that generation, or even of that millennium. Instead, they were shown events which would take place well in the future, in what Scripture refers to as the "last days,"[197] the "latter days,"[198] or the "time of the end."[199]

The prophet Daniel, for example, was given great detail about the "time of the end" when a false Messiah would arise on the world stage and deceive many Jews into thinking he was their long-awaited Yahusha (Savior), when in fact he would be their worst enemy.

In this prophecy, Daniel was told of an imposter who will eventually bring war against Israel, annihilating two-thirds of the Jewish people.[200]

> "And at that time shall Michael (GOD's Warring Archangel) stand up, the great prince which standeth for (as a guardian) the children of thy (Daniel's) people (the Jewish people): and there shall be a time of trouble, such as never was since there was a nation even to that same time: and at that time (the end of the battle of Armageddon) thy people shall be delivered (saved by Yahusha), every one that shall be found written in the book (those who had accepted Him)." (Daniel 12:1)

Afterward, Daniel was instructed to, "…shut up the words, and seal the book, even to the time of the end," for this prophecy would not become relevant for many centuries.[201] Scripture later reveals in the New Testament that the generation that witnesses peace in the Middle East and the rebuilding of the Temple in Jerusalem will be the same generation which will experience the Great Tribulation.[202] This interval will be so horrific that only one-third of Israel will actually survive. Those that are fortunate enough to survive will also see the return of the Messiah.[203]

> "Now learn a parable of the fig tree; When his branch (Israel) is yet tender, and putteth forth leaves (a young nation), ye know that summer (the final harvest of souls) is nigh: So likewise ye, when ye shall see all these things (signs, particularly the rebuilding of the Temple), know that it is near, even at the doors. Verily I say unto you, This (that) generation (who sees these events unfold) shall not pass, till all these things be fulfilled." (Matthew 24:32-34)

See Appendix B—The Olivet Discourse, a study of the seven years of Jacob's Trouble.

---

197 Genesis 49:1; Isaiah 2:2; Micah 2:4
198 Numbers 24:14; Deuteronomy 4:30, 31:29; Jeremiah 23:20, 48:47, 49:39; Ezekiel 38:16; Daniel 2:28, 10:14; Hosea 3:5
199 Daniel 8:17, 11:35, 11:40, 12:4, 9
200 Daniel 7:20-26, 8:23-26, 9:26-27; Zechariah 14:3; Ezekiel 39-40
201 Daniel 8:26, 12:4
202 Matthew 24:34
203 Zechariah 13:9

> Note: In the book of Daniel is concealed a protracted interval of time, commonly referred to as a dispensation. A dispensation is defined as a divine ordering of the affairs of the world. The order or age we currently find ourselves in has already lasted several thousand years and is frequently spoken of as the "Dispensation of the Church." It refers to the present time when GOD has turned HIS attention to the Gentiles and the creation of His Church, or figuratively His Body. It spans the time between Yahusha's first coming and His next coming, or more precisely, until the removal of His Church. This is presented in the timeline of Appendix C—Daniel's Vision of Seventy Weeks.[204]

The Holy Scriptures, Volume 2

With each new generation, another succession of prophets came and went. During the period known as the era of Kings and Prophets the historical accounts of the Hebrew nation were carefully chronicled. As time went on GOD shared more of HIS plan about Israel's restoration and redemption. But then, about 430 BC the last of the prophets spoke and the Hebrew Holy Scriptures officially ended…or did they?

Why would Elohim suddenly stop communicating with HIS people and remain silent for nearly twenty-five hundred years? Or, has GOD continued to speak? What of all the unfulfilled promises and prophesies? What is this new Covenant which HE promised the Jewish people in Jeremiah 31:31? Could it have already been made available to us in another volume… another testament?

> "Behold, the days come, saith the Lord, that I will make a new covenant with the house of Israel, and with the house of Judah: Not according to the covenant (the Mosaic covenant) that I made with their fathers in the day that I took them by the hand to bring them out of the land of Egypt;… But this shall be the covenant that I will make with the house of Israel; After those days, saith the LORD, I will put my law in their inward parts, and write it in their hearts; and will be their God, and they shall be my people." (Jeremiah 31:31–33)

Are there two volumes to the Holy Scriptures? Have we been persuaded not to accept or believe the second volume which offers the promised new covenant…and eternal life?

> "Search the scriptures; for in them ye think ye have eternal life: and they are they which testify of me (Yahusha-Jesus)." (John 5:39)

Neither the Old nor the New Testament are exclusive or independent of the other. The New Covenant (the *Brit Chadashah*) does not change the Old Covenant but completes it by offering the promised New Covenant through the atoning sacrifice of Messiah.

---

204 Daniel 9:22-27

Yahusha Himself said, "Think not that I am come to destroy the law, or the prophets: I am not come to destroy, but to fulfil. For verily I say unto you, Till heaven and earth pass, one jot or one tittle shall in no wise pass from the law, till all be fulfilled (in Me and what I will do at the Cross)."[205]

> Note: The law was "fulfilled" (satisfied) in Yahusha-Jesus by His having lived a perfect sinless life,[206] and by His substitutionary death[207] which satisfied the Law by atoning for mans' sin. And lastly by defeating death in a glorious resurrection,[208] thereby opening the doors of heaven to His own.[209]
>
> Note: The law made nothing perfect but the bringing of a better hope by which we are able to draw near unto GOD.[210] The Aaronic priesthood was temporary,[211] the Messiah's priesthood after the order of Melchizedek, eternal.[212] The profession made six hundred years after the conferring of the law was spoken by David and as such abrogates the Aaronic order.[213] Because the Son's priesthood is eternal[214] the covenant upon which it operates is also eternal. The old covenant is superseded by the new covenant only when the new is internalized and accepted by the individual!

"But now hath he obtained a more excellent ministry, by how much also he is the mediator of a better covenant, which was established upon better promises." (Hebrews 8:6)

> Note: When scriptures from the Old and New Testament are examined and compared, they form a complete picture which would otherwise be incomplete. Take for example, Israel's final seven years of this dispensation. In the first three chapters of the Old Testament Book of Joel, we are given a general outline of what will occur during that time. In the New Testament Book of the Revelation, chapters 6–19, we have been given fourteen comprehensive chapters which detail the events in Joel. The same is true regarding the details concerning our Messiah. He is concealed in the Old Testament and revealed in the New Testament.

---

205 Matthew 5:17–18
206 Hebrews 7:26
207 Isaiah 53:6, 10, 12
208 Psalm 16:10
209 Isaiah 53:11
210 Hebrews 7:19
211 Hebrews 7:23
212 Hebrews 7:17
213 Psalm 110:4
214 Psalm 110:4

Always with Us

As we move through the pages of Scripture we see Yahusha presented in numerous ways. At times He visited us as a man and other times as an angel.

It was Yahusha the Son; one of the three men who visited Abram on the plains of Mamre, and to who Abraham said, "The Lord (Jahovah) appeared..," and "My Lord"(My Adonai) referring specifically to his GOD.[215]

It was Yahusha the Son who Jacob wrestled with throughout the night and afterward named him Israel; of whom Jacob exclaimed, "...for I have seen GOD (Elohiym) face to face and my life is preserved."[216]

And, it was Yahusha, the fourth man in the fiery furnace with the Hebrew children, of which it was said, "the forth is like the Son of GOD (Elahh)."[217]

Yahusha appeared and spoke many more times to the appointed man or woman of the hour. At times, instead of taking a human form He manifested Himself in an image which would become permanently emblazoned into the minds of men.

He was the Word of the Lord which came from the burning bush who commissioned Moses "...GOD called unto him..."[218]

He was the Shekinah Cloud (Hebrew, *anan*) and the Pillar of Fire (Hebrew, *amud esh*) that guided the Hebrew children throughout their wilderness journey—"And the LORD went before them by day as a pillar of cloud to lead them the way." [219]

He came as the guiding "angel" who led the exodus into the Promised Land.

> "Behold I send an angel before thee, to keep thee in the way, and to bring thee into the place which I have prepared. Beware of Him, and obey His voice, provoke Him not; for He will not pardon your transgressions; for MY name (YAHUAH) is in Him (Yahusha)." (Exodus 23:20-21)

> Note: One can well appreciate in the scripture above that a created angel, even one sent by YAHUAH HIMSELF—did not have the name of GOD in him or the ability to pardon.

---

215 Genesis 18:1, 3
216 Genesis 32:30
217 Daniel 3:25
218 Exodus 3:4
219 Exodus 13:21

7

GOD'S PICTURE BOOK

Yahusha in Manifestations and Types

The Holy Scriptures illustrate that GOD has a unique way of teaching. HE taught first by speaking HIS Word, which was recorded and became Scripture. But HE also taught by providing a model, a type. A model or type given in the Old Testament takes the form of an object, (e.g. the Tabernacle in the wilderness, its instruments and furnishings), or with a person (e.g. Moses, Aaron, Joseph, or David). These representations or representatives were a pre-figure of the actual, the authentic, and the promised. They were a progressive revelation of what was forthcoming. Each type would be a similitude of the genuine (antitype). Our understanding of scripture is expanded exponentially when we recognize that this is one of the ways GOD is teaching us of HIS redemptive plan.

At times Elohim would appear to the Israelites in the heavens. HE came at Sinai as a thunderous voice, a storm of smoke, fire, and a thick cloud.[220] HIS presence electrified the atmosphere and made the earth shake. HE instilled a holy fear into the people that they might know and obey HIS every Word. HE told the people through Moses that they were to sanctify themselves before they could even observe HIM from a distance. HE set a boundary around the base of the mountain to illustrate the great gulf which exists between creature and Creator.

No man or beast, then or now, can venture up GOD's Holy Mountain or come into HIS Holy presence and live unless he is first sanctified and then invited. That day only Moses, a redeemer (prefiguring Yahusha) and Aaron, a high priest (prefiguring Yahusha) were invited to cross the boundary at the foot of the mountain. Similarly, only the sanctified and the invited were permitted to enter the Holy of Holies. Today we must still go through the actual Redeemer and High Priest in order to approach the great "I Am."[221]

It is GOD that sets the boundaries. It is GOD who determines who may approach HIM and come into HIS presence! It is a Cross that allows us to cross that boundary!

---

220 Exodus 19: 1-25
221 Exodus 19:9-24, 20:18-21; 28:38

The Tabernacle in the Wilderness

The Torah abounds with typology, the greatest concentration of which is in the book of Exodus. "The Tabernacle is the greatest of all the Old Testament types of Christ and one of the great object lessons of spiritual truth. In its wonderful furniture, priesthood, and worship we see with a vividness we find nowhere else, the Glory and grace of the atonement purchased by Jesus, and the privilege of His redeemed people."[222]

When the Lord commissioned Moses to build this sanctuary, HE told him it was to be "after the pattern of the tabernacle."

> "And let them make me a sanctuary; that I may dwell among them. According to all that I shew thee, after the pattern of the tabernacle, and the pattern of all the instruments thereof, even so shall ye make it." (Exodus 25:8-9)

A pattern of course is only an outline or silhouette of the genuine and the authentic. The original "a greater and more perfect tabernacle (Yahusha), not made with the hands of men," was yet in heaven and still to appear.[223]

The pattern, we are told, was to be a sanctuary, a place of safety and a refuge. It would be set in the midst of HIS people so HE might dwell with them, and they with HIM. It would be the place where they were to bring their sins in order for them to be restored though not entirely expunged.[224] But this was only a pattern. The genuine Tabernacle, the living Tabernacle, the eternal Tabernacle, would delay His actual coming until the proper time.

> "But when the fullness of time was come, GOD sent forth HIS Son, made of woman, under the law, to redeem them that were under the law (the Jewish people), that we might receive the adoption of sons." (Galatians 4:4, 5)

> "And I heard a great voice out of heaven saying, Behold, the tabernacle of God is with men, and He will dwell with them, and they shall be his people, and God himself shall be with them, and be their God." (Revelation 21:3)

In typology, Yahusha would become the sacrifice; the atoning substitute for the man or woman who allowed Him to be offered in their stead. In type an animal would be slain; its blood poured out upon the ground and its lifeless and quartered body tied to the horns of the brazen altar. The smoke of the offering would then rise, becoming a sweet savor to the Father.[225]

---

222 Expositor, Arthur W. Pink
223 Hebrews 9:11
224 Hebrews 10:4
225 Ephesians 5:2

Yahusha was envisaged in the furnishings; the table and shew bread, the bread of life (the Word) which fed the priests (the Believers).[226] He was the lamp stand which brought light into an otherwise dark tent (the world).[227] He was the great vail in front of the Holy of Holies which hung between the Creator and creation and which needed to be passed through in order to approach YAHUAH. Yes, Yahusha was then, and is now the great vail which every man must pass through in order to enter into the Holy of Holies and the presence of the Almighty. And, like a veil that obscures ones' view of what lies beyond, so too is He the vail that one must approach before one can get a glimpse and understanding of GOD.

The Mercy Seat

The tablets of the Law which condemn the sinner were contained within the Ark. On top of the Ark was a golden cover known as the Mercy Seat. In type, the cover represented Yahusha—the mercy of GOD which covers the Law (the ten commandments) and shields GOD's people from the Law which otherwise condemns them.[228]

To this day, the physical Ark has been divinely and intentionally hidden to prevent men from making an idol from what is only a type. Rather, it is GOD's intent that in its absence they might discover the genuine Ark.

GOD's Mercy seat is still there and able to shield us from the law. Even now it can be found as "HE is nigh unto them that search for Him with a contrite heart."[229]

The Ark of the Covenant and the Mercy Seat (Image Source: GOODSALT)

> "The Lord is nigh unto all them that call upon Him, to all that call upon Him in truth. He will fulfil the desire of them that fear him: He also will hear their cry, and will save them." (Psalm 145:18, 19)

> "And ye shall seek me, and find me, when ye shall search for me with all your heart." (Jeremiah 29:13)

> Note: The vail (veil) which separated the Holy Place from the Holy of Holies was torn in two by the hand of GOD at the moment of Yahusha-Jesus' death on the Cross.[230] This was GOD's way of saying, now all men may have access to ME.

---

226 John 6:31-35
227 John 8:12
228 Exodus 25:21-22
229 Psalm 34:18
230 Mark 15:38

Recommended reading concerning typology; *Gleanings in Exodus*, Arthur W. Pink, Moody Press, 1981

Redeemer and Priest

In chapter 16 of the Book of Numbers, a Levite named Korah stirred up the Israelites against Moses and Aaron accusing them of assuming too much authority.

What Korah and his accomplices Dathan and Abiram did not understand was that Moses and Aaron were not self-appointed but that their appointments had come from the Most High GOD.

One grave mistake Korah made was thinking that because he was a Levite he could assume the role of the high priest and that it was simply a matter of taking a censor in hand and walking into the Holy of Holies. Korah publicly challenged Moses for leadership, and Moses responded, "it shall be that the man whom the Lord doth choose, he shall be holy (set apart)."[231] Moses then called for a showdown and told the rebels to appear the next day with their strange fire and incense.

The following day Korah, his accomplices, and the two hundred and fifty tribal princes who allied with Korah appeared before the Tabernacle. It was then that GOD spoke through Moses and afforded the people who were siding with Korah one final opportunity to separate themselves from the rebel leaders. Then, when Moses had finished speaking to the congregation, the three instigators, their families and all they owned were suddenly swallowed up by the earth. Immediately upon seeing the horrific fateful end of their leaders the two hundred and fifty tribal princes fled and cried in fear, but it was too late. They had been given one last opportunity to repent but had declined. Suddenly GOD unleashed fire from on high, and they were incinerated where they stood.

> "And the earth opened her mouth, and swallowed them...They and all that appertained to them went down alive into the pit, and the earth closed upon them: and they perish among the congregation. ...And there came out a fire from the Lord, and consumed the two hundred and fifty men that offered incense." (Numbers 16:32-33, 35)

It became exceedingly clear to those who had remained loyal to Moses and witnessed GOD's response that day that no one can just come into HIS presence or take the place of the appointed Redeemer and High Priest. To those who had watched the earth swallow men whole and saw fire from heaven consume the flesh of rebels, hell was no longer a theory or abstract concept.

> "For there is one God, and one mediator between God and men, the man Christ Jesus..." (1 Timothy 2:5)

> "Jesus said unto them, I AM the way the truth and the Life, no man cometh unto the Father, but by me." (John 14:6)

---

231 Numbers 16:7

"To him give all the prophets witness, that through his name whosoever believeth in him shall receive remission of sins." (Acts 10:43)

"Neither is there salvation in any other: for there is none other name under heaven given among men, whereby we must be saved." (Acts 4:12)

> Note: It needs to be understood that the rituals and sacrifices were all types and symbols. In and by themselves they don't accomplish anything. They were instituted "in type" to point us to the genuine article. It would be Messiah Yahusha-Christ Jesus who would fulfill all the roles of the sacrificial system. Not only would He be the High Priest that could free man of his sins, but also his scapegoat, his pascal lamb, and his final atonement.

Immanuel—GOD With us!

The Prophet Isaiah was sent by GOD to speak prophetically to Judah's King Ahaz. Syria had allied with Ephraim (the ten northern tribes) to defeat Judah.[232]

Centuries earlier YAHUAH had promised King David that HE would plant HIS people in their own land and afford them divine protection;[233] that is, so long as they remained faithful.

So it was that Isaiah went to a skeptical Ahaz to assure him Judah's enemies would not succeed. Ahaz remained cynical, so GOD, speaking through Isaiah challenged him. "Ask thee for a sign of the Lord thy God…"[234]

Ahaz could not bring himself to tempt GOD by asking for a sign, but GOD decided that HE was going to give him a sign regardless and it would be in the form of a prophecy. Though this prophecy would be well into Judah's future it would be established in Scripture as a Messianic covenant. It would also demonstrate that when GOD makes a promise, it will come to pass.

"The Lord himself shall give you a sign; Behold a virgin (Hebrew, המלע *almah*) shall conceive, and bear a son, and shall call His name Immanuel." (Isaiah 7:14)

This was to be the most profound and insightful prophecy in the Hebrew Scriptures, for it spoke of GOD HIMSELF coming to Earth. Not as a burning bush, nor as a Shekinah cloud or even as an angelic being, but as Yahusha (GOD of Salvation). He would be our Mashiach, coming to us in the virgin-born flesh of a man; Immanuel GOD with us!

Israel had not heeded the prophets and had even murdered some of them. Now GOD determined it was needful for HE HIMSELF to leave His throne in heaven, come down to earth and put on the flesh of a mortal man.[235]

---

232 Isaiah 7:2
233 2 Samuel 7:8-10
234 Isaiah 7:11
235 Luke 20:13

> Note: Point 1. A betrothed Jewess maiden (Hebrew, *almah*), under Jewish law would be unmarried and chaste; in a word—a virgin. If she were not a virgin, she might very well be stoned to death upon being found pregnant.[236] As shown in Isaiah 7:14, only a virgin would be the vessel which GOD would use to bring forth our Messiah. In contrast, the Masoretic text recognizes the Hebrew word *"almah"* but then forces the Hebrew word *"bethulah,"* which simply means an unmarried girl. But even if one imposes the word bethulah it doesn't change the fact that under Levitical law the maiden would still be a virgin or be subject to death by stoning.
>
> Point 2. The word "almah" is used just seven times in Scripture. The word virgin was first used when Hebrew scholars translated the word *almah* from the Hebrew into Greek. The Greek word the Hebrew scholars chose was *"parthenos,"* which correctly translated into English is "virgin."
>
> Note: An extensive list of eminent Jewish scholars who believed the word "almah" is best translated virgin would have to include: Dr. Leopold Cohen, Dr. David L. Cooper, Dr. Henry J. Heydt, Dr. Arthur W. Kac, Author Milton B. Lindberg and Dr. Sanford C. Mills.
>
> Point 3. A married woman who had "known a man" and become pregnant would not be an extraordinary "sign," nor would it be in keeping with the question posed to ask for a "sign." In contrast, a virgin becoming pregnant would certainly be an extraordinary sign. Only a divine conception where a virgin was "overshadowed" by GOD [237] would qualify as a "sign" (Hebrew, *owth*); definition: beacon, monument, evidence, mark, miracle.
>
> Point 4. The first prophecy in the Scriptures which Moses wrote or dictated concerning the coming of Messiah was Genesis 3:15. In this verse he spoke of Messiah as the "seed of the woman," not the seed of a man, which would be more appropriate. The reference to the women's seed underscores the virgin birth, indicating no earthly man was involved. Furthermore, the Lord would not be born from an act of sin, as David and Bathsheba learned when their child's life (conceived in sin) was forfeited.

With the prophets having only marginal successes in conveying GOD's will to the people; with the people in doubt of the veracity of the Scriptures, and with their continuous straying from the "old paths", there was no better way than for the Lord to come to earth as a man. Only in this way could He speak to them directly: teaching, confronting and comforting them while personally inviting them to come to Him and be restored.[238]

---

236 Leviticus 20:10
237 Luke 1:35
238 Matthew 21:33-39

8

PRECIOUS BLOOD

The Sacrificial Lamb

Did you ever wonder why YAHUAH would require the Israelites to sacrifice a firstborn male lamb before their departure from Egypt? Was this strange ritual meant to be an object lesson?

On the night of the first Passover (*Pesakh*), physical death came upon the firstborn male of any household which had not applied the lamb's blood to the doorframe of their abode.

Our Lord wasn't simply punishing Pharaoh and the Egyptians for not heeding Moses and refusing to give the Israelites their freedom. The consequence for not applying the blood was for the Egyptians (Gentiles) and Hebrews alike. That is, for any who would not apply the atonement's blood!

The application of the blood was the first and most important lesson the Israelites would be required to learn if they were to be GOD's chosen people. That fateful night the Israelites would come to understand that only the blood of the innocent purges the sins of the guilty. That night physical death would become symbolic of eternal death, and only the application of the blood would save the obedient life that night. Only the application of the blood will save the immortal soul!

"When I see the blood I will Pass over you." Apply the Blood and Live! (Image Source: GOODSALT)

Taking hyssop in hand,[239] dipping it in the lamb's blood, and then applying the blood to one's own door frame (figuratively one's self), was in type, the only way eternal death could thereafter be avoided.[240]

This Paschal lamb was in type the substitutionary object (Hebrew, *Korban Pesakh*), which Yahusha would afterward become.

> "For the life of the flesh is in the blood: and I have given it to you upon the altar to make an atonement for your souls: for it is the blood that maketh an atonement for the soul." (Leviticus 17:11)

An act of faith on an object of love
(Image Source: GOODSALT)

Let us look even closer at what took place during that first Passover. Just prior to the Exodus, the Lord commanded that a firstborn, male lamb; without blemish (figuratively without sin) be taken into each home and kept for several days.[241] In a very real sense, the animal became a family pet. This emotional attachment was part of YAHUAH's object lesson. Just as it was necessary for one to become attached to the animal before it was sacrificed, so must one become emotionally attached to their Savior! Only then can He be made an offering for (their) sins.[242]

This entire experience, from selecting the perfect lamb to adopting it into their home and heart, to the final act of sacrificing it was far more than a mere annual ritual. Like Abram preparing to sacrifice Isaac, it was an act of faith on an object of love meant to convey the need for a blood sacrifice. "And almost all things are by the law purged with blood; and without shedding of blood (there) is no remission." (Hebrews 9:22)

YAHUAH (as the father) did no less than what HE asked Abraham to do; even completing the sacrificial act. HE proved HIS love to each of us, not hesitating to sacrifice HIS own beloved son on a Roman Cross.[243]

---

239   Psalm 51:7
240   Exodus 12:13
241   Leviticus 22:19
242   Isaiah 53:10
243   John 3:16

That day—the day of His execution, Yahusha was made a spectacle in front of the world. Naked, bleeding, in indescribable agony and slowly suffocating to death, He hung between heaven and earth as the *Korban Pesakh*—that all might see the cost of their sin and redemption.[244]

Only by the Blood

We are all familiar with the story of Adam and Eve and how man fell from GOD's grace and was banished from HIS presence all because of one seemingly small act of disobedience. But if we look closely at Genesis 3:21 we see something exceedingly important which is often overlooked. Upon eating the forbidden fruit Adam and Eve immediately knew good from evil and realized they were naked. So, we are told, they tried as best they could to hide their shame by making aprons from fig leaves. The fig leaf aprons were in type the invention of man not unlike his religion, which he practices believing that it will in some way hide his sins and make him acceptable. However, we see that GOD did not acknowledge a covering of fig leaves as a sign of their repentance. The leaves were not adequate to cover the couple's sin from HIS pure eyes. So, GOD HIMSELF took innocent animals and slew them.

> "Unto Adam also and to his wife did the Lord God make coats of skins, and clothed them."
> (Genesis 3:21)

No doubt Adam and Eve were horrified at what GOD was doing. They had never seen blood spurting from a living creature, watching as its life drained out of it as the ground drank its blood. GOD had made the first sacrifice for man. In that one act Adam and Eve must have suddenly realized the cost of their disobedience; something would have to die in order for them to go on living. But the story is not over. We are then told that GOD covered their shame with the untanned flesh of an animal; its bloody hide covered their naked bodies. Blood became their covering.

Next, we read in Genesis of Eve's two sons; Abel, a keeper of sheep and Cain, a tiller of the ground. When it came time to make an offering to GOD Abel took the best of his flock and sacrificed it to the Lord. Abel's offering was acceptable to our Lord because it contained blood. Cain offered the work of his hands and the fruit of the ground, which was cursed. The work of his hands GOD found unacceptable. The fruit of the ground is comparable to what man can produce by works and mitzvah; the best of which are by comparison to the blood atonement "as filthy rags."[245]

We have been "justified freely (without cost) by HIS grace through the redemption that is in Christ Jesus: whom GOD hath set forth to be a propitiation (atoning victim) through faith in His blood, to declare His righteousness for the remission of sins that are past, through the forbearance (mercy) of GOD…"[246]

---

244 Isaiah 52:14-15; 53:5-12
245 Isaiah 64:6
246 Romans 3:25

On the night in which He was betrayed Yahusha said, "for this is my blood of the new testament, which is shed for many for the remission of sins."[247]

In another example we blend blood with faith. GOD tested Abraham's faith by asking him to take his only son Isaac, who Abraham loved more than anything else in the world and offer him as a burnt offering to HIM. Abraham remembered and believed GOD who had promised that he and his wife Sarah (Sarai) would have a son,[248] and that through that seed (Isaac) would come forth a nation.[249] Somehow by a faith; a faith which would go beyond all reason, Abraham believed that Isaac would somehow live on or be resurrected even if he were then to die by his own hand. Taking only a knife, wood and a fire pot, Abraham lead Isaac up Mount Moriah. Once the wood was prepared and the moment was at hand to offer the sacrifice, Isaac asked his father,

> "Behold the fire and the wood: but where is the lamb for a burnt offering? And Abraham said, My son, God will provide Himself a lamb for a burnt offering..." (Genesis 22:7, 8)

Consider the unique way this scripture is worded; "GOD will provide "HIMSELF a lamb." This is just what GOD did. HE provided Himself as the sacrificial lamb.[250]

Preserved by the Blood

> "For the life of the flesh is in the blood: and I have given it to you upon the altar to make atonement for your souls: for it is the blood that maketh atonement for the soul." (Leviticus 17:11)

In our imperfect state we cannot enter into GOD's Holy presence or HIS Holy kingdom any more than the High Priest could enter the Holy of Holies while sin was yet unatoned for.

When that one day each year; the Day of Attornment arrived, the high priest underwent exhaustive preparation and purification before entering into the sanctuary of the Tabernacle.

Yes, he had prayed. Yes, he had selected the animal for a sin offering. Yes, he had put on immaculate garments exclusive for that occasion. Yes, he had readied the costly incense and the censer with which to send up a sweet savor to the heavens. Yes, he washed in the cleansing laver to remove the filth of his humanity. Yes, he had passed the brazen altar and remember that a sacrificial victim had to be offered and lashed to the horns. But was there anything he had forgotten to do? Just one omission or departure from the divine instructions could have dire consequences.[251]

---

247 Matthew 26:28
248 Genesis 18:10
249 Genesis 13:16
250 Genesis 22:8-13
251 Numbers 3:4

With some anxiety he proceeds into the antechamber—the Holies. Carrying the censer with its glowing coals taken from the brazen altar and the aromatic incense that GOD had prescribed, he anxiously advances toward the Great Vail. Before the curtain stands the Altar of Incense–prefiguring a mortal Christ who stands between GOD and man. There he pauses to burn the incense. The smoke rises with the prayers of the priest who dares not proceed until he has expressed his love for his maker and begs forgiveness for himself and a penitent people; a prerequisite for entry.

Though knowing GOD had not yet descended into the Holy of Holies; still with apprehension he takes censer in hand and passes through the tapestry into the Holy of Holies. The smoke and vapors envelope the small chamber; its fragrance likened to a prayer petitioning an audience with the King. The priest then leaves as he had entered. There he breathes a sigh of relief; he has made the appeal to connect with *El 'Elyon*—GOD Most High.

Only by the Blood (Image Source: GOODSALT)

But now he must return with the offering itself and come into the presence of the Great I AM. If all has been done in accordance with divine order and with the utmost reverence, he would find YAHUAH HIMSELF awaiting his return. A transcendent GOD would be hovering between the wings of the cherubim figures atop the golden Mercy Seat. The Ark itself would reflect the glow of GOD, as had Moses' face when he came into the presence of the great I AM.[252]

Returning to the outer courtyard, he collects the warm blood from the ceremonial bullock. He returns to the tent and again enters the antechamber. There he stands, pausing for a moment to gather himself with only the glow from the lampstand to befriend him. The thought must have raced through the priest's mind; will GOD accept what I offer? If HE does not, I will likely not survive.

Before him, separating him from the GOD of all creation hangs the Great Curtain of blue (celestial heaven), purple (royalty), scarlet (glory) and white (purity and grace). The priest pauses again at the Altar of Incense to pay homage to his Maker. Then, stepping forward, he dips his fingers into the basin of sacrificial blood and sprinkles it on the Vail. He must now lift the Vail and pass through this maze of multilayered fine linen which obscures and separates man from the Great I AM.[253]

---

252 Exodus 34:29, 30
253 Exodus 3:14

I can envision the priest as he moves ever so slowly through the Vail. With his arms extended he holds the basin of blood in trembling hands. Again, the thought races through his mind. Will GOD except his offering? As he precedes through the curtain it will be the sacrificial blood which enters the Holy of Holies before he himself has passed through.

The windowless chamber is aglow with the light of GOD. The Father's holy eyes fall upon the basin of blood. The man is eclipsed by what he presents. It is the blood offering which GOD finds acceptable and allows the priest to come into HIS luminous presence. In some inexplicable way the mortal man, born in iniquity–along with all his past sins have somehow been masked by the blood.[254]

As the priest approaches the Ark and having already applied the blood to his own flesh, he immediately sprinkles the blood on and before the Mercy Seat. The blood applied and now finding himself standing in the aura of the Almighty. He is suddenly transfixed by the thought, "HE has accepted my offering. I am still alive! The blood has preserved me! My sins and the sins of the people have been pardoned."

When YAHUAH's eyes fell upon the basin of blood HIS thoughts were immediately projected into the future where HE would see HIS Son's efficacious blood offered for the man or woman who had put their life and faith in His priceless blood.

The priests suddenly remember what Moses had heard from GOD at the first Passover, "and when I see the blood I will pass over you."[255]

Now it all made sense! Now he understood why GOD slew an innocent animal to cover Adam and Eve's guilt and why Abel's sacrifice was acceptable and Cain's failed. Now he understood why Abraham was told to sacrifice Isaac and was then restrained, and how in his stead GOD provided the sacrifice. Now he understood why that preceding Passover an innocent lamb had to die, and why its blood had to be painted on the lintel and door posts of ones' abode. Now he understood why the prophet Isaiah had prophesied the "righteous servant" would need to come to earth as a man and die, and in doing so "shall bare the sins of many."[256]

The Great Vail was in type symbolic of Yahusha–Jesus,[257] when at Calvary, at the moment of His death the vail was rent in two from top to bottom by the hand of GOD. Access to GOD suddenly became available to all men. But like the priest, each one of us must pass through the Vail (Jesus) alone and apply His blood to themselves in order to enter into the presence of the Great I Am.

> "…He (Yahusha) hath poured out his soul unto death: and he was numbered with the transgressors; and he (Yahusha) bare the sin of many, and made intercession for the transgressors." (Isaiah 53:12)

---

254 Isaiah 1:18
255 Exodus 12:13
256 Isaiah 53:12
257 Hebrews 10:20

The Sheep Gate

On the day of His execution, moments before the paschal lambs were slain, Yahusha was forced to carry the crossbar on which He would be nailed and hung. On this route to a hill called Golgotha, He passed through what was called the "sheep gate."[258] The sheep gate was the only gate where the sacrificial lamb would have to pass through on the way to its atoning death. This time that lamb would be manifested in the personage of a Savior. He would have to become the Paschal lamb.

Eternal life is attainable, but only when one is reconciled to GOD through the blood. Our only hope as stated in the Torah and which was never rescinded still lies in the sacrificial blood of an unblemished lamb.[259]

The Aphikomen

At Pesach seder it is customary for the head of house (usually the father) to take three matzos and place them on the table, one on top of the other. He then breaks the middle one into two unequal parts, wrapping the larger piece in a clean cloth and hides it. Then at the close of the meal he recovers it from its hiding place and shares it among the members of the family. That piece of matzo is the called the *Aphikomen*.

The *Shulchan Aruch* (the most widely accepted compilation of Jewish law) bids the Aphikomen to be treated with special reverence because it represents the Korban Pesach. Now, by faith each of us must find that which was broken and hidden from view. Then it is to be consumed with special reverence.

Yiddish linguist and Hebrew paleographer Solomon Birnbaum wrote, "there is a derivative of a word in the Greek, *erchomia*,[260] which has exactly the same meaning as our Aphikomen; it means, I CAME".[261]

The Seder—Remembrance

The Lord's Supper which Christians today celebrate as "Communion" is the carry-over of the Jewish seder. It was instituted at the time of the Messiah's crucifixion. Before that time the only Passover was the one inaugurated by Moses and which Talmudic sage Hillel observed at the crossroads of the millennia. After Yahusha's death and while the Temple stood, his disciples being devout Jews observed both memorials. When the Temple was destroyed and the sacrificial system ended, His followers continued with what was the fulfilment of the Passover—the Lord's Supper.

---

258 Nehemiah 3:1
259 Leviticus 17:11
260 *Strong's Exhaustive Concordance*, Gk., #2064; Thayer Greek-Lexicon
261 Solomon Birnbaum, *The Story that could not be forgotten*, Hermon House Pub. 1953, Lynbrook, NY

> "...and when he had given thanks, he brake it, and said, Take, eat: this is my body, which is broken for you: this do in remembrance of me. After the same manner also he took the cup, when he had supped, saying, This cup is the new testament (B'rit Chadashah)—paid for in my blood: this do ye, as oft as ye drink it, in remembrance of me." (1 Corinthians 11: 24-25)

Yahusha-Jesus's words ring out,[262] for remembrance of the sacrifice of the Lamb is why the Passover is a permanent decree!

The Brit Milah—The Circumcision

While the illustration of types in the Scriptures sometimes appear to be abstract, illogical, and even bizarre, they paint lasting images in our minds. They are meant to compel us to look for the spiritual representation, meaning, or requirement. Comparisons are a fundamental way the Lord uses to allow us to see what HE is ultimately attempting to show us. Such was the mandatory Brit Milah.

Beginning with Abram, a people would be set aside for YAHUAH and a nation was established. Abram's name would thereafter be Abraham, meaning the father of a multitude. Such an auspicious occasion would require a covenant, and not only a covenant, but a blood covenant. The purpose of circumcision was to ratify this promise and simultaneously illustrate several requirements needed to become a child of the Most High.[263]

First, there is a need for one's flesh (our human desires and tendencies), and even the way in which we think to be cut away. Second; when the male foreskin is cut, a drop of blood is shed, making this act a blood covenant with YAHUAH. Third, as Moses told us in the Torah, physical circumcision is a type; a prelude to the spiritual circumcision of the heart.

> "And it shall come to pass, when all these things are come upon thee, the blessings and the curse, which I have set before thee, and thou shall call them to mind among the nations, whither the Lord thy GOD hath driven thee, And thou shalt return unto the Lord thy GOD, and shall obey HIS voice according to all that I command thee this day, thou and thy children, with all thy heart, and with all thy soul; that then the Lord will turn thy captivity, and have compassion upon thee, and will return and gather thee from the nations, wither the Lord hath scattered thee... And the LORD thy GOD will bring thee into the land which thy fathers possessed and thou shalt possess it; and HE will do thee good, and multiply thee above thy fathers. And the Lord will circumcise thy heart, and the heart of thy seed, to love the Lord thy GOD with all thy heart, and with all thy soul, that thou mayest live." (Deuteronomy 30:1-6)

---

262 1 Corinthians 11:24-25
263 Genesis 17:10-14

The circumcision of the heart is the authentic circumcision. In reality GOD cares little about a small piece of skin, but everything about our heart toward HIM.[264] This spiritual circumcision will take place (nationally) during Israel's final restoration. At that time the "stony heart" (a hard-remorseless heart) will be removed. A "new heart" (a heart for GOD) and a "new spirit," (the Holy Spirit—the Rauch H'Qodesh) will be divinely implanted in those who receive Yahusha as their personal Savior.[265]

But one does not have to wait for this to happen. Any individual who earnestly seeks HIM (YAHUAH) "with all of their heart" can find Him (Yahusha) and receive Him and the Holy Spirit at any time.[266]

The Star of Jacob—Our National Emblem!

> "...There shall come a Star out of Jacob and the scepter shall rise out of Israel. Out of Jacob shall come He that shall have dominion..." (Numbers 24:17, 19)

It is He the Star of Jacob that adorns our flag and testifies to the world that it is He—our Messiah in whom we put our trust.[267] It is the Star of David—our coat of arms that adorns our battle tanks and fighter aircraft when we go to war. It is the Star which brings the victory. It is this Star that will come out of the East and vanquish our enemies in the end of days.[268] It is the Star who emancipates those that belong to Him from death to life. It is this Star—our sovereign king on whom the government of the world will one day rest.[269]

He has come in the flesh;[270] being born from the seed of Jacob[271] and from the tribe of Judah.[272] He came from the stem and root of Jesse,[273] and from the bowels of David.[274] He is the original of that which is represented in the sacrifices, the offerings, in our feasts, and in our Holy Days. He is the "Rose of Sharon," the "Lily of the Valley," the "Chiefest among ten thousand," and "the Bright and Morning Star."[275] He was David's, "Rock," "Fortress," and "Deliverer."[276] In Him did he trust.[277]

---

264 Romans 2:28, 29
265 Ezekiel 36:26; Jeremiah 4:4; Zechariah 12:10
266 Jeremiah 29:13
267 Psalm 21:7; 91:2
268 Matthew 24:27; Zechariah 14:3, 12
269 Isaiah 9:6, 7
270 Isaiah 7:14
271 Numbers 24:17
272 Genesis 49:10
273 Isaiah 11:1, 10
274 2 Samuel 7:12
275 Song of Songs 2:1; 5:10; Revelation 22:16
276 Psalm 18:2
277 Psalm 143:8

Yahusha can be your "City of Refuge, the Rock of your Strength," "The GOD of your Salvation;" "Your portion in the land of the living," "Your dwelling place." All you need do is, as David did—invite Him into your heart.[278] "Blessed are all they that put their trust in him…"[279]

> "For thy Maker is thine husband; thy Lord of Hosts is His name; and thy Redeemer, the Holy One of Israel; The GOD of the whole earth shall He be called." (Isaiah 54:5)

The Jewish Feasts

The feasts described in Leviticus were meant to be observed by the Jewish people so they could recognize their Mashiach by linking the events of the past with the expectation of prophecy.

In Leviticus 23 we have an account of seven great feasts. These feasts were a prophecy and a foreshadowing of future events. Some have been fulfilled while others are yet to come. As with all of scripture, the centerpiece is Yahusha-Jesus,[280] and each feast has a correlation to and with Him.

These feasts were holy memorials or celebrations instituted by the Lord. HE promised that if the males of each family would go up at a set time to Jerusalem to keep these feasts HE would look after their families. When the people and particularly their religious leaders became excessively orthodox and cared more about their image, phylacteries, and their seats in the synagogue than in the Lord HIMSELF,[281] HE was repulsed. Isaiah, speaking for the Lord seven hundred years earlier had made it abundantly clear "Your new moons and your appointed feasts My soul hateth; they are a trouble to Me; I am weary to bear them."[282]

> Note: It is for this reason that New Testament scripture refers to the feasts as the Feasts of the Jews, rather than the Feasts of the Lord.[283]

The Feasts are seven in number and if we include the weekly Sabbath, we have eight. But the Sabbath was to be observed at home every week while the other feasts were observed annually at Jerusalem. So, the Sabbath stands apart, with the Passover being foremost because of what it represents.

The feasts may be divided into two sections of four and three. The first section includes the Passover, the Feast of Unleavened Bread, First Fruits, and Pentecost. Then there was an interval of four months, followed by the Feast of Trumpets, the Day of Atonement, and Tabernacles. The first four feasts foreshadow truths connected with this present dispensation and Yahusha's first coming; the last three concern themselves with Yahusha's next coming and the future blessings in store for the Jewish people. Between the two comings is the "interval" of the present dispensation—"the Church Age."

---

278 Psalm 46:1; Isaiah 17:10; Psalm 142:5; Psalm 90:1
279 Psalm 2:12
280 Matthew 13:35
281 Mathew 23:1-7
282 Isaiah 1:4
283 John 5:1

A correlation (types and anti-types) between the feasts of the Old Testament (OT) and their fulfillment in the New Testament (NT) are presented in their progressive order.

The Passover Feast was the memorial of the Israelites' redemption from Egypt. The Passover Lamb that was slain is symbolic of Christ who was slain for the redemption of man.

The Feast of Unleavened Bread began the day after Passover and lasted seven days. It marks the journey of faith taken by the Israelites. The New Testament fulfilment is the walk of faith that begins immediately upon ones' redemption. A new life has begun, and a sanctified walk begins.

> Note: The bread, being unleavened means that sin (leaven) has been removed. When Christ died the New Covenant went into effect. The totality of it was that sin could be removed and man could be sanctified.

The next feast is First Fruits which began after the first day of the Feast of Unleavened Bread. The Feast of First Fruits foreshadowed the resurrection of Christ. Paul spoke of the Lord as "the First fruits of the resurrection of the dead." That is, Christ became the first flesh offering to GOD. By His redemption and resurrection, He opened heaven's gates for a harvest of those souls who would thereafter follow Him.[284]

Pentecost is the English transliteration for the Greek *pentekonta hemeras*; hence penta—as in pentagon, is a five-sided geometric figure. The Hebrew *ha'missim yom* means fifty days. It would be fifty days after the feast of First Fruits that the Jewish people celebrated the Feast of Pentecost. The fifty days refers to the number of days (seven weeks) from the offering of barley sheaves at the beginning of the Passover until the next feast. The next day (the fiftieth day) the people would celebrate the Feast of Pentecost. Since seven weeks elapsed between the two feasts, it was called, Hebrew *hag sabu ot*, Feast of Weeks.[285] It marks the completion of the barley harvest which began when the sickle was first put to the grain[286] and the sheaf were waved—"the marrow of the Sabbath."[287] It is also called *hag haqqasir*, most appropriately named the Feast of the Harvest and *yom habbikkurim*, Day of First Fruits.[288]

At the appointed feast two baked loaves of new, fine, leavened flour were ground from the grain and brought out of each home to wave before the Lord.[289] The two loaves represented the Jews and Gentiles who would inaugurate the Church the day of Pentecost. On that day hundreds must have heard the word and three hundred accepted it and were "born again."[290] "For by one Spirit are we all baptized into one body, whether Jew or Gentile, whether we be bond or free; and have been all made to drink into one Spirit."[291]

---

284 1 Corinthians 15:23
285 Exodus 34:22; Deuteronomy 16:10
286 Deuteronomy 16:9
287 Leviticus 23:11
288 Exodus 23:16; Numbers 28:26
289 Leviticus 23:17–20
290 Acts 2:41
291 1 Corinthians 12:13

To simplify the teaching, the following is offered illustrating their Types (OT) and their corresponding Anti-Types (NT):

Feast – Type:	Symbolizes:	Anti-Type:
1. "Passover" (Leviticus 23:4, 5; Exodus 12:1–14)	Atonement Jesus Death	(1 Corinthians 5:7)
2. "Unleavened Bread" (Leviticus 6:8; Exodus 12:15–20)	Sanctification	A believer's holy walk (1 Corinthians 5:8)
3. "First Fruits" The marrow after the Sabbath (Leviticus 23:10–12)		Yahusha-Resurrection (1 Corinthians 15:22, 23)
4. "Pentecost" (Leviticus 23:15–20)	The Birth of the Church	(Acts 2:1–4, 41)

The interval between Pentecost and Trumpets typifies the present dispensation where the Holy Spirit, the Rauch Ha Qodesh is in the process of gathering out the Church.

The Feast of Trumpets (the first day of the seventh month) ushers in the Jewish New Year which began with the blowing of the trumpets. The trumpets were a call to assemble and for the journeying of the camps.[292] The span between Pentecost and Trumpets was a time when the "Harvest of Vintage" was gathered in. It typifies a future time after the Lord returns when the Jewish people will be summoned back to Jerusalem by angelic trumpeters to celebrate the Feast of Trumpets.[293]

> "And he shall send his angels with a great sound of a trumpet, and they shall gather together his elect (the Jewish people) from the four winds, from one end of heaven to the other." (Matthew 24:31)

5. "Feast of Trumpets" (Leviticus 23:24, 25)	Calling the Assembly, The gathering of Israel. (Matthew 24:29–31)	
6. "Day of Atonement" (Leviticus 23:26–32)	Redemption Israel recognizes their Messiah. (Zechariah 12:10)	
7. "Feast of Tabernacles" (Leviticus 23:33–39)	Sabbath Rest Israel's Millennial Rest. (Amos 9:13–15; Zechariah 14:16–21)	

---

292 Num. 10:1–10
293 Jeremiah 16:14, 15; Isaiah 11:11; Amos 9:14, 15; Matthew 24:29–31

At the outset of this topic of the "Feasts" I spoke of there being an eighth feast that stands apart from the others—referring to the weekly Sabbath. The Feast of Tabernacles began on the Sabbath. It continued seven days, followed by a Sabbath.[294] This Sabbath took place on the eighth day and speaks of the time which will follow the one thousand years (Yahusha's Millennial Reign). This will be the eighth and final dispensation when GOD will create a New Heaven and a New Earth for HIS own.

> 8. The Sabbath, The Fullness of Time The New Heaven and the New Earth.

"And I saw a new heaven and a new earth: for the first heaven and the first earth were passed away; and there was no more sea. And I John saw the holy city, new Jerusalem, coming down from God out of heaven, prepared as a bride adorned for her husband. And I heard a great voice out of heaven saying, Behold, the tabernacle of God is with men, and he will dwell with them, and they shall be his people, and God himself shall be with them, and be their God. And God shall wipe away all tears from their eyes; and there shall be no more death, neither sorrow, nor crying, neither shall there be any more pain: for the former things are passed away. And he that sat upon the throne said, Behold, I make all things new. And he said unto me, Write: for these words are true and faithful. And he said unto me, It is done. I (Yahusha-Jesus) am Alpha and Omega, the beginning and the end. I will give unto him that is athirst of the fountain of the water of life freely. He that overcometh shall inherit all things; and I will be his God, and he shall be my son." (Revelation 21:1-7)

Cross the Jordan

Yahusha—like Joshua, has taken the Jewish people to the edge of the Jordan River.[295] There on the distant shore lies the promise of rest and joy; the Promised land. But one must first cross the Jordan just as one must cross physical death to enter eternal life, and the only way for an individual to cross is by the Cross. I speak of the spiritual awakening of the individual and of the nation of Israel.

In terms of approximately when in the end times the nation of Israel will spiritually "cross over" is not an enigma. We may have been made privy to a secret. "Yet there shall be a space between you and it, about two thousand cubits by measure: come not near unto it, that ye may know the way by which ye must go: for ye have not passed this way (from death to life) heretofore."[296]

I dare say it has been a space of nearly two thousand years since the Savior gave His life for us and showed us that the way is the way of the Cross!

Each of us stands on the brink of the Jordan. We have never passed this way before; from life to death, to eternal life or eternal death. Now it is crucial, that just as Joshua's followers followed

---

294 Leviticus 23:39
295 Joshua 3:8
296 Joshua 3:4

the priests (Believers) who carried the Ark (Yahusha) before the people and proceeded into the Jordan, so are we to.[297] Today, He stands on the other side of that distant shore in the Promised Land, beckoning His people to recognize Him and Cross over.

> "Whom having not seen, ye love; in whom though now ye see Him not, yet believing, ye rejoice with joy unspeakable and full of glory." (1 Peter 1:8)

> Note: A cubit (Hebrew *ammah*), is a measurement which describes a distance or a span.[298] It can be presented as a metaphor.

---

297 Joshua 3:11
298 Gensenius Hebrew – Chaldee Lexicon of the Old Testament, Baker, Hebrew #520

9

THE KINGDOM OF DAVID

David Found His Mashiach

Scripture tells us that when the Messiah returns He will be King over all the earth.[299] He will set up His kingdom in Zion and rule from His Jerusalem.[300] He will appoint kings over the nations, and David shall be His king over the nation of Israel.

(Image Source: GOODSALT)

> "But they shall serve the Lord their GOD and David their king, who I will raise up." (Jeremiah 30:9)

> "Behold the days come, saith the Lord, that I will perform that good thing which I have promised unto the house of Israel and to the house of Judah. In those days, and at that time, will I cause the Branch of righteousness (a descendent of David,) to grow up unto David; and He (Yahusha) shall execute judgment and righteousness in the land." (Jeremiah 33:14-15)

Did you ever wonder why, while YAHUAH will give dominion of the earth to Yahusha and that afterward Yahusha will appoint David king over the nation of Israel? Simply stated it is because David had an incredible heart for GOD which we see amplified in many of the Psalms. We gather from these love sonnets that as a young shepherd boy tending his father's flock David

---

299 Psalm 2:6; 47:2, 6
300 Psalm 48:2

must have spent countless hours communing with GOD and developed a deep and intimate relationship with HIM. David found what escapes most of us; it is possible to have a personal relationship with the Almighty.

Well in advance of the time when a replacement for King Saul would be needed, GOD sent the Prophet Samuel to search out and anoint a young shepherd boy who would one day become Israel's greatest king; and why? Hear the words the Lord spoke to Samuel.

> "Look not on his countenance, or on the height of his stature; because I have refused him: for the Lord seeth not as man seeth; for man looketh on the outward appearance, but the Lord looketh on the heart." (1 Samuel 16:7)

It would be David's incredible heart for GOD and the relationship he developed with GOD which gave him the confidence to take on and defeat the giant Goliath.[301] It would be the same heart which recognized that GOD had appointed Saul king that compelled David to spare Saul's life on two occasions.[302]

At times David would fail his Lord miserably as when enamored with beautiful Bathsheba he impregnated her and then arranged the death of her husband.[303] Though he would pay for his various mistakes numerous times and in numerous ways, he never gave up on his Lord, and his Lord never gave up on him. Neither will the Lord give up on any man or woman so long as they, like David, keep their heart for GOD and follow David's example.

The 5 "R's": Realize, Repent, Return, be Restored...

Did you know that David was a crier? Yes, he would cry out to the Lord,

> "Have mercy upon me, O God, according to thy loving kindness: according unto the multitude of thy tender mercies blot out my transgressions. Wash me thoroughly from mine iniquity, and cleanse me from my sin. For I acknowledge my transgressions: and my sin is ever before me." (Psalm 51:1-3)

REALIZE: One day David suddenly had an epiphany when the prophet Nathan showed him his sins. He had been having an affair with Bathsheba and arranged for the death of her husband Uriah.[304] Suddenly David realized what he had done.

> "I acknowledged my sin unto thee, and mine iniquity have I not hid. I said, I will confess my transgressions unto the Lord; and thou forgavest the iniquity of my sin. Selah." (Psalm 32:5)

---

301 1 Samuel 17:26-32
302 1 Samuel 24:6; 26:9-11
303 2 Samuel 11:15
304 2 Samuel 12:1-13

REPENT: Unlike some who would dismiss the convicting voice of the Holy Spirit when their conscience incriminates them, David accepted responsibility and allowed the Holy Spirit to convict him. He admitted his guilt and begged for forgiveness. He did not ask Nathan or the High Levite priest to forgive him but sought it from the only one who can forgive, GOD his Savior. In an act of desperation, he cried out,

> "Create in me a clean heart, O God; and renew a right spirit within me. Cast me not away from thy presence; and take not thy Holy Spirit from me. Restore unto me the joy of thy salvation; and uphold me with thy free spirit." (Psalm 51:10-12)

RETURN and be **RESTORED:** Once David earnestly sought forgiveness, he felt the grace of GOD settle upon him. He knew he was restored and once more in a right relationship with GOD.

> "The Lord is my shepherd; I shall not want. He maketh me to lie down in green pastures: he leadeth me beside the still waters. He restoreth my soul: he leadeth me in the paths of righteousness for his name's sake." (Psalm 23:1-3)

David realized something many of us were either never taught or have chosen to ignore. Sin does not go away, nor can it be paid for with good intentions, good deeds, or an apology. According to Scripture, unless one can keep GOD's law and the 613 mitzvot perfectly, (and of course no one can), then we have failed to meet the divine criteria to attain heaven.

> "Behold, all souls are Mine; as the soul of the father, so also the soul of the son is Mine: the soul that sinneth, it shall die." (Ezekiel 18:4)

> "Therefore by the deeds of the law there shall no flesh be justified in HIS sight: for the Law is but the knowledge of sin." (Romans 3:20)

There is a fifth "R" in the Psalms. It is a **REVELATION** of the Messiah. David, with a searching heart was given this revelation early on. He was able to see a thousand years into the future and see not only Yahusha's coming, but His death and resurrection.

David saw his Messiah. Can you see Him in these Psalms?

> "Kiss (an expression of Love) the Son (Yahusha), lest HE (YAHUAH) be angry, and ye perish from the way... Blessed are all they that put their trust in Him (Yahusha)." (Psalm 2:12)

> "Have mercy upon me, O Lord; consider my trouble which I suffer of them that hate me, thou that liftest me up from the gates of death: that I may shew forth all thy praise in the gates of the daughter of Zion: I will rejoice in thy Salvation (Yahusha)." (Psalm 9:13-14)

> "Therefore my heart is glad, and my glory rejoiceth: my flesh also shall rest in hope. For thou wilt not leave my soul in hell; neither wilt thou suffer thine Holy One (Messiah Yahusha) to see corruption (decay in the grave)." (Psalm 16:10)

David knew that because he loved and placed his trust in the Holy One of Israel, he would one day be resurrected from the grave as would the Messiah after his death. David knew by faith in the mercies of GOD that he would become a partaker of the glorious promise of spending eternity with his Lord.

> "The Lord (Yahovah) said unto my Lord: (Adon- Sovereign- Messiah) Sit thou at MY right hand (at the right hand of the GODhead) until I make thy enemies thy footstool." (Psalm 110:1)

> "Thou will shew me the path of Life:... at thy right hand (GOD's right hand—sits Messiah Yahusha) there are pleasures for evermore." (Psalm 16:11)

David knew of the second person of the GODhead and called Him both "Lord and Savior."

> "We will rejoice in thy salvation (Yahusha), and in the name of our GOD we will set up our banners: the Lord fulfil all thy petitions. Now know I that the Lord saveth his anointed; he will hear him from his holy heaven with the saving strength of his right hand (Yahusha)." (Psalm 20:5-6)

> "The Lord is my light and my salvation (Yahusha); whom shall I fear? the Lord is the strength of my life; of whom shall I be afraid?" (Psalm 27:1)

> "Oh that the salvation (Yahusha) of Israel were come out of Zion! When God bringeth back the captivity of his people, Jacob shall rejoice, and Israel shall be glad." (Psalm 53:6)

David's salvation began with his admission of guilt. He then cried out to GOD in desperation, knowing the penalty for sin was eternal death.

We do not read in 2 Samuel 12 that David went to the human priest after acknowledging his sin, nor do we read that he brought a sin offering to the Tabernacle, though he undoubtably did. Still, if that were all that was needed to absolve one of his sins it would be most convenient and expedient. But, in reality there is no forgiveness without repentance,[305] and even with repentance, a ransom must be paid. David's recompense would be that though his own life would be spared, his first child's life would be forfeited.[306] His child was conceived in sin; but then all of us are sinners and "shapen in iniquity."[307]

---

305 Luke 13:5
306 2 Samuel 12:13, 14
307 Psalm 51:5

> Note: GOD can and does forgive sin, but the consequence of having sinned remains while we are on this earth. If man sins against his body for example, smoking, he will likely pay a price. If man sins against his spouse or loved ones, sooner or later his heart will be broken, even though he has been forgiven. Like a wound to the flesh, the scar remains.

The Sacrifice

Each and every year like clockwork, Jewish men went to the Tent of the Congregation or to the Temple leading their choice animal to be sacrificed. The animal was his ransom, his replacement, his scapegoat. Still, it was an annual offering. The blood of a sheep, goat, or bull ox was only a temporary remedy; it could not permanently eradicate the sin. Each year the solemn ceremony had to be repeated for its intent was to teach that a greater blood atonement was needed. Only a flawless sacrifice; a human for a human could permanently absolve a persons' sin once and for all and forever!

> "To what purpose is the multitude of your sacrifices unto me? saith the Lord: I am full of the burnt offerings of rams, and the fat of fed beasts; and I delight not in the blood of bullocks, or of lambs, or of he goats." (Isaiah 1:11)

> "For he (YAHUAH) hath made him (Yahusha) to be sin for us, who knew no sin; that we might be made the righteousness of God in Him." (2 Corinthians 5:21)

Though still in the future, there would be only One who was worthy; only One that was capable, and only One that would be provided. David projected his faith into the future to this saving figure—GOD Himself. It would be his Messiah who would one day come and provide the lifesaving blood which sealed the new and greater covenant.[308]

> "Neither by the blood of goats and calves, but by His (Yahusha's) own blood He entered in once into the holy place, having obtained eternal redemption for us." (Hebrews 9:12)

> "And for this cause He (Yahusha) is the mediator of the New Testament that by means of death, for the redemption of the transgressions that were under the first testament (Old Testament), they which are called might receive the promise (through the New Covenant) of the eternal inheritance." (Hebrews 9:15)

---

308 1 Corinthians 11:25

The Missing Temple

(Image Source: ALAMY)

Scripture tells us, "For the life of the flesh is in the blood: and I have given it to you upon the altar to make an atonement for your souls; for it is the blood that maketh an atonement for the soul."[309]

YAHUAH ordered the Tabernacle and afterward the Temples to be built according to HIS explicit design and dimensions. These structures would be a sanctuary where HE would visit and dwell among HIS people. It is the Temple where we are told to make our offerings, and yet there is no Temple today! This then begs the question: How can we make an atonement since the Temple no longer exists?

The answer remains an enigma which baffles the rabbinic who refuses to look beyond the Old Covenant to the New—wherein the answer lays in plain sight. Pride stands in their way. Fear of being disloyal to traditional beliefs has kept the Jewish people from looking beyond to see what else GOD has done.

We previously learned from Exodus 25:9 that the Tabernacle in the wilderness (a forerunner of the Temple) was only a "pattern" of the actual sanctuary which at that time was still in heaven.

> "But Christ being come a high priest of good things to come, by a greater and more perfect tabernacle, not made with hands, that is to say not of this building…" (Hebrews 9:11)

---

309 Leviticus 17:11

It is not the Temple of stone hewn by the hands of men which was laid to waste by a pathetic Roman army; for no army could remove a single brick unless it was GOD's intent. The demise of the Temples was part of HIS plan so we might see the authentic. The Living Temple has replaced the Old stone temple just as the New Covenant has replaced the Old. It now is where the penitent must go in order to have his sins removed.

The Living Temple

When Yahusha-Jesus came to Jerusalem for the Passover, he went to the Temple and found it a marketplace for profiteers. In righteous anger He overturned the merchants' tables and drove out the money changers.[310] His actions and words raised the ire of the Sanhedrin, but the prophetic words of a Psalm were already fulfilled.[311]

> "For the zeal of thine house hath eaten me (Yahusha) up; and the reproaches of them (the Sanhedrin) that reproach thee are fallen upon me." (Psalm 69:9)

Jewish onlookers asked Him for a "sign" (miracle) to establish by what authority He had taken it upon Himself to cleanse the Temple, to which He replied, "Destroy this temple, and in three days I will raise it up."[312] The hearers replied that it had taken forty-six years to build the Temple, how then could He build it back in three days? "But He spake of the temple of His body..."[313] a body which would indeed be raised from the grave in a mere three days. That would be the sign!

> Note: A word about the Temples. The Israelites were no different than other men, for they too shared the propensity to place great emphasis, even venerate the physical. Temples of all religions are alleged to be the place where GOD dwells. Sacred scrolls, statues, and shrines litter the planet. Muslims have their *Kaaba* in Mecca and their *Qubbat As-Sakhrah* in Jerusalem. The Catholics have their Basilicas and Cathedrals in Rome and throughout the world. The Buddhists have their *Mahabodhi*, their *Angkor Wat*, and their *Borobudur* temples. And the Jews... they will soon have their Temple again in Jerusalem.

The Tabernacle in the Wilderness and the Jewish Temples in Jerusalem are the only temples which GOD HIMSELF instructed to be built. GOD knew HIS people would require a visible and physical place around which to center their spiritual life; without which they would repeatedly slip into declension, or worse apostasy. Temporal as they were meant to be, these Temple were and are still needful for the time being.

---

310   Matthew 21:12
311   John 2:17; Romans 15:3
312   John 2:19
313   John 2:17-22

> Note: Zechariah is referred to as the prophet of the Messianic age, for no prophet in the OT was more concerned with the Messianic hope or was given more specific prediction about His coming. He lived at the time when the Temple lay in ruins. GOD moved Haggi and Zechariah, and Zerubbabel (governor) and Joshua (high priest) to rouse the people to rebuild. It had to be rebuilt in order to keep the peoples' spiritual life intact and preserved. It was however in our Lord's providence that the Temple would eventually be destroyed for the people would place too much adoration on the temple itself. It would be the temple of the human heart that would become the dwelling place of GOD the Holy Spirit.[314]

There are still two Temples yet to be built in Jerusalem. One will be quite temporary, in the fashion of Solomon's Temple and will be built before the Messiah returns. Like the Temple before it, it too will be desecrated.[315] The next Temple, the Millennial Temple[316] will be built upon Yahusha's return. It will cover an area of a square mile, from where Yahusha-Jesus will rule and rein for one thousand years. During that time the sacrificial system will be reinstated and continue for the duration of the millennium. Afterward it too will be replaced when heaven comes down and adjoins planet Earth.[317] This final temple is referred to in Scripture as the Eternal City—the New Jerusalem. It will be a mountain sixty times higher than Mount Everest; fifteen hundred miles high at its summit and fifteen hundred miles wide at its base.[318] It will stretch from the Mediterranean Sea eastward, encompassing the entire royal land grant the Lord gave to Abraham and his seed.[319] Thereafter no physical temple will be needed or ever exist, "for the Lord GOD Almighty and the Lamb are the Temple of it."[320]

We would do well to remember that our GOD is too enormous and too magnificent to reside in a building of any proportion, no matter how glorious. The heavens and universe itself can not contain HIM.

> "Thus saith the Lord, The heaven is my throne, and the earth is my footstool: where is the house that ye build unto me? and where is the place of my rest? For all those things hath mine hand made, and all those things have been, saith the Lord: but to this man (the believer) will I look, even to him that is poor and of a contrite spirit, and trembleth at my word." (Isaiah 61:2)

Being omnipresent (simultaneously being in multiple places) GOD may reside when, where, and with whomever HE chooses. Currently and literally HE takes up residency in each genuine believer, who then becomes a temple where HIS Holy Spirit resides.[321]

---

314 1 Corinthians 6:19, 20
315 Daniel 9:27; Matthew 24:15
316 Ezekiel chapters 40-48
317 Revelation 21:1-3, 10
318 Revelation 21:16
319 Genesis 15:18
320 Revelation 21:22
321 1 Corinthians 3:16; 2 Corinthians 6:16

"What? Know ye not that your body is the temple of the Holy Ghost which is in you, which ye have of God, and ye are not your own? For ye are bought with a price: (speaks of Jesus's going to the Cross) therefore glorify God in your body, and in your spirit, which are God's."
(1 Corinthians 6:19-20)

10

HELL IS FULL OF GOOD PEOPLE

SALVATION—Saved from Sin

The fabled Sword of Damocles is poised ominously over our heads, held only by a single strand of horsehair. Though only a legend, the imagery depicts the precarious place we are all in as unregenerate sinners. We are but one breath and a single heartbeat away from either eternal life (heaven), or eternal death (hell).

> "And as it is appointed unto men once to die, but after this the judgment..." (Hebrews 9:27)

If we are to believe the Bible is the inspired and inerrant Word of GOD,[322] then we must believe that salvation is for the sinner, not the righteous.[323]

The sinner is the individual who realizes he is a sinner and is unable to save himself. So, like the publican, in the parable of the Pharisee and the publican, he acknowledged that he was a sinner and cried out for a merciful Savior. "GOD be merciful to me a sinner."[324]

Sword of Damocles, Richard Westall (1779) (Image Source: ALAMY)

The righteous is the man or woman who is under the illusion that they have attained sufficient righteousness as to qualify them to enter heaven. The rich and religious man in the above referenced parable said, "God, I thank thee that I am not as other men are, extortioners, unjust,

---

322 2 Timothy 3:16
323 Matthew 9:13
324 Luke 18:9-14

adulterers or even as this publican. I fast twice a week and give tithes of all that I possess."[325] As the parable continues we find that the man believing himself to be righteous would be resigned to hades, while the humble publican who admitted he was unworthy and sought forgiveness, was forgiven and redeemed.

Only a sinner realizes he needs a Savior, and only a sinner can find One.

The opinion of the righteous that they believe qualifies them is no more than an opinion; an opinion which fails to take into account that GOD's standard and criteria is absolute perfection. Even one sin left unatoned for is punishable by death.

"Cursed be he that confirmeth not (does not accept) all the words of the law to do them…" (Deuteronomy 27:26)

"For whosoever shall keep the whole law, and yet offend in one point, he is guilty of all." (James 2:10)

Our Lord is so holy as to be beyond human comprehension. So flawless is He that the royal seraphim angels who find themselves before His throne can only cover their faces and cry, "… Holy, holy, holy is the Lord of host: the whole earth is filled with His glory."[326]

In a scriptural account, the Prophet Isaiah, when caught up in a vision was all but speechless when he saw Yahusha-Jesus in His unfettered glory and could only utter, "Woe is me… for I have seen the King, the Lord of Hosts."[327]

Imitators and Imitations

Some individuals assume that one good deed negates one bad deed. As such they believe that if their deeds were to be weighed on the balances of an apothecary scale, and their good deeds outweighed their bad, then they will be admitted into a flawless heaven.

This assumption is pure conjecture and has no connection with scripture whatsoever. However, it is a perception often fostered by spiritual leaders and teachers of Judaism, Buddhism, Hinduism, Islam and what may only be described as imitation Christianity. Morals, ethics, and good works are taught and stressed to the point that they have replaced the need for the Cross and the blood.[328]

Mormons for example, are taught salvation comes by virtuous living and belonging to and remaining in good standing with the Church of Latter Days Saints.

Jehovah's Witnesses believe their salvation is based on acknowledging Jehovah as GOD and proselytizing. Jesus is acknowledged merely as one of Jehovah's agents and a created being; not as Immanuel on who ones' salvation is entirely predicated.

---

325 Luke 18:12
326 Isaiah 6:3
327 Luke 6:5
328 Ephesians 2:8-9

Romanism has a litany of heretical doctrines, among which was one perpetuated by their sainted Augustine. He claimed that grace is channeled through the Church of Rome and their sacraments, and that apart from this there can be no salvation or bestowal of grace.[329]

Then too, there are Protestant denominations who do not understand what it means to be "born again."[330] While they may be professing Christians, wear a chain with a cross around their neck and be faithful church-goers, they do not meet the Biblical (GOD's) criteria, and according to the Word of GOD are not "saved" any more than a religious Jew who wears the star of David. While the former individual believes in Christ, they have never entered through the narrow gate, walked the narrow path, and come into His presence. More will be said on this subject and on the difference between knowing "of Christ," and actually "knowing Christ."

When Yahusha-Jesus told His disciples that He was to soon die and that they would shortly follow Him, the Apostle Thomas asked Jesus, how do we follow you to your heaven? "How can we know the way?" Jesus answered him, "I AM the Way, the Truth and the Life: no man cometh unto the Father, but by Me."[331]

He is the Way—the only Way! He (being the Word of GOD) is Truth—the only Truth! And He is Life—the only way to Eternal Life!

Some individuals believe they are heaven-bound by virtue of the fact that they are of a particular ethnicity, or a particular faith, and that this somehow entitles them to enter into GOD's Eternal Kingdom.

One religion has strayed so far from Scripture as to teach the perversion that by confessing their sins to a man and reciting a few prayers, the penitents' sins are suddenly absolved. This fabrication elevates man to that of GOD, for only GOD has the power to forgive sin. The Bible teaches there is only one mediator. "For there is one GOD and one mediator between GOD and men, the man Christ Jesus…"[332] The Roman lie of a human conferring absolution is peddled to millions of Catholics who are unaware that the Bible teaches that our salvation is predicated on one thing and one thing only.

> "He that believeth on the Son hath everlasting life: and he that believeth not the Son shall not see life; but the wrath of GOD abideth on him." (John 3:36)

By altering the meaning of a single scripture, the Church of Rome (until recently) held their subjects' hostage, for they had said that unless a person is a Catholic and confesses to a priest they are doomed to hell.

The scripture they used to substantiate their ability to forgive sin says, "Whosoever sins ye remit, they are remitted unto them; and whosoever sins ye retain, they are retained."[333]

---

329 John W. Kennedy of India, *The Torch and the Testimony*, Christian Books Publishing House, Auburn, ME, 1965, pp. 101-102
330 John 3:3
331 John 14:6
332 1 Timothy 2:5
333 John 20:23

So, who is this the scripture is actually speaking of and what does it actually mean? It is the Bible Believing Born Again Christian who can unequivocally tell the individual that their sins have been remitted (forgiven) if they have accepted Yahusha-Jesus as their personal Lord and Savior. Likewise, it is the same Born Again Christian who can unequivocally warn that individual that their sins are retained (unforgiven) if they continue to place their faith and trust in a religion, a sacrament, or in a man who claims he can forgive sin. In a sentence, it is those who the Gospel acquits—that are acquitted, and those who the Gospel condemns—that shall be condemned!

By intentionally maligning scripture and instilling fear, this cult has managed to gain incredible power, wealth, and control over the masses.

> Note: The invention of the confessional gave the Catholic Church control over the laity. Like frightened children, Catholics are told and have come to believe that they will go to hell, or at least to a contrived place called purgatory if they die without having had their sins absolved by a priest. Absolution (the ability to absolve someone of their sins) is the epitome of sacrilege. Vatican II requires "loyal submission of the will and intellect" to the Pontiff. They teach that no Catholic can assume to obey GOD and HIS Word but must give absolute obedience to the church which acts for GOD.

As portrayed in the movie *The Godfather*, a Catholic mobster can be seen in good standing with his church so long as he is devout and generous to his church. The Catholic hitman can execute someone on Tuesday, go to confession on Wednesday, say one Our Father, three Hail Marys and an Act of Contrition and walk out believing that his sins have been forgiven. How convenient!

Believing himself absolved of his sin, this hit man can hypothetically proceed to execute another thug the following Tuesday, just making certain that he gets to confession on Wednesday. Likewise, the pedophile priest believes he can violate a youngster and afterward confess to his fellow priest and be immediately restored to a state of grace. How ludicrous![334]

Yahusha-Jesus warned that from the very beginning Satan was a liar, "and the father of lies."[335] The cleverest liar will say things which sound as if they were true, or better still, mix lies with truth in order to make them believable. In any theological assertion, the one making the claims can only be disproven if the one being lied to has studied (not simply read) GOD's Word for themselves.[336] Without having actually studied the Bible, (and not a Catholic rendition of the actual Bible), man is at the mercy of Satan—and Satan has no mercy! This dark angel has cleverly produced a false collection of lies in the form of religious doctrines which pose soft arguments to reasonable men by appealing to their love for GOD.

Theologian and author, David Breese in his book, *Satan's Ten Most Believable Lies*, said it well. "No one who does not know the Scripture in detail can claim to know the Scripture at all."[337]

---

334 Luke 13:3-5; Romans 6:1-3
335 John 8:44
336 2 Timothy 2:15
337 David Breese, *Satan's Ten Most Believable Lies*, Moody Press, Chicago, 1974, p. 14

However, the Lord said it best, "...If you continue in my Word, then ye are My disciples: And ye shall know the truth, and the truth will make you free."[338]

We would do well to reflect on the first lesson taught in the Bible; "the serpent was more subtil than any beast of the field which the Lord GOD had made."[339]

Most theologians seem to agree that the serpent was not some snake-like or vile looking creature. More than likely Satan appeared as an attractive, even angelic-looking figure for Eve was not at all repulsed by him but rather gladly listened to him. We know that this appealing figure managed to beguile her by twisting GOD's word and causing doubt.

One lesson which needs to be taken away from this is that the more appealing, the more charming, the more pious a person appears to be, the more guarded and the more suspect we need to be. "Beware of false prophets, which come to you in sheep's clothing, but inwardly they are a ravening wolves."[340]

Unlike Yahusha-Jesus who wore the simple garments of a commoner, each Sunday the religious clergy don their chasuble vestments to add an aurora of piety to their religious performance.

The Apostle Paul gave a grave and prophetic warning in his letter to the Corinthians pertaining to the likes of these charlatans.

> "But I fear, lest by any means, as the serpent beguiled Eve through his subtilty, so your minds should be corrupted from the simplicity that is in Christ. For if he that cometh preacheth another Jesus (or an alternate person with saving power- i.e. Mary), whom we have not preached, or if ye receive another spirit (a lying spirit), which ye have not received, or another gospel (another way to be saved), which ye have not accepted, ye might well bear with him (be easily lured and taken in)... For such are false apostles, deceitful workers, transforming themselves into the apostles of Christ (His earthly representatives and claiming apostolic authority). And no marvel; for Satan himself is transformed into an angel of light. Therefore, it is no great thing if his (Satan's) ministers also be transformed as the ministers of righteousness; whose end shall be according to their works." (2 Corinthians 11:3-4, 13-15)

Recognizable to any practicing Catholic is that they are in jeopardy of being eternally lost were it not for the so-called "mysteries" and "workings" of their church. Such vague words can mean virtually anything their fabricators want or need them to mean in support of their assertion.

Romanism has, by virtue of having existed for seventeen hundred years, gained credibility with the world at large and drawn an alleged 1.2 billion followers into her web. By convincing its adherents that it has been given a divine endowment it has cajoled otherwise rational people from seeing that it is the perpetrator of the most egregious hoax ever played on the masses. In any other sphere but religion the sheer lunacy of what they claim would be laughed at as being too preposterous to be taken seriously.

---

338 John 8:31
339 Genesis 3:1
340 Matthew 7:15

I realize that to one born and raised in Catholicism such an assertion seems unthinkable. How could the gentle, warm, and soft-spoken priest, bishop, or pope, and the good sisters of compassion (nonspecific order) be used as instruments of deception? However, according to the aforementioned scripture, using a cleric (priest, minister, or rabbi) is Satan's modus operandi (mode of operation). If indeed Satan can capture the shepherd, then he has captured the flock over which that shepherd has oversight. This gives great emphasis to the scripture, "Now the serpent was more subtil than any beast of the field which the Lord GOD made."[341]

The majority of Catholic clergy and particularly the lower echelon (priests and nuns) subconsciously know that they are living a lie. Inwardly they are likely little children, uncertain and fearful as to whether they themselves are saved. Some are merely actors who must perpetually be in character when they leave the privacy of their bedrooms. But when in private they clutch their talisman rosary, fondling each little bead between their thumb and forefinger as they petition Mary, "pray for us sinners, now and at the hour of our death." They are in the truest sense of the word in bondage to vain repetitious prayers and good deeds.[342] At the same time they cling to the hope that their acts of devotion and piety are being credited to their account in heaven.

Most of these people are sincere, dedicated, and love GOD. Still they do not realize that it doesn't matter how dedicated you are, it only matters to who you are dedicated. Breaking with Rome and being pronounced a heretic takes more courage than most can muster; so it is that its devotees go on much like religious Nicodemus, uncertain as to whether or not they themselves are saved.[343] Listen to this admission from one of their esteemed and supposedly knowledgeable representatives.

> "Church teaching is, that I don't know, at any given moment, what my eternal future will be. I can hope and pray, do my very best—but I still do not know..." (New York Cardinal O'Conner, *New York Times*, February 1, 1980, B4)

Seminarians and priests are skilled in Catholic creed, code, principal, and policy and have memorized scripture, but in reality, know very little of the Bible. If that were not the case, they would see the disparity between what they believe and the truth. As pawns in Satan's employment, their loyalty to the institution keeps them from daring to compare Rome's teaching with GOD's own Word much less dispute the teaching as heresy.[344] Without knowledge and understanding of the Word of GOD, we like Eve are no match for Satan, and likewise are easily beguiled.

Mariolatry (worship of Mary) is another falsehood and an insult to GOD. According to the Bible, one cannot—I repeat, cannot—pray to, or be heard by any deceased person—including Mary. Furthermore, it is an abomination and forbidden to even try. In ancient times a person who would attempt to communicate with the dead would be stoned to death.[345]

---

341 Genesis 3:1
342 Ephesians 2:9
343 John 3:1-2
344 2 Timothy 2:15; 3:16
345 Leviticus 20:27

"There shall not be found among you any one that maketh his son or his daughter to pass through the fire, or that useth divination, or an observer of times, or an enchanter, or a witch, or a charmer, or a consulter with familiar spirits, or a wizard, or a necromancer (one who communicates with the dead). For all that do these things are an abomination unto the Lord: and because of these abominations the Lord thy God doth drive them out from before thee." (Deuteronomy 18:10-12)

For fourteen centuries Catholics and many offshoots of Romanism not only pray to Mary and to dead saints but deify them. And for the deceased Catholic, masses are said, candles are lit, plenary indulgences and novenas are made; all in disobedience to the Word of GOD.

A noticeable characteristic shared by pagan religions and cults of all kinds, including satanic cults, is that they are fixated on, or venerate the dead. They seek to communicate with the dead or tap into dark powers.[346]

"...it is clear that GOD takes a far more serious view of the theology and morality of false religion than is common among Christians today. The Word of GOD strips the apostates of any veneer of respectability, sincerity of motives or worthy purpose, and reveals them for what they are, tools of Satan and enemies of Christ and of all who love Him."[347]

September 27, 2008, Cardinal Miloslav Vikinin carries the skull of Saint Wenceslaus, patron saint of the Czech nation in in Stara Boleslav Czech Republic. (Image Source: ALAMY)

---

346 Jeremiah 2:8
347 John F. Walvoord, *The Church in Prophecy*, Zondervan Publishing House, 1964, p. 59

11

WHO?

Who Paid the Price? To Whom do We Owe?

While the Church of Rome says that Christ is its central figure, He is kept just beyond reach and made nearly unapproachable. Instead it is Mary who is said to be our intercessor and mediator with Jesus. It is Mary who receives the majority of prayers (e.g., the rosary). It is Mary who is given the adoration due Him. ...And what does GOD have to say about this?

> "I am the Lord: that is my name, and My glory I will not give to another, neither My praise to graven images." (Isaiah 42:8)

> "For there is one God, and one mediator between God and men, the man Christ Jesus..." (1 Timothy 2:5)

By promoting the lie that Mary, not Christ, is the one they are to approach, Satan has managed to keep Catholics from discovering that they can indeed have a deep intimate "one on one" relationship with their Savior; a relationship which Jesus referred to as being "born again."[348]

By using his favorite tool—religion—Satan has kept God-fearing Catholics from taking that one last crucial step necessary to be saved. That step happens only when one fully internalizes what Jesus did for them by taking their sins upon Himself and then paying for them with His life.[349]

God-fearing Catholics are under the false assumption that the gospel taught by the Church of Rome is the same gospel Yahusha-Jesus and the Apostle Paul presented. It most certainly is not! Paul summed it up when he said, "I determined not to know anything among you, save (except) Jesus Christ and Him crucified."[350] Romanism has perverted "the message of the Cross," which is total reliance on Christ and what He alone accomplished for the believer, to the exclusion... I repeat, to the exclusion of all else!

---

348 John 3:3
349 Romans 3:10, 23-24; 5:8, 12; 1 Peter 2:24
350 1 Corinthians 2:2

"Millions profess that Jesus is the son of GOD, yet He is not Lord of their lives… for if He is not Lord of all, He is not Lord at all."[351]

Listen to how Paul warned of another gospel infiltrating the Church; even repeating the warning for emphasis!

> "But though we, or an angel from heaven, preach any other gospel unto you than that which we have preached unto you, let him be accursed. As we said before, so say I now again, If any man preach any other gospel unto you than that ye have received, let him be accursed. For do I now persuade men, or God or do I seek to please men? for if I yet pleased men, I should not be the servant of Christ." (Galatians 1:8-10)

To Know of GOD, or To Know GOD?

If you were asked do you know the president of the United States or the Prime Minister of Israel, you might—without giving it much thought—answer yes and give his or her name. However, if you were walking down Main Street and the president or prime minister was walking toward you, while you might recognize him or her, he or she would not know you. So you wouldn't be entirely correct in saying that you actually know him or her. In reality you know "of" him or her, but you have never actually had an encounter with them.

So it is that many who refer to themselves as Christians know "of" Christ. They believe that He existed, and died on a cross for them, but they still do not actually know Him. They have never had a personal encounter; furthermore, they were never told that such an encounter was possible.

In the Gospel of Matthew, we have the Lord's own words on the matter. Allow these foreboding words to reverberate in your mind and settle into your soul:

> "Not every one that saith unto me, Lord, Lord, shall enter into the kingdom of heaven; but he that doeth the will of my Father which is in heaven. Many will say to me in that day (when they appear before Him), Lord, Lord, have we not prophesied in thy name? and in thy name have cast out devils? and in thy name done many wonderful works? And then will I profess unto them, I never knew you: depart from me, ye that work iniquity." (Matthew 7:21-23)

> "Thus saith the Lord, Let not the wise man glory in his wisdom, neither let the mighty man glory in his might, let not the rich man glory in his riches: but let him that glorieth glory in this, that he understandeth and knoweth Me, that I am the Lord which exercise loving kindness, judgment, and righteousness, in the earth: for in all these things I delight, saith the Lord." (Jeremiah 9:23-24)

---

351 Leonard Ravenhill, *America Is Too Young To Die*, Bethany House Publishers, Michigan, p. 98

What then is the will of the Father? "That they might know thee, the only true God, and (know) Jesus Christ, whom thou has sent."[352]

Missing GOD

There is an old riddle which makes the distinction between knowing Him and knowing of Him. It goes like this. Did you hear about the fella who missed heaven by just sixteen inches? It was the difference between his head and his heart!

It may sound like a rhetorical question, but is it possible to miss GOD even as a devout and religious person? The Bible indicates it is not only quite possible but probable, for we are told in scripture that there is a very narrow gate through which one must enter, and only that gate leads to heaven.[353] In contrast we are told that the majority disregard this narrow and unpretentious gate which was meant for the sheep to pass through; sooner choosing to go through a wide inviting gate which takes one to a broad road that everyone else seems to be taking.

The proud theologian, the philosophical thinker, and the religious (the pharisees, past and present) may go to extraordinary lengths to come up with plausible explanations to their pupils about GOD or how to attain heaven. The master or minister may have spent a lifetime studying, searching, and analyzing the Scriptures and still never grasp the essence of them; "ever learning and never able to come to the knowledge of the truth."[354] He or she may speak five languages, authored seventeen books, and been the chancellor of a prestigious theological institution and still not know GOD.[355] For despite all his getting, the Bible tells us the Lord can only be found by the meek, the humble, and the sincere pursuer of HIM—not the pursuer of knowledge.[356]

> "For thus saith the high and lofty One that inhabiteth eternity, whose name is Holy; I dwell in the high and holy place, with him also that is of a contrite and humble spirit, to revive the spirit of the humble, and to revive the heart of the contrite ones." (Isaiah 57:15)

> "And ye shall seek ME, and find ME, when ye shall search for ME with all your heart." (Jeremiah 29:13)

The great majority of those practicing a given faith have determined in their minds that the measure to which they acknowledge GOD is the extent to which HE can be known.

As previously stated, believing that GOD exists and practicing ones' religion is not the same thing as knowing Him. The vast number of Jews believe in GOD, but they have not known HIM. The vast number of those who believe themselves to be Christians believe in Jesus, but

---

352 John 17:3
353 Matthew 7:14
354 2 Timothy 3:7
355 Romans 2:14
356 Isaiah 35:5

they have never taken the time to actually know Him, which only comes from reading His Word, listening to His Word and internalizing that it was their sin that sent Him to the cross. Many only pursued GOD to the limit of their mind without taking that final crucial step and moving beyond where a grateful heart cries out to a beckoning Savior.[357]

> "But GOD commendeth HIS love to us, in that, while we were yet sinners, Christ died for us." (Romans 5:10)

> Note: T. Austin Sparks in his book, *The School of Christ*, wrote, "Christians can be in one of two classes. There is that very large class whose Christianity is objective—outward. It is a matter of having adopted a Christian life that they now do a lot of things which they once would not do. They go to meetings, they go to church, they read the Bible. It is a matter of doing or not doing, not going or going; being a good Christian outwardly. That is a big class with its various degrees of light and shade. Then there are others who are in this School of Christ, for whom the Christian life is an inward thing of walking with the Lord and knowing the Lord in the heart. There is a great deal of difference between those two classes."[358]

Prevenient Grace

The scriptures tell us that the Father sent the Holy Spirit to search the earth for that man or woman who is desperate for more of HIM.[359] When the Holy Spirit finds such a one, He engages that individual in such a way as to draw them to the Savior.

> "For thus saith the Lord God; Behold, I, even I, will both search my sheep, and seek them out. As a shepherd seeketh out his flock in the day that he is among his sheep that are scattered; so will I seek out my sheep, ...I will seek them which is lost, and bring them back which was driven away, and will bind up that which is broken, and will strengthen that which is sick..." (Ezekiel 34:11-12, 16)

Christendom recognizes Prevenient grace. "No man can come to Me (Yahusha-Jesus), except the Father which hath sent Me draw him..."[360] From this scripture and numerous others,[361] we recognize that before a man or women receives the Savior, the Father, and the Holy Spirit, perceiving that heart to be tender and the moment opportune, invite that individual into the heavenly family. The individual is given the ability to see themselves in their

---

357 Revelation 3:20
358 T. Austin Sparks, *The School of Christ*, World Challenge Inc., Lindale, TX, pp. 86-87
359 Amos 9:9
360 John 6:44
361 John 3:8

unregenerated state and blackened with sin. Then suddenly they see the extent of GOD's love by His having taken their sins upon Himself on a Cross. So it is that GOD's prevenient (coming before) grace is extended and precedes the human decision.[362] As the Bible teaches, it is GOD's will that all men be saved,[363] but the invitation is fleeting and likened to a wind passing by.[364] Still, as with any invitation, it is up to the one invited to either accept it,[365] or to dismiss and reject it.

Sadly, "many are called… (invited at some point in their life, but dismiss the offer) but few are chosen" (become partakers—accepting the Spirits invitation and become saved).[366]

David said, "Today if you will hear His voice, harden not your heart…" (Psalms 95:7)

"Seek ye the Lord while he may be found, call ye upon him while he is near…" (Isaiah 55:6)

"Let him who is athirst come. And whosoever will, let him take of the waters of life freely." (Revelation 22:17)

> Note: It has been said that the Holy Spirit is a gentleman and will never impose Himself on anyone. It is however scriptural that once one has comprehended what Christ has done for them on the Cross and becomes saved, that afterward, should that individual then reject Christ and the gospel, or even become complacent and return to worldly ways, he or she has rejected the Holy Spirit's offer of adoption into the family of GOD. They have committed the unpardonable sin; they will not be given another invitation and will be eternally lost.[367]

"For if after they have escaped the pollutions of the world through the knowledge of the Lord and Saviour Jesus Christ, they are again entangled therein, and overcome, the latter end is worse with them than the beginning. For it had been better for them not to have known the way of righteousness, than, after they have known it, to turn from the holy commandment delivered unto them." (2 Peter 2:20-21)

This does not include the backslider. As long as one retains faith in Christ and His atonement and repents (reverses course), he or she can be renewed and restored.

There are Roman Catholics, Eastern Orthodox Catholics, Ukrainian Catholics, Episcopalians, and various Protestants who have such a deep and abiding love for Jesus that they have received the Holy Spirit and been "born again" in spite of their affiliations. Still, their fidelity to their

---

362 A.W. Tozer, *The Pursuit of God*, Christian Publications, Inc., Harrisburg, PA, 1948, p. 11
363 1 Timothy 2:4-6; Hebrews 2:9; 2 Corinthians 5:14; Titus 2:11-12
364 John 3:8
365 John 3:16; Acts 10:34-35
366 Matthew 20:16; Romans 10:20; Luke 13:22-30
367 Hebrews 6:4-6; 10:26-30; Hebrews 2:3; 2 Peter 1:10; Mark 3:28-29

Catholicism or their religion is so strong that it dominates them. Consequently, their spiritual discernment has been overridden and kept them from appropriating the majesty of truth. While they might argue this point, it is self-evident; as for example, they will not give up their Mariolatry (idolatry).

How much more specific could the Lord have been, when through Paul, He described the latter day apostasy that would challenge the genuine Church.

> "Now the Spirit speaketh expressly, that in the latter times some shall depart from the faith, giving heed to seducing spirits, and doctrines of devils; Speaking lies in hypocrisy; having their conscience seared with a hot iron; Forbidding to marry, and commanding to abstain from meats, which God hath created to be received with thanksgiving of them which believe and know the truth." (1 Timothy 4:1-3)

Speaking of the end time apostasy that will proceed the coming of the Lord, Paul said, "Let no man deceive you by any means; for that day shall not come except there come a falling away (from genuine Christianity) first, and that the man of sin (the Antichrist) be revealed, the son of perdition."[368]

The Apostle Paul Pleads with the Church for Separation

Today, ecumenical gatherings of different faiths and diverse beliefs are joining together in what they believe to be a spirit of unity. At these interfaith symposiums they emphasize common beliefs and principles while ignoring vital doctrinal differences. Subsequently they mix the heretical with the biblical and the holy with the profane.[369] Scripture is clear that believers are to have nothing to do with the likes of such, or with these charlatans that infect and sicken the body of Christ with a heretical disease. Still, this diabolical movement grows as prominent evangelical ministers having attained celebrity status lead as Judas goats—their trusting sheep to slaughter. These so-called ministers who attempt to unify are doing nothing less than the work of Satan.

> "And what concord hath Christ with Belial (Satan)? or what part hath he that believeth with an infidel (one who rejects truth)? And what agreement hath the temple of God (true believers) with idols? for ye are the temple of the living God; as God hath said, I (the Holy Spirit) will dwell in them, and walk in them; and I will be their God, and they shall be my people. Wherefore come out from among them, and be ye separate, saith the Lord, and touch not the unclean thing; and I will receive you." (2 Corinthians 6:15-17)

---

368 2 Thessalonians 2:3
369 Ezekiel 22:26

To Believe in His Existence...or Believe in Him!

Perhaps the most frequently quoted verse in the New Testament is John 3:16.

"For God so loved the world that he gave his only begotten Son, that whosoever believeth in him should not perish, but have everlasting life."

We need to examine the word "believeth" more closely, for its meaning was diminished when it was translated from Greek into English in the New Testament. As this scripture is crucial to where one will spend eternity, we need to look at the Greek definition.

To believe or believeth does not mean simply to believe in something—as one may believe that Jesus came to earth and is the Christ. The word for believe in the Greek is "*pisteuo*."[370] It means to entrust and commit. So, when it is used in John 3:16 it means to trust and commit one's entire salvation and subsequently where one will spend eternity to Christ.

Of equal importance is the word "faith," as used in Ephesians 2:8. "For by grace are ye saved through faith; and that not of yourselves: it is the gift of God…" If we skip over just one word after the word believe (Greek, *pisteuo*) in the Strong's Exhaustive Concordance we arrive at the word for faith, (Greek, *pistis*).[371] Both words have the same origin and nearly identical meanings. In the concordance faith is defined as conviction and a reliance on truth, especially our reliance upon Christ for our salvation.

GOD's formula for salvation is predicated on the conjoined meanings of both words. It is tested by accepting what the natural eye cannot see. Faith and believing are based on what ones' spirit internalizes and the conviction that follows when having heard or read the Gospel account.

"Faith cometh by hearing, and hearing by the Word of GOD." (Romans 10:17)

"For we walk by faith, and not by sight." (2 Corinthians 5:7)

"Faith is the substance of things hoped for, the evidence of things not seen." (Hebrews 11:1)

"Whom having not seen, ye love; in whom, though now ye see him not, yet believing, ye rejoice with joy unspeakable and full of glory…" (1 Peter 1:8)

One can now see that "believing," "faith," and "hope" is the essential trinity in order to receive Christ as Lord and secure a place in eternity with Him.

"Jesus said unto her, I am the resurrection, and the life: he that believeth in me, though he were dead, yet shall he live: And whosoever liveth and believeth in me shall never die. Believest thou this?" (John 11:25-26)

---

370 *Strong's Exhaustive Concordance*, Gk., #4100
371 *Strong's Exhaustive Concordance*, Gk., #4102

12

BUT GOD HAS A PLAN!

Covenants and Dispensations

"A covenant is not merely a system of demands and promises; demands that ought to be met, and promises that ought to be realized; but that it also includes a reasonable expectation that the external legal relationship will carry with it the glorious reality of a life in intimate communion with the covenant GOD."[372]

Over the past six thousand years the Lord has made numerous covenants with certain men like Abraham, Isaac, Jacob, David, and Solomon. HE has also made covenants with certain groups; in particular, with the Hebrew people and the nation of Israel. GOD has also covenanted with a faithful group of believing Jews and Gentiles (a.k.a. the Church). This particular covenant or promise opened heaven's gates by faith in what He accomplished with His resurrection. Because Yahusha-Jesus became the first "flesh" to be actually resurrected to heaven He was symbolized and celebrated in the Jewish feast of First Fruits.[373] Before that, all "saints" (Old Testament, and New—prior to the Cross) were detained within the earth after they had died in what was called Abraham's bosom or Paradise.[374] Old Testament saints were those who like Abraham, David, and Job were sold-out to GOD. They believed, had faith, and staked their destiny on GOD their Savior even though He had not yet come in the flesh. "For I know my redeemer liveth, and shall stand in the latter day upon the earth…"[375]

Perhaps the best way to explain it is to point out that those who are saved today have to by faith look back to the Cross, and those who were saved before Christ came had to look forward to the Cross. Both required faith in the unseen. The scripture below speaks to those of both pre- and post-dispensations.

> "That the trial of your faith, being much more precious, though it be tried with fire, might be found unto praise and honor and glory at the appearing of Jesus Christ: Whom having not seen, ye love; in whom, though now you see Him not, yet believing, ye rejoice with

---

[372] Professor L. Berkhof, *Systematic Theology*, 4th Rev., Eerdmans Publishing, p. 287
[373] Leviticus 23:9-14; 1 Corinthians 15:22-23
[374] Luke 16:22
[375] Job 19:25

joy unspeakable and full of glory: Receiving the end of your faith, even the salvation of your soul. Of which the salvation the prophets have enquired and search diligently, who prophesied of the grace that should come unto you: Searching what, or what manner of time the Spirit of Christ which was in them did signify, when it testified beforehand the sufferings of Christ, and the glory that shall follow." (1 Peter 1:7-11)

The act of GOD's forgiving one of their sins is nothing less than undeserved favor and mercy on HIS behalf. It is referred to in Scripture as grace. Appropriately defined, it is a covenant (a promise of the highest order) made between the individual and his Creator. It cannot be earned, and no man is worthy of it. It is a gift which must be graciously accepted.[376]

In the early Church there were Jewish Christians who felt it simply could not be that easy and insisted that converts were saved by both faith and observing the Mosaic Law.[377] Later, when a religion (Romanism) usurped the name of Christianity and perverted the genuine, it supported penances, self-punishment (e.g., flagellation), kneeling pilgrimages, and self-abasing pagan rituals by which devotees believed would make them more acceptable. The premise of both of these beliefs says that GOD is not gracious, and since man is not righteous, man must make himself righteous in order to make GOD gracious.

Grace Came Before the Law

Though grace is generally thought of as being central to the New Covenant, it has in reality preempted all other covenants including the Sinaitic Covenant.

In ancient times it was extended to the individual who had sought YAHUAH with all his heart. "And ye shall seek Me and find Me when ye shall search for me with all your heart."[378] So it is that grace is inextricably linked to ones' heart for GOD.

Noah was one such individual, "But Noah found grace in the eyes of the Lord."[379] Moses was another, "and thou hast also found grace in My sight."[380] Many others; Enoch, Abraham, and later David would all be recipients of HIS grace. And while, "the law was given (presented) by Moses, …grace and truth came by Jesus Christ."[381]

When the Savior first came, He offered His grace freely to the "Lost sheep of the House of Israel,"[382] and indeed many accepted that grace and were justified in the eyes of GOD.[383] Others however, felt it was necessary to retain, and in some cases remain under the Law in order for one to be saved.

---

376 Ephesians 2:8
377 Acts 15:1, 5
378 Jeremiah 29:13
379 Genesis 6:8
380 Exodus 33:12
381 John 1:17
382 Matthew 15:24
383 Romans 3:24

Even though Messianic Judaism (a.k.a. Christianity) had originated from Biblical Judaism, there were still in the first assemblies pious Jewish Christians who could not fully appreciate the totality of what Yahusha had done at the Cross. They argued that even Gentile converts must adhere to Torah with its ordinances, prohibitions and observances—which included dietary, circumcision, and the keeping of an explicit Sabbath. The Apostle Paul opposed this position, even publicly challenging the Council at Jerusalem where afterward it was settled that these observances were not a requirement.[384] The Sabbath observance (holy days, new moons, and festivals) were instituted by GOD for the Jewish people[385]—prefiguring the coming of their Messiah. None of these observances are required in the New Covenant, so Christians have the freedom to remember, observe and celebrate that which elevates Christ as they choose, so long as it coincides with the New Covenant and the New Testament.[386]

Paul would remind us that Yahusha-Jesus, "blotted out the handwriting of ordinances that was against us (the Law)…and took it out of the way nailing it to the Cross. Let no man therefore judge you in meat or in drink, or in respect of the holy days, or of the next moon, or of the Sabbath days: Which are a shadow of things to come; but the body is of Christ."[387]

The question that remained was whether Jewish-Christians themselves were to retain the laws and ordinances. This were put to rest when at Antioch, Paul would say,

> "Knowing that a man is not justified by the works of the law, but by the faith of Jesus Christ, even we have believed in Jesus Christ, that we might be justified by the faith of Christ, and not by the works of the law: for by the works of the law shall no flesh be justified. But if, while we seek to be justified by Christ, we ourselves also are found sinners, is therefore Christ the minister of sin? God forbid. For if I build again the things which I destroyed, I make myself a transgressor. For I through the law am dead to the law, that I might live unto God. I am crucified with Christ: nevertheless I live; yet not I, but Christ liveth in me: and the life which I now live in the flesh I live by the faith of the Son of God, who loved me, and gave himself for me. I do not frustrate the grace of God: for if righteousness come by the law, then Christ is dead in vain." (Galatians 2:16-21)

Paul was in essence saying that everything the Jewish people were doing in the way of observances and rituals would not justify them. Faith in Christ is the total sum of what it takes to be justified in the eyes of GOD. And if they persist in their belief that they need to do more and continue in the works of the law in order to justify themselves or absolve themselves of their sins, then Christ would have died in vain. Since they have been delivered from the law by faith, he asserted, do not return to it and stumble over it again.

---

384 Acts 11:1-2; 15:1-28
385 Leviticus 23:1; 1 Chronicles 23:31
386 Colossians 2:14-17; Romans 14:5-6; Galatians 4:9-10
387 Colossians 2:14-17

It stands to reason that if just one individual since the beginning of time, could have been good enough, done enough benevolent deeds, gave enough philanthropically or kept enough of the of the law to meet GOD's criteria by which to obtain heaven, then that individual would have "set the bar" to which others would have to reach in order to attain heaven. This would then mean that Yahusha-Jesus would never have needed to come to earth and die an agonizing death for us. A single mortal man or woman would have set the standard. Others would thereafter only have to rise to meet that standard and level of perfection.

But that was not the case. As the song "Jesus Paid It All," by lyricist Kristian Stanfill, expresses, "Jesus paid it all / All to Him I owe / Sin had left a crimson stain / He washed it white as snow."[388]

Admittedly it is understandable, even appropriate, for Jews to remain loyal to their heritage and committed to its preservation. Their roots are older and deeper than any surviving culture or nation on earth. Furthermore, it was YAHUAH HIMSELF who instituted each and every commemorative practice and instructed that they be preserved and perpetuated.[389]

Each ritual and celebration (with the exception of those added by men and not specified in the Holy Scriptures) was presented in type as a witness and an expectation of Yahusha. The sabbaths, the sacrifice, the feasts and fasts, the mikvah, the circumcision, the bar mitzvah, the worship, the music, and the hymns (psalms), were all meant to be an expression of love for, and fidelity to the one and only GOD, and to the Mashiach.

In the coming restoration and throughout Yahusha's millennial reign these same rituals and types (mentioned above) will be reinstituted in celebratory fashion. They will be a witness to the nations of GOD's faithfulness and graciousness to a people HE called to HIMSELF.

It may be said, and correctly so, that the New Covenant, has superseded the Old because the promises of the Old Covenant have been fulfilled and satisfied in the New.

> "In that he saith, A new covenant, he hath made the first old. Now that which decayeth and waxeth old is ready to vanish away." (Hebrews 8:13)
>
>> Note: The word "waxeth," (Greek, *palaioo*) above in Hebrews 8:13 means; "abrogate, annul, no longer in force, out of date, declared obsolete."[390] The word "vanish," (Greek, *aphanismos*) means; "a making away with, a disappearance, vanish away."[391]

The Sabbath for example took on a new meaning under the New Covenant; for not a single command was given by Yahusha-Jesus to His disciples to dedicate a specific day of the week as the Sabbath. In contrast, He spoke and reinforced the other scriptures in the Decalogue (ten commandments) that we are expected to keep. True believers live and celebrate the Sabbath and the Lord of the Sabbath each and every day of their lives.

---

388 "Jesus Paid It All", Lyricist Kristian Stanfill
389 Exodus 31:13, 16
390 *Strong's Exhaustive Concordance, Gk., #3822*
391 *Strong's Exhaustive Concordance, Gk., #854*

Celebrating Jewish practices such as Pesach Seder by Jewish Christians is good, worthwhile and beneficial (as a teaching tool), so long as it is done to portray the true Paschal Lamb. Likewise, other celebratory practices can be a teaching tool and a testimony to GOD's faithfulness. But care must be taken not to return to Torah or to emphasize the associated practices as if still governed by them. Done judiciously and kept in perspective there is purpose. Done imprudently, they make the work of the Christ of "none effect."[392]

> Note: Some argue that the Mosaic Sabbath was to be eternally observed because of phrases like "throughout your generations," "for a perpetual covenant," or "a sign forever."[393] There are however words in the scriptures having to do with time which apply to a given dispensation or dispensations. The sacrificial system will for example be purposeful during the Millennial reign when Yahusha presides over the planet and men will still be learning the ways of the Lord. However, once the thousand years has ended, the first heaven and the first earth will pass away, and New Jerusalem will descend from the cosmos. At that time all the rituals will be obsolete and discontinued, as will the physical Temple itself. At that time "GOD Almighty" (the entire GODhead) will be the Temple (the dwelling place).[394]

"And I saw no Temple therein, for the Lord GOD Almighty and the Lamb are the temple of it." (Revelation 21:22)

A New Assembly and a Greater Covenant

We read in the Gospel of Matthew (16:13–20) that upon coming to the coast of Caesarea, Philippi, Yahusha-Jesus asked His disciples, "Who do men say that I am?"

After the disciples offered what others had said, Peter was suddenly given a divine revelation of who Jesus actually was. I believe that Peter was himself astonished at what he had just then realized, for he immediately blurted out, "Thou art the Christ, the son of the living GOD." "The Lord replied, 'Blessed art thou Simon Barjona: for flesh and blood hath not revealed it unto thee, but My Father which is in heaven. And I say unto thee that thou art Peter, on this rock (single truth), I will build My Church.'"

"On this rock" means on this foundational truth which Peter had just testified, shall Yahusha-Jesus build His Church. It was predicated on the belief that Yahusha-Jesus was and is "The Christ, The Son of The Living GOD!" The Apostle Paul would later make that abundantly clear when he said, "That Rock was Christ."[395]

In that same passage is mentioned the keys to the Kingdom of Heaven. The keys Jesus would give Peter were not just given to him, but to all His disciples. They were the keys of truth; the

---

392 Romans 4:13-17; 1 Corinthians 1:17
393 Exodus 31:13, 16-17
394 Revelation 21:1-2, 22
395 1 Corinthians 10:4

gospel unto salvation; the message of the Cross! These are the keys which unlock heavens gates to all who believed on Him.

> "...whosoever believeth in Him shall not perish, but have everlasting life." (John 3:16)

> "I am the way, the truth and the life: no man cometh unto the Father, but by Me." (John 14:6)

Of great significance were the words Yahusha-Jesus used, "I will build My Church." The Lord was saying that He was about to build something new. No longer (at least for the next two thousand years) was He going to try to reform the nation of Israel who had largely rejected Him. He was going to build a new assembly; a body of believers for Himself, and it would be built on the revelation and proposition (the Rock) which Peter had just been given by the Father.

This new body of this New Testament (testament means witness) would not be like the Old Testament, which was directed to a single ethnic group. Neither would it be confined to geographic boundaries, as had been promised Abraham's descendants.[396] This new Covenant would be "no respecter of persons."[397] It would be worldwide, and it would be available to anyone who placed their faith and trust in Him. This body would become His true disciples and take His title—followers of the Christ—Christians.[398]

In the Gospel of John we are given a revelation about what takes place the moment one accepts Christ and becomes a Born Again believer.[399]

> "Peter rose up and said, referring to the Gentiles '...a good while ago that GOD made a choice among us that the Gentiles by my mouth shall hear the word of the gospel and believe. And GOD which knoweth the hearts bare them witness, giving them the Holy Ghost, even as HE did unto us." (Acts 15:7-8)

> "At that day ye shall know that I am in My Father, and ye in Me, and I in you." (John 14:20)

I want to emphasize the words "and I in you," for these words need to be taken literally! At the exact moment one accepts Yahusha-Jesus, that individual becomes "born again." It is a spiritual conception; the Holy Spirit actually enters into the Believer and fuses with the individuals' spirit. This means that the same Spirit that Jesus received at conception, and that entered into Him a second time after being baptized by John the Baptist in the Jordan river (in preparation for His ministry)[400] likewise enters into the believer.[401] And, just as the voice of GOD declared

---

396 Genesis 15:18
397 Acts 10:34
398 Acts 11:26
399 John 3:3
400 John 1:10
401 Romans 8:11

from heaven at that moment, "this is My beloved Son," so too at that moment is the adoption and sonship of the individual ratified.[402]

> "For ye have not received the spirit of bondage again to fear; but ye have received the Spirit of adoption, whereby we cry, Abba, Father. The Spirit itself beareth witness with our spirit, that we are the children of God..." (Romans 8:15)

With the Holy Spirit endowing the believing Church the new believer would have even more than the covenant relationship that was offered to the Israelites; they would have spiritual unity with GOD HIMSELF!

For the Jewish believer the New Covenant has another wonderful benefit. The endowment of the Holy Spirit gives them the ability to—(as it were) walk in the Torah.[403]

Speaking of the day when Israel will recognize their Messiah, the Lord said through the prophet,

> "And I will put My spirit within you, and cause you to walk in my statutes, and ye shall keep my judgments, and do them." (Ezekiel 36:27)

> "That the righteousness of the law might be fulfilled in us, who walk not after the flesh, but after the Spirit." (Romans 8:4)

"Walking in the statutes" becomes a matter of the heart. It is seeking to live according to GOD's will. It is born in love and from the desire to do all that pleases HIM.

> Note: Messianic Believers may keep their heritage alive and celebrate that which GOD has purposed, for in doing so they are a unique witness to the Gentiles of GOD's faithfulness and HIS Lordship over them.[404] Still, there are some Messianic Jews who though they have received their Messiah have retained certain practices which are in stark contrast to what it means to be in Christ. For example, there are many born again male Jews who practice customs as if they are still under the law, such as the wearing of the yamaka (skull cap). Under the old covenant the Jews believed man is unworthy to have an open face before GOD and must, in an act of submission and humility cover himself. In contrast Christianity is an open-faced relationship based on intimate fellowship. Man is to be uncovered,[405] unabashedly coming before his Lord as one would a friend.[406]

---

402 John 8:14-17
403 John 8:1-5
404 Zechariah 8:23
405 1 Corinthians 11:7
406 John 15:15

> Caveat: There are many varied types of Messianic congregations should one choose to attend. Some put a great deal of emphasis on their Judaism and the Torah as if they were still under the Law rather than Grace. This can diminish the New Covenant; a comparison of which is presented in the letter to the Hebrews, chapters nine and ten. In the course of accentuating and overemphasizing their Jewishness, some Messianic congregations may actually be segregating themselves from the body of Believers, which is scripturally discouraged. We need to remember that "there is (now) no difference between Jew and Greek: for the same Lord over all is rich unto all that call upon Him."[407]

"For He is our peace, who hath made both one, and hath broken down the middle wall of partition between us; having abolished in His flesh the enmity, even the law of commandments contained in ordinances; for to make in Himself of twain one new man, so making peace; And that He might reconcile both unto God in one body by the Cross, having slain the enmity thereby." (Ephesians 2:14-16)

> Note: The "middle wall" was a reference to the barrier in the Temple which separated the Jews, who were permitted into the inner court, from the Gentiles who had to remain in the outer court. Yahusha has eliminated that wall.
>
> Note: Gentiles and their food were thought unclean. Rabbinical law prohibited Jews and Gentiles from sharing meals together which would otherwise represent mutual acceptance. A certain sect of pharisees who had become believers still argued that circumcision was a requirement for any Gentile wanting to be saved, or even have fellowship with Jews. Yahusha had made an end to this when at the Council of Jerusalem, the Apostle Peter and James settled the question.[408]
>
> Note: The weekly Sabbath celebrated from Friday sundown through Saturday sundown is a covenant sign between the Lord and Israel (not the Church), "Speak thou unto the children of Israel (not the Church or the Gentiles), saying, "Verily My sabbaths ye shall keep: for a sign between Me and you throughout your generations…"[409] One should take special note of the word "sign" for a sign is not a law. Today under the New Covenant one is given freedom of observing and commemorating any day and should in fact dedicate and commemorate every day to the Lord.[410] We should not be fixated on any particular day.[411]

---

407 Romans 10:12
408 Acts 15:5-14
409 Exodus 31:13
410 Romans 14:5-6; Galatians 4:9-11; Colossians 2:16-17
411 Colossians 2:16; Romans 14:8

The Sabbath Under the Law, and the Sabbath Under Grace

There are some who misinterpret the commandment to keep the Sabbath (Exodus 20:8), taking it to a fault. They are fixated with a Saturday (the Jewish) Sabbath and believe if it is not celebrated on that day of the week—one is breaking GOD's commandment-Law.

Sadly, they do not understand that the word Sabbath (Hebrew, *Shabbath*) is a command for the Jewish people to both rest and to remember. Remembering (Hebrew, *Zakar*) the Sabbath means to recall something from the past, and to meditate on it.

This begs the question, what is it that our Lord is telling the Jewish people to remember? The answer is found in Exodus 13:3. There we read, "And Moses said unto the people, Remember this day, in which ye came out from Egypt, out of the house of bondage; for by strength of hand the Lord brought you out from this place: there shall no leavened bread be eaten." And so, it was that the ordinance of the Passover—the Sabbath of Sabbaths was established.

All streams of Judaism know this, celebrate the Passover, and are faithful to remind their children.[412] At each Passover seder the story of their emancipation from Egypt is read aloud from the Haggadah as they eat foods symbolic of their time in the wilderness. This never-to-be forgotten practice was to serve as a reminder of the Lord's goodness and faithfulness.

The word "remember" was changed to the word "keep" (Hebrew, *shamar*) in Deuteronomy 5:15 to ensure that future generations never forget that the Lord is their redeemer and deliverer, and that all homage is owed Him. So it is that the two words, "remember" and "keep," are in fact synonymous.

> "And remember that thou wast a servant in the land of Egypt, and that the Lord thy God brought thee out thence through a mighty hand and by a stretched out arm: therefore the Lord thy God commanded thee to keep the Sabbath day." (Deuteronomy 5:15)

The first time the commandment was given to be observed on a particular day is found in Exodus 16:22, 25, 26. There we read, "And it came to pass, that on the sixth day they gathered twice as much bread, two omers for one man: and all the rulers of the congregation came and told Moses….And Moses said, Eat that today; for today is a Sabbath unto the Lord: today ye shall not find it in the field. Six days ye shall gather it; but on the seventh day, which is the Sabbath, in it there shall be none."

The purpose of the Sabbath was to compel man not only to remember, but also to rest. While in Egyptian bondage the Hebrew slaves were worked seven days a week; their mortal bodies, just as ours, need a day to rejuvenate. So it is that "The Sabbath was made for man, and not man for the Sabbath."[413]

Those who maintain that the Sabbath must be kept on Saturday base their supposition on Genesis 2:2–3 which denotes GOD resting after HIS work was done on the sixth day. As GOD

---

412 Deuteronomy 6:7
413 Mark 2:27

does not get tired, the word rested in this scripture is better translated ceased or finished. Attempting to draw a correlation between HIS Creative work in Genesis and the Passover or Sabbath in Exodus has no scriptural foundation. Furthermore, nowhere in scripture is there a command for the six days of creation to be remembered any more than any of the other various acts of GOD.

With the Lord's coming to Earth and His subsequent death, a new and greater covenant came into effect. The Jewish believers stepped out from underneath the shadow of the law and into the light of grace along with the liberty that comes with it. In reality, any day and every day should be devoted to the Lord of the Sabbath. Just as important is that those who "worship Him, must worship Him in spirit and in truth."[414]

For the Believing Jew, the Law was replaced by a Redeemer, and with Him went the mandate to rest and remember on a specific day. "Christ has redeemed us from the curse of the law…"[415] Yahusha-Jesus and what He accomplished at the Cross became the completion of what the Jews were told to remember, "for by strength of hand the Lord (Yahusha) brought you out."[416] Similarly, "by strength of hand" He opened prison doors to them that were bound by the law and brought them out of captivity—proclaiming liberty to the captives.[417] The focus thereafter was to be on the Lord of the Sabbath, rather than the day of Sabbath.

> Note: Christians (be they Jew or Gentile) are now free to observe any Sabbath they choose.[418]
>
> Note: Satan is incredibly shrewd and will do whatever he can to take the focus off Yahusha-Jesus and the Cross and to pervert the Scriptures. It was to this end that he took advantage of a pagan festival which was observed long before Christ came to earth in the flesh. It was the Egyptians who worshiped "Ra" the Sun god. Later the Romans would adopt Ra, call him Sol, and dedicate a day each week to this god, calling it Sol-day or Sunday. What the pagans did does not have any bearing on what the believers did on the first day of the week when they celebrated the Resurrection and the Sabbath on that same day. As a child of GOD, life in the Spirit gives us glorious liberties, of which one is to celebrate the Sabbath when one elects to.[419]

Once a year the pagans celebrated a spring festival called (Greek: Πάσχα) – translated Eastre, which almost always coincided (astrologically) with Passover. Eastre, became Easter. The name Easter was associated with pagan goddesses connected with fertility; Eastre, Ishtar, Astarte, Ashtoreth. Today we have the prolific rabbit, the "Easter bunny" which would become a fitting secular symbol of fertility.

---

414 John 4:23-24
415 Galatians 3:13
416 Exodus 13:3
417 Isaiah 61:1
418 Romans 14:5-6; Galatians 4:9-10; Colossians 2:14-17
419 Romans 8:1

In Acts 12:4 of the King James Bible we read the name Easter, not Passover. In the development of the KJB, fifty-four of the greatest Biblical scholars in Britain painstakingly translated the ancient languages into English. In the process they did not err in using the name Easter instead of the Passover for the two have no relationship other than astrologically. This has not been the case with all modern versions (from the NIV to the NKJV). They have erred, substituting the word Passover for Easter. In the biblical account, the pagan holiday Easter followed the days of unleavened bread, and the days of unleavened bread followed the Passover.[420] They are not the same! In fact, if the King James translators would have translated the Greek word Passover as Easter they would have been in error since the Passover came before the days of unleavened bread. They intentionally were speaking of the pagan holiday.

The Roman Catholic Church and other closely associated religions claiming to be Christian make no distinction between the pagan day Easter and the Lord's Day. So it is that Easter has been associated and celebrated in place of what Christians should be celebrating and referring to as Resurrection Day, not Easter.

> "And because he saw it pleased the Jews, he proceeded further to take Peter also. (Then were the days of unleavened bread.) And when he had apprehended him, he put him in prison, and delivered him to four quaternions of soldiers to keep him; intending after Easter to bring him forth to the people." (Acts 12:3-4)

---

420 Leviticus 23:5-6

13

COVENANT PROMISES AND APPLICATION

A covenant (Hebrew, *b'rit*) means "to cut" and was so named when a solemn pact was made between two parties. In this ceremony the two individuals passed between the flesh of a blood sacrifice which had been cut and divided into pieces.[421] This shedding of blood ratified the agreement making it a blood covenant. In ancient times if either party failed to keep their part of the agreement grave consequences would follow.

Like a contract of the highest order, a covenant is made between two participants and unless otherwise stated is specific to them, or to the people or nation with whom that individual was representing—as with Moses. In the Old Testament these covenants applied to the Israelites and to their descendants (the Jewish people). In some instances, as with the Adamic/Edenic covenant there were two applications or two parts. The first part was specific to Adam and Eve,[422] while the second part was unilateral and universal and applied to all mankind[423]

GOD made the first covenant (Adamic Covenant) with a couple.[424] GOD made the Noahic Covenant after HE had cleansed the earth, and said this covenant would apply to all living creatures.[425] GOD made the Abrahamic Covenant with Abraham,[426] Isaac,[427] Jacob,[428] and with their descendants. GOD made a covenant with the Hebrews after the Exodus.[429] GOD made a covenant with King David, promising that one of his descendants would be the Messiah.[430] And then, in the book of Jeremiah, GOD said that HE would make a New Covenant with Israel.[431]

---

421 Genesis 15:10, 18
422 Genesis 1:26-39; 2:16-17
423 Genesis 3:14-21; Romans 5:12-15
424 Genesis 2:15-17
425 Genesis 9:8-17
426 Genesis 15:8; 17:9
427 Genesis 17:19, 21
428 Genesis 28:16
429 Exodus, chapters 20-23
430 2 Samuel 7:11-16
431 Jeremiah 31:31-33

> "Behold, the days come, saith the Lord, that I will make a new covenant with the house of Israel, and with the house of Judah: Not according to the covenant that I made with their fathers in the day that I took them by the hand to bring them out of the land of Egypt; which my covenant they brake, although I was an husband unto them, saith the Lord: But this shall be the covenant that I will make with the house of Israel; After those days, saith the Lord, I will put my law (Torah) in their inward parts, and write it in their hearts; and will be their God, and they shall be my people." (Jeremiah 31:31-33)

The New Covenant promise was originally made with and for the people of Israel, not instead of them. Afterward and by extension, Christians are made partakers of this covenant promise [432] but they do not replace Israel as GOD's covenantal people.[433] Romans 11:17–18 makes this abundantly clear as it tells us the Gentiles are but grafted branches while Israel is the root.

Each dispensation had or has a different divine program. The dispensation of Law came by Moses and was to the Jew. The dispensation of Grace and truth was given to the New Testament Church and came through Jesus Christ.[434] However, covenant promises made with one group or found in one of the testaments (i.e. the Old Testament) cannot be summarily appropriated and applied to another group. It is not appropriate for example for the Church to claim to be Spiritual Israel; a trend which has become quite common today in evangelical circles and is called Replacement Theology, or more appropriately, Supersessionism.

Replacement theology's foundational belief is that because the Jewish people rejected Christ at His appearing and failed to fulfil their commission of bringing the GOD of Abraham and the Messiah to the nations, they have forfeited their divine appointment and lost the opportunity to be GOD's ambassadors. They maintain that now the Church has—spiritually speaking, replaced Israel. In the process it believes it has inherited their covenants as well. They also believe the Old Testament has been replaced by the New Testament and is now only remotely relevant. As a result, the staunch Replacement advocates have minimized the need to study the Old Testament and dismissed the plan GOD has for the Jewish people. Supporters of this doctrine rely heavily on the scripture that addresses the "seed of Abraham."

While the term "seed of Abraham" is used in Galatians 3:6–9 to represent any Jew or Gentile who followed Abraham's deep faith in the GOD of Abraham, the terms Jew, Israel, or Spiritual Israel are never used in scripture of Gentile believers.

An example of misapplying a scripture to support their position and taking it out of context can be seen when Paul said of Abraham that he "was the father of all them that believe."[435] The word "father" can only be taken figuratively. Believers do not owe their spiritual life to Abraham, but to Christ. The association Paul was making was simply one of comparison between Abraham

---

432 Romans 11:17
433 Ephesians 2:12
434 John 1:17
435 Romans 4:11

"by which his faith was accounted unto him for righteousness"[436] and with that of Christians who are "saved by grace through faith."[437]

Both Abraham and those who lived before the Law and the Christians who came after the Law established their faith and hung their eternal security in the one and same Creator and on the promised Messiah.

Replacement theology adherents will use scriptures like Romans 2:28–29 to support their claim to be spiritual Israel. "For he is not a Jew, which is one outwardly; neither is that circumcision, which is outward in the flesh: But he is a Jew, which is one inwardly; and circumcision is that of the heart, in the spirit, and not in the letter; whose praise is not of men, but of God."

Subscribers to Replacement theology somehow miss the fact that the passage (Romans 2:17–29), is speaking to the Jew with regard to the law. It is simply saying that a true Jew is not one who is circumcised in the flesh, for circumcision of the flesh avails nothing without a circumcision of the heart. A true Jew is more than one who has had a physical cutting of the flesh. He is of the seed of Abraham (a Jew) and who through faith has undergone a spiritual transformation!

The New Testament covenant of Grace is universal and embraces all who become spiritually "born again."[438] In conclusion, it is inappropriate for the Church to apply promises afforded to the Jewish people to themselves.

Romans 11:1–5 makes it abundantly clear that the Jewish people have not been disowned or lost their commission. Paul said, "I say then, Hath GOD cast away HIS people (Israel)? GOD Forbid. For I also am an Israelite, of the seed of Abraham, of the tribe of Benjamin. GOD hath not cast away HIS people…"[439]

To further emphasize the tendency to misapply scripture as it pertains to covenants let us take a look at 2 Chronicles 7:14. There we read the Lord, speaking to King Solomon, made a promise saying, "If my people, which are called by my name, shall humble themselves, and pray, and seek my face, and turn from their wicked ways; then will I hear from heaven, and will forgive their sin, and will heal their land."

The Lord's reference to "My people who are called by His name" was a reference to the Jewish people during Solomon's reign who were called (or known) by the Gentiles—by His name—Yahovah or YAHUAH. And while it may be said that such a promise has a general application, "His people" does not refer to the Church. It was meant for the rebellious Israelites who had "forsook the Lord GOD of their fathers… and laid hold to other gods, worshipped them, and served them."[440] In verse 7:14 they were being encouraged to return to HIM and what HE would do if they returned.

---

436 Galatians 3:6
437 Ephesians 2:8
438 John 3:3
439 Romans 11:1-2
440 2 Chronicles 7:22

> Note: A number of familiar Greek-Roman philosophers, apologists, and so-called Church fathers waged a polemic against the Jews and Judaism and became the propagators of Replacement theology. Examples are plentiful:
>
> Justin Martyr said, "How is it you repent not of the deception you practice on yourselves, as if you alone are Israel? ...We who have been carried out from the bowels of Christ are the true Israelite race."[441]
>
> Origin (Origines Adamantius) said, "The Jews were abandoned altogether, and possess now none of what were considered their ancient glories, so there is no indication of any divinity abiding amongst them."[442]
>
> Augustine and Thomas Aquinas were in concert with their predecessors and furthered the postulate.[443]
>
> Roman Catholic priest Martin Luther believed that the destruction of Jerusalem was proof that the Jews were rejected of GOD and no longer HIS people, and neither is HE any longer their GOD. Adolf Hitler adopted Luther's conviction, and on that ignoble assertion persuaded many Germans (particularly Lutherans) to support his stand on the eradication of the Jewish race.[444]
>
> Even the Reformed Church (Calvinism) leaned in the direction of Replacement theology, as it fit nicely with their interpretation of predestination.
>
> In the twentieth century Replacement theology was advanced by Christian philosopher Karl Barth who was in the vanguard of modern liberal theology. Pope Pius the twelfth acclaimed him to be the greatest theologian of the century. The pope's praise was to be expected, as the Church of Rome has always embraced Replacement theology. Such improper interpretation of scripture demonstrates that even an acclaimed apologist who writes a magnum opus (e.g., Barth's six million word, the *Church Dogmatics*) can err. This is precisely why scripture instructs each of us to study and to rightly divide the Word.[445]

---

441   Justin Martyr, *Dialogues*, Chapter CXXIII, 130 AD
442   Origen, "De Principiis," *The Anti-Nicene Fathers*, A. Roberts and J. Donaldson, vol. 4 (1885; reprint, Grand Rapids: Eerdmans, 1994), 4.1.22
443   Augustine, *The City of YHVH*
444   William L. Shirer, *The Rise and Fall of the Third Reich*, NY, Simon & Shuster, 1960, p. 236
445   2 Timothy 2:15

Protestantism and its Branches

There are within Protestantism today two fundamental streams of thought that have divided Believers which began even before the Protestant Reformation. These divergent thoughts and distinctions have given rise to the numerous denominations we see today. While their doctrinal differences do not in any way leave the exclusivity of Christ's centrality or the authority of the Bible, they do diverge on lesser points of interpretation.

One of these divergent opinions that has been passionately debated between theologians for centuries concerns salvation and the fate of the soul (soteriology). The scripture and one of the larger points of the divide is Romans 8:29–30 and is focused on the word "predestinate" (pre-selection). That is to say, who is heaven-bound and who is hell-bound.

With my interpolations it reads, "For whom he did foreknow (the saints—the Believer), he also did predestinate to be conformed to the image of his Son (to be like Jesus), that he might be the firstborn among many brethren. Moreover, whom he did predestinate (knowing who would accept Him), them he also called (invited): and whom he called, them (who accepted) he also justified: and whom he justified, them he also glorified."[446]

One of these views is frequently referred to as Calvinism (John Calvin), and the other, Arminianism (Jacobus Arminus).

Calvinism is today what is Reform theology. Calvin's interpretation was premised on the belief that salvation was entirely of GOD and that man had nothing to do with it. He maintained that believing, repentance, and becoming saved are all because of the drawing power of GOD which is so great that one is unable to resist it; hence their destiny is assured. Calvin's theology, "Once in grace, always in grace," teaches that GOD's grace is irresistible and so the recipient can never be lost. This prompts the belief in the "eternal security doctrine" which uses John 10:28–29; 17:6; Romans 8:35; 11:29; Philemon 1:6; and 1 Peter 1:5 to support the position.

Arminianism, the other stream of theology, maintains that GOD's will is that all men can be saved because Christ died for all. Yes, Divine Grace is indeed free, but so is mans' will free to resist HIS Grace.[447]

Grace elects to save all who will believe. Grace does not discriminate or preselect. No one is predestined (Greek *proorizó*, predetermined; ordained) to go to a glorious heaven, nor is another person predetermined to go to a horrific hell. GOD beckons "all" men to accept HIS plan of Salvation. "The Lord is not slack concerning his promise, as some men count slackness; but is longsuffering to us-ward, not willing that any should perish, but that all should come to repentance."[448]

Being omniscient (all-knowing), GOD is able to see into the future in what is called foreknowledge (Greek *prognósis*), "For whom he did foreknow…"[449] That is to say, HE knows (not ordains) who will ultimately accept and who will ultimately reject HIS Son. GOD's grace is ever-present.

---

446 Romans 8:29-30
447 John 6:40; Hebrews 6:4-6; 10:26-30; 2 Peter 1:10; 2:21
448 2 Peter 3:9
449 Romans 8:29

To the assembly of Believers in the churches of Asia Minor—(Revelations chapters two and three) who had drifted away from Him, He beckons them back. "Behold I stand[s] at the door and knock (beckons): if any man hear[s] my voice (beckoning), and open[s] the door (his heart), I will come in to him…"[450] The choice is left to each individual.

The other word used in Romans 8:29–30 and elsewhere in the New Testament which is often misinterpreted is the word "called." The Greek word is *"klētos"*[451] and means invited, as opposed to selected. As with any invitation, it becomes necessary for the invited to accept it.

There are many more verses that support the Arminian position, but I'll rest my defense on just one example; "For whosoever (anyone-who) shall call upon the name of the Lord shall be saved."[452]

The Last Days and the Latter Rain

Another example of a misapplication and dislocation of scripture may be seen in Joel 2:23, Hosea 6:3 and in Acts 2:16, which all apply to the Jewish people and to Israel and are specific to the last days, not to this present dispensation (the Church dispensation). At that time the Lord will turn HIS attention back to Israel and HIS executive, the Holy Spirit, will begin the harvest referred to as the "latter rain."[453]

> "Be glad then, ye children of Zion, and rejoice in the Lord your God: for he hath given you the former rain moderately, and he will cause to come down for you the rain, the former rain, and the latter rain in the first month." (Joel 2:23)

Take special note of who it is that is being referred to "ye children of Zion" (the Jewish people).

Though the outpouring of the Holy Spirit was introduced at Pentecost, the final revival (the latter rain)[454] will not take place until after the Church dispensation has ended. It will begin during the Tribulation and build to a crescendo at the Lord's return.[455] According to the scriptures, at that time the Jewish people will be roused from their spiritual slumber by the Holy Spirit and "shall live."[456]

When Peter in Acts 2:16 said, "But this is that which was spoken of by the prophet Joel," and then proceeded to quote Joel,[457] he said, "And it shall come to pass in the last days… I will pour out My Spirit upon all flesh."[458] Peter, like Joel, was clearly speaking of the last days, referring to the Time of Jacob's Trouble and beyond. "And ye shall know that I am in the midst of Israel… And it shall come to pass afterward that I will pour out My Spirit upon all flesh…"[459]

---

450 Revelation 3:20
451 *Strong's Exhaustive Concordance*, Gk., #2821
452 Romans 10:13
453 Zechariah 10:1; 12:10-13
454 Hosea 6:3
455 Ezekiel 36:21-28
456 Ezekiel 37:9, 14
457 Joel 2:28-32
458 Acts 2:17
459 Joel 2:27, 28

Suffice to say we are not in the last days, the latter days, the end times, or the end of days. All references to these days and times are either found in the Old Testament and apply to the Jewish people, or when presented in the New Testament are specific to the Jews and the nation of Israel during the Time of Jacob's trouble, the millennial reign and beyond.[460]

Take special note of the word "afterward." Also take note that the scriptures in Joel have a direct application to the Jewish people. This same outpouring of the Spirit anticipated for Israel spoken in the books of Joel and Acts dovetails with Ezekiel 36:24–27. What Peter was sharing with his audience in Acts after receiving the Baptism of the Holy Spirit was that what had just happened at Shavuot (Pentecost) was "a kin and a kind" of what will happen in the last days.

We also need to reexamine the word "all," as applied to "all flesh." There are words used in scripture and elsewhere which are often taken (too) literally when in fact they are meant generally. This is a figure of speech called synecdoche. When applied to a word such as the word "all" it will often have a measured meaning. It can in fact be used to describe a part of a whole.

We see an example of synecdoche elsewhere in scripture such as in Romans 11:26. "And so all Israel shall be saved…" The word "all" does not mean that every Jew will, unequivocally or automatically be saved simply because they are of Israel. This is validated among other places in Matthew 25:1–13 (the parable of the ten virgins) and in 25:24–30 (the parable of the talents and the unfaithful servant). So, when in Joel, scripture speaks of the Spirit being poured out on "all" flesh its meaning must be mitigated. The scholarly student looks at how the word is being applied and then compares it with other scriptures which either support it or give cause to challenge the interpretation.

Lastly, if this Scripture which Peter was referring to was a promised revival for the Church we have a conundrum, for if it began at Pentecost then it has already been going on now for nearly two thousand years and subsequently we have already been in the last days for nearly two thousand years.

Revival GOD's Way

Expecting a move of GOD is fine, but genuine heaven-sent revival comes only through the lost art of prayer, followed by the acknowledgement of sin and brokenness.[461] The louder the music and the bigger the extravaganza and the more speakers strut and parade across the stage hollering into their microphones the further away revival is. When the human asserts himself and becomes the focus, the Holy Spirit takes His leave.

In his book *Azusa Street*, Frank Bartleman wrote, "If ever men shall seek to control, corner or own the work of GOD, either for their own glory or for an organization, we shall find the Spirit refusing to work. The glory will depart. Let this (speaking of the Azusa Street revival) be one work where GOD shall be given His proper place, and we shall see such a work as men have never dreamed."[462]

---

460 Joel 2:28-32
461 Daniel 9:3-13
462 Frank Bartleman, *Azusa Street*, Bridge Publishing, Inc., South Plainfield, New Jersey, 1980, p. 90

In the past, "Awakenings" (national or global awakenings to GOD) usually occur against a backdrop of very serious spiritual and moral decline. Frequently a catastrophic event like the great San Francisco earthquake of 1906 in which no less than ten thousand lives were lost would leave the survivors numb. Thinking the world was coming to an end many were jolted from their pursuits and preoccupations and sought GOD in communal prayer by gathering in homes. Churches which previously had few attendees began to fill with those looking for answers. So, it may be said that sometimes peril can be our friend as GOD has been known to mercifully dispatch the Holy Spirit to wrench men from their complacency, convict them of their depravity, and compel them to earnestly seek HIM.

As the word revival implies, men are to be revived. Many times, after a genuine awakening the multitude that were before hostages of organized religion or who sat like manikins in dead churches, leave their mortuaries and are forever changed.

Frequently, Awakenings come just before judgement. In 1905, Bartleman wrote, "In 1859, a great revival wave visited our country, sweeping a half a million souls into the fountain of salvation. Immediately the terrible carnage of the War Between the States, 1861–1865, followed. We anticipate that a coming revival, which is already begun—will not judgment follow mercy, as at other times. The present warlike attitude and distress of nations makes us wonder if the judgment to follow may even plunge us into tribulation, the Great one."[463]

That was Bartleman's thought in 1905 and as fate would have it the Azusa Street Revival faded out in 1911 when men began taking it over making it into a church service. Shortly after the Awakening ended judgment came. On June 28, 1914, Archduke Franz Ferdinand was assassinated which is widely acknowledged as the spark that started World War I.

Today there is a move of the Spirit. A groundswell has begun around the world as hundreds of thousands are discovering their Savior. From what the past has shown us, I dare say this outpouring is a precursor of coming judgment on a global scale. "…for when the judgments are in the earth, the inhabitants of the world learn righteousness."[464]

> Note: The terms "revival" and "awakenings" are both moves of GOD. They are however frequently misapplied. Revival (to revive) is for the Church who has become lethargic and passive to the things of GOD. An Awakening is a supernatural intervention for the country. It is a merciful act that brings conviction and repentance and has bearing on the unsaved.
>
> Note: Though it is the fervent hope of the Church today for a heaven-sent revival, there is nothing actually stated in scripture guaranteeing a global revival at the end of this current (Church) dispensation. The Great Revival promised in the "latter days" is named "the Latter Rain" and is promised to the children of Zion (the Jewish people in Israel) during the time of Jacob's trouble.

---

463 Frank Bartleman, *Azusa Street*, Bridge Publishing, Inc., South Plainfield, NJ, 1980, p. 21
464 Isaiah 26:9

> Note: This dreaded time of Jacob's Trouble, the Great Tribulation—the last half of the Seventieth Week of Daniel are all one and the same. The catastrophic events recorded in the book of the Revelation will be the very catalyst needed to bring the Jewish people to their knees, to repentance, and ultimately to their Savior. This will be the beginning of the genuine "Latter Rain" Awakening.

Dependency on GOD's Grace

Whether we are speaking of an Awakening or a Covenant promise, they are each dependent on GOD's grace. Some covenants require man to fulfill his part of the contract in order for the promise to become active or attainable. The Sinaitic Covenant was a covenant of works in which legal obedience (and much more) was the initial step on the road to salvation. Ultimately, even in the Sinaitic Covenant we find that faith and dependency on GOD's grace would be the crucial element.

> "Behold, his soul which is lifted up is not upright in him, but the just shall live by faith." (Habakkuk 2:4)

> "For as many as are of the works of the law are under the curse: for it is written, Cursed is every one that continueth not in all things which are written in the book of the law to do them. But that no man is justified by the law in the sight of God, it is evident: for, The just shall live by faith." (Galatians 3:10, 11)

The supposition that one can somehow earn his way to heaven by keeping the law to perfection is not only implausible but impossible. And, if GOD demands absolute perfection in order to acquire heaven, then heaven is vacant, and the Law would have been a cruel scheme by GOD to punish HIS creation. In reality the Law was meant to show us our inability to keep it. Unable to save ourselves, we are compelled to seek, find and graciously accept the New and everlasting covenant.[465]

> "Incline your ear, and come unto me: hear, and your soul shall live; and I will make an everlasting covenant with you, even the sure mercies of David." (Isaiah 55:3)

> Note: The "sure mercies of David" refer to the gracious promise (the Davidic Covenant) that the Messiah would be a descendent of David. Isaiah is telling us that the everlasting covenant will be, (and now has been) instituted by the Messiah.

---

465 Jeremiah 31:31

The Law and Grace

The first covenant, the Old Covenant, would be useful, even needful. The Israelites would have to learn that GOD is not to be trifled with. They would be forced to acknowledge their indomitable rebellious spirit and they would have to learn that they are to be totally trusting, reliant and dependent on HIM. Victories—past and future, were not and will not be had because of mans' prowess or military might; they are HIS and HIS alone.

> "Be strong and courageous, be not afraid nor dismayed for the king of Assyria, nor for all the multitude that is with him: for there be more with us than with him: With him is an arm of flesh; but with us is the Lord our God to help us, and to fight our battles. And the people rested themselves upon the words of Hezekiah king of Judah." (2 Chronicles 32:7-8)

> "Some trust in chariots, and some in horses; but we will remember the name of the Lord." (Psalm 20:7)

> "For they got not the land in possession by their own sword, neither did their own arm save them: but thy right hand, and thine arm (Yahusha), and the light of thy countenance, because thou hadst a favour unto them." (Psalm 44:3)

> "Not by might, nor power, but by My Spirit, saith the Lord of Hosts (Yahusha)." (Zechariah 4:6)

It was pride and self-reliance which led the Israelites to believe they were capable of keeping the Law, and so they exclaimed, "The Lord our GOD we will serve, and HIS voice we will obey…"[466] However instead of keeping this vow they did just the opposite; they broke the covenant, disobeyed GOD, worshiped idols, and sought other gods. So it was that the Law would remain in effect. Even now the Law remains in force for those Jews who persist in trying to live under it.[467] They have chosen to be judged by the very Law which condemns them rather than accept GOD's grace which would otherwise free them from the "Law of sin and death."[468]

> "For as many as have sinned without law (Gentiles) shall also perish without law (if they do not receive the New Covenant): and as many as have sinned in the law (Jews), shall be judged by the law…" (Romans 2:12)

> "For the law was given by Moses, but grace and truth came by Jesus Christ." (John 1:17)

---

466 Joshua 24:24
467 Romans 2:12
468 Romans 8:2

In some cases, there are covenants GOD makes with man which don't require a response.[469] This is not to say that when men violate such a covenant there aren't ramifications.[470] Often it would be through painful ordeals that man would learn valuable lessons as forewarned in Leviticus 26:14–28 and Deuteronomy 28:15–68.

In the final analysis, the purpose of covenants was and is to bring man into a close relationship with their creator and to become a "peculiar treasure…a kingdom of priests and a holy nation."[471]

If we look at the covenants as a whole, we see both a lesson and a great plan. Each is another rung on the ladder to mans' redemption and restoration. These covenants and our inability to live the law are in a manner of speaking, "a schoolmaster" whereby we learn from our collective mistakes.

> "But before faith came, we were kept under the law, shut up unto the faith which should afterward be revealed. Wherefore the law was our schoolmaster to bring us unto Christ, that we might be justified by faith. But after that faith is come, we are no longer under a schoolmaster. For ye are all (Jew and Gentile) the children of God by faith in Christ Jesus." (Galatians 3:23-26)

The function of the Law was to define sin, and yet it can do nothing whatever to cure it.

Seven Dispensations

Most of the covenants were put in place for a specific period of time. These intervals of time, perhaps lasting a thousand or even two thousand years are referred to as "classical ages" (Gk. *Aions*—period of time) or "dispensations"—meanings vary. In each age, GOD would introduce yet another paradigm by which we could get to know and understand HIM better. These dispensations could be compared to the way a parent might raise up a child, applying a graduated behavior plan as the child matures.

Initially, the infant child is innocent, and nothing is expected of them. Later the toddler begins to develop a conscience and is given promises or rewards in order to bring about the desired behavior. As the child gets older, rules (laws) are put in place and punishments are applied when the child disobeys. The parent has expectations that with discipline the proper behavior is learned. Still later as the individual becomes a young adult and corresponding with their development and behavior, more latitude (grace) is given. At the same time that latitude or license is given more is expected of that young adult.

The Dispensations (particularly the premillennial view) of man from Adam to the present time may be condensed into the following four ages: Innocence and Conscience (Adam and Eve), Promise (Abraham, Isaac and Jacob), Law (Moses and the Israelites), and Grace (The

---

469 Genesis 9:8-17
470 Genesis 18:10
471 Exodus 19:5-6

Church—by the New Covenant).[472] Each dispensation is unique and yet they all have at their core; recognition of GOD, a relationship with GOD, a faith in GOD, and obedience to GOD.

Following these four ages will come three more. The first is a dispensation of Correction and Judgment. It may be compared to what generally happens if the adolescent remains defiant, arrogant, and rebellious. Refusing to heed the parent and/or the public authorities, law enforcement steps in and a judicial decision is handed down for a prescribed (seven year) sentence—the Tribulation Dispensation.[473]

After the seven years are served, those who have endured to the end will be judged.[474] Those who sought and accepted the Lord during this time will be liberated into a Millennial Dispensation; a thousand-year theocracy under the sovereign reign of Yahusha-Jesus.[475] At the conclusion of the thousand years a final tribunal will be held.[476] The "books," in which are recorded the names of all who have ever lived will be opened. Those found in the "Book of Life" will enter into a glorious Dispensation of Perfection (the Eternal Kingdom—Heaven on Earth).[477] Those who are not in the Book of Life will be cast into an eternal lake of fire.[478]

Let us proceed to look at each of the Ages more closely and see that GOD had a plan!

The Age of Innocence and Conscience

Adam and Eve were meant to be the caretakers of the earth, beginning with the Garden of Eden.[479] They failed when they disobeyed GOD and ate the forbidden fruit. Sin and death came into being and all men became its subjects. Born in innocence they lived in the Age of Conscience.[480]

> "Wherefore, as by one man (Adam) sin entered into the world, and death by sin; and so death passed upon all men, for that all have sinned..." (Romans: 5:12)

But GOD had a plan by which to redeem man back to HIMSELF. In spite of mans' failure, HE would send Yahusha. The following message attributed to have been spoken by Moses is a definitive prophesy of the coming Messiah and His defeat over the curse that sin and disobedience otherwise exact.

> "Because thou (Satan) hath done this, thou art cursed... and I will put enmity (hate) between thee and thy seed (figuratively—the children of Satan) and the Women and between thy

---

472   2 Thessalonians 2:16
473   Jeremiah 30:3-7
474   Joel 3:12-14; Matthew 25:31-34
475   Jeremiah 30:9; Revelation 20:4
476   Revelation 20:11-12; Daniel 2:35
477   Revelation 21:1-2
478   Revelation 20:12-15; Isaiah 66:24
479   Genesis 2:15
480   Genesis 2:7

seed and her (Marian's seed); it (He, Yahusha-Jesus) shall bruise thy head (bring a fatal wound to you Satan), and thou (Satan) shall (only) bruise his heel (Satan was only able to bring a fleeting suffering to Christ)." (Deuteronomy 3:15)

The Age of Promise

Abram was the father of the Covenants of Promise; three in total. He was given a land for his descendants. He would be the father of a great nation, and through him all the nations of the earth would be blessed.[481] However, Abram disobeyed GOD and had a son by Sarai's handmaiden Hagar and named him Ishmael. Though the covenant would remain in place, Abram's descendants would pay dearly for his decision. Ishmael would become the progenitor of the Arab-Islamic nation who would thereafter be "against" the descendants of Isaac.

"And he (Ishmael's descendants) will be a wild man; his (their) hand will be against every man, and every man's hand against him (them); and he (Ishmael's descendants—the Arab nations) shall dwell in the presence of all his (Isaac's) brethren (the Jewish people)." (Genesis 16:12)

But GOD had a plan by which to bless Isaac's descendants. HE would send Yahusha through Isaac's seed.

"And there shall come forth a rod out of the stem (stock) of Jesse (the Father of David), and a Branch (the Messiah) shall grow out of his roots: and the Spirit of the Lord (the Rauch HaKodesh) shall rest upon Him (Yahusha-Jesus), the spirit of wisdom and understanding, the spirit of counsel and might, the spirit of knowledge and of the fear (reverence) of the Lord..." (Isaiah 11:1-2)

The Age of Law

Moses was given a covenant at Sinai and instructions to lead the people into the "Promised Land." It could have been a mere twelve-day journey if they had gone directly to Canaan from Egypt, but they did not yet know this GOD of whom Moses spoke, neither did they know HIS ways.[482]

HE would need to take them into the arid desert; to a place where they would learn to be dependent upon HIM. They would need to learn to trust HIM and obey HIM, but they stumbled with each new trial. They murmured constantly and built a golden calf. Then, when reaching the threshold of the Promised Land, ten of the twelve spies balked at taking the land GOD had told them to possess. As a result, the Hebrews would wander forty more years in the wilderness while a generation of murmurers and disbelievers aged out and died off.[483]

---

481 Genesis 12:2-3; 17:2, 8; 22:17-18
482 Hebrews 3:7-11
483 Numbers 13-14

But GOD had a plan. GOD would give them His Word in Law,[484] and four decades in which to learn HIS ways until they understood the measure of divine obedience. HE would also tell them of the coming Messiah and that He shall fulfill the law.

> "The Lord thy God will raise up unto thee a Prophet from the midst of thee, of thy brethren, like unto me (a redeemer); unto Him ye shall hearken..." (Deuteronomy 18:15)

> "And it shall come to pass, that whosoever will not hearken unto my words which He (Messiah) shall speak in My (GOD's) name, I (YAHUAH) will require it of him." (Deuteronomy 18:19)

The Age of Grace

Yahusha arrived on earth as promised and on time. A new dispensation began. He came for the "lost sheep of the house of Israel" and offered Himself as their Savior.[485] Afterward, He would send a Jewish convert, Sha'ul (Paul) of Tarsus to the Gentiles. Some of them would accept the Jewish Messiah as their Savior and the genuine Church; an assembly of Jew and Gentile was born.

The Lessons of the Law had been taught, the school term (the Age of the Law) had ended; it was graduation day. From that time forward the penalty attached to all the broken laws were paid in full for those who accepted Yahusha-Jesus and what He accomplished on a Cross. For them, not only had the wrath of GOD been averted but they would afterward appear sinless in HIS eyes.

> "But GOD commendeth HIS love toward us, in that while we were yet sinners, Christ died for us. Much more then, being now justified by HIS blood, we shall be saved from wrath through HIM." (Romans 5:8, 9)

> "...though your sins be as scarlet, they shall be as white as snow; though they be red like crimson, they shall be as wool." (Isaiah 1:18)

> Note: The grace of GOD may not be taken lightly. While forgiveness is offered to the truly penitent, one cannot continue in their sin and expect an endless stream of forgiveness. Though we all will slip on the slope of sin from time to time, we are to strive to walk upright on the path of virtue. A holy fear of GOD is the beginning of wisdom and so we must walk warily, for where there is no fear there is no grace either.

> "For if we sin wilfully after that we have received the knowledge of the truth, there remaineth no more sacrifice for sins, but a certain fearful looking for of judgment and fiery indignation, which shall devour the adversaries." (Hebrews 10:26-27)

---

484 Deuteronomy 5:1-6
485 Matthew 15:24

Note: Dispensations may be framed differently and therefore the number of dispensations may be viewed differently. The Dake Annotated Reference Bible list (on page 817) nine dispensations: It includes, Angels—Pre-Adamic, Innocence, Conscience, Human Government, Promise, Law, Grace, Divine Government (Millennial), and the eternal Dispensation of the Redeemed (Kingdom Age). He leaves out the brief Tribulation which is a dispensation as well.

14

THE NEW COVENANT

The New Covenant unlocks the Promises of the Old (Image Source: GOODSALT)

The B'rit HaChadeshah

The New Covenant (Hebrew, *B'rit HaChadeshah*) is the promised and final covenant which GOD said HE would make with Israel. It was already extended and is even now available to the individual who earnestly seeks it. It is hidden in plain sight in the New Testament.

Though refused and in some cases even spurned, the New Covenant will become front and center at the conclusion of the Gentile Age. At that time the Holy Spirit will breathe spiritual life into those Jewish people[486] who have survived the sword, famine and fire of the time of Jacob's Trouble.[487]

> "Behold, the days come, saith the Lord, that I will make a new covenant with the house of
> Israel, and with the house of Judah. Not according to the covenant that I made with their

---
486 Ezekiel 36:27
487 Isaiah 66:15-16, 19

fathers... But this shall be the covenant, that I will make with the house of Israel; After those days, saith the Lord, I will put My law in their inward parts, and write it in their hearts; and will be their GOD, and they shall be My people." (Jeremiah 31:31-33)

This spiritual awakening (the new birth) is a divine impartation of the Holy Spirit which enters into a man or women the moment they accept the Savior as their own.

"Jesus answered and said unto him, If a man love me, he will keep my words: and my Father will love him, and We (the Godhead) will come unto him, and make our abode with him." (John 14:23)

The B'rit HaChadeshah had been in effect for nearly two thousand years when what appeared to some to be just an ordinary man was put to death on a Cross. As His blood streamed from His body from hundreds of inflicted wounds, and His soul deserted His mortality, a blood covenant went into effect.[488]

But this covenant like many is only ratified when both parties enter into it. Many have already done so. Some have thought about it but have postponed it, and then there are those who recognize that they are sinners, desperately want to be forgiven and have sought for an intimate relationship with their creator. In so far as the Jewish people are concerned we are told that there is now and will afterward be a remnant who fall into this wonderful category.[489] However, as with a carpet, a remnant is only a small piece; which speaks of a relatively small number of the Jewish people who will seek, find, and accept the New Covenant during the current dispensation.[490] In the next dispensation this will reverse, and many of those living at that time will enter in.

"Thus saith the Lord of hosts; If it be marvelous in the eyes of the remnant of this people in these days, should it also be marvelous in Mine eyes? Saith the Lord of hosts. Thus saith the Lord of hosts; Behold, I will save my people from the east country, and from the west country; and I will bring them, and they shall dwell in the midst of Jerusalem: and they shall be my people, and I will be their God, in truth and righteousness." (Zechariah 8:6-8)

"After this I will return, and will build again the tabernacle of David, which is fallen down; and I will build again the ruins thereof, and I will set it up: That the residue of men might seek after the Lord, and all the Gentiles, upon whom my name is called, saith the Lord, who doeth all these things." (Acts 15:16-17)

There are some who believe that the New Covenant has not yet come into existence. They read the promise in Jeremiah 31:31–34 and interpret it to mean that it is solely to and for the

---

488 1 Corinthians 11:25
489 Isaiah 11:11; Jeremiah 23:3
490 Romans 11:5

House of Israel and will be given to the Jewish people during the thousand-year reign of Christ. Furthermore, they believe that the Church has no covenant with GOD, or that it is encompassed in the Abrahamic covenant. This premise has no merit. Those who believe the New Covenant is just for Israel have erred because they have been looking for the word "covenant" (Hebrew: *brit, beyrith*).

When the translators translated the Hebrew into the Greek (the Septuagint), the word "brit" was taken over by the word *diatheke, diakheke*. Its conventional meaning is "testament." The *Strong's Exhaustive Concordance* gives the same meaning to both words (Heb.#1285; Gk.#1242), indicating that they are essentially synonymous depending on how they appear in the Scriptures and how the words are attached to verbs. While indeed the New Covenant will be offered during the millennium to the Jewish people, it will be for the second time.[491] The New Covenant was offered to them at His first appearance as He came for the lost house of Israel, where many missed the time of His visitation. As GOD is no respecter of persons, HE turned HIS attention to the non-Jew and on the day of Pentecost offering HIS New Covenant to them.[492] So, while Jeremiah 31:31–34 makes it clear that the New Covenant will be offered to the Jewish people, it never states that this New Covenant was not, nor will not be made available to all who believe. John 3:16 clearly tells us that the covenant promise of eternal salvation is now available to all.

An example of the two covenant offerings and the application of the word "testament" being applied is seen in Hebrews 9:15: "And for this cause he is the mediator of the new testament, that by means of death, for the redemption of the transgressions that were under the first testament, they which are called might receive the promise of eternal inheritance."

Clearly, we see our Lord using the term testament at the Last Supper when He said to his disciples, "After the same manner also he took the cup, when he had supped, saying, this cup is the new testament in my blood (making it a blood covenant): this do ye, as oft as ye drink it, in remembrance of me."[493] He was saying that very soon He would go to the Cross and in doing so, His death and His blood would inaugurate a New Covenant for those who placed their faith in His sacrifice.

I would do well to point out that the weightiest covenants, as with the Sinaitic[494] and the Passover[495] were ratified by a death and a blood offering. The first "testament" (under the law) was the covenant promise of eternal life by faith and fidelity to Elohim. Jesus would establish the New Covenant or second "testament" at Calvary and so stated it when He said, "For this is my blood of the New Testament (Covenant), which is shed for many for the remission of sins."[496] As with the first testament, so is the second testament a covenant promise based on faith and fidelity.

---

491 Isaiah 11:10-12
492 Acts 2:39
493 1 Corinthians 11:25
494 Exodus 24:5-6
495 Genesis 12:13
496 Matthew 26:28

The Serpent on the Pole—Numbers 21:4–9

On what would become their four-decade long wilderness journey to the land GOD had bequeathed Abraham's seed,[497] some of the newly emancipated Hebrews having left Egypt began to speak against GOD and HIS appointed emancipator Moses. They murmured about their travel and complained about the provisions GOD had miraculously blessed them with.[498] So it was that GOD would give them an object lesson in type and by example. HE would send poisonous snakes which inflicted painful bites on the complainers; many of whom died.

"Look and Live" (Image Source: GOODSALT)

The people, having realized that the snakes were brought by GOD because of their insolence went to Moses acknowledging their sins, "We have sinned."[499] They begged Moses to pray to GOD to remove the snakes. However, GOD chose not to remove the snakes but instead show them how they could be saved even when bitten (by sin).

GOD instructed Moses to fashion a serpent of brass and set it on a tall pole where it could be seen from all parts of the camp. Then he was to tell the people that those who were bitten and who would look upon this emblem of their sin would live. Whoever refused would most certainly die. This would be a strange decree whereby one had to envision that an object could bear ones' sin and be hung on a pole in his stead. It would require believing in something beyond reason; something totally illogical. It would require believing GOD. It would require faith!

"If someone guilty of a capital offense is put to death and their body is exposed on a pole, you must not leave the body hanging on the pole overnight. Be sure to bury it that same day, because anyone who is hung on a pole is under God's curse. You must not desecrate the land the Lord your God is giving you as an inheritance." (Deuteronomy 21:22-23)

"Cursed is every one that hangeth on a tree..." (Galatians 3:13)

---

497 Genesis 15:18
498 Exodus 16:4, 15; 17:3
499 Numbers 21:7

It is hard to imagine that any of the Hebrews truly understood how looking at a brass serpent could possibly save them, but they had taken the first step by having acknowledged their sin. Now, by faith they would believe Moses who had believed and obeyed GOD.

That day, some thirty-four hundred years ago, the serpent depicted the emblem of sin. The pole became the emblem of the Cross on which the sin substitute (the Suffering Servant) was hung. That day those individuals who by faith believed and obeyed were saved from death.

> "And as Moses lifted up the serpent in the wilderness, even so must the Son of man be lifted up (on a Cross): That whosoever believeth in him should not perish, but have eternal life." (John 3:14-15)

Sadly, we learn from the Scriptures that as a nation, Israel will continue denying her Savior and consequently her national redemption until the last days of the human era. Only then are we told, when her military might has been expended and she finds herself on the verge of annihilation will she cry out in desperation and plead to Yahusha to rescue her.[500]

The many prophets; Moses,[501] Joel,[502] Hosea,[503] Isaiah,[504] Zephaniah,[505] Jeremiah,[506] Ezekiel,[507] Daniel,[508] Zechariah,[509] Malachi,[510] and before them the patriarch Jacob, spoke of Yahusha and of His rescuing and vindicating His people in the last days at the momentous Battle of Armageddon.[511]

The blind have led the blind, and while many who profess to know and teach may hold the book of Truth in their hands, they are yet spiritually sightless. Proudly relying on their knowledge, intellect, and natural wisdom, they claim to have taken hold of the divine; "Ever learning, and never able to come to the knowledge of the truth."[512]

In Jesus' day it was largely because the religious leaders placed little importance on the prophetic scriptures that they failed to recognize Him when He came. Likewise religious leaders of today who disregard prophecy will not be ready when the Church is translated to heaven.

For one to obtain even a glimpse of GOD or to understand HIS Word and ways, it must come from HIM.[513] "The natural man receiveth not the things of the Spirit of GOD: for they

---

500 Psalm 14:7; Isaiah 59:19; Revelation 19:11-15
501 Deuteronomy 4:30
502 Joel 2:1-10, 20-21
503 Hosea 10:14-15; 14:4
504 Isaiah 63:1-6
505 Zephaniah 6:14-15; 3:14-15
506 Jeremiah 30:5-7, 10-11
507 Ezekiel 38:16
508 Daniel 12:1
509 Zechariah 14:2-3, 11-12
510 Malachi 3:3
511 Genesis 49:1, 18-19
512 2 Timothy 3:7
513 Matthew 16:17

are foolishness unto him; neither can he know them, because they are spiritually discerned."[514] Only the humble are given sight for "the Lord openeth the eyes of the blind: the Lord raises them that are bowed down…"[515] He will only be found by those who earnestly seek Him in this way.

"And ye shall seek Me and find Me, when ye search for Me with all your heart." (Jeremiah 29:3)

> Note: By all the many and varied events which we now see occurring in the Middle East; the most significant being the progression of a Peace Plan between Israel and the Arab nations, we now find ourselves on the brink of the "last days." These days will begin shortly after the Church (the last guardian of truth) has been translated to heaven.[516] At that time the Jewish people and Israel will find themselves abandoned and alone. This underscores the title of this manuscript, *"For Such a Time as This"* which has been written, I dare say designated, for that hour when the Jewish people will be ready to receive the message of the Cross and accept their Yahusha.

The Jew First

Many Christians are under the assumption that every verse in the Bible has a direct application to the Christian Church, when in fact four-fifths of the Bible (all of the Old Testament and most of the New Testament) was written to the Jewish people by Jewish scribes.

The entire Old Testament is an historic account of GOD's dealings with the Hebrew/Israelite/Jewish people. It is unarguably a collection of chronicles, covenants, and prophecies to them. However, we also need to recognize that even the vast majority of the New Testament was written to the Jew. The first assemblies (Hebrew, *qahal*) of believers were largely comprised of Jews with only (at first) a small fraction comprised of Gentiles who were drawn in by the Holy Spirit when they bore witness to the truth.[517] Upon examination one will discover that in fact only about forty percent of the New Testament was actually directed to the fledgling Church recorded in letters (Hebrew, *iggerots*) known today as the Pauline epistles. These letters were written by a Benjaminite rabbi named Saul of Tarsus (Paul) who had studied under Rabbi Gamaliel.[518] Paul began writing these letters a number of years after the Messiah had been put to death when he began his missionary journeys around the eastern Mediterranean (circa, 45 AD).[519]

---

514   1 Corinthians 2:14
515   Psalm 146:8
516   2 Thessalonians 2:7
517   Acts 2:47
518   Acts 22:3
519   Acts 13

Though Paul had been divinely appointed to minister to the Gentiles[520] we see that his heart was still very much focused on the Jews, for when he went into various cities he would first go to the synagogues and speak to them on their Sabbaths.[521] He was "bound by his hope for Israel" in that they would come out of their trance and recognize their Messiah.[522]

It is also noteworthy to see that Paul's success in bringing Jews and Gentiles to recognize that Yahusha-Jesus was indeed the promised Mashiach came entirely from the Hebrew Holy Scriptures (Old Testament), as the New Testament was yet to be written. Paul's writings were to present the Jewish Messiah to the Gentiles, not the Gentile Messiah to the Jews!

Not only were the four Gospels which record Yahusha-Jesus's words directed to "the lost sheep of the house of Israel"[523] (not to the Gentiles or a fledgling Church) but so would the last book of the Bible be to the Jews.

The Book of the Revelation of Jesus Christ[524] was written to the Jews who will be alive shortly before the Lord's return (Second Coming). Of the twenty-two chapters of this apocalyptic book, only the first three chapters have an application to the Church. The next fifteen chapters (4–18) are largely about the Jews and Israel who will find themselves caught up in the Great Tribulation. The last four concluding chapters of Revelation (19–22) pertain to all people (Jews, Believers, and Gentiles) at the conclusion of the earth age and thereafter.

It had been GOD's initial plan that the Israelites were to take the GOD of Israel to all the nations (Gentiles) and initiate the Great Commission.[525] However, when they turned away from YAHUAH, compromised with the heathen world and fell into idolatry, that commission was for the time being, passed on to the Believers (the Church). After this Age of Human Government ends and the Millennial Age begins, it is GOD's plan that the Jewish people will become HIS principal ambassadors and teachers.[526] The Apostle Peter speaking to Jewish Christians about the Jewish people[527] said of them, "they will be a chosen generation, a royal priesthood and a holy nation, (Hebrew, *mamlechet kohan vegoy kadosh*), that ye show forth the praises of Him who hath called you out of darkness into the marvelous light."[528]

"And in thy seed shall all the nations of the earth be blessed." (Genesis 22:18)

"And in that day there shall be a root of Jesse, which shall stand for an ensign of the people; to it shall the Gentiles seek: and his rest shall be glorious." (Isaiah 11:10)

---

520 Acts 22:21
521 Acts 13:14; 14:1; 17:1, 10, 17; 18:4; 19:8
522 Acts 28:20
523 Matthew 15:34
524 Revelation 1:1
525 Luke 24:47; Mark 16:15
526 Zechariah 8:23
527 Deuteronomy 7:6; Exodus 19:6
528 1 Peter 2:9

"Thus saith the Lord of hosts; In those days it shall come to pass, that ten men shall take hold out of all languages of the nations, even shall take hold of the skirt of him that is a Jew, saying, We will go with you: for we have heard that God is with you." (Zechariah 8:23)

See Appendix B, *The Olivet Discourse*. A scant outline of the book of the Revelation as it pertains to the Jewish people and Israel during the time of Jacob's trouble and the coming of the Lord Yahusha-Jesus.

15

THE RAUCH H'QODESH

GOD, the Holy Spirit

The Rauch H'Qodesh, or HaRuach HaKodesh, (the Lord Holy Spirit) is the third person of the GODhead mentioned in the Scriptures. He, like the Father and Son, has existed from eternity past, and He, like the Father and the Son has been a co-creator of the universe.

> "...the Spirit of GOD moved upon the face of the waters." (Genesis 1:2)

He is mentioned eighty-nine times in the Bible but in the first person of the Old Testament only three times. His dynamic operations however are undeniable for He is the agent of the GODhead who is the actuator; carrying out the will of El Elohim.

The Rauch H'Qodesh (Image Source: GOODSALT)

He works on the physical plane here on earth as it concerns all the facets of nature and events, but His greater work is done on the spiritual plane. Like a surgeon, He operates on both the individual's heart and mind in tandem in order to draw them to the Creator.

Why haven't we heard more of Him in the Old Testament, one might ask?

The Holy Spirit remained largely in obscurity during the early dispensations. However, His work is clearly visible in the life and ministry of the prophet Samuel and the other prophets who, under His inspiration,[529] were given to speak for the Lord as recorded in Scripture. His purpose then, as it is now, was not to take center stage but to divert attention to the Savior. He would begin the restorative process by awakening men to "Yah" יָהּ (the GOD of Israel)[530] and

---

529 2 Timothy 3:16
530 *Strong's Exhaustive Concordance*, Heb., #3050; Exodus 51:2; 17:16; Psalm 68:5, 19; 77:12; 89:9; 94:7, 12; 102:19; 105:45; 106:1; Isaiah 12:2; 26:4; 38:11

then to Yah the Savior (Yahusha-Jesus). As the Savior is the only Way to GOD[531] since His initial visit,[532] the Holy Spirit's primary objective has been to bring Him into focus.[533]

All the prophets were visited by the Holy Spirit who not only motivated them to speak for GOD, but who had inspired them to speak about the promised Savior.[534] Micah, for example, said, "Therefore I will look unto the Lord; I will wait for the GOD of my salvation (Yesha-Yahusha)."[535]

Just before His earthly departure, Yahusha-Jesus spoke to His disciples in order to assure them they were not going to be left alone in His absence. He told them that He would ask the Father to send another—the Comforter (Greek, *Paraklesis*)—the Holy Spirit, and that He would abide with them forever.[536]

> "Howbeit when He, the Spirit of Truth (the Holy Spirit) is come, He will guide you into all truth: for He shall not speak of Himself; but whatsoever He shall hear (from the Father and Son), that He (shall) speak: and He will shew you things to come. He shall glorify Me: (Yahusha); for He shall receive of Mine, and shew it unto you." (John 16:13-14)

It has been the Rauch H'Qodesh who has been the chief agent of the GODhead on earth for the last nearly two thousand years since Yahusha's resurrection and temporary return to His heavenly throne at the Father's right hand.

> "The Lord said unto my Lord, Sit thou at my right hand, until I make thine enemies thy footstool." (Psalm 110:1)

During this present dispensation (the Church Age), the Holy Spirit has been given oversight of the believing body known as the Church.[537]

> "And I will pray the Father, and he shall give you another Comforter, that he may abide with you forever; even the Spirit of truth; whom the world cannot receive, because it seeth him not, neither knoweth him: but ye know him; for he dwelleth with you, and shall be in you." (John 14:16-17)

The Apostle Paul would afterward say, "But if the Spirit of HIM (GOD) that raised up Jesus from the dead dwell in you, He (the Holy Spirit) that raised up Christ from the dead shall also quicken (make alive) your mortal bodies by HIS Spirit that dwelleth in you."[538]

---

531 John 14:6
532 Acts 4:12
533 Acts 16:13
534 2 Timothy 3:13
535 Micah 7:7
536 2 Timothy 14:16
537 2 Timothy 14:16-26
538 Romans 8:11

> "For by one Spirit are we all baptized into one body, whether we be Jews or Gentiles, whether we be bond or free; and have been all made to drink into one Spirit." (1 Corinthians 12:13)

Upon Yahusha-Jesus' return the Holy Spirit will relinquish oversight of the Church back to Yahusha who will assume His role and title as "Lord of the whole earth."[539]

Unlike men who seek to be acknowledged, there is no envy between the persons of the GODhead. Human tendencies like pride and jealousy simply do not exist. Neither is there position or rank among them; they are entirely co-equal as expressed in the composite unity of *Echad*.

> Note: There are sadly certain sects, e.g., the Jehovah's Witness, who do not see Yahusha-Jesus as GOD and coequal with the Father. Rather they see Jesus as a created being, even as the angelic brother of Lucifer. Their teachers frequently will take and interpret a single word or a fragment of a verse from a scripture and formulate an opinion or an entire doctrine from it, even when it conflicts with the volume of scripture. For example; Colossians 1:15, referring to Yahusha-Jesus reads, "Who is the image of the invisible God, the firstborn of every creature..." Focusing on a single word, "firstborn" (as it might apply to natural birth), instead of first in authority, they have perverted the meaning of the verse. Then they have no choice but to dismiss the next two verses which go on to say, "For by Him were all things created." And "by Him all things consist."[540] From this one error a cult has evolved, leading its unwitting followers to a Christ-less grave.[541]

Citing Colossians 1:15, Dake's Annotated Reference Bible makes the following assertion: "The person we now know as Jesus Christ, the only begotten son of GOD, existed as an equal member of the GOD head from all eternity.[542] Before He became the son of GOD (sonship refers to humanity, not deity; Dakes commentary, note f, Acts 13:33). He was a spirit being and direct agent and carried out the divine plan of creation. He was the direct agent of the GODhead who carried out all creative work. (v.16; Isa.9:6; Jn.1:3; Eph.3:9; Heb.1:3)"[543]

Citing Romans 1:20, and Colossians 2:9, in Thayer's Greek-English Lexicon, the publisher's introduction, Thayer speaks of this misinterpretation as appears in the Jehovah Witnesses New World Translation bible. After giving the correct Greek, he follows it (referring to Romans 1:20 and Colossians 2:9) by saying, "If there were no other proof in the Bible of the fully deity of the Lord Jesus, every Christian should believe on the strength of these two verses alone."[544]

---

539 Psalm 97:5; Micah 1:2-3
540 Colossians 1:16-17
541 Acts 4:12
542 Isaiah 7:14; 9:6-7; Micah 5:2; John 1:1-2; Hebrews 1:8; Revelations 1:8-11
543 Dake's Annotated Reference Bible, KJB, Dakes Publishing, Lawrenceville, GA, 2001, p. 384
544 *Thayer's Greek Lexicon of the New Testament*, Fourth Edition, Baker Book House, Grand Rapids, MI, p. viii

The validation of Jesus being GOD and one with the father is made infinitely clear in Romans 10:13 where it is written, "For whosoever shall call on the name of the Lord shall be saved." Paul referring to Jesus uses the Greek word for Lord, *Kurious*, which is the Hebrew word for Yahovah/Jehovah; (cf. Joel 2:32). This proves that the subject (Jesus), referred to as "Lord" in Romans 10:9 and 10:13 is Jehovah. Thus, there is more than one Jehovah personage spoken of in the O.T. (cf. Gen.19:24). Compare also Psalm 110:1 with Matthew 22:44, and Acts 2:34 where the same word Kurious is used for both GOD and Christ. Kurious has been translated Lord in the Septuagint 667 times as the equivalent of O.T. Jehovah.

The Indwelling Holy Spirit

David was only a shepherd boy when the Lord sent the Prophet Samuel to anoint a future replacement for King Saul. In obedience the prophet went to the house of Jesse, and when he saw David, the Lord confirmed to Samuel this was to be Israel's next King. Samuel then took the horn of oil and anointed David. It was at that moment the Rauch H'Qodesh entered into GOD's young appointee and overwhelmed him.

> "Then Samuel took the horn of oil, and anointed him in the midst of his brethren: and the Spirit of the Lord came upon David from that day forward." (1 Samuel 16:13)

Indeed, from that day forward David was given victories over Goliath, the Philistines, and many other enemies of GOD's people. It was not David the man, his sling, or his sword. It was not his skill or strength that defeated his adversaries. It was GOD's own Spirit who "indwelled" and used an unpretentious young man to fulfill HIS will. "…Not by might, nor by power, but by my Spirit, saith the Lord of hosts."[545]

Later, we read in Psalms that when David recognized his great sins he felt that he might be in jeopardy of losing the Spirit and so cried out to GOD, "Cast me not away from thy presence; and take not thy Holy Spirit from me."[546]

In the same way the Spirit came upon David, so did the Spirit come upon the prophets and prophetesses. It was the Spirit who animated these men and women and by which He transmitted the Will and Word of GOD to that generation and to wayward kings.[547]

> "I have not spoken in secret from the beginning; from the time that it was, there am I; and now the Lord GOD, and HIS Spirit, hath sent me. Thus saith the Lord, thy Redeemer, the Holy One of Israel (Yahusha); I am the Lord thy GOD which teacheth thee to profit, which leadeth thee by the way that thou shouldest go." (Isaiah 48:16-17)

---

545 Zechariah 4:6
546 Psalm 51:11
547 2 Timothy 3:16

It is the same Rauch H'Qodesh who searches the hearts of men like David, and when He finds such a man or woman whose heart is tender for GOD and who is earnestly seeking Him that He then reveals the Savior to them.

> "As a hart (deer) panteth for the water brooks, so panteth my soul after thee, O GOD." (Psalm 42:1)

In that one fleeting moment that an individual accepts his Savior, GOD's Spirit instantly enters into the individual and bonds to that individual's spirit. Immediately the scales which previously obscured GOD from the natural eye of the natural man, along with any lingering uncertainties and doubts as might pertain to GOD suddenly vanish. In the time it takes to pledge a heartfelt prayer of acceptance of Yahusha-Jesus as their Savor the individual receives their spiritual birth. He is "born from on high," "Born anew," "Born again;" now and forever "eternally saved."[548]

The New Birth

> "Now if any man have not the Spirit of Christ, he is none of His." (Romans 8:9)

There is a term found in the third chapter of the Gospel of John which originated with Yahusha-Jesus Himself. It is there that a phrase is recorded only once and repeated only once in the entirety of Scripture, but these words are so crucial that everything else written concerning where one will spend eternity is dependent upon this simple verse.

> "Verily, verily, Except a man be born again he cannot see the kingdom of GOD." (John 3:3)

If we are to take the Lord at His Word, and in particular the word "Except," we should be exceedingly concerned with just what He was referring to when he uses the term "born again."

In this passage (John 3:1–15) where the term is used, we read of a man named Nicodemus who was looking for answers about spiritual concerns he had regarding his own salvation.

Nicodemus was a Pharisee, a Doctor of Judaic law and a member of the High Council of the Sanhedrin. He had spent the greater portion of his life searching the Scriptures in an attempt to derive meaning and truth. Though he was among a handful of men who were supposed to know more about GOD than others, it appears he was apprehensive and unsure of his own eternal destiny.

Nicodemus had stood in the background listening to Yahusha speak to the multitudes. What he heard was not theological jargon or classic sermons, but simple and profound truth; truth so plain and obvious that it went to the very core of ones' soul. Intuitively Nicodemus knew that this Nazarene rabbi had been sent by GOD and had an intimacy with Elohim that he just did not have.

With all his attempts to live according to the Law of Moses, with all his learning, with all his fasting, tithing, oblations, and praying, he was still unsure whether he had done enough to

---

548 Romans 10:9–13

attain heaven. Intuitively he knew that something was missing, something more was needed... That something was that he was still not a child of GOD.[549]

Knowing the scriptures as he must have, Nicodemus should have known what the prophets deemed as the imperative; it is in the creation of a new heart that a man is made right with GOD and that allows the individuals' spirit to be reborn.[550] Nicodemus' Judaism had become his idol, and yet when he heard Yahusha speak, his heart was stirred.

We see that Nicodemus sought out the Lord at night, presumably to avoid being seen by his fellow Pharisees. He saw Jesus not only as a teacher, but also as a miracle worker come from GOD. "Rabbi, we know that thou are a teacher come from GOD for no man can do the miracles that thou doest, except GOD be with him."[551] Little did Nicodemus realize at that time that Jesus had not only come from GOD, but that He was GOD! He was standing in the presence of Immanuel Himself.[552]

Then, just as Nicodemus was about to present his concerns, the Lord, knowing what Nicodemus was about to ask, spoke first. "Verily, verily, Except a man be born again he cannot see the kingdom of GOD."[553]

Nicodemus was understandably baffled with this imperative and replied, "How can a man be born when he is old? Can he enter a second time into his mother's womb?" Jesus' response was to point out the dissimilarity between the two births; one being natural, the other spiritual. "Except you a man be born of water and the Spirit, he cannot enter the Kingdom of GOD. That which is born of flesh is flesh, and that which is born of Spirit is spirit. Marvel not that I said unto thee, Ye must be born again."[554]

The water of which the Lord spoke represents the ambiotic fluid which comes from the mother's womb during the natural birth. This physical birth does not qualify a man for heaven, regardless of what he does in the flesh. Because man possesses a spirit, that also must have a birth... a spiritual birth!

Jesus then spoke again, "The wind bloweth where it listeth, and thou hearest the sound thereof, but canst not tell whence it cometh, and whither it goeth: so is every one that is born of the Spirit."[555]

The wind represents the Holy Spirit who passes (bloweth) where He chooses in a constant search for the individual who is earnestly seeking GOD. Those who are intensely searching will hear the voice of the wind speaking to them in the recesses of their own mind, and yet they will not at first understand where this beckoning is coming from.[556]

It is nothing less than an invitation; the call of the Holy Spirit to come and to receive Yahusha-Jesus as their personal Savior. In reality everyone is beckoned at some point in their life[557] but

---

549 Romans 8:9
550 Jeremiah 29:13; 31:33; 32:39; Ezekiel 11:19; 18:31; 36:25-27; Psalm 51:10
551 John 3:2
552 Isaiah 7:14
553 John 3:3
554 John 3:5-7
555 John 3:8
556 1 Kings 19:12
557 John 3:8; Revelation 22:17

sadly only a few actually hear the sound of the wind, respond, and accept GOD's invitation.[558] Most are consumed with the cares of the world and dismiss the fleeting invitation. As with the wind, it soon passes by and is gone.

> "And the Spirit and the bride say, Come. And let him that heareth say, Come. And let him that is athirst Come. And whosoever will, let him take the water of life freely." (Revelation 22:17)

Each and every individual must be sensitive to the beckoning of Holy Spirit, and when one hears and bears witness to the truth presented in the Scriptures that Yahusha-Jesus is indeed the Savior, it is then up to them to walk toward the light of truth and respond to the divine offer.[559]

> "Today if ye will hear His voice, Harden not your heart..."[560] "I have heard thee in the in a time accepted, and in the day of salvation have I succored thee: behold now is the accepted time; behold now is the day of salvation." (2 Corinthians 6:2)

The new birth of which Jesus spoke was still a mystery to Nicodemus at that time, for he was reaching for understanding with his cerebral mind. "But the natural man receiveth not the things of the Spirit of God: for they are foolishness unto him: neither can he know them, because they are spiritually discerned."[561]

Jesus, knowing how perplexed Nicodemus was, challenged him with a question which would force him to think hard about his salvation. "...Art thou a master of Israel, and knowest not these things?"

What Jesus had said to Nicodemus as to how one is born again should have resonated with him, for he knew the scriptures well. However, like so many, he was preoccupied with the law and tradition and put less emphasis on what the prophets had said about attaining salvation and becoming regenerated.[562] Nicodemus was among the vast majority of the scholarly, "Ever learning, and never able to come to the knowledge of the truth."[563] Like many he had been satisfied to put his faith in his religion rather than his redeemer.

The earnest seeker must approach GOD from his heart, not his head!

> "And ye shall seek me, and find me, when ye shall search for me with all your heart." (Jeremiah 29:13)

What the Lord was to say next began with the words "Verily, verily," (which means Truly, truly), and because He repeated the word verily twice, it places great importance on what was about to be said.

---

558 Matthew 7:13-14; Luke 13:23-30
559 Hebrews 4:7
560 Psalm 45:7
561 1 Corinthians 2:14
562 Jeremiah 31:33; 32:39-40; Ezekiel 11:19; 18:31; 36:25-27; Psalm 51:10
563 2 Timothy 3:7

"Verily, verily, I say unto thee, We speak that we do know, and testify that we have seen; and ye receive not our witness. If I have told you earthly things, and ye believe not, how shall ye believe, if I tell you of heavenly things?" (John 3:11-12)

Man has a propensity to believe only that which he can see, understand, or prove. Man clings to the natural world and hesitates at what requires faith, even in light of the witness of the Word. Nicodemus was a victim of his own mind and making. His faith was in his Judaism and predicated on his own attempts to live a righteous life. Isaiah spoke plainly when he said, "all our righteousness (efforts to be righteous) are as filthy rags."[564]

The Law of Faith

"For we all have sinned, and come short of the glory of GOD; Being justified freely by his grace through the redemption that is in Christ Jesus: Whom God hath set forth to be a propitiation (an atoning victim) through faith in his blood, to declare his righteousness for the remission of sins that are past, through the forbearance of God; To declare, I say, at this time his righteousness: that he might be just, and the justifier of him which believeth in Jesus. Where is boasting then? It is excluded. By what law? of works? Nay: but by the law of faith. Therefore we conclude that a man is justified by faith without the deeds of the law. Is he the God of the Jews only? is he not also of the Gentiles? Yes, of the Gentiles also: Seeing it is one God, which shall justify the circumcision (the Jew) by faith, and uncircumcision (the Gentile) through faith. Do we then make void the law through faith? God Forbid: yea, we establish the law." (Romans 3:23-31)

Permit me to pose the question to the professing Christian and church-goer that may have sat for forty or fifty years in a pew, been a worker in their church, and even been a children's Bible teacher. Have you ever heard your pastor or your priest give a sermon about this imperative for a spiritual birth or the necessity about having to be "born from above"?

Millions in churches today, including the ministers themselves do not know what the new birth is and have never experienced it. One can be a theological scholar and have graduated from a prestigious seminary yet never had this essential soul saving experience. In the final analysis it doesn't matter one iota to GOD whether you call yourself a Baptist, a Lutheran, a Methodist, a Presbyterian, a Catholic, or a Christian. None of these make you a "Born-Again Christian." A Born-Again Christian is one who has by faith, placed his entire destiny on what Yahusha-Jesus did on the Cross, and then in humble adoration surrenders his life to Him and to Him alone!

"Marvel not that I say unto thee, Ye must be Born Again!" (John 3:11)

---

564 Isaiah 64:6

16

ISAIAH RECEIVES THE FIRE!

A Vision of the King, the Lord of Hosts (Isaiah-Esaias 6:1–13)

The Holy Spirit comes to the man who will admit he is "undone."

> "Then said I, Woe is me! For I am undone; because I am a man of unclean lips... for my eyes have seen the King, the Lord of hosts." (Isaiah 6:5)

Isaiah had a divinely imposed vision. Already a prophet, he was given a glimpse of the Lord of Hosts in His unfiltered glory. At that same moment he came under conviction and saw himself through GOD's holy eyes. What he saw was an unworthy sinner; a man undone.[565]

His unclean lips had undoubtedly spoken many vile things. How and why, he must have thought, could I even have been summoned to appear before the Lord of Hosts?

GOD sees through the veneer to the inner man. HE reads our thoughts and knows the intents of our heart.[566] It was Isaiah's recognition and admission of his deplorable self which pleased GOD, for it spoke of the man wanting to be forgiven and willing to be purified.

Undone (Image Source: GOODSALT)

So, we are told, that the Lord ordered a seraphim angel to take tongs and remove a live coal from the heavenly altar and touch Isaiah's lips with it. The obedient angel complied and speaking for the Lord said, "Lo, this has touched thy lips; and thy iniquities are taken away, and thy sins purged."[567]

---

565   Isaiah 6:5
566   Isaiah 66:18
567   Isaiah 6:7

The live coal was symbolic of that which sterilizes and cauterizes the flesh, and if one acknowledges their undoing, it incinerates their sin. But in Isaiah's case it was more, for having both fear[568] and faith, he was already a child of GOD. Now he would be offered a commission[569] and with it would come an endowment of boldness; a baptism that would put fire in the prophet's bones in order to carry out the assignment. It would be a second baptism; a baptism for service!

The Hebrew nations (Israel and Judah) had fallen into declension; "from the foot to the head there is (was) no soundness."[570] An audible voice, the voice of a prophet was needed to confront the people of their depravity and afford them an opportunity to repent and return to HIM.

It was then that the Lord spoke, "Whom shall I send, and who will go for us?" Never did a man answer the call more quickly. "Here am I send me!"[571] The Lord spoke again, "Go and tell these people, Hear ye (you) indeed, but (you) understand not, and see ye indeed, but perceive not."[572]

The glowing coal that touched the prophet's lips and reinvigorated him was a second baptism; the baptism of fire. This special endowment would be essential for the difficult tasks that laid ahead.

For the next forty years the prophet would confront an apathetic people. He would chide them for their moral laxness, their lust and lewdness, their covetness, idol worship, conceit, and drunkenness. He would denounce the long succession of ungodly kings and spiritual shepherds and he would foretell of the destruction of the kingdom of Judah by the Assyrians and the captivity of the people. Most significant was that he would prophesy of GOD Himself coming to earth in the flesh and then giving up His life as an atonement for the many who would receive Him.[573] From an apocalyptic vision[574] he would describe the judgement of the nations and the punishment of the wicked, but how in the end the Lord would vindicate His people, find a faithful remnant,[575] and establish His kingdom on earth. All this was given to a man who was willing to admit he was undone.

The New Birth Experience

If one truly grasps the fact that they are a sinner, and that the consequence of sin is by divine decree a sentence to an eternal hell,[576] they will suddenly realize the gravity of what Jesus did for them in the substitutional act of giving up His life for theirs. If in that fleeting moment they are suddenly overwhelmed with gratitude, a love for Him will explode within their heart. They can then be certain that the Holy Spirit has entered into them and has melded with their spirit.

---

568 Proverb 14:27
569 Mark 16:16
570 Isaiah 1:6
571 Isaiah 1:8
572 Isaiah 6:9
573 Isaiah 53:12
574 Isaiah, chapters 24-27
575 Isaiah 61:6; 65:9
576 Romans 3:23-26; 6:23

At that moment that individual is accepted as a child of GOD[577] and a glorious transformation begins. Though born once in the natural, they have now experienced a second birth; the birth of their spirit. They have become, as it were, "born again."

> "That which is born of the flesh is flesh; and that which is born of the Spirit is spirit. Marvel not that I said unto thee, Ye must be born again." (John 3:6-7)

In this new birth experience the individual goes through a life changing metamorphosis. The "old man" (the natural man) goes through a dying process.[578] With this death go the natural inclinations and aspirations which dominated the individual all his or her life; "and the things of the earth grow strangely dim, in the light of His glory and grace."[579]

When GOD the Holy Spirit enters into an individual it is as if a switch was thrown. Voltage and amperage surge through a dormant wire, and like a lifeless incandescent lamp it suddenly bursts forth with life and light. With this divine birth the person instantly awakens to the things of GOD. A new mind suddenly acquires a new revelation of the Savior. Before, GOD was vague and unperceivable, now HE is not only perceivable but perceptible.

Suddenly the individual knows beyond any doubt that every past sin and transgression have been forgiven; "cast into the depths of the sea;"[580] blotted from GOD's mind as if they never existed;[581] "as far as the east is from the west."[582]

With this transformation, GOD immediately becomes preeminent and takes center stage in that person's life. At the same time a process of sanctification begins to change the individual who now seeks to please and glorify GOD instead of self. He has met a GOD he never imagined he could know; on such a plane as thought to be impossible. He knows intuitively that he has been saved from eternal death and is overcome with gratitude; a sense of peace and joy engulf him. He has become a member of the heavenly family, assured of spending eternity with his Creator.[583]

> "Therefore if any man be in Christ, he is a new creature: old things are passed away; behold, all things are become new." (2 Corinthians 5:17)

A glorious fountain of grace has flowed down from above, "like the precious ointment upon the head, that ran down upon the beard, even unto Aaron's beard: that went down to the skirt of his garments."[584] GOD's love bathes the newborn from head to toe. He has been justified, regenerated and now begins his walk of sanctification; each day drawing closer to the One who purchased his salvation.

---

577 Romans 8:11-17
578 2 Corinthians 5:17
579 Lyrics of the hymn, "Turn Your Eyes Upon Jesus," by Helen Lemmel, 1922
580 Micah 7:19
581 Isaiah 43:25; Jeremiah 31:34
582 Psalm 103:12
583 Romans 8:16-17
584 Romans 133:2

> Note: Because man was made in the image of GOD,[585] and GOD is spirit, so too was man endowed with a spirit.[586] The Creator places the spirit in man at the moment of his conception and the soul and spirit become fused together. Scripture reveals that at that instant, life is established.[587] Just as GOD implants the spirit into man, HE is also capable and desirous of renewing it.[588] This HE does when HE hears a sincere cry from the heart.[589]
>
> Note: The natural unregenerated man has been a servant of his own soul (the natural mind, will, instincts and emotions). The soul is greatly influenced by his flesh (his physical desires for gratification and pleasure). These two entities (soul and flesh) are two of the three components which make up his being. The third is his spirit, which along with his soul is the essence of who he is.
>
> Note: Mans' spirit is born with an inclination towards his Creator and wants fellowship and intimacy. His spirit wants to please and obey but mans' soul and flesh seek independence. Soul and flesh work in tandem, constantly warring against mans' spirit for supremacy.[590] It is not until mans' spirit is co-joined with GOD's Spirit in the spiritual birth that mans' spirit becomes energized and empowered to rule over his soul and flesh.[591] Mans' spirit, when indwelt by GOD's Spirit[592] receives as it were, a new conscience and a new love for truth.[593] It opens a direct line of communication to GOD through prayer[594] not unlike that which the patriarchs and prophets had when they spoke and heard from GOD.

The Message of the Cross!

"But GOD commendeth his love toward us, in that, while we were yet sinners, Christ died for us." (Romans 5:8)

"For HE (YAHUAH) hath made Him (Yahusha) to be sin for us, who knew no sin; that we might be made the righteousness of God in Him." (2 Corinthians 5:21)

"That if thou shall confess with thy mouth the Lord Jesus, and shall believe in thine heart that GOD hath raised Him from the dead, thou shall be saved. For with the heart man

---

585 Genesis 1:26
586 Numbers 27:16
587 Jeremiah 1:5
588 Psalm 51:10
589 Psalms 34:18
590 1 Peter 2:1; James 4:11
591 1 John 4:4
592 Romans 8:16
593 John 4:23-24
594 1 Corinthians 4:15

believeth unto righteousness; and with the mouth confession is made unto salvation." (Romans 10:9-10)

Acknowledge that you are a sinner and destined for hell. In desperation cry out from the depths of your heart for a Savior who willingly took your sin upon Himself and paid the price with His life. Believe and receive with a grateful heart the invitation and offer of adoption. Make Him your personal Savior and the centerpiece of your life. Learn of Him and seek to walk in obedience to His Word. Share the gospel with others, that they too may enter into His presence. If this is done in humble adoration and with utmost sincerity, you can be assured that according to His promise, you are now and forever righteous in the eyes of GOD and will join Him for eternity.

Admission, repentance, and acceptance of the Savor = forgiveness, salvation, and a blissful eternity with GOD.

The Baptism of Fire

Something more was needed. Something more was available.

The dynamic work of the Holy Spirit in a believer's life begins with the Spirit's indwelling at the moment they receive Christ as their savior. However, GOD has much more which HE is willing and wanting to give to the individual who is desperate for more of Him.[595]

In Full Gospel Christendom (which believes the Bible in its entirety), a second baptism, the "Baptism of the Holy Spirit," also known as the "Pentecostal experience" is made available to the Believer. In this supernatural event the Believer receives an impartation of the Holy Spirit exceeding that which they received at the time they were Born Again. It differs dramatically from the initial indwelling in its intensity as it engulfs the individual in such a way as to be felt. In this miraculous experience the individual suddenly becomes totally saturated with the Holy Spirit and is empowered for service.[596] One would be correct if they referred to this experience as an overwhelming, rather than the indwelling which comes when one first accepts Christ. We read in the gospel of Luke,

> "And, behold, I send the promise of my Father upon you: but tarry ye in the city of Jerusalem, until ye be endued with power from on high." (Luke 24:49)

We then read in the book of the Acts of the Apostles, "And, being assembled together with them, commanded them that they should not depart from Jerusalem, but wait for the promise of the Father, which, saith he, ye have heard of me. For John truly baptized with water; but ye shall be baptized with the Holy Ghost not many days hence."[597]

---

595 1 Corinthians 42:1-2
596 Acts 1:8
597 Acts 1:4-5

> "...But ye shall receive power, after that the Holy Ghost is come upon you: and ye shall be witnesses unto me both in Jerusalem, and in all Judea, and in Samaria, and unto the uttermost part of the earth." (Acts 1:8)

> "For the promise is unto you, and to your children, and to all that are afar off, even as many as the Lord our God shall call." (Acts 2:39)

The last thing Jesus spoke to His disciples before He ascended to the Father was for them to go to Jerusalem and wait for the impartation. The disciples were obedient, and in Acts 2:1–4 they received the full measure of the Spirit and afterward went out empowered for ministry. The tongues of fire which descended upon the disciples at Pentecost was the fire that was to burn within them; compelling them to leave their nets and "Go ye into all the world, and preach the gospel to every creature"[598] "...and these sign shall follow them that believe; In My name shall they cast out devils; (and) they shall speak with new tongues."[599]

> "While Peter yet spake these words, the Holy Ghost fell on all them which heard the word. And they of the circumcision (the Jews) which believed were astonished, as many as came with Peter, because that on the Gentiles also was poured out the gift of the Holy Ghost. For they heard them speak with tongues, and magnify God." (Acts 10:44-46)

> "He that believeth on me, as the scripture hath said, out of his belly shall flow rivers of living water (tongues). (But this spake he of the Spirit, which they that believe on him should receive.)" (John 7:38-39)

This promised Baptism of the Holy Spirit cannot be described in human language, for it is simply too intense and too personal to be imagined.[600] It washes over one like a glorious wave. Greater understanding and insight of spiritual matters are conveyed, and spiritual gifts often accompany the impartation for the glory of GOD and for the edification of the body of believers.[601] This infusion exceeds the initial bonding experience of the Spirit when one is first "born again."[602] It is an empowerment for witness and service. It was described at Pentecost as cloven tongues of fire which descended singly on each individual. Perhaps the clearest illustration which proves the baptism of the Holy Spirit (the overwhelming) is a separate impartation from the initial baptism (the indwelling) is seen in Acts 19:1–7. It is there we read that Paul asked the believers at Ephesus, "Have you received the Holy Ghost since you believed?" They replied, "We have not so much as heard whether there be any Holy Ghost." Paul then proceeded to lay hands upon them; and the Holy Ghost was imparted, "and they spoke in tongues and prophesied."

---

598 Mark 16:15
599 Mark 16:17
600 Luke 24:49
601 1 Corinthians 12:4, 7, 8, 11
602 John 7:39

This second baptism cannot be ignored, for the Lord's disciples were already believers (indwelled) at conversion, when afterward Paul invited them to receive the Baptism of the Holy Spirit. Some disciples had even previously been sent out to preach, heal, and deal with demonic spirits,[603] yet the Lord knew they would require more if they were to carry on in His absence and fulfil the Great Commission.[604]

The power of the Spirit with the outward manifestation of tongues (Greek, *Glossolalia*; defined as un-acquired) was considered the normal occurrence of the Christian experience. Unlike the heady and highminded who retreat from what they can't explain, (for "GOD hath chosen the foolish things of the world to confound the wise"[605]) the new believers, in their childlike innocence simple received the impartation by faith. The result was always an immediate, supernatural, outward expression which convinced not only the receiver of the gift, but also the people who heard it (tongues) that a divine power had indwelled the person.[606] In every case there was (and is) an ecstatic speaking in a language that the person has never learned. What indeed could have been a more unique "sign" that something supernatural had taken place and that the Spirit was now active in the believer?[607]

It is this baptism first eluded to by the prophet Joel[608] which is offered and available to those who: "believe for it,"[609] "repent,"[610] "obey,"[611] "desire it,"[612] and who "want to be engaged in the service of their Lord.[613] Like salvation and the gifts of the Holy Spirit,[614] the Baptism and accompanying tongue is only received by faith. It requires one to begin to verbalize what they sense is a foreign word, and then by faith, muster the courage to speak it forth.

It is most regrettable that after the first century when the Spirit was recognized by His manifestations, that His work, leadership, and gifts began to be seen as irrelevant by the new rule and order of an evolving ecclesiastic church. Soon afterward, and even to this present time, His glorious baptism, tongues, and gifts[615] have been summarily dismissed from denominational assemblies which once moved in them and subsequently flourished. By virtue of this mandate to seek the Baptism being the Messiah's final words to His disciples before He ascended to the Father emphasizes its importance.[616]

Avoiding and deemphasizing the transcendence of the Holy Spirit, His Baptism, and what He desires to do through us with this supernatural endowment not only hinders the carrying

---

603 Matthew 10:1; Mark 3:15
604 Mark 16:15
605 1 Corinthians 1:27
606 1 Corinthians 14:22
607 Acts 14:22
608 Joel 2:28
609 Acts 1:5-8; 2:3-4; 19:2-6
610 Acts 2:38
611 Acts 5:32
612 Acts 8:15-17
613 Acts 2:8; 4:31; 9:17-18; 10:42-47; 19:2-6
614 1 Corinthians 12:4-7
615 1 Corinthians 12:1-11
616 Luke 24:49-51

out of the Great Commission but is a direct insult to GOD. It is no wonder His glory has departed from many of the assemblies that had once believed and received the enduement. Today they are a mere shell of what they once were.[617] The modern roots of Pentecostalism which reached back to the days of George Fox and the Quakers, John Wesley and Methodism, and William Booth of the Salvation Army, were too radical for the cerebral Church. Many Baptists, Lutherans, Presbyterians, Methodists, Wesleyans, Nazarenes, Missionary Alliance, and even a number of today's Pentecostal assemblies which had grown out of the Holiness movement and once advocated for the Baptism lost their fervor and became deniers and dissenters of the promise.

Since Christianity became organized, institutionalized, and sophisticated, (another word for prideful) denominations have disengaged themselves from the Lord Holy Spirit. Their understanding is limited to intellectual knowledge. They have little inspiration, illumination, or revelation to offer. They preach to please the party rather than to raise the standard. And so today, the Holy Spirit looks for the Church where the welcome mat says, "Come Holy Spirit, we need thee. Come sweet Spirit we pray. Come in thy strength and thy power. Come in thy own gentle way."[618]

> Note: The Holy Spirit and His "overwhelming" of the believer is presented in great detail and in numerous accounts in the New Testament scriptures, especially in these books: the Acts of the Apostles, the Letters to the Corinthians, and the Letter to the Ephesians. The Holy Spirit is currently the principal agent of the GODhead here on earth during this dispensation.[619] His primary mission is to draw men to Yahusha-Jesus.
>
> Note: There are some who teach in error that the Baptism of the Holy Spirit and the evidence of tongues, and the gifts of the Spirit were meant for the Morning Star Church of the first century and have since passed away. These teachers base their assumption on two scriptures; most prominent being 1 Corinthians 13:8. Regrettably, they have failed to see that in this scripture, where it is said that these signs would one day cease, Paul was referring to the Eternal Age when "that which is perfect is come."[620] Indeed, at that time, in that Perfect Age, the signs and spiritual gifts[621] will no longer be needed, for we will then be "face to face"[622] with the Lord. All that will continue afterward and eternally is Charity (love).

---

617 1 Samuel 4:19-22
618 Gloria and William J. Gaither, Song, "Come Holy Spirit," 1964 William J. Gaither, Inc.
619 John 16:7-15
620 1 Corinthians 13:10
621 1 Corinthians 12:1-11
622 1 Corinthians 12:12

Note: A second scripture that is often misinterpreted and causes some to deny the Baptism of the Holy Spirit is Ephesians 4:4-5; it reads, "There is one body, and one Spirit, even as ye are called in one hope of your calling; One Lord, one faith, one baptism." The phrase "one baptism" refers to being baptized into the body of Christ and into His death by means of the Cross.[623] This scripture pertains to the salvation experience and ones' adoption into the family of GOD.[624] Neither is it speaking of water baptism which is an outward and public confession of ones' faith and a decision to become a follower (disciple).

Note: Tongues are spontaneous spiritual utterances of a language never learned which always accompany the Baptism of the Holy Spirit. This ecstatic manifestation is the initial evidence which confirms to the individual that they have indeed received this enduement associated with service. This conveyance of "power" (Gk. *dunamis*, Acts 1:8) is different from anything they may have had or experienced before. If gifts were resident in the individual before (such as teaching), they are exponentially magnified. The individual is then and thereafter equipped for service.

Note: Scripturally speaking, there are "diverse" (different) kinds of tongues,[625] each with a different purpose. Principally tongues are used for a "sign" to unbelievers so that they may witness the manifestation of the supernatural and earnestly seek for this gift.[626] Occasionally, though sparingly, tongues are used to transcend language barriers when testifying of Jesus Christ.[627] Tongues are also among the "gifts of the spirit" used for the edification of the body of Believers, such as the prophetic tongue which is used in conjunction with the gift of interpretation.[628] There is a tongue used in impassioned prayer (devotion and worship)[629] and for praise,[630] and for supplication.[631] There is a tongue for when the natural mind knows not what to pray for, and when interceding for others.[632] And, there is a powerful tongue used when engaging in demonic warfare.[633]

Note: The modern Church rests in having obtained salvation and is content with having received a measure of the indwelling; that endowment being regeneration. They dismiss the mandate that our Lord spoke to His disciples not to undertake their mission until they had first received this empowerment.

---

623 Romans 6:3
624 Romans 8:15; Galatians 4:5
625 1 Corinthians 12:10
626 1 Corinthians 14:22; Acts 8:15-18
627 Acts 2:6
628 1 Corinthians 12:4, 10, 28-30; 14:12; Romans 12:6-8
629 1 Corinthians 13:14
630 1 Corinthians 14:15
631 Ephesians 6:14
632 1 Corinthians 14:14
633 Mark 16:17

"Christ has explicitly informed us that it is the indispensable provision required to perform the work assigned each. No one has at any time any right to expect success unless he first secures the enduement of power from on high. Both the promise and the admonition apply equally to all Christians of every age and nation."[634]

Then and Now

In those days when GOD's Spirit visited assemblies, the people came together to meet with Him; not to hear a feel-good sermon. According to the revivalists, the people would even avoid greeting one another with little more than a nod of the head. They wanted to first meet with GOD and went directly to their knees. The ministers spoke little and hid much. Men would spend hours in silence, in expectation that they might hear a word from heaven.

In the barns and warehouses where saints often met there was no sermonizing, no choir, no organ or bands. No church business was discussed, no announcements made, no programs offered, and no activities publicized. No collections were taken. Perhaps an old coffee can might be found near the back door for any who wanted to give voluntarily. If songs were sung at all they were spontaneous hymns sung acapella about the Cross, the blood, and HIS grace. Unlike much of the music today, the old hymns carry an anointing which is simply missing from modern compositions.

Early on there was no platform or pulpit, everyone was on the same level. In control was the Holy Spirit, and no man dared usurp Him. Spontaneous messages would come forth under powerful anointing and then praises would ring out as tears rolled down cheeks. What a departure from what we once were. Now we have "a form of godliness, but deny the power thereof."[635]

As the late English evangelist and author Leonard Ravenhill wrote, "GOD's house today is neither a house of prayer nor a house of power... I'm sure the main reason we do not have national revival beginning with personal revival is that we are content to live without it."[636]

I would add to the evangelist's assertion that our neglect includes not recognizing the Holy Spirit, His Baptism, and the conveyance of His power to witness Christ.[637] We have made ourselves spiritually impotent. The Holy Spirit now stands outside many churches and knocks on their doors. He calls, waiting to be invited in,[638] but the sanctimonious church has bolted the doors and sings louder so as to drown out His beckoning.

---

634 Charles G. Finney; *The Enduement of the Holy Spirit,* Independent of New York, December 21, 1871
635 2 Timothy 4:5
636 Leonard Ravenhill, *America Is Too Young To Die,* Bethany House, Minneapolis, MI, 1979, pp. 120, 109
637 Acts 1:8
638 Revelation 3:20

> Note: The Baptism of the Holy Spirit will be poured out upon the Jewish people in the "last days" as revealed to the prophet Joel.[639] The time of Jacob's Trouble will be so horrendous that the Lord will empower His own so that they may not only bravely abide in their faith, but speak the word of GOD with boldness.[640] In that day the gifts of the Spirit[641] will be in full operation[642] as the Lord will raises up a standard against the enemies of His people.[643]

"I have set watchmen upon the walls, O Jerusalem, which shall never hold their peace day or night: ye that make mention of the LORD, keep not silent…Go through, go through the gates; prepare ye the way of the people: cast up, cast up the highway; gather out the stones; lift up a standard for the people. Behold, the LORD hath proclaimed unto the end of the world, Say ye to the daughter of Zion, Behold thy salvation (Yahusha) cometh; behold His reward is with Him, and His work before Him." (Isaiah 62:6, 10-11)

The Only Hope!

"And this is life eternal, that they might know thee the only true God, and Jesus Christ, whom thou hast sent." (John 17:3)

America needs revival, for it is already engaged in a war and is losing. This war to which I refer is unconventional and its enemy invisible. It is a spiritual war; a war its people know little or nothing about.

It is not fought with guns or missiles, and its lethality is not evidenced by graves or crumpled buildings but rather in a decay of morality, ethics, and godliness. A praying people armed with spiritual weaponry and endowed with the Holy Spirit are its elite soldiers, able to destroy the enemy's strongholds. But they must engage in fervent prayer to unleash a barrage from heaven which can ultimately manifest as a heaven-sent revival or a Great Awakening.[644]

---

639 Joel 2:28-29
640 Acts 4:31
641 1 Corinthians 12:1-11
642 Joel 2:28, 29
643 Isaiah 59:19
644 Ephesians 6:12; 18; 2 Corinthians 10:4

17

GOD PROVES BY PROPHECY

"Faith does not mean a leap in the dark, an irrational credulity, a believing against evidence and against reason. It means believing in the light of historical fact, consistent with evidence, on the basis of witnesses." George Eldon Ladd—Professor of New Testament exegesis[645]

"All Scripture is given by inspiration of GOD…" (2 Timothy 3:16)

Prophecy is a most tried witness and an indicator of the divine authorship of Scripture. Moses qualified this when speaking of false prophets.

"And if thou say in thy heart, How shall we know the Word which the Lord hath not spoken? When a prophet speaketh in the name of the Lord, if the things follow not, nor come to pass, that is the thing which the Lord hath not spoken." (Deuteronomy 18:21-22)

Divine Authorship (Image Source: GOODSALT)

Conversely, the opposite is also true. When that which a prophet has spoken comes to pass, that individual may indeed have spoken a word from the Lord.

We are most fortunate that not only did GOD's prophets present HIS Word to the people but that scribes recorded them for all posterity. What greater evidence and witness could GOD have given us by which to authenticate the promised Messiah? What greater evidence could GOD have given us to attest to His authorship than to put prophecy into script?

---

645 George Eldon Ladd, *I Believe in the Resurrection of Jesus*, Josh McDowell, *A Ready Defense*, Here's Life Publishing, San Bernadino, CA, p. 219

Foretold and Fulfilled

I mentioned previously that the book of Isaiah has as its centerpiece the Ha'Mashiach. I now want to illustrate that Yahusha-Jesus is not only the centerpiece of the book of Isaiah but of the entire Bible and that He has filled all the Messianic prophecies predicted up to this moment in time. Here are just a few of the hundreds of prophecies He fulfilled at His first coming.

1. He would be the Seed of a Woman.

    Prophecy: Genesis 3:15
    "...and I will put enmity between thee and the woman, and between thy seed and her seed; it shall bruise thy head, and thou shalt bruise his heel."

    Fulfilled: Galatians 4:4
    "...but when the fullness of the time was come, God sent forth his Son, made of a woman, made under the law."

2. He would be the Seed of Abraham.

    Prophecy: Genesis 22:18
    "...and in thy seed shall all the nations of the earth be blessed; because thou hast obeyed my voice."

    Fulfilled: John 11:51-52
    "And this spake he not of himself: but being high priest that year, he prophesied that Jesus should die for that nation; And not for that nation only, but that also he should gather together in one the children of God that were scattered abroad."

3. He would come through Isaac.

    Prophecy: Genesis 21:12
    "And God said unto Abraham, Let it not be grievous in thy sight because of the lad, and because of thy bondwoman; in all that Sarah hath said unto thee, hearken unto her voice; for in Isaac shall thy seed be called."

    Fulfilled: Hebrews 11:17-19
    "By faith Abraham, when he was tried, offered up Isaac: and he that had received the promises offered up his only begotten son, of whom it was said, That in Isaac shall thy seed be called: accounting that God was able to raise him up, even from the dead; from whence also he received him in a figure."

4. He would come through Jacob and Judah.

   Prophecy: Genesis 28:14; 49:10

   "...and thy seed shall be as the dust of the earth, and thou shalt spread abroad to the west, and to the east, and to the north, and to the south: and in thee and in thy seed shall all the families of the earth be blessed."

   "The scepter shall not depart from Judah, nor a lawgiver from between his feet, until Shiloh come; and unto him shall the gathering of the people be."

   Fulfilled: Revelation 5:5

   "And one of the elders saith unto me, Weep not: behold, the Lion of the tribe of Juda, the Root of David, hath prevailed to open the book, and to loose the seven seals thereof."

5. He would come through David.

   Prophecy: 2 Samuel 7:12-13; Jeremiah 23:5

   "And when thy days be fulfilled, and thou shalt sleep with thy fathers, I will set up thy seed after thee, which shall proceed out of thy bowels, and I will establish his kingdom. He shall build a house for my name, and I will stablish the throne of his kingdom for ever."

   "Behold, the days come, saith the Lord, that I will raise unto David a righteous Branch, and a King shall reign and prosper, and shall execute judgment and justice in the earth."

   Fulfilled: Acts 13:22-23; Romans 1:3-4

   "And when he had removed him, he raised up unto them David to be their king; to whom also he gave testimony, and said, I have found David the son of Jesse, a man after mine own heart, which shall fulfil all my will. Of this man's seed hath God according to his promise raised unto Israel a Saviour, Jesus."

   "...concerning his Son Jesus Christ our Lord, which was made of the seed of David according to the flesh; and declared to be the Son of God with power, according to the spirit of holiness, by the resurrection from the dead..."

6. Immanuel would be born to a virgin.

   Prophecy: Isaiah 7:14

   "Therefore the Lord himself shall give you a sign; Behold, a virgin shall conceive, and bear a son, and shall call his name Immanuel."

   Fulfilled: Matthew 1:18, 21

   "Now the birth of Jesus Christ was on this wise: When as his mother Mary (Miriam) was espoused to Joseph (Yosef), before they came together, she was found with child of the Holy Ghost...And she shall bring forth a son, and thou shalt call his name JESUS (Yahusha): for he shall save his people from their sins."

7. He'd be born in Bethlehem of Judea.

    Prophesy: Micah 5:2

    "But thou, Bethlehem Ephratah, though thou be little among the thousands of Judah, yet out of thee shall he come forth unto me that is to be ruler in Israel; whose goings forth have been from of old, from everlasting."

    Fulfilled: Matthew 2:1

    "Now when Jesus was born in Bethlehem of Judæa in the days of Herod the king, behold, there came wise men from the east to Jerusalem..."

8. Wise kings and men shall worship Him, and offer gifts.

    Prophecy: Psalm 72:10

    "The kings of Tarshish and of the isles shall bring presents: the kings of Sheba and Seba shall offer gifts."

    Fulfilled: Matthew 2:1- 2, 4-6, 10-11

    "Now when Jesus was born in Bethlehem of Judæa in the days of Herod the king, behold, there came wise men from the east to Jerusalem, saying, Where is he that is born King of the Jews? for we have seen his star in the east, and are come to worship him. And they said unto him, In Bethlehem of Judæa: for thus it is written by the prophet, And thou Bethlehem, in the land of Juda, art not the least among the princes of Juda: for out of thee shall come a Governor, that shall rule my people Israel. When they saw the star, they rejoiced with exceeding great joy. And when they were come into the house, they saw the young child with Mary his mother, and fell down, and worshipped him: and when they had opened their treasures, they presented unto him gifts; gold, and frankincense, and myrrh."

9. He shall come into His Temple.

    Prophecy: Malachi 3:1

    "Behold, I will send my messenger, and he shall prepare the way before me: and the Lord, whom ye seek, shall suddenly come to his temple, even the messenger of the covenant, whom ye delight in: behold, he shall come, saith the Lord of hosts."

    Fulfilled: Luke 2:27, 30-32

    "And he came by the Spirit into the temple: and when the parents brought in the child Jesus, to do for him after the custom of the law... (Simeon a devout Jew spoke) for my eyes have seen my salvation, which thou hast prepared before the face of all people; a light to lighten the Gentiles, and the glory of thy people Israel."

10. He will be preceded by a messenger.

   Prophecy: Malachi 3:1

   "Behold, I will send my messenger, and he shall prepare the way before me: and the Lord, whom ye seek…"

   Fulfilled: Luke 1:11, 17

   "And there appeared unto him an angel of the Lord standing on the right side of the altar of incense (and spoke)…And he (John the baptizer) shall go before him in the spirit and power of Elias (Elijah), to turn the hearts of the fathers to the children, and the disobedient to the wisdom of the just; to make ready a people prepared for the Lord."

11. He will have the Spirit of GOD upon Him.

   Prophecy: Isaiah 11:2; 61:1

   "…and the spirit of the Lord shall rest upon him, the spirit of wisdom and understanding, the spirit of counsel and might, the spirit of knowledge and of the fear of the Lord…"

   "The Spirit of the Lord God is upon me (Messiah Yahusha-Jesus); because the Lord hath anointed me to preach good tidings unto the meek; he hath sent me to bind up the brokenhearted, to proclaim liberty to the captives, and the opening of the prison to them that are bound…"

   Fulfilled: Matthew 3:16; John 3:34; Acts 10:38

   "And Jesus, when he was baptized, went up straightway out of the water: and, lo, the heavens were opened unto him, and he saw the Spirit of God descending like a dove, and lighting upon Him…"

   "For he whom God hath sent speaketh the words of God: for God giveth not the Spirit by measure unto Him."

   "…how God anointed Jesus of Nazareth with the Holy Ghost and with power: who went about doing good, and healing all that were oppressed of the devil; for God was with him."

12. He will be like a prophet similar to Moses.

   Prophecy: Deuteronomy 18:15

   "The Lord thy God will raise up unto thee a Prophet from the midst of thee, of thy brethren, like unto me; unto him ye shall hearken…"

   Fulfilled: Acts 3:20-22

   "And HE shall send Jesus Christ, which before was preached unto you: Whom the heaven must receive until the times of restitution of all things, which God hath spoken by the mouth of all his holy prophets since the world began. For Moses truly said unto the fathers, A prophet shall the Lord your God raise up unto you of your brethren, like unto me; him shall ye hear in all things whatsoever he shall say unto you."

13. He will enter into public ministry.

Prophecy: Isaiah 61:2

"The Spirit of the Lord God is upon me (Yahusha); because the Lord hath anointed me to preach good tidings unto the meek; HE hath sent me to bind up the brokenhearted, to proclaim liberty to the captives, and the opening of the prison to them that are bound (by the Law); To proclaim the acceptable year (now salvation is available) of the Lord, and the day of vengeance of our God; to comfort all that mourn..."

Fulfilled: Luke 4:16-19

"And he came to Nazareth, where he had been brought up: and, as his custom was, he went into the synagogue on the Sabbath day, and stood up for to read. And there was delivered unto him the book of the prophet Esaias (Isaiah). And when he had opened the book, he found the place where it was written, The Spirit of the Lord is upon me, because he hath anointed me to preach the gospel to the poor; he hath sent me to heal the brokenhearted, to preach deliverance to the captives, and recovering of sight to the blind, to set at liberty them that are bruised, To preach the acceptable year of the Lord."

14. His ministry would begin in Galilee.

Prophecy: Isaiah 9:1-2

"Nevertheless the dimness shall not be such as was in her vexation, when at the first he lightly afflicted the land of Zebulun and the land of Naphtali, and afterward did more grievously afflict her by the way of the sea, beyond Jordan, in Galilee of the nations. The people that walked in darkness have seen a great light: they that dwell in the land of the shadow of death, upon them hath the light shined."

Fulfilled: Matthew 4:12, 16, 23

"Now when Jesus had heard that John was cast into prison, he departed into Galilee; And leaving Nazareth, he came and dwelt in Capernaum, which is upon the sea coast, in the borders of Zabulon and Nephthalim: That it might be fulfilled which was spoken by Esaias the prophet, saying, The land of Zabulon, and the land of Nephthalim, by the way of the sea, beyond Jordan, Galilee of the Gentiles; The people which sat in darkness saw great light; and to them which sat in the region and shadow of death light is sprung up... And Jesus went about all Galilee, teaching in their synagogues, and preaching the gospel of the kingdom, and healing all manner of sickness and all manner of disease among the people."

15. He would be hailed King and Savior by the Jewish people.

Prophecy: Zechariah 9:9

"Rejoice greatly, O daughter of Zion; shout, O daughter of Jerusalem: behold, thy King cometh unto thee: he is just, and having salvation; lowly, and riding upon an ass, and upon a colt the foal of an ass."

Fulfilled: Matthew 21:5
"Tell ye the daughter of Sion, Behold, thy King cometh unto thee, meek, and sitting upon an ass, and a colt the foal of an ass."

16. He would come as a commoner and live in poverty.

    Prophecy: Isaiah 53:2
    "For he shall grow up before him as a tender plant, and as a root out of a dry ground: he hath no form nor comeliness; and when we shall see him, there is no beauty that we should desire him."

    Fulfilled: Mark 6:3; Luke 9:58
    "Is not this the carpenter, the son of Mary, the brother of James, and Joses, and of Juda, and Simon? and are not his sisters here with us? And they were offended at him."

    "And Jesus said unto him, Foxes have holes, and birds of the air have nests; but the Son of man hath not where to lay his head."

17. He shall be meek and unpretentious.

    Prophecy: Isaiah 42:2
    "He shall not cry, nor lift up, nor cause his voice to be heard in the street."

    Fulfilled: Matthew 12:15, 16, 19
    "But when Jesus knew it, he withdrew himself from thence: and great multitudes followed him, and he healed them all; and charged them that they should not make him known... He shall not strive, nor cry; neither shall any man hear his voice in the streets."

18. He shall be tender and compassionate.

    Prophecy: Isaiah 40:11; 42:3
    "He shall feed his flock like a shepherd: he shall gather the lambs with his arm, and carry them in his bosom, and shall gently lead those that are with young."

    "A bruised reed shall he not break, and the smoking flax shall he not quench: he shall bring forth judgment unto truth."

    Fulfilled: Matthew 12:15, 20; Hebrews 4:15
    "But when Jesus knew it, he withdrew himself from thence: and great multitudes followed him, and he healed them all... A bruised reed shall he not break, and smoking flax shall he not quench, till he send forth judgment unto victory."

    "For we have not a high priest which cannot be touched with the feeling of our infirmities; but was in all points tempted like as we are, yet without sin."

19. He was not to be believed by His own.

   Prophecy: Psalm 69:8
   "I am become a stranger unto my brethren, and an alien unto my mother's children."

   Fulfilled: John 1:11; 7:3, 5
   "He came unto his own, and his own received him not."

   "His brethren therefore said unto him, Depart hence... For neither did his brethren believe in him."

20. He would be hated for no cause.

   Prophecy: Psalm 69:4; Isaiah 49:7
   "They that hate me without a cause are more than the hairs of mine head: they that would destroy me, being mine enemies wrongfully."

   "Thus saith the Lord, the Redeemer of Israel, and his Holy One, to him whom man despiseth, to him whom the nation abhorreth..."

   Fulfilled: John 15:24-25
   "If I had not done among them the works which none other man did, they had not had sin: but now have they both seen and hated both me and my Father. But this cometh to pass, that the word might be fulfilled that is written in their law, They hated me without a cause."

21. He would be rejected by Jewish rulers.

   Prophecy: Psalm 118:22
   "The stone which the builders refused is become the head stone of the corner."

   Fulfilled: Matthew 21:42
   "Jesus saith unto them, Did ye never read in the scriptures, The stone which the builders rejected, the same is become the head of the corner: this is the Lord's doing, and it is marvelous in our eyes?"

22. Jews and Gentiles would combine against Him.

   Prophecy: Psalm 2:1-2
   "Why do the heathen rage, and the people imagine a vain thing? The kings of the earth set themselves, and the rulers take counsel together, against the Lord, and against his anointed (Messiah)..."

   Fulfilled: Acts 4:27
   "For of a truth against thy holy child Jesus, whom thou hast anointed, both Herod, and Pontius Pilate, with the Gentiles, and the people of Israel, were gathered together..."

23. He'd be betrayed by a friend.

Prophecy: Psalm 41:9

"Yea, mine own familiar friend, in whom I trusted, which did eat of my bread, hath lifted up his heel against me."

Fulfilled: John 13:18, 21

"I speak not of you all: I know whom I have chosen: but that the scripture may be fulfilled, He that eateth bread with me hath lifted up his heel against me...Verily, verily, I say unto you, that one of you shall betray me."

24. He would be sold for thirty pieces of silver.

Prophecy: Zechariah 11:12

"And I said unto them, If ye think good, give me my price; and if not, forbear. So they weighed for my price thirty pieces of silver."

Fulfilled: Matthew 26:15

"And said unto them, What will ye give me, and I will deliver him unto you? And they covenanted with him for thirty pieces of silver."

25. He'd be spit upon and scourged.

Prophecy: Isaiah 50:6

"I gave my back to the smiters, and my cheeks to them that plucked off the hair: I hid not my face from shame and spitting."

Fulfilled: Mark 11:65; John 19:1

"And some began to spit on him, and to cover his face, and to buffet him, and to say unto him, Prophesy: and the servants did strike him with the palms of their hands."

"Then Pilate therefore took Jesus, and scourged him."

26. He'd be nailed to the Cross.

Prophecy: Psalm 22:16

"For dogs have compassed me: the assembly of the wicked have enclosed me: they pierced my hands and my feet."

Fulfilled: John 19:18; 20:25

"...they crucified him..."

"The other disciples therefore said unto him, We have seen the Lord. But he said unto them, Except I shall see in his hands the print of the nails, and put my finger into the print of the nails, and thrust my hand into his side, I will not believe."

27. He'd be numbered with the transgressors and ask His father to forgive His executioners.

   Prophecy: Isaiah 53:12
   "...He was numbered with the transgressors; and He bare the sins of many, and made intercession for the transgressors..."

   Fulfilled: Mark 15:27-28; Luke 23:34
   "And with him they crucify two thieves; the one on his right hand, and the other on his left. And the scripture was fulfilled, which saith, And he was numbered with the transgressors."

   "Then said Jesus, Father, forgive them; for they know not what they do."

28. He will rise from the dead, be resurrected to life and ascend to heaven.

   Prophecy: Psalm 16:10; 68:18
   "For thou wilt not leave my soul in hell; neither wilt thou suffer thine Holy One to see corruption."

   "Thou hast ascended on high, thou hast led captivity captive: thou hast received gifts for men; yea, for the rebellious also, that the Lord God might dwell among them."

   Fulfilled: Luke 24:6, 31, 34, 51
   "He is not here, but is risen... And their eyes were opened, and they knew him; and he vanished out of their sight...The Lord is risen indeed...And it came to pass, while he blessed them, he was parted from them, and carried up into heaven."

29. He shall reveal Himself to the Gentiles and many shall accept Him.

   Prophecy: Isaiah 11:10
   "And in that day there shall be a root of Jesse, which shall stand for an ensign of the people; to it shall the Gentiles seek: and his rest shall be glorious."

   Fulfilled: Acts 10:45
   "And they of the circumcision which believed were astonished, as many as came with Peter, because that on the Gentiles also was poured out the gift of the Holy Ghost."

30. Having returned to His heavenly throne with the GODhead, He now awaits the culmination of the earth age, when He will return as King of Kings and Lord of Lords.

   Prophecy: Hosea 5:15; Psalm 110:1
   "I will go and return to my place, till they acknowledge their offense and see My face: in their affliction they will seek Me early."

   "The Lord said unto my Lord, Sit thou at my right hand, until I make thine enemies thy footstool."

Fulfilled: Hebrews 1:2-3; John 14:29

"Hath in these last days spoken unto us by his Son, whom he hath appointed heir of all things, by whom also he made the worlds; Who being the brightness of his glory, and the express image of his person, and upholding all things by the word of his power, when he had by himself purged our sins, sat down on the right hand of the Majesty on high..."

"And now I have told you before it come to pass, that, when it is come to pass, ye might believe."

As already presented, the Hebrew Holy Scriptures tell us the Messiah would come from the tribe of Judah,[646] the house of David,[647] and of the root of Jesse.[648]

The Shabbat evening chant used in Temple Service is one of many chants and prayers by which we are encouraged to acknowledge our Mashiach. In it we recognize that He would be a descendant of Jesse, Boaz, and David. Today there are no surviving genealogical records which could be used to verify the linage of anyone who claimed to be the Messiah. But there were in the days of his initial coming and they have been preserved in the gospel record.

Sabbath Evening Chant

"Shake off the dust; Arise O my people
Adorn thyself with thy beautiful attire.
By the hand of Jesse's Son,
The Bethlemite, draw,
Draw nigh to my soul, redeem it.
Awake, awake, rise and shine,
For the Light has come.
Awake, awake, utter a song;
For the Glory of Jehovah Upon thee is revealed."

---

646 Genesis 49:10
647 Jeremiah 23:5
648 1 Samuel 16:1; Isaiah 11:10

18

THE LAW OF PROBABILITY

One Hundred Thousand Trillion

There are some who argue that any man with the name Yahusha-Jesus could simply decide to fulfil several of the prophecies of the Bible, thereby making himself out to be the Messiah. To them I offer the following by Professor Peter W. Stoner as presented in the publication *Science Speaks; a Scientific Investigation of the Old Testament*, Chicago, Moody Press, 1969.

> Note: Dr. Peter W. Stoner was Professor Emeritus of Mathematics and Astronomy, Pasadena City College and Professor Emeritus of Science, Westmont College.

Dr. Stoner calculated the probability of one man fulfilling the major prophecies of Scripture concerning the Messiah. Using the science of probability to rule out coincidences the professor determined; "If any person in recorded history had fulfilled just eight of the Messianic prophecies, it would be a 1 in a 1017 probability." This is: 1 chance in 100,000,000,000,000,000 (1 in 100 Thousand Trillion).

Described another way; if 100 Thousand Trillion silver dollars were placed upon the state of Texas, it would cover the entire state to a depth of two feet. To complete this probability, a blindfolded man would then have just one chance to find a previously marked silver dollar.

Not only did Messiah fulfill all eight prophecies, but hundreds more.[649] In addition, Dr. Stoner went on to say, "If one were to fulfill, the first forty-eight (48) major prophecies, it would be a probability of 1 in 10^{157} or 10 followed by 157 zeroes."

"GOD so thoroughly authenticated Jesus as Yahusha that even mathematicians and statisticians who were without faith had to acknowledge He was the Christ—the Anointed One, the Promised Messiah."[650]

Only the Jewish Messiah—Yahusha ha Meshiach (Jesus the Christ) unmistakably fulfilled the many prophecies, which Scripture told us would positively identify Him.

---

649 *All the Messianic Prophecies of the Bible*; Herbert Lockyer, Zondervan Publishing House, 1973
650 *Science Speaks; A Scientific Investigation of the Old Testament*, Chicago, Moody Press, 1969

When pressed by the Pharisees who questioned his authority Yahusha-Jesus said to them, "Search the Scriptures; for in them ye think ye have eternal life: and they are they which testify of ME."[651] "Then said I, Lo, I am come: In the volume of a book it is written of ME."[652]

At the time of Yahusha's earthly ministry all the ancestral records of the Jews living in Palestine dating back centuries were archived in the Temple Mount. The Pharisees of that day were obsessed with trying to find evidence which would discredit this unorthodox teacher and thereby eliminate even the most remote possibility that this one called Yahusha-Jesus could have been the Messiah. However instead of discrediting Him these same records would later authenticate that He possessed the genealogical credentials necessary to be the Promised One.

Nearly forty years after His death all the records were destroyed by fire and lost forever when Titus' army sacked the Temple in 70 AD. This would have made it impossible for anyone afterward to authenticate Yahusha's linage, except for the fact that His ancestry had been previously transcribed by his disciples and circulated before the fire destroyed the archived originals.

Today we have complete uninterrupted documentation of both His maternal (Miriam), and His surrogate paternal parent (Yosef) in Matthew 1:1–17 and in Luke 3:23–38 of the New Testament. It would certainly be an anomaly for GOD, who intentionally supplies us with an abundance of evidence in the Scriptures to expect us to verify who the Mashiach was or is without this record.

How for example could we otherwise verify if He was from the house of David or the tribe of Judah?

Of all the prophecies recorded in Scripture, one in particular is absolutely astounding for it tells of a specific time when the Messiah would be born and when He would die. The phrase "… shall Messiah be cut off…" is supplied in the Messianic prophecy in the book of Daniel to indicate that he will be killed.[653] According to this passage, the time of His death would occur before the destruction of the Temple in Jerusalem, which Jews acknowledge each year at Tisha B'Av.

See Appendix C for a comprehensive study of Messiah's first Coming—*Daniel's Seventy Weeks*.

In an article entitled, "Why I believe Jesus Christ is my Jewish Messiah," Bible teacher and author, Dr. Arnold Ross summarizes the dilemma of disbelief.

"The Bible is GOD's message to man. Holy men of GOD spoke as they were led by the Holy Spirit. The Bible is a spiritual book. You understand it, you get GOD's message only as the Holy Spirit of GOD opens it to you. Because of disbelief in divine authorship of our Holy Scriptures, neither our rabbis nor their followers could recognize their Messiah when He came. Neither could they grasp the message and guidance GOD gives through our prophets so that we can recognize our Messiah."

Suggested Reading; *All the Messianic Prophecies of the Bible*, Herbert Lockyer, Zondervan Publishing House, 1973. Over 300 predictions about the Messiah are to be found in the Hebrew Holy Scriptures (p 17).

---

651 John 5:39
652 Psalm 40:7
653 Daniel 9:26

Behold thy King Cometh!

In Yahusha-Jesus' day, thousands upon thousands of Jews who heard Him speak and witnessed the miracles He performed accepted Him as their Messiah. Their shouts of praise and recognition were alluded to a thousand years earlier by the psalmist who in Psalm 118:26 exclaimed, *"Baruch Haba B`shem Adonai,"* "Blessed is He who comes in the name of the Lord."

This prophetic psalm pointing to the Savior's initial coming was fulfilled when just before Pesach, Nisan 9–March 29, 33 AD. Yahusha rode into Jerusalem on a donkey as the Jewish people publicly acclaimed Him to be their Messiah using that very phrase, *"Baruch Haba B`shem Adonai."*[654] In addition, not only were these very words of acclamation used but so too was the manner of His coming. For it was foretold by the Prophet Zechariah over five hundred years earlier and by the prophet Isaiah over seven hundred years earlier,

> "Rejoice greatly, O daughter of Zion; shout O daughter of Jerusalem: behold thy King cometh unto thee: HE is just and having salvation; lowly and riding upon an ass, and upon a colt, the foal of an ass." (Zechariah 9:9)

> "Behold, the Lord hath proclaimed unto the end of the world, Say ye to the daughter of Zion, Behold, thy salvation cometh; behold, His reward (Salvation) is with Him, and His work before Him." (Isaiah 62:11)

Zechariah's and Isaiah's prophesy would see their fulfillment when Yahusha-Jesus entered into Jerusalem on a donkey as recorded in the gospel of Matthew.

> "Tell ye the daughter of Zion, Behold, thy King cometh unto thee, meek, and sitting upon an ass, and a colt the foal of an ass. And the disciples went, and did as Jesus commanded them, and brought the ass, and the colt, and put on them their clothes, and they set him thereon. And a very great multitude spread their garments in the way; others cut down branches from the trees, and strewed them in the way. And the multitudes that went before, and that followed, cried, saying, 'Hosanna to the Son of David: Blessed is he that cometh in the name of the Lord; Hosanna in the highest.'" (Matthew 21:5-9)

---

654 Matthew 21:5-9

> Note: Students of Scripture recognize that it is characteristic of GOD when speaking to and through the prophets to use nouns or verbs which eliminate any doubt as to whom or what GOD is referring to. This is especially important when transitioning from Testament to Testament. Phrases like "daughter of Zion, Behold thy King" are used in both Old and New Testaments; a form common to ancient Midrashim expositor preaching. In the two preceding passages, Zechariah 9:9 and Matthew 21:5-9 we take note that the King brings with Him salvation. He did not come as a conqueror, riding a white steed, but as a humble servant king riding a small donkey. His message was all about salvation and what one must do in order to attain heaven.[655]

So we read in Zechariah 9:9 the King will "come lowly and riding on an ass,"[656] but then we are also told in Zechariah 6:12, 13 that Messiah "The Branch" (from the seed of David presented in Jeremiah)[657] will be the same person who will build the Temple of the Lord and will rule from His throne. Unquestionably we have two Messianic appearances!

> "...and speak unto him, saying, Thus speaketh the Lord of hosts, saying, Behold the man whose name is The BRANCH; (the Son of David—in the above passage) and he shall grow up out of his place, and he shall build the temple of the Lord: even he shall build the temple of the Lord; and he shall bear the glory, and shall sit and rule upon his throne; and he shall be a priest upon his throne: and the counsel of peace shall be between them both." (Zechariah 6:12-13)

A study of the rabbinic writings from the early centuries illustrates that many of the rabbis were convinced that Jesus was indeed the promised Messiah. While the miracles He did first caught their attention, it was the evidence of Scripture they could not deny. The closer they scrutinized the scriptures the more convinced they became.[658] Messianic Judaism flourished throughout the Roman Empire and beyond because it was predicated on the authority of Hebrew scripture.

Approximately fifty percent of Holy Scripture are devoted or relative to prophecy. In contrast, prophecy is completely missing from the Koran, the Hindu Vedas, the Baghavad Gita, and the Ramayana.

Other belief systems such as Mormonism (the Church of Latter-Day Saints) have based much of their belief on and in The Book of Mormon and the Doctrine and Covenants, both of which are associated with Joseph Smith. They are replete with prophecies (howbeit flawed). These additions are alleged to have been given by spiritual messenger entities on behalf of GOD. The purpose of these supposed angelic visitations was to add to and update prophecies of the Bible. Sadly, Mormon disciples have dismissed the last and final admonition of the Bible, which by virtue of it being Yahusha-Jesus' final words to us should be given the greatest emphasis. It says—nothing shall be added to His Word!

---

655 Acts 16:30-31
656 Zechariah 9:9
657 Jeremiah 23:5, 33:15
658 John 12:42

"For I testify unto every man that heareth the words of the prophecy of this book, If any man shall add unto these things, God shall add unto him the plagues that are written in this book: And if any man shall take away from the words of the book of this prophecy, God shall take away his part out of the book of life, and out of the holy city, and from the things which are written in this book." (Revelation 22:18-19)

Prophecy and its flawless fulfillment is the indelible stamp of divine authorship which is only contained in the Judeo-Christian testaments.

Lying Spirits, Familiar Spirits, Seducing Spirits

While a prophecy not coming to pass is an indication of a false prophet, even a prophecy coming to pass needs to be measured against HIS written Word.

GOD has on occasion permitted lying spirits to entice an evil doer.[659] Today lying spirits and familiar spirits, both of which are demon spirits[660] use mediums and channelors who profess to hear from the dead in order to prey upon the gullible living.

These spirits are referred to as familiar spirits because they are familiar with generations of the particular family to whom they have been assigned. Because they know all too well what took place in the lives of the deceased family members, these spirits can speak to the psychic or anyone else who attempts to contact the dead and pretend to be the voice of their deceased loved one. The popular Ouija board is an example of just how easy it is to communicate with demonic spirits if one wants to dabble in the occult. These spirits adore such opportunities. Demonic spirits (ghosts or specters) can and do occasionally appear as well—particularly to those looking to communicate with the dead or those fascinated with the supernatural.

In 1 Samuel 28 we read that King Saul, frustrated that GOD would not answer him by dreams, vision, by prophet, or the Urim concerning an impending battle with the Philistines, sought out a witch in the city of Endor. Saul knew full well he was seeking out a spirit, which was against GOD's law and was punishable by death. Still he persisted, hoping to contact and get advice from the Prophet Samuel who had died at least two years earlier. In subscribing to this witch (a necromancer—communicator with the dead) he invited in a familiar spirit who was only too happy to impersonate Samuel. This familiar spirit knew Samuel and Saul's past relationship and could easily mimic the prophet. Though demons cannot know the future, except for what GOD has predicted in bible prophecy, they can and do make predictions based on likelihood.[661]

There is no record of GOD ever allowing communications between the living and the dead. When GOD speaks, He speaks through the Holy Spirit; never through unscriptural and unlawful ways, as was the case with the specter impersonating Samuel. Therefore, if men believe they can communicate with or pray to any deceased human they are being deceived. Not only is it

---

659 1 Chronicles 18:19-21
660 Deuteronomy 18:10-12; 1 Samuel 28:7; 1 Chronicles 10:13
661 1 Samuel 28:19

not possible to communicate with the dead, it is forbidden.[662] This includes praying to Jesus' deceased earthly mother, Mariam (Mary)!

As Paul warned Timothy, "seducing spirits" will become more prevalent in the last days.[663] Though we are not yet (as I write) in the last days, this is still true even in the Church today. There are many professing prophets and prophetesses who believe they are hearing from GOD but are in reality hearing another spirit. Believers should remember that the spirit of prophecy is not about men and their issues. The Bible tells us that the "testimony of Yahusha-Jesus is the spirit of prophecy."[664] This means prophecy testifies and glorifies Him and while it may edify the Church, it still must glorify Him.

> Note: Prophecy is among the spiritual gifts given and distributed by the Holy Spirit.[665] The Spirit does not speak for Himself, but for the entire GODhead, and when He does speak, what He speaks glorifies Yahusha-Jesus.[666] Furthermore, though the gift of prophecy is indeed active today, it is also counterfeited. There is relatively little need for GOD to continue to add to what He has already presented in His written Word— for the Bible is complete! One should also be mindful that when a biblical prophet spoke in times past it was primarily a warning to a king or to that generation of what GOD had already spoken to a former generation. For all these reasons Paul warned that tongues and prophecy should be evaluated as genuine (or not) by the hearers.

> "How is it then, brethren? when ye come together, every one of you hath a psalm, hath a doctrine, hath a tongue, hath a revelation, hath an interpretation. Let all things be done unto edifying. If any man speak in an unknown tongue, let it be by two, or at the most by three, and that by course; and let one interpret. But if there be no interpreter, let him keep silence in the church; and let him speak to himself, and to God. Let the prophets speak two or three, and let the other judge." "Wherefore breathern, covet to prophecy, and forbid not to speak with tongues. Let everything be done decently and in order."
> (1 Corinthians 14:26-29, 39-40)

Be aware that GOD may allow lying spirits[667] to lie, and lying signs and wonders to prove (test) HIS people in order to see if they will act contrary to HIS Word; hence we pray, "And lead us not into temptation, but deliver us from evil."[668] The real test of a prophetic word is not only to see if the prophecy comes to pass but moreover, if it coincides with the Word of GOD. Anything however the least bit contrary to the Word is false! One shall know the false prophet from the

---

662 Deuteronomy 18:9-14
663 1 Timothy 4:1
664 Revelation 19:10
665 1 Corinthians 12:4-7, 10
666 John 16:13-14
667 1 Kings 22:21-23
668 Matthew 6:13

genuine by their teachings; therefore it is imperative for each of us to study HIS Word for ourselves.[669] For like a roaring lion, Satan lies in wait, ready to pounce and consume little lambs.[670]

When Yahusha-Jesus said, "you shall know them by their fruits," He was speaking about how one can recognize false prophets. "Beware of false prophets, which come to you in sheep's clothing, but inwardly they are ravening wolves. You shall know them by their fruits."[671] The fruits to which He was referring had nothing to do with their outward conduct or virtues, as with the fruit of the Spirit.[672] Outward conduct can be a pretense or a performance. Our Lord was first and foremost referring to knowing them by their doctrine and whether it coincides with or is contrary to Scripture. Do they speak the gospel that faith in Christ and what He accomplished at the Cross as being all sufficient[673] or do they speak another gospel which requires fidelity and conformity to a religious institution? The Apostle Paul was emphatic when he said,

> "I marvel that ye are so soon removed from him that called you into the grace of Christ unto another gospel: Which is not another; but there be some that trouble you, and would pervert the gospel of Christ. But though we, or an angel from heaven, preach any other gospel unto you than that which we have preached unto you, let him be accursed. As we said before, so say I now again, if any man preach any other gospel unto you than that ye have received, let him be accursed." (Galatians 1:6-9)

What gospel is it that Paul preached? "For I determined not to know any thing among you, save Jesus Christ, and him crucified."[674] "God forbid that I should glory, save the Cross of our Lord Jesus…"[675] "For I am not ashamed of the gospel of Christ: for it is the power of God unto salvation to every one that believeth; to the Jew first, and also to the Greek."[676]

---

669 2 Timothy 2:15
670 1 Peter 5:8
671 1 Peter 7:15-16
672 Galatians 5:22
673 Galatians 2:16
674 1 Corinthians 2:2
675 Galatians 6:14
676 Romans 1:16

19

BIBLICAL JUDAISM AND RABBINICAL JUDAISM

The Jewish Revolt

After Yahusha-Jesus' coming, Messianic Judaism (a.k.a. the Church—Acts 11:26), circa 41 AD, rapidly spread throughout the Roman Empire.

Initially the Romans did not distinguish between orthodox Jewry and Messianic Jewry. A succession of Roman emperors; Caligulia, 37–41 AD, Claudius, 41–54 AD, and Nero, 54–68 AD, saw the Church simply as a Jewish sect which invited Gentiles to become proselytes.

The Roman emperors' single major contention with the Jews and the Messianics was that neither group was willing to accept Roman pagan ideology or recognize the divine status which the emperors asserted they possessed. Nero in particular claimed this to be treasonous and became one of the earliest and most notorious persecutors of Christians. Historians state that he would have these Messianic believers (a.k.a. Christians) captured, dipped in oil or tar, and then set on fire to light his garden at night.[677]

During the early part of the first century tensions were common between the Greeks and Jews to the point that the Romans became exasperated with the continuous disturbances. Issues such as Roman taxation were imposed and hostilities escalated, especially when even the Temple treasury was taxed.

In 66 AD the Roman army responded by plundering the Temple and executing as many as six thousand Jews in Jerusalem. The Jews responded with a full-scale rebellion and so began the first of three Jewish-Roman wars; the Great Revolt (66–73), the Kitos War (115–117), and the Bar Cochba revolt (132–135).

So it was that there were three groups of people who would not compromise their beliefs and bow to their Roman oppressors. The first group was the Jewish national zealots and the revolutionary faction—the sicarii, who would not accept Roman domination.[678] The second group

---

677 Tacitus XV, (then Roman senator and historian), The Annuls, 44
678 Josephus, *The War of the Hebrews*, Vol.2, 254-257

was the devout Jews who clung tenaciously to their Torah. The third group were the Jews who, along with their converts, had studied the Tanakh and realized that Yahusha-Jesus was indeed their Messiah.

The Split

There were essentially two reasons for the divergence between Biblical Judaism, which held that Jesus was the Mashiach, and Pharisaical (later Rabbinical) Judaism which denied Him and His divinity.

While the Temple stood and the sacrificial system was in place, there existed a schism between the Messianic and the Rabbinic Jews—but there wasn't intense animosity. However, after the Temple was destroyed and there was no longer a way to continue the sacrificial system, the rabbinic felt the need to come up with an alternative. That alternative was to assert that by keeping the commandments and acts of kindness—*mitzvahs* (secondary meaning)—sins could be exonerated. The Messianic believers would have none of this and the divide widened.

Many Orthodox and Charedim would not compromise either, for they understood that only by the shedding of blood is atonement made.[679] Orthodoxy held strictly to the Torah while others began following the Rabbinic—*Halachah* (traditional Jewish legal interpretation). In any event, without the Temple each individual had to decide how they were going to atone. Would they keep Torah and become passive to the Tanakh which bore witness to the Messiah? Would they accept the rabbinic alternative of works and deeds? Or, would they search the entire body of Scripture and recognize that the atonement had already been made?

There were some who tried to find some middle ground and somehow keep blood in the atonement. This gave rise to the *Kaparot* ritual performed by the Orthodox Charedim. This ritual, done just prior to *Yom Kippur* is performed by taking a live rooster, reciting a penitent prayer, "a soul instead of a soul, or a rooster goes to death but I go free"—as they rotated the bird over their head. Their hope was that their sins were transferred to the fowl which was then slaughtered by slitting its throat. It does not surprise me that not so ironically, the Hebrew word for rooster "*geber*" may also be used for (a) man.

It is a human tendency that when faced with a dilemma for man to invent some seemingly reasonable alternative, even if it goes against that which has been divinely prescribed. A stark example was Aaron's concession to placate the people and permit them to fashion a calf of gold.[680]

The genuine article must not be imitated. Just as no strange fire was to be used [681] and no strange altar was to be built;[682] neither is it left to man to come up with an alternative to expunge sin. GOD despises imitations, and all the more when they are meant to represent or replace HIM.

---

679 Leviticus 17:11
680 Exodus 32:1-4
681 Exodus 10:1-2
682 Exodus 20:25

There is an inborn trait among Jews to debate and argue the meaning of Scripture. This was especially true with the rabbinic. Each new generation of disciples became consumed with discovering new meaning in the scriptural narratives. Studying the thoughts and assertions of the sages became central to rabbinic preparation and would later give rise to the 6,200-page Talmud of today. Numerous commentaries, compendiums, and even traditions were blended with the Holy Writ until the Hebrew Scripture began to be considered a guiding principle rather than a series of divine instructions. This became the basis of what is today Reform Judaism; the focus of which is universal peace, social justice, and personal morality.

In the mid-nineteenth century, Conservative Judaism, or Reconstructionism became popular. Its adherents held to the universal teachings of Judaism; however, they believed there needed to be changes. Conservative Judaism (of which there are many nuances) felt the need to evaluate each subject against the sources and Jewish tradition. While both Conservative and Reform Jews believe that GOD is real, some believe the Torah and Tanakh are not necessarily the inspired Word of GOD or that scripture should be taken literally.

Intellectual defenses have their place, but Theology (Theo-GOD, ology-Science) is not one of them. Theology deals with our knowledge of GOD and HIS relationship with man and has but one fountainhead—Scripture!

As science is a systematic and logical arrangement of certified facts, so is Theology; leaving no room for suppositions. If one is to believe the Bible is GOD's Word to man, then it must also be accepted that everything that disagrees with the Scriptures is but opinion.

> Note: The word religion comes from the Latin, meaning "to bind." While it should pertain to things which bind man to GOD in relationship. Not so mysteriously is the fact that it has become something that simply—binds men!
>
> Note: The early Talmudic writings (second century and afterward) have themselves undergone many alterations. In 1264 AD the first of many censorships were undertaken at Barcelona by a commission of Roman Catholic friars called Dominicans. The Dominicans had come into existence in 1216 when they were approved by Pope Honorius III who deemed them the scholastic order of the Church of Rome and charged with combating heresy and heretics. The Dominican Order made it part of their mission to remove passages from sacred writings considered objectionable from the Roman Christian perspective. As centuries came and went more papal bulls and disputations were enacted, and while much Talmud has been retained, much has been lost to antiquity.

Returning to the subject of "the split" between Rabbinic Judaism and Messianic Judaism, we will move forward on the timeline to the beginning of the second century.

In 132 AD a Jewish revolt led by Simeon Ben Kosiba (Cochba) occurred against the Roman Empire. At the beginning of the revolt, the Messianic Jews, having strong national convictions joined in; that was, until Rabbi Akiva (Akiba) declared Bar Cochba to be the Messiah who would lead the Jews to defeat their Roman oppressors. The Messianic believers found Akiba's assertions completely unacceptable which ultimately led to a schism which continues until this day.

The psalmist and the prophet Isaiah both predicted that when Yahusha-Jesus would first come He would be the "sanctuary" for those Jews who would accept Him. But He would be a stumbling stone for others who refused to believe. Those who rejected Him would be taken in Satan's *gin* (snare), (Hebrew, *moqesh*), and their fate forever sealed.

> "I will praise thee: for thou hast heard me, and art my salvation. The stone which the builders refused is become the head stone of the corner." (Psalm 118:21-22)

> "And He shall be for a sanctuary; but for a stone of stumbling and a rock of offense to both the houses of Israel, for a gin and a snare to the inhabitants of Jerusalem. And many among them shall stumble, and fall, and be broken, and be snared, and be taken." (Isaiah 8:14-15)

Authentic Judaism

Over the centuries Satan has been very successful in advancing a disdain for Jews who have accepted Jesus as their Messiah. He knows they (Believers) hold the keys (truth) to the kingdom of heaven and can steal his quarry if they can propagate the Gospel. Those adhering to mainstream Judaism have even marked their family members who have accepted Jesus as apostates (Hebrew, *meshummand*) and in some cases pronounced them dead. Their unwillingness to delve into the Holy Scriptures and investigate for themselves the possibility that Jesus is the Messiah is largely because of the relentless persecution from those who for centuries touted themselves as Christians and claimed to be followers of Jesus!

This is a true contradiction, for the genuine Christian Church (Believers) shares a great love for the Jewish people and even feels indebted to them. True Christianity recognize it was the Jews who were GOD's first chosen people and were HIS appointed custodians of HIS Word. The true Church sees the Jews as the first bearers of the "Good news" (Hebrew, *Besorah*) and the first evangelists to the Gentiles. In so far as what may be referred to as a "religion," Judaism is the foundation and fountainhead of Christianity.

It appears to elude the Jewish people today that what is authentic Christianity was originally Biblical Judaism. It was not until the sheer numbers of Gentiles who joined this Jewish sect (then called Nazarenes) outnumbered their Jewish brethren that this movement was even thought of as something other than a Jewish sect.

The Gentile believer who comes to Yahusha must accept the God of *Avraham* (Abraham), *Yitzchak* (Isaac), and *Ya'acov* (Jacob). The Gentile convert must accept the *Kitvei HaKodesh*, (Hebrew Holy Scriptures). The Gentile convert must believe the Torah, and that which was spoken by the prophets. And, the Gentile must accept the Jewish Messiah as his substitutionary sacrifice. In reality the Gentile must accept Biblical Judaism and become grafted in, hence becoming part of the commonwealth of Israel.[683]

The Messianic Jew—or if you prefer, the Hebrew Christian, or simply Christian—is fulfilling his destiny and bringing the GOD of Abraham to the Gentile nations just as YAHUAH told Abram he would.

"...and in thee shall all the families of the earth be blessed." (Genesis 12:3)

"And in that day there shall be a root of Jesse, which shall stand for an ensign of the people; to it shall the Gentiles seek: and his rest shall be glorious." (Isaiah 11:10)

In the eleventh chapter of the book of Romans, beginning with verse thirteen, the Gentiles which have become part of the Church are portrayed as "wild olive branches," while Israel is portrayed as the "lump" and the dormant "root." Like a root, it is hidden; buried in darkness beneath the soil—it has not (as yet) seen the light of the "Son." Nevertheless, like the dormant root it has retained its life.

This living root has been the source of life and nourishment which has fed the seemingly sleeping trunk. The Great Husbandman has grafted in branches of the wild olive tree (the Church) and they have taken hold.[684]

In one day, at the commencement of the Kingdom Age, the root and trunk will burst forth with its own natural olive branches and bear tremendous fruit as it shares its Messiah with the nations.[685] The Church has not replaced Israel in the plan of GOD but rather has become a part of that plan!

One of the most outstanding Jewish Christians of the nineteenth century was Britain's Prime Minister Benjamin Disraeli. He was both a great Jew and a great Christian and never thought it a compromise to be both. Asserting Christianity was the fruit of Judaism he wrote, "In all church discussions we are apt to forget the second Testament is avowedly only a supplement. Jesus came to complete the law and the prophets." Christianity is completed Judaism, or it is nothing. Christianity is incomprehensible without Judaism, as Judaism is incomplete without Christianity."[686]

---

683   Romans 11:17
684   Romans 11:17
685   Zechariah 8:23; Isaiah 66:19
686   Jacob Gartenhaus, *Famous Hebrew Christians*, Baker Book House, Grand Rapids, Michigan, 1979, p.73

20

ENTER THE HOLY SPIRIT

The Comforter

> "And I will pray the Father, and he shall give you another Comforter, that he may abide with you forever..." (John 14:16)

Shortly after Yahusha-Jesus had completed His earthly mission and returned to His heavenly throne[687] there came another member of the GODhead—the promised "Comforter"—GOD the Holy Spirit.[688]

Fifty days had passed since the waving of the barley sheaf at the beginning of the Passover. It was now the Feast of Pentecost (Hebrew, *Shavouth*). There in Jerusalem, the first assembly of Yahusha's disciples had obediently gathered as He had commanded them.[689] As they were all in one mind, focused and absorbed with their now risen Savior, there suddenly came a mighty rushing wind which filled the house. Then, with what could only be described as cloven tongues of fire, the Holy Spirit descended, settling upon each individual Believer.[690]

As promised the Spirit had been given, ensuring that even in Jesus' absence a member of the GODhead would be with His disciples thereafter.[691] This would be a prelude of what the prophet Joel spoke of eight hundred years earlier. This transcendent event would be a divine endowment to Believers in this the Church dispensation, and afterward to the Jewish people in the latter days; just prior to[692] and immediately following the Lord's second coming.[693]

On that particular Pentecost His disciples would be the first to receive this supernatural gift when the magnificent Holy Spirit took up His post on earth. He would enter into each of them, fusing Himself to the Believer's own spirit. This would aptly become called the Baptism

---

687 Psalm 110:1
688 John 16:7; Luke 3:16; 24:49
689 Acts 24:49
690 Acts 2:2-4
691 John 14:16-18
692 Revelation 7:3
693 Joel 2:28-32; Acts 2:16

of the Holy Spirit. Afterward this endowment would be freely given to those who, from their innermost being, repented;[694] obeyed;[695] prayed;[696] sought;[697] and believed.[698] The Holy Spirit came just as Yahusha-Jesus had promised and continues to be available to all Believers who are earnestly intent on living for and serving the Lord.[699]

That day and thereafter, the Holy Spirit ignited the spirit of men and women who dared believe for it. Once empowered they went out sharing the Gospel of Salvation with others who themselves then received the Baptism.[700] Like a flame which comes in contact with dry hungry wood, the Holy Spirit leaped from one Believer to another.[701] The Church became so energized it could not be constrained or contained. Having been endued with the power from of high, the limitations of the ordinary man became infinite…GOD had entered in![702] GOD was now in control![703] Suddenly and gloriously emancipated from the cares and concerns of this temporal world, the Believers' focus, which had before been on earthly pursuits changed; Yahusha-Jesus became their all in all!

The one characteristic that distinguishes the genuine born-again Christian from one who claims they are a Christian is that the genuine Believer lives a life enthralled with Yahusha-Jesus and whose every desire is to attain more of Him.

> "I am crucified with Christ: nevertheless I live; yet not I, but Christ liveth in me: and the life which I now live in the flesh I live by faith in the Son of GOD, who loved me and gave Himself for me." (Galatians 2:20)

> "My life is no longer my own; it belongs to Him. It is His life that I am now partaking in." (Finis Jennings Dake, the Dake Annotated Reference Bible, Gal. 2:20, comment "w," paraphrased.)

The Jewish believers were freed from the bondage of the Law and the boundaries of traditional Judaism. The Gentiles believers were freed from all the distortions associated with polytheism, Gnosticism, and Hellenism. In keeping with His promise, He came to set the captives free; which are today His Church.[704]

> "For by one Spirit are we all baptized into one body, whether we be Jews or Gentiles, whether we be bond or free; and have all been made to drink into one Spirit." (1 Corinthians 12:13)

---

694 Acts 2:38
695 Acts 5:32
696 Acts 8:15
697 Acts 9:17
698 Acts 19:2-6
699 Acts 2:39
700 Acts 1:8; 10:42-43
701 Acts 19:2-6
702 1 John 4:4
703 1 Corinthians 12:10, 28-29; Galatians 3:5
704 Isaiah 61:1

The Church Victorious

Although there is relatively little historical documentation of the spread of the Church until the latter part of the second century, still there is evidence as we read in Paul's letter to the Church at Thessalonica.

> "For from you sounded out (went out) the word of the Lord not only in Macedonia and Achaia, but also in every place your faith to God-ward is spread abroad; so that we need not to speak any thing. For they themselves shew of us what manner of entering in we had unto you, and how ye turned to God from idols to serve the living and true God; and to wait for his Son from heaven, whom he raised from the dead, even Jesus, which delivered us from the wrath to come." (1 Thessalonians 1:8-10)

In the year 112 AD, Governor Pliny of Bithynia wrote to Roman Emperor Trajan of the economic effect Christianity was having on the empire. In the narrative he spoke of how temples (pagan temples) were nearly empty as were the markets, as the selling of sacrificial animals had diminished significantly.[705]

Rome's response to this messianic contagion was more persecution. Those alleged converts who had merely been swept up in the fervor of what was then in vogue but who had not experienced a genuine conversion soon abandoned their newfound faith to escape their persecutors. The genuine Church continued on in obedience to their commission to spread the Gospel message to the nations in spite of the threat.[706]

In so far as Judaism was concerned, the human nature loves its orthodoxy and clings resolutely to law and tradition rather than to promise. Even the Jewish apostles James, Barnabas and Peter had occasion to make concessions and observe practices such as dining restrictions that were common to Jewish orthodoxy.[707] In the beginning, and likely in hope of making converts, they believed that some accommodation could be struck.[708] Their spiritual judgment was for a moment misplaced; their earthly loyalty to Judaism challenged their spiritual loyalty to their Lord. Later all this would change as Paul especially became emphatic that no one is justified by the law and there is no room at all for concession.[709]

Herein is the dilemma we all faced or will face. In whom or in what do we believe and put our trust? Is it ourselves, man and religion, or is it GOD and HIS Word?

> "No man can serve two masters: for either he will hate the one, and love the other; or else he will hold to the one, and despise the other. Ye cannot serve God and mammon." (Matthew 6:24)

---

705 John W. Kennedy, *The Torch of the Testimony*, Christian Book Publishing House, Auburn, ME, 1965, p.49
706 Mark 16:15; Luke 24:47; Matthew 5:14-16
707 Galatians 2:11-14
708 Acts 15:3; 21:24, 27; Galatians 2:11-14
709 Galatians 3:11-13

"Let thy mercies come also unto me, O Lord, even thy salvation, according to thy word. So shall I have wherewith to answer him that reproacheth me: for I trust in thy Word." (Psalm 119:41-42)

21

MINISTERS OF RIGHTEOUSNESS?

Truth and Travesty

"Is not my word like as a fire? saith the Lord; and like a hammer that breaketh the rock in pieces? Therefore, behold, I am against the prophets, saith the Lord, that steal my words every one from his neighbour. Behold, I am against the prophets, saith the Lord, that use their tongues, and say, HE (GOD) saith." (Jeremiah 23:29-31)

Twenty-one of the twenty-seven books of the New Testament have scriptures warning us of "false teachers," "false prophets," "false doctrines," "deceitful workers," "Satan's ministers of righteousness," "wolves in sheep's clothing," "another gospel," "the great falling away," etcetera. The truth be told, apart from the scriptures that concern themselves with our salvation, no other subject is spoken about or given more emphasis in the New Testament than the warnings of fakes.

"Beware of false prophets, which come to you in sheep's clothing, but inwardly they are ravening wolves." (Matthew 7:15)

"For I am jealous over you with godly jealousy: for I have exposed you to one husband that I might present you as a chaste virgin to Christ. But I fear, lest by any means, as the serpent beguiled Eve through his subtilty, so your minds shall be corrupted from the simplicity which is in Christ Jesus..." (2 Corinthian 11:2-3) "...For such are false apostles, deceitful workers, transforming themselves into apostles of Christ. And no marvel; for Satan himself is transformed into an angel of light. Therefore it is no great thing if his ministers also be transformed as the ministers of righteousness..." (2 Corinthians 11:13-15)

Additional warnings are found in: Matthew 10:28; 15:8–9; 23:27–28; 24:5; Mark 13:6, 22; Luke 21:8; Acts 20:28–32; Romans 16:17–18; 2 Corinthians 4:2–4; Galatians 1:6–9; Ephesians 4:14; Philippians 2:16–18; 3:2; Colossians 2:8; 2 Thessalonians 2:10–12; 1 Timothy 4:1–3; 2 Timothy 3:1–5; 1 Peter 5:8; 2 Peter 2:1–3; 3:17; 1 John 2:18–19; 4:1; Jude 3, 4; Revelation 18:4.

Versions and Perversions

Satan would not wait until the New Testament was completed to assail the Word of GOD. Unable to destroy the writings themselves, which were meticulously transcribed and preserved by GOD's custodians, Satan would find another way. He would use the teacher; the alleged "ministers of righteousness" to pervert and distort the Truth. This would not be difficult at all, for most—whether Jew or Gentile—have never been taught from the Word (the Bible) itself, but rather from the deductions, fabrications, and the contrivances of men.

A Jewish disciple, Shimon, better known as the Peter the apostle, wrote,

> "But there were false prophets also among the people, even as there shall be false teachers among you, who privily shall bring in damnable heresies, even denying (Greek, *arneomai*, contradicting) the Lord that bought them, and bring upon themselves swift destruction. And many shall follow their pernicious ways; by reason of whom the way of truth shall be evil spoken of." (2 Peter 2:1-2)

While this passage was directed to the Church at large and no false teachers were specifically identified, the words "even denying the Lord that bought them" suggest that there were teachers who had joined the assemblies who were contradicting what Christ had said. This satanic strategy of manipulating GOD's Word has gone on unabated since His first coming. And, what better way for the imposters to establish their own postulations than to write it in a book and call it a Bible?

Today all modern versions of the Bible have deleted, altered, or raised doubt concerning multiple hundreds of scriptures, even those spoken by Yahusha Himself. These are not trivial omissions or alterations but are of such significance as to undermine His deity, His virgin birth, salvation by faith alone, His efficacious blood, and His bodily resurrection. Collectively these perversions put into question the inerrancy, infallibility, and literal truths of the Word. What's more I dare say, is that the majority of ministers today accept and teach from these perversions and believe them to actual be the Word of GOD. Quite possibly a generic, ecumenical-Universal bible, perhaps called the New World Bible, may emerge and become universally accepted as it will integrate the doctrines of various belief systems.

Implanting a seed of doubt is a favorite trick of Satan which he employs in modern versions. Often found in footnotes or bracketed adjacent to a scripture is a lie—meant to give the reader cause to doubt the veracity of the scripture. For example, the New International Version, Zondervan Publishing, 1978–84, has such a notation next to the corresponding verse—Mark 16:9–20. There it reads, "The most reliable early manuscripts and other ancient manuscripts do not have Mark 16:9–20." What they are actually saying is that two, fourth-century codices, the Codex Vaticanus and the Codex Sinaiticus (circa 313 AD)—both of which support the long family tree of Roman bibles leave out the last twelve verses of Mark 16:9–20; which just so happens to be the Great Commission. The publisher's accusation is unfounded, for there is not another manuscript, either uncial or cursive that omits this passage. In fact, there are eighteen other uncials, and six hundred cursive manuscripts that do include these verses.

Try and imagine the consequences if there was any credence to this assertion made in the NIV. Who then could defend one truth or doctrine? Who then could speak of salvation by faith, or on what scriptures our salvation is predicated? Alas, how could GOD even hold HIS creation accountable if the Word itself were deficient or defective?

Today with thousands of alterations in an array of versions we would be hard pressed as to which one is the genuine Word of GOD. Is it the New World Translation of the Jehovah Witnesses? Is it the Latin Vulgate or the Catholic Douay complete with Apocrypha? "I trow not!"

> Note: The Apocrypha, meaning, "hidden away," is a collection of eighteen non-canonical books written during the intertestamental period known as the "four-hundred"—"Silent Years," (400 BC–1 BC) between Malachi and Matthew. These writings were rejected by the Church fathers as being unworthy and unsupported by Byzantine codices and excluded them from the cannon of scripture. In their defense and while untrustworthy some can be useful historically, theologically, and even to a point, scripturally, so long as the reader knows how it fits or clashed with divine truth. Jewish and Protestants theologians reject these writings (as presented in the Belgic Confession [1561] and the Westminster Confession of Faith [1647]) as non-scriptural and in part heretical. They have been used to support the saying of masses, prayers to the dead, almsgiving as a meritorious act of penance, and the existence of Purgatory. Roman Catholicism accepts most of the books (excluding First and Second Esdras, Letters of Jeremiah, Prayers of Manasseh, and Third and Fourth Maccabees) as canonical.
>
> Note: Today there are a plethora of modern versions of the Bible. Unwitting ministers have disregarded the admonitions of Scripture and left the verbally inspired Textus Receptus (Received Text) which is based on quantum amounts of manuscript evidence, as found in the King James Bible (KJB). The writers have supplemented what is referred to as the dynamic equivalence; a process where writers express their own thoughts, using what they believe to be an equivalent expression in contemporary language for readability. The KJB uses what is referred to as formal equivalence, keeping literal fidelity to the lexical details and grammatical structure of the original language. In contrast the dynamic equivalence tends to a more natural rendering at the cost of literal accuracy.

In synagogues and churches alike, congregants are obliged to sit like mannequins for an hour or so each week; a captive audience to the orator. There, like little school children they occupy a seat; their scholarly teacher expecting them to accept whatever he spoon-feeds them. To question, to challenge is taboo; accept, be still, and say Amen.

Some six years before Peter gave his warning, a converted Pharisee, Paul the apostle, while writing his second letter to the Christian assembly at Corinth, Greece, remarked that at that time there were already many engaged in corrupting the Word.

> "For we are not as many, which corrupt the word of God: but as of sincerity, but as of God, in the sight of God speak we in Christ." (2 Corinthians 2:17)

The word "corrupt" in Greek is "*kapeleuo*" and means adulterate. This particular word is used only once in scripture. However, in Isaiah 1:22 we have a similar word in Hebrew, "*mahal.*" There it refers to the tavern keepers who mixed water with wine. When it comes to new Bible versions, Satan is consistently adding a cup of poison into a lake of truth.

In 58 AD the Apostle Paul would write these passionate words to the assembly at Galatia.

> "I marvel that ye are so soon removed from him that called you into the grace of Christ unto another gospel: which is not another; but there be some that trouble you, and would pervert the gospel of Christ. But though we, or an angel from heaven, preach any other gospel unto you than that which we have preached unto you, let him be accursed. As we said before, so say I now again, If any man preach any other gospel unto you than that ye have received (Jesus Christ and Him Crucified), let him be accursed (damned)." (Galatians 1:6-9)

This was not to say it was a new gospel but a perversion of the real gospel. Paul brings great emphasis to this warning by repeating the word accursed; meaning damned.

In 2 Timothy 4:3–4 we learn that Satan not only seduces the biblically unlearned; but strives to capture the spiritual leaders who teach. It is the rabbi, priest, and minister who Satan considers the finer trophy, for if he is successful in leading the flock into heresy then the sheep will unwittingly follow the Judas goat into the "great ditch" (a metaphor for hell).[710] Scripture warns that as time goes on men will put less credence in the Bible, become more Bible illiterate, and seek (Greek, *episoreuo*) teachers who are able to persuade them to believe a false gospel.

> "For the time will come when they will not endure sound doctrine; but after their own lusts shall they heap to themselves teachers, having itching ears; and they shall turn away their ears from the truth, and shall be turned unto fables." (2 Timothy 4:3-4)

Leaven in the Loaf

During the first century, the Greco-Roman world was laden with philosophical theorists consumed with themselves and their new theories. The Greeks believed that knowledge was the key to all things whether natural or spiritual. *Gnosis*, the Greek word for knowledge and enlightenment

---

710   Matthew 15:14

soon infiltrated Christianity and became what is today Gnosticism—of which there are many shades. Today we might put Gnosticism into the same phylum with psychology or secular humanism.

Paul, in his letter to the Church at Colosse attempted to correct this heretical disease which had infected the Church. It had been created largely by combining Jewish legalism and mysticism with Hellenistic intellectualism, but it came from many other vectors as well. Some had their foundation in the oriental beliefs; others in astrology and polytheism.

> "Touch not; taste not; handle not; which all are to perish with the using; after the commandments and doctrines of men? Which things have indeed a shew (show) of wisdom in will-worship, and humility, and neglecting of the body; not in any honor to the satisfying of the flesh." (Colossians 2:21-23)

Before the ink was dry on the parchment of Paul's letters to the Christian assemblies, forgeries were already being made.[711] Unregenerated minds had been influenced by celebrated philosophers and free thinkers going back to Socrates, Plato, and Aristotle.[712] The generations of academics and philosophers who followed would strain the Word of GOD to come up with new theories and discoveries—eventually bringing man into the so-called Age of Enlightenment. By the time the twentieth century dawned there was no shortage of modern liberal theologians. Eventually humanism came into vogue and put man on a still higher pedestal. It was then that Liberation theology became the new paradigm of modern Christianity.

> Note: Liberation theology has grown into an international and inter-denominational movement, which began within the Catholic Church in Latin America in the 1950s and 1960s. It arose principally as a moral reaction to the poverty caused by social injustice. Liberal Christianity of the early 20th century has morphed into what is today modern Christianity. Its promoters believe that it is the future of the Christian Church to follow what may be best described as the Christian Social (Socialist) Gospel. In true Marxist fashion it identifies individualism, capitalism, nationalism, and militarism as America's spiritual evils which need to be replaced respectively with collectivism, socialism, internationalism, and pacifism.

Cults

From its conception Satan hatched and hurled an unending surplus of false gospels at the Church. Docetism was one early gnostic cult which the Apostle John refuted.[713] It was characterized by the view that Christ was an apparition and had not come in the flesh.

---

711   2 Thessalonians 2:2
712   Acts 17:19-21
713   1 John 4:1-3

In the second century circa 144 AD, a bishop named Marcion (Marconism) drew away many of the Christian faith with gnostic speculations. Marcion believed in dualism, and that the law-giving God of the Old Testament (Jehovah) was evil and rivaled the good and merciful God of the New Testament. He also rejected all suggestions that Judaism was the foundation of Christianity.[714]

About 240 AD a Persian born near Bagdad named Mani was also a believer in dualism and became the founder of Manichaeism.[715] He presented a form of Gnosticism that in many ways resembled Zoroastrianism, even calling himself the Paraclete (the one who comes along side).

Some cult heresies resembled Far Eastern religions ranging from Theosophy, believing that man is innately divine and has insight into the nature of GOD and the world either through direct knowledge or through some physical process.

Then there were Neoplatonists (founder Plotinus) in the third century. Plotinus' beliefs were a carryover from Plato's mystical theology (of which Augustine ascribed); some of which linger in some of the "mysteries" of Catholic theology.

There were also the Cabalists who are considered to be types of theosophists, having divine insight into GOD and nature by mystical study.[716] Cabalism is thought to have derived from a revered second century scholar, Simon ben Yohai, whose teachings established the basis for the Zohar (the Cabalistic bible).[717] Cabala involves a numerical interpretation of the narrative of scripture and dabble in the magical and mystical, to include the doctrine of mans' evolution. To this we can add a sect of Universalism which teaches that there is a final salvation of all souls.[718]

By the fourth century Epiphanius (315–403 AD), Bishop of Salamis, in his Greek treatise *Penarion* indicated there were no less than eighty heretical parties at the time; each attempting to further their own end.[719]

In His omniscience Yahusha-Jesus knew that various spurious teachings and perversions would be introduced and would continue until His return. So it was that He instructed the Apostle John to write seven letters to seven churches in Asia Minor. All would be admonished, and all but two would receive harsh reprimands.[720]

What was to happen next would set a course for the next seventeen hundred years and have unimaginable consequences on Jews, Gentiles, and Christians alike. Satan would initiate his most cunning plan by which to blind men from truth and steal their very souls. It would come in the form of a religion; an apostate church that would call itself Christian. It would draft hundreds of millions of unwitting Gentiles into its web while slaughtering the followers of Christ and attempting to annihilate the Jewish race.

---

714 *The Columbia Encyclopedia*, 2nd Edit., Columbia University Press, NY, 1956, Marcion, p. 1219
715 *The Columbia Encyclopedia*, 2nd Edit., Columbia University Press, NY, 1956, Manichaeism, p. 1210
716 *The Columbia Encyclopedia*, 2nd Edit., Columbia University Press, NY, 1956, Theosophy, p. 1967
717 *The Columbia Encyclopedia*, 2nd Edit., Columbia University Press, NY, 1956, Cabala, p. 288
718 *Random House Webster's Dictionary*, Random House, Inc., 1990, Universalism, p. 1458
719 Philip Schaff, *History of the Christian Church*, Vol. 1, Hendrickson Publishers, 1985, p. 187; *The Colombia Encyclopedia*, 2nd Edit., Columbia University Press, NY, 1956, Epiphanius, p. 625
720 Revelation, Chapters 2 and 3

22

WINDS OF CHANGE

Winds of Change and the Human Propensity

Six thousand years ago, in a garden called Eden, the serpent tempted the first humans with an offer. It wasn't fruit he offered Eve, but the power for her and Adam to become as gods. "Ye shall be as gods."[721] To this day he dangles the same fruit before the eyes of hungry men and women.

Satan's jealous and egocentric heart fostered a hate for GOD which compels him to destroy anything that is good, righteous, or godly. And because mankind is GOD's most cherished creation and the dearest thing to HIS heart,[722] Satan is obsessed with keeping men and women from discovering their Savior.[723] He accomplishes this using the lust of the flesh, the lust of the eyes, and the pride of life.[724] Then, by enlisting human agents [725] he stalks the vulnerable,[726] exporting heresy, propaganda, and lies.

At the pinnacle of mans' aspirations, beyond fame and the attainment of wealth, lies his appetite for power. Whether it is politics, industry, an empire, a government, or a religious community, man is obsessed with controlling it. In his bid for headship, he, like all good salesmen, markets himself as the one who is best qualified for the position. He claims to have the knowledge, the ability, and the credentials to efficiently and effectively carry out the (his) agenda. The Church would be no exception.

Over time this human propensity found its way into the assemblages of Believers. Not only did the most charismatic and persuasive secure leadership, but once in position they would begin to see themselves as having not just a divine appointment but divine authority.[727] With

---
721   Genesis 3:5
722   Jeremiah 31:3
723   John 10:10
724   1 John 2:16
725   2 Corinthians 11:14
726   1 Peter 5:8
727   3 John 9-10

titles came prestige and wealth; power would follow. Eventually some who had once been unpretentious elders became presbyters; then full-time clerics, then bishops. Then by political gerrymandering a monarchial bishop would be elected from their ranks. With mans' propensity to have a leader or a human figurehead[728] even in matters pertaining to GOD, a special social class of ecclesia was born.

A political organization with all the components of a religious government took shape, and through its electoral process established its hierarchy. Once the esteemed candidate for the post of bishop of bishops (a.k.a. the Pontif) had been voted into office, he received his coronation and was enthroned. Then, like a king from his golden chair set upon a lavish stage above the throng, he is venerated as his vassal priests lie prostrate before him. He sits shamelessly, assuming leadership over the body of Christ whose headship belongs to Christ alone.[729]

In stark contrast, those who have been truly appointed by GOD as His sub-shepherds and given oversight of one of His small flocks understand they are not over or above those they teach but equal.[730] They recognize that only the Holy Spirit leads the Church and needs no human magistrate.[731]

How did this come about, one may ask? In the first century small assemblies would cautiously meet in homes throughout cities and hamlets. Each assembly was independent of the other. Each had its own eldership. The elders were tasked with giving oversight, but no one person had authority over another. The Lord Himself had warned the Apostle Peter,

> "Feed the flock of God which is among you, taking the oversight thereof, not by constraint, but willingly; not for filthy lucre, but of a ready mind; Neither as being lords over God's heritage, but being examples to the flock." (1 Peter 5:2-3)

The authentic eldership was tasked with not only teaching, but because each assembly was like a close-knit family, the elders looked out for the earthly needs of the group as well.[732] So the eldership was committed to the spiritual and physical needs of their own assembly but had no authority over another assembly. The Bible indicates that neither the Church at Jerusalem nor the Apostle Paul was in a position to do any more than attempt to bring a correction by a letter of advisement (an epistle) if they felt something was amiss.[733]

Slowly at first, a transition from eldership to authoritarianism began to evolve as men distanced themselves from the biblical model of the book of Acts. This evolution would have serious consequences, eventually setting the stage for the monarchial institution. Tragically the pristine innocence and scriptural order of the Primitive Church, which can only work through subjection to the Lord and His Word, was usurped.

---

728 1 Samuel 8:6, 19
729 Ephesians 1:22-23
730 1 Peter 5:2-5; 1 Corinthians 12:12-26
731 Acts 20:28
732 Acts 2:44-47
733 1 Corinthians 1:10-11

By the early second century men like Ignatius of Antioch were advocating for an apostolic line which GOD had established solely for the founding of the Church.[734] Once the biblical record was established (which would later become the New Testament) and the foundation of the Church laid, the office of the apostle would be unnecessary and would end with the death of the Apostle John. The Bible record was plentiful and complete and would need no more apostolic leadership. Adding or deleting from His Word was thereafter forbidden by the Lord Himself.[735] Today, the nearest thing we have to an apostle (one sent by the Holy Spirit) is (like Paul was) the missionary.

Ignatius felt otherwise. Having been schooled by the Apostle John he may have believed he was to be part of the next generation of leaders. His motivation may have been well-intended as he had firsthand knowledge of how John had written seven letters to seven churches in Asia Minor; two of which (Pergamos and Thyatira) had allowed heresy into their assemblies.[736] Perhaps Ignatius thought that by establishing an overseeing authority (a.k.a. a government) truth would be safeguarded from heresy and the tenets of faith on which the Church had been established would be preserved.

It was at that earlier juncture (perhaps 96 AD) that the Church began wearing two faces. On one hand was the Church of Philadelphia[737] whose strength was not their own,[738] who kept the Word with diligence and kept Christ preeminent. On the other hand were the Churches of Ephesus and Laodicea; churches of works and form;[739] churches where individuals claimed to be apostles, "and are not and have found them liars."[740]

From Smyrna and Troas, Ignatius wrote letters to assemblies in Ephesus, Magnesia, Tralles, Philadelphia, and Rome. In these letters he attempted to unite the Church under the auspices of elected leaders. It was from these writings that he is believed to have been the first one to have used the word for "Universal," which is synonymous with the word Catholic. In his zeal Ignatius apparently overlooked the fact that the Church being one body[741] implies a spiritual unification, not a physical unionization. Still, his alter ego may have played a role in his vision, for having been a protégé of the Apostle John and perhaps believing that he was among the providentially appointed, he not only advocated for an apostolic line but even referred to himself as Ignatius *Theophorus* (God Bearer).[742] Whether his motives were self-serving or whether he was simply trying to guard the Church from heresy remains uncertain. However, by the end of the second century his writings had gained support and the authority of the office of bishop grew more powerful, setting the stage for the next evolution.

---

734 Ephesians 2:20
735 Revelation 22:18-19
736 Revelation 2:12-15, 20
737 Revelation 3:7-10
738 Revelation 3:8
739 Revelation 2:1-2; 3:14-18
740 Revelation 2:2
741 1 Corinthians 12:12-14
742 *The Columbia Encyclopedia*, 2nd. Edit., Columbia University Press, NY, 1956, p. 944

John W. Kennedy of India, in his book *The Torch of the Testimony*, wrote, "Christianity has always been open to heathen influences to the extent that it has departed from the divine pattern, and the departure which Ignatius so zealously encouraged fitted in admirably with the aura of mystery which surrounded the fashionable cults of the day. It is easy to understand how, to pagans who assume the Christian faith, a regime of clerics could take on a much different significance from what was ever intended by Ignatius and others of his persuasion. From being a special class of people it was a short step to their being considered a class with special powers, and the ceremonies which they officiated, baptism and the Lord's table, naturally became associated directly with the powers they were supposed to employ. The power of the Spirit having gone, these rites took its place; baptism came to be understood as a means whereby regeneration was miraculously conferred, and the Lord's table, with bread and wine miraculously transformed into the actual flesh and blood of Christ through the power of the bishop, became a further means of magical impartation of divine grace. All this was a direct inheritance from heathenism, for nowhere in the New Testament is there any hint."[743]

---

[743] John W. Kennedy, *The Torch of the Testimony*, Christian Book Publishing House, Auburn, ME, 1965, p. 55

23

BAIT, SWITCH, AND FOOL

Two Masters, but Only One Choice!

> "Open rebuke is better than secret love. Faithful are the wounds of a friend, but the kisses of an enemy are deceitful." (Proverbs 27:6)

Dear Catholics, who love GOD and who GOD loves, and Catholic priests and nuns who out of your love for GOD have allowed yourselves to become both pawns and victims; hear what the Lord is saying to you.

> "No man can serve two masters: for either he will hate the one, and love the other; or else he will hold to the one, and despise the other. Ye cannot serve God and mammon (man)." (Matthew 6:24)

Do we Love and Trust GOD more than we Love and Trust our Religion, or do we Love and Trust our Religion more than we Love and Trust GOD?

> "Then said Jesus to those Jews which believed on him, If ye continue in my Word, then are ye my disciples indeed; and ye shall know the truth, and the truth shall make you free... If the Son therefore shall make you free, ye shall be free indeed." (John 8:31-32, 36)

When one hears the word "church" it typically forms an image in one's mind. To many it simply means a building or house of worship. To others it represents a religious service, and to still others, an organized religion. However, in the Bible the term has a very clear and specific meaning which has no relationship with any of the above.

In the fifth book of the New Testament immediately following the gospels is a book titled, The Acts of the Apostles, (Hebrew, *Ma'aseh Shilichim*)—commonly referred to as the book of Acts. It is there we have the historic account of the development of the early Church.

In the seventh chapter, beginning with the thirty-eighth verse we read that Israel is described as "the church in the wilderness," for it was put upon Israel to be "called out" from other nations and to be set apart for GOD. So, it was only natural that when the Testaments were translated from Hebrew to Greek, that the Greek word *"ekklesia,"* meaning ones called out and set apart, was used. Another Greek word, *"kurike,"* from which the English word for "church" was derived, also came into use. It meant "that which belongs to the Lord." Both words are most appropriate to describe those who chose to follow Christ and Christ only! The Bible also refers to these called out ones as: The Elect, the Brethren, Believers, Saints, Disciples, Christians, the Saved, and the Body of Christ.

We should keep in mind that the Lord never created a single religion. He did not build an organization or a religious government. He would appoint overseers (elders), not overlords. He formed a body which would be an extension of Himself and through which He could give to mankind the simple gospel message which leads to eternal life.[744]

It would be the Apostle Paul who would have a prophetic foreboding word from the Lord. He said that after his departure from the congregation at Ephesus "grievous wolves" (purveyors of heresy) would not only enter into the Church but evolve from within and draw away followers after themselves.[745] Truer words were never spoken.

> "Take heed therefore unto yourselves, and to all the flock, over which the Holy Ghost hath made you overseers, to feed the church of God, which he hath purchased with his own blood. For I know this, that after my departing shall grievous wolves enter in among you, not sparing the flock. Also of your own selves shall men arise, speaking perverse things, to draw away disciples after them. Therefore watch, and remember, that by the space of three years I ceased not to warn every one night and day with tears." (Acts 20:28-31)

The true Church would retain its modest form and order. She would hold fast to the unpretentiousness Gospel of salvation, which is the message of the redemptive power of the Cross.

Paul would say it so well, "For I am jealous over you with godly jealousy: for I have espoused you to one husband, that I may present you as a chaste virgin to Christ. But I fear, lest by any means, as the serpent beguiled Eve through his subtilty, so your minds should be corrupted from the simplicity that is in Christ.[746]

In contrast to the simplicity which is seen in Christ is the opulent counterfeit of the Church which would put on royal trappings and regale herself in imperial fashion. Her thirst for power would become unquenchable as she made her way to becoming a religio-political government. Her single biggest threat was truth and the genuine Church which exposed her as a fraud.

> "Having a form of godliness, but denying (rejecting) the power thereof: from such turn away. For of this sort are they which creep into houses, and lead captive silly women laden with sins, led away with divers lusts, ever learning, and never able to come to the knowledge of the truth." (2 Timothy 3:5-7)

---

744 1 Corinthians 12:12
745 Acts 20:29-31
746 2 Corinthians 11:2-3

It is a part of the human disposition that man looks for some visible god to worship. If not a golden calf, a plaster statue, or a wooden totem, then a golden man.

The evolution of an ecclesiastical institution was never GOD's plan, nor was it in the minds of the apostles. During the first and second centuries autonomous local churches, each with their own eldership continued to govern themselves without interference. A study of the writings of the early church fathers also confirms that there was no rigid overseeing body, no apostolic lineage, and certainly no Roman authority. Only later did a dictatorial, overbearing religious government materialize.

In the true Church, Christ alone is the head. In the counterfeit, a human in a costume would prey on the gullible by all manner of fear.

During the first century, what is today called Christianity was in fact Biblical Judaism. What is now

A Golden Man (Image Source: ALAMY)

referred to as "the Church" began as a small Jewish congregation which originated in Jerusalem. Its founders were all Jews who had recognized the Messiah from the overwhelming evidence provided in the Hebrew Holy Scriptures from which the Apostle Paul taught. It needs to be appreciated that the Hebrew Scriptures were all that existed at the time. Furthermore, there were no printing presses, so copies were handwritten and limited. Those wanting to learn were largely reliant on the oral teachings of their elders or later from letters copied and passed from assembly to assembly.

The first Jewish assemblies were not comprised of individuals who had been proselytized by Gentiles and who had somehow managed to convert them to another faith; quite the reverse. It would be the Jews who would proselytize the Gentiles!

These Jewish disciples were not particularly pious men and women, nor were there but a few true scholars. They were simple ordinary men (e.g., fishermen) and ordinary women who intuitively knew what they were hearing was the truth.

As an unpretentious rabbi (Yahusha-Jesus) spoke, they recognized that His words were much different than other masters. As He explained the scriptures His words came alive with meaning and eternal promise. The words He spoke and those spoken afterward by His disciples penetrated hearts, went into souls, and awoke the spirits of men.[747] Almost without realizing it those that heard these words suddenly understood that Judaism was not the observances of laws, rituals or traditions. It is all about having an intimate relationship with Him, and so it was appropriately recorded, "in Him, we live, and move, and have our being."[748]

---

747   John 7:46; Acts 2:37, 41
748   Acts 17:28

Perhaps for the first time, those who heard the scriptures explained without all the theological jargon realized that the GOD of all creation actually loved them. "The Lord hath appeared of old unto me, saying, Yea, I have loved thee with an everlasting love: therefore with loving kindness have I drawn thee."[749] Love was and remains the foundation on which a genuine relationship is built. These ordinary men and women of Judea had connected with the GOD of Abraham; a God which the heady and high-minded could not find and could not know.[750]

> "In that hour Jesus rejoiced in spirit, and said, I thank thee, O Father, Lord of heaven and earth, that thou hast hid these things from the wise and prudent, and hast revealed them unto babes: even so, Father; for so it seemed good in thy sight." (Luke 10:21)
>
> "GOD resisteth the proud, but giveth grace to the humble." (James 4:6)

Four hundred and seventy years before GOD called Moses from a burning bush and before the Law was ever given, Abram had met GOD by simply seeking HIM from the recesses of his heart.[751] If this was the way that a man could connect with GOD, then why shouldn't any man be able to do the same? Why then shouldn't you and I be able to?[752]

> Note: I am quite certain had Isaiah been a contemporary of Yahusha-Jesus he would undoubtedly have been a follower as well. So too would have Moses, King David, and the major and minor prophets, for they all had messianic revelations and exhortations. Their collective contributions to the canon of Scripture advanced and enhanced the identity of Yahusha-Jesus as the Messiah. This is precisely why He was recognized by many Jews at his appearing!

It has been said, and rightfully so, that "the manipulators of history are not the ones who lived it, but rather the ones who wrote it." "History does not lie; only people lie." Those who accept what they are taught and will not verify it by delving into history or even examining encyclopedias are among the majority. Just as a mathematician or an accountant must justify each column before advancing, so must each searcher of truth. And, if the figures don't add up, then one must find the error and recalculate before advancing.

Any student of history can follow the bloody footprints from century to century, from country to country, from crusade to inquisition, or from the pogroms to the holocaust. Likewise, he or she can, if they choose, turn a blind eye to or excuse the theological differences which caused a Reformation, and which have since dissolved in an unfiltered pool of so-called brotherly love.

---

749 Jeremiah 31:3
750 1 Peter 5:5
751 Hebrews 11:10
752 Psalm 34:4, 6

I cannot help thinking of a brainwashed Catholic friar of the Augustinian order named Martin Luther who in 1517, despite recognizing and exposing ninety-five heretical doctrines of the Church of Rome (which helped birth the Protestant Reformation), had at the same time been so indoctrinated by the teachings of Rome and Augustine that he continued to spurn the Jews, even advocating for the burning down of Jewish homes.

> Note: Patristics is the study of the church fathers and their writings and is taught in Catholic seminaries. In their teachings it can be observed that numerous genuine Christian bishops, scholars, and historians who opposed the fallacious teachings of the Church of Rome were rebranded by Rome as "their own" church fathers. Many of these genuine Christians were summarily sainted by the very institution they had rejected. Satan needs only a pen and a scribe to charm the unstudied.

24

CATHOLICISM VS. CHRISTIANITY

For Catholics, salvation does not come from a deep and abiding relationship with Yahusha-Jesus on whom their salvation is entirely predicated. Rather, it is through a lengthy process which begins with an obligatory infant baptism—without which the parents are warned the child cannot enter heaven. Then, Catholic proxies; a godfather and godmother are charged with the responsibility of seeing to it that the child is raised in Romanism, further ensuring the child remains an indentured servant for life.

In Catholicism, heaven is accessed through participation in numerous non-biblical practices: sacraments, confessions, penance, plenary indulgences, and absolutions. It continues with the mandatory attendance of masses, holy days of obligation, novenas, and the reciting of vain repetitious prayers—which are repudiated in scripture.[753] The repetitious prayers are made all the more egregious by the fact that in the reciting of the "rosary" (prayer beads which had their origin in ancient pagan practice) the majority of the prayers are said to a deceased human (Mary) to whom they have given goddess status. She is claimed to have been immaculately conceived,[754] and that she was sinless[755]—both of which is contrary to scripture.[756] It is also stated that she had a glorious assumption (been taken up physically to heaven). These doctrines have absolutely no scriptural basis but are meant to deify a young Jewish woman who was simply used of GOD to birth and nurture the child Yahusha-Jesus. The Catholic, Anglican (Episcopal), Greek (Eastern) Orthodox churches, and other offshoots are all complicit in fostering the same and similar heretical doctrines.

Here are just three admonishments of which there are scores that the Bible is emphatic about, but which Catholics and other pseudo-Christian religions disregard.

Think of this if you pray the rosary.

> "But when ye pray, use not vain repetitions, as the heathen do: for they think that they shall be heard for their much speaking." (Matthew 6:7)

Think of this when you pray and invoke Mary to mediate or intercede with GOD on your behalf.

---

753 Matthew 6:7
754 Papal bull, *Ineffabilis Deus*, by Pope Pius IX in 1854
755 Encyclical Mystici Corporis, 110, Pope Pius XII
756 Romans 3:23

"For there is one God, and one mediator between God and men, the man Christ Jesus..." (1 Timothy 2:5)

Think of this when you refer to your priest as father.

"But be not ye called Rabbi: for one is your Master, even Christ; and all ye are brethren. And call no man (spiritually speaking) your father upon the earth: for one is your Father, which is in heaven. Neither be ye called masters: for one is your Master, even Christ." (Matthew 23:8-10)

> Note: Mary is purported to be the Mother of GOD. However, GOD is from everlasting to everlasting and has no mother. Mary was simply the mother of Jesus. Her motherly role was limited to be the vessel which would give birth to the infant and nurture him through childhood. Prayers and adoration given to Mary are in direct violation of the Second Commandment.[757] Furthermore, "GOD is no respecter of persons."[758] HE loves each of HIS creations equally.[759] He loves you just as much as he loved Mary.[760]

Ghostly Specters

The Apostle Paul warned that, especially in "latter times," ghostly specters—"seducing spirit"[761] would become prevalent. Their objective is to seduce the gullible who would dismiss the teachings of the Bible for the teachings of men. The Apostle Paul warned that Satan has the ability to materialize and disguise himself even as an "angel of light" or take on the appearance of an angelic being (even one that might be perceived as Mary).

"And no marvel; for Satan himself is transformed into an angel of light. Therefore it is no great thing if his ministers also be transformed as the ministers of righteousness; whose end shall be according to their works." (2 Corinthians 11:14-15)

In his prophetic predictions of the end time apostasy, Paul gave his protégé Timothy a most revealing prophecy. In it he accurately described the Catholic Church. It would be Romanism that would endorse the seducing spirits (e.g., Mary) as legitimate; who would themselves believe and teach lies; who would impose a life of celibacy on themselves, and who would at times (on Fridays, until just two generations ago) command their parishioners to abstain from eating meat.

---

757 Exodus 20:5-6
758 Acts 10:34
759 2 Peter 3:9
760 Mark 3:31-35
761 1 Timothy 4:1-2

> "Now the Spirit speaketh expressly, that in the latter times some shall depart from the faith, giving heed to seducing spirits, and doctrines of devils; speaking lies in hypocrisy; having their conscience seared (from the truth) with a hot iron; forbidding to marry, and commanding to abstain from meats, which God hath created to be received with thanksgiving of them which believe and know the truth." (1 Timothy 4:1)

Paul went on to tell the Church of Thessalonica that Satan will manufacture "signs and lying wonders" with which to deceive the unregenerated (unsaved) during the last days. It will be the False Prophet in support of the Antichrist who will be credited for many of these seemingly supernatural miracles.[762]

The appearance of celestial lights and ghostly forms are evidence of just who it is that is in disguise. Furthermore, these apparitions often instruct their devotees to do something which is a direct violation of GOD's commandments.[763]

One such specter the Church of Rome alleges to have been Mary is said to have visited a young girl, Catherine Labouré in 1830. The specter instructed her to describe the image of the apparition to her father confessor, and to tell him that they should put her image on medallions and that "All who wear them will receive great graces." [764] This graven image[765] worn by Catholics is commonly referred to as the "miraculous medal."

> "Thou shalt not make thee any graven image, or any likeness of any thing that is in heaven above, or that is in the earth beneath, or that is in the waters beneath the earth..." (Deuteronomy 5:8)

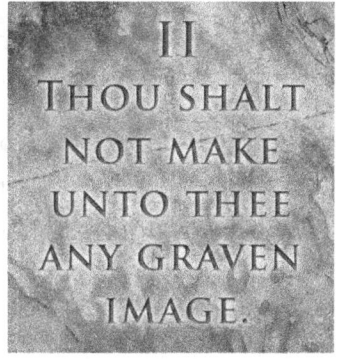

Thou Shalt Not! (Image Source: GOODSALT)

With increasing focus and the elevation of Mary, Christ and the Cross become diminished and the way to heaven obscured. Often, I have heard people when suddenly surprised, exclaim, "Jesus, Mary, and Joseph!" Mary and Joseph do not deserve to even be mentioned in the same breath with our Lord Jesus, much less equated with Him. But Romanism canonizes them; making demigods out of mere mortals and determining that they should be venerated.

Another example of a ghostly visitation professing to be Mary purportedly came with a message for Catholics to pray for world peace. This request is contrary to what the Bible tells us as to how the earth age will end. The scriptures clearly tell us that the earth age will end in a cataclysmic war, in a battle called Armageddon.[766] The Bible also teaches that in the last days it will be under the guise of peace that many will be deceived.[767] Such an appeal (were it not for the fact that the story was a total fabrication) would be a clear indicator

---

762 2 Thessalonians 2:9
763 Exodus 20:4
764 Joseph Glass, "Miraculous Medal," The Catholic Encyclopedia, Vol. 10. NY, Robert Appleton Co., 1911. 20 Dec. 2012
765 Deuteronomy 5:8
766 Daniel 12:1; Ezekiel 38:16, 18; Jeremiah 30:7; Zechariah 14:2-3, 12-14; Revelation 19:11-21
767 1 Thessalonians 5:3

of a demonic entity posing as a representative of GOD. Were a genuine appeal to be made, as in a prophetic word, it must align with scripture! Here is what was alleged to have taken place.

Medjugorje Today News: In September 2012, in Turin, Italy, Catholic visionary Ivan Dragicevic alleged to have been visited by the specter in which she (the specter) petitioned her followers to join her in prayer for peace in the world.

Title: "Mary strongly calls to pray for peace," Jakob Marschner, September 18, 2012, Dragicevic quotes Mary: "Dear children, also tonight I want to help you. Pray for peace. Pray with me for peace in the world. Peace, dear children! Only peace! I am praying with you for peace in the world. For this reason, I say to you, dear children, persevere in prayer! Thank you, dear children, because also today you have responded to my call."

Once again; the only peace which the Bible speaks of before Christ's return is a false peace.[768] This peace will be a deception orchestrated by the religious figure—the False Prophet and the Antichrist as depicted in Revelations chapters 13 and 17. There will be no peace on earth until the "Prince of Peace"[769] (the Lord Yahusha-Jesus) returns and establishes His Kingdom on earth![770]

> "For yourselves know perfectly that the day of the Lord so cometh as a thief in the night. For when they shall say, Peace and safety; then sudden destruction cometh upon them (Israel), as travail upon a woman with child; and they shall not escape." (1 Thessalonians 5:3-4)

> "And the great dragon was cast out, that old serpent, called the Devil, and Satan, which deceiveth the whole world: he was cast out into the earth, and his angels were cast out with him." (Revelation 12:9)

> Note: Reported by a former Jesuit priest, Alberto Rivera—who died mysteriously after three failed attempts on his life—gave an account of what was told to him by his mentor, Jesuit Cardinal Augustine Bea. Bea told him that the apparitions of Mary such as at Fatima, Portugal in 1917 were contrived by the Vatican to cause a resurgence of Romanism in what was becoming an anti-Catholic nation as it moved to socialism. Later made into a touching movie, it depicted three children; Lucia deSantos, Franco Marco, and Jacinta Maro (and no one else) who were said to have had visions of a luminous lady (allegedly Mary—the "Blessed Mother"). The scheme worked like a charm as pilgrimages continue to Fatima to this day to worship Mary. Though I believe this, and the dancing orbs later seen only by Pope Pius XII, to be a total hoax, it would not be contrary to scripture if a specter did appear. In addition, what appear to be miraculous healings can manifest if Satan tells his minion "spirits of infirmity" to release its victim in order to maintain the hoax that it was because of petitions made to Mary that a participant was healed.

---

768 Daniel 8:25
769 Isaiah 9:6
770 Isaiah, 2:4; Micah 4:3

> Note: Catholicism is based on blind submission, indoctrination, and heretical teaching. They teach that the Bible alone is insufficient and must be accompanied with "tradition" and "magisterium" (the teaching authority) which only the pope and his priests can provide. They claim that only when all three; tradition, magisterium, and the Bible are joined together do we have the Word of GOD. In contrast the Lord said, "if any man add or take away from His book (the Revelation)—He shall take away that his part out of the Book of Life."[771] Unless these embezzlers of souls recognize, repent, and come out of what is a cult, they have sealed their destiny in an eternal Lake of Fire.

Fallacies and Fabrications

The Catholic and the Episcopal Church, among others, have been quite successful in convincing (and thereby governing) their followers by making the assertion that they have been given divine appointment and divine authority through an uninterrupted apostolic line via a succession of popes and bishops going back to the original twelve apostles. This contrivance worked well during the Dark Ages when ignorance and superstition were prevalent, but amazingly it still works well today. This claim is a total fabrication, as no such line exists. The one they purport to be the first pope (Peter) was nothing of the kind and was alleged to have been put to death by their Roman namesake. The Church of Rome took shape in 323 AD and became the state religion of the Roman Empire. If they insist that their popes can be traced to the first century, then their apostolic line would have been the line of Caesars' who claimed the title Pontiff Maximus and were among other things, the religious heads of government.

> Note: The title "Pontifex Maximus" or Supreme Pontiff was one of the numerous titles Roman Emperors appropriated for themselves. Under imperial law they were the head of all religions in their empires. It wasn't until several decades after Constantine (272-337 AD) that the title and office of Pontifex Maximus would be appointed by a reigning emperor to another individual. Eventually Emperor Flavius Gratianus Augustus—"Gratian" assumed the throne in 378. Emperor Gratian favored Christianity over traditional Roman religions. He felt because he wasn't a clergyman it was not right to hold the title of Pontifex Maximus and so he renounced it. He bestowed the office and title upon a Portuguese deacon named Damasus who became the first official religious pontiff when the Edict of Thessalonica was issued in 380. The Edict ordered all subjects of the Roman Empire "to profess (adopt) the faith of the bishops of Rome and Alexandria." This reinforced Roman Christianity until the East and West Schism in 1054 when the Eastern—Greek Orthodox Church severed all ties with the Western—Church of Rome.

---

771   Revelation 22:18-19

> Note: The title "Pontifex Maximus" is mentioned numerous times by early church historians (particularly by Tertullian), but it was not applied to a Christian bishop. The early church believed that the Pontifex Maximus was the King of Heathendom; the evil high priest of the pagan mystery religions of Rome.[772]

Romanism has slowly evolved over nearly seventeen hundred years, adding new heretical doctrines and inventing scores of practices which are contrary to GOD's Word. To protect and indemnify themselves from being exposed as charlatans they instituted what would be the first prohibition of the Bible to laymen at the Council of Toulouse (Cannon 14) in 1229: "We prohibit also that the laity should be permitted to have the books of the Old or New Testament; unless anyone from motive of devotion should wish to have the Psalter or the Breviary for divine offices or the hours of the blessed Virgin; but we most strictly forbid their having any translation of these books." Source: *Heresy and Authority in Medieval Europe*, Edited with an introduction by Edward Peters, Scholar Press, London, copyright 1980 by Edward Peters, ISBN 0–85967–621–8, pp. 194–195, citing S. R. Maitland, *Facts and Documents* (illustrative of the history, doctrine and rites, of the ancient Albigenses & Waldenses), London, Rivington, 1832, pp. 192–194.

Finding that they were unable to crush the truth and stem the growing tide of Bible literacy after the printing press came into existence in 1440, Romanism was forced to come up with something which would neutralize the advance of the Reformation. So it was that "Tradition" was declared of equal authority with the Bible by the Council of Trent in 1545. Then Pope Pius IX, proclaimed the "Syllabus of Errors," which was later ratified by the Vatican Council in 1864. This document condemned freedom of religion, conscience, speech, press, and scientific discoveries which are not condoned by the Roman Church. This same edict asserted the pope's temporal authority over civil rulers.

Here are just some of the numerous fabrications which Popes and Councils adopted over the centuries:[773]

- The making of the sign of the Cross and prayers to the dead. (circa 300 AD)
- The veneration of angels, dead saints and images. (375 AD)
- The Mass as a daily celebration. (394 AD)
- The beginning of exalting Mary—the term "Mother of God" was first applied at the Council of Ephesus. (431 AD)
- The sacrament, Extreme Unction—Death bed absolution of sin. (526 AD)
- Prayers directed to Mary and saints. (circa 600 AD)
- Title "Universal Bishop" given to Boniface III by Emperor Phocas. (607 AD)
- The worship of the Cross, images, and relics authorized. (786 AD)
- The use of Holy water. (850 AD)
- The canonization of dead saints, Pope John XV. (995 AD)

---

772 Mark Bonocore, Article, *Title Pontifex Maximus*, www.philvaz.com/apologetics/a104.htm
773 Loraine Boettner, *Roman Catholicism*, The Presbyterian Reform Publishing Co., Phillipsburg, NJ, 1962

- The Mass made obligatory. (11th century)
- The Rosary beads—introduced by Peter the Hermit. (1090 AD)
- The Inquisition—instituted at the Council of Verona. (1184 AD)
- The sale of Indulgences. (1190 AD)
- Auricular Confession—Confessing to a priest instead of to GOD, Pope Innocent III at the Lateran Council. (1215 AD)
- Adoration of the Host (communion wafer), Pope Honorius III. (1220 AD)
- The doctrine of Purgatory, Council of Florence. (1439 AD)
- The Bible forbidden to layman, the index of Prohibited Books. (1559 AD)
- Infallibility of the pope in matters of faith and morals, Vatican Council. (1870 AD)
- The Assumption of Mary (bodily ascension to heaven), Pius XII (1950 AD)
- Mary proclaimed Mother of the Church, Pope Paul IV. (1965 AD)

Masks and Makeup

The Church of Rome has worn many masks over the centuries, changing its appearance as needed when the tide of its power surged and ebbed depending on the religious conviction of the then reigning monarch of a realm. Historically, when tyrannical dictators rose to power and war was imminent, Rome would, in order to preserve her power, align herself with whichever side she believed would ultimately be victorious.

In the twentieth century, believing Hitler and the axis powers would ultimately be the victor, she befriended Europe's tyrants. After the defeat of Germany, she abetted the Nazi war criminals by smuggling them to Argentina, Brazil, and other South American countries. Catholic priests, bishops and archbishops ran an underground network known as the "Ratline" through which a steady stream of war criminals escaped. This was done with the full knowledge and silent blessing of Pope Pius the XII.[774]

> Note: For almost forty-six years after Israel's rebirth in 1948 the Vatican refused to acknowledge her statehood and right to exist. Later Rome would revisit the issue and for pragmatic and political reasons concede that Israel was the Jewish homeland. She still insists that Jerusalem is an international city.

For the better part of her existence, and into the nineteenth century, as with the Spanish Inquisition (1478–1834), she would, in order to maintain her supremacy be an aggressor; hostile, violent, and murderous. However, over time she learned that far more can be achieved by pretending to be docile, charitable, and assume the aura of holiness. This was especially true in countries where she was in the minority and had little influence as it concerned the levers of power.

---

774 Mark Aarons and John Loftus, *Unholy Trinity: How the Vatican's Network Betrayed Western Intelligence to the Soviets*; St. Martin's Press, NY, 1991, Preface, pp. xii-xiii

During the last century she has waited patiently for the appropriate time in which to take her place on the world stage while proclaiming her desire to be a broker for peace (Latin, *Pax Romana*, "Roman Peace"). Today as her numbers have grown, so too has her political stature. Even now the Pontiff steps from behind the religious pulpit, travels to the United States, steps behind the United Nations Assembly podium, and takes on global issues.

> Note: The Spanish Inquisition 1478-1834, was an era of severe censorship, death, and ghastly torture initiated by Spain's emperors Ferdinand V and Isabella. The inquisitions were public tribunals perpetrated against Jews, Moors, and Protestants; anyone who disagreed with the principals of the Church of Rome and would not convert to Catholicism. This was done by permission of Pope Sixtus IV. Though the Encyclopedia Britannica states the pope gave "reluctant approval," further research shows that was not the case. The pope appointed the first inquisitor general; a Castilian Dominican Friar, Tomas de Torquemada. The Catholic encyclopedia itself states that according to Jewish historian, Graetz, "in the course of Torquemada's fourteen years as Inquisitor general (1485-1498), at least 2000 Jews alone were burnt alive as impenitent sinners"[775] Estimates go as high as 8,800 who died by fire and 9,654 that were punished in other ways (Histoire de Inquisition, IV, p.252, Llorente). If non-Catholics agreed to recant their faith under the threat of torture, they had to name other alleged heretics in order to escape an agonizing death. The inquisition became a witch hunt that lasted over 350 years. Cruelty in scope and intensity far surpassed the Medieval Inquisition from which Catholic monarchs took the idea.[776] The Catholic encyclopedia goes on to say this was necessary in part "for the preservation of Catholic Spain." The contemporary Spanish chronicler, Sabastian de Olmedo, in his work, *Chonicon magistrorum generalium Ordinis Praedictorum*, (fol. 80-81) calls Torquemada, "the hammer of heretics, the light of Spain, the savior of his country, the honor of his order."

On the surface, the Church of Rome appears to foster some worthwhile programs. These charitable works are of course paid for by their donor's monies which are collected each week in an offering basket overtly passed in front of each pew sitter. This obligates each congregant to give; making it something of an embarrassment should one not have the resources or choose not to contribute.

The monies designated for the poor or relief funds are a pittance of what the church takes in from their profits derived from commodity trades and from business investments. The charitable programs they sponsor are intended to give the illusion of generosity, while a tireless sisterhood of nuns gives sacrificially of themselves to the orphaned, poor, and sick.

The current pope (Francis) is lauded as "the peoples' pope;" the pope of the poor, the downtrodden, and the common man. However, mingling with the people does not make him either a man of the poor, nor does it demonstrate true humility. Rather, as any politician will tell you,

---

775 *History of the Jews*, Philadelphia, 1897, IV, p. 356
776 *The Columbia Encyclopedia*, 11th Edit., Columbia University Press, NY, Inquisition, p. 962

shaking hands with constituents and kissing babies, or washing and kissing the feet of Muslims, provides an excellent photo op. One never sees the Pope write a check for a few hundred million dollars to an area where the people (often with a large Catholic population) have been devastated by an earthquake or tsunami.

> Note: Over the centuries, popes have been murdered by their successors. Others in the Holy See have arranged the murder of pontiffs that would otherwise diminish their control. Some popes have committed incest, and numerous have had illegitimate children by mistresses. Believing that the priesthood is a hereditary line, most priests throughout the Middle Ages were the sons of other priests and popes. (Some examples: Pope Sylverius [536] was the son of Pope Hormisdas [514-523], Pope John XI [931-935] was the son of Pope Sergius III [904-911].) All popes lived in royal comfort, furnished by the alms of the poor or business investments. Today the pope continues to live in splendor; every need met, while his devotees continue to claim him to be a "man of the poor."

The Catholic institution has openly taken a biblical position against abortion which is indeed GOD's position.[777] They have also said that homosexuality is a sin, as GOD has decreed.[778] However, leniency and permissiveness toward sin is selective and discretionary. Such hypocrisy can be seen when they turn a blind eye and fail to condemn and excommunicate Catholic candidates and Catholic politicians who excuse, tolerate, or support abortion. They will accept the sinner into their fold without the sinner recanting his sin or amending his life. They are passive to the sin, lest they convict themselves for their long history of concealing their pedophile priests and bishops, who, when exposed by their victims, are hurried away to a monastery instead of paying the consequence prescribed by criminal law. Only when scores of victims come forward and it becomes public knowledge do they denounce their own and make a gesture of financial restitution.

The same may be said about their perspective of homosexuality.[779]

In an interview aboard a flight back to Rome following a visit to Georgia and Azerbaijan, when questioned about his stance on homosexuality the Pope (Francis) said, "When a person (who is gay) arrives before Jesus, Jesus certainly will not say, "Go away because you are homosexual."

Trusting Catholics who have placed their faith in their leader and who would sooner believe a man rather than GOD are like lambs made ready for the slaughter. Hear GOD's clear position on the subject, for nothing could be more contrary to what the Pope asserted.

> "For the wrath of God is revealed from heaven against all ungodliness and unrighteousness of men, who hold the truth in unrighteousness; Because that which may be known of God is manifest in them; for God hath shewed it unto them." (Romans 1:18-19)

---

[777] Jeremiah 1:5
[778] Leviticus 18:22
[779] October 2, 2016; Reuters, by Phillip Pullella

> "Wherefore God also gave them up to uncleanness through the lusts of their own hearts, to dishonour their own bodies between themselves: Who changed the truth of God into a lie, and worshipped and served the creature more than the Creator, who is blessed for ever. Amen. For this cause God gave them up unto vile affections: for even their women did change the natural use into that which is against nature: And likewise also the men, leaving the natural use of the woman, burned in their lust one toward another; men with men working that which is unseemly, and receiving in themselves that recompence of their error which was meet. And even as they did not like to retain God in their knowledge, God gave them over to a reprobate mind, to do those things which are not convenient..." (Romans 1:24-28)

> "Without understanding, covenant breakers, without natural affection, implacable, unmerciful: Who knowing the judgment of God, that they which commit such things are worthy of death, not only do the same, but have pleasure in them that do them." (Romans 1:31-32)

As repulsive as a homosexual lifestyle is to a genuine Christian; only superseded by atrocious infanticide, the most egregious "assertion" that Catholicism teaches its followers is that they are the representatives of Christ who hold the keys to heaven and that their followers are heaven bound (saved)—when, according to the Word of GOD they are not! By this one lie they are resigning their trusting followers by the millions to hell.

Salvation has absolutely nothing to do with them, but everything to do with having a deep personal relationship with Yahusha-Jesus. "Believe on the Lord Jesus Christ and thou shall be saved..."[780] "For by grace are you saved through faith; (in Yahusha-Jesus) and that not of yourselves: It is the gift of GOD: Not of works (efforts and good deeds), lest any man shall boast."[781]

Salvation is entirely predicated on what Christ has done on the Cross—for those who are solely reliant on Him. It has absolutely nothing to do with blind obedience and submission to the Catholic institution, her pope, her heretical doctrines, and her other contrivances.

> "Jesus answered and said unto him, Verily, verily, I say unto thee, except a man be born again, (have a spiritual birth) he cannot see the kingdom of God." (John 3:3)

> "Verily, verily, I say unto you, He that heareth my word and beleiveth on HIM that sent ME, hath everlasting life, and shall not come into condemnation, but be passed from death to life. Verily, verily I say unto you, the hour is coming and now is, (as the gospel is being offered) when the dead (spiritually dead) shall hear the voice of the SON of GOD; and they that hear (and respond) shall live." (John 5:24-25)

> "He that believeth (trusts exclusively in) the Son of GOD hath everlasting life: and he that believeth not the Son, shall not see life; but the wrath of GOD abideth on him." (John 3:36)

---

780 Acts 16:31
781 Ephesians 2:8-9

25

ROME AND ROMANISM

A History Lesson

In the second, third, and during the beginning of the fourth century, while the gospel was spreading throughout the Roman Empire, so too was persecution. The Romans, having dealt with numerous Jewish rebellions beginning with the Maccabean Revolt (168–164 BC), and lasting until the Jewish-Roman War (132–135 AD), decided that the eradication of the Jews and their various sects was the appropriate solution to ensure that there would be no more uprisings. Adolf Hitler would later call it, "the Final Solution."

But GOD had a different plan, for even the Diocletian Persecution, the most severe of that era, failed to stem the growth of this messianic phenomena. Conversely, persecution appeared to do just the opposite. The second century historian, Quintus Septimus Florens Tertullian, a Carthaginian, and himself a convert to Messianic Judaism, wrote of this extensively in his famous work the *Apologeticus*. In it he said, "the blood of the martyrs is the seed of the Church."[782]

When men saw that Believers were prepared to suffer and die for their faith while having a calming peace, it caused them to become Believers themselves; for if our faith cost nothing, men will value it as having little value.

During this same period the various Roman emperors lived in constant fear of being assassinated or losing their empery to their own generals and political rivals. Consequently, they ruled by fear, not hesitating to put to death anyone they perceived as a threat, including their own family members. Most of these emperors relished the

Roman demigod statue, Emperor Claudius (Tiberius C. Caesar Augustus Germanicus), 41-54 AD, Jupiter displayed in the Vatican Museum. (Image Source: ALAMY)

---

[782] *Apologeticus*, Chapter 50

torture and death of Jews and Christians and sponsored atrocities for public entertainment. Today these mass murderers would be classified as certifiably deranged or demon possessed.

As the numbers of Messianics grew and the catacombs were filling with corpses, the Romans became increasingly concerned at the seeming unstoppable growth of the Church. They were obviously just as puzzled as the Pharisees who thought this messianic movement would quickly fade away after crucifying its leader.[783] However, not only did it not diminish, it grew exponentially. What the Caesars' failed to realize was that the kingdom of which the Lord's followers spoke was not of this earth;[784] neither did it pose a direct threat to them, only to their pagan ideologies. Still, to ensure that there would never again be another revolution they decided to eliminate any possibility and found ways to draw those they considered dissidents out into the open.

To accomplish this, the emperors demanded universal sacrifice to themselves and their gods.[785] For the next two hundred and eighty years, those who refused or would not recant were killed. Under excruciating torture some renounced the Messiah, but a vast number of the Jew and Gentile Believers remained faithful and instead chose martyrdom.

Persecution came in waves, reaching a climax in the third and fourth century. Emperor Trajan Decius (circa 250 AD) martyred thousands of Christians and Jews who would not ascribe loyalty to the Roman ancestral gods and offer sacrifices to their idols.[786] Decius required everyone under penalty of death to produce certificates (*libellius*) proving they had made the annual sacrifice to the Roman gods.[787] Decius was followed by Valerian (253–260 AD) and the hunt for Christians and Jews escalated across the empire. "Not a town or village escaped."[788] This was followed by the "Great Persecution" under Emperor Diocletian; "an incalculable bloodbath," which lasted until 304 AD.[789] The torture and slaughter intensified under Emperor Galerius Valerius Maximinus until just two years before his death in 311 AD when he withdrew his executive order and issued an Edict of Toleration.[790]

Then as the fourth century was yet dawning, there came what appeared to be a GOD-sent emperor who would bring an end to persecution and inaugurate religious freedom. Believing they were finally emancipated, Jews and Christians understandably breathed a sigh of relief. Little did they know that what was coming next would be much more perilous than the death of one's mortal body; that being the death of one's immortal soul.[791] Satan had a new scheme, he would birth a counterfeit Christianity to compete alongside the authentic. Not only that, but his counterfeit would have the endorsement of the state, thereby giving it legitimacy. The contest was on!

---

783 Acts 5:38-39
784 John 18:36
785 H. Chadwick, *The Early Church*, Wm. B. Eerdmans Publishing, 1967, p. 118
786 William Byron Foxbush, ed. *Foxe's Book of Martyrs*, Zondervan, 1962, p. 17
787 H. Chadwick, *The Early Church*, Wm. B. Eerdmans Publishing, 1967, p. 118
788 Philip Hughes, *A History of the Church*, London, 1934, Vol. 1, p. 165
789 Philip Hughes, *A History of the Church*, London, 1934, Vol. 1, p. 172
790 Arthur Chushman McGiffert, Translated from, *Church History*, 2nd Series Vol.1, Chapter 14, Edit Schaff & Wace, Christian Literature Publishing Co., 1890
791 Matthew 10:28

Enter the Universal Church

In 312 AD the Roman Empire was in great turmoil as opposing generals and regents of different territories vied for control. That same year, Roman general, Flavius Valerius Aurelius Constantinus (Constantine the Great), prepared to engage a rival at the Tiber River.

Just prior to the battle he claimed to have seen a sign from GOD in the heavens. He described it as being not unlike the Egyptian "Ankh;" a symbol which represented enduring life to the Egyptians. The Ankh was anything but a sign of life, for it would closely resemble what had been the epitome of Roman torture—the Roman cross.[792]

> Note: The Ankh was an ancient Egyptian symbol (the actual hieroglyphic sign) associated with magical protection. It remains an enduring icon today in the occult where it is recognized as a style of the Christian cross.
>
> Note: The Christian apologist Lactantius wrote that the Christian monogram Constantine emblazoned on his legion's shields looked roughly like the letters X and P printed on top of each other: ☧. This same monogram is often seen on the vestments worn by Catholic clergy today. Many archeologists believe that the Roman Cross used to crucify the Lord actually resembled the letter X, not the letter T.

In this same vision and accompanying this instrument of agony, Constantine claimed he was given a message, *"In hoc signo vinces"*—Latin for, "In this sign conquer." In a battle that ensued with his rival Maxentius at the Milvian (or Mulvian) Bridge, Constantine defeated his adversary and adopted the cross as his sign "and did conquer magnificently."[793] In 315 AD Constantine took control of Greece and the Balkans, and in 324 AD he defeated the last of his enemies and became the uncontested Emperor of the Empire.

As sole ruler he sought to unite a divided and disintegrating realm. Previously, "He not only tolerated paganism but even encouraged the strictly anti-Christian imperial cult."[794]

The sword had worked well against his military adversaries but not against the Jews and Christians. Persecution and attempts to eradicate them by his predecessors had failed, but toleration had not been tried except for a feigned attempt by predecessor Emperor Galerius two years earlier. Galerius late

The Egyptian Ankh (Image Source: ALAMY)

---

792 Ramsey MacMullen, *Constantine, Crosscurrents in World History Series*, Dial Press Publishing, NY, 1969, p. 72
793 *The Columbia Encyclopedia*, 2nd Edit., Columbia University Press, NY, 1956, p. 447
794 *The Columbia Encyclopedia*, 2nd Edit., Columbia University Press, NY, 1956, p. 447

effort showed promise. Constantine reasoned this might be a far more effective way to attain his goal. He would bring the empire together by convincing his subjects that religious persecution was at an end. While the Edict of Milan—an edict of tolerance—had been issued in 313 AD, now it would be broadened to include acceptance.

Recognition and legitimacy of Christianity was to begin. The sword would for a time be put back in its sheath. So it was that he conceived a new plan—a reign of peace.

A narcissist, Constantine now dubbed "the Great," perceived himself to be the leader of a new era, and time would prove he was; but to what end? What began as a period of toleration would eventually morph into a state religion and become a religious caliphate, the Universal Church of Rome.

> Note: An edict of toleration is a declaration by a ruler or government which states that members of a given religion will not be persecuted for their religious practices and traditions. To Christians and Jews this meant an end to their persecution. Later this freedom would be used to induce them into joining what would become the unifying or Universal religion of the empire.

Author David Hunt in his book *Global Peace and the Rise of the Antichrist*, wrote of Constantine, "A brilliant commander also understood that there could be no political stability without religious unity. Yet to accomplish that feat would require a union between paganism and Christianity. How could that be accomplished? The Empire needed an ecumenical religion that would appeal to all citizens in a multicultural society. Giving Christianity official status was not enough to bring internal peace to the Empire: Christianity had to undergo a transformation so that pagans could 'convert' without giving up their old beliefs and rituals."[795]

It was traditional for Roman emperors to appropriate multiple titles other than Caesar—a family name which later came to mean the imperial head of government. The monarchs would also be titled Imperator—Military Commander of the armies and navy. They would also appropriate a title which linked them with their gods and elevated them as the head of all religions, Pontifex Maximus. The title Pontiff Maximus had been adopted by Roman emperors prior to Constantine and can be seen on Roman coins from the time of Caesar Augustus.

For Constantine this was a perfect fit, for *Pontifex* in Latin means "bridge builder." *Maximus* means the greatest; hence Pontifex Maximus—"the greatest bridge builder."

It would take a few more decades for this new brand of Christianity to evolve and solidify, but eventually in 380 AD it would become official and become the religious arm of the

Roman coin: Aureus of Tiberius, 14-37 AD - inscribed Maxim Pontif (Image Source: GETTY)

---

795 David Hunt, *Global Peace and the Rise of the Antichrist*, Harvest House, 1990, p. 106

government. The word "Catholic" is synonymous with the word "Universal," hence the name, Roman Catholic Church.[796]

> Note: The word "catholic" is a transliteration of the Greek word καθολικός (katholikos), which, in turn, is derived from two Greek words: κατά (kata), meaning "according to" and ὅλος (holos) meaning "whole, entire." Thus, καθολικός means "about or regarding the whole." In English, the word "catholic" literally means "universal in extent, involving all, or of interest to all." In the context of Christianity, it means "pertaining to the whole Christian body or church." Thus, the term "catholic church" literally means the "universal church."
>
> Note: The word "Universal" cannot be understated for it reveals what this religious empire's goal was, is, and ultimately intends to be. The objective is a Universal World Church over which it will preside with absolute impunity. Today she has her own satellite television station and calls herself the Universal Church or the Church Universal. By referring to herself with this title she is acclimating people all over the world to accept her global status and reigning authority.

Just as Constantine integrated various belief systems to unite his empire, so will Satan's proxy the Antichrist and his False Prophet (the bridge builder) unite the world religions under their governing authority. So important is this for us (and particularly for the Jewish people) to understand, that our Lord devoted an entire chapter in the Bible describing "her" in great detail.[797] (Appendix D—*Mystery Babylon*, Revelation 17)

From Emperor to Imposter

Constantine would need to build an infrastructure for his religio-political government. To that end he would appoint prelates and bishops over cities and designated regions which today are referred to as dioceses. These political appointments have been used down through the centuries with the awarding of the highest appointments (archbishops and cardinals) going to the monarch's most favored and trusted allies. These clerical offices were highly sought after as they were extremely lucrative positions which enabled these papal governors to easily exact money from the laity, asserting they were collecting a tithe for GOD.[798]

There were believed to have been other appointments to high clerical offices of individuals who may have had no understanding of Christianity. In such cases trusted politicians and military officers needed only to exchange their senatorial robes and military uniforms for clerical robes. In this way the emperor could ensure his control over the religious wing of his government.

---

796 Lorraine Boettner, *Roman Catholicism*, Presbyterian and Reform Publishing, 1962, p.287
797 Revelation chapter 17; and 13:8-15
798 Frederick Nolan, *Integrity of the Greek Vulgate*, pp. 17-18

In order to form a unified belief system and give it legitimacy, Constantine had to enlist and appoint clerics from congregations throughout the Mediterranean. Their beliefs however were quite wide and varied and needed to be merged and codified into a single canon (standard). To this end he would appoint a bishopric and form a centralized government now called the Holy See. He would then periodically call these bishops together to council in convocation. Certain bishops known as the Curia would be the emperor's advisors and were asked to vote on weighty matters. These were referred to as synods or conclaves (secretive assemblies). The first of these formal rule setting assemblages was the Council of Nicaea (325 AD); the most recent was Vatican II which concluded in 1965.

> Note: Vatican II did not liberalize Catholicism; rather it reaffirmed the cannons and decrees of previous councils including the Second Council of Nicaea, the Council of Florence, and the Council of Trent—with its 100-plus anathemas against non-Catholics.[799]

---

799   Paraphrased from: Austin Flannery, *Vatican Council II: Concillar and Post Concillar Documents*, rev, ed., Contello Publishing, 1988, pp. 379, 380, 412

26

WHICH BIBLE?

As with forming any new government, once a hierarchy has been established a charter is created which formalizes its purpose. In a religious government, instead of a charter or constitution the crafters would require some kind of sacred document, even a bible. Such an instrument would serve as a basis from which they could then add the necessary encyclicals (bulls), and decretals (doctrines), and formulate a canon of rule.

Constantine realized that these resources were already in existence. The Hebrew Holy Scriptures and the collection of New Testament writings which had begun to be collected would serve nicely. By adopting and combining the two testaments he and his schemers were able to entice many who had accepted these as sacred writings to join this replica of Christianity.

To lend credence to their new religion they would first need to prepare a new bible. Such a bible would have to appear to have been derived from ancient manuscripts. So the first step was to create spurious manuscript evidence. Once legitimized by these forgeries they could then tailor their bible in such a way as to serve their interest and give them authority over their subjects. To this end Constantine employed a gnostic scholar, Eusebius of Caesarea (260–340 AD). Eusebius and his accomplice Pamphillus were commissioned to produced fifty bibles for Emperor Constantine which would eventually become the Roman Latin Vulgate.[800] Jerome (340–420 AD) would later add the finishing touches to it.

> Note 1. *Vulgate* means that which is best known. The Roman Vulgate does not come from the Old Latin (pre-Jerome) which was in harmony with the authentic vulgates of the first and second century. The authentic New Testament writings emanated from the primitive (genuine) Church in Syria. This included the Greek Vulgate, the Syrian Peshitta, and in the Old Latin—the Italic Vulgate. These authentic writings, undergirded by a voluminous amount of manuscript evidence, would in 1624 become the *Textum Receptum*—or Textus Receptus; more commonly referred to as the "Received Text" or the "Traditional Text." It is from these manuscripts that the Authorized King James Bible originated.

---

800 David Otis Fuller, *Which Bible?*, Grand Rapids International Publications, 1975, p. 3

Note 2. The New Testament, as found in the King James Bible (not in modern bible versions) was developed from the Traditional Greek Byzantine Text, most closely associated with the writings of the Apostle Paul which originated in Antioch, Syria and Asia Minor. The Byzantine Text is far and away supported by the vast majority (2,864—whole or in part) of Greek manuscript evidence which was handed down by the early church. In contrast, the Church of Rome relied heavily on the Alexandrian manuscripts, referred to as the Alexandrian Text which was written by gnostic Greek philosophers in the region of Alexandria, Egypt.

Note 3. In constructing these manuscripts, changes from the Byzantine manuscripts were introduced. Two of these Alexandrian manuscripts, the Codex Vaticanus ("B") and Codex Alexandrinus ("A") coincidently appeared (circa 331-332 AD) and became the central uncial (written in upper case letters) reproductions which would become the Revised Latin Vulgate. Many notable linguists (Dr. Edward Hill, Dr. Robert D. Wilson, Dr. David O. Fuller, Dr. D.A. Wait, Dean John W. Burgon) believe the two uncial manuscripts were conveniently fabricated for the occasion just as Constantine's new Bible was taking shape. The Latin Vulgate was proclaimed the official Bible of the Roman Catholic Church at the Council of Trent (1545-1563)[801] as part of the Counter-Reformation. It was also at the Council of Trent that Rome would add to its Bible the spurious non-canonical books known as the Apocrypha. The Alexandrian manuscripts have only forty-three other manuscripts (whole or in part) on which to lend support to "B" and "A".

Note 4. To add credibility to the Roman counterfeit the Curia (the papal court and governing body) sort to affiliate themselves with the original apostles and the genuine Church fathers. To accomplish this the Magisterium (Roman Catholic authority to teach religious doctrine) fabricated writings and letters to that end. They also manufactured decrees at numerous councils to serve as a basis for much of Roman canon law. Thereafter, false decretals' (papal letters) were revised and expanded upon by each new pope, increasing pontifical authority.[802] Catholics have, in much the same way as Jews, been baited and fooled as a result of leaving the exclusivity and authority of GOD's pure Word for a religious alternative. I dare say, that it is unlikely that not more than one Catholic layman in a thousand knows the true history of their own church, nor do they know what the scriptures say Catholicism will become in the "last days." (Appendix D- *Mystery Babylon*) Sadly for Catholics, they have been taught from childhood that their salvation is dependent on their obedience to the Church of Rome to such an extent that even contemplating the possibility that they may have been

---

[801] Jasper James Ray, *GOD Wrote Only One Bible*, The Eye Opener Publishers, 1955, p. 19; Burgon & Miller, The Traditional Text, p.163; Edward F. Hill, *The King James Defended*, The Christian Resource Press, 4th Edit., 1984, p. 126

[802] J.H. von Dollinger, *The Pope and the Council*, London 1869, pp. 83-85

> cajoled and controlled is not an option. In the final analysis, subconsciously—the fear of missing heaven and being eternally damned to hell for leaving "Mother Church" makes them obedient subjects.
>
> Note 5. The Latin Vulgate is Revised Latin. Many of the transcriptions were based on corrupt Alexandrian manuscripts which originated from the fifth column of Origen's Hexapla (six column bible). Egyptian born Origen Adamantius (185-254 AD) taught that Christ was a created being (Greek, *kitisma*) and was not divine.[803] Origen attempted to synthesize Greek philosophy with Christianity and illustrate that Christianity is compatible with Greek thought.[804] Latin Vulgate transcriber, Eusebius of Caesarea was a great admirer of Origen and his Hexapla.
>
> Note 6. Latin was originally a common language of the Empire, but later became the language of the scholars and the ecclesiastics. Handwritten bibles were costly and in short supply until the invention of Johannes Gutenberg's printing press (circa 1439) with moveable type. Before then, Catholic laity were entirely dependent on their priests to read to them and interpret the scriptures. The Renaissance changed all that, accelerating the vernacular languages of Europe to the detriment of Latin's status as *lingua franca* (the language used for communication between people not sharing a native language). Literacy woke Europe to GOD's Word and birthed the Reformation. This threatened the power of Romanism and broke their monopoly causing them to initiate the Counter Reformation.

Roman Catholic Church leaders at all levels were opposed to the laity having access to the Bible in the local languages. It would be a major factor in the arrest and execution of the likes of England's bible transcriber William Tyndale in 1536.

As legitimate Bibles were produced, and in an effort to keep Catholics from being able to rightly divide the Word of GOD for themselves, a prohibition was ordered. Bibles written in the common languages of the people were, in 1559, officially placed on the *Index Librorum Prohibitorum*—the list of prohibited books by Pope Paul IV. A year later at the Council of Trent it was replaced by the *Tridentine Index*. This index remained in effect until the final version (the twentieth edition) appeared in 1948. It was only formally abolished on June 14, 1966 by Pope Paul VI when defending it became untenable.

A complete list of the authors and writings present in the successive editions of the *Index* is given in J. Martínez de Bujanda, *Index Librorum Prohibitorum, 1600–1966*.

---

803 Encyclopedia Britannica, 1936, Vol. 16, pp. 900-902
804 *The Columbia Encyclopedia,* 2nd Edit., Columbia University Press, NY, 195, p. 1451

Note 7. An excerpt from *Foxe's Book of Martyrs*, reads, "The simple and unlearned people, being far from the knowledge of the Holy Scriptures, thought it quite enough for them to know only those things which were delivered them by their pastors; and those who followed Romanism, from their priests. The priests taught nothing else, but such things as came forth from the court of Rome; whereof the most part tended to the profit of their order, more than to the glory of Christ."[805]

Note 8. Modern Catholic Bibles included the: New American Standard Bible (NASB); Revised Standard Bible (RSV); Ignatius Bible; Jerusalem Bible; and the Douay-Rheims Bible. The Church of Rome currently has control of several Bible publishing companies and with it the ability to adjust the Word of GOD to accommodate their interests. Managing Catholic thought means managing what Catholics believe to be GOD's Word.

Note 9. Satan's scribes and modern corruptions: Two heretical textual critics, Brooke Foss Westcott (1825-1903) and Fenton John Anthony Hort (1828-1892) were responsible for replacing the Traditional Text; a core of the Authorized King James, with the local text of Egypt, which has since been adopted by the Roman Catholic Church. These alterations have become the basis for the many modern versions. These versions are just that—versions, scripted from the New Greek Text of Westcott and Hort. This New Greek Text was later to become the basis for the English Revised Version (1885) and the American Standard Version (1901). This was followed by the Revised Standard Version (1946, 1952); the Living Bible (1967, 1971); the New International Bible (1973, 1978); the Good News Bible (1976); and the New Revised Standard Version (1990).

Note 10. Modern versions have changed the Greek Textus Receptus in about six thousand places. There are over two hundred omissions alone which have a bearing on Christ's deity, His efficacious Blood, and His virgin birth. Whole phrases have been bracketed or italicized, suggesting that their authenticity is questionable. These are tell-tale indicators of tampering and what is referred to as higher criticism (an approach that assumes a secular perspective and denies the supernatural inspiration of scripture). Today higher criticism is passed off as scholarship.

For accuracy, including an admirable commentary, I personally recommend, *The Holy Bible, Authorized King James Version, Expositor's Study Bible*, Jimmy Swaggart Ministries, Baton Rouge, Louisiana (www.jms.org). Suggested reading: *Let's Weigh the Evidence*, by Barry Burton, and *New Age Bible Versions:* by G.A. Riplinger. Riplinger gives an in-depth account of the history and corruption of the Bible and how through the acceptance of modern versions Christians are being dummied down.

---

805 John Fox, *Foxe's Book of Martyrs*, Whitaker House, 1981, p. 51

"For the time will come when they will not endure sound doctrine; but after their own lusts shall they heap to themselves teachers, having itching ears; And they shall turn their ears from the truth, and shall turn unto fables (fiction)." (2 Timothy 4:3-4)

> Note 11. Translator John Wycliffe (1324-1384) lived when the Church of Rome dominated Europe and (Roman) authorized bibles were to be written only in Latin. He loved the Bible so much that he wanted to share it with his English countrymen. He began translating the Latin Vulgate NT into Middle English, writing by hand; each copy taking ten months. These translations were banned and burned as quickly as the Catholic church officials could find them. So hated was he that the Catholic church, by decree of the synod of Constance in 1415, called for his bones to be exhumed and thrown well away from any church cemetery. Wycliffe had been an instrument of GOD which helped to spark the Protestant Reformation and unshackle the minds of men from Roman domination.[806]
>
> Note 12. Constantine's alleged conversion to genuine Christianity is quite unsupported. Unlike the untold thousands who had laid down their lives for their testimony and refused to serve false idols, he never renounced his Roman gods. In addition to practicing Christian rituals, he also celebrated pagan rites and used pagan cultic practices to insure good rain and good farm crops. He supported worship to the Sun God—"Sol" and declared Sunday to be an imperial holiday, even before setting the birth of Christ on the winter solstice (the birthday of the sun), which is entirely incorrect. Based on Luke 2:3-5, male Jews (e.g., Joseph), Jesus's surrogate father, had to return to the city of their lineage (e.g., the city of David—Bethlehem) for the taking of a census in compliance to a Roman decree (Luke 2:1-2). Most scholars agree that this registration was required in the autumn; likely the month of October. This places Jesus's birth in September or October, not in December on the winter solstice.

In what must be the most ingenious plot ever hatched, Romanism has persuaded its billion-plus devotees to accept its claim that it is GOD's representative, spokesman, and authority on earth. By distancing itself from the Bible and cloaking itself in robes of righteousness[807] it has captured minds and enslaved followers. It has been Satan's Judas goat, to lead the sheep to slaughter.

---

806 John Fox, *Foxe's Book of Martyrs*, Whitaker House, 1981, p. 68
807 Luke 20:46

27

PAGANISM 101

Sunday, "Dies Solis," the day of the sun (from the Latin, *Sol Invicticus,* Unconquered Sun) was named after an ancient Babylonian/Persian deity, "Mitra," god of the sun. Sometime around the fifth century BC the name was altered to "Mithra." Later the Greeks and the Romans, both polytheistic, would recognize Mithra or Sol and add him to their collection of gods. By the time the Christian era began, this heathen cult was well established and became known as "Mithraism."

History records that in "the middle of the third century Mithraism seemed on the verge of becoming the universal religion," and subsequently became the greatest antagonist of Biblical Christianity. This growing ideology was adopted by the Caesars and embraced by the nobility, especially in Alexandria and Rome.[808]

(Image Source: GETTY)

When Emperor Constantine, himself a sun worshiper, began the process of uniting the disintegrating empire he needed to include the priests of the numerous pagan religions in his realm. They, along with genuine Christian leaders were summoned in an effort to integrate the various beliefs into a universal standard; blending pagan teachings, practices, and customs with elements of Christianity. The Sunday festival of Mithraism was one such adaptation.

Seen today, the officiating priest, bishop, cardinal, or pope reverently elevates the monstrance, also known as ostensorium, which represents the sun. The vessel is used in Roman Catholic, Old Catholic, and Anglican churches to display the consecrated Eucharistic host during Eucharistic adoration or Benediction of the so-called "Blessed Sacrament."

What was not found in the Hebrew Holy Scriptures or the New Testament (such as the Blessed Sacrament) was explained away as the "mysteries of the faith." A number of mystical

---

[808] *The Columbia Encyclopedia*, 11th Edit., Columbia University Press, NY, *Mithra*, p. 1297

sacramental forms were adopted as well as other pagan rituals, including ringing of bells, lighting of votive candles, and the use of holy water.

"In the 19th century there was a revival of interest in this religion (Mithraism), partly because of supposed borrowing by Christianity, but with the wider knowledge of comparative religions it is seen that the features common to Mithraism and Christianity are common to many other religions as well."[809]

Constantine also retained the Altar of Victory in the Roman senate, and the continuation of Vestal Virgins as part of Temple practice. He was not baptized into his own Roman brand of Christianity until just before his death by Eusebius. Eusebius, a devotee of Origen Adamantius, (head of the catechetical school of Alexandria), who from his hundreds of writings blended pagan philosophy with Christian theology.[810]

One only need to look at the fruit of the Holy Spirit resident in the followers of Yahusha-Jesus of which the Apostle Paul spoke of in Galatians 5:22–23, or the virtues he spoke of in Philippians 4:8 to see that Constantine was anything but a Christian. He murdered a son Crispus, a nephew, and other members of his family who he feared might have occupied his throne.

A historian and Catholic priest, Philip Hughes wrote, "In his manner he (Constantine) remained to the end, very much the pagan of his early life. His furious tempers, cruelty which once aroused, spared not the lives even of his wife and son…are unpleasing witness to the imperfection of his conversion."[811]

Emperor Constantine had begun a new form of imperialism. A succession of pontiffs would follow with a predisposition to expand their empire by forced colonization, eventually leading to the crusades and inquisitions.

Each pope would broaden his alleged divine authority beyond that of their predecessor by issuing an Apostolic Constitution (the highest ranking document), an Encyclical Letter (second in importance), or a Papal bull (named after the lead seal—*bulla*).

> Note: Papal bulls are elaborate papal documents issued in the form of a decree or privilege. They have been in use at least since the sixth century, but the term was not used until around the middle of the thirteenth century.

As mentioned in the preceding chapter, the Papacy's success in getting their followers to believe they have been given divine authority has been achieved by convincing their subjects that through some mystical association with the Apostle Peter they have become his successors. They refer to this contrivance as "the apostolic line." It was engineered by simply perverting the meaning of a single scripture (Matthew 16:18–19) and has been accepted by the biblically unschooled who have been limited to Rome's teachings and assertion.

---

809 *The Columbia Encyclopedia* 11th Edit., Columbia University Press, NY, Mirth, p. 1297
810 *The Columbia Encyclopedia* 11th Edit., Columbia University Press, NY, Origen, p. 1451
811 Ramsay Mac Mullen, *Constantine*, p. 12;

> Note: The first indication of a pope asserting infallibility is thought to have been in a declaration by Pope Gregory I (590–604 AD), which was later quoted in the twelfth-century *Decretum Gratiani*. However, the doctrine was defined dogmatically and ratified in the First Vatican Council of 1869–1870. Today the Catholic Church still makes the assertion of the Pontiff's infallibility when speaking (Latin, *ex cathedra*) in matters of faith and morals; which as a general term can be applied to virtually anything they choose.

Replace and Rename

In merging the various religions of his empire, each of which had their own deities, Constantine came up with a practical solution. He would simply rename the various pagan gods and goddesses and match them to the Christian Jesus. He would do the same with Jesus's earthly mother Mary, His earthly surrogate father Joseph, to the various apostles, and to a myriad of other so-called "saints."[812]

Hathor, for example, was considered to be the Egyptian "mother of god, friend of sinners, and protectress of the dead."[813] Both she and Isis (also an Egyptian goddess) were associated with her infant baby Horus. Isis in particular could be explained as Mary and her baby as Jesus. Lesser pagan gods who were normally prayed to for special needs would be renamed and canonized as saints who could then be prayed to for more specific needs.

Isis and Horus, Mary and Jesus
(Image Source: ALAMY)

Steeped in idolatry, statues and graven images would become icons of adoration. Kneeling before them, praying to them, and kissing their stone feet were common practices of many cults. Candles were lit and prayers and petitions were made to these carved or marble idols for the sick, dying, or dead. The very act of such practices is a direct violation of the first two of the Ten Commandments wherein GOD speaks that HE and HE alone is to receive our recognition and homage.[814]

The Roman Catholic practice of invoking the spirits of the dead (a.k.a. deceased saints) has an application to spiritualism and divination; both of which are condemned in scripture.[815]

How utterly contemptuous to make any graven images (Hebrew, *pesel*; meaning to hew-carve), or to bow, or to worship anything but GOD HIMSELF! Only a Satanic cult would

---

812 W.H.C. Frend, *The Rise of Christianity*, Philadelphia, 1984, p. 773
813 Joseph Zacchello, *Secrets of Romanism*, Loizeaux Bros. Pub., Neptune, NJ, 1948, pp. 15-16
814 Exodus 20:4
815 Deuteronomy 18:10-11

delight in such spiteful defiance of GOD's commandments. GOD reviles the worship of divine females in the strongest terms!

> "Thou shalt not make unto thee any graven image, or any likeness of anything that is in heaven above, or that is in the earth beneath, or that is in the water under the earth: thou shalt not bow down thyself to them, nor serve them: for I the Lord thy God am a jealous God, visiting the iniquity of the fathers upon the children unto the third and fourth generation of them that hate me..." (Exodus 20:4-5)

> Note: One of the most revealing indicators that a religion is pagan (an occult) is that they have a divine feminine or "queen of heaven"[816] to which they recognize and pay adoration to. Hinduism has Shakti. Buddhism has Tara. Islam has Sophia. Catholicism has Mary.

> "The children gather wood, and the fathers kindle the fire, and the women knead their dough, to make cakes to the queen of heaven, and to pour out drink offerings unto other gods, that they may provoke Me to anger." (Jeremiah 7:18)

Apostate Icons

As the Roman religion was taking shape certain of their prelates and scholars began writing treatises which would later be used to undergird Roman theology. These individuals would be recognized by the Catholic Church as the Early Church Fathers. In reality many were gnostic theorists and admirers of such Greek philosophers as Socrates and his students Plato and Xenophon.

One such example of how easily an apostate from biblical Christianity is made into a "Church Father" can be seen in Augustine of Hippo—a.k.a. Saint Augustine (354–430 AD).

Augustine lived in the Roman Province of Algeria, North Africa. He was later sainted by Rome and became Saint Augustine. In his early years he was heavily influenced by Manichaeism and afterward by Neo-Platonism. He converted to Roman Christianity in 387 AD.

A gifted intellect, Augustine developed his own approach to philosophy and made theology accommodations; introducing a variety of methods and perspectives. Former president of Dallas Theological Seminary, Dr. John F. Walvoord expounded on Augustine's beliefs: "Augustine and subsequent theologians in the Roman Catholic Church maintained that grace was channeled through the church and the sacraments and, apart from this medium there could be no true salvation or bestowal of grace. As a result, the great doctrine of justification by faith, the truth of the fullness of the power the Holy Spirit, and the truth that believers had immediate access to the throne of grace without an earthly priest as mediator became dim. Soon the authority of the Scriptures as the Word of GOD became subordinate to the authority of the church, and the interpretation of the church took precedence over the teaching ministry and illumination of

---

816   Jeremiah 7:18; 44:17-19, 25

the Holy Spirit. The Word of GOD, thus shackled and to a large extent kept from the people, cast its restrictive light on the darkness of the Middle Ages."[817]

Today Augustine is an icon of Romanism and the patron saint of brewers, printers, theologians, and for the alleviation of sore eyes.

Sainting became a tradition of Rome and each saint was conferred a special area to which adherents could pray for special needs. The Roman Church's teaching on the invocation and veneration of saints is defined in the Council of Trent, Session XXV (1563).

Another Catholic scholar who was made into a Catholic icon was Thomas Aquinas. Aquinas began writing his philosophical treatises *Summa Theologica* in 1265, which among other things approved the sale of indulgencies (the purchasing of forgiveness); a lucrative scam which lead to blanket corruption. He also taught that good works mitigate evil deeds and can reduce imprisonment in a factious prison called Purgatory.

Catholicism teaches that Purgatory is a place where most everyone is said to have to spend time suffering a penance for their earthly sins.[818] This is of course pure heresy as there is no such intermediary place where souls go in the whole canon of Scripture. The Bible teaches only two places exist for an individual after death—Heaven for the saved and Hell for the unsaved. Purgatory is an additive invented in the spurious Apocrypha.

"And as it is appointed unto men once to die, but after this the judgment..." (Hebrews 9:27)

Aquinas also taught that being subject to the pope is necessary for salvation, and heretics (non-Catholics) could, after the second warning be killed. His precise (translated) words were, "they have merited to be excluded from the earth through death."[819]

It also became quite common for the Church of Rome to espouse and exploit individuals for their own purposes by sainting them, even when those individuals had in reality defected or repudiated Catholicism. This was easily accomplished for Rome knew that only a studied few would ever learn of their charades.

Francis Bernadone was one such example. Bernadone, better known as St. Francis of Assisi was born a son of a cloth merchant in 1182. In 1209 he became convicted in his heart when he heard Matthew 10:7–14 read aloud by an evangelist and became a debtor to Christ.

In this passage from the gospel of Matthew, Yahusha-Jesus directs his disciples to go about preaching to the Jewish people the "Good News" that their Messiah had already come to earth so they could be forgiven and live eternally with Him, and that one is saved by faith.[820]

Francis soon set out as a simple missionary to preach repentance, humility, and poverty. He went to Egypt and Syria and preached Christ to the Muslims. Over time he developed followers and wrote a list of rules, the *Regula primitive*—Primitive Rule.

---

817 John F. Walvoord, *The Church in Prophecy*, Zondervan Publ. House, Grand Rapids, MI, 1964, p. 52
818 John W. Kennedy of India, *The Torch of the Testimony*, Christian Book Publishing, 1965, p. 120-121
819 Lousi Guerin, Barri Ducis, *St. Thomas of Aquinas, Summa Theologica*, 1857, vol. 4, p. 90
820 Ephesians 2:8

These rules were based on the teaching of the four gospels and were not entirely in harmony with the Church of Rome. However, as a good Catholic he sought and received the reluctant approval of the pope in order to continue with the Great Commission.[821]

The pope at that time, Innocent III, granted him permission to continue so long as he stayed within the confines of Roman teachings. Later in 1210 the pope sanctioned a monastic order of his disciples, aptly named the Franciscan Order. In 1223 Pope Honorius III reorganized the Order, modifying Francis's rules with the "Second Rule" or "Rule With a Bull." This rule encumbered the Franciscans with new regulations, restrictions, and disciplines. The changes were a deep grief to Francis, but with no choice he reluctantly accepted them. He afterward went into semi-seclusion and died three years layer on October 3, 1226.

The Franciscan Order would later undergo a metamorphosis and, along with the Dominican Order, become Roman inquisitors. One hundred and fourteen Franciscans who would not renounce their vow of poverty and conform to Pope John XXII's papal bull, *Cum inter nonnullos* (1323), were condemned to death and burned at the stake.[822]

Missionary and author John W. Kennedy of India wrote, "We do not deny the devotion of Francis and his early followers, nor their desire to see a revival of true spiritual values within the Roman Church, but when any spiritual movement can be contained within the confines of a worldly, ecclesiastical system, it will soon be dragged down to the same level as the system it tried to reform."[823]

> Note: Sainting (Canonizing) individuals is an unbiblical and heathen practice whereby the papacy elevates an individual to a demigod. This is a carryover from Pharaohs, Babylonian Emperors, and Roman Emperors—all of whom claimed to possess a measure of divinity. Saints are referred to thirty-five times in the Old Testament and sixty times in the New Testament, each time referring to all true and faithful Believers.

Pious Pirates and Magicians

Rome's religious bandits stole piecemeal whatever pagan objects enhanced their image. It didn't matter if it was the fish head mitre (religious headpiece) of the Philistine god Dagon, which has been worn by bishops and popes for centuries, or the Phoenician prayer beads use to pray to the goddess Astarte (Astoreth).

It didn't matter if it were the 83-foot-high, 320-ton stone Egyptian obelisk which once stood at the Temple to the Sun in Egypt and was transported to the center of Saint Peter's Square where it now stands. These pious pirates would appropriate whatever they felt would serve their purpose, not only from the pagans but from Judaism as well.

---

821 Mark 16:15-16
822 John W. Kennedy of India, *The Torch of the Testimony*, Christian Book Publishing, 1965, p. 120-121
823 John W. Kennedy of India, *The Torch of the Testimony*, Christian Book Publishing, 1965, p. 121

Just as Judaism had its high priest beginning with Aaron, so too does Rome have its high priest (their pontiff). And, as with the Aaronic priesthood which was based on a Levitical hereditary line, these counterfeiters claim to have a continuous apostolic pedigree going back to one of Yahusha's Jewish disciples (Hebrew, *Shimon Cephas*, Greek, *Simon Bar-Jona*, English, *Simon*, surname *Peter*).

The Roman ecclesia would copy from the Levitical priestly garments and the royal colors.[824] They would burn incense as Levitical priests had been directed to by GOD, and they would use a replica of the unleavened shew bread for their communion rite. So brazen have they become as to claim to be able to say that ones' sins had been forgiven—a privilege once reserved for the Levitical high priest, until Christ came.

They control their subjects by fear. Not the fear of the sword of a dictatorial tyrant, but worse, "Excommunication:" resulting in the loss of heaven and the pain of hell. Even many of Europe's monarchs believed the claim and like frightened children, when directed, put their armies and navies at the pope's disposal—which made possible the Crusades.

To this day they have no real explanation about why they put hideous and grotesque gargoyles (portrayed in art as demons) to garnish the facades of their hundreds of Gothic cathedrals. Neither can the Episcopal Church explain why they would use gargoyles to adorn their Washington National Cathedral that began construction in 1907. These conjured figures are a carryover from the Medieval period when fear was a means to obedience. Why would demon figures be used to decorate the façade of what these fraudsters' claim to be the house of GOD?

The ultimate blasphemy however can hardly be imagined. These priests, like some shaman witch doctor, claim the magical power to transform the GOD of the universe into a bite-sized commercial wafer and then serve Him up from a brass goblet. The absurdity of this stymies the mind, yet each Sunday all over the world followers form lines and reverently step forward to consume GOD. Romanism and its offshoots have taken paganism to a new level.

---

824 Exodus 28:5

28

TOLERANCE, PEACE, AND UNITY

Today, under the guise of tolerance and world peace, an attempt is being made to again (as in Constantine's day) merge the world's religions into one homogenous belief system. Religious unity is becoming the new mantra and is seen as essential to the global initiative and in establishing a one world order. Today ecumenicalism is in high gear; commonalities are being emphasized and differences deemphasized. Prominent television evangelicals surrender their tenets and unite with Catholic bishops and cardinals just as the Apostle Paul had prophesied when he spoke of the great "falling away" of the Church.[825]

Commenting on this phenomena, Christian theologian, pastor, and once president of Dallas Theological Seminary, Dr. John F. Walvoord wrote, "It is a sad commentary on Contemporary Christendom that it shows an overwhelming desire to return to Rome in spite of Rome's evident apostasy from true biblical Christianity. In fact, modern liberalism has far outdone Rome in its departure from theology of the early church, thus has little to lose by a return to Rome. Apostasy which is seen in its latent form today will flower in its ultimate form in the future super church which will apparently engulf Christendom in the period after the rapture (removal) of the Church."[826]

There is only one religious institution capable of assuming the role of the World Church. With sovereign nation state status, a government infrastructure in place, ambassadors and consulates in virtually every country; with global acceptance, with a billion followers, and with trillions of dollars in currency, gold, art, business investments, stocks, bonds, and real estate, the Church of Rome prepares to realize its ultimate goal—leader of the Universal-World Church.[827]

Citing an example, how after 960 years a schism has dissolved and amalgamation begun: The following quote was the opening paragraph of the "Common Declaration" signed by both Orthodox Patriarch Bartholomew and Pope Benedict at the conclusion of the Divine Liturgy for the Feast of St. Andrew in 2006, "This fraternal encounter which brings us together (Pope

---

825 2 Thessalonians 2:3
826 John F. Walvoord, *The Revelation of Jesus Christ, A Commentary*, Moody Press, Chicago, 1966, p. 248
827 Daniel 11:36-37; Revelation 13:4; 17:1-18

Benedict XVI of Rome and Ecumenical Patriarch Bartholomew I), is God's work, and in a certain sense his gift. We give thanks to the Author of all that is good, who allows us once again, in prayer and in dialogue, to express the joy we feel as brothers and to renew our commitment to move towards full communion. This commitment comes from the Lord's will and from our responsibility as pastors in the Church of Christ. May our meeting be a sign and an encouragement to us to share the same sentiments and the same attitudes of fraternity, cooperation and communion in charity and truth. The Holy Spirit will help us to prepare the great day of the re-establishment of full unity, whenever and however God wills it. Then we shall truly be able to rejoice and be glad."

Renewal and Unification (Image Source: GETTY)

> Note: At the time of this writing (2017) the Anglican (Episcopal) Church and numerous naive Evangelical sub-denominations (The Emerging Church, the Seeker Sensitive Church, and others) have compromised the doctrines which the Reformers denounced as heretical and have embraced a benign view of Romanism. These gullible or disingenuous leaders are now in the process of overturning the Reformation. In growing numbers they are recognizing the Roman pontiff as the official "Head of the Christian Church." Reflective of this attitude was a statement made in 1987 by televangelist and pastor Robert Schuler of the Crystal Cathedral who said, "It's time for Protestants to go to the shepherd (Pope) and say what do we have to do to come home?"

> Note: An extensive survey (2008) of 3,500 adults by the Pew Forum on Religion and Public Life, details statistics on religion in America exploring the shifts taking place in the U.S. religious landscape. The survey found that Americans are quite accepting of religions other than their own. Seventy percent of those with a religious affiliation agreed that "many religions can lead to eternal life." Among mainline Protestants that figure jumped to 83 percent, and among Catholics to 79 percent. As would be expected, the response among evangelical Protestants was lower. Still, over half of evangelicals 57 percent agreed that "many religions can lead to eternal life." More than 80 percent of Jews, Hindus, and Buddhists agreed with the statement, and more than half of Muslims did.

To illustrate just how apostate Romanism has become, here is its view on faith and salvation: On September 11, 2013, Pope Francis wrote an open letter to Eugenio Scalfari, the founder of the Italian newspaper *La Repubblica* in which the pope made this statement negating the need for the Cross of Christ, "First of all, you ask me if the God of Christians forgives one who doesn't believe and doesn't seek the faith. Premise that—and it's the fundamental thing—the mercy of God has no limits if one turns to him with a sincere and contrite heart; the question for one who doesn't believe in God lies in obeying one's conscience. Sin, also for those who don't have faith, exists when one goes against ones' conscience. To listen to and to obey it means, in fact, to decide in face of what is perceived as good or evil. And on this decision pivots the goodness or malice of our action."

According to this poor deluded man, if one abides by his conscience, even if he has no saving faith, GOD will forgive him. Blatantly missing is any reference to the wage of Sin, the need for a Savior, any reliance on the blood and the Cross of Christ, or any need to be Born Again. The Bible is clear and emphatic as to what an individual must do to be saved. We should pray for this poor man for he apparently doesn't believe the Bible and he truly needs to get saved!

> "Seeing that there is one GOD, which shall justify the circumcision (the Jew) by faith, and uncircumcision (the Gentile) by faith." (Romans 3:30)

> "Neither is there salvation in any other: for there is none other name (but Yahusha-Jesus) under heaven given among men, whereby we must be saved." (Acts 4:12)

> "He that believeth on the Son hath everlasting life: and he that believeth not the Son shall not see life; but the wrath of God abideth on him." (John 3:36)

> "Jesus answered and said unto him, Verily, verily, I say unto thee, Except a man be born again, he cannot see the kingdom of God." (John 3:3)

"Jesus saith unto him, I am the way, the truth, and the life: no man cometh unto the Father, but by me." (John 14:6)

"And he (Jesus) said, Take heed that ye be not deceived: for many shall come in my name, saying, I am Christ (more appropriately—of Christ); and the time draweth near: go ye not therefore after them." (Luke 21:8)

"Ye hypocrites, well did Esaias (Isaiah) prophesy of you, saying, This people draweth nigh unto me with their mouth, and honoureth me with their lips; but their heart is far from me....But in vain they do worship me, teaching for doctrines the commandments of men.... But He (Yahusha-Jesus) answered and said, Every plant, which my heavenly Father hath not planted, shall be rooted up. Let them alone: they be blind leaders of the blind. And if the blind lead the blind, both shall fall into the ditch." (Matthew 15:7-9, 13-14)

The true Church is not a religious institution; it is a living organism with Christ as its head. It may be said, and rightfully so, that anything having two heads (e.g., Christ and a pope) is a freak.

The Church is alive with the life of Christ, each member sharing the same Spirit which Jesus possessed when on earth. Established in faith, it is rooted and grounded in GOD's Word, to the exclusion of all else![828]

---

828 John 17:11, 21-22; Romans 8:9

29

WHICH CROSS?

Crusaders take Jerusalem (Image Source: ALAMY)

Satan's ruse on the Jewish people has been to convince them that Roman Catholicism and Biblical Christianity are one and the same.

Historically there has never been an ethnic group whose unabated sufferings approached that of the Jewish people. What's more is that the worst practitioners of this cruelty were led by those who called themselves Christians, supposedly followers of the Jewish Messiah. It would be the Roman Catholic popes who would take persecution and cruelty to a level which surpasses human creativity and required demonic tutoring.

"The Crusaders held a cross in one hand and a sword in the other. At times they herded Jews into synagogues and then set fire to the buildings, burning them to the ground."[829]

---

829 Paraphrased from Gibb, H. A. R., *The Damascus Chronicle of the Crusades*: Extracted and Translated from the *Chronicle of Ibn Al-Qalanisi*, Dover Publications, 2003, pg. 48

From earliest times Jews and Gentile Believers died together. Some were butchered by gladiators for sport and others were fed to the lions for entertainment. Together they were hung on poles on the highways that lead to Rome. Coated with tar, they were lit on fire and burned alive becoming human torches to light the roads at night. And why? Because they refused to deify the Roman Emperor and would not disavow the GOD of Abraham or their exclusive relationship to their Messiah.

Like the three Hebrew children Hananiah, Mishael, and Azariah (Shadrach, Meshach, and Abednego) they would not bow to any self-proclaimed deity or compromise their belief.[830] Many Jews and their Protestant counterparts chose to die, rather than deny.[831]

> "He (Yahusha-Jesus) shall redeem their soul from deceit and violence: and precious shall their blood be in his sight." (Psalm 72:14)

Satan's successful ruse on the Jewish people has been to convince them that "Roman Catholicism" and "Biblical Christianity" are one and the same, when in fact they are polar opposites!

Genuine Christians follow the humble teachings of the Jewish Messiah who preached "love thy neighbor as thyself" as if it were the eleventh commandment.

> "A new commandment I give unto you, That ye love one another; as I have loved you, that ye also love one another. By this shall all men know that ye are my disciples, if ye have love one to another." (John 13:34-35)

> "Jesus said unto him, Thou shalt love the Lord thy God with all thy heart, and with all thy soul, and with all thy mind. This is the first and great commandment. And the second is like unto it, Thou shalt love thy neighbour as thyself." (Matthew 22:37-39)

> "Let all bitterness, and wrath, and anger, and clamour, and evil speaking, be put away from you, with all malice: and be ye kind one to another, tenderhearted, forgiving one another, even as God for Christ's sake hath forgiven you." (Ephesians 4:31-32)

Why would the genuine Church—the followers of Yahusha-Jesus—EVER embrace the names: "the Holy Roman Empire," "the Church of Rome," or the "Roman Catholic Church," when it was the Roman Emperors, the Roman Army, and the Roman Empire who have been the greatest persecutors of Jews (and Christians) in history? Only Satan would choose, adopt, and flaunt the name The Church of Rome! Satan gloats at mans' naivety in the face of the obvious, as even now he assembles the Revised Roman Empire and brings the religious arm and the political arm together as they once were.

---

830 Daniel 3:10-12
831 Revelation 12:11

30

FROM ASHES TO EMPEROR

It is common knowledge that the Hebrew people and the nation of Israel have experienced relentless persecution for over thirty-five hundred years. But let us continue to follow the bloody path, the escalation of religious dominance, and the unbending faith of Jews and Gentile Believers who would not bow their knees to Baal.[832] I refer to that period of time appropriately called the Dark Ages (476–1000 AD), so named because of the intellectual darkness, ignorance, warfare, barbarianism, famine, and the first bubonic plague (541–542 AD) which killed multiple millions throughout Eastern and Western Europe.[833]

There are of course historians who shy away from the term Dark Ages because of the connotation, preferring Early Middle Ages; but no matter what it is called—it was a time of war and conquest which began when Germanic Visigoths and Vandals sacked Rome in three assaults over a period of sixty years. In fact, any city with anything of value was stripped and plundered, especially for its gold and silver. The Western Roman Empire finally collapsed in 476 AD when the Germanic military leader Flavius Odovacer removed the last Western Roman emperor, Romulus Augustulus, and declared himself King of Italy.

With their cities in ruins the people had no alternative but to leave the urban cities and move to the country to either farm or starve. The Church of Rome was not seen as a threat at that time by its new rulers as it had no military or military aspirations. The mighty Roman army had been thrashed and broken over the course of numerous battles. So it was that this religious souvenir of Rome's defeat was permitted to continue in its religious role.

In the absence of a central government the Papal Church was looked to by the people as the last vestige of Roman order. Over time it took on the character of a quasi-civil government, and as with all civil governments it became ambitious, legalistic, corrupt, and finally—dictatorial.

With each new pope came new claims of divine authority which fed her insatiable appetite for more power and wealth. Compliance and allegiance became mandatory and dissenters became heretics. In the narcissistic fashion of their Roman emperor predecessors, popes retained the title Pontifex Maximus and proceeded in their quest to extend their realm. They would coronate

---

832 1 Kings 19:18
833 Jeremy Norman, HistoryofInformation.com, "The Plague of Justinian"

kings and conquerors that would cross the channel to England for their new papal emperor.[834] One by one, Europe's monarchs fell under her spell as she convinced these temporal royals that they too were her subjects and under a divine mandate to submit to her. Under the threat of excommunication, which they believed would damn them to hell, most complied.[835]

One of the most diabolical tactics to ensure compliance by government officials was to place a town or even an entire country under interdict, which was a blanket refusal to provide communion to all in the affected area. Even kings who were opposed to the doctrines of the church would often capitulate over legitimate concerns that their terrorized subjects, who were fearful of going to hell because they couldn't take communion, might revolt.

Pledging their obedience and surrendering their sovereignty, these monarchs placed their armies and navies under the Pontiff's authority. This gave the popes new opportunities to take by sword what was not donated to Holy Mother Church, or more appropriately to this new Empire—The "Holy Roman Empire."[836]

It should be of no surprise that GOD would, as HE has done previously in the Holy Scriptures, foretell of the impending doom of an empire.[837] When doing so HE describes that empire in such a way that it could later be identified.

Those who have read the Apostle John's apocalyptic vision of the final religious empire in the book of Revelation can recognize the religious system who, for the last seventeen hundred years has, "with the kings of the earth committed fornication," "decked herself in gold," "having a golden cup full of abominations," and been "drunken with the blood of martyrs of Jesus."[838]

> Note: The term Holy Roman Empire (Latin, *Sacrum Imperium Romanum*) was not officially used until 962 AD when Otto I was crowned emperor, fashioning himself as the successor of Charlemagne. This would begin the uninterrupted presence and expansion of the Church of Rome.

Holy Wars

As time marched on the kings of Europe fought among themselves to lay claim to territories which were previously part of the Old Roman Empire. Between the fifth and fifteenth centuries virtually every nation in Europe, the Middle East, North Africa, and Asia, from Afghanistan and India to Britannia (Latin, Roman Britain), would have their boundaries drawn and redrawn through an endless succession of wars.

At the same time the papacy was expanding her empire. No longer was she simply an extension of an empire—she now was the empire! With the passage of time and by virtue of her

---

834 Lawson, M. K., *The Battle of Hastings: 1066*, Stroud, UK: Tempus, 2002
835 Sidney Z. Ehler and John B. Morra, *Church and State Through the Centuries*, London 1945, pp. 299, 314
836 Edward Augustus Freeman, *The History of the Norman Conquest of England*, p. 320, cited in, David Hunt, *A Woman Rides the Beast* p. 232
837 Daniel 5:22-27
838 Revelation 17:2, 4, 6

durability and longevity she gained more standing as kings adopted Catholicism for themselves. As went the king, so went the kingdom. Her strategy was working like a charm, except that is, for those unyielding Jews and Believers.

The reigning Catholic monarchs not only gave her tremendous tracts of land and unimaginable treasure, but most importantly the power she so craved. Until the sixth century the papacy held sway over the Mediterranean, North Africa, most of Europe, and the Baltics. However, in the seventh century after the death of the prophet Muhammad, his caliph (successors) took up the cause to spread Islam and expand their empire. The contest was on! Which empire would become the world's empire and reign universally?

Initially, the crusades were a power struggle for Jerusalem, which for the majority of time had been under the Muslim caliphate. The popes, wanting the Holy Land for religious, economic, and political reasons issued proclamations pitting the Church of Rome against Islam. These Holy Wars were directed at Arab Muslims (Saracens), the North Africans (Moors), and the Seljuks (Turks) who had converted to Islam. Later the Church of Rome would turn against the Eastern Byzantine (Greek) Empire as well.

The Arab-Islamic nation grew so rapidly that they soon occupied the Arab Peninsula and much of the Middle East. Damascus fell to the Muslim invaders in 635 AD, and afterward other bastions of Romanism; Antioch, Alexandria, and Jerusalem succumbed. Where churches once stood, mosques took their place. Islamic armies from North Africa (Moors) swept into France and Spain. Then at the Battle of Tours in 732 AD the Islamic army met defeat by the Frankish army of Charles Martel and retreated to the Pyrenees Mountains. According to some historians, this was a turning point which saved Western Europe from becoming a Muslim Caliphate.

Martel had realized that the Muslims could be repelled; perhaps even defeated. This inspired the papacy to become even more vigorous in encouraging Frankish knights to seek armed confrontation with Moorish "infidels"—justifying the war on religious grounds.

Frankish King Charles I (French, *Charles Le Grand*—Charlemagne) was the grandson and namesake of his grandfather Charles Martel. He assumed the throne in 768 AD and became the undisputed ruler of the Frankish Kingdom which would form the foundation for modern France and Germany. Charlemagne would continue his grandfather's legacy of fidelity to the papacy, becoming its protector. At the request of Pope Adrian I, Charlemagne removed the Lombards (a Germanic tribe) from power in northern Italy, becoming King of Italy in 774 AD. In his acquisition he gave what is now the Papal State—Vatican City, to the Papacy. He then led an incursion into Muslim Spain. Afterward, in 782 AD he would take his cavalry to slaughter forty-five hundred Saxons at the Massacre of Vaerden, in what is now Verden, Germany. He reached the pinnacle of his power in 800 AD, when on Christmas Day at the Old St. Peter Bascilica he was crowned Emperor of Rome by Pope Leo III. The religious and political union of Church and State (Pope Leo III and Charlemagne), was—after three tumultuous centuries—once again solidified into a unified Roman Empire.

With an insatiable appetite for wealth and power the papacy continued to grow. In 1064 AD Pope Alexander II, wanting to dominate all of Europe, called for the conquest of the Muslim Moors who had retained a foothold in Europe. He would call this a "Christian Emergency" and was said to have promised any Catholics who participated a collective indulgence.[839] And so, the bloody quest went on. With a large population of Moors in the Iberian Peninsula (Spain and Portugal) it would become the epicenter of war. In the city of Barbastro it has been estimated that after surrendering, perhaps as many as fifty thousand Moors were massacred in what became known as the Siege of Barbastro. With each victory the papacy became even more emboldened and energized.

The Holy Roman Empire's re-conquest of the land occupied by the Muslims had begun in earnest at the end of the ninth century. The Reconquista as it was called was originally a war of conquest and only later became a religious war of liberation. Though the French were first stirred by their religious duty to the Papal Church to retake the land, they were even more motivated by the prospect of material wealth in the way of plunder.[840] Hundreds of thousands of pious Catholic zealots from across Western Europe enlisted.

"It would be thirty years later that Pope Urban II would give an inspiring speech at the Council of Clermont (1095) calling for an armed force by Latin—Roman Christians (Catholics) to mount a Holy War against the Muslims in order to recapture the Holy Sepulcher and the Holy City Jerusalem. To his Catholic conscripts the Pope promised full penance for the journey; which would be perceived as a virtual guarantee into heaven."[841]

Just as Constantine had done almost eight hundred years earlier, *cruxes* (crosses) from which the name Crusaders is associated, were distributed among the pontiff's unholy army. This was to be a "Just War" (Latin, *bellum iustum*), having GOD's full approval. The dye had been cast.

From that point forward impassioned devotees of Rome would slaughter indiscriminately in the name of the Christ, massacring the infidels, who included Muslims, Jews, and genuine Christians. In other words, anyone who would not convert to Romanism.

The First Crusade ignited a long tradition of organized violence against Jews in Europe who were perceived to be as much of an enemy as the Muslims. "To satisfy their conscience and give credence to their cause these mercenaries of Rome would hold the Jews responsible for the crucifixion of Christ. Because Jews were immediately distinguishable in contrast to the distant Muslims, crusaders wondered why they should travel thousands of miles to fight non-believing Muslims when there were already Jews closer to home."[842]

Persecution was not confined to the Muslims and Jews. Just as much vengeance was aimed at Biblical Christians who, like many Jews, refused to convert or recognize a self-proclaimed Vicar of Christ. These Believers who protested would later earn the name "Protest-ants."

---

839 Charles J Bishko, *Studies in Medieval Spanish Frontier*, Study II, p. 62
840 H.J. Chaytor, *History of Aragon and Catalonia*, (The Reconquest), 1933, The Library of Iberian Resources, p. 37
841 E.H. Broadbent, *The Pilgrim Church*, London, 1931, pp. 88-89
842 Sidney Z. Ehler, John B. Morrall, eds., *Church and State through the Centuries*, London, 1954, p. 7

> Note: The word Vicar (Latin, *Vicarious*) has been applied to an ecclesiastical representative of certain prominent religions. It is predominant in the Anglican/Episcopal Church, referring to a clergyman in charge of a parish. In Roman Catholicism it not only applies to bishops, but to the "bishop of bishops." Popes are commonly referred to as the Vicars of Christ. The word *vicarious* means a substitute. So, a pope is in essence saying that he is the substitute for Christ.[843]

"Their persecution of Christians actually surpassed that of Jews, for it was the true Christians who refuted Catholicism and exposed their heresy. The names of these clusters of European Christian are recorded in encyclopedias, but their persecution and sufferings have been relegated to dusty history books rarely visited."[844]

"Around 1000 AD, one of these European protestant groups was called the Berengarians. They would be followed in 1147 by the Henericians, the Bogomills (friends of GOD) and the Waldenses or Poor Men of Lyons. Afterwards came the Cathars (Puritans), and the Albigenses."[845]

Not only did Christians not persecute GOD's chosen people, they themselves were persecuted and killed in even greater numbers than were the Jews!

Nine major crusades and numerous minor ones continued intermittently for two hundred years (1096–1291). While the crusades had largely been about reclaiming territories held by Muslim dynasties, it was also about which of the two religious empires—the Western (Latin) Holy Roman Empire with its capital in Rome, or the Eastern (Greek) Byzantine Empire with its capital in Byzantium (later named Constantinople; today, Istanbul, Turkey)—would ultimately dominate the Middle East.

The experiences of the first two crusades had thrown into stark contrast the vast cultural differences between these two religious empires. The Church of Rome viewed the Byzantines as having betrayed the faith because they were more interested in trade than conquest and had adopted a policy of tolerance and assimilation toward Muslims.

It was originally Rome's intention to conquer Muslim-controlled Jerusalem and take it for themselves. Though they failed, despots are never satisfied and like the addict they crave more: so it was that the campaign took another turn. Tensions continued to escalate between the West (Rome) and the East (Constantinople); so began the Fourth Crusade in 1202.

In April 1204, the Crusaders of Western Europe invaded and sacked Constantinople. This was the final act of divide which had begun with the "Great Schism" in 1058 over political and theological differences between the Eastern Byzantine Church and the Western Church of Rome. These events became key turning points in the decline of both the Eastern and Western empires, with Rome suffering the greatest embarrassment.

---

843 *Merriam Webster's Collegiate Dictionary*, Random House, NY, 1995, p. 1484
844 David Hunt, *A Women Rides A Beast*, pp. 254-255
845 John W. Kennedy of India, *The Torch of the Testimony*, Christian Book Publishing House, 1965, pp. 115-123

Catholic Europe would mount no further significant response against the Muslims. Eventually three of the four principal khanates (a political entity ruled by a Khan; e.g., Genghis Khan) embraced Islam. The Mongolian Empires and the Ottoman Empire would afterward rule most of Eurasia for the next four hundred years.

> Note: The First Crusade kindled what would become a long tradition of organized violence against Jews in European culture. Even as they were being victimized (though not on the scale of the attacks of 1096), Jewish money was seized and used in France for financing the Second Crusade. During the Second Crusade in 1320, Jews in Aragon (Spain) were attacked and slaughtered.[846] The two Shepherds Crusades in 1251 and 1320 also saw attacks on Jews in France. In England, the Third Crusade was the pretext for expulsion of the Jews and confiscation of their money. Today, as a result of Roman popery, France, Spain, and Italy remain largely Catholic.

As the Crusades were drawing to an end the Holy Roman Church's obsession with exterminating Christians and Jews was just beginning. A new reign of terror began in 1291.

The Medieval Inquisitions were born, and Romanism would redefine the meaning of cruelty for the next four hundred years. Anabaptists (Mennonites), Hussites, Puritans, Camisards, Huguenots, Moravians, Plymouth Brethren, Reformists: protesting Christians all, went side by side with their Jewish companions and met death together.

> Note: "It is the consensuses of most historians who have made a study of martyrdom that between sixty and seventy million Christians were put to death for their faith from the first century until the mid-nineteen hundreds." John B. Wilder, *The Other Side of Rome*. Wilder agrees with Ex-Roman Catholic Jesuit priest Dr. Alberto Rivera "that at that time the total number of victims approached 68 million."[847]

---

846 R.W. Thompson, *The Papacy and the Civil Power*, New York, 1876, p. 418
847 John B. Wilder, *The Other Side of Rome*, Zondervan Publishing House, p. 153

31

LEST WE FORGET!

During the Reformation and Rome's response (the Counter-Reformation) of the sixteenth and seventeenth centuries, historians looked back at the Crusades through the prism of their own religious beliefs. Catholics viewed the Crusades as a noble effort for GOD, and centuries later only as "a regrettable occurrence." Protestants and Jews recognized it for what it was—the horrific work of the devil.

With the invention of the printing press translators were able to make the Scriptures available to the people. Church congregations could each have their own Bible: Truth (the "Good News") that proclaims that one is totally and complete justified by faith and faith alone, set men free while unmasking the doctrinal lies which for centuries had held the people in bondage.

"Being justified freely by his grace through redemption that is in Christ Jesus..." (Romans 5:24)

"For by grace are you saved through faith; and not of yourselves: it is the gift from GOD: Not of works (deeds) least any man shall boast." (Ephesians 2:8-9)

Rome's Curia was infuriated as its authority was not only being challenged but undermined. In retaliation they unleashed a Counter-Reformation at the Council of Trent and formed the Society of Jesus (the Jesuit Order) to halt the Protestant contagion. With the exception of most of Ireland and Southern Europe, Europe turned predominantly Protestant, leaving Catholic Central Europe to become the epicenter of persecution.

Years before the French Wars of Religion officially began scores of massacres were taking place in rural France. In 1545 the Massacre of Mérindol took place when Pope Francis I ordered the punishment of the Waldensians (Protestants) of the city of Mérindol for their dissenting religious activities. Historians have estimated that homegrown troops killed thousands, both there and in some twenty-eight neighboring villages.

Afterward Catholic King Henry II of France continued the persecution with more ferocity, believing that the Protestants were pure heretics. On June 27, 1551, Henry II issued the Edict of Châteaubriant which sharply curtailed Protestant rights to even assemble, much less worship.

Between 1562 and 1598, bloody campaigns of the French Wars of Religion were waged as Catholic popes urged Catholic kings to rid their realm of French Huguenots (Calvinist Protestants). French Catholic troops began the massacres at Vassy, France and summarily slaughtered worshipers while they were holding religious ceremonies in a barn which was their church.

One of the most diabolical, premeditated massacres was to become known as the St. Bartholomew's Day Massacre; so named as it was staged on the eve of the Catholic feast of the Apostle Bartholomew.

On August 23–24, 1572, a prearranged predawn massacre began as a church bell sounded. Appointed Catholic assassins broke into Protestant homes as the bell tolled and slaughtered men, women, and children. The butchery lasted several weeks, spreading throughout Paris, then to other cities, and on to rural villages. Historians estimates the number of Protestants murdered across France may have been as many as thirty thousand. Though by no means unique, it "was at the time, the worst of the century's religious massacres."[848]

> Note: After the Massacre in 1572, Pope Gregory XIII sent the king a Golden Rose. The accompanied Latin inscription read, "for the slaughter of the Huguenots." The medal depicted an angel bearing a cross and sword next to butchered Protestants.

The genocide marked a turning point in the French Wars of Religion. The Huguenot Reformation movement was severely crippled by the loss of many of its leaders. Jews and Protestants fled to countries like Holland, Switzerland, and the Netherlands to escape. Many then made their way to England and on to America. Most of those who remained in France were later hunted down during the Camisard War (1702–1705). Conservative estimates of those Camisards (French Protestants) who were killed range between four hundred thousand and one million. In many ways it resembled the Nazi campaign against Jewish citizens.

> Note: Among those who fled France was the author's father's family progenitor and his father's namesake, Joost (Joseph) DeBaun. He was born in Beaune, Cote d'Or, France about 1642. A few years before the Revocation of the Edict of Nantes (1685), he saw his family tortured and massacred; victims of the dreaded Inquisition. He was reported to be the only member of his family to have escaped. He moved to Middleburg, Holland, and in 1683 emigrated to Brunswick, Long Island, New York. There and afterward, he became a town clerk, school master, elder and Churchmaster of the Hackensack, New Jersey Dutch Reform Church. Joost DeBaun died between 1718 and 1722 and is believed to have been buried in the Huguenot Cemetery, in Cherry Valley, North Hackensack, New Jersey, or the Hackensack Church Cemetery.

---

848 H. G. Koenigsberger, George L. Mosse, G. Q. Bowler (1999), *Europe in the Sixteenth Century*, 1999, Second Edition, Longman

> "...due to his bitter experiences and suffering that Joost had known in France, he was imbued with the spirit to spread Protestantism as much as he could...who wished so much more for the religious freedom of his posterity. Joost DeBaun's decedents are for the most part Protestants. A few intermarried into Roman Catholic families."[849]

With the eighteenth and nineteenth centuries came the dawning of Romanticism. The harsh view of the crusades was being deemphasized and somewhat mitigated as people became distracted by the visual arts, music, and literature. However, at the same time, history became an independent discipline and historians recorded in detail the crusades and the persecution of those like Wycliffe, Hus, Savonarola, and Tyndale. In the twentieth century (circa 1950) Sir Steven Runiciman wrote his epic work, *A History of the Crusades,* where he called out the Crusades for what they were, "High ideals were besmirched by cruelty and greed… the Holy War was nothing more than a long act of intolerance in the name of God."

By the twentieth century the world was changing at unprecedented speed. Anti-Semitism and then extermination lead tyrannical dictators in military uniforms to raze Europe. Two World Wars had killed approximately eighty-eight million people. In 1945 the world went nuclear, giving man the ability to annihilate the planet; but in the aftermath of World War II a global economy emerged. International corporations were formed. Air travel and communications shrank the world and with it, memories of religious persecution. Few wanted to look back and remember what men are capable of, and fewer still wanted to investigate the role Rome had played.

Today in the twenty-first century—eight hundred years after the Fourth Crusade—recorders of persecution have become fewer and fewer. Memory fades as history books are erased. A new paradigm of global oneness is emerging. Old enemies are being repatriated with a simple apology. Still there are some who, like the holocaust survivors, refuse to forget the genocide of multiple millions in Europe, or how the "Catholic Ustachi (1940) lead the most barbaric raids upon the Serbians (Jews and non-Catholics) and practiced Satanic torture that made even the Gestapo wretch."[850]

The Master Race and the Master Church

The papacy has for centuries worked in partnership with despotic kings and tyrannical dictators. In each case the Church of Rome would be the religious arm of the secular state. In a symbiotic relationship each obtained what they wanted from the other.

As the ruthless Third Reich extended its empire, the Vatican told its cardinals and bishops, who in turn told their laity, to profess loyalty to the Reich. German Catholics were made to believe the lie that loyalty to the Fuehrer, who was born Catholic and considered becoming a priest,[851] would spare the country from the terror of war and the horrors of Bolshevism. At the same time the populist were told it would secure order

---
849 William H. Wallace, *Genealogy of the DeBaun Family,* Oceanside, NY, Copyright 1974, Library of Congress 74-15394, pp. 24-26
850 Jack T. Chick, *Smokescreens,* Chick Publications, Chino, CA, 1983, p. 28
851 William Shirer, *The Rise and Fall of the Third Reich,* Simon and Schuster, NY, 1960, pp. 10-11

Vatican ambassador and Adolf Hitler (Image Source: GETTY)

and raise employment. Catholic countries like Austria not only refused to contest the loss of their sovereignty but enthusiastically welcomed Hitler's army when they marched into Heldenplatz in Vienna, Austria.[852]

Even after Hitler's intent for domination was evidenced by the invasion and conquest of Poland, resulting in between 5.47 million and 5.67 million Polish deaths[853] (about 20 percent of the country's total population, and over 90 percent of its Jewish minority) the Vatican continued their support of this maniacal "son of the Church."

The Lateran Concordant was a reciprocal agreement between Mussolini and the Vatican. In this agreement Roman Catholicism would become the sole state religion of Italy. In exchange, the pope would require Catholics (many of whom opposed Mussolini) to back him and the National Fascist Party. It is the consensus of historians that without the Catholic Church's support, Mussolini would not have been elected. The Church of Rome remained loyal to Il Duce throughout World War II, believing that he and the Axis powers (primarily German) would ultimately be victorious, and they would be on the winning side of history.

The Vatican aligns with Mussolini. Cardinal Pietro Gasparri, Cardinal Secretary of State under Pope Benedict XV and Pope Pius XI signs the Lateran Treaty, 1929, with Italian dictator, Benito Mussolini. (Image Source: GETTY)

The dictator in turn gave the pope whatever he wanted, including making Catholic education in public schools' compulsory and using only teachers and textbooks approved by the Catholic Church. Furthermore, any criticism against Catholicism would be a penal offense. The collaboration between church and state had been a proven formula by which to subjugate the citizenry over the centuries. What's more, according to Scripture, this evil alliance will be used again.[854] It shall be in Christ's name that Rome will reestablish her reign over the kings of the earth.

---

852 David Hunt, *A Women Rides the Beast*, Harvest House Publishers, 1994, p. 223
853 AFP / Expatica. 30 July 2009. (Polish experts lower WWII deaths tolls, Retrieved 4 November 2009)
854 Revelation 13:12

> Note: The Lateran Agreement (February 11, 1929) included a political treaty which created the state of the Vatican City and guaranteed full and independent sovereignty to the Holy See. The Vatican agreed perpetual neutrality regarding international relations and to abstain from involvement in international relations. Italy reaffirmed its position taken in 1848 (Statute of the Kingdom of Italy) that the Catholic, Apostolic, and Roman Religion is the only religion of the State.[855]

In 1933, Italy and Germany signed a Concordant with the Vatican. Author and lecturer David Hunt wrote, "Pope Pius XII was outspoken to his faithful (Catholics) about human rights while silent about the Holocaust and Hitler's systemic extermination of the Jews, because to do so would have condemned his own church for similar deeds."[856]

By his silence the pope gave Romanism tacit approval to the annihilation of Christ's natural brethren the Jews. German Bishops and Cardinals joined the throng extolling the virtues of National Socialism. Hitler, Himmler, Goering, and Hoess (Commandant of Auschwitz) were seen as Catholics in good standing with the Vatican. Seeing Rome sanction the genocide and enter into concordats with Hitler, gullible German Catholics became swept up in the national hysteria largely through the effective propaganda campaign of Joseph Goebbels.

Guenter Lewy, an American author, political scientist, and professor emeritus at the University of Massachusetts, Amherst, was born in Breslau, Germany in 1923. He immigrated to Palestine after the coordinated assault on the Jews known as the Kristallnacht (German, *die Kristallnacht*) which occurred on November 9–10, 1938.

During the two-day siege at least ninety-one Jews were killed and thirty thousand were arrested and incarcerated in concentration camps. Jewish homes, hospitals, and schools were ransacked as the attackers demolished buildings with sledgehammers. Over one thousand synagogues were burned and over seven thousand Jewish businesses were destroyed or damaged. Later, Lewy voluntarily took up arms against Germany, serving in the Jewish Brigade. He summarized the position of the Catholic Church at that time in his book, *The Catholic Church and Nazi Germany*:

The Vatican Concordant with Nazi Germany. Seated center is Cardinal Pacelli (later to become Pope Pius XII). Second from the left is Hitler's star diplomat, Nazi, Roman Catholic Franz Von Papin, who helped bring Hitler to power. Standing to the far right was a little-known prelate at the time, Giovanni Battista Enrico Antonio Maria Montini, later to become Pope Paul the VI. (Image Source: GETTY)

---

855 Lateran Agreement, Article 1
856 Dave Hunt, *A Woman Rides a Beast*, Harvest House, 1984, p. 284

> "When thousands of German anti-Nazi were tortured to death in Hitler's concentration camps, when the Polish intelligentsia was slaughtered, when hundreds of thousands of Russians died as a result of being treated as Slavic Untermenschen (sub-humans), and when six million human beings were murdered for being 'non-Aryan,' Catholic Church officials in Germany bolstered the regime perpetrating their crimes. The Pope in Rome, the spiritual head and supreme moral teacher of the Roman Catholic Church, remained silent. In the face of these great and moral depravities which mankind has been forced to witness in recent centuries, the moral teachings of a Church (of Rome) dedicated to love and charity could be heard in no other form but vague generalities."[857]

To this day, the vast majority of Jews fail to differentiate between Roman Catholicism and authentic Christianity; tragically, they are seen as one. Because of the perpetual hatred and mistreatment Satan has managed to keep the Jewish people from even considering, much less investigating, their own Hebrew Holy Scriptures and realizing that the one the Catholics call their Savior could actually be the Jewish Mashiach. It is for this same reason that Yahusha-Jesus challenged the Pharisee class, "Search the scriptures; for in them ye think ye have eternal life: and they are they which testify of me."[858]

In reality and contrary to what many believe, though He is the Savior, "I am the Way, the Truth and the Life; no man cometh unto the Father but by Me."[859] He is not, automatically or inevitably everyone's Savior. Yahusha-Jesus made the distinction as to whose Savior He is when He said,

> "That which is born of the flesh is flesh; and that which is born of the Spirit is spirit." (John 3:6)

> "GOD is Spirit; and they that worship HIM, must worship HIM in Spirit and in Truth." (John 4:24)

In contrast, speaking through the prophet Isaiah and reiterated in the gospel of Mark regarding the Jewish people, the Lord said,

> "Well hath Isaiah prophesied of you hypocrites, as it is written, This people honoureth Me with their lips, but their heart is far from Me. Howbeit in vain do they worship Me, teaching for doctrines the commandments of men." (Mark 7:6-7)

To this day the Jewish people believe the lie that Roman Catholicism is authentic Christianity. Here is an example of how Roman Catholicism is perceived as being one and the same as genuine Christianity. In an indictment from a scholarly rabbinical treatise on the Holocaust, *Mass*

---

857 Guenter Lewy, *The Catholic Church and Nazi Germany*, McGraw-Hill, 196, p. 341
858 John 5:39
859 John 14:6

Murder of Jews, written by Rabbi Yoel Schwartz and Rabbi Yitzchak Goldstein, the authors, and in all likelihood their Jewish readers, fail to make the distinction between the two diametrically opposed groups. The following is a quote from the chapter titled, "The Christian Role in the Holocaust":

"...without Christianity, the success of Nazism would not have been possible...Were it not for the fact that dozens of generations in Europe had been imbued with religious hatred, the growth of racist hatred toward Jewry in modern times could not have taken place. Furthermore (all) through the Holocaust, the Vatican refrained from protesting the murder, and by and large stood aside, rescuing only a tiny few. To this day the Vatican refuses scholars' full access to the documents of the period. It has been established, however, that the Vatican was among the first in the world to know about the genocide, and it did nothing to publicize the information. Walter Laquer, The Terrible Secret."

"It is difficult to avoid the conclusion that the Pope's inaction indicated tacit approval... Even when the Church participated in isolated rescue activities, the motives seem to have been to bring the rescued Jews into the bosom of Christianity. Thousands of Jewish children were taken into monasteries, and after the war, many were not returned to their people and faith even after relatives pleaded for their release...With unparalleled cynicism, many Christians still see the Holocaust as a heavenly punishment for the Jews' failure to accept Christianity."[860]

---

860 Yoel Schwartz and Yo'el Ben Aharon Shvarts, *Shoah: A Jewish Perspective on Tragedy in the Context of the Holocaust*, Mesorah Publications Ltd., 1990, pp. 159-161; David Hunt, *A Woman Rides A Beast*, Harvest House, p. 266

32

THE FUTURE COLLABORATION OF THE TWO BEASTS

Scripture teaches that in the end times there will come not one, but two World Leaders. One will be a political figure, the other a religious figure. Both are appropriately referred to in Scripture as "beasts" (Greek, *therion*—dangerous animals), which serve the same "dragon" (Greek, *derkomal*—serpent—Satan).

The first beast will be the Antichrist.[861] He will be a political figure and rise to prominence on the world stage before the time of Jacob's Trouble actually begins. He will be a brilliant statesman; captivating the masses, the epitome of a diplomat. He will make his debut as a mediator and peacemaker, bringing sectarian fighting between Shia and Sunni and between the Islamic-Arab nations and Israel to (a temporary) detente.

He will be a Muslim, as Islam does not recognize Christ as GOD and therefore, he is so named Anti–Christ, and of course as a Muslim he will have sway over the nations of Islam. Isaiah referred to him as the King of Assyria—which was then part of ancient Syria.[862] This was a Greek term derived from *Assyrios* (Assyria).[863]

The Assyrian (Syrian) empire once stretched from Eastern Asia Minor and North Syria across Babylon to Persia, to the border of India. Special attention should be given to the fact that the Babylonians overran what is referred to as neo-Assyria (900–612 BC); so the Babylonian empire once encompassed what is today largely the nation of Islam. The association with regard to "the Assyrian" (Antichrist), the nation(s) of Islam, and to literal Babylon[864] is crucial to understand. All are implicated in the establishment of the seventh (the World Government) and the eighth kingdom (the World Dictatorship) that will attempt to annihilate the Jewish people and bring about the end of the age of human government (covered in detail in Appendices C and D).

---

861 Revelation 13:1-10
862 Isaiah 10:12; 14:25
863 F. Rosenthal, *Die Aramaistische Forschung*, 1939, p. 3
864 Revelation 14:8; 18:2

> Note: When the Antichrist makes his debut on the world stage, many Jews may see and accept him as their Messiah—believing him to be eligible as a Muslim-Jew based on Deuteronomy 26:5-6. It is in this one scripture that Jacob is spoken of as a Syrian (Arammity). The Hebrew linage is verified through Arphaxad, a son of Shem (Genesis 11:10-32). Hebrew ancestry (via Abram) indicates that the Jewish race stemmed from what were Syrians. Abram was in fact a Syrian and lived in Syria (Padan-Aram). This association is widely accepted, as Jewish males are required to say at the feast in Jerusalem before the Lord GOD,

"And thou shalt speak and say before the LORD thy God, A Syrian ready to perish was my father, and he went down into Egypt, and sojourned there with a few, and became there a nation, great, mighty, and populous: And the Egyptians evil entreated us, and afflicted us, and laid upon us hard bondage..." (Daniel 8:8-9)

In Daniel's vision (in the above scripture), the Assyrian was seen as a "little horn" which came out of one of the "four notable horns" of the "He Goat"—"*Grecia*".[865] Scripture reveals that this horn from which the little horn grew was from the Syrian division of Alexander's Grecian Empire.[866] This establishes the region from which the Antichrist will come. The eastern part of the Seleucus (Syrian) empire during the time of Daniel was part of the great Babylonian Empire. Today this would include Israel, Turkey, Lebanon, Jordan, Syria, Iraq, western Iran, northern Saudi Arabia, and even the Nile region of Egypt. So, it is most fitting that the last great "city"[867] (center of world government, commerce, and finance) be named Babylon.

> Note: Muslims and Muslim nations will one day unify under the Antichrist and stage an all-out war against Israel during the time of Jacob's Trouble. Since the defeat of the Ottoman Empire in World War I the Islamic nations have been unable to unify. But this is rapidly changing. The Turkish state with its ministry of religious affairs oversees the religious organization Diyanet. Diyanet has an ominous agenda. With the mass migration of Muslims into Europe the demographics have changed dramatically. The Diyanet has established an estimated two thousand outposts in Europe primarily in mosques; setting up a cohesive network throughout the European Union. While Arab leaders may presently despise the Turks, they would much sooner see a Muslim Europe than one comprised of various nation under occidental authority. Diyanet sees the opportunity to unite the Muslim people under the Turkish banner into a political, national, and religious neo-Ottoman empire and take back the continent. President Tayyip Erdogan sees the Turks as heir to the empire. The head of the Diyanet, Dr. Ali Erbas, tweeted on April 6, 2018, "The fundamental purpose of our existence is to dominate the world."

---

865 Daniel 8:21
866 Daniel 8:21-23
867 Revelation 18:10, 16

> Note: As the Antichrist comes to power he will manage to gain the confidence of the Jewish people by supporting the rebuilding of the Temple in Jerusalem.[868] This means that before this could possibly occur, a two state solution between the Palestinians and the Israelis over Jerusalem will have taken place. It also suggests that other Arab (Muslim) nations will also recognize and make peace with Israel.

The second beast will be a religious leader who will have a "lamb like" (gentle) appearance.[869] He will be the pope and will preside over the emerging World Church. We are told he will conspire with the first beast, seemingly putting to rest centuries of war between Islam and Roman Christianity.[870] This was portrayed in Daniel's vision of the statue Colossus made up of various metals. The feet were a blend of iron (Romanism) and clay (Islam). Like the two elements, they can never truly blend together.[871]

> "And as the toes of the feet were part iron (Romanism), and part clay (Islam), so the kingdom shall be partly strong and partly broken. And whereas thou sawest iron mixed with miry clay, they shall mingle themselves with the seed of men: but they shall not cleave one to another, even as iron is not mixed with clay." (Daniel 2:41-42)

> Note: Castelnuovo di Porto refugee center, Italy; March 24, 2016 (picture omitted according to the terms of use by owner Reuters; paragraph 13, Reputation). However, in the photograph is seen Pope Francis, who like some of his predecessors, knelt and kissed the feet of others. In this instance he is washing and kissing the feet of Muslim, Orthodox Jew, Hindu, and Catholic refugees during a foot-washing ceremony declaring them "children of the same God." His gesture was said to be that of welcome and brotherhood at a time when anti-Muslim and anti-immigrant sentiment has spiked following the Brussels attacks.

This poses the question; how could this pope say "we are all children of the same God," and why would he say such a thing in light of scripture?[872]

There are three prominent monotheistic religions (the belief in one God); Christianity, Judaism, and Islam. By convincing the people that all three faiths worship the one and same god, and that he is simply called by different names (Jehovah or Allah), the pope is priming the masses for religious unification. In contrast it is the One and Only GOD (the GOD of the Jews and the GOD of the Bible) that makes one a child of the One and Only GOD!

---

868 Daniel 9:27
869 Revelation 13:11-18
870 Revelation 13:12
871 Daniel 2:42-43
872 2 Corinthians 6:14-18

Renewing Old Alliances and Forming New Ones

Shortly after Muhammad's death in 632 AD, the Vatican made an alliance and financed a massive Islamic army in North Africa for the purpose of eliminating the Jews and true Christians from Jerusalem in order to acquire the Holy City for itself. In the initial agreement it was established that Jerusalem and Europe would go to the Church of Rome while the Muslims would have the Arabian Peninsula (Medina and Mecca), including Turkey and the East; but this would soon change.

By 637 AD, Islam had grown exponentially and conquered Palestine in the Siege of Jerusalem. Jerusalem became part of the Islamic Caliphate and would remain such for centuries. Rome of course wanted to regain the city but had no army. The Muslims began encroaching on Europe which infuriated the pope even more. War is mans' way to get what he wants when diplomacy fails. So it was that war was declared not only against the Muslims, but against the Jews and Christians who would not submit to the Church of Rome. In 1099 the crusades officially began under the same banner—the bloody red cross, that centuries before Emperor Constantine claimed gave him by divine right to conquer for GOD.

Believing they could purge Eurasia of all infidels, the pontificate began a series of military campaigns which would span the length and breadth of the Old Roman Empire.

Wars have come and gone, alliances have been made and broken between Rome and the nation of Islam, but the day is fast approaching when two beasts will again unite. Under the guise of unity and harmony, it will appear as though peace is finally at hand.

> "For when they shall say, Peace and safety; then sudden destruction cometh upon them, as travail upon a woman with child; and they shall not escape." (1 Thessalonians 5:3)

Following his meeting with Pope Francis in Vatican City, Muslim World League (MWL) Secretary General Muhammed al-Issa met with the head of the Pontifical Council of the Vatican, Cardinal Jean-Laurent Tauran. A latter meeting was held in the presence of the secretary of the Council of Archbishops, Miguel Isosu, and Archbishop Khalid Akasha. Cardinal Tauran said the meeting with the pope opened a new chapter of friendship and cooperation between the Vatican and the Islamic world in the face of global challenges and risks. Al-Issa thanked the Vatican and Tauran and expressed appreciation for the work undertaken by the Pontifical Council,

(Image Source: ALAMY)

which he said enhances coexistence and cooperation. Secretary General Muhammad al-Issa lauded the historic meeting with the pope, and the pope's rejection of claims that Islam is linked to extremism and terrorism. Al-Issa went on to say that the MWL has communicated and cooperated with the Vatican via the Pontifical Council in all areas to achieve common goals, notably the spread of peace and harmony. The president expressed pleasure over the MWL's historic visit, which he said carries a new vision of peace and coexistence.

Current Events and Alliances

The Prophet Ezekiel had a word from the Lord that in the latter days there would be a provisional collaboration between an enemy of Israel from the north and a dominant power from what was ancient Syria.[873]

The Deception

Jews unfamiliar with what the scriptures say about the False Prophet and the False Messiah will become enamored with two enigmatic figures.[874] The vast majority of the rabbinic will be so enthralled with being permitted to finally rebuild the Temple that they will turn a blind eye to the many prophecies that speak of this deception. Likewise, Gentiles who believe the teaching that there must first be world peace and that only then will the Savior return (Dominionism/Kingdom Theology) shall also be among the deceived if they have not themselves previously been translated as part of the Church.

In addition to the granting permission to rebuild the Temple in Jerusalem, Satan will enable the False Prophet to perform amazing miracles, making it appear that this religious figurehead is unquestionably GOD's appointed spiritual leader.[875] Once he has been perceived as a demigod

Tehran, Iran, November 23, 2015: Russian President Vladimir Putin and Iran President Hassan Rouhani sign join documents following Russian-Iranian talks after the nuclear deal framework with Iran had been drawn. Afterward, on January 26, 2016, when the nuclear agreement was signed Pope Francis held private talks at the Vatican with Iranian President Hassan Rouhani. Their friendship and their meeting was an effort to allow Iran to take a more prominent place on the world stage. (Image Source: ALAMY)

---

873   Ezekiel 38:1-7
874   Matthew 24:24
875   Revelation 13:13

by the different faiths, he will present the Antichrist as the Savior to the Catholics, the Mahdi to the Muslims, and the Mashiach to the Jews. Afterward he will command everyone to exalt and worship this planetary leader under penalty of death.[876]

After forty-two months from the time the accord to rebuild the Temple has been ratified, the Antichrist will set up an image (the "abomination of desolation," as spoken by Daniel the prophet) in the Temple.[877] This act will dispel any doubt as to who he is and expose his true identity as the "King of Fierce Countenance,"[878] "The Prince that Shall Come,"[879] "The Willful King,"[880] "The Man of Sin," "The Son of Perdition."[881]

> "Then I saw another beast come up out of the earth. He (the Pope) had two horns like those of a lamb (gentle lamb-like appearance), but he spoke with the voice (authority) of a dragon (Satan)—(His commands will be demanding, fierce and cruel). He exercised all the authority of the first beast (the Antichrist). And he (the Pope) required all the earth and its people to worship the first beast, whose fatal wound had been healed (his ancient empire restored; he as a demonic prince from the past being reinstated)." (Revelation 13:11-12)

> Note: The "first beast" (the Antichrist) mentioned in the verse above represents a man, a satanic prince, and the empire that he (the prince) previously ruled over. The wound he is said to have incurred speaks of the empire (not the man) that was defeated just prior to the rise of the Roman empire. (More explanation follows and is also provided in Appendix D.)

> "And he (the Pope) doeth great wonders, so that he maketh fire come down from heaven on the earth in the sight of men, and deceiveth them that dwell on the earth by the means of those miracles which he had power to do in the sight of the beast; saying to them that dwell on the earth, that they should make an image to the beast, which had the wound by a sword (appeared to have been destroyed), and did live." (Revelation 13:13-14)

> "And he (the False Prophet) had power to give life unto the image of the beast, that the image of the beast should both speak, and cause that as many as would not worship the image of the beast should be killed. And he causeth all, both small and great, rich and poor, free and bond, to receive a mark in their right hand, or in their foreheads: and that no man might buy or sell, save he that had the mark, or the name of the beast, or the number of his name." (Revelation 13:15-17)

---

876 Revelation 13:12, 15
877 Daniel 9:27; Matthew 24:15; Revelation 12:6
878 Daniel 8:23
879 Daniel 9:26
880 Daniel 11:36
881 2 Thessalonians 2:3

"When ye therefore shall see the abomination of desolation (the image), spoken of by Daniel the prophet, stand in the holy place (the Temple), whosoever readeth let him understand..." (Matthew 24:15)

> Note: The references to "beast" or "beasts" in scripture (and particularly in the books of Daniel and the Revelation) have three different meanings depending on where and how the word is used. The referral to a "beast" in the first order applies to a living thing, like an animal (Chaldee, *cheyva*), as in Daniel's visions,[882] or as presented in Revelation chapter 13, (Greek, *theoreo*).[883] These references refer to a living/spiritual/demonic entity such as the beast which ascends from the bottomless pit.[884] A second application is that it can refer to a man (the beast out of the sea)—the Antichrist[885]—or (the beast out of the land) the False Prophet;[886] both of which are controlled by a beast of the first order—a spiritual entity—Satan. The "sea" refers to the sea of humanity—the people, not the ocean. The third application refers to an empire or empires, as in Daniel 7:3 or in Revelation 13:3. There it refers to both the empire and the satanic prince ("the Prince that shall come"[887]) over that empire. There in Revelation 13, one of the heads of the seven-headed beast (a vanquished ancient empire) comes back to life. This will amaze the world and the world will worship both Satan and his representative—the Antichrist. The Antichrist is both a man and demonic prince that has occupied (possessed) the man. Also take note that in Revelation 17:7 the beast is depicted as empires. There we are shown a mystery woman having ridden on the backs of ancient empires supported by the dragon (Satan) himself.

For scriptural evidence which identifies the Church of Rome as Mystery Babylon, see Appendix D, "*Mystery Babylon*"—Revelation 17.

Recommend reading: *A Woman Rides the Beast*, David Hunt; Harvest House, and *Roman Catholicism*, Loraine Boettner, the Presbyterian and Reform Publishing Company.

---

[882] *Strong's Exhaustive Concordance*, Heb., #2423
[883] *Strong's Exhaustive Concordance*, Gk., #2342
[884] Revelation 11:7
[885] Revelation 13:1
[886] Revelation 13:11
[887] Daniel 9:27

33

THE NEW PARADIGM

Scripture warns that the most effective enemies of Yahusha-Jesus are not those who speak against Him, but those who pretend to be His ministers and ensnare the biblically naïve.[888]

Today, entire mainline Protestant denominations are being drawn into the end time apostasy foretold by Paul the Apostle in a letter to the Church at Thessalonica. Scripture refers to this as "the falling away."[889]

Of course, it only stands to reason that in order to fall away from something there first must be something to fall away from. That something is Truth, and that truth is the Word of Life—the Holy Scriptures—the Bible! It is that truth and that faith once delivered unto the saints[890] which Paul warned would be abandoned. In the gospel of John the Lord made it clear as to who indeed are part of the genuine Church when He said, "But the hour cometh, and now is, when the true worshipers (the genuine Church) shall worship the Father in spirit and in truth; for the Father seeth such to worship HIM."[891]

Just prior to the Antichrist coming to power[892] many Protestants, Evangelicals, and whole denominations will be persuaded to leave the foundation of the Bible and their once held fundamental beliefs. They will be romanced by the pleas of a pope and his bishops who will twist the scriptures making the unwary believe it is GOD's will for them to return to the Universal Church from which they long ago left for truth.

Romanism is that departure from the truth which began in earnest with the great falling away in the fourth century and afterward metastasized. In the latter days, of which we are now on the threshold, whole assemblies of believing Christians will leave the Truth and be swept into the Roman cult.

> "Now the Spirit speaketh expressly, that in the latter times some shall depart from the faith, giving heed to seducing spirits, and doctrines of devils; Speaking lies in hypocrisy; having their conscience seared with a hot iron…" (1 Timothy 4:1-2)

---

888   Acts 20:28-31
889   2 Thessalonians 2:3
890   Jude 3
891   John 4:23
892   2 Thessalonians 2:3

The biblically naïve evangelical church has been taken-in by slick charlatan ministers of mega-churches who thrive financially on the premise that GOD is doing a new thing. Their very name, and the umbrella under which they collect "the Emerging Church" is in itself informing. In accepting a new paradigm, they are in essence saying that, "Old time Religion, ain't good enough for them." Once again, the admonitions of scripture which forecast "another gospel,"[893] and a "falling away"[894] have been disregarded.

> "But though we, or an angel from heaven, preach any other gospel unto you than that which we have preached unto you, let him be accursed. As we said before, so say I now again, If any man preach any other gospel unto you than that ye have received, let him be accursed (Greek, *anathematize*, cursed by GOD). For do I now persuade men, or God? or do I seek to please men? for if I yet pleased men, I should not be the servant of Christ." (Galatians 1:8-10)

The gospel which Paul was referring to: the only gospel Paul preached, and the only authentic gospel is told us in 1 Corinthians 1:23–24, "But we preach Christ crucified, unto the Jews a stumbling block, and unto the Greeks foolishness; But unto them which are called (the true Church), both Jews and Greeks, Christ the power of God, and the wisdom of God."

The late Dr. S. Maxwell Coder, vice president and Dean of Education at Moody Bible Institute, wrote,

> "In churches all over the world where the gospel was once preached faithfully, sermons are now devoted to subjects that have no foundation in the truth of God. Any teaching which denies or substitutes something else for the clear declarations of the Word, is likely to be what Paul calls the doctrine of demons."[895]

> "Take heed that no man deceive you.... And many false prophets shall rise, and shall deceive many... For there shall arise false Christs (alleged Christians), and false prophets, and shall show great signs and wonders; insomuch that, if it were possible, they shall deceive the very elect." (Matthew 24:4, 11, 24)

The "Emerging Church" is only one of many names given to an ecumenical movement which downplays or negates the Cross and the Blood of Christ. Instead, it replaces them with experience-driven faith, human involvement, charitable works, and the acceptance of non-bible-based beliefs. It teaches that one may acquire heaven regardless of what he believes or to whatever god he ascribes. In their premise there is a god who graciously accepts anyone no matter what they believe so long as they are following their conscience. Such an assertion makes the need

---

893 Galatians 1:8
894 2 Thessalonians 2:3
895 S. Maxwell Coder, *The Final Chapter*, Tyndale House publishing, 1984, p. 146

for a Savior having to have come to earth, be spit upon, scourged and nailed to a cross totally unnecessary. The following scripture illustrates how GOD deplores the unification of other belief systems with Biblical Christianity.

> "What fellowship hath righteousness with unrighteousness? And what communion hath light with darkness? And what concord hath Christ with Belial? Or what part hath he that believeth with the infidel?" (2 Corinthians 6:14-15)

In the early years of Israel's development YAHUAH forbad HIS children from having anything to do with the Gentiles, knowing that exposure would lead to their contamination and their being drawn into paganism. However, YAHUAH also knew that after Yahusha-Jesus would come to earth that many Jewish followers (Believers) would lead the Gentiles into the fullness of their Messianic faith.

> "That the blessing of Abraham might come on the Gentiles through Jesus Christ; that we might receive the promise of the Spirit through faith." (Galatians 3:14)

The day is fast approaching when Yahuah will separate the wheat from the chaff and the sheep from the goat nations.[896] Just as HE demanded in time past, so HE demands now—a holy people, sanctified (set apart) for HIMSELF. We are to be separate from all other belief systems and pledge our fidelity—heart, mind, and strength exclusively to HIM.[897]

Passive acceptance and acknowledgment of Yahusha-Jesus is the antithesis of deep love for Him, and it is that deep love which is the hallmark of what it means to be a true Believer.

Perhaps the finest expression of gratitude apart from the Word itself for what our Savior did for us on the Cross was written by John Bunyan in his epic novel, *The Pilgrim's Progress*. There we read of a woman named Christina—the wife of her husband Christian, who like her husband left the world and all its hollow treasures behind her and sought her Savior. It was on her journey to the Celestial City that she was overwhelmed with gratitude and said,

> "True; methinks it makes my heart bleed to think that He should bleed for me. Oh! thou loving One! Oh thou blessed One! Thou deservest to have me, thou hast bought me: thou deservest to have me all; thou hast paid for me ten thousand times more than I am worth..."[898]

For more information regarding "The Emerging Church" and other deceptive movements ushering the Church into apostasy, "The Seeker Sensitive Church," "The International House of Prayer—IHOP," "The Passion of the Presence," "The Apostle and Prophet Reformation," etc., visit www.discernment-ministries.org and www.jsm.org

---

896 Matthew 25:31-33; Isaiah 11:4
897 Deuteronomy 6:4-9
898 John Bunyan, *The Pilgrim's Progress*, Whitaker House, 1973, p. 154

The Repackaging of Defective Teachings

There is a great deal of defective teaching going on in the Church today which has capitalized on the believers' love for GOD, coupled with their desire to experience a supernatural move of GOD. The promoters of what has come to be called "movements," tell their subscribers that as dutiful Christians it is their responsibility to enter into a new revelation that GOD just gave them. In reality these movements are not new. They are nothing but resuscitated copies of various movements that began after World War II, such as, "The Sons of Destiny," "The Kansas City Prophets," "Joel's Army," and "The Tabernacle of David." There was and remains today the "Reconciliation Movement"—its forerunner, "The Manifest Sons of GOD" whose doctrines includes Christian Universalism. This doctrine (Universalism) teaches that eventually the whole world will be saved through the atoning sacrifice of Christ and that ultimately every human being will be restored and be in harmony with GOD.

Such movements cannot accept biblical teaching which describes the declension of the Church, the falling away, and an eternal hell. They refuse to accept a dark outcome but force a triumphant eschatological finale, emphasizing the Church as overcoming and victorious. While such a statement as overcoming and victorious is biblical, it has a spiritual application: not one that must take place in the natural realm. Furthermore, overcoming and victorious pertain solely to the true Church of believers, not to the religious order.

Movements like those mentioned above begin when so-called ministers abandon sound teaching, strip portions of scriptures from their context, and formulate a new paradigm (a new thing). The gullible sheep, believing their leader has been given a prophetic revelation, jam auditoriums to be part of this new phenomena. These pitchmen author one book after another once they have made the best-sellers list with their initial offering. Their eager publishers then crank out their goods and rake in the money as fast as the presses will roll. Their books have promoted the "Purpose Driven Church," the "Kingdom Now" theology, and the "New Apostolic Reformation."

We need a Faith-driven Church, not a Purpose-driven Church. The Purpose-driven author vaguely speaks of sin or the need for repentance; or that unatoned sin is a sentence to an eternal lake of fire. The Purpose-driven author doesn't mention the need to be born again, or the need to live the spirit filled life. He teaches that to teach Jesus is the only way to heaven is intolerant of other faiths. He avoids the controversial or reactionary that segregates Biblical Christianity from pseudo-Christianity. He even refers to the pope as, "our pope." Such rationale has become characteristic of the modern church, who like flies are drawn to what is decaying.

Clergy turned authors reveal so-called hidden passages from the Hebrew Scriptures that previously went undiscovered and are alleged to have application to America today. While these luminaries are consumed with prognosticating, those truly called of GOD are consumed with soul-winning, elevating Christ, and delivering the gospel.

Today celebrity pastor-prophets, often with huge churches, are perhaps a little more suave and sophisticated than their predecessors but their messages are largely the same: "We can take the earth back from the enemy and transform it into the Kingdom of GOD."

This "Kingdom Now" theology has been repackaged, for we are now to take back "the seven mountains" of our culture (Economy, Government, Family, Spirituality, Education, Media, and Celebration). The promoters believe that GOD's strategy is to transform society largely through the workplace or through each believers' GOD-given talent. In this way each believer can dominate one of these mountains and usher in the Kingdom.

Their formula begins by first shouting out a declaration at the top of ones' lungs, exclaiming that it is their destiny to take control: ascend the mountain that has an application to their skill set, rise to leadership in that venue, and in doing so transform the nations bringing the Kingdom of GOD into existence. These same masterful speakers tell their audience that if they neglect their responsibility, then they own the failure, and GOD's plan will be delayed.

Such movements have numerous cousins, with promising names such as the "Azusa Now," or the "Second Pentecost" which proposes "they" can recreate sovereign moves of GOD like the authentic 1906 Azusa Street Awakening through their bravado.

Today, charismatic ministers/promoters believe they can manipulate the sovereign GOD of the universe into bringing revival by scheduling large ecumenical revival gatherings with a scripted program, a succession of prominent motivational speakers, and a half a dozen or so guest prophets. Sometimes these attempts are accompanied with theatrics as with the Toronto movement where participants cackled like chickens, barked like dogs, or erupted in outbursts of unwarranted laughter. Of course, such antics are completely opposite to what compelled the Lord to bring heaven-sent revivals in the past. Instead, this theater is reminiscent of the priests of Baal who tried to coerce their god in a contest on Mount Carmel.[899] In the past, genuine heaven-sent Awakenings began when a small group of saints came together with barely any human involvement and sought HIM, not the miraculous. It was often when these saints quietly prayed, interceded, and petitioned HIM for a lost nation that the Holy Spirit would visit, and a genuine revival would manifest.

There is no rationale behind attempts to move GOD other than that which is scriptural. One can go back and see how Solomon prayed[900] or how revival began under Ezra[901] to see what compels GOD to visit those who seek Him properly.

In the recent past (the first half of the twentieth century) GOD shut down the great tent revivals when the ministers turned into showmen and their focus was on who had the biggest tent, or how many miracle healings were counted at the event.

Because of their lack of humility, their showmanship and exploitation of the gift, GOD retracted the healing gift and the Holy Spirit took His leave. The evangelist, no longer experiencing

---

[899] 1 Kings 18:20-29
[900] 1 Kings 8:22-39
[901] Ezra 9: 1-9, Nehemiah 8:1-12

the authentic, brought in their own actors, crutches, and wheelchairs to the theatre.[902] With the passing of the likes of Wigglesworth and Kuhlman, and without the genuine, the culpable ministers sought other ways to keep their credibility and the money flowing in.

In so far as revival is concerned, perhaps A.W. Tozer said it best:

> "Our mistake is that we want God to send revival on our terms. We want to get the power of God into our hands, to call it to us that it may work for us in promoting and furthering our type of Christianity. We want still to be in charge, guiding the chariot through the religious sky in the direction we want it to go, shouting glory to God, it is true, but modestly accepting a share of the glory for ourselves in a nice inoffensive way. We are calling to God to send fire to our altars, completely ignoring the fact that they are our altars and not God's. And like the prophets of Baal we are working ourselves into a frenzy as if we could by violence command the arm of God."[903]

> Note: The Great Awakenings (generally accepted as three in number) have over the last three centuries awakened Europe, America, and many other continents to our transcendent GOD. These moves of the Holy Spirit began by first reviving the Church and afterward the unchurched. All of the authentic revivals were accompanied by powerful preaching that gave listeners a sense of personal guilt, inculcated a plea for forgiveness, and a commitment to a live a higher standard of personal morality. Most apparent was that it infused a desire to draw closer to the Savior.

Powerful preaching initiated many revivals as it disquieted men to see that they very well may be "Sinners in the hands of an angry GOD." It was also through the publishing and preaching of the truth that brought about the greatest of all Awakenings—the Reformation! We must follow that time-tested model. We must have another reformation of our hearts before we can expect to have another heaven-sent revival.

> Note: "Sinners in the hands of an angry GOD" was the title of a sermon preached by revivalist Jonathan Edwards on July 8, 1741, to his congregation in Northampton, Massachusetts. Edward's sermon was based on scripture and painted such a vivid picture of Hell that it caused the hearers to cry out in fear of where they actually stood in light of GOD's Holiness and their human condition. Repentance is the required action that touches GOD and moves HIM to birth a Great Awakenings.

I would be remiss as an apologist if I didn't address a misnomer associated with revival and awakenings. There are some that believe that as we approach the end of the Church Era; that a

---

902 David Edwin Harrell, Jr. *All Things Are Possible: The Healing and Charismatic Revivals in Modern America*, Indiana University Press, 1975, pp. 139-140
903 A.W. Tozer, *Revival Conditions*

great worldwide revival has been promised. They believe that the Holy Spirit which was given to the Church at Pentecost was the "former rain." Some believe that the move of the Spirit which became evident in the Great Awakenings of the past three centuries has been escalating and that a worldwide revival is scriptural and about to manifest as the "latter rain." They err in the fact that just as the "former rain" belonged to Israel (not the Church), so too, as Joel emphasized,[904] will the "latter rain." Jewish prophets[905] also recognized that the "latter rain" pertains to the Jewish people during the Time of Jacob's Trouble and at Christ's appearing. Having said that, let us continue to pray and pray fervently that although a Great Awakening is not guaranteed in scripture prior to the Church being removed, that our GOD will nonetheless honor our prayers and bestow us with HIS presence.

---

904 Joel 2:23
905 Jeremiah 3:3; 5:23-25; Hosea 6:3; Zechariah 10:1

34

CHEAP GRACE AND COSTLY GRACE

Make no mistake, the "gospel of grace" (His love and unmerited mercy toward us) is not cheap grace, commonly marketed by so-called pastors in stadiums they call churches.

German-born Dietrich Bonhoeffer, a Lutheran pastor who joined the underground during World War II was convinced it was his duty as a Christian to work for Hitler's defeat. He was murdered by the Nazis in the Flossenberg concentration camp in Bavaria in 1945 at the age of thirty-nine. In his book *The Cost of Discipleship* (translated from German, *Nachfolge*, 1939) he wrote,

"Cheap grace is the deadly enemy of our Church. We are fighting today for costly grace... Cheap means grace sold on the open market like cheap wares...Cheap grace is an inexhaustible treasure, from which she showers blessings from generous hands, without asking questions or fixing limits. Grace without price; grace without cost! ...The essence of grace, we suppose, is that the account has been paid in advance; and, because it has been paid, everything can be had for nothing. Cheap grace is preaching of forgiveness without repentance...Cheap grace is the denial of the Living Word. Cheap grace means justification of sin, without the justification of the sinner."

"Costly grace is a treasure hidden in a field; for whose sake a man will gladly go and sell all that he has. It is the pearl of great price to buy for which the merchant will sell all his goods. It is the kingly rule of Christ, for whose sake a man will pluck out the eye which causes him to stumble. It is the call of Jesus Christ at which the disciple leaves his nets and follows Him... Such grace is costly because it calls us to follow, and it is grace because it calls us to follow Jesus Christ. It is costly because it cost a man his life, and it is grace because it gives a man the only true life... Above all it was costly because it cost GOD the life of HIS Son: "Ye are bought at a price," and what has cost GOD much, cannot be cheap for us... GOD did not reckon HIS Son too dear a price to pay for our life, but delivered Him up for us. Costly grace is the incarnation of GOD."[906]

---

906 Dietrich Bonhoeffer, *The Cost of Discipleship* (excerpts), Collier Books, Macmillian Publishing Co., NY, p. 45-48

Choices

Isaiah was the first to tell us that when the Messiah would come to earth, the vast majority of His people (the Jewish people) would not recognize or at first accept Him. He would be, as it were, a stumbling block and an offense to many of them.[907] They were awaiting a savior who would save them from their enemies—not from their sins.

In the letter to the congregation in Rome the Apostle Paul reiterated what Isaiah had said, adding that GOD had one thing in mind and one crucial message for which He had come to earth to personally convey. That message was that an atonement for their sins was first and foremost and still required. This message would become the gospel unto salvation—the gospel of Grace, the gospel of Christ, referred to by true believers as "the message of the Cross." To state it another way, His love for us was so great that He willingly took our sins upon Himself and paid for them on that Cross.

If any truly penitent individual who internalizes what He did for them and why, and then turns their life over to Him, they shall be "born again:" adopted into the family of GOD and be with their Savior forever more.[908]

> "For the Jews require a sign, and the Greeks (Gentiles) seek after wisdom: But we preach Christ crucified, unto the Jews a stumbling block, and unto the Greeks foolishness; But unto them which are called (Believers), both Jews and Greeks, Christ (is) the power of God, and the wisdom of God." (1 Corinthians 1:23)

> "For I am not ashamed of the gospel of Christ: for it is the power of GOD unto salvation to everyone that believeth; to the Jew first, and also to the Greek." (Romans 1:16)

> "For I am determined not to know (esteem important) anything among you, save (except) Jesus Christ and Him crucified." (1 Corinthians 2:2)

> "But God commendeth his love toward us, in that, while we were yet sinners, Christ died for us." (Romans 5:8)

The Cross has been a stumbling block and an offense to many, even bringing division among members of ones' family. And while heartbreaking as this is and contrary to HIS will, it was nevertheless predicted.

> "Think not that I am come to send peace on earth: I came not to send peace, but a sword. For I am come to set a man at variance against his father, and the daughter against her mother, and the daughter in law against her mother in law. And a man's foes shall be they

---

907 Isaiah 8:14
908 Romans 6:40

of his own household. He that loveth father or mother more than me is not worthy of me: and he that loveth son or daughter more than me is not worthy of me. And he that taketh not his cross, and followeth after me, is not worthy of me. He that findeth his life shall lose it: and he that loseth his life for my sake shall find it." (Matthew 10:34-39)

Mans' pride and belligerence are to blame for his rejecting GOD's clear offer and reprieve. Over the course of the individual's lifetime,[909] the Holy Spirit looks for those moments when the individual is sensitive or searching for answers or seeking for GOD Himself. It is in those fleeting moments that the Spirit draws attention to the Savior, leaving man without excuse, for the invitation was extended.[910] Still a gentleman, the Holy Spirit will not impose Himself or GOD's will on anyone. Each of us is free to choose what he will believe and who he will serve.

"The Lord is not slack concerning his promise, as some men count slackness; but is longsuffering to us-ward, not willing that any should perish, but that all should come to repentance." (2 Peter 3:9)

Opposing GOD's attempts to woo man to HIMSELF are demons of every sort: familiar spirits, lying spirits, spirits of hate and murder, and spirits of lust and vain glory. These spirits specialize in mans' personal weakness and concentrate on where his susceptibilities lie. Once they discover his weakness, they set a snare—baited with enticements specific to that individual's natural appetite—"the lust of the flesh, the lust of the eye, and the pride of life."[911] Besides the preoccupation with the pursuits of this world, let us not fail to include the most subtle: the convenience of religion.

"For all that is in the world, the lust of the flesh, and the lust of the eyes, and the pride of life, is not of the Father, but is of the world." (1 John 2:16)

"Howbeit in vain do they worship me, teaching for doctrines the commandments of men." (Mark 7:7)

The Narrow Gate

"Enter ye in at the strait (narrow) gate: for wide is the gate, and broad is the way, that leadeth to destruction, and many there be which go in thereat: because strait (narrow) is the gate, and narrow is the way, which leadeth unto life, and few there be that find it." (Matthew 7:13-14)

Man's pride feeds his ego; his deductions give ascent to his lofty opinions.[912] So confident is he in his conclusions as to disbelieve what GOD has so graciously provided us with…HIS written Word.

---

909 Genesis 6:3
910 Romans 1:17-22
911 1 John 2:16
912 1 Corinthians 1:22

"But if our gospel be hid, it is hid to them that are lost: in whom the god of this world (Satan) hath blinded the minds of them which believe not, lest the light of the glorious gospel of Christ, who is the image (stature) of God, should shine unto them." (2 Corinthians 4:3-4)

> Note: The "Gospel of Grace" is the message of the Cross, also referred to as the "Gospel of Christ," and as the "Good News." It is the message and offer of salvation won by His death and resurrection.

"But none of these things move me, neither count I my life dear unto myself, so that I might finish my course with joy, and the ministry, which I have received of the Lord Jesus, to testify the gospel of the grace of God." (Acts 20:24)

> Note: The Gospel of Grace is one of two gospels spoken of in Scripture. The other is the "Gospel of the Kingdom" which refers to the time when Jesus was present on earth and the Kingdom was first being offered to Israel. John the Baptist would say, "Repent for the Kingdom of GOD is at hand," meaning the Lord is here now.[913] The Gospel of the Kingdom (the nearness of His Second Coming and eminent return) will be preached by those who become Believers during the Time of Jacob's Trouble. They will have looked to the scriptures and recognized how near His return is. The "Gospel of the Kingdom shall be preached in all the world for a witness unto all nations…"[914] Here the word "preached," (Greek, *kerusso*) is best interpreted, proclaimed; not, as so often taught, published.[915]

Begging the Question

Would the Bible which has described each and every empire which persecuted the Jewish people from the Egyptian to the Assyrian, from the Babylonian and Medo-Persian, to the Grecian, and on to the Roman [916] somehow neglect to mention the most nefarious empire of all? "I trow (think) not."[917]

> "Surely the Lord GOD will do nothing, but (unless) HE revealeth HIS secret unto HIS servants the prophets." (Amos 3:7)

> "And he said, Behold, I will make thee know what shall be in the last end of the indignation: for at the time appointed the end shall be." (Daniel 8:19)

---

913   Matthew 4:17, 23; 10:7
914   Matthew 24:14
915   *Strong's Exhaustive Concordance*, Gk., #2784
916   Daniel 7:16-17
917   Luke 17:9

This empire which GOD will and has made known to the studied, is far more sinister than the former empires whose leaders were identifiable by a crown or a soldier's uniform. Instead, this empire will be ruled by two seemingly benign leaders. One will wear a suit, the other will cloak himself in a frock—"a wolf in sheep's clothing."[918]

Our Lord has identified the religious arm of the future empire which stole His name and claims to be His earthly representative. He has revealed "her" identity by her deeds and associations. She is aptly named the "Whore" who has been "drunk with the blood of the saints and with the blood of martyrs."[919]

Historic accounts of the centuries of genocide of non-Catholics, and even their Catholic counterpart (the Eastern Orthodox Church) have been ignored or forgotten, even recently referring to the assault on Constantinople as an "unfortunate period."

In 2001, Pope John Paul II wrote to Christodoulos, Archbishop of Athens, and said, "It is tragic that the assailants, who set out to secure free access for Christians to the Holy Land, turned against their brothers in the faith. The fact that they were Latin [Roman] Christians [crusaders] fills Catholics with deep regret."[920]

It wasn't to give "free access" of the Holy Land to the Christians that compelled the Church of Rome to send crusaders to invade the land GOD had bequeathed to Abraham and his descendants; it was to seize the land for themselves, expand their empire, force the Muslims to retreat and rid the land of the Jews. With the voracious and insatiable appetite of the shrew, she will eat her own, as the Eastern Church discovered.

In 2004, while Bartholomew I, Patriarch of Constantinople, was visiting the Vatican, Pope John Paul II asked, "How can we not share at a distance of eight centuries, the pain and disgust?"[921]

This gesture of humility has been regarded as an acceptable apology to the Greek Orthodox Church for the terrible slaughter perpetrated by the Rome's Crusaders during the Fourth Crusade. Bartholomew accepted the apology and responded in a liturgy attended by Roman Catholic Archbishop Philippe Barbarin.

> "We receive with gratitude and respect your cordial gesture for the tragic events of the Fourth Crusade. It is a fact that a crime was committed here in the city 800 years ago. The spirit of reconciliation of the resurrection... incites us toward reconciliation of our (two) churches."[922]

Attesting to their goal of an ecumenical World Church, Pope John Paul II's immediate predecessor, Paul IV, when giving his blessing to the Second World Conference on Religion and Peace in Louvain Belgium said,

---

918   Matthew 7:15
919   Revelation 17:6 (see also Appendix D)
920   Austin Cline, *Apology Accepted*, April 16, 2004. http: //atheism.about.com/library/FAQs/christian/blfaq rcc index.htm
921   Austin Cline, *Apology Accepted*, April 16, 2004. http: //atheism.about.com/library/FAQs/christian/blfaq rcc index.htm
922   Alan Geyer, *Religious Isolationism: Gone Forever?, The Christian Century*, October 23, 1974, pp. 980-981

"Buddhists, Christians, Confucianists, Hindus, Jains, Jews, Muslims, Shintoists, Sikhs, Zoroastrians and still others, we have sought here to listen to the spirit within our varied and venerable religious traditions... we have grappled with the towering issues that our societies must resolve in order to bring about peace... We rejoice that the long era of prideful and even prejudiced isolation of the religions of humanity is, we now hope, gone forever."

Murderous assaults contrived by the Vatican against Jews and Protestants in Ireland and France, as well as Muslims in Europe were often preceded by not only acceptance, but by warmth and friendship. This ploy has been used many times in an effort to cause non-Catholics to let their guard down assuming the Vatican has reformed. This has been a fatal mistake and has cost millions of people their lives. Her Latin maxim, "*semper eadem*" ("always the same,") has never changed.

35

A DIFFERENT CROSS

The Cross has Different Meanings to Different People

To the unsaved Jew, the Cross is a symbol of death and pain; a reminder of the cruelty of those who called themselves Christians.

To the Church of Rome the Cross is a symbol of their power and control. It is not an empty Cross testifying of a risen and victorious savior, but a crucifix, depicting a lifeless and defeated Jesus. Like Nebuchadnezzar's golden image,[923] its devotees are expected to bow their heads or genuflect before it as their overlords pass among them holding a graven image on a shepherd's staff. Satan undoubtedly relishes seeing such acts of submission in direct defiance of the second commandment.[924]

Today under the current pope the emphasis of Catholic theology is actually a political movement known as Liberation Theology. What is now being emphasized is an even greater distortion of an already distorted doctrine. It now implies that Christ's emphasis was on liberating the poor from unjust economic, political, or social conditions. Of course, this was not the Lord's purpose, neither was redistribution of wealth, or social transformation. These are fundamental principles of Marxism-Leninism and are not coincidental, but a deliberate step in advancing the Global Agenda.

A defeated Jesus (Image Source: GETTY)

To the genuine Christian—the Believer—the Cross is an empty Cross. No longer is there pinned the figure of a man in agony. No longer is there draped a lifeless corpse. Instead, it speaks of a Savior who paid a debt He did not owe; of a risen Christ who defeated death, and of a resurrected Christ who now sits on His throne waiting to welcome all who have staked their salvation on what He accomplished for them on that beloved Cross.

---

923   Daniel 3:5-6
924   Exodus 20:4

> Note: While relieving the sufferings of the poor is most worthy, the central purpose of the Christian Commission is to bring the lost to the saving knowledge of Christ by explaining what He accomplished by His death and resurrection.[925] "For GOD so loved the world..."[926]

In or On?

The level of "saving" faith is not simply believing "in" what Christ did, but believing "on" what Christ did. He took on Himself our sins and paid our debt. So, we must trust wholly and completely on Him and on nothing but Him!

Let us look at the frequently quoted passage John 3:16, where we read, "For God so loved the world, that he gave his only begotten Son, that whosoever believeth in him should not perish, but have everlasting life."

There we see the words "believeth in." However, if we were to take a closer look at these two words, we will gain a greater understanding of the passage; for the word "in," as we shall see, essentially means "on."

The first word, "believeth," actually has a much more profound meaning in Greek than in English. The Greek word for believeth is "*pisteuo*."[927] It implies "entrusting" rather than simply believing in. So, John 3:16 is better interpreted: He who entrusts one's salvation to the Son and what He accomplished on the Cross.

The next word used in John 3:16 to consider is the word "in" (actually, it is "into").[928] The Greek word used for "in" or "into," is "*eis*" and it happens to be the same Greek word for the word "on."[929]

We also see the word "*eis*" in another scripture having to do with salvation. It is used just a few verses later in John 3:36. "He that believeth on *(eis)* the Son hath everlasting life: and he that believeth not the Son shall not see life; but the wrath of GOD abideth on *(eis)* him." In this verse the translators used the more appropriate English word "on" instead of "in" or "into."

So again, the basis for salvation is to entrust that all your sins were put on Jesus, and that He bore them for you on the Cross—if you can fully internalize the magnitude of His love for you then the debt on your account has been paid in full.

We would do well to point out that John 3:16 reads "GOD so loved," which is past tense. Shortly after we read in John 3:36 "but the wrath of GOD abideth (present tense) on him that believeth not..." This stresses the dire need to accept Yahusha-Jesus at that moment (in the present) when the Holy Spirit extends the invitation, for like the wind, it is not certain that it will pass by again.[930]

---

925 Mark 16:15-16
926 John 3:16
927 *Strong's Exhaustive Concordance*, Gk., #4100
928 *Strong's Exhaustive Concordance*, Gk., #1519
929 *Strong's Exhaustive Concordance*, Gk., #1519
930 John 3:8

"For he saith, I have heard thee in a time accepted, and in the day of salvation have I succoured thee: behold, now is the accepted time; behold, now is the day of salvation." (2 Corinthians 6:2; Isaiah 49:8)

"Behold, I stand at the door, and knock: if any man hear my voice, and open the door, I will come in to him, and will sup with him, and he with me." (Revelation 3:20)

"And the man said to Paul, 'What must I do to be Saved?' And Paul answered, '…Believe On the Lord Jesus Christ and thou shalt be Saved…'"[931]

Not on or through Mary.
Not on or through Peter.
Not on or through Mass.
Not on or through Infant Baptism.
Not on or through Confession.
Not on or through Communion.
Not on or through Penance.
Not on or through Absolution.
Not on or through Novenas.
Not on or through Holy Days of Obligation.
Not on or through Last Rites.
Not on or through Good Works.
Not on or through Tithing.
Not on or through Sabbaths.
Not on or through Purgatory.
Not on or through Rosary.
Not on or through Pilgrimages.
Not on or through Poverty.
Not on or through Catechism.
Not on or through Suffering.
Not on or through Holy Water.
Not on or through Candles.
Not on or through the Law.
And not on or through Romanism!

"He that believeth on the Son hath everlasting life: and he that believeth not the Son shall not see life; but the wrath of God abideth on him." (John 3:36)

---

[931] Acts 16:31

36

WHO IS A JEW? WHAT IS A MESSIANIC JEW? WHAT IS A JEWISH CHRISTIAN?

It is amazing how few people can correctly characterize a person who says they are a Jew. Stereotypical definitions are numerous:

A Jew is a person who is born of a Jewish mother.

A Jew is a person who practices a form of Judaism.

A Jew is a person who claims their ethnic identity as a citizen of the nation of Israel.

In similar fashion, a stereotypical definition for a Christian is a Gentile who may be a Catholic or any one of a range of Protestants.

These definitions are incomplete. Both terms have Bible-based meanings. The term Jew is derived from Jacob's fourth son. In general usage the term Jew came to represent all of the people of Israel—the descendants of Abraham, Isaac, and Jacob. The term Christian is derived from the term "Christos," the Greek equivalent for Messiah. Christian simply means "Messiah-like" or "follower of the Messiah." So, one being a Jew is an ethnic term, and the other is descriptive of what one believes—hence the word "Believer."

The Scriptures speak of a third group, the Gentile (Hebrew, Yiddish—*Goy* גּוֹי, regular plural *goyim* גּוֹיִים or גּוֹיִם). It is also the standard biblical term for a nation. The word is often used disparagingly to describe those not of Jewish descent.

The difference then between a Jew and Gentile is clear-cut. A person who is a Gentile will die a Gentile. A person who is a Jew will die a Jew. Neither the Jew nor the Gentile can lose their ethnicity, but one who becomes a Christian (a Believer) has to choose to become such. Being

(Image Source: ALAMY)

a Christian is completely voluntary. Ethnically speaking, it may be said there are Jewish Christians, Russian Christians, Chinese Christians, etc.

A Jew who exercises his faith and places his salvation in the Messiah may be free to call himself a Messianic Jew, a Hebrew Christian, a Christian, or simply a Believer. Regardless, he or she remains a Jew. Similarly, a Gentile who accepts our Messiah will, regardless of his ethnicity, be a Gentile Christian.

No one is born a Christian, nor are they a Christian because their parents had them baptized into a religion. Becoming a Christian (a genuine Christian) is voluntary and must begin with one having a spiritual birth—or "born anew."

Marvin Lutzker, a twentieth century Hebrew Christian, wrote an article which appeared in the *Los Angeles Times* many years ago. Here is an excerpt from that article.

> "As a Christian what part of my Jewishness have I given up? The One true GOD, the GOD of Abraham, Isaac and Jacob? Certainly not! Have I given up any part of the Old Testament? No. So then what have I been converted from, and to what have I been converted? No, I haven't been converted from anything. I am more a Jew now than ever before, because I now read the Old Testament with understanding and belief."

Dr. Arthur Kac pointed out in *The Spiritual Dilemma of the Jewish People*,

> "The modern Hebrew Christian movement is about one hundred years old. Its origin coincides with the time of the national awakening of the Jewish people in the nineteenth century. Its separate and distinctive existence is marked by a deep consciousness of its kinship with the Jewish people and the awareness of the unique character of the mission, being to maintain in the midst of the Jewish people a candlestick of witness of the Messiahship of Jesus."

Among the great Hebrew Christians of the nineteenth century was British statesman, writer, Prime Minister of Britain, Benjamin Disraeli (1804–1881). In 1868 he emphasizes Christianity's dependence on Judaism:

> "In all church discussions we are apt to forget the second Testament is avowedly only a supplement. Jesus came to complete the 'law and the prophets.' Christianity is completed Judaism, or it is nothing. Christianity is incomprehensible without Judaism, as Judaism is incomplete without Christianity. He hopes that Jews 'will accept the whole of their religion instead of only the half of it,' as they gradually grow more familiar with the true history and character of the New Testament."

> Note: The nineteenth century saw at least 250,000 Jewish accept Christ according to existing records of various societies. Data from the Pew Research Center (2013) indicates that 1.6 million adult American Jews identified themselves as Christian; most aligned with Protestant (Biblical) Christianity. According to the same data most of the Jews who identified themselves as some sort of Christian (1.6 million) were raised as Jews or are Jews by ancestry. According to a 2012 study, 17 percent of Jews in Russia identified themselves as Christians.

I would like to a repeat a caveat which I presented earlier in the subchapter of "A New Assembly and a Greater Covenant."

Messianic Believers may keep their heritage alive and celebrate that which GOD has purposed, for in doing so they are a unique witness to the Gentiles of GOD's faithfulness and HIS Lordship over them. However, in doing so the emphasis is no longer on hope and expectation but on fulfilment.

There are many varied types of Messianic congregations should one chose to attend. Some are truly liberated by the promise of the New Covenant, while others put extraordinary emphasis on their Judaism, tradition and the keeping of Torah as if they were still under the Law rather than Grace. This significantly diminishes the New Covenant and makes grace an adjunct to the law.

A clear example of this tendency is given to us in Acts 15 where Jewish (Messianic) Believers, after becoming saved, still maintained it was necessary for proselytes to keep the Law of Moses and be circumcised. To this day, by exaggerating and accentuating their Jewishness some Messianic congregations are actually segregating themselves from the body of Believers. We need to remember that "there is (now) no difference between Jew and Greek: for the same Lord over all is rich unto all that call upon Him."[932]

A Word to Jews who Accept Yahusha-Jesus as their Savior

Once truly liberated from the law, Biblical Jews did not return to the law and go on with all the Jewish rituals, ceremonies, and traditions which some Messianics tenaciously cling to today. The mature realize that the purpose for which these observances and formalities were instituted was to point us to the Messiah and to the Cross.

> "Think not that I have come to destroy the law, or the prophets: I am not come to destroy, but to fulfill (it)." (Matthew 5:17)

Now we need only to exert our faith, accept Him as our ransom, receive His grace, make Him Lord of our lives and follow after Him. He is to be celebrated, not our Jewishness.

---

[932] Romans 10:12

> Note: There are some Messianic teachers who stumble with the above passage (Matthew 5:17); specifically, with the word "fulfill." They interpret this to mean that the law is still in effect. Were they to look up the word used (Greek, *"pleroo"—Strong's*, #4137) they would realize that the word fulfill in this passage translates to "satisfy." Hence the Lord's death has satisfied the Law!

A Word to Gentile Believers

There are some Gentile Believers who take issue with the name Messianic Jews or Hebrew Christians, saying that they should just refer to themselves as Christians. I would do well to point out that the name Christian is the modern (English) name for Messianic, which evolved from Greek word, Χριστός (*Khristós*) or Christos. The word became Crist (Old English) and was only later standardized to Christ during the eighteenth century. The word Christian (follower of the anointed one) was a natural language progression, translated from the Hebrew word מָשִׁיחַ (*Māšiaḥ*) for Messiah. In the final analysis, if those who call themselves Christians (followers of the Messiah) actually want to refer to themselves correctly, they should (in reality) be referring to themselves as Messianics or Masiahians; not Christians. They (the Gentiles Believers) are the wild branches who have been grafted into the good olive tree and a partaker of the root. "Boast not against the branches."[933] Gentiles are warned not to boast of their being accepted by GOD when for a time HE has taken leave of the Jewish people who are likened to the branches that were broken off because of their unbelief. Rather they are to reverently fear HIM, less they also not be spared! We are all to walk circumspectly before the Lord less we be overtaken with pride.[934]

> "For if GOD spared not the natural branches, take heed lest HE also spare not thee."
> (Romans 11:21)

---

933 Romans 11:18
934 Ephesians 5:15

37

A RABBI'S TESTIMONY

What kind of a Jew would I be if I did not search the Scriptures for my Mashiach and when I had found Him, accept Him? I have an obligation both to GOD and to myself to discover for myself who He is and how I can know Him. I must know of who the Scriptures speak, for my eternal destiny depends on my acceptance or rejection of Him.

The great majority of Jews, regardless of their religious orthodoxy or lack thereof, are passionate about their ethnicity and culture and cling tenaciously to it. This loyalty to Judaism is entrenched in them. Their rabbis have taught them, and rightfully so, that their Scriptures abound with admonitions about intermingling or intermarrying with Gentiles and adopting their beliefs. Example after example is provided in the Scriptures of how GOD punishes such infidelity. Fear of being cajoled and drawn into a pagan ideology, shunned by the Jewish community, or losing their identity as a Jew has paralyzed them. They believe that by becoming Messianic they have abrogated their Judaism. To this end they choose to be objective rather than subjective. They are satisfied with the external aspects of being Jewish instead of the internal, which is all about intimacy and relationship with HIM. Love is an emotion, and an emotion is subjective. Scripture indicates that GOD is an emotional being and that HE first loved us (1 John 4:18–19). Love—not heritage, not culture, not tradition—is the stimulus and the catalyst by which HE draws an individual to HIMSELF, and by which we are drawn to HIM. Sometimes GOD will even use adversity to save a soul or launch a ministry.

One Orthodox rabbi: a graduate of Hebrew Union College, Cincinnati, Ohio, who became a Jewish Christian expressed his experience and undoubtedly that of thousands of other Jews. His name was Rabbi Max Wertheimer.

His first appointment was the B'nai Yeshorun Synagogue in Dayton, Ohio, where, like many of his contemporaries he focused on social issues, ethics, culture, and Jewish Law. As a dutiful representative of his faith in the community he attended ecumenical gatherings with other clergy in the area, becoming an honorary member of the Ministerial Association.

Rabbi Wertheimer lived well, having a beautiful home with all the amenities, two servants, a daughter Rose, and a beautiful baby boy. But then his life suddenly changed. His young wife was taken seriously ill and despite the efforts of numerous physicians and specialists, she died.

Confounded as to why the GOD he served would take away his beloved and leave him a heartbroken widower with two small children left him distraught. In his grief, everything of any importance suddenly became subordinate to understanding.

What had GOD done to him and why? What did GOD want of him? How could he as a rabbi speak comfort to others when he found himself crippled with grief? How could he give others hope when he himself had not answers to relieve his own despair?

So it was that with nothing to comfort him, he resigned his post as rabbi and went to the Holy Scriptures to find the answers… And, if not answers, perhaps he could find resolution. Study would become his escape.

His exposure to the others in the ministerial association had brought into question the one they believed to be the Messiah. So, in the privacy of his home he began a study: a study which became a preoccupation of an alleged Savior of which he had boastingly rejected.

In his writings, he explained that he began reading the New Testament and comparing it with the Old.

> "One chapter in the Hebrew Scriptures, Isaiah 53, made a definite impression on me, especially in the last clause of the eleventh verse, '…by His knowledge shall my righteous servant justify many, for He shall bear their iniquities.'"

Here was the only mention in the whole of Scripture of "My righteous servant."

> "We have David my servant, but here it is: 'My Righteous Servant.' I said to myself: 'who is that righteous servant? To whom does the prophet refer?' I argued, whoever that righteous servant of Jahovah is, one thing I am sure: he is not Israel, because the same prophet, in an earlier chapter, declares Israel to be a sinful nation, a people laden with iniquity, a leprous nation. The righteous servant of Jahovah must be one who is holy. If it is not Israel, who could it be? So it was that I began a study of the fifty-third chapter of Isaiah, and afterwards decided to begin at the first chapter of Isaiah and read it through.[935] Gradually the scales fell from my eyes, and I discovered what many other rabbi had also found."[936]

Rabbi Wertheimer's experience stemmed from the loss of his wife. He could not have understood at the time how such a tragedy could have ever prompted such a discovery. GOD's ways are beyond us,[937] but HIS promises and purposes never waver. With the Father of lights, there is no variableness, neither shadow of turning.[938] GOD had broken a haughty spirit and made a seeker's heart tender. Rabbi Wertheimer would go on until his death in 1941 teaching, exclaiming, and leading many Jews to their Mashiach.

---

935 Arnold M. Ross, *A Rabbi's Testimony*, A Hermon House Publication, World Messianic Fellowships, Inc. Lynbrook, NY
936 Steven Schwartz, *Dear Rabbi*, Chosen People Ministries, Orangeburg, NY, p. 19
937 Isaiah 55:8-9
938 James 1:17

What Jew would not accept his Messiah if he learned His identity?

"Ye are MY witnesses, saith the Lord, and MY servant whom I have chosen: that ye may know and believe Me... I, even I AM the Lord; and beside Me there is no Savior (Yahusha)." (Isaiah 43:10-11)

"...there is no God, else beside ME; a just God and a Savior (Yahusha); there is none beside ME. Look to Me and be saved, all the ends of the earth: I AM God and there is none other." (Isaiah 45:21-22)

"Behold, the Lord hath proclaimed unto the end of the world, Say ye to the daughter of Zion, Behold, thy salvation (Yahusha) cometh; behold, His reward is with Him, and His work before Him." (Isaiah 62:11)

See Chapter 53—*The Suffering Servant of Yahovah*—Isaiah 53 for a verse-by-verse analysis.

38

JUST ONE SIN!

Without the Scriptures, it is impossible to understand the magnitude and implications of the three-letter word "Sin." In our imperfect state, we cannot enter into HIS Holy presence or HIS Holy kingdom any more than the High Priest could enter the Holy of Holies while sin was yet unatoned for.

> "And the Lord said to Moses, Whosoever hath sinned against ME, him will I blot out of My book." (Exodus 32:33)

To a perfect GOD sin is the antithesis of holy and pure. Even sins we would call negligible, trivial, and insignificant cannot be allowed in the presence of absolute perfection, otherwise perfection becomes imperfection. It must be erased from the book of record[939] or judgment as prescribed by Law must and will prevail!

> "Thou (GOD) art of purer eyes than to behold evil, and canst not look on iniquity..." (Habakkuk 1:13)

> Note: The holiness of GOD has two branches: perfect righteousness and perfect justice. HE is absolute righteous and absolutely just. As such it is impossible for HIM to do anything contrary to HIS Word, or to have fellowship with anything that is less than perfect.

"As for GOD, HIS way is perfect..."[940] (Hebrew, *Ha'EL Tamim Darko*—The Lord perfect is HIS Way.)

Perfection demands perfect justice. GOD cannot be partial or unfair to any man, or for that matter to any nation. HE must deal with each of us and our sin with perfect justice.[941]

All that is unrighteous, sinful or unclean, must, just as the leaper had to, go to the high priest in order to be declared healed; so must the individual. And if the leper was healed, a dove was

---

939 Revelation 20:12-13
940 Psalm 18:30
941 Psalm 119:137-138; 145:17; Habakkuk 1:13; Romans 2:5-6, 11

killed, and its blood poured over a second dove that was given to live and set free.[942] Substitution and the blood were the redeeming factor. To be set free was the result.

Scripture tells us that the penalty for having just one unatoned sin is a sentence to an eternity in hell.

> "Behold, all souls are mine; as the soul of the father, so also the soul of the son is mine: the soul that sinneth, it shall die (eternal death)." (Ezekiel 18:4)

> "For the wages of sin is death; but the gift of God is eternal life through Jesus Christ our Lord." (Romans 6:23)

And who is a sinner?

> "…There is none righteous, no not one… For all have sinned, and come short of the glory of God…" (Romans 3:10; 3:23)

We would do well to remember that it only took a single bite of a seemingly innocuous piece of fruit for Adam and Eve to be cast out of a pristine garden of perfection. Their personal relationship with YAHUAH was severed; no longer would they meet with HIM face to face as they had. An Earth which was endowed to them went by default to the governorship of a demonic adversary.[943]

> "So HE drove out the man; and HE placed at the east gate cherubim, and a flaming sword." (Genesis 3:24)

We would do well to remember too that Moses himself was prohibited from entering the Promised Land and died alone on Mt. Nebo for what appeared to be a small act of disobedience. In a moment of frustration, prompted by his people murmuring he failed to obey GOD's instruction to the letter. So it was that he smote a rock twice with his staff instead of speaking to the rock.[944]

I ask you, if GOD could justify doing this to HIS righteous servant Moses, where then does that leave the rest of us?

Few realize that their failed attempts to live a moral, ethical, or righteous life are not sufficient to enter into the presence of our Holy, Holy, Holy GOD.[945]

> "They are all gone aside, they are all together become filthy there is none that doeth good, no not one." (Psalm 14:3)

---

942 Leviticus 14:1-7
943 Ephesians 2:2
944 Numbers 20:8, 11
945 Isaiah 6:3

Though we may hope upon hope that our good deeds, prayers, tithes, and philanthropic giving will open heaven's gates for us, the Scriptures declare they will not! All our mitzvahs do not erase a single sin and our Yom Kippur prayers are but a plea for forgiveness. No bread cast upon the outgoing tide can carry our sins away and no amount of fasting buys us forgiveness. The reciting of repetitious prayers accomplishes little. Only brokenness even gets GOD's attention.[946]

> "But when the righteous turneth away from his righteousness, and committeth iniquity, and doeth according to all the abominations that the wicked man doeth, shall he live? All his righteousness (good) that he hath done shall not be mentioned: in his trespass that he hath trespassed, and in his sin that he hath sinned, in them shall he die." (Ezekiel 18:24)

> "...but your iniquities have separated between you and your God, and your sins have hid his face from you, that he will not hear." (Isaiah 59:2)

> "The Lord is nigh unto them that are of a broken heart; and saveth such as be of a contrite spirit." (Psalm 34:18)

> "For all those things hath mine hand made, and all those things have been, saith the Lord: but to this man will I look, even to him that is poor and of a contrite spirit, and trembleth at my word." (Isaiah 66:2)

Where, I ask you, is the required blood in any of our rituals? The kosher kill in a slaughterhouse does not fulfil the Temple law or apply its blood to our sin! And, if there is no blood sacrifice, where then is there atonement?[947] Just one sin will separate us from GOD for eternity. Just one sin condemns us to a scalding lake of fire for eternity.[948]

---

946 Isaiah 57:15
947 Leviticus 17:11
948 Revelation 20:11-15

39

THE HUMAN TRINITY—
SPIRIT, SOUL, FLESH

To better understand who and what we are we must look at HIS Word. Scripture tells us man was made by GOD "in HIS own image, and after HIS's own likeness."[949] It is clear that GOD is a spirit being, therefore man, being in GOD's likeness has the distinction of also possessing a spirit. Unlike GOD, mans' spirit is confined to a body as long as he's alive; afterward his spirit leaves the corruptible body to live on in eternity.[950] For this reason man is actually more a spirit being than a mortal being.

So, what is a spirit? It is the authentic person, the self, the fundamental essence of who we actually are. It is our immortal being which occupies a temporal shell.

Because a spirit is given by GOD to each of us, it could be likened to the seed of GOD which has been implanted in man; much like the seed of life which produces an offspring. It is implanted in us at the moment of conception and becomes joined to the soul, thereafter, making the two inseparable. It is at the moment of conception that life begins and becomes eternal!

> "Before I formed thee in the belly I knew thee; and before thou camest forth out of the womb I sanctified thee, and I ordained thee a prophet unto the nations." (Jeremiah 1:5)

Having come from GOD, mans' spirit is not only conscious of GOD but has the inclination to love, worship, and serve HIM. Once GOD implants the spirit in a human it then becomes the exclusive property of that person; free to be as it were, "a free spirit;" having a free will and free choice. It may then serve the soul and flesh, or it may surrender itself to its parent creator.[951]

This free spirit may be likened to a kite tethered to its handler by a string. Although tethered, it is still able to move freely in the wind, darting where it may. However, should the string

---

949 Genesis 1:26
950 Isaiah 66:24; Mark 9:43-44
951 Luke 16:13

break it falls to earth, its life is over. It must remain tethered and under tension to its master to remain alive. Likewise, the free spirit must concede its control to GOD's Holy Spirit, lest it too will fall and die—eternally.

Staying connected is the exclusive choice and the conscious decision of the individual.[952] When a decision to totally surrender ones' spirit to the Spirit of GOD a spiritual unification, a spiritual baptism, a second birth takes place. Scripturally speaking, this is what it means to become "born of the Spirit or born again."[953]

It stands to reason that if a person is to be born a second time there must first take place a death of the person. So, death or the process of surrendering and dying to self is an imperative.

The Apostle Paul said, "Know ye not, that so (as) many of us as were baptized into His death… even so we should walk in newness of life… Knowing our old man (our former self) is crucified (put to death) that the body of sin might be destroyed, that hence forth we should not serve sin."[954]

> "I am crucified (I figuratively died) with Christ: nevertheless I live; yet not I, but Christ liveth in me: and the life which I now live in the flesh I live by the faith of the Son of God, who loved me, and gave himself for me." (Galatians 2:20)

So, what is it that must die? It is our self-will which must be crucified; wherein one willingly and wantingly says, "nevertheless not as I will, but as thou wilt."[955] Our old man (self) is put to death and then out of love and gratitude, not unlike the same love that compelled our Lord to go to the Cross for us—we are spiritually compelled to want to follow after Him. Hence a follower of Christ is a disciple of Christ—a.k.a. a Christian.

The spirit in man, unlike that of an animal has a conscience with which to differentiate right from wrong and good from evil. It is this consciousness by which GOD makes man accountable for his actions.

> "For as many as have sinned without law (Gentiles) shall also perish without law: and as many as have sinned in the law (Jews) shall be judged by the law; For not the hearers of the law are just before God, but the doers of the law shall be justified. For when the Gentiles, which have not the law, do by nature the things contained in the law, these, having not the law, are (have become) a law unto themselves: Which shew the work of the law written in their hearts, their conscience also bearing witness, and their thoughts the mean while accusing or else excusing one another; In the day when God shall judge the secrets of men by Jesus Christ according to my gospel." (Romans 2:14-16)

---

952 John 15:1-6
953 John 3:6
954 Romans 6:3-4, 6
955 Matthew 26:39

> Note: Mans' conscience bears him witness of that which is right or that which is wrong, so that even without knowing the law (as a Jew might) he still intuitively knows right from wrong. GOD has not left men without light. The above scripture does not imply however that following ones' conscience makes him sinless any more than ones' attempts at following the law. Both leave men in want, and "come short of the glory (Greek, *doxa*—due honor)[956] of GOD."[957] Scripture (Romans, chapter two) tells us that Jews who maintain that they can live by and under the law will ultimately be judged by the very law which they are unable to keep unto perfection. Therefore, the law will judge and condemn them. Gentiles who don't ascribe to the law, but who have lived according to their conscience and their opinions will also be judged and perish, for though they didn't know the law, they could not live a perfect life either.

The Believer recognizes his vile condition and inability to do anything to save himself, and so in desperation he or she cries out for a Savior.[958] And when the cry comes from the depths of ones' heart, the person will find one waiting.[959]

The soul can best be described as the holder of life and is often used in scripture as "life," which is why we can say that when the soul is gone from the body, life is gone from the body. The soul animates the body. It uses the body's senses in exploration and expression. It is the natural mind from which feelings, thoughts, and emotions are created, and from where man's choices are born. Sin for example, is born in the mind.

Both animals and man have a soul which is stimulated and influenced by what the individual comes in contact with. The soul is intrinsically connected with the physical body. It is stimulated by its surroundings and by the five senses whether good, bad, positive, or negative. Like the animals which have a soul but no spirit, the soul gives us our survival instinct as well as our physical inclinations. It possesses a carnal nature and has carnal appetites. Without the governorship of the spirit it roams unbridled.

Left on its own—without the Holy Spirit's indwelling—the natural man obeys the natural senses wherein the soul will often override the spirit and take dominion. Sin is the net result of the soul dominating the spirit, rather than the spirit dominating the soul.

Our soul and its cohort, the flesh, are in a constant war for supremacy against our spirit.[960] Only when the Holy Spirit indwells a believer does that individual's spirit become infinitely greater: even greater than demonic spirits which seek to draw men away from GOD.[961]

> "Dearly beloved, I beseech you as strangers and pilgrims, abstain from fleshly lusts, which war against the soul..." (1 Peter 2:11)

---

956 Thayer Greek-English Lexicon, 4th Edit., Baker House (Gk. #1391, p. 155)
957 Romans 3:23
958 Luke 18:13
959 Jeremiah 29:13
960 Galatians 5:17
961 1 John 4:4

The flesh is the third member of the human trinity. It is corruptible (subject to decay), having a limited duration and an expiration date. It is the accomplice of the soul and will serve the soul unless the Holy Spirit has been endowed to the individual and the individual has given it dominion. To the believer it is said,

> "Ye are of God, little children, and have overcome them: because greater is he (the Holy Spirit) that is in you, than he (Satan) that is in the world." (1 John 4:4)

40

THE THREE DEATHS; PHYSICAL, SPIRITUAL, ETERNAL

The Bible speaks of three kinds of death. The first we all know; that being the physical death of ones' body, but the scriptures also speak of two other forms of death. The second type of death is referred to as "spiritual death." If one has not received Christ as Savior and received the Holy Spirit (the Spirit of Christ), even though they are physically alive they are dead spiritually. If they were to die in that unregenerated condition they will be excluded from the family of GOD. "Now if any man have not the Spirit of Christ, he is none of His."[962]

> "Jesus answered, Verily, verily, I say unto thee, except a man be born of water and of the Spirit, he cannot enter into the kingdom of God." (John 3:5)

Spiritual death is separation from GOD for eternity. It also means being relegated to a place of torment which we have come to call Hell.[963] At the end of this present age—the Age of man—Christ will reign sovereignly for one thousand years on earth. The souls and spirits of the spiritually dead will have been held prisoners in a subterranean abyss (Hades) and will afterward be summoned and appear before GOD at the Great White Throne of judgement.[964] There, books will be open in which the record of their life was recorded. Another book, the "book of Life" which records only the names of those who have received Christ and whose sins have been expunged will also be opened. Those who are found in that book will enter into a glorious new heaven on a transformed earth. Those not found in the book of life and having no mediator and without an atonement having been made for their sins, will hear a verdict of guilty pronounced over them. Their former bodies will rise from the grave and with their soul and spirit they will be cast into an indescribable place of agony, the Lake of Fire.[965] As they had

---

962 Romans 8:9
963 Deuteronomy 32:22; Psalm 9:17; Isaiah 5:14; Matthew 5:22; 10:28; Luke 16:23
964 Revelation 20:11
965 Revelation 20:10, 14

once died physically they now are now officially declared dead spiritually. This the Bible refers to as the "second death."[966]

> "And death and hell were cast into the lake of fire. This is the second death. And whosoever was not found written in the book of life was cast into the lake of fire." (Revelation 20:14-15)

Each of us has been afforded a time—we call a lifetime—in which to find and accept our Savior and avoid spiritual death.

> "My Spirit shall not always strive with man, for that he is also as flesh: yet his days shall be a hundred and twenty years." (Genesis 6:3)

> Note: A maximum of 120 years.

> "The days of our years are threescore years and ten; and if by reason of strength they be fourscore years, yet is their strength labour and sorrow; for it is soon cut off, and we fly away." (Psalm 90:10)

> Note: An average life expectancy.

The third type of death spoken of in the Scriptures is "eternal death." It is referred to as such because it is endless. It begins immediately after physical death if one dies without having accepted Christ as their Savior (spiritual dead). At the moment the fate of the individual is sealed forever. There is no appeal, no reprieve, no amnesty, no second chance. The mortal body, along with their soul and spirit[967] will be relegated to a never ending, indescribable place of torment.[968]

> "And as it is appointed unto men once to die, but after this the judgment..." (Hebrews 9:27)

Pertaining to the pious who have depended on their religion to save them, the Lord said, "Many will say to me in that day, Lord, Lord, have we not prophesied in thy name? and in thy name have cast out devils? and in thy name done many wonderful works? And then will I profess unto them, I never knew you: depart from me, ye that work iniquity."[969]

> "Then shall he say also unto them on the left hand, Depart from me, ye cursed, into everlasting fire, prepared for the devil and his angels..." (Matthew 25:41)

---

966 Revelation 20:14
967 1 Corinthians 15:53
968 Revelation 20:15; Matthew 25:41
969 Matthew 7:22-23

The alternative of course is to receive the Savior while He may be found and join Him in His glorious heaven on earth forever.[970]

"He that believeth on the Son hath everlasting life: and he that believeth not the Son shall not see life; but the wrath of God abideth on him." (John 3:36)

"Seek ye the Lord while he may be found, call ye upon him while he is near..." (Isaiah 55:6)

---

[970] Revelation 21:1–22:5

41

HELL AND BEYOND

"For the wrath of God is revealed from heaven against all ungodliness and unrighteousness of men, who hold the truth in unrighteousness..." (Romans 1:18)

"The war is real, the battle hot and the time is short...to the FIGHT!!!" (Image Source: Artist, Geoffrey Grider. www.NowTheEndBegins.com)

The most neglected and avoided subject in the Bible is the one which needs to be squarely confronted. The prospect that a place of torment such as is described in Scripture could exist causes the mind to recoil in denial. However, we need to understand that a God who loves HIS creation as our GOD does, would do everything possible without infringing on an individual's free choice to keep that individual from the punishment his sins impose on him and what the Law prescribes. To this end GOD speaks nearly as much in Scripture about the existence of hell (the lake of fire,) as HE does of HIS glorious heaven. What Yahusha-Jesus said to his disciples about the splendors of heaven, "if it were not so, I would have told you,"[971] might just as easily be said of the horror that await the damned.

Even those who believe in the New Testament Jesus and accept the fact that there is a place of torment, have a difficult time believing that the God who loves HIS creation enough to allow His Son to die for it, could be the same God that created a place of eternal punishment and who would resign souls to it. But just as the weight of our sin escapes us, so does the consequence. We are but to believe HIS Word, and to accept that Hell exists.

Religious leaders of virtually all belief systems tend to avoid the subject, either because they have never studied it, find it too foreboding, or simply refuse to believe the Lord would allow such a place to exist. The alternative is for them to gloss over the subject, deny its existence, or formulate non-biblical opinions such as these:

1. Some believe their religion is the one true faith. They believe men have been given the authority to forgive sin through the provisions of confession, penance, or on their death bed by a contrived sacrament of absolution they call extreme unction.

2. Some believe that simply believing in Jesus is enough. They have no idea what the term being "born again" means and what a spiritual birth is.

3. Some believe their birthright is their legacy to heaven; supported by good works, prayer, and observances.

4. There are also individuals who have difficulty accepting the authority of Scripture. They often dismiss the possibility of Hell based upon the presumption that if Hell does exist, it is only for the truly evil. They argue that reasonably good people don't go to Hell.

5. Some say GOD is love, and a loving God would never send the ordinary man to such a place as described in the scriptures.

6. Some teach reincarnation, and that man is in some perpetual cycle until his essence becomes united with the universe or he reaches a god-like state of perfection.

7. Universalism teaches that eventually all humankind will, regardless of their religion, be saved and enter into heaven—claiming Christ died for everyone.

8. And lastly, there are those who simply reject the existence of Hell, believing that when you die it is over. There is no afterlife.

---

[971] John 14:2

In the final analysis, Hell remains an enigma to most people by demonic design, aided and abetted by religious leaders who will not teach the Scriptures.

> "And fear not them which kill the body, but are not able to kill the soul: but rather fear him which is able to destroy both soul and body in hell." (Matthew 10:28)

In describing the torments of the damned, even words like terror and horror are not graphic enough. Only by the word "fire" are we able to get even a sense of the pain and agony that awaits those who have refused HIS grace. Should one find himself standing before the Great White Throne of judgment and hear a verdict pronounced over him that he is sentenced to the Lake, it will be too late to plead, "Have Mercy upon me, Lord!" Once the sentence is issued, there will be no appeal.[972]

> "And as it is appointed unto men once to die, but after this the judgment..." (Hebrews 9:27)

The following passages speak of the "Lake of Fire" as the "second death." It is the fate of all who will not recognize their sins, repented and accepted GOD's only provision—Yahusha (Savior).

> "Depart from Me, ye cursed into everlasting fire prepared for the devil and his angels." (Matthew 25:4)

> "And the devil that deceived them was cast into the lake of fire and brimstone, where the beast and the false prophet are, and shall be tormented day and night for ever and ever." (Revelation 20:10)

> "As therefore the tares are gathered and burned in the fire; so shall it be in the end of this world. The Son of man shall send forth his angels, and they shall gather out of his kingdom all things that offend, and them which do iniquity; and shall cast them into a furnace of fire: there shall be wailing and gnashing of teeth. Then shall the righteous shine forth as the sun in the kingdom of their Father. Who hath ears to hear, let him hear." (Matthew 13:40-43)

If at this moment you are gripped by a holy fear,[973] then you can believe that it is GOD the Holy Spirit beckoning you to respond.

> "And others (will be) save with fear (of hell), pulling them (escaping) out of the fire..." (Jude 23)

---

972 Revelation 20:11
973 Jude 23

"Behold, I (Yahusha-Jesus) stand at the door, and knock: if any man hear My voice, and open the door, I will come in to him, and will sup with him, and he with me." (Revelation 3:20)

"...behold, now is the accepted time; behold, now is the day of salvation." (2 Corinthians 6:2; Isaiah 49:8)

> Note: The terms Sheol in the Old Testament and Hades in the New Testament never refer to the eternal state of punishment; therefore, these words should not be translated into the word hell. Hell properly refers to the eternal state of punishment described as the Lake of fire, or Gehenna. English dictionaries incorrectly define Hell as Sheol or Hades, often as an abode of evil spirits. A clear distinction should be made between Hades (a place of internment)[974] prior to the Great White Throne judgement, and the eternal punishment in Gehenna (Hell).

There are eight Hebrew and Greek words translated "hell" and "grave" in Scripture:

1. Sheol—world of the dead—as subterranean (used as Hell: incorrectly)[975]

2. Hades—place of departed souls—grave (used as Hell: incorrectly)[976]

3. Tartaroo—place of eternal torment (used of Hell: correctly)[977]

4. Gehenna/Ge-Hinnnom—place of everlasting punishment—lake of fire (used as Hell: correctly)[978]

5. Geber—the grave or sepulcher[979]

6. Limnen tou puros—eternal lake of burning (used of Hell: correctly)[980]

7. Qeber/Qeburah—sepulcher—grave[981]

8. Mnaymion—pertaining to the grave[982]

---

974 Luke 16:22-28
975 *Strong's Exhaustive Concordance*, Heb., #7585
976 *Strong's Exhaustive Concordance*, Gk., #86
977 *Strong's Exhaustive Concordance*, Gk., #5020
978 *Strong's Exhaustive Concordance*, Gk., #1067
979 *Strong's Exhaustive Concordance*, Heb., #6913
980 *Strong's Exhaustive Concordance*, Gk., #3041-#4451
981 *Strong's Exhaustive Concordance*, Heb., #6900
982 *Strong's Exhaustive Concordance*, Gk., #3419

Each word clearly differentiates the place or subject to which it is being applied so there is no doubt as to its meaning. Having said this, the Bible exhausts human language in describing Heaven and Hell. The former is more glorious, the latter more horrifying than even the language of scripture is capable of expressing.

> Note: Misapplication of Scripture. There are some (as with Seventh Day Adventists) who teach that at the end of the one thousand years, GOD will utterly destroy (Greek, *katesthio*) the flesh, soul, and spirit of all those who were not found in the Book of Life. They draw their conclusion largely from Malachi chapter four which speaks of the destruction of the ungodly. They err in perceiving that the "great and dreadful day of the Lord"[983] refers to the Great White Throne Judgment when instead it refers to the Second Coming (the return) of the Lord. It is descriptive of the battle of Armageddon. It is spoken of as well in Ezekiel 38:17-23 when flaming fire will go out before Christ and His army, consuming (destroying in the flesh) all that opposed Israel on that day and on that battleground. It is also referenced in Revelation 19: 14-19. The burning up spoken of in Malachi refers to the bodily destruction of GOD's enemies at Armageddon; the "devouring" of these enemies spoken of in Revelation 20:9-10 is post-millennial. The word "devoured" (Greek, *katestho*), if translated into today's English would mean to eat—as in consume His enemies; not permanently obliterate them.

At the end of Christ's millennial rein, Satan and his angels will be loosed from the abyss where they were confined after the battle of Armageddon. This same scenario is presented in Isaiah 24:21–22. Upon being loosed, Satan and his rebels will have a brief opportunity to go through the earth once more, deceiving the nations and all those who hated the strict laws of living under the Lord's theocracy. Satan's forces will briefly mobilize in the land of Gog and Magog as they did one thousand years earlier. This time they will be soundly and permanently defeated and cast (body, soul, and spirit) into the everlasting lake of fire; not to be burned up, but be tormented day and night forever in their indestructible form.[984]

"The righteous of God is as inexorable as the love of God is infallible. The love of God is not free to express itself to those who have spurned Jesus Christ. Their torment is not a momentary one, for it is described as continuing forever; literally into the 'age of ages,' the strongest expression of eternity of which the Greek is capable. To emphasize the idea of continued suffering, they are declared to have no rest day or night…. their torment is not interrupted when repentance is too late. How dangerous it is for men to trifle with false religion, which dishonors the incarnate Word and contradicts the written Word."[985]

---

983 Malachi 4:5
984 2 Thessalonians 1:9; Isaiah 66:22-24; Matthew 25:41; Mark 9:41-49; Revelation 14:9-11; 20:11-15
985 John F. Walvoord, *The Revelation of Jesus Christ - a Commentary*, p. 219

42
THE SUBSTITUTE

The Substitute

You live in a country with exceptionally strict laws and where the law is carried out to the letter.

One day you are driving your car when the traffic light turns yellow. You are in a hurry and instead of slowing down you accelerate, and the light turns red. At that very moment a six-year-old girl is rushing to get to school and darts out into the street in front of you. You slam on your brakes, but to no avail. Your car hits the child and she is killed.

You are arraigned on manslaughter. The court has appointed you an attorney and the two of you appear before the magistrate. You tell your story and your attorney makes an appeal for leniency. The judge listens to both of you and then looks down at an open Law book in front of him; a Law book which he has vowed to uphold. A moment goes by. The judge lifts his head and looks up. His eyes are fixed on you, and he begins to speak.

"Sir, I believe your story, but we have strict laws concerning manslaughter. You admitted accelerating and going through a red light. Our law requires, 'an eye for an eye and a tooth for a tooth.' The child died and therefore according to our law, a life must be forfeited for her life. I have no choice; the law is the law. In three days, you will be hung by the neck until you are dead."

You are taken away to death row. After two days your lawyer comes to your prison cell and says that he has a plan to save your life. He will plea bargain for your soul.

He gets you a stay of execution on a legal technicality. The day of your appeal arrives, and your lawyer presents his case.

"Your Honor, we are not here to argue the merits of the law, for we understand the law is irrevocable. However, in reading the law it only stipulates 'an eye for an eye;' or in this case, a death for a death. It does not say who has to die. So Your Honor, I am willing to take this man's sentence. I wish to be executed in his place."

Silence descends over the courtroom like a shroud. The judge peers down at the Law book again and carefully reviews the familiar law.

After what seems like an eternity, he looks up and directly into your eyes and speaks. "It seems your attorney is correct. He has made an offer which I cannot refuse. Are you willing to allow this innocent man to take your sentence and be hung in your stead?"

The room again grows eerily quiet. You are confounded by what the attorney has just proposed and what the judge is allowing. A hundred thoughts race through your mind, settling on a question: If I say yes, this innocent man will die and I will be set free, for under the law one cannot be tried twice for the same crime. But how can I allow this wonderful man to die for me? It is unfathomable that he would make such an offer… yet I heard his words with my own ears.

The judge breaks the silence once more. "Mister, I need an answer; it is up to you? Give me your answer."

If you answer yes, the punishment for your crime—your sin is transferred to another. He dies and you live. Can you say yes? Will you say yes? Yahusha-Jesus wants you to say yes! The moment you do He has already done it when he hung on a Cross two thousand years ago! His last words just before He died are just as relevant now as they were then, "it is finished!"[986]

> Note: The last words uttered by the Yahusha-Jesus before He died on the Cross were, "It is finished." He was not referring to the end of His life or ministry, but what He accomplished and completed by His substitutionary sufferings and death for you!

We speak of "the finished work of Christ"[987] because there is nothing left to be done to provide man with salvation but to accept it by faith. The work of GOD in Christ is a once-and-for-all offer for "whosoever will."[988]

Provisionally speaking, it provided redemption "for all."[989] It is an opportunity of reconciliation "for every man"[990] and "for the world."[991] His life for ours was the propitiation (the appeasement of GOD's justice for the sins of men).[992] It is the provision in the law[993] for the sins of every person who by faith accepts it.[994]

"Look unto me, and be ye saved, all the ends of the earth: for I am God, and there is none else." (Isaiah 45:22)

---

986 John 19:30
987 John 17:4
988 John 3:16
989 1 Timothy 2:6
990 Hebrews 2:9
991 2 Corinthians 5:19
992 Habakkuk 1:13
993 Isaiah 1:18
994 1 John 2:2

43

THE CONTEST FOR YOUR SOUL

"For we wrestle not against flesh and blood, but against principalities, against powers, against the rulers of the darkness of this world, against spiritual wickedness in high places." (Ephesians 6:12)

If you pause to consider that since the fall of man the earth has been largely controlled by Satan[995] then you can better understand famine, disease, hate, murder, war, depravity, and mans' inhumanity to man.

Man finds himself as it were on the chess board of life; on the playing field called earth. Two competitors, Yahusha-Jesus and Satan, vie for each chess piece. Whether one is a pawn or a king; whether one is a bishop or a queen, he or she occupies a space on this board.

As in the game of chess there are rules to be followed. One rule is that Satan can take any unprotected piece which randomly moves into the open. Another rule is, if a man seeks GOD with all his heart, GOD will sacrifice a substitutionary chess piece (Yahusha-Jesus) for that pawn, rook, knight, bishop, king, or queen. GOD then puts that human chess piece in a safe position where he or she remains for the remainder of the game. Without Yahusha-Jesus we are destined to be taken by Satan. With Yahusha we are destined to be saved!

The War We Face

One should be aware that during each dispensation GOD has dealt with man differently. It would be a process of educating him in order to bring him into a full and right relationship.

During Old Testament times Jews were instructed in obedience to GOD, and so Law was put in place, and with it the need for atonement. After Christ came, His atonement made those Jews and Gentiles who accepted Him justified in the eyes of the Father and placed them under another covenant; a covenant of Grace.

It wasn't long however, after the Apostle Paul taught that we are "justified by faith without the deeds of the law,"[996] that teachers from within the foundling Church began perverting the

---
995 Job 1:12
996 Romans 3:28

gospel of Grace and lead gullible believers into heresy.[997] We now have a name for this spurious facsimile of Christianity, for it pompously adopted its name from the capital city and the empire from which it evolved. It has abandoned "costly grace" and taught its followers that sin is easily absolved with a confession, apology, and a prayer.

Scripturally speaking, the pardon of sin has always existed, but it is GOD, not man, who forgives, and who does not require a human interloper. The only meditator between GOD and man is GOD our Savior. "For there is one God, and one mediator between God and men, the man Christ Jesus…"[998]

Pardon has always been based on justice: "an eye for an eye," a human for a human, a Savior for a sinner. In contrast, those who claim to have the power to absolve a person of their sins have made the grace of GOD of no effect by denying the totality of what Lord Jesus accomplished on the Cross.[999] They have in essence replaced Him, for they have taken on the role of mediator between GOD and man and fabricated their own rules and requirements by which one can attain heaven. They claim to possess the keys to the Kingdom of heaven, when in reality the keys they hold fit the keyhole of the gate of a subterranean prison.

The Bible teaches that in so far as salvation is concerned, we are to "earnestly contend for the faith…"[1000] A contender, as with a prizefighter, is one who fights doggedly to win the prize. Jesus made this exceedingly clear when He said, "And from the days of John the Baptist (who was still within the confines of the O.T dispensation) until now, the kingdom of heaven hath suffered violence (satanic attacks), and the violent (those who are desperate to attain heaven) take it by force (press in with all determination to assure their destiny)."[1001]

> "Wherefore, my beloved, as ye have always obeyed, not as in my presence only, but now much more in my absence, work out your own salvation with fear and trembling."
> (Philippians 2:12)

Satan has been resolute in his efforts to keep men from seeking and finding their Savior.[1002] He has an arsenal of weaponry with which he distracts and dissuades. Using the pleasures of life, the cares of this world, and a host of other fascinations—he dangles them in front of our noses as a carrot before a donkey. But by far, his favorite and most successful tool is religion. Religion is Satan's placebo, and like a placebo it does nothing. The unwary and trusting, believing the religious pill they have been handed is the authentic, swallow it. And of course, it has no effect.

Like a spider, Satan and his human minions inject poison (false doctrine) into the captives caught in their web. Once entangled, victims are first anesthetized, then paralyzed, and afterward consumed.

---

997 Acts 20:28-32
998 1 Timothy 2:5
999 Galatians 5:4
1000 Jude 3
1001 Matthew 11:12
1002 1 Peter 5:8

The man or woman who stakes their hope in religion is placated and unlikely to study GOD's Word for themselves wherein they would see the disparity between heresy and truth. Only those desperate (violent) enough to shake off the stupor of the drug (heretical doctrine), turn from the sin which so easily besets them,[1003] accepts the Savior and strives to live a sanctified life—will ultimately enter the kingdom of heaven.[1004]

So long as man is kept distracted and absorbed with earthly things, he is not likely to "earnestly contend for the faith which was once delivered to the saints."[1005] The man or woman who has accumulated so much wealth that they can afford virtually anything they want and who are consumed with the treats and toys of the world has, in all likelihood, been left unhindered by Satan. The Deceiver (Satan) is careful not to rock the canoe of the passive with adversity as this might otherwise cause them to seek and find their Savior; for they are already on their way to a Christless grave.

> "And again I say unto you, It is easier for a camel to go through the eye of a needle, than for a rich man to enter into the kingdom of God." (Matthew 19:24)

The same applies to the man or woman preoccupied with sports and entertainment or any one of a thousand seemingly benign pursuits.

> "And the cares of this world, and the deceitfulness of riches, and the lusts of other things entering in, choke the word, and it becometh unfruitful." (Mark 4:19)

The Lord made it clear that obtaining heaven is not for the passive, but the desperate. The Truth (the Word) has been under attack since Eve had her first encounter with Satan, but all the more since Jesus made his debut, brought us the truth and purchased our redemption. Yes, only the violent: those who press in and are desperate to be saved, will indeed be saved!

1003 Hebrews 12:1
1004 Galatians 5:16-21
1005 Jude 3

44

THE REAL ENEMY: SATAN

> "For we wrestle not against flesh and blood, but against principalities, against the rulers of darkness of this world, against spiritual wickedness in high places." (Ephesians 6:12)

To understand the real enemy of the Jewish people, we need to understand who Satan is. To understand the "whys and wherefores" of their tumultuous past, we need to recognize who Satan is. To understand the fast-approaching threat to Israel and the real and present danger, we need to recognize Satan's role in orchestrating Israel's next holocaust.

Be assured that Satan is not some hideous cloven-footed beast with horns; an impression taken from pagan mythology. He is not some ill-defined spiritual being who oversees hell, waiting for the wicked to check in at his subterranean desk. Quite the contrary: scripture paints a different picture when it refers to him as "the prince of the powers of the air,"[1006] "the god of this world,"[1007] and "an angel of light."[1008]

Since the fall of Adam and for a limited time, Satan has by default been given dominion over our planet. In his capacity as interim governor he is constantly influencing and to a large extent controlling "the children of disobedience."[1009] Yahusha-Jesus speaking to these children of disobedience, "You are of your father the devil, and the desires of your father you want to do. He was a murderer from the beginning, and does not stand in the truth, because there is no truth in him. When he speaks a lie, he speaks from his own resources, for he is a liar and the father of it."[1010]

Know Your Enemy

Military officers' study historic battles and tactics at war colleges. So too does the wise general who expects to confront a particular enemy commander study his opponent.

[1006] Ephesians 2:2
[1007] 2 Corinthians 4:4
[1008] 2 Corinthians 11:14
[1009] Ephesians 2:2
[1010] John 8:44

While engaged in an epic tank battle with Germany's Field Marshal Erwin Rommel in North Africa during World War II; U.S. Army General George S. Patton, sensing victory as he peered at the battlefield from his command post, and referring to Rommel's book, *Infanterie Greift An* (Infantry Attacks), was purported to have said, "Rommel, you magnificent bastard, I read your book."

Patton had studied his adversary and subsequently won the day. Even today this book is required reading by all Marine Corps NCOs and officers. Should we not study our enemy, his objectives and tactics from the one and only book which exposes him?

Here is a historic synopsis from Scripture about our adversary: In a distant age, in eternity past, well before Adam and Eve made their debut on earth, a rebellion took place in the heavens. In creating HIS angels, GOD made one of them exceptional. He was given the name Lucifer, meaning "the son of the morning or light bearer," and he was given the rank of archangel. His task was to hover over the throne of GOD not unlike a halo.

We are told in Ezekiel 28:11–19 that he was perfect in beauty, full of wisdom, robed in every precious stone; even having a magnificent voice. He was the epitome of perfection—that is until the day when pride and envy began to grow inside him.[1011]

He became so smitten with himself that he believed he deserved the exaltation and adulation that his Creator alone deserves. Driven by envy and using his rank and superior intelligence he was able to persuade one third of heaven's angels into following him in an insurrection against GOD.[1012]

> "For thou (Lucifer) hast said in thy heart, I will ascend into heaven, I will exalt my throne above the stars of GOD: I will sit also upon the mountain of the congregation, in the sides of the north: I will ascend above the heights of the clouds; I will be like the most High." (Isaiah 14:13-14)

In the end the rebellion failed as only it could have and those same angelic beings were cast out of heaven and from the presence of Almighty GOD.[1013] Their fate was forever sealed and their destiny is to be consigned to a lake of fire for all eternity.[1014]

It was at the onset of the rebellion that Lucifer was given a new name, Satan—which is to say Adversary.[1015] Though he no longer has his position in heaven, he still has not been completely constrained. He has been permitted to go "to and fro" between heaven and earth accusing the brethren (those in Christ) when they slip and sin.[1016] It is then that he is reminded—that Jesus has already purchased them and that their sins were washed away by His indelible precious blood.

1011 Ezekiel 28:13-15
1012 Revelation 12:4
1013 Revelation 12:9
1014 Revelation 12:7-9; 20:10-14; Matthew 25:41
1015 Job 1:6
1016 Job 1:7; Revelation 12:10; Luke 22:31

> "Be sober, be vigilant; because your adversary the devil, as a roaring lion, walketh about, seeking whom he may devour..." (1 Peter 5:8)

With Satan's superior intelligence which dwarfs that of humans, those who have no knowledge or understanding of Scripture and who are not indwelled with the Holy Spirit are no match for this nefarious immortal.

It is my personal belief, though not stated in the Bible, that it is GOD's intention to replace the one-third of heaven's fallen angels with loving, faithful, and obedient men and women. Men and women that GOD can be assured would never rebel. By giving man the same opportunity that was afforded the angels to either love and remain faithful to HIM, or to disregard HIM and be independent, all creation becomes a witness to GOD's fairness and impartiality.

Like the angels, GOD has given man free will and the liberty to choose who he will serve and who he will worship. Will he choose to serve *El ELYON* (the Most High GOD),[1017] or will he turn against his Creator, follow Satan's example, and serve himself?

> "No man can serve two masters: for either he will hate one, and love the other; or else he will hold to one and despise the other. You cannot serve GOD and mammon (man or self)." (Matthew 6:24)

1017 Genesis 14:18; Psalm 78:35

45

KILL THE MESSIAH

From Egypt's pharaohs to Europe's kings, to the tyrannical dictators of the last century, the Jewish people have been subject to endless persecution. Such hatred defies human logic but serves to illustrate the power and influence Satan has over men. How mystifying indeed (were it not for demonic influence) that many of those persecutors are thought to have come from those claiming to be followers of the Jewish Messiah.

Satan knows the scriptures better than any human who has ever lived. He knows that according to Genesis 3:15 he has already been defeated by the atoning work of the Messiah. He knows his fate as predicted in Revelation 20:10 is to be cast into the dreaded Lake of Fire for eternity. Perhaps in a state of denial he clings to the faint hope that if he can change just one predicted event, he can somehow change his destiny.

Could he stop the Messiah from ever being born by destroying the Jewish people and the seed line of David?[1018] Could he destroy the Messiah once He was born?[1019] Could he cause Him to fail in His redemptive plan by causing Him to sin?[1020] All his efforts have met with failure; but in desperation he continues to try.

Long ago, in order to keep the Messiah from ever being born Satan attempted to exterminate the Hebrew race through which the Savior was promised to come.[1021] To accomplish this he prompted an Egyptian pharaoh to destroy all Hebrew male infants—of which Moses was one.[1022] However, GOD's plan cannot be altered. Just as GOD would divinely protect the infant Moses, so too would he protect the infant Yahusha-Jesus.[1023]

Soon after the Messiah was born, Satan attempted to have the infant slain while He was yet a toddler. To that end he would use a Roman client king of Judea named Herod to put out an edict to slaughter all Jewish males in Bethlehem less than three years of age.[1024] When

---

1018 Exodus 1:22
1019 Matthew 2:16; Acts 7:19
1020 Mark 1:13
1021 Genesis 12:3
1022 Exodus 1:22; Deuteronomy 18:15
1023 Matthew 2:16
1024 Matthew 2:12-18; Jeremiah 31:15-17

Satan's attempt failed, and some thirty years later Yahusha rose from the dead and the plan of redemption went into effect, Satan wanted revenge.

Having failed in all his attempts to prevent Yahusha-Jesus from fulfilling His destiny, Satan sought retribution. Knowing how dear to GOD's heart the Jewish people are,[1025] Satan directed his hatred against them by having an endless succession of kings, emperors, and tyrants persecute them. However, his greatest retaliatory achievement has not been in persecuting them, but rather in keeping them from discovering their Yahusha and seeing their souls eternally lost.

1025 Deuteronomy 32:10

46

DECEIVER, DISTRACTOR, DISSUADER

Permit me to review some of Satan's successes.

By substituting the name Jesus instead of Yahusha in the New Testament, Satan has separated the Old Testament references to Yahusha from the New Testament personage of Jesus. This makes it expedient to deny that they are one and the same! Imagine how many Jewish people might have been inclined to accept Jesus of the New Testament and the message of salvation had His name been retained in the Hebrew, Yahusha? By using the name Jesus instead of Yahusha, the prefix Yah (GOD) is lost, and with it His divinity!

Satan has managed to deceive GOD's people by having them believe that their persecutors were genuine Christians—and that genuine Christianity is synonymous with Catholicism!

He has put into question the divine authorship and authority of the Hebrew Holy Scriptures, giving them parity with other writings (e.g., the Talmud) or relegating them to a book of stories and platitudes!

He has counterfeited the Bible with scores of modern versions (variations) which are replete with omissions and which cast doubt on the Savior's divinity and other foundations of our faith!

He has been successful by convincing the Jewish people, largely through their rabbis, that their Messiah has not yet appeared, despite the overwhelming evidence provided in the Scriptures which identifies Him!

He has convinced man that good deeds, tithing, philanthropic giving, prayers, and an alternate atonement can absolve their sins and that all decent people go to heaven!

He has managed to convince Jews that believing in Jesus the Christ is not Jewish!

He has been able to keep man distracted; absorbed and enticed with the pleasures, cares, and concerns of this fleeting experience we call life with hardly any thought as to where he will spend eternity!

He has used religion to replace relationship!

He has been able to keep man from realizing that GOD has extended him a personal invitation to join HIM forever in the promised New Covenant of the New Testament!

"But if our gospel be hid, it is hid to them that are lost: In whom the god of this world (Satan) hath blinded the minds of them which believe not, lest the light of the glorious gospel of Christ, who is the image (stature—Hebrew, *eikon*) of God, should shine unto them." (2 Corinthians 4:3-4)

47

DOUBT, DISTRUST, DISBELIEF

In an article entitled, "Why I believe Jesus Christ is my Jewish Messiah," Bible teacher and author Arnold Ross elaborated on what scripture tells us.

> "The Bible is GOD's message to man. Holy men of GOD spoke as they were led by the Holy Spirit. The Bible is a spiritual book. You understand it, you get GOD's message only as the Holy Spirit of GOD opens it to you. Because of disbelief in divine authorship of our Holy Scriptures, neither our rabbis nor their followers could recognize their Messiah when He came. Neither could they grasp the message and guidance GOD gives through our prophets so that we can recognize our Messiah."

The natural man with his soulish instincts has the tendency to reject that which constrains him. In its place he gives ascent to his own thoughts and opinions which supersede GOD's injunctions. If he recognizes the Bible at all, it is more as a general guide rather than the literal, emphatic, and all-inclusive message from GOD to men. This gives the natural man the freedom to interpret it however he chooses and to live accordingly.

Subscribing to ones' own suppositions as it concerns matters of faith is itself an admission of ones' disbelief in GOD's authorship of the written Word. On the other hand, if one can say that he believes that GOD has indeed spoken, and that man has indeed recorded it, then he has no other choice but to disregard the teachings and conclusions of dissenting philosophers.

> "Because that, when they knew God, they glorified him not as God, neither were thankful; but became vain in their imaginations, and their foolish heart was darkened. Professing themselves to be wise, they became fools..." (Romans 1:21-22)

It was quite deliberate that GOD began HIS written Word with an illustration of just how vulnerable we are to Satan's most successful ploy; planting a seed of doubt. Satan's methodology has not changed; create doubt, misquote, or deny. By a mere inference, the changing of a single word or by a false assertion, the truth is put into question.

In man's first encounter with Satan in the Garden of Eden, the deceiver's first objective was to create doubt by asking Eve, "Yea, hath God said?" Once he had planted the seed of doubt his next step was to misquote GOD's word, "Yea ye shall not surely die." Then, he would introduce a lie, "…then your eyes will be opened, and ye shall be as gods."[1026] It is also worth noting that Eve responded by repeating GOD's command not to eat of the fruit but then added, "neither shall ye touch it, lest ye die."

> "Now the serpent was more subtle than any beast of the field which the Lord God had made. And he said unto the woman, Yea, hath God said, Ye shall not eat of every tree of the garden? (the misquote of verse 16) And the woman said unto the serpent, We may eat of the fruit of the trees of the garden: but of the fruit of the tree which is in the midst of the garden, God hath said, Ye shall not eat of it, neither shall ye touch it, lest ye die (GOD's true Word). And the serpent said unto the woman, Ye shall not surely die (the lie): for God doth know that in the day ye eat thereof, then your eyes shall be opened, and ye shall be as gods (another lie), knowing good and evil." (Genesis 3:1-5)

In a similar fashion, Satan has succeeded in deceiving the Jewish people, Catholics, and the world at large. They, like innocent and trusting Eve have been persuaded into believing the lie that the Bible is less than divine, less than complete, and less than emphatic.

> "As for God, his way is perfect; the word of the Lord is tried: he is a buckler to all them that trust in him." (2 Samuel 22:31)

Indeed, the Word of GOD is tried, and all He does is perfect. Though mans' interpretation of GOD's Word is subject to error, the Bible remains inerrant and is our clearest and most objective means of hearing the voice of GOD.[1027]

A key strategy of Satan is to get men to trust and accept the teachings of men—rather than the teachings of the Bible.

Hear what GOD spoke to the Prophet Jeremiah centuries ago, for it remains just as applicable today.

> "My people hath been lost sheep: their shepherds have caused them to go astray, they have turned them away on the mountains: they have gone from mountain to hill, they have forgotten their resting place." (Jeremiah 50:6)

By using shepherds to dismiss or refute what is so apparent in Scripture, Satan has managed to keep the Jewish people from even considering, much less accepting their Messiah. It is the religious teacher who is the most culpable for causing disparity between the Jews who don't believe in

---

[1026] Genesis 3:5
[1027] Romans 15:4; 2 Timothy 3:16-17; Hebrews 4:12

their Messiah and those who do. The fear of being labeled as a *Meshumodim* (traitor), ostracized, or spoken of as dead has caused many Jews from publicly proclaiming Yahusha-Jesus as their Messiah. With regard to salvation, Satan uses religion to complicate what is fundamentally simple.

> "But I fear, lest by any means, as the serpent beguiled Eve through his subtilty, so your minds should be corrupted from the simplicity that is in Christ." (2 Corinthians 11:3)

> "That if thou shalt confess with thy mouth the Lord Jesus, and shalt believe in thine heart that GOD hath raised Him from the dead, thou shalt be saved. For with the heart man believeth unto righteousness; and with the mouth confession is made unto salvation." (Romans 10:9-10)

Yahusha-Jesus added,

> "And fear not them which kill the body, but are not able to kill the soul: but rather fear HIM which is able to destroy both soul and body in hell....Whosoever therefore shall confess Me before men, him will I confess before My Father which is in heaven. But whosoever will deny Me (Yahusha) before men, him will I also deny before My Father which is in heaven." (Matthew 10:2, 32-33)

Early in the introduction of this book I spoke of leading you to a gate and to a narrow path, and that it would be your choice to enter in or bypass it. The Way is the path to heaven, and it is a very narrow path. There is only one "gate" (Yahusha) which one must choose to go through which puts them on this path. If you believe the enormous amount of scripture which has been presented and the witness of history, then you have come to understand that wittingly or unwittingly false teachers in sheep's clothing have succeeded in dissuading the masses.[1028] Isn't it time to break the chains that bind you? "If the Son therefore shall make you free, ye shall be free indeed."[1029]

> "Jesus saith unto him, I am the way, the truth, and the life: no man cometh unto the Father, but by me." (John 14:6)

> Note: There are Catholics who have been "born again" and are heaven bound and eternally saved. This is not because they have realized the fraud which has been perpetrated on them, or because they rejected their Catholicism, but in spite of it. Their love for Yahusha-Jesus has eclipsed their trust and dependency on their religion. Howbeit, for everyone who has become saved, there are thousands who remain content in their Catholicism and have a false sense of salvation. Consequently, their end is death.

[1028] Matthew 7:13-15
[1029] John 8:36

"There is a way which seemeth right unto a man, but the end thereof are the ways of death." (Proverbs 14:12)

The love of GOD and the work of the Holy Spirit transcends ecclesiastical boundaries just as HE transcends ethnicities and cultures. In the times of His visitations (heaven sent revivals and awakenings), whole Protestant denominations (Lutherans, Presbyterians, Methodists, and Baptists) who had become passive and indifferent to the Pentecostal experience were suddenly jolted from their pews, and all their sanctimonious dignities went out the church windows. When the Neo-Pentecostal/Charismatic movement began in the 1960s it swept through the Episcopal and Roman Catholic community as well. Caught off guard, their sanctimonious leaders were in a quandary as their formality and structure gave way to undignified expression. Fearful of losing their constituents they were forced to either to accept and join in, downplay the supernatural, or wait for the movement to pass and then resume with their theater.

To some extent the Catholic Charismatic movement was a pretense of the authentic born-again experience, as participating Catholics were never released from their beliefs and dependency on "mother church" or their fidelity to Mary their intercessor. Some did receive the Baptism of the Holy Spirit; others believing they had received it merely mimicked it. Were the baptism legitimate, and had the Holy Spirit overwhelmed them, that individual would recognize the travesty of Romanism and been set free.

48

THE PEACE PLOY AND THE NEXT HOLOCAUST!

(Image Source: SHADOW BOX)

Of the Holocaust we say, Never Again!—but that is not what Scripture says.

Satan has one more devious plan in store for the Jewish people. A plan which the prophets warned will overtake Israel after the people have returned to their ancient homeland leading up to the latter days.[1030]

It will follow a global economic recession which will leave national economies reeling and necessitate an economic reset. In many countries civil chaos will become the order of the day. A war weary world with ideological differences may be put on hold, for wars cost money. Politicians will be confounded as to what to do to set the world back on its feet. Who they will ask can solve the unsolvable? A superhuman is needed, and a superhuman will emerge.

The words attributed to Paul Henri Charles Spaak, a socialist politician, statesman, former Premier of Belgium, who was instrumental in the founding of the EEC (later the European

---

1030 Daniel 8:19, 23-25; Joel 2:1-2; Zechariah 14:2

Union) and who became Secretary-General of NATO (1957–1961) had expressed the view which will set the stage for this superhuman.

> "What we want is a man of sufficient stature to hold the alliances of all people and to lift us out of the economic morass into which we are sinking. Send us such a man, and be he god or devil, we will receive him."

The Anti-Messiah (Antichrist)

At that time, when the world is in confusion, a captivating, charismatic, and persuasive leader will arise out of the Middle East and ascend to prominence on the world stage. His platform and motives will appear to be for the good of all mankind. In reality they will profit and empower him and the global elite while making indentured servants of the people.

> "And through his policy also he shall cause craft to prosper (wealth gained by fraud) in his hand; and by peace (Hebrew, *shalvah*, catching off guard) shall (he) destroy many." (Daniel 8:25)

The New World Leader (Image Source: CRYSTAL GRAPHICS)

Advocating peace and tolerance this rising star will captivate the masses who will fall under his spell. Ascending in the hierarchy of the New World Order he will quickly be elected to the office of World leader. As chief executive he will preside over the armies and navies[1031] of a ten regional-nation confederacy.[1032]

In this global government all controversies between nations will be settled by a world parliament and world court over which he will have the final say. His decisions will be decisive and his mandates without appeal. He will gradually evolve from World leader to World dictator. Wheeling such power he will broker a concord between Israel and the Islamic nations. It will appear that the threat of war has finally been eliminated and that peace will at last have become a reality. It is this very ploy which Satan will use to lull and lure Israel into the dreaded time; the "Time of Jacob's Trouble."[1033]

> "Alas! For that day is great so that none is like it: it is even the time of Jacob's trouble..." (Jeremiah 30:7)

1031 Revelation 6:2, 4
1032 Revelation 17:12
1033 Jeremiah 30:7

The Jewish people have been taught from the Holy Scriptures that one day the Messiah will come to earth, establish His kingdom, and bring in a lasting peace—which indeed He will; however not before the false messiah makes his debut. Without having accepted the New Testament or studied the prophetic books of the Bible many will be deceived.

The single most convincing act of treachery by which this impostor will delude the Jewish people will not only be brokering a peace accord with the Muslim nations, but in granting the Jewish people permission to rebuild the Temple and to reinstate animal sacrifice.[1034] It will be this one act that will cause many Jews to see this as the fulfilment of a Messianic promise.[1035] They will ask themselves; "Could this individual then be the Messiah?" For a brief time, all will appear well.[1036]

> "Let no man deceive you by any means: for that day shall not come, except there come a falling away first (an apostasy within Christendom), and that man of sin be revealed, the son of perdition (the Antichrist); Who opposeth and exalteth himself above all that is called God, or that is worshipped; so that he as God (posing as the Messiah, and to the Muslim the Mahdi) sitteth in the Temple of God (in Jerusalem), shewing himself that he is God. Remember ye not, that, when I was yet with you, I told you these things? And now ye know what withholdeth that he might be revealed in his time. For the mystery of iniquity (that which is against GOD's laws) doth already work: only he (the empowered Spirit filled Church) who now letteth will let, until he (the true Church) be taken out of the way (the rapture of the Church). And then shall that Wicked (the Antichrist) be revealed, whom the Lord (Yahusha-Jesus) shall consume with the spirit of his mouth, and shall destroy with the brightness of His coming: Even him, (the Antichrist) whose coming is after the working of Satan with all power and signs and lying wonders, And with all deceivableness of unrighteousness in them that perish; because they (the unbelieving) received not the love of the truth, that they might be saved. And for this cause God shall send them strong delusion, that they should believe a lie (and be taken in by the Antichrist): That they all might be damned who believed not the truth, but had pleasure in unrighteousness." (2 Thessalonians 2:3-12)

Today in America's government there are scores of representatives, both Jewish and those who believe themselves to be Christians who are either oblivious to or unwilling to believe the Bible is GOD's emphatic Word. Consequently, they are globalists and support the formation of a New World Order. They will applaud the one world monetary system and in their ignorance they will support the taking of the mark of the beast.[1037] They are among the vast majority referred to in the preceding scripture of which it is said, "they receive not the truth."

1034 Daniel 9:27
1035 Malachi 3:1
1036 Matthew 24:37-38
1037 Revelation 13:16

The Time of Trouble

> "And at that time shall Michael (GOD's archangel) stand up, the great prince which standeth for the children of thy people (Israel): and there shall be a time of trouble, such as never was since there was a nation even to that same time:[1038] and at that time (at the very end) thy people (the Jewish people) shall be delivered (at Yahusha's return), every one that shall be found written in the book (book of life, through their acceptance of Yahusha)." (Daniel 12:1)

In the 38th and 39th chapter of the book that bears his name, the Prophet Ezekiel informs us of another event which will occur during the first half of the Tribulation.

Presumably in a quest for energy dominance (oil), an emboldened superpower will have alienated itself from the global union and gone rouge. Though there has been considerable debate as to who is being alluded to by their ancient names, a vast army described as coming from the north[1039] could only be the former Soviet Union. Geographically, Moscow is due north of Jerusalem.

Ezekiel tells us that the land (Israel) will be recovering from war and dwelling safely in their own land. The Temple will have been built and sacrifice reinstated when another war breaks out involving the Soviet Union and the nations the Antichrist presides over.[1040] This will be but one of three tri-continental wars that take place during that time in the Middle East.

> Note: While it seems impossible for the Temple to be built where the Al Aqsa mosque is presently situated, it will nevertheless occur, as the actual ancient Temple site is adjacent to the mosque. Still many Jews will perceive this as nothing less than a miracle of GOD, not realizing that soon after its completion it will be desecrated by this same man (Antichrist) who made it possible.[1041] Scripture tells us this will begin the final three-and-a-half years of Daniel seventieth week—the Great Tribulation; which will make the Holocaust pale by comparison.[1042]

The False Prophet

The Antichrist will have a religious collaborator (the False Prophet—the Roman Pontiff). He will extol the Antichrist as the world's savior, and like a Judas goat he will lead the multitude of Catholics who see him as GOD's representative on earth to worship this counterfeit.[1043]

There will also be many other faiths which will have come to accept the Roman pontiff as head of the World Church; especially when he performs astounding miracles. Where else will they think,

---

1038 Revelation 20:12
1039 Ezekiel 38:15
1040 Ezekiel 38:8, 14
1041 Daniel 9:27; Matthew 24:15
1042 Daniel 12:1
1043 Mark 13:5-6; Revelation 13:8, 12

could such power come from except from GOD.[1044] It will however be none other than Satan, the great deceiver, who will be the engine behind these miracles and supernatural phenomena.[1045]

At the same time, there will be at least 144,000 Jews, as well as Gentiles, who will have read the scriptures, realize what is being perpetrated, and attempt to warn others of the masquerade.[1046] These believers will be "sealed"[1047] (divinely preserved), and after they have been afforded the time in which to deliver the gospel message, they will be "caught up" to heaven in what may be termed a second rapture.[1048] This will occur before the "vials of GOD's wrath"[1049] are poured out upon the earth which occur during the second half of the seven years, referred to as the Great Tribulation.

Others, who afterward become believers (during the last three and one-half years of Daniel's seventieth week) will become tribulation saints. Many will be "overcome"[1050] by the Antichrist, and perish as martyrs.[1051] Still, some will manage to survive these last horrific judgments[1052] and the battle of Armageddon.[1053] Those who have come to believe as well as those who have not, but managed to survive, will, on the last day of the battle, witness the Lord's return.[1054]

Prior to the Tribulation, the believing Church will have been divinely removed; "caught up" to meet their Savior in the air.[1055] Having received total forgiveness and being seen as spotless in the eyes of GOD, there is no reason, nor does it serve any purpose for the Church to be left on earth and incur GOD's wrath. This brief period of forty-two months will be a time of judgment.

> "For God hath not appointed us (the genuine Church) to wrath, but to obtain salvation by our Lord Jesus Christ, Who died for us, that, whether we wake or sleep, we should live together with him. Wherefore comfort yourselves together, and edify one another, even as also ye do." (1 Thessalonians 5:9-11)

Even Now

Even now, Palestinian factions Fatah and Hamas war with Israel while Iran continues undeterred and barely unhindered in developing its nuclear capability. ISIL has had its setbacks and lost some territory, but jihadists have simply moved to neighboring regions as jihadism metastasizes throughout the world.

1044 Revelation 13:13
1045 Revelation 13:4
1046 Revelation 7:3-8
1047 Revelation 7:3-4
1048 Revelation 14:3
1049 Revelation 16:1
1050 Revelation 13:7
1051 Revelation 6:9-11; 13:15; 14:13
1052 Revelation 8:1-13
1053 Revelation 14:15-20
1054 Matthew 24:22; Zechariah 12:8-10; 13:8
1055 1 Thessalonians 4:14-18

The Middle East is becoming a "seething pot;"[1056] an indicator as to just how near we are to a rapture of the Church. Afterward will come war, and finally a peace accord will be offered in troubled times.[1057]

In the meantime, we hear the drumbeat for global peace getting louder and louder. A statue at the United Nations Headquarters in New York City depicts a man swinging a hammer, beating a sword into a plowshare. This symbolizes mans' desire to put an end to war and convert the implements of destruction into creative tools for the benefit of all.

The abbreviated scripture from Isaiah inscribed on the base of the monument will likely become a mantra of the New World Order.

"...and they shall beat our swords into plowshares, and spears into pruning hooks..."
(Isaiah 2:4)

The United Nations (Image Source: GETTY)

The problem is that this scripture is chronologically misused. It will not occur during the present dispensation. It refers to a time after Yahusha returns to earth when He has vanquished Israel's enemies and set up His earthly kingdom.[1058] It is an illusion promoted by oligarchs who seek to dominate the planet and bring in a One World Government.[1059]

1056 Jeremiah 1:13
1057 Joel chapters 1 and 2
1058 Micah 4:3
1059 Ezekiel chapters 38, 39; Joel 2:18-3:17; Zechariah 14:1-17; Revelation 16:14-17

49

PROPHECY, PROPHET, AND TEACHERS

The Lord has given us prophecies in part so that all may know that "the Lord—He is GOD," and there is none other.[1060] A second reason is so those who choose to believe His Word might know just what to expect, prepare themselves spiritually, and educate others for what lies ahead. A third reason is that in seeing prophecy unfold, men will realize the Bible is the Word of GOD and make a decision to seek and find their Savior while they still have time.[1061]

> "Surely the Lord GOD will do nothing, but HE revealeth his secret unto HIS servant the prophets." (Amos 3:7)

Sadly, there are more than a few ministers today who believe prophecy and eschatology (the study of end-time events) either irrelevant or too difficult to decipher and teach their congregants. Consequently, they circumvent the prophetic which leaves their flock in want of what GOD felt important enough to expound upon. Clearly the lack of teaching of the book of the Revelation is just one glaring example of their dereliction.

By virtue of the fact that GOD deemed it important to put literally hundreds of prophecies in HIS Word makes avoiding them a direct insult to HIM. Furthermore, those who evade prophecy cannot possibly have a command of the Scripture and do not deserve the title of teacher, rabbi or minister.

> "And this voice which came from heaven we heard, when we were with him in the holy mount. We have also a more sure word of prophecy; whereunto ye do well that ye take heed, as unto a light that shineth in a dark place, until the day dawn, and the day star arise in your hearts..." (2 Peter 1:18-19)

1060 Isaiah 45:5-6, 14; 46:9; Mark 12:32
1061 Genesis 18:17

> Note: We are told in Ephesians 4:11 that the Holy Spirit has endowed the Church with what is become known as the fivefold ministry. Two of these offices are "pastor" and "teacher." The word pastor refers to a shepherd (Hebrew, *ra'ah*) and is one who is given to care for, teach, and safeguard the flock from heresy. However, if we look closely at scripture, we see that the pastor is primarily a teacher. In the King James Bible, there is no comma after the word pastors in this scripture. This indicates that the word "teachers" is not part of the series, but rather that pastors are (or are supposed to be) the teachers.

Three times in just one verse the Lord said to Peter, "If you love Me, feed (teach) My sheep."[1062] In fact, if we look at 1 Corinthians 12:28, which also speaks of the ministries of the Church we see that the office of the pastor is omitted, and the office of the teacher has replaced it. While a teacher is not necessarily a pastor, as he may not have direct oversight of a flock, the pastor must always be—first and foremost—a teacher. The two offices (pastor and teacher) are nearly identical; teachers teach truth and pastors preach and teach the truth as they care for their wards. A shepherd who doesn't feed or know enough to feed GOD's flock isn't worthy of the office or the title.[1063] Zeal without knowledge does not qualify one for ministry any more than does knowledge without understanding.[1064]

> "Let the elders that rule well be counted worthy of double honor, especially they who labor in the Word and doctrine." (1 Timothy 5:17)

Insofar as apostles and prophets are concerned, we are told that they were provided for the establishing of the Church.[1065] Their mission was to form "the foundations" on which the Church was to be built. Now that the Word is complete and bound in a single book (the Bible) the need for the apostle is no longer necessary and has subsequently ended. Still there remains the office of the prophet; but once again, with the written Word complete the office is largely used in reassuring and encouraging the Body of Christ, or—and most important (as in ancient times)—to warn a generation to repent and return as judgment follows opportunity. Today the true prophets of GOD may be likened to the late David Wilkerson, who like Isaiah, Jeremiah, and Ezekiel were harbingers of judgment. Today prophets of GOD are few and far between, while the pseudo-prophets are plentiful.

> "If any man think himself to be a prophet, or spiritual, let him acknowledge that the things that I write unto you are the commandments of the Lord." (1 Corinthians 14:37)

The office of the prophet is still needed to guide each new generation especially when they begin to wavier and follow some new doctrine or movement. The genuine teacher brings forth

---

1062 John 21:15-17
1063 1 Peter 5:2
1064 Romans 10:2
1065 Ephesians 2:20

and gives understanding to the recorded Word and like the prophet rightly divides it.[1066] The GOD sent teacher is a defender of the Word from those who would twist and pervert it.[1067] The genuine prophets of old, the prophets of late, and the GOD appointed teachers all share the same Word, and as such are all ministering under the same inspiration of the same Holy Spirit.[1068] All that is taught, or all that the prophesied must, without exception, align with the Word.

In conclusion, no man can dub another man or woman an apostle or a prophet because they spout some purported prophecy or speak of a dream they were alleged to have had. Likewise, the real test of a minister is not whether one has gone to seminary, attained a degree, taken a vow, gone through an ordination ceremony, or been awarded a church or title.[1069] A minster (a servant) of the Most High is one that has actually received His Spirit, knows His heart and who He has called.[1070]

1066 2 Timothy 2:15
1067 Philippians 1:17
1068 2 Timothy 3:16
1069 Romans 10:2
1070 Ephesians 4:4

50

UNFOLDING PROPHECIES

Let us look at a few of the most glaring prophecies which indicate in what hour of GOD's prophetic clock we now find ourselves.

1. Israel Returns to the Promised Land and Becomes a Nation Once Again

> "For I will take you from among the heathen, and gather you out of all countries, and will bring you into your own land. Then will I sprinkle clean water upon you, and ye shall be clean: from all your filthiness, and from all your idols, will I cleanse you." (Ezekiel 36:24-25)

The aforementioned scripture is just one of many which mention the establishment of the state of Israel in the latter days. However, this passage has been fulfilled (only) in part. Even though Israel has been recognized as a nation and many Jews have returned to their ancient homeland, the final gathering and cleansing presented in the above scripture and in Isaiah 11:12 will not take place until after the Lord has returned.[1071] At that time, GOD will dispatch his angels and Jews from around the world who survived the Great Tribulation will be supernaturally marshalled and brought back to the vast land grant promised to Abraham's descendants.[1072] It is then we are told that the "spiritual birth" of the nation, described in Ezekiel 36:24–28 and Daniel 9:24 will take place. However, the return of the people to their ancient land and the establishment of the nation of Israel is the precursor, and the most significant indicator of just how close we are to "The Time of Jacob's Trouble."

2. The Jews will be Hated of all Nations

Some 3,600 years ago, for no justifiable reason, an Egyptian Pharaoh (likely Thutmose II, 1479–1425 BCE) developed an inordinate hatred for the Hebrew people and enslaved them.[1073] Since that time one empire after another has followed suit in an endless procession of persecution.

1071 Deuteronomy 30:3; Jeremiah 16:14-18
1072 Matthew 24:31; Genesis 15:18; Ezekiel 39:28; Zechariah 8:12
1073 Matthew 24:9; Mark 13:13; Luke 21:17

However, never before has this hatred become so apparent. Today it is visible on every continent as the nation of Islam spreads its tentacles across the globe. Today some thirty plus major militant Islamic groups around the world have pledged allegiance to ISIL fulfilling what they believe will be a worldwide jihad that will usher in their Mahdi.

By all accounts we are today approaching what the prophets referred to as the latter days. According to Scripture, "The Time of Jacob's Trouble" will be the worst assault ever unleashed on Israel by a confederacy of her ancient enemies. Their names may have changed from Babylon to Iraq and from Persia to Iran or from Grecia to Syria, but their hatred for their Jewish half-brothers has only intensified.

This hatred was first spoken by an angel of the Lord who prophesied to Sarai's bondmaid Hagar after she had conceived Abram's first-born son, Ishmael.

> "And the angel of the Lord said unto her (Hagar), I will multiply thy seed exceedingly, that it shall not be numbered for multitude. And the angel of the Lord said unto her, Behold, thou art with child, and shalt bear a son, and shalt call his name Ishmael; because the Lord hath heard thy affliction. And he (referring to his Arab descendants) will be a wild (warlike) man; his hand will be against every man, and every man's hand against him; and he shall dwell in the presence (the same land) of all his brethren (the Jew)." (Genesis 16:10-12)

Abraham was further instructed to "Cast out the bondwomen and her son (Ishmael): for the son of the bondwomen shall not be heir with the son of the freewoman (Isaac)."[1074] This prophecy was underscored in Paul's words "But he (Ishmael and his decedents) who was of the bondwomen (Hagar) was born after the flesh; but he (Isaac and his descendants—the Jews) of the freewomen was by promise."[1075] "But as then he (Ishmael) that was born after the flesh persecuted him (Isaac) that was born after the Spirit, even so it is now."[1076]

We are not told of any confrontation between Issac and Ishmael during the course of their lives, but rather of that which would arise between their offspring. The Ishmaelites became known as Arabians.[1077]

We also see in Scripture an example of how not only the descendants of stepbrothers, but also descendants of brothers may become adversaries. This was made apparent in the very next generation which divided Isaac's sons Esau and Jacob. We are told that, "Esau hated Jacob" because he felt robbed of the blessings his father had bestowed on his brother. "Esau said in his heart, the days of mourning for my father are at hand; then will I slay my brother Jacob."[1078]

Esau's descendants became known as the Edomites and grew to be hardened enemies of Israel. Referring to the Edomites Ezekiel said, "Because thou hast has a perpetual hatred, and

---

1074 Genesis 21:10, 12
1075 Galatians 4:23
1076 Galatians 4:29
1077 2 Chronicles 17:11
1078 Genesis 27:41

has shed the blood of the children of Israel by the force of the sword.... I will make thee (a) perpetual desolation."[1079]

In the end, Edom of old and the Arab nations to the south and east of Israel, along with other nations which have sworn or attempted to destroy Israel will unify and form a coalition—only to be destroyed at the Lord's return.[1080]

Repeatedly, as predicted in scripture, their leaders have vowed to obliterate Israel, annihilate the Jewish people and make Palestine part of their caliphate.[1081] Today the borders between Iraq and Syria have been erased as jihadist like the Islamic State of Iraqi and Levant—ISIL, Da'esh (ISIS), Harakat Al-Muqawama Al-Islamia (HAMAS), and Iran's proxy—Hezbollah, along with the Palestine Liberation Army (PLO) are grouping. Elsewhere jihadists like Boko Haram in Nigeria, the Houthis in Yemen, Al Shabaab in Somalia, and the Islamic separatist group Abu Sayyaf in the Philippines are connecting and conspiring together. Al-Qaed and its Syrian affiliate, the Al Nusra Front have recruited large numbers from the Free Syrian Army, which means America has actually been arming and financing Israel's enemy.[1082] This planetary hatred for Israel is but another prophetic indicator of just how close we are to the end of this age.

Numerous times since the Babylonians first wrenched the Judeans from the land of Palestine, they would return only to become dislodged and repeatedly scattered. The Jewish prophets had long ago predicted this, but so too did these same prophets predict that the people would one day return to their rightful homeland and thereafter remain. In these prophecies these prophets described the last battle in human history would be fought over this small piece of real estate (referring to Israel). The prophet Zechariah spoke,

> "And in that day will I make Jerusalem a burdensome stone for all people: all that burden themselves with it shall be cut in pieces, though all the people of the earth be gathered together against it." (Zechariah 12:3)

The kings of nations and the emperors of empires long buried beneath the sands of time mocked the Hebrew prophets and spoke of Israel's demise as a foregone conclusion. Yet today there sits Israel on the very land GOD bequeathed her, and although she finds herself in the midst of a seething cauldron, encircled by her ancient Arab adversaries, it is they who are doomed to disappear.[1083] Were they only to believe what Zechariah or Ezekiel had prophesied or what GOD spoke to Abram, they would cease and desist with their plans and beg for forgiveness.

> "And the heathen shall know that I the Lord do sanctify Israel, when My sanctuary shall be in the midst of them forever more." (Ezekiel 37:28)

1079 Ezekiel 35:5, 9
1080 Obadiah 1:15, 18; Isaiah 34:5-9; Zechariah 14:3
1081 Ezekiel 36:4-5
1082 Matt Druge, *Druge Report*, November 24, 2015
1083 Obadiah 15-18

"In the same day the Lord made a covenant with Abram, saying, Unto thy seed have I given this land, from the river of Egypt (the Nile) unto the great river, the river Euphrates:" (Genesis 15:18)

"And I will establish my covenant between me and thee and thy seed after thee in their generations for an everlasting covenant, to be a God unto thee, and to thy seed after thee. And I will give unto thee, and to thy seed after thee, the land wherein thou art a stranger, all the land of Canaan, for an everlasting possession; and I will be their God." (Genesis 17:7-8)

"Sojourn in this land, and I will be with thee, and will bless thee; for unto thee, and unto thy seed, I will give all these countries, and I will perform the oath which I sware unto Abraham thy father; And I will make thy seed to multiply as the stars of heaven, and will give unto thy seed all these countries; and in thy seed shall all the nations of the earth be blessed;" (Genesis 26:3-4)

"And the land which I gave Abraham and Isaac, to thee I will give it, and to thy seed after thee will I give the land." (Genesis 35:12)

"Which covenant he made with Abraham, and his oath unto Isaac; And confirmed the same unto Jacob for a law, and to Israel for an everlasting covenant…" (Psalm 105:9-10)

3. Who is Gog and What is the Land of Magog?

What is presently going on with Russia's invasion of Ukraine has many students of the Bible wondering if this is a foreshadowing of a battle described in Ezekiel 38 and 39 about Gog and Magog.

Some teach that Gog will be the Russian oligarch in the end times who will assault Israel, and that Russia is the land of Magog. So, it behooves the student of Scripture to dig deep and look at all the scriptures in prophetic books, such as Ezekiel, Daniel, and the Revelation where the evidence is made infinitely clear that this is not what the scriptures are saying.

Many prophetic scriptures are first alluded to in the O.T. and then revisited in the N.T. where they are then expounded upon. So it is that the battle depicted in Ezekiel is the same battle expanded upon in the Revelation. A line-by-line comparative reading of the battle and the aftermath illustrates that they both are describing the Battle of Armageddon—e.g., birds eating the dead bodies of Israel's enemies (Ezek. 39:17-18 and Rev. 19:17).

There are numerous other parallel verses—e.g., the methods by which GOD will destroy Israel's enemies … the overflowing rain, blood, fire, brimstone, hailstone, etc., all of which occur only at the Battle of Armageddon. Numerous prophets—Ezekiel 38:18-22, 39:2-7, 17-20), Isa. 63:1-8, Joel 2:3; Zech. 14:1-15; Mt. 24:27-31; 2 Th. 1:7-10; 2:8-12; Jude 14-15; and Rev.16:17-21—are specific to this one battle, which culminates with Messiah's second advent.

I would argue that Gog is not going to be a Russian oligarch, nor is Russia (proper) the land of Magog. In support of my premise, I bring to mind that in Daniel 8:8-9, 20-25, we are told that the Antichrist (Gog) will come from one of the four divisions of the ancient Grecian Empire (Greece, Turkey, Syria, Egypt) once under Alexander the Great that were divided into providences between his generals after his death. All these providences were later conquered by the Romans and became part of the Roman Empire. This clearly affirms that Gog will not come from Russia, but from one of these divisions. Daniel 11:35-45 narrows down which of these four divisions he will come from, for it is there we are told he will come from the Syrian division. Syria (Syrian Arab Republic) is located immediately north of Israel and just south of Turkey. It is, therefore, not a coincidence that the Antichrist has as one of his names, "the Assyrian" (Micah 5:5). Gog (Antichrist) is also referred to in Daniel 11:40 as the "king of the north" (Syria) who is "pushed at" (pressed into war) by a nation from the south (Ethiopia – Egypt).

Daniel 7:8, 23, 24 indicates that the Antichrist (the little horn) will arise out of one of the ten horns (kingdoms) of what will be the new G10 of the Revised Roman Empire. This excludes the rouge nation of Russia that never was part of the Old Roman Empire. So, Gog is not a Russian, and neither is Russia Magog.

Scripture further reveals that the Antichrist will be troubled by "tidings from the north" (presumably Turkey) and that he leaves Palestine where he will set up his image in the Temple and then engage and destroy this northern enemy (Daniel 11:44). If Russia was Magog and Gog the Russian oligarch, we then need to concede that there is no formidable nation north of Russia, only oceans and icebergs. So, Russia must be discounted, as well as its leader as land of the north in Daniel 11:44.

Syria and Turkey are, on the other hand, nations directly north of Israel and the ones that come into focus. Being that Syria and Turkey were two of the four divisions of the Grecian Empire, and that the Antichrist will rise from this region, offers a reasonable explanation why Satan will appoint the Prince of Grecia as his theater commander of the eighth and final empire (Revelation 17:11). See Appendix D, p. 572, "Vision of the Eighth Kingdom Expounded" in *For Such a Time as This: The Spiritual Wakening of Israel*.

> Note: The Prince of Grecia is a satanic prince that Satan appointed and that allowed Alexander the Great to be so successful in just thirteen years and able to destroy the entire Medo-Persian Empire. Now confined in the abyss this prince will be loosed in the last days and empower the Antichrist to revive the old Grecian Empire.

A Muslim—not a Russian. We see from the body of Scripture that the Antichrist rises to power and makes peace (albeit temporary) with Israel and confirms an agreement (Daniel 9:27) between the Muslims and the Jewish people, allowing them to rebuild the Jewish Temple on the Temple Mount next to the Qubbat al-Sakhraha (Dome of the Rock). So, we can readily see it is not a Russian monarch but a Muslim or Syrian Jew who confirms détente between the Jews and the Muslim-Arabs. It is an individual of the Islamic faith who is able to unite the Islamic nations in the Middle East into a federation or caliphate that becomes his principal army who will lead the assault against Israel.

We also read in Revelation of the False Prophet (a pseudo-Christian, a.k.a. a pontiff) who is in league with the Antichrist. In Daniel chapter 2, Nebuchadnezzar has a dream and sees a statue where various empires are depicted by depreciating metals and elements. The feet and toes we read, were a "mingling," of iron and clay (Daniel 2:42-43). Just as these two elements cannot mix, only "mingle," neither can these two ideologies—iron (The Universal Church of Rome's own brand of Christianity—Roman Catholicism) and clay (Islam). This underscores the fact that the Antichrist is not a Russian, but a Muslim.

One needs to also take note that Gog is also mentioned and is the subject of Revelation 20:8 where he (the Antichrist)—the principal human enemy of GOD is defeated at Armageddon and is later along with Satan, relegated to the Lake of Fire. So, we see that Gog is none other than the Antichrist and from the same scripture that Magog is not a single nation (e.g., Russia) but speaks of all the nations that will align themselves with Gog to destroy Israel.

Other supportive facts:

Gog is the same individual referred to elsewhere as: "the Little Horn" (Daniel chapters 7 and 8); "The Prince that shall come" (Daniel 9); "the King of the North" (Daniel 11); "the Man of Sin," "the Son of Perdition," "the Wicked" (2 Thes. 2); "the King of Babylon" (Isaiah 13 and 14), and "the Assyrian" (Micah 5).

The land(s) of Magog, along with Meshech and Tubal and other regions spoken of in Ezekiel 38 and 39, can be traced from Genesis 10, where we read that they were descendants of one of Noah's sons, Japheth. His name means extension, which was fitting, for his progeny extended throughout Euro-Asia. These sons and grandsons became the progenitors of various races whose ancient names give rise to where they lived.

Magog are largely the European nations that will align themselves with Gog, who were all within the boundaries of the Old Roman Empire at its zenith. Russia proper was never a part of the Old Roman Empire, which excludes it from being Magog. Only a very small fraction of what is today Russia, centered around the Black and Caspian Seas, is included in the land(s) of Magog. That small fraction of Russia may also be the Lord's way of telling us that only a fraction of a once great Russian Army will be left from either an early unmentioned war or another occurrence leading to its demise. By biblical chronology Russia is predestined to be defeated or loses it superpower standing before the Euro-Asia nations lose their autonomy and are reduced to ten regions. This ten-region unification would be impossible otherwise.

> Note: Numerous maps available on the Internet are in error if they depict Magog as Russia, as are the Bible teachers who teach of an attempted Russian invasion of Israel. If one thinks about it, Russia has no interest or extraordinary hatred for Israel and is not bent on her annihilation. Contrarily, the Arab nations are.

Gomer was the progenitor of the Galatians and Phrygians, natives of Northern Europe who became known as the Gauls and Celtics and who later became German, French, Welch, Irish Britons and other Anglo-Saxon races.

Magog, Meshech, and Tubal were sons of Japheth who, along with others, were predominate in Northern Europe and Eastern Asia. Magog was the progenitor of Scythians and Tartars. They resided in Russia and predominantly in what is today Southern Russia and Georgia, just north of the Caucasus Mountains between the Black and Caspian Seas.

Meshech, the Muscovites, did inhabit Russia in the fourteenth century but originally were in what is today the southern region of Russia, the same regions ascribed to Magog.

Tubal were the progenitors of Iberians (Spain and Portugal), Georgians, Cappadocians (Turkey), and other Asiatic and European nations. Tarshish is on the Southern Atlantic Coast of Spain. Sheba & Dedan were Arabs of Southern Arabia near the Persian Gulf.

In Genesis 10, the sons of Japheth, the Septuagint, adds Rosh to the list, which some commentators—Young, Rotherham, and Moffatt—claim to be Russia. Even if they were correct, it does not prove that Russia will be the predominating power in the last days or that Gog will emerge from Russia.

Insofar as wars are concerned, scripture indicates that there will be three tri-continental wars (Europe, Asia, Africa) and two invasions of Palestine. The first occurs when the Antichrist occupies Israel in the first three and a half years— the lesser-Tribulation, and sets up an image desecrating the Temple, which marks the middle of the Tribulation.

We are then told of two nations—one north (presumably Turkey) and one from the south (Africa/Ethiopia/Egypt)—that will threaten him and his global aspirations. Tidings from the north (presumably Turkey) will cause Gog to leave Palestine and engage and decimate this enemy (Dan. 11:40). The defeat of these nations will need to occur before the ten kingdom regions (the ten toes of the metallic image of Daniel 2) can solidify. Afterwards three of the original ten will be eliminated (Dan. 7:23, 24; Rev. 17:12-17).

Far more is said of the third tri-continental war that culminates with the Battle of Armageddon than of the first two wars. The third tri-continental war will begin in the middle and second half of Daniel's seventieth week. Gog and the six kingdom-states will war against a country to the east (Daniel 11:44). The nation of the north in this verse is a reference to Gog himself, not an enemy nation to his north.

We are given an indication as to who the land to the east is, for in Revelation 15:12 we are told that the Euphrates River dries-up "that the way of the kings of the east might be prepared". The Euphrates River speaks to Iraq but does not limit it to Iraq, for just east of Iraq lies the Arab nations of Iran, Afghanistan, and Pakistan.

While this is taking place, and in Gog's absence from Jerusalem, the Jewish people will attempt to regain their land. Gog will return with a vengeance and invade Israel for the second time during the second three and a half years (the Great Tribulation) in an attempt to destroy the Jewish people (Rev. 12:13) and add the state to his empire.

In so far as Russia is concerned and the possibility of it invading Israel, this could only occur when what is left of a decimated Russian Army would be conscripted to join the European nations and others who, along with the Arab confederacy form a coalition becoming part of Gog's gigantic army, (Arabic, Hamon-Gog; multitude of Gog; hence Magog). Gog and the goat nations (Magog) will invade Israel and then be destroyed by our Lord at the Battle of Armageddon.

Summation: As stated, Gog will be a Muslim or a Syrian Jew, either overtly or covertly. Hence, he is Anti (against) Christ. He will rise to power and begin by uniting the Muslim nations who will have all the resources, including nuclear, to overwhelm Russia, either before, or during the first half of the Tribulation.

> Note: As a point of interest, the USA left some eighty billion dollars' worth of state-of-the-art military equipment to the Arabs when they abandoned Afghanistan that could be used against Russia, and later, against Israel by Gog. What's more is that with the surrender of Afghanistan, three Arab-Islamic nations—Afghanistan, Iran, and Pakistan—all of which have, or will have, nuclear weaponry and delivery systems, now have shared borders creating (at least geographically) an Islamic caliphate.

4. A Global Government and the Migration to Babylon

A one world monetary system is virtually upon us as the United States dollar is on the verge of losing its standing as the dominant World Reserve currency. History bears witness to mans' long dream and insatiable appetite to rule the planet. Whereas in the past nations were conquered by swords, guns, missiles, or bombs, today man has learned that financial indebtedness of nations is a far more effective way to take planetary control while leaving national assets and infrastructure intact.

In the words of Mayer Rothschild (1744–1812), referred to as the founding father of international finance, "Let me issue and control a nation's money and I care not who writes the laws." The International Banking syndicate has in true Keynesian fashion, coordinated the fiat fiasco. Debt-ridden, entitlement-driven economies and the incalculable global credit bubble will most certainly collapse under their own ponderous weight.

The world's largest market, the financial exchange market (FX), also referred to as the currency market is the largest market in the world. It is forty times larger than the U.S. stock market and trades four trillion dollars between banks, financial institutions, governments and mega-investors every single day. Its immense size literally controls currencies, stocks, bonds, commodities; everything traded on the planet. Because it doesn't trade in "real money" but borrowed money, it is greed driven. It is cheap money with which banks make speculative investments during extended bull market runs. This has created a massive bubble and set in motion an inevitable sequence of events that will suddenly tumble all the other markets like a column of dominos. Bubbles or Bubble Dynamics are a result of speculation fueled by the illusion that deficits don't matter, excesses don't matter, mispricing and risks don't matter; even geopolitical events and looming threats don't matter just as long as money (borrowing/interest) is cheap.

According to Bill Bonner of the Bonner Research firm, Agora Inc., the global credit debt in trillions of dollars is astronomical. The outstanding credit debt incurred by American citizens alone is approximately six trillion dollars. As there is only 1.2 trillion in physical (fiat) money on the entire planet, one can readily see that when the dollar plummets and the markets crash, bankruptcies and forfeitures will skyrocket, banks will fail, and all credit will come to an abrupt halt. Unable to use credit cards the public will stampede to their banks and ATMs only to find the doors closed and machines out of cash.

As credit is based on a promise to pay, it only exists as long as people believe they are going to be paid. Since the 1950's America has developed into a credit economy; buying on credit has become its addiction. As credit is the life blood of our economy, it stands to reason that when the blood stops, the patient dies.

When the day of reckoning occurs, and financial markets collapse the domino effect will be systemic and unstoppable. People will bolt to withdraw their savings and sell whatever assets they have to no avail. All government electronic generated checks, social security, and welfare will abruptly stop. Pensions, retirement funds, and 401Ks will dissolve into thin air. Every venue and vector of every economy and every life will be affected. Producers, suppliers, wholesalers, and retailers, including food, fuel, and staples (everything)—will require physical cash making cash king and the cashless beggars. However even this is not the end, for what will take place afterward will be nothing short of global pandemonium.

A World government has coalesced under the auspices of the International Bank of Settlements—a syndicate of internationalists, global bankers, and financial combines. With members including the Federal Reserve, Central banks, and the International Monetary Fund, this hegemony controls all governments. When the collapse takes place or just before it takes place, in order to prevent the free-fall and in order to mediate the damage, a global monetary restructuring or reset will be initiated. This preemptive measure will be a provisional measure as the world moves toward an international electronic currency, which will at some point involve the taking of the mark.[1084]

> "And that no man might buy or sell, save (except) he that hath the mark, or the number of the name of the beast or the number of his name." (Revelation 13:17)

> Note: The United Nations High Commissioner for Refugees (UNHCR) has high hopes and is moving forward with its plan to use biometric technology (the Biometric Identity Management System) to be able to universally identify and track the global population by the year 2030. The Identification for Development (ID4D) initiative was originally launched by the World Bank and they are proud to be working with the UN to bring it to fruition.

1084 Revelation 13:16

> Note: The Bank of International Settlements (BIS) was founded in 1930 as an outgrowth of Rockefeller trustee Owen D. Young's so-called "Young Plan" which was implemented to chain German payments for the unpayable WWI reparations to a consortium of financiers led by J.P. Morgan. The BIS is located in Basel, Switzerland, but is above Swiss law by terms of a treaty which makes the bank untouchable and free from search, seizure or interference by Swiss authorities. Any nation that has a central bank tied to the Bank of International Settlements and the International Monetary Fund is a controlled nation. Economic dictums are handed down from on high by the global cartel.[1085] The BIS knows full well what is coming as a result of these central banking manipulations. They know what results when you print money without collateral, implement fractional reserve banking, and combine the biggest bond bubble in history along with a ten-year bull run in stocks.
>
> Note: According to Boston Consulting Group, the nation's largest banks have been found guilty of breaking the law and were required to pay more than $178 billion in legal claims since the financial crisis. In 2013, J.P. Morgan paid $410 million for manipulating the electricity market. Later that year, it paid $13 billion to settle claims that it knowingly sold toxic loans. In 2014, Bank of America paid a $6.3 billion fine for selling faulty mortgages. And in 2015, five big banks paid $5.8 billion for rigging the currency markets.

Dr. Carrol Quigley in his 1,348-page book, *Tragedy and Hope*, published in 1966, wrote,

> "This system was to be controlled in feudalist fashion by the central banks of the world acting in concert, by secret agreement arrived at in frequent private meetings and conferences. The apex of the system was to be the Bank of International Settlement in Basil, Switzerland."[1086]

Though the majority of the earth's citizenry remain blissfully unaware or willfully ignorant, the day is already here that the cabal of the Elite rule and the rest follow and serve. A world president, a world parliament, and a world constitution already exist and only wait for the right moment to replace sovereign nation autonomy and their respective constitutions. America's teeth were being removed one at a time by its puppet Muslim president who was installed by the global cartel and whose agenda has been the destruction of our constitution, our free society and our way of life.

With a deliberate plan to create a global economic collapse, the oligarchs in control of the New World Order will be begged to take planetary control and repair the system which will eventually lead to a cashless society.[1087]

1085 "Ruling the World of Money," Edward Jay Epstein, *Harper's Magazine*, article, November 1983
1086 Carrol Quigley, *Tragedy and Hope*, MacMillian and Co., NY; Collier—MacMillian, London 1966 p. 134
1087 Revelation 13:17

Author and lecturer, Willard Cantelon wrote in his book, *The Day the Dollar Dies,*

> "The world system will be praised and promoted by brilliant men. With elegance and apparent logic they will persuade men that this is the path to peace and security. The world leader (Antichrist) will rise to power with flattery and gain complete control of the military and monetary powers of all nations."[1088]

5. Instituting 666

The mystery of 666 has puzzled man ever since it was first declared to the Apostle John by the Lord Himself over nineteen hundred years ago.[1089] Theologians and numerologists have strived to unravel the enigmatic number and speculated ad nauseam as to who it might be. Caesars and popes, kings and despots have all been proposed. Now as we approach the time of the end, that which has been hidden can now be understood. For knowledge has increased (as with computer technology) and much of that which was sealed[1090] is now revealed.

In line with transfer technology, Near Field Communications has in concert with the communications carriers like T-Mobile, AT&T, Sprint, Verizon, and Google, put in place software which permits transactions and money transfers between the latest mobile cell phone recipients and merchants, banks, and our government agencies (IRS, Social Security, Welfare, FEMA, etcetera). At the moment of their choosing the globalist cabal will pull the plug on cash and "no one will be able to buy or sell" without using their individual designated number. The number referred to in Revelation 13:17–18 we are told is "666" and we are also told that it is the number of the man. The number 666 (a computer algorithm—a computer generated number) is the digital assigned number/mark of the beast (being a transaction system) associated with an individual's own name and identity. This is made clear when one recognizes that the word "the" was added by the translators; "as the number of the man." In the Greek, the word "for," not the word "the" is used in Revelation 13:17. The word "the" was supplied by the translators to clarify the meaning, even though there was no specific Greek word to express it. However, the word "for" is presented in the Greek New Testament in this verse; hence the scripture may be understood as: it is the number "for," or assigned to each particular individual / "for" each man. One should also keep in mind that these verses are specific to buying and selling, and that a number, as with a digital number will be required in order to transact business—hence a digital currency! This technological method of buying and selling is already in wide use today. Blockchain technology and digital currency (e.g., bitcoins) has not entirely replaced fiat yet, however it is gradually being implemented. The day will come when cash will be eliminated altogether and one will have no choice but to use the digital system if he wants to buy or sell.

1088 Willard Cantelon, *The Day the Dollar Dies*, Logos International, 1973, p. 145
1089 Revelation 13:17-18
1090 Daniel 12:4

6. The World Church and the "Falling Away"

One-hundred-and-fifty years ago essentially two books, the Bible and McGuffey's Reader(s) were the principal schoolbooks found in America's classrooms. As time went on other books gradually replaced McGuffeys in the academic marketplace and the Bible was summarily relegated to the school library. The desire for distinct grade levels, less overt religious content, and greater profitability helped bring about their decline.

Prestigious divinity schools which had been founded on traditional Christian theology afterward morphed into Universalism and Unitarianism. Today they accommodate faculty and students from a variety of religious backgrounds including Muslim, Hindu, Buddhist, Sikh, etcetera. Their academic programs attempt to balance theology and religious studies with secular perspectives of religion. Today churches seeking pastors specify in their searches that they are looking for applicants that are "culturally sensitive," which may be interpreted as looking for a pastor who is accepting of other beliefs.

Somewhere between the nineteenth and twenty-first centuries a contemporary church stopped believing that the Bible was the inerrant Word of GOD. In the past the major Protestant denominations, though divided on marginal theological points were still united in their core beliefs: the deity of Christ, His atoning sacrifice, and the narrow path to heaven. Then psychology and rationalism came into vogue and gained a foothold.

The Apostle Paul warned us that at the end of the earth age, as we approached the latter days apostasy would characterize the Church, thereby making it yet another indicator of the late hour in which we now find ourselves.

> "Let no man deceive you by any means: for that day shall not come, except there come a falling away (apostasy) first, and that man of sin be revealed, the son of perdition..."
> (2 Thessalonians 2:3)

The development of the World Church (one required leg on the three-legged stool of the New World Order) is rapidly evolving. A growing number of Neo-orthodox Protestants, Evangelicals, Greek Orthodox, and the Anglican Church are recognizing the Pontiff as the head of Christendom. At the same time other faiths outside of Christendom are being drawn into what has been called the Emerging (Emergent) Church and the Peace in a Globalized Society movement. The P.e.a.c.e Plan is designed to involve every Christian and every church in every nation in the task of serving people in areas of the greatest global needs. The Three-Legged Stool refers to bringing together the different sectors in society; the public sector of effective governments, the private sector of effective businesses, and the social sector of effective community organizations, including faith-based organizations. Ecumenicalism is also an essential part of "Agenda 21" (the global initiative and agenda for the twenty-first century).

7. The Middle East—the "Seething Pot"

While wars in Europe, the Pacific, Korea, and Vietnam have been momentous—they are not mentioned in the Bible, nor are they associated with the prophetic. It is the Middle East which prophecy tells us will be the epicenter of the world's attention in the end times, and Israel its most sought-after prize. And while wars have been fought on its ancient battlefields for millennia they have never before (directly or indirectly) involved all of mankind while the Jewish people occupied their homeland.

> Note: The United Nations Educational, Scientific, and Cultural Organization (UNESCO) is a specialized agency of the United Nations. Its declared purpose is to contribute to peace and security by promoting international and cultural reforms in order to increase universal respect for justice, the rule of law and human rights in concert with fundamental freedom proclaimed in the United Nations Charter. In a resolution passed on October 13, 2016, it used its majority of its fifty-six voting members (the majority being Islamic member nations) to erase the Jewish peoples' rightful connection to their land. UNESCO condemned Israeli actions at Jerusalem's holy sites and its ties to the Temple Mount and the Western Wall. In a sentence, it delegitimized Israel's heritage. Instead of recognizing the return of the Jewish people to their land (which was stolen from them during Arab occupation) it denounced Israel as an occupying power and affirms that it is the Palestinians who are the rightful heirs. This underscores the dangers of the Palestinian statehood initiative. In the passage of the resolution, only six nations voted against it: the United States, Germany, the United Kingdom, the Netherlands, Lithuania, and Estonia). Twenty-six nations abstained! UNESCO's anti-Israel agenda has long been apparent as it has been characteristic of other policy positions of the U.N. Human Rights Council. It is one more harbinger of what the Bible predicts would take place as we approach the end times.

8. The Guise of Peace

The United States (under its previous presidents) was the spearhead for the United Nations to force Israel to accept a two-state solution. At the present time Prime Minister Benjamin Netanyahu is resisting, but for how long we do not know. With pressure mounting daily, with Iran's escalating control over the region, a desperate Israel may be forced by the United Nations to concede to the "two-state solution" and a return to pre-1967 borders (which never existed but were invented and claimed by anti-Israeli factions). This is very worrisome for such an agreement as a two-state solution could become a precursor of the false-peace accord mentioned in the scriptures.[1091] This being the case, it could be the most significant indicator of just how near we are to the beginning of the Tribulation.[1092]

1091 Daniel 9:27
1092 Daniel 12:1; Joel 2:11

If Israel is recognized as an autonomous nation by Arab nations that previously would not recognize her, if alliances and trade agreements are made and commerce begins between Israel and former adversaries, then we can readily see peace on the horizon and another prophecy of the late hour in the process of being fulfilled.

> "For yourselves know perfectly that the day of the Lord so cometh as a thief in the night. For when they shall say, Peace and safety; then sudden destruction cometh upon them, as travail upon a woman with child; and they shall not escape." (1 Thessalonians 5:2-3)

> Note: Daniel 9:27 states that the Antichrist will "confirm" (Hebrew, *gabar*—strengthen) an existing peace covenant, not establish one! So according to the scripture a "peace agreement" will have been established prior to the beginning of the "one week" (seven years) Tribulation.

9. Tolerance, Merging Beliefs, and A One World Religion

> "And I beheld another beast coming up out of the earth, and he had two horns like a lamb… and he deceiveth them that dwell on the earth." (Revelation 13:11, 14)

In his visit to the United States during the week of September 21, 2015, Pope Francis was given the unprecedented opportunity to address the White House, the U.S. Congress, and the United Nations General Assembly. In what became the most extravagant and costly reception ever given to a dignitary, the pope spoke to millions of Catholics and non-Catholics in the cities of New York, Washington D.C., and Philadelphia. Whole business districts were corded off and traffic rerouted; even the United Parcel Service suspended delivery for two days. The largest police forces and secret service details ever were employed as the pope roamed in virtual unscripted autonomy wherever he chose.

Speaking largely on global issues, he entwined love, tolerance, acceptance, respecting one another on the personal level, and on the planetary level. His meteoric rise on the political stage caught the world by surprise as did his ability to captivate the adoring masses who venerated him as one might a divine. Everywhere he went worshipful crowds strained to touch any part of him as if something spiritual and holy could be imparted to them by doing so. People wept, cried, and held up their sick children in the hopes their infirmities would be healed as had the crowds when Jesus walked among the people.

All of this is a prelude to what the Bible warns will occur at the conclusion of the human era when a religious figure seduces the world at large[1093] and brings to a climax the great "falling away."[1094] The seduction began soon after Christ's resurrection as Satan and his minions infiltrated the young Church bringing in heretical doctrines and leading those who would believe in Christ further away from the faith and the gospel once delivered to the saints.[1095] This malignancy will

---

1093 Revelation 13:14
1094 2 Thessalonians 2:1-3
1095 Jude 1:3

escalate exponentially once the Church—the restrainer—has been translated (raptured) and the defenders of truth have been removed.[1096]

> "Also of your own selves shall men arise, speaking perverse things, to draw away disciples after them." (Acts 20:30)

10. Society a Sign

The New Testament is rich with prophetic narratives describing the sociological condition which will exist during the closing days of the earth age, both prior to the Lord catching out His Church and afterward.

Just as Yahusha-Jesus forewarned Abraham that He was about to destroy Sodom and the cities of the plain, "Shall I hide from Abraham that thing which I do?"[1097] So it is that the Lord has given us yet another sign showing us what society will be like prior to His return.

Scripture tells Believers that we are to be, "exhorting one another (in the things of the Lord), and so much more, as ye (we) see the day approaching."[1098] This verse indicates that Believers will indeed be able to recognize (by signs) the end of the present age. The word "exhorting" (Greek, *parakaleo*) implies inviting; suggesting that Believers should be actively evangelizing and warning others of the coming apocalypses while there is still time.[1099]

The Apostle Paul wrote prophetically to his pupil Timothy of a perilous time which would precede the coming of the Lord. In it he described the predominant characteristics of men living at that time. Today we see the escalation of these behaviors within our society, our government, and the professing church. Disobedience, ungodliness, pleasure seekers, greed, liars, traitors, trucebreakers, and a replica of the genuine Church (but one which has no foundation in the truth) leaves us with little choice but to recognize the late hour in which we presently find ourselves.

> "This know also, that in the last days perilous times shall come. For men shall be lovers of their own selves, covetous, boasters, proud, blasphemers, disobedient to parents, unthankful, unholy, without natural affection, trucebreakers, false accusers, incontinent (lacking self- control), fierce, despisers of those that are good, traitors, heady, highminded, lovers of pleasures more than lovers of God; having a form of godliness, but denying the power thereof: from such turn away." (2 Timothy 3:1-5)

There has always been a "final straw," an act so egregious that it brought an end to GOD's patience and long-suffering and unleashed the full measure of HIS judgement. Sodom and Gomorrah had their day of reckoning. America has not only matched but exceeded all the

---

[1096] 2 Thessalonians 2:8
[1097] Genesis 18:17
[1098] Hebrews 10:25
[1099] 2 Timothy 4:5

graphic examples of depravity and debauchery presented in the Scriptures.[1100] For over forty years (since 1973), nine unelected men and women on the Supreme Court have played god with innocent human life and condemned more than sixty-one million babies to excruciating deaths for convenience. Today their body parts are being dissected and sold for profit on the open market; debauchery has reached a new level.

Because no fire and brimstone has plummeted down from heaven; no pandemic disease or catastrophic event has yet occurred; no visible retribution has yet to befall the country; it may appear that GOD is indifferent to what we do, or that HE is simply a figment of mans' imagination, for what moral and virtuous god could possibly stand for the murder of tens of millions of infants. So it is that without divine judgment the people continue in their sin and their perversions escalate.

On June 26, 2015, the U.S. Supreme Court ruled in favor of same-sex marriages for all fifty states. Once again, the court of man and the law of man defied the Court of GOD and the Law of GOD.[1101] These spiritually destitute men and woman in black robes shall one day stand before the only real Supreme Court Judge, in the only real Supreme Court and say as Paul did, "What was I that I could withstand GOD?"[1102]

The city of Sodom (a metaphor for sodomy) had once been compared to the Garden of Eden, "a land well-watered fruitful and green."[1103] Today nothing remains of her; she has been smelted into the sands of the Dead Sea basin.

To paraphrase the English evangelist Leonard Ravenhill, Sodom had no Bible; America has millions. Sodom had no churches; America has hundreds of thousands. Sodom had no radio and television gospel preachers; America has had thousands. Sodom had no seminaries; America has hundreds. I ask you, who then is to be held more accountable, Sodom or America?[1104]

GOD has no obligation to give favor or grace to a nation which has relegated HIM to some generic, nebulous three letter word g.o.d. The nonspecific word may be taken to mean whichever god one chooses to ascribe to. HIS identity, YAHUAH, the GOD Abraham has been relegated to a neutral noun, God. His Son, Yahusha-Jesus, the one and same GOD to whom the whole earth has been bequeathed is no longer (as our founders proclaimed Him to be) our sovereign king. Today, instead of being reverenced, His name is profaned, and He has become the article of witticisms.

We have thought it enough to emboss our coinage with "In God We Trust," while we are passive to both HIM and HIS commandments; even denying the divine authority of HIS Word. We have become a lukewarm nation and like the Laodicean church where many proclaimed themselves Christian, we too have abrogated that which is sacred. We have forgotten the terror of the Lord and the consequence, "I will spew (spit) thee out of my mouth."[1105] Indeed, it is a

---

1100   2 Kings 23:10; Leviticus 18:21
1101   Leviticus 18:22, 29
1102   Acts 11:17
1103   Genesis 13:10
1104   Luke 10:12-14
1105   Revelation 2:14-17

travesty to sing "GOD bless America and shed your grace on thee," for HIS grace to an impudent nation is over! We have been "weighed in the balances and found wanting, GOD hath numbered thy kingdom, and finished it."[1106] We have written our own epitaph!

If indeed I sound like a doomsayer, then I am at least in the company of men like Noah, Jonah, Isaiah, Jeremiah, and Ezekiel; all who tried to warn the people of what lay ahead. We have lost our compass. We have lost our conscience. We have lost our way.

Everything which is now happening in America has historical precedence, as the life cycle of most empires has only been about two hundred years. Even with democracies it can be seen that once they have reached maturity their people become passive to GOD. The progression of GOD's cherished Israel was from bondage (in Egypt), to spiritual faith (under Moses), to great victory (under Joshua), to liberty (under David), to abundance under Solomon. Then from abundance, to complacency,[1107] and from complacency back to bondage.[1108] Mercy is Judgment postponed. Judgment is mercy exhausted.

America's hope, however fleeting, lives in only one word—Repentance! And it is only in repentance that a man or a nation can discover their Messiah; be emancipated from the wage of their sins, and avert tyranny, captivity, and destruction. When His sovereignty is acknowledged and homage is paid Him, despotism and oppression stand little chance and the nation prospers. He (Yahusha-Jesus) and He alone is our hope—our only hope—our Blessed hope!

But can such a proud and godless people become a broken people? What is the prospect of them crying out…Jesus! Jesus, I love you! Jesus, I want you! Please Lord, take your backslidden and covenant country America back! Be our sovereign King once more as in the days of our founding. We have no GOD but thee! Forgive me of my own transgressions that lead you to hang on a cross in my stead. I proclaim you Lord over me, Lord over my family, Lord over my America, Lord over all!

The door of the Ark which has remained open from the time of Christ until now, bidding "whosoever will" to enter in, is rapidly closing. Prophetically speaking, rain clouds; black and thunderous, driven by tempest winds from on high are no longer on the distant horizon but on the edge of our own fruited plain. The light from the Son will soon be obscured by an eerie shadow as men are no longer choosing to endure sound doctrine.[1109] Darkness will cover the land; day will be as night.[1110] One must enter into the Ark before the gangplank is raised and the hatch sealed and the waters of judgment prevail over the earth.[1111]

I do not believe it coincidental that the last and shortest epistle in the New Testament—the book of Jude, just happens to precede the book of the Revelation and was randomly placed there. Jude describes the escalation of social decadence leading to the Tribulation. Like a tsunami, whose mass and energy grows as it is about to make landfall, it first draws back the tide and exposes

---

1106 Daniel 5:26-27
1107 Deuteronomy 8:11-14
1108 Deuteronomy 28:15-68
1109 2 Timothy 4:3-4
1110 Joel 2:2
1111 Matthew 24:36-39; Genesis 7:18-19

what was before submerged. Likewise, are the sign of social depravity and corruption exposed as we approach the last days. And while history illustrates that deviant behavior has been prevalent in every age, when all the societal signs coincide in one generation and are concurrent with all the other prophetic indicators, it is more than coincidental; it is the perfect storm!

A catalog of declension would include rampant government, business, and banking corruption; social and cultural moral bankruptcy; a national educational system devoid of and even anti-GOD; a culture whose majority believes in evolution instead of creationism; and an anemic Christianity with all the trappings, but with little substance.

The only prophetic event in Scripture which must take place before the Tribulation begins will be the disappearance of all true Believers.[1112] I mention this because it will be the most irrefutable occurrence in all of history which will underscore the authority of the Bible. May all the unpersuaded, be they Jews, Catholics, Muslims, etcetera, reexamine their beliefs if they find themselves earthbound and a witnesses to this supernatural event.

Like the Apostle John was told, so have I been given to "Write the things which thou has seen, and the things which are, and the things which shall be hearafter…"[1113] Let him who "hath an ear, let him hear what the Spirit saith unto the churches."[1114] See: Appendix A—The Judgment of America.

11. The Resurrected and the Remnant

After Jesus' resurrection and since Pentecost,[1115] for the last nearly two thousand years, the Holy Spirit has indwelled those who have received Christ as their personal Savior.[1116] It is He who has guided[1117] and empowered the Church of Believers.[1118] It is He who through the collective body of the Church that has been the restraining factor, confronted heresy, held back the sea of deception and exposed the enemies of the Cross.[1119] Once the Church has been removed the World Church will rise to dominate and subjugate.[1120] Still, the Holy Spirit (capable of being omnipresent) will continue to operate here on earth, gathering and sealing a remnant for our Lord during the final seven years of the earth age.[1121]

The next great prophetic event awaiting fulfilment will be the "resurrection of the just"[1122] when the true Church consisting of all Born-Again believers will be suddenly…

1112 2 Thessalonians 2:6
1113 Revelation 1:19
1114 Revelation 2:7, 11, 29; 3:6, 13, 22
1115 Acts 2:1-4
1116 John 14:16-17
1117 Romans 8:14
1118 2 Corinthians 10:4-5
1119 2 Thessalonians 2:7
1120 Revelation 13:15-16
1121 Revelation 7:3, 9, 14
1122 Luke 14:14

> "...caught up together... to meet the Lord in the air....We will not all sleep (die physically), but we shall all be changed. In a moment...at the last trump (denoting the end of the Church Age)...the dead shall be raised incorruptible, and we (the living) shall be changed...put on immortality...then...death is swallowed up in victory." (1 Corinthians 15:51-56)

Scripture tells us this "catching away"—commonly referred to as the rapture (the source of which is Latin, *rapturo*) will precede "the Seventieth Week of Daniel."[1123]

During those final seven years purposed by GOD, many Jewish people will cry out to YAHUAH in desperation. It will be at that time that many Jews will come to recognize their Mashiach, is their GOD[1124] and that it is He who is making an end of their transgressions.[1125] Those who awaken and turn to Him with all their heart will be among the elect; the remnant of Israel.[1126]

> "Therefore say thou unto them, Thus saith the Lord of hosts; Turn ye unto Me, saith the Lord of hosts, and I will turn unto you, saith the Lord of hosts." (Zechariah 1:3)

> "And it shall come to pass in that day, that the remnant of Israel, and such as are escaped of the house of Jacob, shall no more again stay upon him that smote them; but shall stay upon the Lord, the Holy One of Israel, in truth. The remnant shall return, even the remnant of Jacob, unto the mighty God." (Isaiah 10:20-21)

Insofar as the Tribulation is concerned, we would do well to remember that the Old Testament saints and the blood bought Church have already been reconciled to GOD and Christ. Therefore, there is no need whatsoever, and it serves no purpose for them to incur the judgments and wrath of GOD during the Tribulation; hence they will not have to.[1127] This is emphasized in 1 Thessalonians where Paul, after describing the catching away concludes with,

> "For GOD hath not appointed us to wrath, but to obtain salvation by our Lord Jesus Christ, who died for us, that, whether we wake (are alive) or sleep (those having previously died), we should live together with Him. Wherefore comfort yourselves together, and edify one another, even as also you do." (1 Thessalonians 5:9-11)

Abraham's nephew Lot and his family were divinely escorted out of Sodom by GOD's election, selection, and mercy because they feared and reverenced the GOD of Abraham. Their removal occurred just before HE rained destruction on the cities of the plain. So, will HE remove His own just before judgement begins in earnest.

1123 Daniel 9:24-27
1124 John 17:11
1125 John 9:24
1126 Micah 5:7-8; Zephaniah 3:9-17; Romans 11:5
1127 Revelation 6:16-17

We would also do well to remember that the Church of Philadelphia, which was both an existing church in Apostle John's day and is also symbolic of the true Church today, was told,

> "Because thou hast kept the word of my patience (Greek, *hupomone*—hopeful), I also will keep thee from the hour of temptation, which shall come upon all the world, to try (Greek, *petrazo*—discipline) them (the unregenerated) that dwell upon the earth." (Revelation 3:10)

It will likely be the sudden disappearance of millions of Believers which will compel many who had previously been told of the rapture to suddenly realize this was a biblical promise for the truly saved Church. Finding that they have been left behind, it will become apparent just who were the true believers and who thought they were. This will compel, I pray, many to turn to Christ and become part of the remnant.[1128]

How appropriate that those individuals who receive this revelation are found in a book so named, "The Revelation (the unveiling) of Jesus Christ."[1129]

The present direction of mainline denominations as well as a substantial part of the evangelical Christendom has been to abandon the full gospel and fine solidarity with Rome. This is a huge step toward apostasy; however, it is only the beginning. Once the Church has been divinely removed from the earth, nothing will hinder the advancement of heretical doctrine.[1130]

Presently the Church of Rome's hold on its subjects is far greater than that of any secular government which is why the New World Order will take advantage of Rome's ambition to head a One World Church. Once Rome has managed to consolidate religions and subjugate the masses, the New World Order will no longer need her and subsequently will see her as a hindrance and abandon her.[1131]

The shift to ecumenicalism which we are presently seeing in the Evangelical and Protestant denominations is itself a sign of the late hour and the nearness of the translation of the true Church.

1128 Jude 23
1129 Revelation 1:1
1130 2 Thessalonians 2:7
1131 Revelation 17:15-18

51

GOD'S CLOCK

GOD's clock is a prophetic clock. Often, HE marks time by signs and events, many of which are confirmed with measurable precision from scripture. HIS clock will not be hurried nor can it be delayed.

The writer of Ecclesiastes tells us "to everything there is a season, and a time to every purpose under the heavens…"[1132] The writer goes on to say, "He (GOD) hath made (or will make) every thing beautiful in HIS time…"[1133]

Isaiah told us that Israel will be the benefactor of this for there is a season coming when HE will bring "Salvation to Zion."[1134] However, before this occurs, a dreaded time "a time of trouble, such as never was"[1135] will overtake a people who have resisted believing the entirety of Scripture and in particular the New Testament.

For those teachers who have never taught prophecy, and for those who have rejected what HE who has "declared the end from the beginning"[1136] has to say about what will occur at the conclusion of this earth age, here is a brief synopsis.

At a time the Bible refers to as the "fullness (summation) of the Gentiles (age),"[1137] when human government has run its course and satanic princes are desperate to change their prophetic destiny, a succession of "signs" will grab the attention of the world. The first will be a supernatural occurrence when instantly GOD will bodily remove all genuine believers from the earth, as they will be "caught up together to meet the Lord in the air…"[1138]

(Image Source: GOODSALT)

1132 Ecclesiastes 13:1
1133 Ecclesiastes 3:11
1134 Isaiah 46:9–13
1135 Daniel 12:1
1136 Isaiah 46:10
1137 Romans 11:25
1138 1 Thessalonians 4:17

With the Church gone, society will quickly deteriorate. There will be "distress of nations and confusion."[1139] In the midst of chaos a world leader (the Antichrist) will emerge.[1140] He will offer solutions and make promises reminiscent of a former German dictator who mesmerized the German people in the twentieth century. However, unlike the German tyrant he will not approach as a conqueror, but a unifier.

Simultaneously, with a global government promising a better world and the end of war, nations will gladly surrender their autonomy. As the new order solidifies a new global economy will be put in place and a world church will bring different faiths together harmonizing ideologies under its banner. Then, when it appears an armistice has finally come between Israel and their foes, an agreement will be ratified by the new world leader allowing the Jewish people to rebuild the Temple. With the Jewish people living under the guise of peace in unwalled cities,[1141] the ruse will have succeeded.

> "When they shall say, Peace and safety has come; then sudden destruction cometh upon them, as a women in travail with child, and they shall not escape." (1 Thessalonians 5:3)

After being restored, the Temple will be defiled[1142] and war will initiate the "beginning of sorrows."[1143] One hundred and forty-four thousand[1144] sons and daughters of Israel will have previously become Messianic Believers and have brought a message of hope, proclaiming the nearness and imminent return of the Lord.[1145] In both desperation and in expectation those who have become believers will cry out, *"Maranatha"* (Arabic), the Lord is coming.[1146]

As the Jewish people see the prophetic unfolding before their eyes, they will begin to understand that the New Testament is part of Holy Scripture and that the one called Jesus was indeed their rejected Mashiach.[1147] As Isaiah was given to say, and the eyes of the blind shall see out of obscurity, and out of darkness."[1148]

During the second half of the seven years of "Jacob's Trouble"[1149] natural disasters of epic proportion will be felt around the world. Bizarre weather phenomenon, the likes of which have never been experienced will blanket the planet. Earthquakes and volcanic eruptions will take place in places where they have rarely or never in recorded history occurred.[1150] In the aftermath

---

1139 Luke 21:25
1140 Revelation 13:5-7
1141 Ezekiel 38:11
1142 Daniel 9:27; Matthew 24:15
1143 Matthew 24:8
1144 Revelation 14:4
1145 Revelation 12:3-8
1146 1 Corinthians 16:22
1147 Isaiah 53:3
1148 Isaiah 29:18
1149 Jeremiah 30:7
1150 Revelation 8:6-13

of war and these events the planet will experience famine, starvation, and pestilence.[1151] Ongoing war will continue unabated for forty-two months as GOD's judgement is carried out by human oppressors[1152] and demonic entities.[1153]

During the final days of this saga Israel will be surrounded by a federation of Arab-Islamic nations. The invaders led by the Antichrist will slaughter all but a third of Israel's Jewish population. Many will have already died by war, famine, disease and natural disasters.[1154] Just as all appears lost the Lord, accompanied by his heavenly army will return.[1155] He will destroy the enemies of Israel, "consuming them with the spirit of his mouth, and with the brightness of his coming."[1156]

The remnant of the Jewish people who survive the wars and planetary holocaust will suddenly recognize and magnify the Lord of the Host, the Holy One of Israel, the King of Kings, the Lord of Lords, the I Am who I Am; the Alpha and the Omega.[1157]

> "Arise shine; for the light is come, and the glory of the Lord is risen upon thee. For, behold the darkness shall cover the earth, and gross darkness the people: but the Lord shall arise upon thee, and His glory shall be seen upon thee." (Isaiah 60:1-2)

At last the Jewish people will come to the realization that their Messiah needed to first come in order to save them from their sins before He would save them from their enemies. Even in the midst of the horrors of that day salvation will be available to the individual who seeks Him with all their heart.

> "And it shall come to pass, that whosoever shall call on the name of the Lord (Yahusha-Jesus), shall be delivered..." (Joel 2:32)

The imperative which Moses first taught in the Torah, and which Jeremiah echoed, is the key that opens the door. Loving GOD is a matter of the heart, not the head.

> "And thou shalt love the Lord thy GOD with all thine heart, and with all thy soul, and with all thy might." (Deuteronomy 6:5)

> "And rend your heart, and not your garments, and turn unto the Lord your God: for he is gracious and merciful, slow to anger, and of great kindness, and repenteth him of the evil." (Joel 2:13)

1151 Matthew 24:7; Revelation 6:4-8
1152 Revelation 12:1-7
1153 Revelation 9:13-19
1154 Zechariah 13:8-9
1155 Revelation 19:11-16
1156 2 Thessalonians 2:8
1157 Revelation 22:13

"And ye shall seek ME, and find ME, when ye search for ME with all your heart." (Jeremiah 29:13)

"Behold, I stand at the door and knock: if any man hear My voice and open the door, I will come into him and will sup with him and him with Me." (Revelation 3:20)

In the verse above the words "I will come in to (into) him" are to be taken literally, for GOD the Ha Rauch Ha Kodesh will enter into the seeker and bond with the seeker's spirit.

Today we see the sands of time have all but drained from HIS divine hourglass. Israel has returned to Palestine, yet in unbelief. And while no man knows the hour of His coming, we have been given an abundance of signs. "He declares from the beginning and from ancient times the things that are not yet done."[1158] The bride to be must quickly trim her lamp and prepare herself; for her betrothed will soon arrive and take her to Himself.[1159]

It has been conservatively estimated that there are now more than one and a half million Jews around the world who have recognized their Messiah and accepted Yahusha-Jesus as their personal Savior.[1160] Hundreds of Rabbis, several Chief Rabbis, and even some Chacham have openly professed Jesus as their Mashiach. Still the Great Shepherd of Israel (Hebrew, *Ro' Eh Yisrael*) searches for the one lost lamb that He might save him or her from the predators and add them to His flock.[1161]

Hear the words of David in the sixth Messianic Psalm where he extols his Messiah.

"The Lord is my shepherd; I shall not want. He (Yahusha) maketh me to lie down in green pastures: He (Yahusha) leadeth me beside the still waters. He (Yahusha) restoreth my soul: He (Yahusha) leadeth me in the paths of righteousness for His name's sake. Yea, though I walk through the valley of the shadow of death, I will fear no evil: for thou (Yahusha) art with me; thy rod and thy staff they comfort me. Thou preparest a table before me in the presence of mine enemies: thou anointest my head with oil; my cup runneth over. Surely goodness and mercy shall follow me all the days of my life: and I will dwell in the house of the Lord for ever." (Psalm 23)

1158 Isaiah 46:10
1159 Matthew 25:1-13
1160 Jacob Gartenhaus, *Famous Jewish Christians*, Baker House, Grand Rapids, MI, 1979, pp. 24-25
1161 Luke 15:4

52

THE TWO VISITATIONS; THE LAMB AND THE LION

I cannot think of any other Messianic prophecies which identify Yahusha and Jesus as being one and the same, as those in the book of Zechariah. There He is depicted as having come to earth twice: first as the Paschal Lamb who would die on a Cross, and second as King of kings and Lord of lords, the Lion of Judah.

Zechariah points out how astonished the Jewish people who survive the Great Tribulation will be when He appears for the Second time, for He will carry in his flesh the wounds of the past. They will see with their own eyes where spikes pierced His hands and pinned Him to a Cross, and where a Roman spear lanced his side. And then… they will weep for the centuries of denial for the one that died for them; for the one they had rejected; for the Holy One of Israel.

(Image Source: GOODSALT)

The Lamb and the Lion

"And I will pour upon the house of David, and upon the inhabitants of Jerusalem, the spirit of grace and of supplications: and they shall look upon me whom they have pierced, and they shall mourn for him, as one mourneth for his only son, and shall be in bitterness (weep bitterly) for him, as one that is in bitterness for his firstborn." (Zechariah 12:10)

"And one shall say unto Him, What are these wounds in thine hands? Then He shall answer, Those with which I was wounded in the house of my friends." (Zechariah 13:6)

But they will also weep for joy and shout, "For this GOD is our GOD forever and ever..." (Psalm 48:14)

The following scripture from Isaiah refers to those from the house of Jacob who will be alive at the time of His Second Coming and enter His Millennium. It speaks to those who had rejected truth but whose eyes will be opened and who will understand.

"And in that day shall the deaf hear the words of the book, and the eyes of the blind shall see out of obscurity, and out of darkness. The meek also shall increase their joy in the Lord, and the poor among men shall rejoice in the Holy One of Israel.... Therefore thus saith the Lord, who redeemed Abraham, concerning the house of Jacob, Jacob shall not now be ashamed, neither shall his face now wax pale. But when he seeth his children, the work of mine hands, in the midst of him, they shall sanctify my name, and sanctify the Holy One of Jacob, and shall fear the God of Israel They also which erred in the spirit shall come to understanding, and they that murmured shall learn doctrine." (Isaiah 29:18-19, 22-24)

53

THE SUFFERING SERVANT OF YAHOVAH

Isaiah 52:13–14 and 53:1–12

The description of the Suffering Servant discussed in Isaiah 53 actually begins in Isaiah 52 when the prophet had a vision of the Messiah. He saw Him in His tortured state, beaten mercilessly, hardly recognizable and hanging from a Roman Cross.

> "Behold, MY servant shall deal prudently, He shall be exalted and extolled, and be very high. As many were astounded at thee; his visage was so marred more than any man, and his form more (mutilated) than the sons of men…" (Isaiah 52:13-14)

Nailed above His head to mock Him was a board that read, "This is Yahusha, the King of the Jews."[1162] Little did His executioners realize that truer words were never written.

Seven hundred years before Yahusha came to earth, Isaiah was told of His coming and what He would endure for those who would receive Him.[1163] What more could GOD have done than to describe the Messiah's life and death, and the purpose for which He had to come, than to present it to us in such vivid detail that we might recognize Him?

Wounded for Our Transgressions—Bruised for Our Iniquities (Image Source: GOODSALT)

1162 Matthew 27:37
1163 Isaiah 53:1-12

Isaiah 53:

1. Who hath believed our report? and to whom is the arm of the Lord revealed?

2. For He shall grow up before HIM as a tender plant, and as a root out of a dry ground: He hath no form nor comeliness; and when we shall see Him, there is no beauty that we should desire Him.

3. He is despised and rejected of men; a man of sorrows, and acquainted with grief: and we hid as it were our faces from Him; he was despised, and we esteemed Him not.

4. Surely he hath borne our griefs, and carried our sorrows: yet we did esteem Him stricken, smitten of God, and afflicted.

5. But He was wounded for our transgressions; he was bruised for our iniquities: the chastisement of our peace was upon Him; and with His stripes we are healed.

6. All we like sheep have gone astray; we have turned everyone to his own way; and the Lord hath laid on Him the iniquity of us all.

7. He was oppressed, and He was afflicted, yet He opened not his mouth: He is brought as a lamb to the slaughter, and as a sheep before her shearers is dumb, so He opened not his mouth.

8. He was taken from prison and from judgment: and who shall declare his generation? for He was cut off out of the land of the living: for the transgression of MY people was He stricken.

9. And He made his grave with the wicked, and with the rich in His death; because He had done no violence, neither was any deceit in His mouth.

10. Yet it pleased the Lord (YAHUAH—Yahovah) to bruise Him; HE hath put Him to grief: when thou shalt make His soul an offering for sin, He shall see His seed, He shall prolong his days, and the pleasure of the Lord shall prosper in his hand.

11. HE shall see of the travail of His soul, and shall be satisfied: by His knowledge shall My righteous servant justify many; for He shall bear their iniquities.

12. Therefore will I divide Him a portion with the great, and He shall divide the spoil with the strong; because He hath poured out His soul unto death: and He was numbered with the transgressors; and He bare the sin of many, and made intercession for the transgressors.

The Suffering Servant described in these verses is the Messiah, not the Nation of Israel as taught by some rabbinic. To help the reader recognize HIM, here is a verse-by-verse commentary.

v.1 "Who hath believed our report? And to whom is the arm of the Lord revealed?"

Who will believe the Scriptures and recognize the Mashach; the arm of Yahovah when He first appears?

v.2 "He shall grow up before him as a tender plant, and a root out of dry ground..."

He shall grow up just like any other child, not with a title or from privileged beginnings.

"...he hath no form or comeliness; and when we shall see him, there is no beauty that we should desire him."

He shall appear as an ordinary man; His majesty concealed.

v.3 "He is despised and rejected of men; a man of sorrows, and acquainted with grief: and we hid as it were our faces from him: he was despised and we esteemed him not."

He knew of the sorrows and sickness of man, and of the centuries of persecution that His people had endured. He felt then, and feels now, our grief. He was despised and rejected by many of His own (the Jewish people), not unlike today.

v.4 "Surely he hath borne our griefs), and carried our sorrows: yet we did esteem him stricken, smitten of GOD and afflicted."

Since the Hebrews became GOD's people, He has carried them. He felt their pain and their sufferings during their captivities. He knows our sickness as He knows our sins and borne them both when He went to the Cross. But when after His trial the people saw Him tied to the scourging post and beaten and then hanging helplessly from the Cross, many who had recognized Him as the Messiah, believed the Father had forsaken Him.

v.5 "But he was wounded for our transgressions, he was bruised for our iniquities: the chastisement of our peace was upon him."

He underwent the brutally beaten and torturous death for our sins, but His eyes were fixed on what His death would accomplish. It would be the Cross where the greatest transaction for mankind would ever be made ... Redemption purchased for all who would graciously receive it.

This was the punishment that GOD imposed upon Himself. Our sins could only be paid for by a faultless human blood sacrifice.[1164]

(Image Source: GOODSALT)

v.6 "All we like sheep have gone astray; we have turned everyone to his own way; and the Lord hath laid on HIM the iniquity of us all."

Every single person on earth has gone astray at some time. We have gone our own way, done our own thing, and we all sinned. So YAHUAH (as the Father) laid our iniquity upon Adonai Yahusha (Lord Jesus) the Son.[1165]

v.7 "He was oppressed, and afflicted, yet he opened not His mouth: He is brought as a lamb to slaughter, and as a sheep before His shearers is dumb, so He opened not His mouth."

Isaiah may have had a vision of Yahusha being seized, imprisoned and appearing in a mock trial before the High Priest and the Jewish High Council. They would try to find accusers who would testify that He said He was GOD so that they could seek the death penalty for blasphemy. But He would not answer them as they had hoped. He knew that whether He admitted that He was Immanuel (God with Us) or not, they would still charge Him accordingly; so He remained silent.

v.8 "He was taken from prison and from judgment: and who shall declare His generation? For he was cut off out of the land of the living (died a vicious death): for the transgressions of my people was he stricken."

He was taken from prison and appeared before Pontus Pilate. He was sentenced to death by crucifixion and kept His appointment with the Cross.

v.9 "And he made his grave with the wicked, and with the rich in his death: because he had done no violence, neither was any deceit in his mouth."

1164 Leviticus 17:11
1165 John 3:16

Yahusha-Jesus was put to death as a criminal but was buried in the sepulcher of a wealthy Jewish believer, Joseph of Arimathea.[1166] He remained peaceful during His trial and would not speak a vile word against His accusers, His judges, or His executioners. He went willingly to the Cross for the sake of those that would one day accept His offering and become His own.[1167]

> v.10 "Yet it pleased the Lord to bruise Him; he had put Him to grief: when thou shall make His soul an offering for sin, He shall see His seed, He shall prolong his days, and the pleasures of the Lord shall prosper in his hand."

Though it pained YAHUAH to have Yahusha endure His cruel end, it was necessary, for He had to become our sin offering. Yahusha's "seed" refers to those who will accept Him by faith as their Savior. To those who will receive Him, He will oversee their lives as they join the parade of saints who have spread the gospel from generation to generation.[1168]

> v.11 "HE shall see of the travail of His soul, and shall be satisfied: by His knowledge shall MY righteous servant justify many; for He shall bear their iniquities."

YAHOVAH was pleased, knowing that what Yahusha had succeeded in doing had all been worthwhile; He had accomplished what was necessary. He had justified many; redeeming the souls of Believers.[1169] Their sins died on the Cross with His humanity.

> v.12 "Therefore will I (YAHUAH) divide him (Yahusha) a portion with the great, and He (Yahusha) shall divide the spoil with the strong (His own); because He hath poured out His soul unto death: and He was numbered with the transgressors; and He bare the sins of many, and made intercession for the transgressors."

Yahusha succeeded in accomplishing His earthly mission. "The government shall be upon His shoulders…"[1170] YAHUAH shall give Yahusha not only Zion, but the entire planet for His Kingdom[1171] and He will graciously share it with His own.[1172] They are "a chosen generation, a royal priesthood, a holy nation, a peculiar people; that ye shall show forth the praises of Him who hath called them out of darkness into His marvelous light…"[1173] This had been GOD's divine plan from the very beginning.

1166 John 19:38; Luke 23:50-53
1167 John 6:39-40
1168 Romans 8:28
1169 John 17:9-10
1170 Isaiah 9:6
1171 Psalm 48:2
1172 Revelation 21:7; 1 Corinthians 2:9
1173 1 Peter 2:9

It is a sad commentary that many Rabbinic choose to interpret Isaiah 53 by inferring the nation of Israel is the subject of the passage. Those who take this passage out of context (as established by the chapter which precedes this passage) distort the meaning and violate hermeneutical discipline.

Rabbi Claude G. Montefiore (1858–1938) made the assertion that the omission of this chapter has been deliberate.

> "Isaiah 53: and quotations from it are rarely read by the Rabbinic because of their Christological interpretation given to the Chapter by Christians. They are omitted from the prophetical lessons (Haftorot) for the Deuteronomy Sabbaths..."[1174]

A deliberate attempt to elude the Messianic meaning becomes blatantly obvious as one considers that Haftorah readings read in synagogues all over the world as they are identical for the designated Sabbath days. Blatantly obvious is the omission of Isaiah 53. These readings leave off at Isaiah 52:12 and resume at 54:1.

- Haftorah for Ekeb: Isaiah 49:14-51:3
- Haftorah for Shofetim: Isaiah 51:12-52:12
- Haftorah for Noah: Isaiah 54:1-55:5
- Haftorah for Sephardi ritual: Isaiah 54:1-10
- Haftorah for Ki Tetze: Isaiah 54:1-10
- Haftorah for Re'eh: Isaiah 54:11-55:5

The eighth century Musaf prayer read on the Day of Atonement, the Talmud, the Midrashim, and the Jewish Prayer Book all support the view that Isaiah 53 refers to the Messiah.

> The Musaf prayer: "We are shrunk up in our misery even until now! Our Rock hath not come to us; Messiah our righteousness hath turned from us; we are in terror, and there is none to Justify us! Our iniquities and the yoke of our transgressions bear, for He was wounded for our transgressions: He will carry our sin upon His shoulders that we may find forgiveness for our iniquities, and by His stripes we are healed. O eternal One, the time has come to make a new creation, from the vault of heaven bring Him up..."

Why would Yahusha allow Himself to be crucified by men? The answer is most profound. It is because HIS own law demands it! Only by the shedding of blood is there remission of sin!

> "For the life of the flesh is in the blood: and I have given it to you upon the altar to make an atonement for your souls: for it is the blood that maketh an atonement for the soul." (Leviticus 17:11)

1174 Claude Goldsmid Montefiore & Herbert Martin James Loewe, *A Rabbinic Anthology*, (op. cit. p. 544)

Speaking figuratively, man did not nail Him to a Cross; His love for us nailed Him to the Cross. He went willing for you and for me. Hear the message of Cross...

"But God commendeth his love toward us, in that, while we were yet sinners, Christ died for us. Much more then, being now justified by his blood, we shall be saved from wrath through him. For if, when we were enemies, we were reconciled to God by the death of his Son, much more, being reconciled, we shall be saved by his life. And not only so, but we also joy in God through our Lord Jesus Christ, by whom we have now received the atonement. Wherefore, as by one man (Adam) sin entered into the world, and death by sin; and so death passed upon all men, for that all have sinned..." (Romans 5:8-12)

> Note: Shlomo Yitzchaki, (Rashi) was the first one to suggest that the "Suffering Servant" of Isaiah 53 represents Israel. Until then the Suffering Servant was almost universally understood by Jews as referring to the Messiah. Rashi's interpretation has been refuted by such sages as: Rabbi Moshe Kohen Ibn Crispin (fourteenth century); Rabbi Elijah de Vidas (sixteenth century); and Chief Rabbi of Salfed, Moshe el Sheikh "Alshech" (1508-1593).

Perhaps the most famous rabbi of all time, Moshe ben Maimon—Moses Maimonides (1135–1204), wrote in a letter to Jacob Alfajumi, wherein he quoted Isaiah 52:15 and 53:2. Even though the rabbi did not recognize that the Messiah had already come, he did recognize that Isaiah 53 pertained to Him, not Israel. The letter read,

"What is to be the manner of Messiah's advent, and where will be the place of His first appearance?...And Isaiah[1175] speaks similarly of the time when he will appear...He came up as a sucker before him, and as a root out of dry earth,...in the words of Isaiah, when describing the manner in which the kings will hearken to Him, at Him the kings will shut their mouth; for that which had not been told them they have seen, and that which they had not heard they have perceived."[1176]

1175 Isaiah 53:2
1176 S.R. Driver and A.D. Neubauer; *The Fifty-Third Chapter of Isaiah According to the Jewish Interpreters*, Translations by KTAV Publishing House, NY, 1969, pp 374-375

54

FOR SUCH A TIME AS THIS

Hosea the prophet was privileged to see thousands of years into the future to the time when GOD would gather HIS chosen people from around the world and bring them back to Palestine. However, giving them a homeland was just the first part of Israel's restoration. As important as this event was to the Jewish people it is subordinate to GOD's primary purpose. That purpose being to restore them spiritually and bring them back into intimate relationship.

> "For the children of Israel shall abide many days without a king, and without a prince, and without a sacrifice, and without an image, and without an ephod, and without teraphim: Afterward shall the children of Israel return, and seek the Lord their GOD, and David their king; and shall fear (reverence) the Lord and HIS goodness in the latter days." (Hosea 3:4-5)

The "Dry Bones" seen by the Prophet Ezekiel in a vision are beginning to put on flesh.[1177] The progressive revelation has now begun in earnest. The time is here; two days (two thousand years), have passed since Yahusha' first visitation. The voice of GOD is speaking, "…O' ye dry bones, hear the Word of the Lord!"

(Image Source: ALAMY)

> "After two days will He revive us: in the third day He will raise us up, and we shall live in His sight. Then shall we know if we follow on to know the LORD, His going forth is prepared as the morning; and He shall come unto us as the rain, as the latter rain and the former rain upon the earth." (Hosea 6:2-3)

[1177] Ezekiel 37:1-14

The third day is about to dawn. The first glow of the Son-rise is breaking on the horizon. The scales are beginning to fall from the eyes of the Jewish people. The veil is beginning to lift.

"To everything there is a season, and a time for every purpose under the heaven: A time to be born..." (Ecclesiastes. 3:1)

It is, "for Such a time as this!"[1178]

1178 Hadassah (Esther 4:14)

55

THE INVITATION

The Adoption

You are a young orphan. You live in a comfortable orphanage with other children who have become your close friends. There is good food and a playground with some wonderful things to play on; you are quite content.

One day a young couple visits the orphanage looking to adopt a child for their own. They meet with the administrator and walk outside to where the children are all playing so they might consider which child they want to adopt.

The administrator calls over to one little girl and says, "Sally, how would you like to be adopted by these lovely people?" Sally looks at them and then looks back to her little girl friends skipping jump rope and says, "No thank you, I want to go back and play with my friends." Sally is excused, turns away, and returns to skipping rope.

The administrator calls little Johnny over who was playing with his friends on the jungle gym and asks him the same question, to which Johnny replies, "No thanks, I like it here and I want to stay and play with my pals." Johnny then is also excused, turns away, and returns to play with his friends.

The administrator then calls to you. You, like the other children were having a good time on the swings but being obedient you come over. He then asks you, "Would you like to be adopted by this nice couple, go home with them, and become part of this loving family?" You look at the man and his wife who are smiling down on you. Suddenly it dawns on you what is being offered. Your lips begin to part, and a small smile begins to form. When the couple sees your response, their smiles become even broader and warmer. Still, in almost disbelief you ask, "You mean you want me to be your child?" The couple looks at one another and then gazes into your eyes and answers, "Yes we do; more than anything else. But do you want to leave this place and live with us?" In that moment the decision becomes entirely yours… and you reply, "More than anything else in the world I do!"

So the question is, do you want to continue as an orphan on this earthly playground, enjoying your friends and being content with what you have and where you are, or do you want—more than anything else—to be adopted into the loving family of GOD?

My friend, as His name Yahusha-Jesus (Savior) declares, He is both GOD and Savior. He can be your garment of salvation and your robe of righteousness, but it is up to you to want this royal robe.[1179]

> "I will greatly rejoice in the Lord, my soul shall be joyful in my God; for He shall clothed me with the garments of salvation, He hath covered me with the robe of righteousness, as a bridegroom decketh himself with ornaments, and a bride adorneth herself with her jewels." (Isaiah 61:10)

(Image Source: GOODSALT)

GOD has offered all this to you for only the price of a heartfelt prayer. If you will say it back to Him; meaning every syllable from the depths of your heart you will receive the "spirit of adoption whereby you may cry, Abba, Father."[1180] Once such a prayer is said, you have His Word that you will join Him in His glorious kingdom for eternity.[1181]

"GOD of Abraham, Isaac, and Jacob, I receive Yahusha-Jesus as my Messiah, who did what the Law cannot do. Yahusha, you are my atonement. You alone have saved me from my sins. Your blood has washed me white as snow and made me Holy in the Fathers eyes. Come into my heart right now as I declare you as my Lord and Savior. From this day forward, I will love you, proclaim you and serve you. I will do my very best to live a life, holy and acceptable to you. Jesus, I am yours and you are mine."

Welcome to the family of GOD. You are now a new creature; "old things are passed away; behold all things are become new.[1182]

Let these verses encourage you as you begin your walk with Yahshua-Jesus.

> "I Am the resurrection, and the life, he that believeth in Me, though he were dead, yet shall he live: And whosoever liveth and believeth in Me shall never die..." (John 11:25-26)

> "I will praise thee, though thou wast angry with me, thy anger is turned away, and thou comfortest me. Behold GOD is my salvation (my Yahusha, my Jesus). I will trust and not be afraid: for the Lord Yahovah is my strength and my song. He also is my salvation (my Yahusha). Therefore with joy ye (you) shall draw water out of the wells of salvation. And

---

1179 Luke 15:21-22
1180 Romans 8:15
1181 Romans 10:9-13
1182 2 Corinthians 5:17

in that day shall ye (you) praise the Lord, call upon His name, declare His doings among the people, make mention that His name is exalted. Sing unto the Lord for He hath done excellent things: this is known in all the earth. Cry out and shout thou inhabitants of Zion: for great is the Holy One of Israel in the midst of thee." (Isaiah 12:1-6)

"It is now time for us to "Blow ye the trumpet in Zion, and sound an alarm in My (His) holy mountain: let all the inhabitants of the land tremble: for the day of the Lord cometh, for it is nigh at hand..." (Joel 2:1)

I will close with the same message which our Lord closed with in His written Word, for it is His message to man, His offer of grace, His invitation to all.

"And the Spirit and the bride say, Come. And let him that heareth say, Come. And let him that is athirst come. And whosoever will, let him take the water of life freely." (Revelation 22:17)

The End ... No, the Beginning!

As we approach the time of the latter rain[1183] may "the trial of your faith, being much more precious than of gold that perisheth, though it be tried with fire, might be found unto praise and honour and glory at the appearing of Jesus Christ: Whom having not seen, ye love; in whom, though now ye see him not, yet believing, ye rejoice with joy unspeakable and full of glory..." (1 Peter 1:7-8)

"For in him we live, and move, and have our being..." (Acts 17:28)

With Love and Blessings,
Bruce and Quenda

[1183] Joel 2:23

ABOUT THE AUTHOR AND HIS TESTIMONY

My mother was a German Jewess. My father was a devout Irish Catholic. After World War II, and after my dad was discharged from the Army Air Corps, the three of us lived with my Yiddish grandparents in the predominately Jewish community of Woodmere, New York.

According to a Catholic mandate, before an interfaith marriage could take place, the non-Catholic would have to concede that any children they had would be raised in Catholicism. Not being a pious Jewess, my mother accepted the terms.

In 1951 we moved a short distance away to Oceanside, New York; however, I still considered Woodmere to be my true home and would return almost every weekend to stay with my grandparents. The one condition my father insisted on however was that my grandfather would have to take me back to Oceanside early Sunday mornings to go to mass with my father.

At age seven, I began twelve successive years of weekly Catholic religious instruction. As I grew older, I began pondering; if there was only one GOD and both Jews and Catholics believed in this same GOD, and even had at the core of their belief the Old Testament, then why were these two faiths so distinctly different? Why was there so much disparity? Why couldn't my grandparents recognize Jesus? And why…why did my grandfather have a noticeable disdain for my father?

Fast forward: Returning from Vietnam, I attended Adelphi University. Required to take English Literature and study the works of philosophical thinkers I began to challenge my religious convictions, for even having been indoctrinated in Catholicism I found it to be largely superficial. Then while taking a sequence of psychology and sociology modules an atheist professor sowed seeds of doubt about the existence of GOD, and those seeds began to germinate.

It wasn't long after that, that I became the personification of the "Prodigal Son."[1184] Subsequently, I went through some tumultuous times, not unlike the wayward son in the parable. I sowed to the wind and subsequently reaped the whirlwind I deserved. I was soon alone, homeless, and loveless.

Then, in the time it takes to look into a mirror and see ones' reflection, I saw myself as I really was. What I saw revolted me and I broke! It was in that moment of total despair that I cried out to GOD seeking forgiveness from the depths of my being.

[1184] Luke 15:11-32

Previously, I had been content in my belief that membership in the Catholic Church and following its rules, rituals, and teachings was enough to attain Heaven. After all I thought, what more could GOD expect from anyone?

My religion portrayed a GOD who resided in a distant place called Heaven where all good practicing Catholics would eventually end up, even if they were to have a layover in a place called Purgatory. Only the truly evil go to Hell, I thought.

In all the years spent in Romanism I had never been urged to read or study the Bible and therefore never did, so I had no idea how it conflicted with what I had been taught. I had been indoctrinated, programmed, and managed. Ignorance was bliss and I was content in my Catholic cocoon.

I had reasoned that GOD simply loved everyone and that he didn't get personally involved with anyone. I was taught and believed that Mary was my mediator. So, I thought, it was enough that GOD was pleased that I was a Catholic and believed in Jesus. And, when I sinned, I believed HE would excuse my sins; even so-called mortal sins if I confessed to a priest, said a few prayers, and resolved not to do it again.

Like many who put their trust in religion I subconsciously used it as a safety net, dangling somewhere between hope, promise, and the unknown. Years came and went as I lived in my delusion; that was until that day when my life fell apart. In that dark moment, like a drowning man choking for air I cried out so earnestly that I literally broke the sound barrier; for the GOD of all creation heard my cry and revealed HIMSELF in a way I had never imagined possible. I had crossed into another dimension. I had traversed death and gone from the physical realm into the spiritual.

After that glorious life-changing moment I visited my father and tried to explain what had happened to me, but the words escaped me. All I could blurt out was, "Dad, HE is real! I mean, HE is really real!"

GOD had come to me in a way that defies the human experience. I had escaped death three times in Vietnam that I recall, never realizing at the time that it was a forbearing God who had kept me from hell—had I died in my unregenerated state. In HIS omniscience HE knew that if HE were to keep me alive that I would one day receive Yahusha-Jesus as my personal savior and be adopted into the family of GOD.

In much the same way HE had sustained me over the years, waiting patiently for me to come to the end of myself. Through my own self-destruction and pain, HE extended me an opportunity we have come to call grace. In my brokenness HE would seize me, save me, and sanctify me solely because I had come to terms with my sin and internalized what He did for me by going to the Cross.

Just as the scriptures urged all of us to do, I had sought HIM with all of my heart and with all my soul, and with all my remaining might, and suddenly—as promised, HE revealed HIMSELF. "And ye shall seek Me and find Me, when ye shall search for Me with all of your heart."[1185]

[1185] Jeremiah 29:13

Before my transformation the Bible was just a fine-looking book with a rich leather cover, gilded with gold leafed pages. It was however little more than an ornament. It had been given a place of prominence on the family bookshelf as if to say to visitors, "see—we're good religious people who believe in GOD." But now as I began reading the scriptures which had before merely been ink and type, they suddenly took on a life of their own. It was as if GOD was speaking not just to me, but just for me. Not only did I hear them in my mind, I felt them penetrate my very being. While I felt conviction, I felt something even greater; I felt forgiveness; I felt loved.

The Lord of all creation was suddenly conversing with me a miserable sinner! The more I sought HIM the more HE spoke. Now I understood. The Bible was not simply another book, it was alive; a living breathing Word to each of us! It was more than hope, it was promise! What had begun as a lifeline to heaven became my passion. Today HIS Word remains my focus and teaching it my delight. As it has grown in me, I have grown in it.

Before GOD made HIS presence known I did not understand why I had been born a Jew and raised a Catholic, but today I do; it was, "For Such a Time as This." Now, I want to bring others to see the disparity between Rabbinic Judaism and Biblical Judaism, and between Catholicism and Genuine Christianity.

I have proudly returned to my roots as a Biblical Jew, which means I have accepted my Messiah and become a follower—a true Jew, and a true Christian. I am now compelled to share with any who will hear the differences and the deceptions which have separated many from our Great and Mighty GOD, and from the King of Glory (Hebrew, *Melech Hakavod*), Yahusha-Jesus.

"How shall we escape, if we neglect so great (a) salvation..." (Hebrews 2:3)

APPENDIX A

THE JUDGMENT OF AMERICA

"...And can the liberties of a nation be thought secure when we have removed their only firm basis, a conviction in the minds of the people that these liberties are of the gift of GOD? That they are not able to be violated but with HIS Wrath. Indeed, I tremble for my country when I reflect that GOD is just: that HIS justice cannot sleep forever." Thomas Jefferson

"The Lord is not slack concerning HIS promises, as some men count slackness, but is long suffering (patient) to us-ward, not willing that any should perish. But that all should come to repentance..." (1 Peter 3:9)

What the Lord has done to other nations and empires, even to HIS beloved Israel when the people blatantly disregarded HIM and HIS admonishments, HE will do to any and to all. America will be no exception for she has no fear of GOD, no trembling heart. Given ample time in which to turn from her sins, revere and return to HIM, with patience exhausted, HIS righteousness demands justice.

Righteousness mandates Justice
(Image Source: ISTOCK)

"The heathen are sunk down in the pit that they made: in the net which they hid is their own foot taken. The Lord is known by the judgment which he executeth: the wicked is snared in the work of his own hands...The wicked shall be turned to hell, and all the nations that forget GOD." (Psalm 9:15-17)

No one knows with certainty at what hour GOD's judgment of America will begin, therefore my deductions—as they may concern time, are provisional. Indeed, it may have already begun as America, has in the past two and a half decades, had a number of evil and ungodly leaders in its highest offices whose goal is the dissolution of the nation as we know it. Now we see its economy faltering: a harbinger of what is coming.

In the past GOD has brought judgment in increments; with a graduating chastening as with the plagues of Pharaoh's Egypt—each increased in severity. So, may we anticipate a progression and an escalation of calamitous events.

However, one thing is certain. We know from HIS Word that once HIS Church has been removed, judgment will begin in earnest and build to a crescendo ending in unimageable suffering.

From what we have learned and observed, as the prophetic becomes the present—HIS patience is nearing an end. If for the sake of a praying Church HE postpones judgment on America, or for the sake of a single soul who HE knows will receive Him, should HE bestow us with one final undeserved Great Awakening—that is indeed HIS unfathomable mercy. But make no mistake and be not taken in should encouraging times return, for they will be brief, and Judgement will come, and Justice will be served! We have sewn to the wind and shall reap a whirlwind.

As a boy growing up in the 1950s, I remember a different America. Though it couldn't be said that it was strictly a Judeo-Christian nation, it was for the most part. A belief in GOD was pervasive and the agnostic was a rarity. I remember one day in 1954 when my teacher told the class that the words "under God" were added to our Pledge of Allegiance. Without any dissent, the nation universally and gladly accepted it, for we believed in GOD. HE had just given us the victory in a world war and now opportunity and optimism swept the country. Premarital sex was wrong. Marriage was a lifetime commitment. Abortion was an abomination. Homosexuality was a perversion, and pornography was an embarrassment. Drugs were called dope, as were those who used them.

Today, all that has changed. HE has been taken out of our schools. Prayer, even silent prayer, has been eliminated so as not to offend the atheist. Today, drugs are rampant; pornography can be found on almost every television channel; premarital sex is accepted; homosexuality is considered a norm and GOD...well, HE apparently doesn't care as no fire and brimstone have been unleashed. Today's ministers, be they rabbis, pastors, or rectors, skirt the Word of GOD with soft sermons. They avoid that GOD is Holy; that Hell is a real; and that unless a man is Born Again, he shall not enter the Kingdom of GOD. The seared minds of many are akin to those of the Sodomites, and still we have the audacity to sing "GOD Bless America."

So what is next? Scripture portrays Israel as being alone in the last days when a consortium of Arab-Muslim nations bent on annihilation converge on her. Strikingly absent are any allies,[1186] including her once closest ally, world superpower—the United States.

Were the United States either still a superpower or still an ally, Israel would never be in jeopardy of being conquered as Scripture forecasts.

I believe that in the not-too-distant future, America will no longer be a force to be reckoned with. One or more events will happen rendering her impotent, for she like Israel has left the old paths and failed to take GOD at HIS Word.

"The wicked shall be turned to hell, and all the nations that forget GOD." (Psalm 9:17)

[1186] Matthew 24:9

"Be not deceived; God is not mocked: for whatsoever a man (or a nation) soweth: that shall he also reap." (Galatians 6:7)

In the years leading up to the 2016 presidential election things were looking bleak for America. A stagnant economy, huge debt, high unemployment, and terrible foreign policy allowed for Israel's and America's adversaries to make great gains under the Obama administration. The country was most certainly in a downward spiral.

During the 2016 primaries leading up to the election, there were a number of conservative candidates claiming to be Christians. Their sincerity and optimism, though commendable, was misplaced, for no matter how well-meaning their intentions and how sound their strategies, they all appear to lack understanding of what GOD has said on the subject. Be it Israel, or America; there is no restoration apart from national repentance! Not one candidate was bold enough to speak this forth.

> Note: Scripture does speak of "sheep nations." This refers to nations who side with Israel positionally or diplomatically in the last days; however, it does not imply that they are military allies who would defender her.[1187]

Learning from Israel's Mistakes

There is a passage from the Old Testament which is often quoted which urges the people to pray and get right with GOD. It includes HIS promise to restore the nation if they will comply. Though spoken to Israel, the general application of 2 Chronicles 7:14 is such that it can be applied to the United States or to any God-fearing nation that complies.

> "If My people, which are called by My name, shall humble themselves and pray, and seek My face, and turn from their wicked ways; then will I hear from heaven, and will forgive their sins, and will heal their land."

What is often overlooked is that when the Lord spoke these words to King Solomon, Israel was in its heyday and things were looking exceptionally bright; so, the covenant promise didn't seem to be relevant. The people were still enjoying the benefits of living in Solomon's wealthy and unchallenged kingdom. These words were given as a warning to a people before the empire disintegrated; a people who did not see themselves as sinners or having turned away from HIM. Only five verses later do we read of the consequence for denial or negligence.

> "But if you turn away, and forsake My statues and My commandments, which I have set before you, and shall go and serve other gods and worship them I will pluck them (the people) up by the roots out of my land which I have given them; and this house which I have sanctified for My name. I will cast them (the people) out of My sight, and make it

---

1187 Matthew 25:32-33

to be a proverb and a byword among the nations. And this house which is high shall be astonished to everyone that passeth by it; so that he shall say, Why hath the Lord done this unto this land and unto this house? And it shall be answered, Because they forsook the Lord GOD of their fathers..." (2 Chronicles 7:19-22)

In the end the people didn't "seek HIS face or turn from their wicked ways" and so their land was divided, and they were eventually overtaken by their enemies. So it is with America that all human effort will not restore her to her former greatness unless the leaders and the people unabashedly acknowledge their sin, repent and seek after the Lord; ultimately recognizing Yahusha-Jesus as their sovereign king.

In so far as America is concerned, there is a biblical precedence which illustrates how GOD chooses to deal with a nation that attempts to put HIM in the same camp with their god. In a word, HE simply topples it!

America's god has become her wealth and economy. Her people worship money. The "Big Board" (the Stock Exchange) is just one example of her many icons. Consequently, GOD can be expected to topple this colossal idol. When this occurs, the United States will be dramatically changed. As her dollar is devalued investors will rush to abandon her currency and place their wealth in more secure assets.

> "And the Philistines took the ark of God, and brought it from Ebenezer unto Ashdod. When the Philistines took the ark of God, they brought it into the house (temple) of Dagon, and set it by Dagon (the statue). And when they of Ashdod arose early on the morrow, behold, Dagon was fallen upon his face to the earth before the ark of the Lord. And they took Dagon, and set him in his place again. And when they arose early on the morrow morning, behold, Dagon was fallen upon his face to the ground before the ark of the Lord; and the head of Dagon and both the palms of his hands were cut off upon the threshold; only the stump of Dagon was left to him. Therefore neither the priests of Dagon, nor any that come into Dagon's house, tread on the threshold of Dagon in Ashdod unto this day." (1 Samuel 5:1-5)

Allow the words, "the head and the hands were cut off" and "only a stump was left" to reverberate in your mind for it may be applied to America… Its head or headship as the world leader and the world's leading economy? Its hands give it the ability to produce and prosper, while a handless America speaks to its helplessness, even to defend itself or its allies.

Freedom of Religion and Cultural Diversity

Born from religious oppression, freedom of religion under our first Amendment is one of our most cherished fundamental rights guaranteed in our Constitution. But what if the nature and intent of one religion is to abolish another? Should that belief system be supported by our Constitution? Does it not become the antithesis of freedom to worship as one chooses if one seeks to eliminate another? Should a religion that promotes such an ideology as Sharia law or for that matter the feudal brand of Romanism be supported and allowed to flourish unrestricted by law? Could such ideologies expand and be the downfall of that nation?

The Holy Scriptures present a lesson as to how GOD views the subject of diversity. In chapter eleven in the book of 1 Kings, Solomon, (accorded to be the wisest man on earth at that time) and a God-fearing Israelite had added multiple foreign wives to his harem. To accommodate his wives, he permitted the building of temples to their gods. In the process these wives were able to turn his heart to their gods. This was an abomination to our Lord. Solomon had broken the covenant he had made only ten years earlier when he had dedicated the Temple to his GOD.[1188] In response to his blatant disobedience Solomon's kingdom was divided and GOD eventually permitted it to be overtaken by others. Were it not for the Abrahamic and Davidic Covenants this might have been the end of the Jewish race altogether.

Under Mosaic Law and the Ten Commandments was the first commandment, "Thou shalt have no other gods before me." The word "before" did not mean putting HIM first and allowing other gods to follow HIM in a descending succession; it meant and means not permitting or acknowledging there were other gods at all! The punishment for breaking any of the Ten Commandments was death.[1189] For this one sin alone GOD would blot out the offender's name from the Book of Life (Hebrew, *Sefer Chayim*).[1190] This then begs the question; Would GOD indeed prescribe death to a nation as HE has to the individual who breaks this commandment? The answer is unequivocally yes. Our Lord affords a person or a nation enough time to repent and return to HIM, but eventually if that person or nation refuses this grace[1191] then death becomes the consequence for infidelity.[1192]

Solomon had dared to oppose the "I AM" but soon learned about GOD's intolerance for cultural diversity. The penalty would be to bring an end to what was then the wealthiest and most invincible empire on earth[1193] GOD would begin the downward spiral by introducing a number of godless kings over the nation that would result in the affliction and subsequent conquest and of the people.[1194]

There would be a total of thirty-three ungodly kings and one ungodly queen of Israel from the time of Saul to the Babylonian captivity…and only nine godly kings. Eventually, as GOD had ordained, and as HIS prophets had warned, both Israel and then Judah would fall to their Assyrian and Chaldean oppressors. So it was that the sins of the father would be borne by their children until there was national repentance.

> "And the seed of Israel separated themselves from all strangers, and stood and confessed their sins, and the iniquities of their fathers." (Nehemiah 9:2)

1188 2 Chronicles 7:12-14
1189 Exodus 20:3
1190 Exodus 32:30-33; Psalm 69:28
1191 1 Kings 11:6-10
1192 Deuteronomy 6:14-15
1193 Deuteronomy 10:14-23; 2 Chronicles 9:22
1194 1 Kings 11:39

Will America acknowledge her sins and her depravity, seek Lord and be forgiven or will she like Israel follow the dark path that leads to consequence?

Insofar as America is concerned, her beginnings were admirable and began with a covenant when believers first came to this land. The Plymouth Brethren (also known as Separatists) had fled to America to escape the mandate to surrender their beliefs to the Church of England (the Anglican/Episcopal Church) by what was called, "the Divine Right of Kings."

On November 11, 1620, having arrived at Plymouth, Massachusetts and while still on the ship the Mayflower, the Puritans covenanted with the GOD of Abraham, consecrating this land to HIM.

In what would be called the Mayflower Compact they vowed this would be a Christian nation, "…having undertaken, for the glory of God, and advancement of the Christian faith…"[1195]

How promising were the words recorded in the personal journal of their leader William Bradford, who wrote, "one candle can light a thousand." Faithful to the call of GOD and steadfast to the teachings of the Holy Scriptures, Bradford crossed an ocean and lit the candle which would afterward make America a Christian nation and the greatest nation ever conceived.

It is also noteworthy that in his book *Of Plymouth Plantation*, Bradford understood the dangers of Satan's counterfeit church. Here is the first sentence of the first paragraph of the first book written on American soil.

> "It is well known unto the godly and judicious, how ever since the first breaking out of the light of the gospel in our honorable nation of England, (which was the first of nations whom the Lord adorned therewith after the gross darkness of popery which had covered and overspread the Christian world), what wars and oppositions ever since, Satan hath raised, maintained and continued against the saints, from time to time, in one sort or other."

This covenant made by the Separatists has remained in effect for centuries. While it did, the nation grew and prospered. It abounded with natural resources and enjoyed freedoms other nations could only wish for. It was the GOD of Abraham who was recognized and acknowledged as our benefactor—"GOD shed HIS grace on thee." But we the people have withdrew from the covenant. Like Israel, we have compromised and condoned the un-condonable. We have relegated GOD to an impersonal, unnamed and unknown entity. Each generation has brought us further and further from our beginnings.

While Americans have been given the freedom to worship as they choose, many have chosen poorly. Failing to remember the lessons of Scripture and history, they, like King Solomon, have permitted heathens to establish their temples in a consecrated land and elected godless leaders to rule them. "When the righteous are in authority, the people rejoice: but when the wicked beareth rule, the people mourn."[1196]

1195 *The Mayflower Compact*, William Bradford, 1620
1196 Proverbs 29:2

One can be certain that after the Lord's return and His millennial reign begins, there will be no political correctness, no temples to imaginary gods, and absolutely no tolerance for other belief systems.

> "I am the Lord, and there is none else, there is no God beside me: I girded thee, though thou hast not known me..." (Isaiah 45:5)

Just as the people are oblivious of Who it is that they have opposed, so have they been oblivious to several of the deviant agenda of their elected leaders. Why for example would a nation seek "hope and change" or want their nation "transformed" from the freest and most prosperous nation on earth is an enigma were it not for the fact that Satan has been given license when the people chose to "change the truth of GOD into a lie, and worship and serve the creature more that the Creator who blessed them."[1197]

We would do well to remember that what may seem right in the eyes of men is rarely right in the eyes of GOD.[1198] America has allowed her liberties to trump GOD's laws and, in the process brought judgment upon herself.

There is no neutrality with GOD when it comes to pluralism, or a pluralistic society. When a nation such as America, established on the foundation of the Bible; a nation which recognized the one and only GOD and HIS Son as their sovereign; a nation whose laws, constitution and government were modeled from HIS Word; should that nation afterward abandon its Biblical roots for pluralism, it is certain to lose the blessings and benefits of a Christian civilization. Inevitably, its moral standards decay, its liberties are constrained by an overbearing government, and it succumbs to some form of tyranny.

Consistent with HIS ways would be for HIM to enact the same judgement HE prescribed for Israel.

> "Behold ye among the heathen, and regard, and wonder marvelously: for I will work a work in your days which ye will not believe, though it be told you. For, lo, I raise up the Chaldeans, that bitter and hasty nation, which shall march through the breadth of the land, to possess the dwelling places that are not theirs." (Habakkuk 1:5-6)

Today the Chaldeans (geographically identified as the Arab-Muslim nations which occupied Babylon in Habakkuk's day) are not yet the majority in America as they are quickly becoming in numerous European countries, but they are now streaming in through porous borders or through the visa lottery system. Muslims from Islamic nations; some under the guise of persecution are being admitted and given asylum without being vetted. Under the Obama administration sanctuary cities sprung up across America's landscape and gave refuge to illegal felons.

1197 Romans 1:25
1198 Jeremiah 8:9; 24:11-12; Habakkuk 1:13; 2 Kings 24:2

In time their numbers will flourish, and with a voting majority they will gradually take more and more control. Inevitably, a Muslim faction will occupy seats in congress and with a strong voice oppose the underpinnings of our Constitution.

Sharia law has already usurped civil law in certain communities like Dearborn, Michigan. Author Martin Mawyer; in his book *Twilight in America: The Untold Story of Islamic Terrorist Training Camps Inside America*, writes that currently, twenty-two villages in nine states have enclaves which are considered to be "no go zones" for the rest of America.[1199] Religious freedom is mutating into religious persecution. Jewry and Christianity are coming under attack as they are forced to accept federal laws which demand they violate their religious convictions.

The Bible and rule of law here in the United States as it applies to those who violate immigration laws (lawbreakers) are now praised by the disloyal for their success in breaking the laws of the land. These advocates further claim the illegals have the same rights as natural born citizens and look to reward them with all the benefits of citizenship. Past President Obama has been the vanguard, as he not only allowed Islamic extremists into our country but did his best to streamline the process.

There is indeed a right way and a wrong way to deal with situations, and that way may be found in the Bible. The Scriptures teach that breaking the law is not acceptable. "Those who forsake the law praise the wicked, but those who keep the law strive against them."[1200] Grace and mercy are to be had only when there is lawful obedience.

Jihadist attacks on American soil may be expected to escalate, but the real threat will be covert as they infiltrate our halls of justice and seats of government. At the same time, a progressive administration took the first step toward totalitarianism by attempting to limit free speech by suggesting anything the slightest bit derogatory is hate speech. Political correctness and the cancel culture have become a growing trend.

> Note: Under the Obama administration tens of thousands of Muslim refugees have been allowed into the country. There are an estimated 5.5 million Jews living in America. According to the Center for Immigration Studies in Washington the Muslim demographic is estimated at about 3 million but is growing much faster due to the acceptance of refugees, via the indulgent immigration policy of the Obama administration and the birth rate associated with Muslim families. This is destined to dramatically change the demographics in America, its culture and America's policy towards Israel. What is happening in Europe is a clear indication of what we can expect to happen in the U.S. if the open-door policy continues. This developing trend could prove a threat to Jewish Americans first and ultimately to Christians as well. Robert Spencer, author of the Jihad Watch blog at the David Horowitz Freedom Center said, "four separate and independent studies since 1998 have found that eighty percent of mosques in the U.S. preach hatred of Jews and Christians and the need to ultimately impose Shariah law here." As the Muslim population has grown, the number

---

1199 The Connors Report – Media Network, February 12, 2017, author Martin Mawyer, *Twilight in America*
1200 Proverbs 28:4

> of mosques sprouting up in the U.S. has multiplied fifteen-fold since the September 11, 2001, terrorist attack that killed nearly three thousand Americans. The number of mosques grew from just two hundred on 9/11 to between 2,500–3,000 by 2015.

By abandoning our immigration policies that have always welcomed foreigners in a fair and equitable manner, the United States has ensured its "transformation" and with it the erosion of Judeo-Christian values and beliefs. With each successive generation we can expect further declension and moral deterioration. In doing so, that which GOD spoke to Israel could become the fate of America as well.

> "And I will set my face against you, and ye shall be slain before your enemies: they that hate you shall reign over you; and ye shall flee when none pursueth you. And if ye will not yet for all this hearken unto me, then I will punish you seven times more for your sins." (Leviticus 26:17-18)

The Holy Scriptures tell us, the most high ruled (rules) in the kingdoms of men, and that HE appointeth over it whomsoever HE will.[1201] From this scripture we recognize that it is none other than GOD who gave America the president (Obama) she deserved. A president who by his policies has followed the manifesto of the global oligarchy who positioned him to take over and take down the country.[1202] And why, one might ask, would GOD permit this to happen? The answer is obvious. Aside from His Church, America has no "trembling heart, no sorrow of mind."[1203] Her transgressions, lack of remorse, and her failure to recognize and venerate her creator and benefactor has brought her before the bench of justice. She has "sown the wind, and shall reap the whirlwind."[1204]

America's Last Saving Grace

America's last saving grace was that she had remained a friend to Israel, but under the Obama administration that too deteriorated. Be assured that when an ally capable of helping Israel fails to defend her from her enemies, then they themselves will be cursed of GOD.

> "Cursed be everyone that curseth thee (Israel), and blessed be he that blesseth thee." (Genesis 27:29)

Such was the fate of the city of Meroz mentioned in the Book of Judges. Meroz was cursed by the angel of GOD in the song of Deborah and Barak when her inhabitants failed to fight alongside the Israelites in a battle against Sisera's army.[1205]

1201 Daniel 5:21
1202 Saul Alinsky, *Rules for Radicals*, and *Reveille for Radicals*, Chicago University Press 1946, Vintage Books, Random House, 1969
1203 Deuteronomy 28:65
1204 Hosea 8:7
1205 Judges 5:23

"Curse ye Meroz, said the angel of the Lord, curse ye bitterly the inhabitants thereof; because they came not to the help of the Lord, to the help of the Lord against the mighty (the enemies of Israel)." (Judges 5:23)

GOD, it appears, has with HIS appointment of President Trump postponed judgment on America; but this should not be interpreted as a reprieve. It is largely for Israel's sake, not for America's sake, that judgment is being delayed. As we approach the end of the Church dispensation our Lord has begun to set the stage for Israel's finale. HE is aligning the nations (friends—sheep nations and foes—goats nations) for what will happen next. It is almost certain that either when the Church is removed or perhaps after the Trump administration ends, that should a progressive administration regain power that America will again align herself with the United Nations which sees Israel as being responsible for the contention in the Mid-East.

> Note: On December 21, 2017, we saw the handwriting on the wall as battle lines were being drawn. One hundred and twenty-eight nations in a vote (128-9) of the UN General Assembly condemned President Trump's decision to move the U.S. embassy from Tel Aviv to Jerusalem and recognize Jerusalem as Israel's capital. In reality, it is GOD who has chosen Jerusalem as the capital of Israel; the president is simply the instrument HE has chosen to bring it to pass.

"But I have chosen Jerusalem, that my name might be there; and have chosen David to be over my people Israel." (2 Chronicles 6:6)

"For Zion's sake will I not hold my peace, and for Jerusalem's sake I will not rest, until the righteousness thereof go forth as brightness, and the salvation thereof as a lamp that burneth." (Isaiah 62:1)

The Perilous Global Economy

A few paragraphs ago I mentioned that GOD is going to topple America's god (a.k.a. her economy). However, it will not only be America's economy that collapses but the entire global economy. America will afterward be crippled; the ramifications will overwhelm the country and civil chaos will likely ensue.

The first harbinger of judgment is already underway. Unbeknownst to most Americans is that the United Stated dollar is on the verge of losing her status as the premier World Reserve Currency. When this comes to pass the dollar will suddenly be greatly devalued; perhaps by as much as seventy percent. The best that can be hoped for is that the devaluation is gradual.

When Alan Greenspan was the Federal Reserve chairman and part of the global syndicate, he made an admission, howbeit camouflaged in rhetoric. "The United States can pay any debt it has because we can always print money to do that. So there is zero probability of default. We can guarantee cash benefits as far out and whatever size you like but we cannot guarantee their purchasing power."

So it may be said, that the value of the dollar is only as good as what one can buy with it. Once the value of the dollar has been degraded, those to whom our Federal government is indebted will not want that debt paid in paper fiat but in tangible assets and a certain yellow precious metal.

Our two-decade long grand experiment in financial bailouts, quantitative easing, debt stimulus, and the massive printing of 4.4 trillion dollars by the Federal Reserve in collusion with the U.S. Treasury has debased the dollar and brought us to this inevitable moment. Only after he retired as Federal Reserve Chairman did Alan Greenspan make a full admission. "Deficit spending is simply a scheme for the confiscation of wealth. Gold stands in the way of this insidious process. It stands as a protector of property rights."

> Note: Former FED chairmen Ben Bernanke, along with many economists have admitted that the U.S. dollar has lost 98% of its value since the Federal Reserve was established in 1914. If one looked at charts, they would see that from 1914 until 1933 (when F.D. Roosevelt fixed the domestic gold price at $35 per ounce) things were relatively stable. From 1933 to 1971, at least the foreign held dollar continued to be backed by gold. Consequently between 1914 and 1971, the world had confidence in the U.S. dollar. During those six decades, the dollar only lost about one or two percent of its purchasing power. As long as there was any connection between the paper dollar and gold the dollar's loss of purchasing power was minimal. Then in 1971, President Nixon took us and foreign held dollars off the gold standard and the connection between gold and the U.S. dollar was—with the stroke of a pen—no more. The dollar became an un-guaranteed promissory I.O.U. note. Since 1971 the fiat dollar has lost at least 96% of its purchasing power! The association is undeniable; as long as the paper dollar was officially redeemable in gold (if only as it related to foreign trade and exchange), then the value of the paper dollar had some stability. But when the fiat dollar was completely detached from gold its purchasing power began and continued to fall. Hence the primary cause of the dollar's decline (purchasing power) is a result of its having no or little gold backing. Meanwhile the Treasury prints more paper fiat. This leads to the obvious conclusion that if governments are forced by the power brokers to have even some of their paper dollars backed with gold then their money may maintain a value. Thus, by reinstating a gold and asset-based monetary system, (in the process of a global reset) things could be expected to somewhat normalize.

Greed has driven the stock market to unprecedented levels which, to a large degree, have decoupled it from the geopolitical events taking place around the world. Financial institutions using fractional reserve banking and leveraging have extended themselves many times beyond what they have in their reserves. Market manipulation (rigging) is blatantly obvious if one looks at how COMEX can control the price of physical gold by selling over eighty ounces of paper (promissory gold) for every ounce of deliverable physical gold. Emerging market companies over-borrowed trillions of dollars.[1206] Looming equity (inflated real estate) created another bubble as the stock market tests new highs. And while the markets flirt with highs, according to Bloomberg, just six stocks account for 98% of the S&P 500: Facebook, Amazon, Apple, Netflix, Google, and Microsoft.

There is now a low-volume participation of market investors who realize the economy is sick. While the U.S. dollar index is up, this might look promising to some but is in fact a bad omen. A strong dollar chokes U.S. exports by making them less competitive and destroying the profits of companies who export their products overseas.

The U.S. national debt is currently approaching 22 trillion dollars. The U.S. debt-to-GDP ratio is 103%, and America's total bank debt is approximately 70 trillion dollars. During the Obama administration, the U.S. federal government added $9 trillion to the public debt, which is more than it had amassed in the previous 246 years. Public unfunded pensions are over 5 trillion. Corporate American has borrowed an estimated 1 trillion dollars but has increased its production by only an estimated 200 billion. The five major banks in the U.S. have north of $340 trillion in derivative exposure with JP Morgan's exposure, properly valued—probably in excess of $100 trillion.

Central banks are compelled to buy stocks and treasury (pension) bonds to keep the juggler's pins twirling in the air. Low interest rates prompted corporate stock buybacks, a substitute of debt issuance for the likes of junk bonds was made in order to make corporate balance sheets appear solvent. Global giants such as Glencore, Petrobras, and Deutsche Bank are in serious trouble as the stock markets of the ten largest economies on the entire planet are tottering. Stock market activity is generated by freshly printed (illusionary) dollars and by expectation, not by growth, which comes much later.

Some of the largest European banks are showing undeniable signs of a looming default. Among them are Credit Suisse, Deutsche Bank, United Bank of Switzerland Group, Royal Bank of Scotland Group PLC, Barclays, Banco Santander, and Hong Kong Shanghai Banking Corporation.

Bad loan defaults have reached towering proportions. Derivative gambles have come home to roost and bogus mortgage practices by the largest banks have forced them to pay out billions in fines to settle their collusion in market manipulations. At the same time, European banks began instituting negative interest rates which crushed margins as these banks are largely affected by Euro nations' diminishing economies.[1207]

Debt is global and there is no end in sight. The loaning of money from central banks to small banks at virtually zero percent interest only exacerbated the situation when those banks loan money to investors and speculators in failing economies. The banks in Italy, for example, are collectively holding $356 billion (U.S. dollar equivalent) of Non-Performing Loans (NPLs). These NPLs are loans in which the borrowers have defaulted. France and Germany jointly have

---

1206 IMF Global Market Stability Report, April 2014, Chapter 2
1207 Mike Larson, *Money and Markets: Investing Insights*, "Do not ignore the Euro-bank Crash," February 4, 2016

$272 billion (U.S. dollar equivalent) of NPLs. Europe's banks collectively have approximately $1 trillion in NPLs.[1208] In an effort to stop what might otherwise become a bank crisis contagion throughout Europe, the European Central bank can only institute more regulations and print more depreciating euros, making the taxpayer responsible for the debt.

We currently live in an economy where we are forced to grow our debt just to keep it from collapsing. America's economy and that of all other countries do not have enough cash or generate enough cash flow to support the untold trillions of debt that has been incurred!

All currencies are in reality debt notes and there are very few assets left to borrow against. This is why the stock market cannot be allowed to fall and why interest rates were not raised for years. But like any Ponzi scheme, there comes a time when the jig is up. The U.S. National Debt* surpassed $21 trillion in the first quarter of 2018. Several states are, for all intent already bankrupt, and others like Pennsylvania and Ohio are in peril. Devastating wildfires in California, the cost of storm damage from five catastrophic hurricanes—Harvey, Irma, Maria, and Michael to the Gulf states, and to the already bankrupt U.S. territory Puerto Rico (the damage of which together is still undetermined)—give one a sense of the magnitude of our dilemma…a dilemma which will necessitate the FED devaluing the dollar by printing more worthless money.

The bond market (the largest market) is the cornerstone of the entire global financial system. When it is realized that the government cannot pay the interest/dividends on its bonds, investors will abandon their positions. Virtually all the market will thereafter unwind, and the economies of every nation will tumble. With an unpayable national debt, skewed data (fake numbers) are essential, as the appearance of minimal inflation must be maintained. The FED inflated its balance sheet (by inventing money) from $900 billion in 2007 to $4.5 trillion today. They recently announced their intention (a feeble gesture) to reduce their balance sheet by auctioning off a pathetic 10–30 billion dollars of treasury bonds each month; however, there are few if any investors willing to purchase these bonds at what the FED purchased them for. If there are any potential buyers, they would likely not pay more than 65% of what the FEDs originally bought them for. Since union and corporate pension funds are enormous holders of treasuries, it means that pension funds may have lost 35% of their value. This may force private and public pension funds which are already insolvent into bankruptcy.

> Note: John Williams (shadowstats.com) claims the true national debt is actually closer to $100 trillion. The Congressional Budget Office and economist Laurence Kotlikoff have said that, including unfunded liabilities, the U.S. government's true national debt is over $200 trillion!

While a national debt doesn't necessarily ever have to be completely paid off, the economy does have to grow faster than the debt and interest. Historically, when a nation's debt exceeds its ability to repay even the interest, it can be assumed that the currency will collapse. Governments

---

[1208] *The International Forecaster*, October 21, 2017, "Where the Next Major Banking Crisis Will Begin," Justin Spittler and Joseph Withrow, p. 9

around the world have followed America's example by printing currency without collateral in an effort to inflate the problem away, or to at least postpone the inevitable. The greater the level of national debt, the more dramatic the level of inflation, and once it reaches a tipping point, inflation escalates quickly into hyperinflation—which no government has been able to control. This then ends in insolvency. When this occurs, America will experience what can only be described as a "credit freeze."

Economic growth that is produced by continually increasing debt is a ticking bomb. The following are real time (October 2018) statistics.

U.S. consumer credit just hit another all-time record high. In the second quarter of 2008, total consumer credit reached a grand total of 2.63 trillion dollars, and now ten years later that number has soared to 3.87 trillion dollars. That is an increase of forty-eight percent in just one decade.

Student loan debt has surpassed 1.5 trillion dollars for the first time ever. Over the last eight years, the total amount of student loan debt has shot up seventy-nine percent in the United States.

According to the Federal Reserve, the credit card default rate in the U.S. has risen for seven quarters in a row.

Real wage growth in the United States just declined by the most that we have seen in six years.

We are in the midst of the greatest "retail apocalypse" in American history. At this point, fifty-seven major retailers have announced store closings so far in 2018.

The size of the official U.S. budget deficit is up 21% under President Trump. It is being projected that interest on the national debt will surpass half a trillion dollars for the first time ever this year.

Goldman Sachs is projecting that the yearly U.S. budget deficit will surpass 2 trillion dollars by 2028.

Cumulatively, the U.S. is 66+ trillion dollars in debt, which makes it the world's largest debtor nation.

An apathetic and naïve citizenry is itself blameworthy. It is said that the average American watches only about fifteen minutes of televised news a day (most of which is false news or dribble), and measures the health of the economy on whether the Dow is green or red. In the meantime, and taking full advantage of their gullibility, the propaganda machine spews out nothing but fabricated statistics with a straight face.

> Note: President Trump's promised Tax Reform has been passed. Unemployment is alleged to have reached a new low at 3.7%. The stock market has broken new highs over eighty-six times since President Trump has taken office. The Dow gained 674 points in one week in December 2017, and then lost 1031 points in October 2018. The banks were up 5.8%; the brokers and dealers gained 4.5%; and the transports jumped 5.9%. The prospect of seeing manufacturing and export sectors come back to life has convinced many that the undeclared recession is over. In what can only be described as hysteria, many amateur speculators abandoned all discipline and risked their savings in the Bitcoin phenomenon. People are once more back to living above their means as they pile on holiday debts to their credit cards. Howbeit, essentially nothing has changed. The

> FED is still inventing invisible money. The 4.5 trillion dollars which drove the markets is still owed. Lent out at artificially low interest rates, the principal of the debt was never touched, and the FED has until recently continued to buy back debt and create new dollars. If they were to stop abruptly, the banks would fail, and the depositors would lose their savings. The economy would grind to a halt. Corporations would default on their loans and unemployment would rocket. Meanwhile, the federal government has continued spending; posting ongoing budget deficits. In the meantime, currency wars are ongoing between the most powerful nations as they undermine one another in an attempt to increase their exports. What is about to occur is a global meltdown, for greed and the quest for power have led all of the industrialized nations to the brink of default.

Believing that the tax overhaul and the bonus giving is a true sign of a recovery while the budget deficit takes another quantum leap is reckless. One cannot fund all the projects (the military, the Wall, Immigration/Deferred Action for Childhood Arrivals, the infrastructure, education, the opioid epidemic, hurricane recovery, etc.) at one time. President Trump did not create the deficit and was left with no choice but to pass another gargantuan budget. Though his efforts are most commendable, and his hope to salvage our country most noble, we have been weighed in the balance and found wanting. We have sown to the wind and will subsequently reap the whirlwind.

Surely "…the love of money is the root of all evil: which while some covet after, they have erred (turned away) from the faith, and have pierced themselves through with many sorrows."[1209]

Creating a New Currency

Since 1971 and on through the 1990s the U.S. dollar (USD) had strength and status as the world's "petro-currency." This meant that countries purchasing oil from one another would first be required to exchange their currency into the USD to complete the transaction. This made the USD the premier world reserve currency. In the 1970s it was used to purchase nearly 100% of crude oil sold on international markets. Today less than 80% of international crude oil sales are made with the USD. So the status of the USD has been eroding for quite some time.

More and more countries are now circumventing the USD and purchasing crude oil using their own currency. To facilitate this, and in order to stabilize the global financial system, the International Monetary Fund (IMF) has, since 2011, expanded the use of intrinsically worthless Special Drawing Rights (SDR). This is done in part because the SDR is a less volatile alternative to the fluctuating U.S. dollar and gives the Central Banks greater control. This new reserve asset (for the central banks) levels the playing field between global economies.

The International Monetary Fund has also proposed the creation of SDR-denominated bonds which could reduce central banks' dependence on U.S. Treasuries. Assets such as oil and gold, which are traded in U.S. dollars could then be priced using SDRs.

[1209] 1 Timothy 6:10

The USD petro-currency hegemony will end when the fiat dollar is no longer the primary petro-currency. This disconnect will cause its purchasing power (value) to plummet. When the dollar loses its perceived value, it will be seen as inflation. Once this inflation begins it is unstoppable and gains momentum, quickly spiraling into hyperinflation.

> Note: Inflation is not in our future; it is here! It has been steadily increasing over the past forty-seven years. Since 1971 the fiat dollar has lost over 95% of its value. Stated another way, a $1,000,000 U.S. bond purchased in 1971 is only worth approximately $50,000 today. The Federal Reserve, our own government, and the so-called television market analysts tell the unwitting public that the current rate of inflation hovers around a modest 2%, when in reality it is 8.66%.[1210] If you purchase groceries, attend college, have a cavity filled at the dentist, pay car insurance or pay taxes you can well appreciate that you have been lied to. The U.S. Dollar Index (USDX) is a measure of the dollar's purchasing power as compared to six other major world currencies. Since January 2017; in less than nine months the USDX has as mentioned fallen nearly 9%. So, a 9% drop in the dollar's purchasing power is tantamount to 9% monetary inflation. In the final analysis the perceived value of the USD is tumbling. All the FED can do is support the stock markets to keep up the charade that the economy is stable for as long as possible. This problem is not limited to the United States; the entire worlds' fiat is based on a debt-based monetary system; howbeit the yuan, euro, or the U.S. dollar.

The debasement of currencies is not happenstance, but intentional. It has been carefully planned by the global money masters for decades. A currency reform and the establishing a global currency cannot be accomplished while national currencies dominate. The U.S. dollar must therefore be usurped, which is exactly what America's previous president (Obama) and his administration (all puppets of the global constabulary) purposed!

With the global collapse and the immediate need to restore order occurs, the "Rescuers" with their new monetary system will jump in. An integrated computer system stands ready; just waiting to be implemented. With the dollar and paper currencies obsolete, cashless electronic currency transfers and a digital monetary system will be instituted.

> Note: For years now governments around the world have despised cash as it is almost impossible to trace, and therefore tax. So it is, that they have attempted to make cash obsolete by implementing restrictions; for example, how much cash you can carry when you go through customs; even how much of your money you can withdraw from the bank at any one point in time. If you deposit or withdraw more than $10,000 from a U.S. bank or other financial institution (either cash or electronically) the bank must file a "currency transaction report" with the U.S. Treasury. As I write; in France, cash

---

1210 ShadowStats.com, John Williams, Shadow Gov., Unemployment Statistics; July 2016

> transactions over 1,000 euros are now illegal. It's also a crime to send any amount of cash by mail. Spain has a limit of 2,500 euros. Violate that law and the government will confiscate 25% of one's cash. Italy has made it illegal to use cash for transactions over 999.99 euros; any amount over that and you must use a debit card, credit card, a non-transferrable check or a bank transfer. Violate the law and the Italian government will confiscate 40% of the amount paid.

In an effort to move to a cashless economy, Swedish banks have begun removing ATM machines, compelling its citizenry to use credit cards and electronic banking. The intent is to drive interest rates into negative territory. As long as cash exists the banks cannot charge their depositors for holding their savings, otherwise their depositors will withdraw their cash. However, if cash were abolished and electronic banking was the only option, the banks could then charge their customers a negative interest rate for managing each transaction. The customer would have no other option. Negative interest rates mean financial institutions charge customers for "the privilege" of letting the bank keep their money in an account.

> Note: A cashless society using new electronic banking technology has taken hold in several countries in Europe and Asia. Legislation and banking policies are phasing out cash and coin. Central banks are enamored with the prospect, as is the U.S. Internal Revenue Service. Several nations including Israel and India have embraced Swish—a digital person-to-person, real-time payment system not unlike PayPal and have designed a framework for its adoption. Sweden's national bank, Riksbanken, and Denmark were the first to integrate the electronic payment system through Bankgiro. A number of Swedish banks have digitalized branches which will simply not accept cash. Spain has just announced that effective January 1, 2017, it would prohibit cash transactions in excess of 1,000 euros (c. U.S. $1,080). But perhaps the most significant news to date came in January 2017 when China announced that the People's Bank of China (PBOC) has successfully completed its digital currency trial run. China is ready to switch to a digital currency.

> Note: While proponents of electronic currency speak of how it will stop money laundering, drug trafficking and the financing of terrorism, its real purpose and effect will be to control the populace. With a simple flip of a switch the financial oligarchs can control all finance by shutting down the internet or extracting a depositor's money at will. With the elimination of cash an individual loses the ability to freely conduct business with whom they wish and when they wish; a cornerstone of our sovereignty. With every electronic purchase or transfer tracked we forfeit our privacy to the banks and the government.

Willard Cantelon, in his book *The Day the Dollar Dies* wrote, "The world system will be praised and promoted by brilliant men. With elegance and apparent logic, they will persuade men that this is the path to peace and security."[1211]

> Note: Since 1970, the first phase of the implementation of a world currency went into effect. It was an outgrowth of the Bretton Woods agreement following WWII which rested on the U.S. dollar as a gold backed reserve currency to which other countries' currencies were pegged at a fixed exchange rate. However, the U.S. fell into a balance of payments deficit while trying to maintain the U.S. dollar at its thirty-five dollar per ounce of gold. Something needed to be done to maintain confidence in the dollar and prevent a gold run on the U.S. treasury. The U.S. had to run a balance of payments surplus in order to keep the world supplied with dollars if it were to remain the reserve currency. When it became apparent that the dollar/gold system would need to be supplemented by a synthetic reserve asset, (another instrument that could serve as a proxy for gold and provide liquidity for central banks) the global engineers came up with a paper asset—the "SDR," or Special Drawing Rights. Few realize that it was British economist John Maynard Keynes who in 1944 at Bretton Woods New Hampshire advocated for a new form of world money (the bancor). The bancor would be backed by a basket of commodities which would include gold; so it was Keyes that may be accredited with the concept of the SDR. At present SDRs must be converted into one of seven major currencies; the U.S. dollar, the Japanese yen, the British pound sterling, the Swiss franc, Australian dollar, the Canadian dollar and the Euro before being used by central banks for foreign exchange operations. Whether one cares to call these SDRs paper gold or simply debt securities, they are a supplemental reserve asset which uses the electronic transfer system.

A menacing China and its renminubi (yuan) is now included in the SDR club. Commerce and foreign investment capital have markedly circumvented the U.S. dollar. A huge paradigm shift of wealth is now occurring. Recently they have sold off $200 billion U.S. Treasury bonds and amassed hundreds of tons of gold to back the Yuan in order to get a strong weighting in the SDR basket. Holding $1.3 plus trillion of U.S. debt, China is poised to devalue the USD. China has been buying an exorbitant amount of gold each month to hedge their massive $3 trillion of foreign exchange reserves, consisting largely of U.S. debt.

To keep up the appearance that the U.S. dollar is strong, the Federal Reserve (the largest Central Bank in the World) has created over 4.5 trillion dollars' worth of liabilities by printing Federal Reserve Notes (paper money) out of thin air, and with no physical backing (gold). They have then used those trillions to purchase U.S. Treasury bonds back from lenders such as China who held them as security for loaning the U.S. money. They are now in the process of redeeming them as China has initiated a treasury bank dump. The United States was once the greatest lender nation on earth; now it is the greatest borrower nation.

1211   *The Day the Dollar Dies*, Willard Cantelon, Logos Publishing, 1973

Disgusted with the United States being the premier World Reserve Currency and having the ability to print as much money as it wants, fifty-seven nations led by Russia and China have entered into an alliance to destroy the U.S. Dollar. The BRICS nations (Brazil, Russia, India, China, South Africa) have initiated what is a "voting reform" in the IMF. Together they now have a voting majority (14.9%) large enough to override the United States veto power. The U.S. has always used its veto power to eliminate the possibility of New World Money being instituted. On January 1, 2017, this became a thing of the past. The U.S. is losing its hegemony and its economy will break down as inflation becomes the order of the day.

China has been working for years to establish global currency status and destroy the U.S. dollar. It is now strengthening the yuan by backing it with gold that cannot be traded in U.S. dollars. This alone could cause a rout and collapse of the American economy.

> Note: According to the Society for Worldwide Interbank Financial Telecommunications, the yuan (officially called the renminbi) overtook the euro in 2013 as the world's second-most used fiat currency in trade finance and became the fifth most popular fiat currency for global payments. China now challenges the U.S dollar for dominance in global trade and finance.
>
> Note: The U.S. treasuries market is one gargantuan bubble that has no way of ever being deflated as the U.S. will never be able to repay its debt. The foreign loan holders (China, Japan, Saudi Arabia and others) hold $6.2 trillion of the U.S.'s $20 (acknowledged) trillion national debt. They are of course aware they will never be repaid with real money. They also know the overvalued dollar will inevitably collapse under its own preposterous weight. Therefore, with their U.S. treasury bills losing value every day, logic tells them to sell before the rout begins and the dollar becomes worthless.

Today the FED's balance sheet has swelled to $4.5 trillion while its total capital, which corresponds to their net worth has collapsed to just 1.3% of total assets. The value of the FED's assets barely exceeds their liabilities.[1212] The universal law of bond markets is that bond prices and interest rates move inversely to one another. When interest rates go up, bond prices go down. This explains why the FED hasn't raised interest rates for the last eighty plus months until just recently. Raising the interest rate will devalue bonds and the FED will go into negative territory. When this occurs, they will be recognized as insolvent causing a global economic stampede.

The next phase of global financial restructuring will be the centralization of power which will require a reset of all fiats—each designated a value in what are basket currencies. This new world exchange will be a precursor to a one world monetary system wherein a global government will institute global taxation which must be paid for in global currency.[1213]

1212 Soveignman.com, article, "The global financial system is now resting on a margin of 1.3%."
1213 Revelation 13:17

> "And he causeth all, both small and great, rich and poor, free and bond, to receive a mark in their right hand, or in their foreheads: And that no man might buy or sell, save (except) he that had the mark, or the name of the beast, or the number of his name." (Revelation 13:16-17)

During the Obama administration, the power mongers tightened the noose, taking control of all commerce as free trade agreements are voted upon by the U.S. Congress. The contents of these agreements were held in the utmost secrecy but were rumored to include hidden sections which will take control of Internet communications, freedom of speech, permit global price fixing, and a multitude of other issues.

America's Gold Reserves in Question

In the 1960s, French President Charles de Gaulle criticized the U.S. government for printing overvalued U.S. dollars to pay for its trade deficits. This had allowed U.S. companies to buy European assets with dollars which were unfairly kept in value by a fixed gold peg. In 1965, the French president took $150 million of his country's dollar reserves and redeemed the paper currency for U.S. gold, worth at the time about $12 billion. The U.S. dollar was then still backed by gold and could be redeemed by foreign governments. Consequently, Fort Knox (U.S. Bullion Depository) was tapped of some of its gold. But France only began what became a trend. Spain soon redeemed $60 million of its U.S. dollar for gold, as did other nations. By March 1968, gold was flowing out of the United States at an alarming rate. The U.S. government had no choice but to give away its reserve in order to defend the U.S. dollar at a fixed rate of $35 per ounce. Before the run had ended in early 1970 it is estimated that about two-thirds of our nation's gold reserves (approximately four hundred million ounces) were gone! In 1950 the U.S. gold reserve was approximately twenty thousand tons; by 1980 it was approximately eight thousand tons.

Many believe the U.S. gold reserve today has only a fraction of what it claims to have. Fort Knox has not had a full audit since 1956. Former Rep. Ron Paul and his son Senator Rand Paul, have, without success, been the vanguard for a complete audit. It seems that it would take an act of Congress or a Treasury crisis to require a full audit.

As if this weren't enough to cause skepticism of what gold remains in the vaults, there has been a demand by several countries led by Germany for a full audit of their gold reserves held here in the United States (for safekeeping) and that their gold be repatriated to them. The New York FED refused a physical audit and agreed to return 674 tons of bullion back to them over the course of seven years! Why it would take seven years raises the level of suspicion. One can only wonder if China (like Europe) may have demanded U.S. gold in lieu of U.S Reserve notes for the 1.3 trillion owed them!

In a vision given the prophet Daniel over twenty-five hundred years ago, the prophet saw a fourth beast (an empire) "diverse (different) from all the others." We read that this empire "shall devour (consume) the whole earth."[1214] The Chaldean word Daniel used was *akal*.[1215] When the

---

[1214] Daniel 7:23
[1215] *Strong's Exhaustive Concordance*, Heb., #399

word is developed as in the New Testament it means to forcibly appropriate,[1216] and demand compliance.[1217] This forth beast is different from former beasts in the method by which it will take control! It will begin by demanding compliance to its monetary policies, thereby controlling commerce and all aspects of the global economy. This is the agenda of the New World Order.

Benefactors and Betrayers

In the past century and a half, America has been greatly used by GOD in accomplishing HIS plan for the Jewish people. No other nation provided them with a safe haven as they fled from their European and Eurasian persecutors. Once they arrived in America, American Jews were free to practice Judaism and share in the liberties given all immigrants. Subsequently, Jewry thrived in America while GOD prepared their ancient homeland for their spiritual restoration.[1218]

The Second Great Awakening that began in the mid 1800's and lasted to the mid 1900's shook small villages and large cities alike as scores of Protestant revivalist crisscrossed the country. Leading throngs of their countrymen to the Cross, these indomitable individuals preached on the nearness of Christ second coming and the reestablishment of the Jewish nation which would precede His arrival.

What was happening in Russia at that time would set the stage for what was to happen next. In the 1870's Russia pogroms and the infamous May laws compelled Jews to seek refuge elsewhere. A small number made it to Palestine but tens of thousands made it to Elis Island and began their new life in America. Genuine Christians sought then, as they do now, to support their Jewish brethren, for they believed in GOD's unwavering promises for the restoration of Israel.[1219] By the 1880's and 1890's Christians in prominent positions in America and Great Britain played a crucial role in preparing the groundwork for the establishment of a national homeland in Palestine.

At the same time Europe and particularly France, which for centuries had been under Roman Catholic monarchs became a hotbed of anti-Semitism against the Jewish people. In Turkey and surrounding countries, the genocide of Armenian Christians and Jews gained momentum and Turkey aligned itself with Germany. The battle lines were being drawn.

During World War I, Britain, afraid of a Muslim-Arab uprising and wanting to protect its holdings in Muslim Africa, India and the Far East, made a pact with Arab Syria guaranteeing independence for a united Arab country east of the Jordan River.[1220] This was Britain's gamble to keep neighboring Syria and the Arabian Peninsula from becoming part of the Ottoman Empire which had already allied with Germany.

At the end of the First World War and with the Western allies' victory over the axis powers, the collaborative efforts of numerous men; some with a vision for a homeland for the Jewish people (Zion) gave rise to the Balfour Declaration, named after British Foreign Secretary Arthur

---

1216 Matthew 23:14; Mark 12:40
1217 2 Corinthians 11:20
1218 Ezekiel 36:27; 37:14
1219 Ezekiel 36:24
1220 Appendix 2, Memorandum drawn up in London by Middle East Department Prior to Palestine Conference, p. 30, Report on Middle East Conference held in Cairo and Jerusalem, 12 March 1921, CO935/1/1

J. Balford. The agreement called for a Jewish homeland in Palestine. In 1919 in the Treaty of Versailles; what was called the "Mandate" appointed the British with the administration of Eretz Yisrael—the Land of Israel. On November 2, 1922, it was ratified by the newly formed League of Nations. Under the Declaration and the Mandate, Britain agreed to manage the lands west of the Jordan and leave the land to the east to a semi-autonomous Arab Levant.

With the Balfour Declaration and a homeland secured under public law, that which was first proposed by Rev. William E. Blackstone in 1878 and later by journalist Dr. Theodor Herzl in 1896, and afterward by chemist Chaim Weizmann, became a reality. Ezekiel's vision had begun.[1221] The "noise" of such men as Blackstone, Herzl, and Weizmann woke the dead dry bones and the bones started to "shake." Five years later the League of Nations gave Britain the mandate to actually establish the homeland and the bones began "coming together."[1222]

Though the Declaration did not grant the Jewish people autonomy or statehood but it did give them their ancient land to return to. With anti-Semitism continuing to escalate throughout Europe and Asia, seventy thousand Jews made their way back to Palestine. "Sinew and flesh" began covering the "dry dead bones."

The Jewish people began arriving and established communities in what had only sixty years earlier been a barren and deserted land.[1223] Samuel Clemens (a.k.a. Mark Twain) who journeyed there wrote, "only two or three clusters of Bedouin tents could be found, but not a single permanent habitation."[1224]

The "Mandate of Palestine" defined Britain's responsibilities and powers of administration over what they perceived as their Commonwealth. It included not only securing and establishing the Jewish national home but safeguarding the civil and religious rights of all the inhabitants. Still, there came stiff Arab opposition against any Jewish immigration. This compelled Britain to make further concessions which restricted Jewish immigration (Hebrew, *aliyah*). Annual quotas were established as to how many Jews could migrate back to the land based on what Britain determined was the country's economic capacity to absorb them. This was still unacceptable to Palestine Arabs who having no voice became angry with British colonial rule and the influx of Jews.

In 1929–1930 came the Great Depression, and in 1933 Adolf Hitler began his earnest ascent to power in Germany. Hostility toward Jews intensified and spread to Poland and Romania. For many Jews, America and Palestine became their only refuge. Still the poison (anti-Semitism) had made its way across the pond to America and with it the creation of the German American Bund (1936), an organization in support of Nazi ideology.

In 1936, Arab guerrillas began attacking Jewish settlements in Palestine; killing their occupants in what was the beginning of the Arab Revolt, which would continue unabated until 1939. In an effort to quell the situation the British sent Charles Wingate to organize a Jewish defense force, but in addition to protecting Jews the British were careful not to inflame the Muslim Arabs in the rest of the region. Britain's concern was if the Arabs believed Britain was solely for

---

[1221] Ezekiel 37:1-14
[1222] Ezekiel 37:7
[1223] Ezekiel 36:34-35
[1224] Mark Twain, *Innocent Abroad*, (Impressions of Palestine – 1867), chapters 45-57

Jewish interests, they would jeopardize losing their assets and influence in the Middle East. In 1937, with tensions escalating, Britain's House of Commons responded by announcing that it was sending a commission to study the unrest in Palestine.

Then on September 30, 1938, President Franklin Delano Roosevelt and Britain's Prime Minister Neville Chamberlain would, in an attempt to appease Hitler, sign the Munich Agreement which conceded Czechoslovakia to Nazi Germany. Roosevelt's concession coupled with Chamberlain's naivety—declaring "peace in our time"—emboldened Hitler in his quest for world domination and the German war machine grew more powerful. In the meantime, Nazi Herman Goring's propaganda campaign convinced the citizenry that the Jews were responsible for just about all of the world's problems.

Lauded and loved to a fault by his generation, President Roosevelt chose to remain an isolationist. Well aware of the Jewish persecution going on in Europe, he stood by. Beyond sending war supplies and provisions to Brittan he would not combat. It wouldn't be until 1941 when Pearl Harbor was attacked by the Japanese that Roosevelt would engage America in the fight against Hitler.

Chamberlain and Hitler (Image Source: GETTY)

> Note: Had President Roosevelt believed or understood the Bible and taken action in defense of the Jewish people when the Reich began its persecution and the imprisonment of them, it is quite conceivable that GOD would have intervened and made the allies victory easier. Listen to what GOD has to say about coming to the aid of the Jewish people.

"Then shall they also answer him, saying, Lord, when saw we thee (the Jewish people) an hungred, or athirst, or a stranger, or naked, or sick, or in prison, and did not minister unto thee? Then shall he answer them, saying, Verily I say unto you, In as much as ye did it not to one of the least of these, ye did it not to me." (Matthew 25:44-45)

In March 1939 Hitler seized Bohemia and Moravia. Britain's Neville Chamberlain saw war on the horizon with Germany and needed to once again appease the Arabs and quickly find a solution. To that end the British government produced the "White Papers" which abandoned the idea of partitioning. Instead it sought to create an independent Palestine to be governed by Palestinian Arabs and Jews in proportion to their population at that time. It also held that Jews were prohibited from buying any more land outside of their existing settlements and that Jewish migrations to Palestine was to be restricted to seventy-five thousand over the next five years (1940–1944). This measure the British believed, would keep the Jews as a permanent minority in

Palestine. After 1944, the quota for further immigration of Jews to Palestine would depend on permission of the Arab majority. The provisions of the White Papers were vehemently opposed by both Palestinian Jews and Arabs. The Jewish people wanted quotas and restrictions lifted and the Arabs wanted an end to all Jewish immigration which they foresaw could lead to statehood.

Once the Holocaust began and the annual fifteen thousand (Jewish) quotas were met, British authorities began turning back ships carrying what they decided were "illegals" (those without immigration certificates). The problem would intensify during the war in Europe as Jews fleeing Nazi persecution and attempting to get to their homeland were denied access. Refugees were held in detention camps or deported to islands off the coast of Africa.

With much of Europe under German domination, France occupied, and Britain under siege, the world at large became less and less concerned about the plight of the Jew.[1225] By the end of World War II, millions of Europeans refugees were living behind barbed wire fences in "displaced persons camps" within Germany and Austria. Lacking adequate provisions and medical care, European Jews organized an underground network known as the "*Brichah*" (Hebrew, meaning flight). They would move thousands of Jews from these camps to ports on the Mediterranean from which they could then get on any ship that would float and make their way to Palestine under the guise of a foreign flag.

The British restrictions implemented in 1936 to stem the tide of Jews fleeing Nazism was one thing, but afterward in a post war exodus of Jews from Europe, Britain would launch a massive naval and military force to turn back the refugees. Over half of the one hundred and forty-two ships which made the attempt to get to Palestine were intercepted by the British blockade and rerouted to internment camps on the island of Cyprus. Of the apprehended, about fifty thousand people ended up in these camps, but more than sixteen hundred drowned at sea. Only a few thousand actually entered Palestine.[1226]

S.S. Exodus, Haifa, 1947 (Image Source: GETTY)

One such ship attempting to reach Palestine was commandeered by the British. Forty-five hundred and fifty-four passengers—sixteen hundred men, twelve hundred eighty-two women, and sixteen hundred and seventy-two children defied the British government and went on a hunger strike which lasted three weeks. The ship was (renamed) the S.S. Exodus. Its cargo consisted of mostly Holocaust survivors who had no immigration certificates for Palestine.

1225 R.S. Lenk, *The Mauritius Affair, The Boat People of 1940/41*, London, 1994
1226 *"SS Mefkure Mafkura Mefkura"* Haapalah/Aliyah Bet, 27 September 2011

The hunger strike brought world attention to the plight of the Jews and the matter was turned over to the United Nations for resolution. Journalists had exposed the dramatic struggle and heartlessness of the British which outraged the post war world. The British were forced to change their policy. However, from the moment Britain instituted the Balfour Declaration in 1917, the once Great British Empire, of which it boasted "the sun never sets" lost its commonwealth and narrowly escaped becoming an annex of Germany. Britain had made the crucial mistake of not taking GOD at HIS Word.

"And I will bless them that bless thee, and curse them that curseth thee…" (Genesis 12:3)

"Unto thy seed will I give this land…" (Genesis 12:7)

Time Marches On

The year was 1947; Harry Truman was president and the United Nations had to take up the issue of the Jewish homeland. The plan brought before the General Assembly was one of partitioning, and while man had thought that such a proposal was a fair and equitable solution, GOD did not!

In the decades which followed, war went on unabated in Palestine as surrounding Arab nations levied their tanks and artillery against the tiny state of Israel. In each instance, against overwhelming odds GOD brought the victory. The enemies of Israel and the world at large, not believing the Bible to be the unwavering and infallible word of GOD, persisted in prescribing and imposing their will and disregarded GOD's emphatic Word.

Fast forward to 1991: George H. W. Bush is president of the United States. He is himself an idealist and a globalist, and so after toppling Saddam Hussein's regime in the Gulf War, proposed a broad "Peace Plan" for Palestine.

The plan calls for a two-state solution between the Palestine Liberation Organization and Israel. Bush believed that such a compromise would bring an end to hostilities in the Middle East. Apparently, he did not know his Bible very well or take GOD seriously, for one does not defy GOD or decide to parley with the land GOD gave to Abraham's descendants.

"When the Most High divided to the nations their inheritance, when he separated the sons of Adam, HE set the bounds of the people according to the number of the children of Israel." (Deuteronomy 32:8)

President Bush's "Road Map to Peace" was tantamount to telling Israel that she must surrender more of what little remained of *Eretz Yisrael*. The Bible is replete with accounts of both Gentile kings, as well as kings of Israel who learned there are severe consequences for disbelieving or disobeying GOD. Nothing changes with time or when the title "king" would be retitled "president" or "prime minister." Disobedience is still disobedience and GOD will have none of it!

> Note: I don't believe it was coincidental that Israel's Prime Minister Ariel Sharon, having initiated Israel's disengagement from Gaza, (Israel's agricultural breadbasket) and forcing the expulsion of ten thousand Jewish residents from Gaza, the Golan Heights, and the West Bank in 2005, suddenly suffered a stroke on January 4, 2006. Thereafter, Sharon would remain in a permanent vegetative state until his death in January 2014.

President Bush pursued his agenda, convening the "Madrid Peace Process" which later evolved into the "Oslo Accords." The Accords were not only a timetable in which Israel was to forfeit her land but also focused on partitioning GOD's Holy City, the City of David, Jerusalem.[1227] At Bush's urging the United Nation passed resolutions 242 and 338 which determined new borders for Israel based on pre-1967 occupation. Bush's successors, William J. Clinton, George W. Bush, and Barack Hussain Obama each continued to advance the surrender of GOD's land to GOD's adversaries.

One of the most notable ways GOD dealt with the children of Israel when they became indifferent to HIM and apathetic to HIS Word; when they recognized pagan gods, and adopted worldly aspirations, was to give them kings they deserved. These kings had no fear of GOD and did "evil in the HIS sight."[1228] They were often cruel men who would overburden the people with taxes.[1229] However, it is "God who ruled in the kingdom of men, and He appointeth over it whomsoever HE will."[1230] Yes, it is GOD who ultimately appoints kings and presidents, and it is GOD who has used and will use evil rulers to chastise the people for their arrogance.[1231] And, if the people still refused to be corrected, it was GOD who would allow them to be overtaken by their enemies and ultimately end up in captivity.[1232]

The Enemies Within Our Gates

In the 2008 presidential election, a young first term senator from Illinois was suddenly catapulted from obscurity to become the forty-fourth president of the United States. His electorate included seventy-four percent of the total Jewish vote. In a second term in 2012, sixty-nine percent of the Jewish vote helped re-elect what was by all indications a Muslim president.[1233]

Born to a Muslim father, raised in his childhood in Islam by a Muslim stepfather, registered in school as Muslim—in a Muslim nation, he suddenly and inexplicably went from being a community organizer to a junior senator, to become the most powerful man on the planet.

Though he never gives the reason why he gave up his name Barry Soetoro (the surname of his Indonesian stepfather) and adopted his African-Arabic-Muslim name, Barack Hussain

---

1227 Joel 3:2; Isaiah 66:16
1228 2 Kings 21:2
1229 2 Chronicles 10:11
1230 Daniel 5:21
1231 2 Kings 21:12
1232 Leviticus 26:17, 36; Deuteronomy 28:25, 62, 64
1233 M. Mellman, A. Strauss, K. Wald, *Jewish American Voting Behavior 1979-2008: Just The Facts*, July 2012

Obama, in his book *Dreams From My Father*, it appears from all accounts that he was at odds with a white-dominated society.[1234] Obama attended the Trinity United Church of Christ in Chicago for twenty years and called the Rev. Jeremiah Wright his pastor. Wright preached black liberation, reparation, and embraced a blanket disdain for America. Only when he became candidate Obama did he disengage himself from the controversial Wright and abandoned his membership at Trinity United.

His eligibility to become president as a natural born citizen of the United States itself has been put into question, as the "certificate of live birth" (not a birth certificate) submitted as proof of his U.S. birth turned out to be photoshopped, and therefore fraudulent.

His ideologies and objectives are no longer in question, for just as he promised the American people that he would fundamentally transform America, so did he do his level best to do just that. His many policy decisions spoke to his objectives which might have been verified by his records and senior thesis from Colombia University—if it weren't for the fact that they remained sealed to this day.

Among the many records Mr. Obama had refused to release are: the marriage license of his father (Barack Sr.) and mother (Stanley Ann Dunham), his name change records—Barry Soetero to Barack Hussein Obama, his adoption records, records of his stepfather and his mother's repatriation as U.S. citizens from Indonesia, his baptism records, his Noelani Elementary School (Hawaii) records, his Punahou School financial aid or school records, his Occidental College financial aid records, his Harvard Law School records, his Columbia College records, his records with the Illinois State Bar Association, his files from his terms as an Illinois state senator, his law client list, his medical records and his passport records.

Obama's Muslim roots are deep; seemingly deeper than his profession of Christianity, for actions speaks far louder than words. After his inauguration he appointed numerous Muslims to his cabinet and operatives of the Muslim Brotherhood to some of the highest and most sensitive posts in America's government.[1235] Most obvious and influential was his senior advisor and confidant, an Iranian-born Muslim, Valerie Jarrett, who guided Obama (particularly) in foreign policy and immigration decisions.[1236]

Even after his presidency ended Obama and the Deep State accomplices continue to do whatever they could to sabotage President Trump, for he had interrupted and obstructed the global cartel's timetable and agenda. But of all Obama's successes, his greatest triumph has been to divide the country into two diametrically opposing factions; autonomy and individualism (nationalism) vs. dependency and conformity (socialism). Obama knew and followed the communist manifesto of "divide and conquer" and that "united we stand; divided we fall."

1234 Richard Wolffe, *Newsweek*, "When Barry became Barack," March 22, 2008
1235 Israeliinternationalnews.com Report, "Egypt's Muslim Brotherhood Infiltrated Obama Administration" January 9, 2013
1236 The Ulsterman Report, Valerie Jarret and the Muslim Brotherhood, February, 2011

> Note: Inexplicably, neither the Democrat, the Republican, or the Conservative party pursued Obama's eligibility as a natural born citizen to any extent in order to become president prior to the 2008 election. All remained eerily quiet. Had they done so, it would have most assuredly disqualified him and given the election to either Hillary Clinton or John McCain. The silence of the parties and the nominees suggests that Obama was not a permissible candidate, but one appointed by a shadow global syndicate that wheels such power as to decide who will be king and who will be president. Their selection is largely based on who can sway the masses and who will obediently carry out their policies and plan of domination. The goal of the global syndicate is to have all heads of state take direction from them. These same powers will continue to do anything they need to do in order to remove President Donald J. Trump from office. Just who some of these Deep State seditionists are is most apparent, for they have revealed themselves by their relentless pursuit of the president by spying, lying and devising a false narrative in order to impeach him.

"Every kingdom divided against itself cannot stand...how can one enter into a strong man's house, and spoil his goods, except he first bind the strong man and then he will spoil his house." (Matthew 12:25, 29)

The Caliphate

To illustrate to the Arab world where his true allegiance rested, Obama freed the worst of the worst of Islamic terrorists from Guantanamo's penitentiary so they could return to the battlefield. He then traded a U.S. Army deserter for five high value Taliban prisoners. Between 2014–2016 the Obama administration may have given over 33 billion dollars in cash and gold to Iran to settle the Iranian nuclear agreement.

To focus attention away from the escalation of radical Islamic encroachment in the Middle East and throughout the world Obama maintained climate change is our biggest threat. Were he truly a Christian and believed the Bible, he wouldn't be concerned with climate change, for he would know that the earth age will end with catastrophic geologic events and the battle of Armageddon—fought largely between Muslim nations and Israel. Even Muslims who believe their Koran believe the world (as we know it) will end with a momentous Islamic war. In the final analysis, by redirecting the world's attention to global warming, he allowed radical Islam the needed time in which to grow, consolidate, and form trade pacts with rogue nations such as the Soviet Union, China and North Korea—who share intelligence, weapon development and weaponry itself.

Arguably the most consequential action Obama took if measured in human lives was to abruptly remove the U.S. military from Iraqi against the recommendation of his generals, and before the government was stabilized. The vacuum allowed ISIS to grow exponentially overnight—indiscriminately butchering an estimated six hundred thousand and taking a foothold in Syria.[1237] In the aftermath, Obama disregarding immigration process and constitutional law and allowed thousands upon thousands of non-vetted Syrian refuges into America. His policies would change the demographic and bring a stronger Sharia influence into our society and government. It appears that his intent was to change our culture to that of an Islamic state and facilitate world Islamic supremacy. In one respect he was at least truthful, for he has done his level best to keep his 2008 campaign promise, "We are five days away from fundamentally changing the United States of America."

> Note: The Holy Scriptures describe the advance of Islam in its quest for world supremacy at the conclusion of the earth age. We can to a large extent determine the late hour in which we now find ourselves as prophecy becomes reality. We can also tell when a civilization is so endangered as to be on the verge of being overtaken. This has become evident as we witnessed previous leaders of the civilized free world: Obama (America), Cameron (Britain), and Merkel (Germany) deny the threat posed by the mass influx of Muslims into their respective countries. Instead they tranquilize their citizens touting the refrain, "Islam is a religion of peace," when history testify otherwise. During his administration Obama allowed the U.S. military to degrade. It was purported that when President Trump took office, only half of the United States military's war planes were flyable; many had been cannibalized for parts to keep the other half flying. According to former Vice Chief of Staff, retired four-star General Jack Keane, our military is the smallest it has been in seventy-five years, and it will take four or five years to bring us to where we need to be.
>
> Note: The origin of Islam began when the warlord Muhammad laid siege to and took what was the Jewish settlement of Yathrib in Hijaz (Arabia). After conquering the city, he renamed it Medina (now claimed as Islam's second holiest city). Before Muhammad and the birth of Islam, during the fifth century, Persian Jews dominated the economic life of Yathrib; held all the best land and must have formed at least half of the population.[1238] Once in control Muhammad proceeded to execute the inhabitants of the Jewish tribe of Quraiza, decapitating seven hundred Jewish men and taking the woman as sex slaves.[1239] After Muhammad slaughtered the Arabian Jews and appropriated their land and property, he announced that it had been according to "Allah's will." He is quoted as saying, "...some you slew and others you took captive. He (Allah) made you masters of their (the Jews) land, their houses and their goods, and of yet another land (Khaibar) on which you had never set foot before. Truly, Allah has power over all things."[1240] Khaibar was another Jewish settlement north of Medina that Muhammad conquered in 628 AD.

1237 The death toll from the war in Syria according to the Syrian Center for Policy Research estimated that at least 470,000 Syrians had died. It stopped counting because of the lack of confidence in the data.
1238 Alfred Guillaume, *Islam*, Penguin Books, 1954, pp. 11-12
1239 Bernard Lewis, *Arabs in History*, Oxford University Press, 1950, pp. 40, 45
1240 *The Quran*, Surah 33, v. 26-32, Dawood translation

Not only does Islam's origin testify of its intent to dominate and subjugate, so does its holy book as numerous verses from the Quran underscore the mandate to slaughter the un-submissive and defiant infidels (Quran 5:33, 8:12, 47:4). So, this self-proclaimed prophet of God; murderer, sex slaver of little girls, and provocateur of barbarism established a religion under cruelty and threat which is now taking over Europe. Sweden for example has now become the rape capital of Europe, and the Muslim demographic in England has grown nine times faster than the native population. It is destined to eventually become the majority—evoking Sharia law.

> Note: The Islamic worldview and collective obligation, which would include domination, is referred to as *"fard kifaya."* Many of the strategies of Jihad involve negotiating with the intent to deceive. The Sahih al-Bukhari, (one of six major hadith—book of the prophet collections of Sunni Islam), Vol. 4, Book 52, Number 269 says the prophet said, "War is deceit." The strategy of *"Hudna"* (is calm or quiet), as with a truce or armistice, and is clarified in Sahih Muslim's Hadith, 15:4057.

Allah's messenger (Muhammad) was given to say,"He who takes an oath but eventually finds a better way should do that which is better and break his oath." A devout Muslim who ascribes to this would have no problem in violating an oath—"I do solemnly swear or affirm that I will faithfully execute the Office of President of the United States, and will to the best of my ability, preserve, protect and defend the Constitution of the United States."

What is so perplexing is that many of Obama's most ardent supporters were Jewish democrats who voted for nearly all of his divisive programs. Social justice; a mantra of Reformed Judaism is the first rung on the ladder of socialism. These supporters have abetted their leader, fundamentally changing and weakening America and putting Israel in great peril. Even as Israel's Prime Minister Benjamin Netanyahu addressed a joint session of Congress on March 3, 2015, imploring the United States not to make a conciliatory agreement with Iran which would eventually lead to her building or buying a nuclear weapon, a number of these progressives aligned themselves with their president and ridiculed the Prime Minister.

Secretary of State John Kerry's signing of the non-nuclear weapon agreement with Iran is reminiscent of Neville Chamberlain's conceding to Hitler. After signing the Munich Accords, Chamberlain gave his ill-famed quote, "We have achieved peace in our time." His declaration turned out not to be a prediction of peace, but of World War II. In ratifying the agreement with Iran, were it not for the pro-Israel position that President Trump has taken and his refusal to affirm the nuclear agreement, I dare say that America would have written her own epitaph, for Israel is still and always will be the apple of GOD's eye.[1241]

With the UN Security Council (UNSC) approval of a nuclear deal, an undeterred Iran has surreptitiously continued its development of a nuclear weapon and its ballistic missile delivery system. Despite sanctions it is openly purchasing weapons and defense systems from Russia and

---

1241 Zachariah 2:8

is sharing nuclear and ballistic technology with North Korea. It was buying time and running out the clock with the "sunset clause" while a world in denial passively watched.

It is now too late for the UN Security Council to take aggressive action against Iran, and were Israel to act independently and conduct a preemptive military strike to take out enrichment facilities, Iran would retaliate and thousands of missiles would rain down on Israel from bordering Muslim nations. Israel would most assuredly be seen as the provocateur and igniting not only a major regional conflict but a planetary war.

America's previous President Obama, Vice President Biden, and his Secretary of State Kerry had been the engineers of the nuclear deal with Iran and betrayed Israel. This had put America in great peril. John P. McTernan in his book *As America Has Done to Israel*, illustrates that in the past whenever our leaders initiated a policy that was detrimental to Israel, some horrific natural disaster occurred.[1242] I believe that should another administration take control of the Executive Branch and, as Obama, Biden and Kerry did, and ally with Israel's enemies, we can expect GOD to be consistent in demonstrating HIS indignation in the way of some tragic event that would effect America and her invincibility.

> "For the day of the Lord is near upon all the heathen: as thou (Gentiles—nations) has done unto thee (Israel) thy reward (judgement) shall return upon thy (their) own head." (Obadiah 1:15)

> "For thus saith the Lord of Hosts; After the glory hath HE sent me unto the nations which spoil (rob) you (Israel); for he that toucheth you toucheth the apple of HIS eye." (Zechariah 2:8)

Executing the Plan

One does not transform a nation such as America without transforming the thinking of its people. Historically transformation is carried out when a charismatic individual (such as Adolf Hitler) rises from the populous disquieting the people and promising them a better life.

When a nation such as America enjoys the benefits of a free society and is relatively content, instigating discontentment is a challenge and requires an individual with extraordinary charm and magnetism. Therefore, the planners had to first find and install an exceptional mutineer who could subtly implant seeds of rebellion.

In so far as how one goes about dismantling a government, we look at the Latin phrase *Ordo ex Chao* ("order from chaos"). This has been the time-tested formula of tyrants to bring a revolution and give themselves control over the populace. A double agent was needed.

As already pointed out Obama was an embittered individual with a Neo-Marxist ideology. He was befriended by Saul D. Alinsky, a community activist and organizer who became his mentor. In 1972 Alinsky authored and published *Rules for Radicals; a primer for realistic radicals*.

1242 John P. McTernan, *As America has done to Israel*, Whittaker House 2008, New Kensington, PA

It capitalized on Vladimir Lenin's plan for world conquest by communist Russia. It focused on inciting revolution; first in low-income communities by capitalizing on the disparity between the "Have and the have-nots." This would be the first step necessary in bringing about social reform which would then metastasize into political reform.

Vladimir Lenin's plan for world conquest emphasized that it was necessary to take control of eight areas of a society:

1. Healthcare: Control healthcare and you control the people.

2. Poverty: Increase the poverty level as high as possible, as the poor are easier to control and will not fight back if you are providing everything necessary for them to live.

3. Debt: Increase the debt to an unsustainable level. Then increase taxes and this will produce more poverty.

4. Gun Control: Remove the ability for the populace to defend themselves from the government; that way you are able to create a police state.

5. Welfare: Take control of every aspect of their lives (Food, Housing, Income).

6. Education: Take control of what people read and listen to (media/internet); take control of what children learn in school.

7. Religion: Remove the belief in GOD from the government and schools.

8. Class Warfare: Divide the people into the wealthy and the poor. This will cause more discontent and it will be easier to then tax the wealthy and so support the poor (The Cloward-Piven strategy).

> Note: The Cloward-Piven strategy: Richard Cloward and Francis Fox Piven were American sociologists and political activist professors. Michael Reisch and Janice Andrews wrote that Cloward and Piven "proposed to create a crisis in the current welfare system by exploiting the gap between welfare law and practice that would ultimately bring about its collapse and replace it with a system of guaranteed annual income. They hoped to accomplish this end by informing the poor of their rights to welfare assistance, encouraging them to apply for benefits and, in effect, overloading an already overburdened bureaucracy."[1243]

1243 Michael Reisch; Janice Andrews (2001, *The Road Not Taken,* Brunner Routledge, pp. 144-146

The Record

The process Obama promised in his pre-election speech to transform (neo-communism) requires the incremental dismantling of the free economy. By doubling the national debt and giving free rein to the Federal Reserve to print trillions of fiat dollars, the country now finds itself on the brink of bankruptcy.

Obama who had sworn an oath of office to uphold the Constitution and its laws did just the opposite. Checks and Balances were overridden by executive orders; confiscation of private property by the Environmental Protection Agency; attempts to overturn the Second Amendment and the bringing of frivolous lawsuits against states who exercised their authority under the Tenth Amendment to defend their borders from illegal aliens, are just a sampling of the dictatorial powers that he employed.

Jihadists bent on terrorizing Americans on American soil went streaming in through virtually open borders.[1244] With refugees fleeing to Europe from Islamic war-torn countries, he proposed that America take in two hundred thousand Syrian refugees of which 98% were Muslim; this without vetting them to ensure that they weren't terrorists posing as refugees. At the same time, he ignored Syrian Christians who are facing persecution from every side in their country. Prime Minister Benjamin Netanyahu has repeatedly warned us, "They will use your laws to get inside the country, then use your freedoms against you!"

Unbeknownst to most Americans, our State Department along with our Treasury has, for the past thirty-five years, been working with the United Nations High Commission (UNHC) which is under the influence of a powerful Muslim organization, the Islamic Conference. Their purpose is to spread Islam by resettling Muslims in enclaves within cities. By overpopulating a country, they will eventually be able to overtake it using their electoral process and institute Sharia Law. This was the strategy of the Prophet Mohammad, who told his followers it was their duty to go to other countries and colonize them. The name he gave this was *Hijra*. America has already taken in one hundred thousand Somalian Muslims and another one hundred thousand Muslims from counties like Iraq, Afghanistan and Pakistan. Once these alleged refugees entered this country they were put on buses, transported to one of 109 American towns or cities and simply left off at courthouses for the local government to integrate.[1245]

We have been told by U.S. intelligence sources that Jihadist sleeper cells are currently in all fifty states. It is also believed that warehouses with caches of weapons and munitions have been stored in anticipation of a "call to arms" whereby Islamic soldiers are to retrieve the weaponry and begin their onslaught on our cities. French police have recently discovered similar caches hidden in French mosques.

The Obama administration had strived for redistribution of wealth through a broad spectrum of policies, ignoring due process and bypassing congress. Federal regulatory agencies like the Internal Revenue Service target conservative groups, businesses and individuals. Agencies like the EPA and

---
1244 Harvey Kushner with Bart Davis, *Holy War on the Home Front*, Sentinel, the Penguin Group, 2004, p. 166
1245 Ann Corcoran, "Refugee Resettlement and the Hijra in America," Center for Security Policy Press, Washington D.C.

executive orders have devastated the coal industry. Twenty thousand coal miners and plant workers lost their jobs in Kentucky in February 2016. At the same time the federal government has grown into a behemoth in its quest to take control away from the states and federalize private industry.

In 2015, the Obama administration had in the Federal Register 81,611 pages of new and proposed regulations; more than the federal government has ever before issued in a single year. According to a study by Harry A. Silverglate, an attorney at law and author of, *Three Felonies a Day: How the FEDs Target the Innocent,* the government has criminalized so many mundane activities that the average American unknowingly commits three felonies a day. Federal criminal laws have become so dangerously disconnected from the English common law tradition that prosecutors can now pin federal crimes on any one of us for even the most innocuous behavior.

Free speech has been bridled by political correctness and the cancel culture and even labeled a hate crime. The national media had become the voice of the administration—feeding a naïve public a trough filled with lies and false statistics. Unemployment is a glaring example as it is nearly four times greater than what the government admits. The nation's actual unemployment figures have been skewed by simply using the U3 model rather than the all-inclusive U6 model. In the first quarter of 2016 there were 7.9 million working age Americans that were "officially" unemployed and another 94.4 million working age Americans that were considered to be "not in the labor force." When you add those two numbers together you get a grand total of 102.3 million working age Americans that did not have a job.

Forty-six million Americans were using food pantries and millions more were on some form of government subsistence. Wages were growing slower than the cost of living. According to the Pew Research Center, the median wealth for middle class households dropped by an astounding twenty-eight percent between 2001 and 2013. The velocity of money (how fast money passes from one person to the next) in the United States dropped to the lowest level ever recorded; even lower than during the depths of the last recession.

Corporate debt in the U.S. has approximately doubled since just before the last financial crisis and defaults have risen to the highest level since the last recession. For each of the past six years more businesses have closed in the United States than have opened, which prior to 2008 had never happened before in all of U.S. history.

The world's largest retail store, Walmart, announced the closing of 154 stores and the laying off of ten thousand employees. Macys and Sears have followed suit.

Beginning in 2018, the Ford Motor Company of Dearborn, Michigan was intending on expand its $2.5 billion facility near Mexico City, Mexico, and invest another billion dollars adding five hundred thousand automobiles to its annual capacity, doubling last year's production. The intended move reflected how such countries as Mexico, Thailand, and Vietnam have become an attractive place for global carmakers and typify how America has outsourced manufacturing (in all sectors), dramatically reducing its Gross Domestic Product.[1246] Whether or not President Trump's corporate tax plan to repatriate American companies is successful remains to be seen.

1246 *Wall Street Journal*, "Ford to More Than Double Mexico Production Capacity in 2018," February 2016

During the Obama presidency an astounding $9 trillion was added to the U.S. national debt, which means we added more than a trillion dollars a year to the debt. When you do the math, the federal government is robbing more than $100 million from our children and grandchildren every single hour of every single day. At the same time the citizenry was told they are in an economic recovery, howbeit slow.

The administration succeeded in ramrodding a mandatory health care bill through a Democrat-controlled Senate using entirely democratic votes during Obama's first administration. Keeping your doctor and your policy and the promise that the Affordable Health Care Act would be affordable were pure lies; just as the promise that it would be self-sustainable. Its architects knew from the beginning that there would not be enough young and healthy registrants (electing to pay exorbitant premiums) to offset the medical costs of the sick and elderly. This was always the endgame of Obamacare. Totally dismantle private insurance through an unworkable system and after it goes bankrupt and with healthcare in total disarray, force the nation into socialized medicine.

This health care bill was never about healthcare, but about control. Socialism is the steppingstone to communism by which the liberal/progressive politicians would advance their goal of transforming our republic. They would win elections by convincing the malcontent that they are entitled to live on welfare, government subsidies, and the success of others.

A House Divided Will Fall

"And if a house be divided against itself, that kingdom cannot stand." (Mark 3:25)

On January 27, 1838, twenty-eight-year-old Abraham Lincoln, having recently passed the Illinois bar exam was asked to address the Young Men's Lyceum; a boy's school in Springfield, Illinois. The topic was "The Perpetuation of Our Political Institutions." In his speech Lincoln spoke against the dangers of slavery and on the recent outbreaks of mob violence. He spoke how the two could corrupt the federal government and the citizenship in a constitutional republic. In the speech, Lincoln spoke well of the political system established by the founding fathers but warned of a destructive force he perceived from within. "Shall we expect some transatlantic military giant to step the ocean and crush us at a blow? Never! All the armies of Europe, Asia, and Africa combined, with all the treasure of the earth in their military chest, with a Bonaparte for a commander, could not by force take a drink from the Ohio or make a track on the Blue Ridge in a trial of a thousand years. At what point then is the approach of danger to be expected? I answer. If it ever reaches us it must spring up amongst us; it cannot come from abroad. If destruction be our lot, we must

Young Lincoln (Image Source: ALAMY)

ourselves be its author and finisher. As a nation of free men, we must live through all time or die by suicide."

Seventy-five years ago America was a God-fearing nation. Churches were full, prayer was recognized in school and in 1954, "one nation under GOD" was added to the Pledge of Allegiance and was unashamedly recited each morning by all students. Today all that has become endangered or is already extinct.

History has proven that the first freedom lost before despotic rule is established is the first amendment. Freedom of speech must first be bridled. Today social justice warriors offended by anything and everything they can dream up have rational people cowering in silence; scared to death of losing their job and being branded with a hate crime. Even the police are afraid to enforce the law for fear of consequences by the officials under whom they serve.

It was not by chance that GOD was taken out of classrooms. Neither did we go from a country noted for its morality, to teaching kids about transgenderism in third grade, by chance. A baby was considered alive in its mother's womb and abortion was murder. No, the decomposition of our country was planned by the globalists over one hundred years ago. They have followed the playbook to the letter. Wait until the WWII generation has died out and capture the next generation or the one to follow. Propagandize the youth before they leave elementary school. Turn colleges into Marxist indoctrination centers with the manifesto that promises social equality. Convince the spoiled youth to hate America by recalling what it did to the native Indians and slaves and call for its government to be dissolved. Infiltrate the halls of justice and all branches of government. Transform the democratic party from the ideologies of a nationalist John F. Kennedy to the line of a progressive left-wing radical (communist) party.

In the social engineering play book, history books over three years old are being removed from school libraries and sent to the landfills. History is being summarily erased as statues of the confederacy and even our constitutional forefathers are being removed from public and private space because a minority finds them offensive. Patriotism is denigrated by the alt-left who provoke a culture war. Even our American flag and our national anthem have, at sporting events, become associated with bigotry as sport icons take a knee. Illegal aliens are given refuge in sanctuary cities as their mayors and governors deify constitutional law.

The United States is in decline economically, morally and spiritually. The further its pillars erode, the greater and more certain are the consequences. The greater the consequences, the worse things get. The worse things get, the greater the likelihood that the citizenry can be manipulated; for fearful and desperate people invariably make the wrong choices.

While political contenders have always had a reputation of saying whatever is required to garnish votes, it is the voter who ultimately chooses to believe the candidate that makes the greater promises. While I believe President Trump was being sincere and honorable when he was elected on such promises as, "We will make America great again," "We will return jobs to America," and "We will grow the economy," optimism alone no longer carries the day. It will have to take divine intervention, for this is not a tangible war but a spiritual war and must be fought on the spiritual plain by spiritual warriors.

> "For the weapons of our warfare are not carnal, but mighty through GOD to the pulling down of stronghold..." (2 Corinthians 10:4)

We are no longer the post war America that towered above a tattered and battered post war world seventy years ago and who held great sway over all nations. The world is vastly different today. Moreover, our country has never been so divided (ideologically, politically, morally, and spiritually); perhaps eclipsing the War Between the States.

It has taken a century, since 1913 when globalist Thomas Woodrow Wilson took the presidency and began taking the country up the One World Government ladder. That progressive ascension has allowed the elite to achieve their goal. Independent and unhindered by regulations or the democratic process, they have built a solid global infrastructure—the Deep State. In a world drowning in debt and with control of the entire financial and commerce sectors, they can; apart from GOD's intervention, do as they please. The old adage, "who holds the purse strings, holds the power" was never clearer. America's own purse is bulging with I.O.U.'s, so that at any given moment it can be declared insolvent. At the moment of their choosing the Cabal can flip a switch and implement "Ice-Nine" which can freeze all private holdings and public assets in every bank and financial institution in the world. It can freeze all markets and exchanges. They can then evoke wealth extraction at will; bring in world taxation, a world monetary currency and a world government.

If America has been granted a temporary stay of judgment—averting its collapse by having elected President Trump, it is only because a praying Church succeeded in petitioning GOD for a righteous president.

> "Only he (the Spirit filled Church) who now letteth (has the power to prevent lawlessness from taking over), will let (continue to prevent lawlessness), until he (the Spirit filled Church) be taken out of the way (translated—raptured), then shall that Wicked (the Antichrist) be revealed..." (2 Thessalonians 2:7)

> Note: To carry out his noble campaign promises to build a wall, capture and evict illegal felons, enlarge and rebuild our military, renovate our infrastructure, give tax breaks to companies who will move back to the United States and to the middle class, President Trump will need to borrow several trillion dollars, up front. In a world swimming and connected by debt, being able to borrow at a low interest rate, (for a country already 21 trillion in debt) is an unknown. Competing with the likes of China whose wage earners makes substantially less than their American counterparts, repatriating American companies remains an uncertainty.

Solving our national debt will not solve our national problem; neither will be solving unemployment or poverty. Solving unaffordable health insurance will not solve our national problem. Solving our porous borders and dealing with illegal aliens will not solve our problems. Even solving our foreign policy and trade issues will not solve our national problems. Only by national repentance, a return to GOD, and proclaiming "Behold the Lamb of GOD, which taketh away the sins of the world"[1247] shall America be spared.[1248] Our only hope lies in a Great Awakening on an underserving nation, by a merciful GOD.

> Note: The American people have spoken and elected the Republican candidate, Donald J. Trump. In the euphoria, few Trump voters paused long enough to consider how, despite all odds, their candidate suddenly came from behind in the final two weeks to take the election from the established democratic candidate; a candidate with a larger party constituency and with much more funding and resources. Both parties were stunned with the outcome. While the commentators and political analysts provided numerous reasons for the victor's success and the loser's failure, the only real reason Mr. Trump won was that GOD deemed it so! The Bible tells us, "the most high God ruled in the kingdom of men, and that he appointeth over it whomsoever he will."[1249] While GOD has demonstrated that HE will, as HE has in the past with Gideon,[1250] raised up a man in time of crisis, it is not the man that will deliver the nation. The man must not be put on a pedestal for if the nation is delivered, it is not his doing. No weapon and no adversary can destroy a nation that puts its faith in GOD and all the attempts of man are futile unless GOD gives the victory.

If by GOD's appointment of President Trump, an hour of grace has been given to America, it is not to "Make America Great Again." GOD is not in the business of restoring an empire or blessing a nation that is largely indifferent to HIM and doesn't take HIM at HIS Word. GOD's only interest is to bring the people [hence the nation] back to HIMSELF and see them redeemed by accepting HIS Son as their sovereign and Savior.

It has been purported that President Trump has recently accepted Christ and been "born again."[1251] Be that the case or not, he now finds himself surrounded, influenced and guided by a team of elder Christians. So, it may well be that like Nineveh in Jonah's day (Jonah 3:5–10), America has been given one last chance to repent and return; which initially Nineveh did. Sadly, history also records that after Nineveh had repented and was spared from GOD's wrath in Jonah's day, the people returned to their heathen ways. Two generations later the once great capital of the Assyrian Empire came to an end. In 612 BC the city was sacked and burned by the allied forces of the Persians, Medes, Babylonians and others who divided the region among themselves. Thereafter the area was sparsely populated until eventually the ancient ruins became buried beneath the sands of Iraq.

1247 John 1:29
1248 2 Chronicles 7:14
1249 Daniel 5:21
1250 Judges 6:11-16
1251 http://www.wnd.com/2016/06/dr-james-dobson-calls-trump-a-baby-christian/

The Herd Mentality, the Millennials, and the Embrace of Socialism

> "America will never be destroyed from the outside. If we falter and lose our freedoms, it will be because we destroyed ourselves." Abraham Lincoln

Seventy years ago, (though in no way perfect) lived a generation of Americans who possessed a moral compass based on the Judeo-Christian faith. Their president, Dwight David "Ike" Eisenhower, having just delivered the world from the most aggressive tyrant of the twentieth century put America on a course of expansion, promise and expectation. Today that has all but vanished as America now flounders to keep its head above water while its pockets are weighted with debt.

The White House had (pre-Trump) a blatant progressive (socialistic) agenda. The Congress (with few exceptions) was run by self-serving politicians, not statesmen. The Supreme Court had a number of justices who believe our Constitution is a "living" document and must change with the times to accommodate the liberal and morally perverted agenda.

For a while (under this democratic administration), America lost its political will to intervene and defend the weak nations that gave muscle and meaning to alliances. The bullies of the world became emboldened by our disengagement and made a mockery of our once feared military. Our sailors were even ordered to surrender and pose as beaten captives at the hands of Iranian sailors, and our naval destroyers were taunted by Russian fighter planes practicing strafing runs on our war ships. Alas, we reached the point where we barely appear to have the backbone to protect ourselves, much less our allies.

There is no question that the character of America had changed, but the blame cannot be entirely laid on our leaders. It is "We the people" who are most culpable, for the vast majority have abandoned our faith in GOD and His redemptive work on the Cross. We, like Israel of old are simply bearing the consequence of our infidelity.

Today in America is a generation born between 1982–2004. Traversing the 1,000-year juncture they are appropriately referred to as the Millennial generation. Those under forty years old have no recollection of the hundreds of millions of deaths which grew from socialistic beginnings, paused at communism, and metastasized into totalitarianism. The promises of Hitler, Stalin, Hirohito, and Mao culminated in unfathomable human tragedy for their own people to whom they promised a better life.

Socialism is an ideology propagated and cultivated by its benefactors. It begins by removing evidence and consequences from history books and re-educating the naïve minds of the young who believe themselves wiser than their parents and predecessors. It promises a fairer better world, either through a political revolution or an actual one. In the end it leaves a greater gap between the haves and the have-nots, and often a swath of human deprivation, starvation and subjugation which frequently morphs into extermination.

Just a short time ago, under the democratic party flag an acclaimed socialist/progressive candidate competed for their party's presidential nomination. He swooned the pampered millennials with promises of free college, free health care, and debt forgiveness. When asked how this will be paid for, he answered, "by extracting the money from the wealthy and the job creators." It is these same job creators and their CEOs who have a responsibility to produce dividends for their shareholders in a free market economy. It is also within their right of industry to outsource manufacturing to foreign countries where labor is cheaper, unions don't exist, and corporate taxes are realistic. By increasing corporate tax to pay for their proposals the socialists destroy "made in America" and the free market incentive.

A social (socialistic) democracy is alleged to be born on the premise of fairness, and that all (including the non-producers) have the right to be supported by the producers. Under the guise of the collective good, socialism disguises itself as social democracy. In the course of the metamorphosis from self-government (by the people) to a larger, intrusive, and more empowered central government, liberties are forfeit and freedoms are lost until what is left bears no resemblance of its former self. Free health care, free education, free everything… except freedom!

> Note: According to retired senator and former presidential candidate Ron Paul, membership in the democratic socialist party jumped 500% between 2017-2018. According to Paul, Senator Bernie Sanders had acquired as much as eighty-four percent of the millennial generation vote.

Common Core curriculum, a global program designed to control the next generation by dumbing down our children, was instituted without a referendum. In the meantime, the education departments, particularly at the local level get away with increasing school budgets after being defeated by continuing to bring the budget up for another and another vote until eventually it passes.

Today it seems school children require artificial turf on their football fields, while those living on social security, unable to keep up with property taxes lose their homes. A typical third-grade class now costs $220,000 a year; $175,000 of it for salaries. Are students today better educated than those were 100 years ago at a fraction of the cost when adjusted for inflation?

"Agenda 21," a global policy initiative for the twenty-first century, was instituted by the global cabal to monitor and control every aspect of a person's life. Agenda 21 includes "sustained development" (a.k.a. planetary population control) which is designed to reduce the global population under the premise that food production and energy resources can no longer sustain the planet's escalating population. The global initiative maintains that according to the Population Division of the United Nations Department of Economic and Social Affairs (who issued the report in June 13, 2013), the world population was then approximately 7.2 billion and is projected to reach (an unsustainable) 9.6 billion by 2050.[1252]

Selective law enforcement and armed government intervention at the local level has been adopted by federal agencies, many of which have their own quasi-military enforcement

---

1252 UN Press Release: United Nations Department of Economic and Social Affairs. June 13, 2013. Retrieved, March 16, 2015

departments. Over 1.6 billion unjustifiable rounds of ammunition, seven thousand automatic assault rifles, and twenty-seven hundred armored vehicles have been purchased; not by the Department of Defense for our military, but by the Department of Homeland Security who manages security inside the U.S. border. Other agencies include; the Department of Education, the Environmental Protection Agency (to the tune of $715 million), and the U.S. Postal Service, all of which have acquired or are in the process of acquiring arms and ammunition.

Various laws and acts such as the Posse Comitatus Act, which were designed to limit the executive branch's use of federal troops on American soil has been repealed and rewritten. At the same time presidential powers have broadened; which in the hands of the wrong individual could support a tyrant. In signing Executive order #13603 Obama gave himself the power to declare martial law at virtually any time with the slightest provocation. He even had foreign soldiers wearing U.S. uniforms specially trained in urban crisis intervention imbedded with U.S. federal troops here on U.S. soil.

Large convoys of military vehicles and equipment have been staged for rapid deployment throughout the country. Frequently incidents are recorded on YouTube videos showing emboldened Transportation Security Agency (TSA) officers stopping law-abiding citizens on U.S. soil and the drivers unlawfully questioned and detained. This harassment is designed to condition the people for a metastasizing police state. It bears a resemblance to the Nazi occupation when German soldiers stopped whoever they wanted and demanded to see their papers.

There was, during the summer of 2015, a "military exercise" dubbed "Jade Helm 15" which deployed combat troops in thirteen states; obviously a rehearsal in anticipation of when the dollar defaults. The U.S. military and the Transportation Security Agency are themselves being conditioned and hardened to employ unconstitutional tactics against American citizens. Jade Helm's distasteful motto is "master the human domain" which they claim refers to their intelligence gathering. President Obama signed Executive Order #13693 in conjunction with the expansion of the National Defense Authorization Act which contains provisions that usurp rights and freedoms guaranteed in our national charter.

In 2009, the 111th Congress proposed H.R. 645, the National Emergency Centers Act which, although defeated, called for the adaptation of federal facilities into National Emergency Centers for use in national emergencies. A reformulation of H.R. 390 was introduced by the 113th Congress in 2013—the National Emergency Centers Establishment Act. Had it passed it would have directed the Secretary of Homeland Security to establish national emergency centers on closed military installations complete with barbed-wire fences, staffed by guards and having all the technologies used in prison containment. The reintroduction of such bills reveals that the establishment anticipates that martial law may be required, and a detention infrastructure needs to be in place as the economy continues to deteriorate and the prospect of civil unrest increases.

In the years leading up to FEMA (camp) legislation, the government prepared for the eventuality of civil and political unrest such as, Rex 84, Operation Garden Plot, and Operation Cable Splicer. It is purported by numerous watchdog organizations that despite H.R. 645 and H.R. 390 not being passed there are now scores of these National Emergency Centers, innocuously called Residential Centers. More appropriately, they are internment camps. These facilities have been transformed from military bases or have been newly constructed to, as needed, accommodate dissidents, anarchists, and/or patriots(?). Presidential power by "executive orders"—without congressional approval—has the ability to eclipse the U.S. Constitution. History attests that the abuse of executive power has been a prelude to totalitarianism.

Internationally, the previous administration (Obama) had offended and betrayed its allies while enabling Israel's enemies to advance across the region. He reduced the size of the armed services and its assets just when Israel was facing its gravest threat, and he discharged flag officers from all the military branches who opposed him. In just seven years of his administration, three of the four Secretaries of Defense had either resigned or been excused.

History will undoubtedly prove that a Muslim president had intentionally allowed the Islamic caliphate to grow and creep closer toward Israel's borders in their stated objective to annihilate the Jewish state. Under the guise of concern for refugees fleeing ISIS, he welcomed undocumented Muslim Syrians into the United States, and threatened to veto any bill that Congress put forward requiring their being properly vetted.

Islam permits lying to an unbeliever, even concealing ones' faith as a Muslim and calling themselves a Christian if it serves the ultimate goal of bringing about their intended objective of world domination! It is called *al-Taqiyya*, which in Arabic means deception. The gullible saw the president as compromising. The discerning saw him as disingenuous. Every move he made was calculated and intentional. Every move was to weaken America and advance Islam. We had taken in a Trojan horse and anointed him president.

What the Arab-Islamic nations were unable to accomplish through warfare, America's elected leader had achieved for them. With presidential power the United States has aided and abetted Israel's enemies. In the process and unbeknownst to most Americans, America was clashing with and opposing GOD HIMSELF! If there be a stay of execution for America it is only for the sake of the Church and the harvesting of a few more souls. It will continue only until the Church is divinely removed![1253]

Portioning Israel

> "In the same day the Lord made a covenant with Abram, saying, Unto thy seed have I given this land, from the river of Egypt (the Nile) unto the great river, the river Euphrates." (Genesis 15:18—ca. 1913 BC)

Despite her benevolence to the Jewish people and Israel in the past, America's ignorance as to who GOD gave the Promised Land to will not be excused if she presses for the partitioning of Israel. Will America defy GOD and bring judgment upon herself; the consequence of which has been written beforehand?

1253 2 Thessalonians 2:7

"I will also gather all nations, and will bring them down into the valley of Jehoshaphat, and will plead (judge) with them there for My (the Jewish) people and for my heritage Israel, whom they have scattered among the nations, and parted (partitioned) My land." (Joel 3:2)

"For it is the day of the Lord's vengeance, and the year of recompenses for the controversy of Zion." (Isaiah 34:8)

The above passages serve to illustrate that under recent former presidents, America nearly reached her tipping point, for she no longer feared GOD, nor did she believe the Bible is HIS unwavering Word.

On December 23, 2016, the United Nations Security Council showed its true colors. With only days remaining before Obama was to leave office, he and his administration gave its biggest denunciation yet to longstanding ally Israel. They allowed the UN Security Council (UNSC) to condemn Israeli settlements and under the auspices of international law force the Israelis to vacate their homes, maintaining that they were built on what constitutes Palestinian territory. It seems the world has forgotten that the very land the Palestinians claim as theirs was known by its Biblical names Judea and Samaria, which dates back to 1400 BC when Joshua crossed the Jordan River after Moses' death.

In July of 2016, the UN and its diplomatic partners, the so-called Middle East Quartet comprised of the UN, Russia, the United States, and the European Union, submitted a report that essentially called for the strictest implementation of the Oslo Accords, spelling an eventual end to the Jewish presence in the 1967 liberated territories. The proposal was brought to a vote in the UN Security Council (USSC). Instead of casting a veto to support Israel, as it almost always has on council resolutions concerning the Israeli-Palestinian conflict, Obama-appointee U.S. Ambassador Samantha Powers abstained. This gave a green light for the council to approve Resolution 2334 by a 14–0 vote.

An unauthorized Israeli official told the Associated Press that Obama and Secretary of State John Kerry "secretly cooked up with the Palestinians an extreme anti-Israeli resolution behind Israel's back, which would be a tailwind for terrorism and boycotts and effectively make the Western Wall of the Temple mount occupied Palestinian territory" (JNi.media, December 24, 2016). By abstaining from voting, instead of vetoing the resolution (which would have protected a portion of the land GOD bequeathed to Abraham),[1254] America has spurned Israel and defied GOD. Obama has been the most anti-Israeli American president on record. In denial of GOD's Word and with intent, he might have brought a curse upon our country.

In light of Benjamin Netanyahu's retort to the UN's decision, which was to ignore the resolution and derail the Arab plan to establish a Palestinian State in the heart of their country, tensions in the Mid-East have intensified. Thousands of Arab militants and terrorists the world over became emboldened, seeing the passage of this resolution as having legitimatized a call-to-arms. The fifteen nations represented in the UNSC disregarded the fact that Israel is a Jewish

---

1254 Genesis 12:1; 15:18; 17:8; 26:3-4; 35:12; Psalm 105:9-10

state by definition. Insofar as Arabs are concerned, Israeli Arabs are citizens of a Jewish state. As such, they enjoy the same rights and freedoms shared by all citizens. What the Israeli-Arabs do not enjoy is the right to their own national homeland!

America under President Trump has no choice but to make the most crucial decision our country has had to make since our decision to defend our European allies against the Axis powers in World War II. This choice has in the short term determined the fate of America, as we are for the time being on the side of GOD as it concerns Israel. From the Biblical accounts we can be assured that GOD cares nothing of state department diplomacy, arbitration, concessions, or detente. President Trump and his administration must continue to oppose and even defy the UN and determine to defend Israel's sovereignty regardless of the consequences. America must commit itself 100% to the Jewish State, abandon pursuing a two-state solution, and be willing to use all her resources in Israel's defense, even if it initiates the inevitable World War predicted in the Bible.

If America believes that a diplomatic solution with nations who refuse to acknowledge Israel as a nation state will ever somehow bring peace, her assumption is an absurdity. Delay and arbitration (as in Iranian nuclear agreement) is a tactic which allows Israel's enemies to form a military coalition and develop their defenses and nuclear capabilities. War is best averted when America has been in a position of strength and willing to use her strength. Three, four, or five years from now, that will no longer be the case, for the enemy will have strengthened their resolve if the "sunset clause" remains in effect.

Twice progressive democratic presidents, T. Woodrow Wilson and Franklin D. Roosevelt, tried to appease encroaching German dictators, the Kaiser and the Führer, while they grew their armies and armament. Had Wilson and Roosevelt acted sooner, two World Wars would likely have been limited if not averted.

"When the situation was manageable it was neglected, and now that it is thoroughly out of hand, we apply too late the remedies which then might have effected a cure. There is nothing new in the story. It is as old as the Sibylline books. It falls into that long, dismal catalogue of the fruitlessness of experience and the confirmed unteachability of mankind. Want of foresight, unwillingness to act when action would be simple and effective, lack of clear thinking, confusion of counsel until the emergency comes, until self-preservation strikes its jarring gong–these are the features which constitute the endless repetition of history." Winston Churchill, House of Commons, 2 May 1935, after the Stresa Conference.

In the final analysis, if the Trump administration defends Israel with the same determination that it would defend America, America might for the present, receive the promise of GOD, who said to Abraham, "I will bless them that bless thee…"[1255]

1255 Genesis 12:3

War not Peace—The Sino-Iran-Soviet-N.Korea Alliance.

Peace on Earth has always been one of mans' elusive dreams, but like a dream it is a departure from reality and more importantly from scripture. The quest for power and control have always been and always will be the bedrock for war. The Bible tells us war will continue and escalate[1256] until the end of human government and the establishment of a divine government.[1257] The Scriptures, by the use of olden names (e.g. Meshech/Rosh—modern Russia, Ezekiel 3:2, 3; and by geography (Persia—modern Iran, Ezekiel 38:5) give us a basis as to what nations will be principals in tri-continental wars against Israel leading up to and during the last days. We now see the main characters emerging.

By definition a dictator is a person who exercises absolute power over the people, often without the free will of the people. It is regularly accompanied with an insatiable appetite to expand what he or she believes to be their empire. This was Lucifer's objective when in a Pre-Adamic age, he sought to overthrow GOD. Like so many Luciferian traits, they have been adopted by his human minions.

One would think that men would have learned from history and two World Wars that appeasement and concession doesn't bring peace but rather allows despots time in which to become stronger and form alliances. Scripture indicates that the final wars—a quest for world domination will begin when a consortium of evil dictators and their nations will gather against Israel.[1258]

Today, dictators having recognized the U.S. has a conciliatory administration; one example being to allow Iran to continue its nuclear ambitions—even after having indicated their intent is to wipe out the tiny nation of Israel.

An axis of adversaries; predominantly China, Russia, Iran, and North Korea have a unified objective. Together they are engaged in neutralizing their common adversary—the United States—which since it became a world power impeded their taking other nations by conquest. Even though each of these dictators has an agenda to rule with autonomy over the others, they have for the time being adopted the axiom, "The enemy of my enemy is my friend."

This quartet of evil—each having nuclear capabilities, are hobbling their continent economically, financially, and militarily. They freely share weaponry, technology, and intelligence. Their joint territorial expansion extends from the Black Sea, to the Sea of China and beyond, even advancing toward the islands of the Pacific. It is uncanny how, reminiscent of what occurred prior to World War II, that history repeats itself. Today politicians and national security leaders appear oblivious to what the Bible has to say or about the harbingers of war. Instead these deniers believe diplomacy and concession toward despots resolves expansionism. Indeed, "those who fail to learn from history are doomed to repeat it."

While Russia aims at taking the Ukraine and absorbing Crimea and the Baltic States of Estonia, Lithuania, and Latvia, Iran's aim is to take control over the Gulf of Hormuz and

---

1256 Matthew 24:6
1257 Psalm 46:9
1258 Zechariah 14:2

control the Suez Canal. At the same time Iran overshadows Syria, Lebanon, and Yemen through proxy terrorists.

North Korea has never wavered in its resolve to absorb South Korea and now has the means to do it. Whereas before South Korea sovereignty was safe under the protection of the United States, today North Korea has an ally in China with a military that rivals the United States. In the meantime, China's leader Xi Jinping has rejected Hong Kong's independent government and seized it along with its trade and commerce. Xi Jinping has also declared Taiwan belongs to Beijing and has sworn to take it by force if necessary. In gaining control of the Taiwan Straits and with their huge navy (which now dwarfs America's navy) China can blockade Taiwan's shipping lanes if the U.S. lose its resolve to defend her. China has also claimed the Japanese Senkaku Islands in the South China Sea and laying claim to international waters has built islands for ocean ports and military installations. At the same time all four of these nations perpetrate cyber-attacks on the U.S., testing our defenses and vulnerabilities, and more importantly our resolve to stop them.

If any of our NATO allies are attacked or overtaken by any of these Sino-Arab-Soviet members it is dubious as to whether the United States will come to their rescue. If the U.S. fails to act and allows any of its allies to fall; be it the Ukraine or Taiwan, the U.S. will lose all credibility. The question then becomes, what will happen to Israel? Will they be abandoned as well? And what would happen if the U.S. had to face a four-front war against adversaries in another hemisphere? If the U.S. had to engage them would the United States be victorious without divine intervention? Not likely!

If we consider that when the Hebrews and the nations of Israel and Judah became passive and indifferent to GOD, or when the failed to take HIM at HIS Word or give HIM exclusive recognition and homage; or when they rejected HIS offer of atonement, HE promised that their enemies would overtake them and destroyed them.[1259] So if we are to believe the written Word and the GOD that cannot lie, then we every reason to believe America will suffer the same fate.

The Apostate Protestant Church

America will be judged for both her godlessness and her gross sins. The most glaring examples of her godlessness are her disregard for the sanctity of life (pro-choice/abortion) and her acceptance of the homosexual lifestyle, with same sex marriages having become socially acceptable and legal. More recently, the federal government is now attempting to enforce "transgender identity," making it a crime to discriminate against the opposite sex (depending on what gender they choose for themselves) and to use whatever bathroom, locker room, or shower area they decide to.

1259 Leviticus 26:14-38

> Note: Transgender and transsexual are terms applied to people whose gender identity is opposite their GOD given assigned sex. Recently the U.S. Federal Courts upheld a ruling that transgender persons (who are so confused as to what sex they are) are now welcome into the U.S. military. No longer is their sexual disorientation an indicator of mental instability put into question, but so is the mental stability of the judicial system that has licensed it.
>
> Note: In a Pew Research Public Opinion Poll, *Changing Attitudes on Gay Marriage*, it was reported that support for same-sex marriage has steadily grown. Based on this poll, a majority of Americans (55%) support same-sex marriage, compared with 39% who oppose it. The Millennial generation (1981>) lead the way at 70%.

We have reached the point where certain sectors of major denominations who profess to be Christian have completely disregarded the prohibitions of Scripture and slid into the cesspool of the unregenerated.

> "Thou shalt not lie with mankind, as with women kind: it is an abomination...For whosoever shall commit any of these abominations, even the souls that commit them shall be cut off from among thy people." (Leviticus 18:22, 29)

> "Wherefore GOD also gave them up to uncleanness through the lusts of their own hearts, to dishonor their own bodies between themselves...For this cause, GOD gave them up unto vile affections: for even their women did change the natural use into that which is against nature." (Romans 1:24, 26)

> "Even as Sodom and Gomorrha, and the cities about them in like manner, giving themselves over to fornication, and going after strange flesh, are set forth for an example, suffering the vengeance of eternal fire. Likewise also these filthy dreamers defile the flesh, despise dominion, and speak evil of dignities." (Jude 7-8)

It was recently declared (March 2015) that the largest Presbyterian denomination (the Presbyterian Church U.S.A.), has expanded its definition of marriage to include a "commitment between two people." After decades of debate over same-sex relationships it now recognizing "gay" marriage as "Christian" in their church constitution.

The Episcopal Church which blazed a trail in 2003 by electing the first openly homosexual Anglican bishop officially joined the Presbyterian Church U.S.A. and the United Church of Christ, becoming the third mainline denomination to embrace gay marriage rites just days after the U.S. Supreme Court legalized same-sex unions.

The Evangelical Lutheran Church in America, which eliminated barriers to gay ordination in 2009 took a similar approach, allowing some discretion by clergy and congregations to officiate at same-sex ceremonies.[1260]

GOD uses a most powerful word in describing these sins. HE declares them an "abomination"![1261] A once GOD fearing nation, America has followed the course of other now extinct empires and will subsequently reap what she has sown.[1262]

On the issue of abortion: Here is a synopsis of Protestant Groups official positions according to the Pew Research Center, Religion and Public Life, January 16, 2013. Strikingly obvious is how these groups try to sanitize and justify murdering the unborn child. The Word of GOD is emphatic; life begins at the moment of conception![1263] All arguments which skirt the sanctity of life and offer concessions oppose GOD and HIS Word! The Word spoken to the prophet Jeremiah should be evidence enough as to when GOD says life begins!

> "Then the word of the Lord came unto me, saying, Before I formed thee in the belly I knew thee; and before thou camest forth out of the womb I sanctified thee, and I ordained thee a prophet unto the nations." (Jeremiah 1:4-5)

As with homosexuality, so too do the denominations try to define the circumstances that make abortion permissible or acceptable.

The Episcopal Church: While the Episcopal Church recognizes a woman's right to terminate her pregnancy, the church condones abortion only in cases of rape or incest; cases in which a mother's physical or mental health is at risk, or cases involving fetal abnormalities. The church forbids "abortion as a means of birth control, family planning, sex selection, or any reason of mere convenience."

The American Baptist Churches in the USA: Recognizing the different views on abortion among its members, the American Baptist Churches' General Board encourages women and couples considering the procedure "to seek spiritual counsel as they prayerfully and conscientiously consider their decision." Though the board opposes abortion "as a primary means of birth control," it does not condemn abortion outright.

The Evangelical Lutheran Church in America: The official position of the Evangelical Lutheran Church in America states that "abortion prior to viability (of a fetus) should not be prohibited by law or by lack of public funding" but that abortion after the point of fetal viability should be prohibited except when the life of a mother is threatened or when fetal abnormalities pose a fatal threat to a newborn.

The Presbyterian Church (USA): In 2006, the Presbyterian Church's national governing body, the General Assembly, reaffirmed its belief that the termination of a pregnancy is a personal

---

1260 Rachel Zoll, New York, AP article, *Presbyterians approve gay marriage in Church Constitution*, March 19, 2015
1261 Leviticus 18:21-22; 20:13; Romans 1:26-28
1262 Galatians 6:7
1263 Jeremiah 1:5

decision. While the church disapproves of abortion as a means of birth control or as a method of convenience, it seeks "to maintain within its fellowship those who, on the basis of a study of Scripture and prayerful decision, come to diverse conclusions and actions" on the issue.

The United Methodist Church: While the United Methodist Church opposes abortion, it affirms that it is "equally bound to respect the sacredness of the life and well-being of the mother and the unborn child." The church sanctions "the legal option of abortion under proper medical procedures" but rejects abortion as a method of gender selection or birth control and stresses that those considering abortions should prayerfully seek guidance from their doctors, families and ministers.

I dare say that were Calvin, Wesley, or even Luther alive today, they would put on sackcloth, cover themselves in ashes and weep and fast, knowing GOD will recompense evil for evil!

What is Next?

By the forces of nature and the crises of history GOD brings judgment upon wicked men. At some point in time after the Church has been translated to heaven, the Bible predicts that judgment will come in the form of catastrophic (so-called natural) events. And while there have always been geological catastrophes—earthquakes and such—the ones which are to come will be of epic proportion…more correctly, of divine proportion, for GOD will have purposed them.[1264]

Divine Judgment (Image Source: ISTOCK)

1264 Isaiah 26:9; Job 9:5-6; Nahum 1:5-6; Isaiah 13:11, 13; Psalm 18:7; Revelation 16:8, 18

These geologic events will occur in areas not generally associated with earthquakes or tsunamis, e.g., the east coast of the United States, and the middle of the country versus the west coast and the Pacific Rim.

When judgment befalls America, and with the devaluation of the dollar, the bond and derivative markets will collapse initiating the collapse of all the markets. Banks and investment houses will close, food will be hyper-inflated, and gangs will take to the streets. Civil anarchy will erupt in all major cities. Martial law will be invoked which will foster a police state; thousands will likely die as a result of the shortages and mayhem.

Over the long term, and at some point, after the global depression has devastated economies around the world, I believe drought and water shortages will occur in many countries and specifically in America. It's quite possible that infestation or blight will devastate crops. Crop failures mean food shortages which will hyper inflate the cost of food. This will trigger food riots which will cause the federalization of farms, the agricultural and food industry, and bring about the implementation of indefinite martial law.

The New World Order

For over a century the world's elite, or if you prefer, the illuminati, have been engaged in putting in place strategic mechanisms for the greatest transfer of wealth and power in human history. Dr. Henry Kissinger called this "a new international economic order." It begins with debt-based economics. That means creating personal, national, and international debt so immense as to become unmanageable and unpayable. This will result in the collapse of the global financial system. This then leaves no alternative but for the oligarchy to create a new system with them in control over all banking, finance and commerce.

Today, the banking cabal lead by the European Central Back, the Bank of Japan, and the Bank of England, with an unlimited supply of digital money are collectively buying $200 billion a month of asset, purchasing debt, propping up corporations and hedge funds, and accumulating stocks. Today, it is the cabal and the mega-corporations (not the public trader) that make over 90% of the trades and are responsible for bringing the market to its seemingly never-ending highs.

Think how simple it is for them to take the world hostage. All they need to do is purchase 51% of the stock in a corporation and become the majority shareholder. They then, for all intents and purposes, own the company. Once in control of the energy, industrial, technological, and pharmaceutical complexes, they can easily force the hundreds of thousands of smaller corporations in the supply chain to sell them controlling interests in their corporations or lose their contracts. So, by digitally producing what is worthless fiat (what some appropriately refer to as "Monopoly" money), they can (as in the game Monopoly) purchase real estate, real companies, and real assets until they ultimately control everything on the Monopoly board.

Socialism is a means for government to gain control of the resources of production by colluding with banks and corporations. Globalism supersedes socialism and circumvents government by taking direct control of financial institutions and mega corporations.

Since 1954, global power players including representatives from government, private industry, media, finance, think tanks, academia, as well as numerous other organizations representing both private and public interests have been meeting annually behind closed-doors in what is one of the most secretive and powerful organization of its kind—the Bilderberg Group. On June 9, 2016, in the Taschenbergpalais hotel in Dresden, Germany, nearly 130 politicians, financiers, and industrialists attended the conference. The guest list included the chief of the International Monetary Fund, as well as the former heads of the CIA and MI6. Under a heavily armed security presence there was no transparency, as journalists were barred.

The Book of the Revelation goes into limited detail about this global government and its financial system, known as Babylon.[1265] At the time of this writing, the stock market is gambling with $303 trillion in derivatives. "The Conglomerate" of the Federal Reserve, the Central Banks, the mega-financial institutions, along with the G20 and the American Congress have made taxpayers personally liable for their crooked bookmaking.

The disregard for what I refer to as Biblical Economics has as one of its fundamental principles, "The rich ruleth over the poor, and the borrower is a servant of the lender."[1266] This proverb is well understood by the power brokers who are now in control of most of the planet's wealth. A new system according to Revelation Chapter 13 will evolve, instituting a cashless system.[1267]

> Note: In reality a cashless society is already here; banking, stocks, commodities, and treasury bonds are all now digital and paper certificates (money) obsolete. Eventually even those who hold physical gold will (in a digital world) have difficulty in redeeming the noble metal.

Those who claim to understand global economics while ignoring what is going on in the spiritual realm are among the great majority of the deceived. Satan, we are told, acquired dominion over the assets of the planet when Adam and Eve forfeited what GOD had essentially given them to manage and possess. Thereafter, Satan became by default, "the god of this world"[1268] and the head of the commercial empire—a.k.a. Babylon. The proof of his having control over the world's governments was made clear when Satan tempted Yahusha-Jesus in the wilderness, offering to give Him all the kingdoms of the world if only He (Jesus) would worship him.[1269]

To this day Satan presides over the planet's economic and religious systems, controlling human puppets that do his bidding in what is the Luciferian economic system. Greed, fraud, deception, and the lust for power are his calling cards. Soon, and with the collapse of the U.S. dollar, the global avalanche of currencies will begin, and once again the prophetic will become the historic.

1265 Revelation 18:2-17
1266 Proverbs 22:7
1267 Revelation 13:17
1268 2 Corinthians 4:4
1269 Matthew 4:8-9

> Note: In the past several years, major institutional banks have been convicted of rigging the markets and fined over $200 billion. They defraud mortgage holders, launder money, fix the labor rate, and manipulate the precious metal market. The gold cartel's alleged price suppression scheme has held gold and silver down in order to help prop up the value of the fiat dollar. Since 2014, Deutsche Bank, Bank of Nova Scotia, Barclays, HSBC, Societe Generale, and UBS were sued civilly in Federal Court for manipulating gold prices. Deutsche Bank, Bank of Nova Scotia, HSBC, and UBS were sued for manipulating silver.[1270] What's more the banksters never see the inside of a prison. But this pales by comparison to what the Federal Reserve has been doing these many years. The Federal Reserve has only been audited once since its inception in 1913, and that was a very, very limited audit ordered by Congress after the 2008 meltdown. One of their discoveries was that the FED had allocated and sent $16 Trillion (with a T) to corporations and foreign banks supposedly for financial assistance they termed "banking relief." During the market meltdown, it took a freedom of information act to find out that the U.S. FED had "lent" $16 Trillion to Europe. That was $16 trillion which congress was never told about. When FED Chairmen Ben Bernanke was asked, "Who got the money?" He responded, "I don't know?" Into what or whose pockets this money went is a mystery, as the money is still unaccounted for. In the meantime, the autonomous Vatican bank, whose depositors are presidents, heads of state, sheiks, and billionaires of every sought swelled. I can't help wondering too if a great deal of the money wasn't used to purchase controlling stock interest in the energy and communication giants that rule the internet with impunity.
>
> Note: Senator Nelson Aldrich was a key figure on the Senate Finance committee in 1906. He oversaw the nation's currency and was referred to by some as "the General Manager of the Nation." It was in this capacity that in 1910 he presided over a secretive Jekyll Island conclave with the nation's richest and most powerful banking moguls. It was that meeting, undertaken in complete secrecy and hidden from the public until decades after, that gave birth to the Central Banking and Federal Reserve itself.[1271]

If history has taught us anything, it is that mainstream economic thinking has failed spectacularly prior to financial crisis. Whether it was the collapse of the markets in 1930, or in 2007–2008, the market gurus were blindsided. They were not just wrong in their prognostications, but infinitely wrong. With rose colored glasses they might have been singing, "happy days are here again" just as the floor of the stock market collapsed.

To summarize; here are just a few reasons why an economic collapse is inevitable:

Creditor countries are beginning to cash in their U.S. Treasury investments, anticipating a bond market collapse. The U.S. dollar has all but lost its status as the petro dollar as more and

---

1270 Silver case is *In re: London Silver Fixing Ltd. Antitrust Litigation*, 1:14-md-02573. The gold case is In re: *Commodity Exchange, Inc. Gold Futures and Options Trading Litigation*, 14-md-2548, U.S. District Court, Southern District of New York (Manhattan).

1271 *Century of Enslavement: The History of the Federal Reserve*, James Corbett

more nations are now circumventing the USD and trading with other currencies and with gold, oil, and natural gas. The Chinese are backing their yuan with physical gold, whereas the U.S. dollar is only a promissory note (an IOU) without backing and as such, has no intrinsic value.

As confidence in the USD continues to diminish, and credit dries up, the interest rates for the government to borrow will rise dramatically. The U.S. having a debt based monetary system must continue to borrow in order to make good on the debts it has already incurred. The U.S. must keep borrowing indefinitely to keep the illusion it is solvent. Going into more debt is not an option but a necessity.

Fractional banking practices are so overextended that in the event of an economic collapse the financial institutions can only pay a small percentage of their investors who have bought into paper gold and the Electronic Fund Transfer (ETF) markets, which as an industry recently surpassed $3.4 trillion. Digital debt-instruments like stocks, bonds, and derivatives cannot be liquidated at their full value. Banks do not have adequate collateral for their loans. Neither is there enough fiat should even a substantial number of their depositors try to extract their money at one time. Banks and lending institutions will have no choice but to claim insolvency and close. Pension funds and 401Ks will disappear.

The global acceptance of a cryptocurrency (e.g., Bitcoin) could create a reset which will put the USD in further jeopardy as the push to a cashless society takes hold. Digital currencies could enable people to load credit in various currencies and store and protect their money by buying shares of gold bullion stored in Switzerland or the Vatican Bank.

> Note: A caveat to the virtual currency investor. There are countries like South Korea who have proposed a ban on cryptocurrencies. Exchanges such as Coinone and Bithumb have been raided by police and tax agencies for alleged tax evasion. Finance ministries all over the world are scratching their heads to come up with ways to tax the illusionary market.

The twenty-first century has produced a global society and a new and untested economic paradigm. The models and trends of the past no longer have integrity. The old templates that once guided prudent investing are side stepped as hedging and stop orders are thought to be infallible safeguards. The world at large and the financial world in particular is a ticking time bomb as the largest financial conglomerates are found guilty of collusion and fraud and fined astronomical fees. Still the greedy ignore the bellwethers and drive the markets to new highs.

Today we have unpayable levels of government debt, banks with multiple sets of books, and over leveraged financial institutions that couldn't possibly fulfill their contracts in the event of a rout. At the same time the Economic Union is in jeopardy of unraveling as Britain prepares to leave the failed experiment. All this is transpiring while rogue nations (Iran and North Korea) with ballistic pursuits promise nuclear retaliation. Russia's Vladimir Putin continues the occupation of Eastern Ukraine and carries on military exercises on the Baltic borders of Poland, Latvia, and Lithuania. America weighs in by providing sophisticated javelin tank busters to the

Ukraine. All this as China continues to build strategic military islands on reefs in international waters and threatens to take possession of Taiwan.

> Note: China and Russia challenge American power, influence, and interests, attempting to erode American security and prosperity. They are determined to make economies less free and less fair, to grow their militaries, and to control information and data that allows them to repress their societies and expand their influence.
>
> Note: While Americans are preoccupied with new stock highs, the bitcoin phenomenon, and the prospect of a new economy under President Trump, the majority seem oblivious to how tenuous things are with Russia, Iran, and especially with China. They have turned a blind eye to the fact that most of the United Nations members oppose us, as evidenced by the voting record.

In the meantime, America has become a divided nation. The nation has not been as polarized as it is now since the War Between the States. What's more, this polarization has been carefully orchestrated by the progressive global management syndicate which has usurped the name democrat in order to carry out its socialistic/global agenda. By capitalizing on generations of family allegiance to a once noble party (e.g., the party of John F. Kennedy) which had integrity and represented the working class, these saboteurs have garnered the support of the unwitting.

Their true colors are demonstrated by their unwillingness to accept the results of the 2016 election and their attempts to impeach the standing president on a contrived conspiracy of Russian collusion. They are, by definition seditionists, attempting to overthrow the nation's lawful government. Abetted by the majority of the news media that spew out fake news (a fifth column tactic) and swoon the gullible. What they are attempting is nothing less than a coup d'état. Whether any of these traitors have knowledge of the Scriptures or not, they know this one maxim: "and if a house be divided against itself, that house cannot stand."[1272] The military maxim is "divide and conquer."

Three of our noble presidents—Eisenhower, Kennedy, and Reagan—recognized and warned us of the Deep State and Shadow Government. In their speeches they spoke of it as being the greatest threat our nation faces.

In January 1961, John F. Kennedy, referring to the Deep State and Shadow government said, "There is a plot to enslave every man, woman, and child. Before I leave this high office, I intend to expose this plot." He was summarily assassinated by the very intelligence agency that he was about expose.

President Trump has attempted to do the exact same thing; expose and dismantle them. He nicknamed the Deep State and Shadow government "the Swamp," and promised to drain it. Realizing he was able to do just that, they martialed all their forces and affiliates to stay in power and keep their magnus empire. President Trump faces the same threat that President Kennedy faced and for which he was murdered.

1272 Mark 3:25

The Climate Change Farce

Mind control and hostage taking. Mind control—the ability to control the thoughts and behavior of the masses is a time-tested strategy. It has worked exceedingly well by dictators, governments, and religious institutions to dominate their subjects. Historically, disinformation, propaganda, and psychological warfare (the use of fear) have been the instruments of totalitarianism.

To illustrate my point: today there are telecommunication giants with integrated computer systems who monitor and track our thoughts and mold our decisions with every click of the mouse. Without our recognizing it our options and thought processes are channeled and focused. By repetitive advertisements our choices are being limited by what is visually offered; our selections are being made for us. So it is that we make decisions as to what we should purchase, what we should eat, or what kind of car we should drive. The same applies to what we believe! The paranoia that surrounds climate change is just one of the oligarch's innovations that threatens to regulate and subjugate the people. Climate change is not about atmospheric change but about power and control!

In order for the global cartel to quickly manage the masses, they must use psychological warfare. The term, "to psych someone out" is to frighten them to the point that they can no longer think rationally. Propaganda and fear mongering are most effective tools. Environmental threats, global extinction, and the destruction of the planet are a perfect smokescreen with which to take the focus off their real agenda—planetary control.

This mechanism has allowed the United Nations to pass global regulations as the people cheer for more. The climate change advocates even insist climate change is the number one threat: greater than Jihadism or the nuclear threat from rogue nations. The fertile minds of the know-it-all youth, who always look for a cause to attach themselves to, are particularly vulnerable to propaganda. This allows their indoctrinators (politicians and professors) to quickly draw them in. The threat of planetary extinction is a most effective way to distract the unwary from recognizing the true agenda.

Climate change due to greenhouse gases and carbon emissions is grossly exaggerated and the burning of fossil fuel has a miniscule effect on global temperatures. At the same time the alarmists ignore evidence of naturally occurring climate change. The premise that fossil fuels are causing carbon dioxide gases insulating the planet, triggering global warming and the melting of polar icecaps is contradicted by empirical evidence. For example, pre-industrial warming has occurred numerous times; even eight hundred years before the first smokestack of the Industrial Revolution was ever erected. The less-than-one degree rise in the earth's temperature over the past century coincides with the doubling of the solar magnetic field over this same period. The earth is in reality a spinning magnet which is the principally cause for geologic and climatic changes.

According to Dr. Patrick J. Michael, science director and senior fellow of the CATO Institute Center for Scientific Study, the planet has warmed only 0.9% Celsius over the last century, and only half of that nine-tenths of a percent could, at best contribute to greenhouse gases. Dr. Michael goes on to say that this slight rise in the earth's surface temperature has actually been beneficial to global agriculture; extending growing seasons by 5%; furthermore, that CO2 has actually been beneficial as it supports vegetation. Both of these factors have increased global food production.[1273]

The fear-based propaganda that is fed to a gullible public by the misinformed has been the invention of the United Nations inter-government panel on climate change whose goal is to unify views and policies—hence the Paris Accord on Climate Change (Dec. 12, 2015). In keeping with the global agenda, the Accord's purpose is autocracy—whereby the few rule the many. The climatological studies which are continuously financed by governments around the world, award institutions such as the Academy of Science and prestigious universities with huge federal grants to produce climate models that support their hyper-political agenda.

Thirty-two families of computer models have been produced for and used by the United Nations. All but one (the Russian model), were based on a false and unscientific premise inconsistent with what has been occurring year by year. It is the subsidized academic scientist, not science, that is behind their foreboding projections.

In 2007, thirty-one models were brought before the U.S. Supreme Court who commissioned the Environmental Protection Agency (EPA) to determine if carbon dioxide was endangering the health and human welfare of the planet. Their consensus was that if they (the EPA) determined it was, they would be given great regulator power and funding. It therefore behooved the EPA to take the position that man was and is destroying the atmosphere and endangering the planet.

The devastation we have seen in the way of hurricanes and typhoons is not the result of weather change, nor is it the frequency or magnitude of storms. Devastation has increased, but it is largely a result of a population who have chosen to live on the water's edge of the oceans coasts—barely above sea level, or in the case of Katrina (as with New Orleans, LA.), building cities behind levees below sea level.

Citing an example: The Netherlands is the main constituent country of the kingdom of Netherlands. It is a highly populous country with a population density of about 1,068 persons per square mile. It is one of hundreds of countries with extremely low-lying populated areas, with over 26% of its land area being below sea level—and only about 50% of the country is even three feet above sea level. The history of flooding in the country dates back to the year 1134 whereby a storm created an island known as Zeeland. In 1287, another flood left over fifty thousand people dead.

Former President Obama took it upon himself and autocratically signed America into the Paris Climate Accord. Using skewed data and false claims, just as he had in 2013, wherein he stated that 97% of scientists agree climate change is real, man-made, and dangerous, he succeeded in hurtling the progressive (globalist) agenda forward.

A global predecessor of Obama was vice president turned environmental scientist Al Gore. He and the Hollywood climate professionals claimed that we will end up drowning the polar bears and snuff out all life on the planet with CO2. Even Pope Francis has become a climatologist

---

1273 "Life, Liberty and Levin", Televised interview, Fox News, Oct. 22, 2018

stating in an encyclical, "the bulk of global warming is caused by human activity and I call on people—especially the world's rich—to take steps to mitigate the damage by reducing consumption and reliance on fossil fuels."[1274] An informed President Trump with authentic facts and the best science at his disposal was not duped and opted out of the Paris Climate Accord.

Climate change is a cyclic event which can take place over a thousand or more years due to the rotation and axis of the earth and its relationship to the sun. In the past this has brought on the ice ages and afterward their disappearance. This natural phenomenon has caused the polar artic to warm and the orbiting winds surrounding the polar continent to alter the ribbon configuration of the jet stream. This caused warm air to stall over certain regions like California and colder air to stall over areas like the Northeast. Unrelenting warm air (as in the west) has caused drought and the drying up of aquifers and reservoirs, giving rise to devastating forest fires and crop failure.

The winds that circumvent the globe are in part shaped by the 7,000-degree superheated liquid core of the planet. This heat is constantly permeating the mantle of the earth, as seen in volcanic eruptions. Huge portals and volcanic eruptions under the oceans are constantly releasing heat through enormous fissures which warm ocean currents, which in turn can melt sections of ice caps that are exposed to these currents. Geologic magnetic fluctuations and the shifting of tectonic plates constantly release immeasurable amounts of heat, methane and other gases, of which carbon dioxide is the most prevalent. The molten core of the earth is the earth's thermostat.

Tidal heating (also known tidal flexing) occurs through the tidal friction processes. Orbital and rotational energy are dissipated as heat in the surface ocean. Over the course of an earth orbit, the friction from this tidal flexing heats up the planet's interior as well. It is theorized that this also contributes to heat variations and the melting of ice caps. At the same time as some sections of the caps are melting others on the opposing side are forming. Other contributors to planetary heating besides tidal heating are radioactive decay, and orbital resonance which occurs when two orbiting planets cyclically pass close to one another exerting a gravitational influence on one another.

What is referred to as the Goldilocks zone is the infinitely small habitable temperature zone which sustains plant and animal life here on earth. There are an extensive number of factors that contribute to the habitable zone of life: the earth's distance from the sun, its axis and rotation, its one moon which rocks the perfectly salted seas and enables it to cleanse itself, its magnetic core and gravitationally energy, and the perfect blend of oxygen, nitrogen, and carbon dioxide. These are just a few of the features which the Creator crafted to provide us with a habitat which remain entirely under HIS control.

As in the book of Exodus, chapters eight through ten, GOD brought a series of escalating plagues and pestilences upon an arrogant Egyptian Pharaoh prior to the Hebrews being emancipated. Such examples reveal how GOD deploys judgment in an attempt to get man to repent and return to HIM. Still man denies that GOD is involved in natural disasters, even referring to them as acts of "mother nature," or now "climate change." I dare say that if man believes climate

---

1274 www.washingtonpost.com/local/an-italian-draft-of-pope-francis-environmental-paper-leaks

change left unchecked will bring an end to civilization, then he has testified of his ignorance or disbelief in the Bible; for if one knew and believed Scripture they would know exactly how this earth age is destined to end.[1275] Those who make the assertion that the planet will be destroyed if environmental issues are not addressed must be discounted as biblical Christians or biblical Jews.

> Note: To accept that human induced factors and not natural factors control our weather, one would have to ignore the real scientific data that has been documented from ice cores, dripstones, tree rings, and deep-sea sediment cores. Cyclic evidence includes the Holocene Warming Period, the Akkadian Cold Period, the Minoan Warm Period, the Bronze Age Cold Period, the Medieval Warm Period, the Little Ice Age, and the Modern Warm Period. It would also include the one thousand year-long Eddy Cycle (seasonal cycles) which ran parallel to solar cycles.

The Deep State and the Shadow Government

What is now taking place in the United States and throughout the world is eerily similar to George Orwell's dystopian novel, *1984*—the formation of the Superstate, the end time One World/New World global government, Babylon the Great.[1276]

The Deep State is a criminal empire and global network. It is an international cabal; composed of the infinitely wealthy and the most powerful people on earth. Its membership includes heads of state, political parties, politicians, pay for play operatives, foreign governments, diplomats, and attachés. It includes industry moguls, central banks, and the largest financial institutions in America, England, Europe, and the world.

It includes the telecommunications and social media giants, who also happen to own not only the major broadcasting companies, but the largest newspapers in the country. It has compromised federal law enforcement, our national security apparatus, the military industrial complex, and the intelligence agencies, where the top echelon and their complicit directors have built a fourth branch of the government; a Shadow Government.

In this alliance secrecy is power and power has given them both control and autonomy which has allowed them to usurp the three branches of government in the United States. It is they who determine whether or not to share or conceal information from Congress. It is they who surreptitiously record and store every electronic communication shared between the citizenry and keep an electronic dossier (metadata) on each and all. It is they who undergird their partner, the drug cartel that pours billions into their pockets and their Swiss, Vatican, and offshore bank accounts.

The Deep State includes regulatory agencies like the Environmental Protection Agency that confiscates private land or attempt to shut down the fossil fuel industry. It is the Deep State that has exacted control of the State Department and Justice system with cover-ups such as Benghazi and the Uranium One deal.

1275 Revelation chapters 4-19
1276 Revelation 18:2

It includes entrenched legislators—"the establishment"—who pass regulations for their own empowerment. Who pass bills that encumber the people with debt. Who attempt to usurp the Constitution to silence free speech or disarm the citizens from the right to bear arms. It includes billionaire traders and industry moguls who hand-pick and sponsor political candidates for congressional offices—including the presidency. Many of these legislators have amassed tens and in some cases hundreds of millions of dollars which would be unexplainable were it not for their being complicit in nefarious deals. It includes the global non-governmental Trilateral Commission, the Bilderberg group, and the Council of Foreign Relations.

The accomplices are innumerable (hence the word Deep) and their reach limitless; for this is a global consortium that works both inside and outside official government channels; circumventing the law when convenient, and the democratic process when necessary. It centralizes control in feudal fashion. It is classic aristocracy, where the few rule the many.

Its tactics are time tested: Infiltrate academia, sway the unwitting with propaganda (the media), entice the electorate with entitlements (the democratic progressive socialist platform), then dismantle the economy with unpayable debt in trillions and make the citizenry dependents of the state. Once the people have become reliant on subsidies, they happily give up their independence for entitlements.

If their politicians can gain control and hold onto the majority in all three branches of government long enough, they believe they can turn our country into a one-party system—another name for communism. The progressive progression is from socialism to communism, and from communism to totalitarianism.

The Global Cartel includes the North Atlantic Treaty Organization (NATO) and its intergovernmental military alliances—a future global police force. It includes the World Trade Organization (WTO), the Bank of International Settlements, the Central Banks, and the largest trading institutions in the world. It includes the Federal Open Market Committee (FOMC)—the governing body of the Federal Reserve which exercises control of the money supply, interest rates, and the availability to credit. It includes the London Interbank Offered Rate (LIBOR)—a syndicate of banks which wields great power over the value of currencies and precious metals. At least $350 trillion in derivatives and other financial products are tied to LIBOR.[1277] And, the Deep State includes its most powerful originators and orchestrators; the enormously wealthy Jesuit-Vatican, the Rothschild Empire (the world's biggest bank), and the house of Windsor (the British Crown).

However, it is the United Nations that is the de facto government of the Deep State. It has since its inception, portrayed itself as the benevolent global organization and the only hope for humanity. Once the Deep State and Shadow Government has been successful in imbedding their policymakers into office, the U.S. Constitution and the Bill of Rights, along with all other national constitutions, will be usurped by the UN's World Constitution. Once established it will control and tax all trade and commerce and implement a world tax on every global citizen.

1277 *The NY Times*, "Behind the Libor Scandal," July 10, 2012

This will allow them to extract money at will through the quantum banking system. With digital blockchain technology it will institute the mark of the beast.[1278]

Today we recognize this evolving New World Order alluded to in the Bible as the Revised Roman Empire and as the fourth beast; a dominating Luciferian empire from which the Antichrist will rise to become world sovereign.[1279]

Recommended reading: *The Deep State: The Fall of the Constitution and the Rise of a Shadow Government*, by Mike Lofgren.

A prophetic Word of encouragement for the Church, given to Pastor Angelina Kiena on September 19, 2016:

> "The beginning of this nation I have used the persecution of the Saints of foreign lands for good, it is what formed the Christian base to be empowered and to generate the impetus of a united power. This Nation was formed by imperfect men however; the Gospel was generated by the freedom which it procreated. Religious Puritans and other persecuted saints of other lands generated the Gospel in this Nation with the freedom established by the founding fathers."

> "The evil which now is showing itself strong has always been; now that evil can be seen which had laid hidden."

> "The evil in the world is rising to its culmination, that the judgment of God will be justified. Its corruption is darkening all nations, some more than others to where the rottenness reaches into heaven provoking the judgment and wrath to come."

> "Within this darkness and stench is that which causes the heart of the saints to shrink but take heart. For a marvelous thing is taking place. The darker the world the brighter the light of My people. The darkness viewed from Heaven shows fourth brightly the light of the true and holy saints like a jewel. This brings a tear of joy for the finish work on the cross. The darkness will endeavor to encroach upon the brightness of My Jewel the Church, but it will not and cannot succeed."

> "You will feel the darkness, you will mourn over it, you will travail, and this in itself will polish you to a gleaming threat to the world even more. How be it, you're very light repels darkness until I reach down and take you to Myself. Draw near to Me, stay pure and clean; let not your light grow dim. As I take delight in looking to and fro upon the earth to evaluate, protect and cherish and prepare my own. Look up, rejoice in knowing your redemption is near."

1278   Revelation 13:16-17
1279   Daniel 7:7-8, 20

APPENDIX B

THE OLIVET DISCOURSE

Mount of Olives (Image Source: GOODSALT)

A Study of the Seven Years of "The Time of Jacob's Trouble"

Apart from the Book of the Revelation, what has come to be called the "Olivet Discourse"[1280] is the most comprehensive prophecy found in the New Testament concerning the end times and the coming of the Lord. It can be seen in its most complete form in the Gospel of Matthew, chapters 24 and 25. It also appears in the Gospel of Mark, chapter 13, and in the Gospel of Luke, chapter 21. The Discourse is sometimes referred to as the "Little Apocalypse," so named because it is descriptive of the suffering which Israel will undergo during the "time of Jacob's

---

[1280] Matthew 24-25

Trouble."[1281] Jacob's trouble is more commonly referred to as the "Tribulation,"[1282] or more correctly, the "Great Tribulation."[1283]

The passage derives its name from the Mount of Olives; a ridge and cemetery situated east of and overlooking Old Jerusalem. The Mount was a place of solitude where Jesus frequently went to pray or explain things to His disciples, especially things that they would need to know in order to carry out their commission.[1284] So it was that this tranquil setting would be where the Lord would reveal to His disciples by what signs they would know that the time of His return was at hand.

As the story begins, we see Yahusha-Jesus and these disciples making their way to Jerusalem for the Passover. The Lord knew that this time He would not live to celebrate this Passover but become the Passover sacrifice for those who would accept Him as their *Korban Pesakh*.[1285] He would meet His appointment with a Roman Cross just as Isaiah had predicted.[1286]

A day earlier, while traveling along the caravan road from Bethany to Jerusalem, Jesus and His disciples reached the crest of the Mount of Olives. There He paused and looked toward the city. To the west, just beyond the Kidron Valley stood Mount Moriah and Herod's Temple. The sun was probably shining that morning with its rays illuminating the white marble fascia and the huge white columns making it appear as if the Temple was made of gold.

Gazing at the edifice the Lord spoke, "O Jerusalem, Jerusalem, thou that killest the prophets, and stonest them which are sent unto thee, how often would I have gathered thy children together, even as a hen gathereth her chickens under her wings, and ye would not! Behold, your house is left unto you desolate. For I say unto you, Ye shall not see me henceforth, till ye shall say, Blessed is he that cometh in the name of the Lord."[1287]

In His ability to see into the future, not only did the Lord know His own fate but also the fate of the Temple, for it would be toppled in a mere thirty-seven years during a Roman siege.

We then read that Jesus began to weep, but He was not weeping for Himself or for the Temple. Instead, He wept for the Jewish people who had missed the time of His "visitation."[1288] He knew what this would mean for them, for now they were destined to continue under the "rod of (GOD's) correction"[1289] for many more years, even until His next visitation.[1290]

What is so heartbreaking is that had the Jewish people remembered what the patriarchs and the prophets had said and recognized their Savior at His coming, things undoubtedly would have been much different.[1291] The Lord would have made Israel the chief of nations, "…the head,

---

1281 Jeremiah 30:7
1282 Deuteronomy 4:30
1283 Matthew 24:21; Revelation 7:14
1284 Mark 16:15; Acts 1:8
1285 John 1:29; Isaiah 53:10-11
1286 Isaiah 53:12
1287 Matthew 23:37-39
1288 Luke 19:44
1289 Ezekiel 20:37
1290 Luke 19:44
1291 Deuteronomy 28:12

and not the tail…"[1292] Instead Israel would experience centuries of chastisement which will only conclude when the "Seventieth Week of Daniel"[1293] has played out. This protracted time between His first and second comings and particular the last three and one-half years would be necessary "to finish the (their) transgression, and make an end of sin, and to make reconciliation for iniquity, and to bring in everlasting righteousness."[1294]

In Deuteronomy we are told that anyone can seek and find Him at any given moment, yet for most Jews it will take a Great Tribulation before they yield, seek and find Him. Moses could not have been clearer then when he said,

> "But if from thence thou shalt seek the Lord thy God, thou shalt find him, if thou seek him with all thy heart and with all thy soul. When thou art in tribulation, and all these things are come upon thee, even in the latter days, if thou turn to the Lord thy God, and shalt be obedient unto his voice; (for the Lord thy God is a merciful God;) he will not forsake thee, neither destroy thee, nor forget the covenant of thy fathers which he sware unto them." (Deuteronomy 4:29-31)

The omniscient Creator knew well before Yahusha was to appear on earth that He would be rejected by His own people.[1295] Fourteen hundred years before Yahusha's arrival, Moses was given a word from GOD admonishing the Hebrew children that GOD was sending His anointed and there would be grave consequences if they wouldn't heed or accept this Promised One.

> "The Lord thy God will raise up unto thee a Prophet from the midst of thee, of thy brethren, like unto me; unto him ye shall hearken…And it shall come to pass, that whosoever will not hearken unto my words which he shall speak in my name, I will require it of him." (Deuteronomy 18:15, 19)

> "But it shall come to pass, if thou wilt not hearken unto the voice of the Lord thy God, to observe to do all his commandments and his statutes which I command thee this day; that all these curses shall come upon thee, and overtake thee…The Lord shall send upon thee cursing, vexation, and rebuke, in all that thou settest thine hand unto for to do, until thou be destroyed, and until thou perish quickly; because of the wickedness of thy doings, whereby thou hast forsaken me." (Deuteronomy 28:15, 20)

The consequence of failing to believe the patriarchs and the prophets would result in the prayers and petitions of the people to go unanswered. "And thy heaven that is over thy head shall

---

1292 Deuteronomy 28:13
1293 Daniel 9:24
1294 Daniel 9:24
1295 Isaiah 53:3

be brass, and the earth that is under thee shall be iron."[1296] Though GOD hears their wailings, still the vast majority refuse to heed Moses' admonition; sooner believing their rabbis' than the evidence provided in their own Holy Scriptures.

The Olivet Discourse, like many Old Testament prophecies suddenly vaults over scores of centuries from the time it was spoken to the "last days" of the earth age. From the time of Jesus' first coming we leap some twenty centuries to His second coming. Between these two advents has been interpolated an entire dispensation which has come to be called the "Church Age." It might better be referred to as the Age of the Believers.

During this dispensation GOD would temporarily suspend HIS dealings with HIS people Israel because of their perpetual disobedience, their passive indifference and their rejection of their Savior. Instead, HE would turn HIS attention to the Gentiles, offering Himself to them as their Messiah just as He had with the Jewish people. GOD tells us HE is no respecter of persons, or for that matter ethnicity. HE is looking for those who are looking for Him.

> "Then Peter opened his mouth, and said, Of a truth I perceive that God is no respecter of people; But in every nation he that feareth (Greek, *phobeo*—reverence) him, and worketh righteousness, is accepted with him." (Acts 10:34-35)

So it is that HE will accept anyone who accepts Him, and who then chooses to follow after Him; becoming as it were, His disciple.

> "How beautiful upon the mountains are the feet of him that bringeth good tidings, that publisheth peace; that bringeth good tidings of good, that publisheth (Hebrew, *shama*—to declare) salvation; that saith unto Zion, Thy God reigneth!" (Isaiah 52:7)

By all indications the Age of the Gentiles (which encompasses the great span of time in which the Israelites were first enslaved or dominated by Gentiles, to the end of Gentile era—the return of the Lord), is nearly at an end. Soon GOD will, as promised, once again focus HIS attention on the people and nation of Israel.[1297] HIS ultimate objective has always been to redeem them and afterward to restore them. The Olivet Discourse is a synopsis of prophetic events soon to unfold during the "Seventieth Week of Daniel."[1298] (Appendix C)

> Note: Abram's descendants had been given unmerited favor as GOD HIMSELF adopted them, protected them, and afforded them every advantage imaginable. All HE asked in return was their love and obedience.[1299]

1296 Isaiah 28:23
1297 Ezekiel 36:17-26
1298 Daniel 9:24-27
1299 Deuteronomy 6:5

It was in Leviticus 26:33 where we read that the Hebrew people were first told that disobedience would result in their being scattered among the heathen. Six other books in the Hebrew Scriptures repeated the warnings which for the most part went unheeded.[1300] The rejection of HIS Son was the final straw; GOD would turn away from them and reveal Himself to another chosen people.[1301]

Not long after the crucifixion when the disciples had recorded the accounts of Christ, the biblical annals of the Jewish people ended. On August 5, 70 AD, the last fortification, the Tower Antonia, that guarded the Temple Mount was overtaken. The Temple was leveled, and the Jewish people entered the great diaspora. So it was once again that their painful journey would continue. Not only would they be dispersed, but they would be despised,[1302] hated, slain,[1303] and left few in number.[1304] But GOD has a reason for permitting ordeals. HE chastises the ones HE loves so that they will see the error of their ways, repent and return to HIM.[1305] The "Time of Jacob's Trouble" will accomplish what the pleas of prophets and the years spent in exile could not.

> "And ye have forgotten the exhortation which speaketh unto you as unto children, My son, despise not thou the chastening of the Lord, nor faint when thou art rebuked of him: For whom the Lord loveth he chasteneth, and scourgeth every son whom he receiveth."
> (Hebrews 12:6)

Rightly Dividing the Word

Before examining the passage itself, it needs to be pointed out that this Discourse is frequently misapplied. Some teachers force the scripture—imposing the Church into them when in fact the Church was yet an unrevealed part of GOD's divine program when the Lord spoke the Discourse. Furthermore, the Church is not mentioned or even alluded to in this narrative, which it most certainly would have if it were present during this time. The reason the Church is not mentioned is because it will have been supernaturally removed before this foreboding time begins.[1306]

The "Time of Jacob's Trouble" is a dispensation unto itself and is not a part of the Church Age. It is actually the resumption of GOD's dealing with Israel; it being the last Week of the Seventy Weeks of the prophecy given to Daniel.[1307]

By misapplying who the Scripture is referring to, the entire prophesy becomes distorted. This distortion is then imposed into the book of the Revelation where the misinformed see the

---

1300 Deuteronomy 28:15, 64; 44:27; Jeremiah 9:16; Ezekiel 12:15
1301 Isaiah 11:10
1302 Obadiah 2; Jeremiah 33:24
1303 Leviticus 26:17
1304 Deuteronomy 28:62
1305 Proverbs 3:11
1306 1 Thessalonians 5:9, 11
1307 Daniel 9:24-27

Church as still being here on earth. As we move forward it will become exceedingly clear that the Olivet Discourse pertains to the Jews and Israel, not to the Church.

It is indeed the Seventieth Week of Daniel, the travail of Isaiah, the birth pangs of Jeremiah, the sword of the Lord in Ezekiel, and the Great and Terrible Day of the Lord in Joel that are lead-ins to the Lord's second coming. Once this is realized the learner will see how effortlessly it dovetails with the revelation given the Apostle John in the book so named the Revelation of Jesus Christ.

When analyzing scripture, it is important to keep in mind that almost four-fifths of the Bible is devoted entirely to the Jewish people. It has become characteristic for the Church to see itself as being of supreme importance and the focal point of scripture in general. In reality only one-fifth of the Bible gives an account of the Church, its origin, development and destiny. Even the great majority of the New Testament and that which Jesus spoke during His earthly ministry (lettered in red in many bibles) did not have a direct application to the Church. One must remember that Jesus came for "the lost sheep of the house of Israel,"[1308] not for the Gentile. Jesus would emphasize this in a passage to a Syrophoenician woman (a Gentile) who sought Him that He might cast a demon from her daughter.[1309] It would be Paul who would afterward address the Church in his epistles,[1310] and Luke who would record the teachings and accounts of the Church in the Acts of the Apostles. So it is that when we look at the New Testament, we see that the Synoptic Gospels (Matthew, Mark, Luke) were all written to the Jews, and are oriented to the Jewish people. The Discourse centers on a series of questions pertaining to Jewish prophecy, asked by Jewish disciples, to their Jewish Messiah.

Disciplines

When one uses standardized hermeneutic disciplines (accepted principles for interpreting writings) it allows those writings—in our case, Scripture—to speak and be interpreted with far less risk of being misinterpreted.

Language (grammar for example) has its general set of rules. These rules and other literary rules need to be included and applied to scripture just as they are to other literary works. Expository hermeneutics involves recognition, validations, historical proofs, theological premise, word and language idioms, etiology, relationships with other scripture, authorship, typology, and eschatological comparison. In this study we must touch lightly on these basic disciplines in order to, as scripture directs us, "prove all things."[1311]

Rules of scholarship are not generally taught, emphasized, or applied in Bible studies today. This neglect has led to many misconceptions and wrong conclusions. Today for

---

1308 Matthew 15:24
1309 Mark 7:24-30
1310 Romans 11:13
1311 1 Thessalonians 5:21

example we have Pre-Tribulation, Mid-Tribulation, Post-Tribulation, and No-Tribulation rapture advocates.

We have Kingdom Theology—Dominionism, and Replacement Theology. We have the Apostles and Prophets, the Emerging Church, Jehovah Witnesses, Latter Day Saints, and a host of other distorted teachings which all allege to have their foundation in the same Book. This would be an enigma if it weren't for the fact that we know the human tendency is to make the Bible conform to our interpretations instead of allowing the Bible, and only the Bible to educate us. So this study will not only give clarity to a prophetic passage but will also serve to demonstrate how one is to analyze scripture.

Church Bible Studies in general offer a hasty interpretation. They are appropriately referred to as Inductive Bible Studies. An inductive study focuses on the general meaning and the basic message; it serves as a framework on which to build. Inductive study is opposite from the deductive process which uses hermeneutic principals. Expository hermeneutics begins with the basic message but then traces it backward to its intended meaning. Exegesis (analysis) seeks for an interpretation which will account for all the features of the passage—both on its own, and in context and in relationship to other scripture.

> Note: When a scripture does not appear to be in harmony with other scriptures, then the studious learner is to delve deeper. There are verses in the Bible that upon first glance, or when singled out from the setting and context of the passage can be easily misconstrued. Jehovah Witnesses' frequently seize a scripture such as John 14:28, where Jesus said, "I go unto my father: for my father is greater than I..." and assert that this statement confirms that Jesus is not GOD or equal with Jehovah. Using only inductive study (a starting point) they develop a theory. Were they to use a deductive approach and compare scripture with scripture (e.g. Philippians 2:5-8, Hebrews 2:9, John 1:1, 14, Colossians 2:9) they would see that it invalidates their allegation. In John 14:28 Jesus was not saying the He was not GOD or that the Father was in fact greater than He, but that He in His temporary role as Son of man and with self-imposed limitations had to, just as we have to, approach the Father with our request (John 14:13).

It is my hope and part of the objective in this study to illustrate several of the fundamental principles and disciplines used to obtain the correct interpretation of scripture. I would encourage you to take a highlighter and make notations of these passages in your Bible as we examine each verse. Highlight those words which have a purely Jewish application such as the "Temple," "Judea," and "Jerusalem." Highlight Jewish idioms (expressions and phrases) such as the "abomination of desolation" and "the beginning of sorrows;" all of which are specific to the Israelites of the Hebrew Holy Scriptures. Do this and it will soon become apparent to whom this discourse applies and in what timeframe it applies.

To summarize:

1. Apply rules and disciplines of interpretation.
2. Be on the lookout for key words and phrases which specify who it is that is being addressed.
3. Compare the scripture we are researching with other supporting scriptures (parallel scriptures) found elsewhere in the Bible.

Key points to keep in mind:

1. The discourse begins with an extended section devoted to Israel; it concludes in Matthew 25:31–46 with a section concerning the fate of the Gentile nations.
2. Jesus met privately with four of His Jewish disciples who ask Him three questions of Jewish expectation.
3. All the questions that were asked were relative to the time when He would return to earth and vindicate His people.

There are fifteen specific mentions of the end or of Christ's coming in just two chapters. More time words, definitive signs or references to Jewish locations are given here than anywhere else within such a brief range of scripture. The Greek word for "coming" is *"parousia"* (*"para,"* with and *ousia*, being) or being with. It denotes arrival in a physical presence.

Speaking of Times

To say as some do, that we are now living in the last days and that "signs" (wars, earthquakes, etc.) spoken of in Scripture depict the present time is coercing scripture and is an unscholarly way of interpreting the Word. References to the last days, latter days, latter rain, etc., refer to the seven years of The Time of Jacob's Trouble, the Battle of Armageddon, the Day of the Lord's Coming, and the Millennium which follows His coming. It does not refer to the end of the Church Age! End time expressions, all of which are found in the Old Testament, are Jewish idioms. These terms are never used with regard to the times leading up to the Tribulation, or to the end of the Church Age. It may be appropriately said we are on the threshold of the later days, but we are not in the latter days. Therefore prophecies—for example, Joel 2:28–29 are still in the future and for Israel.

> **Examples:**
>
> The Last days: The end of seven weeks preceding the millennium. (Daniel 8:19; 2 Timothy 3:1; James 5:3; 2 Peter 3:3; Jude 18)
>
> The Last days: The millennium. (Genesis 49:1; Isaiah 2:1; Micah 4:1)

The Latter days: The millennium. (Job 19:25)

The Latter days: The millennium. (Hosea 3:5)

The Latter days: The future Tribulation. (Numbers 24:14; Deuteronomy 4:30, 31:29; Jeremiah 23:20, 30:24, 48:47, 49:39; Daniel 2:28, 10:14)

The Latter years: Armageddon. (Ezekiel 38:8, 16)

Applying "end time" Scriptures to the Church or to the Church dispensation is a violation of application. It breaks with a standard rule of Systematic and Covenant theology which is to apply scripture to whom or to what that particular scripture pertains. Once the misnomer that we are presently in the "end times" or "latter days" is accepted, an entirely different picture emerges. This error in chronology has led many a reader to the wrong supposition. Randomly taking scriptures and covenants from the Old Testament and applying them to the New Testament Church has become commonplace. Misapplication has given rise to such misconceptions as viewing the Church as "Spiritual Israel" when it is not. Spiritual Israel is forthcoming at the onset of the millennium and refers to the spiritual birth of the nation of Israel.[1312]

The Church is the Church, and Israel is Israel. The everlasting covenant GOD made with Israel applies specifically to them, not to the Church. That which was promised to or covenanted with Israel is applicable only to Israel.[1313]

> "And I will establish my covenant between me and thee and thy seed (Abraham and his descendants) after thee in their generations for an everlasting covenant, to be a God unto thee, and to thy seed after thee." (Genesis 17:7)

> "He that is born in thy house, and he that is bought with thy money, must need be circumcised: and my covenant shall be in your flesh for an everlasting covenant." (Genesis 17:13)

> "And God said, Sarah thy wife shall bear thee a son indeed; and thou shalt call his name Isaac: and I will establish my covenant with him for an everlasting covenant, and with his seed after him." (Genesis 17:19)

> "Every sabbath he shall set it in order before the Lord continually, being taken from the children of Israel by an everlasting covenant." (Leviticus 24:8)

Scripture bears witness to scripture and must effortlessly blend with other passages which address the same subject. This is especially true when interpreting the prophetic. Books like Joel,

---

1312 Ezekiel 36:24-27; 37:13
1313 Psalm 105:9, 10; Genesis 17:7-8; 26:3-4; 35:12

Ezekiel, Daniel, Hosea, and Zechariah, all complement Matthew 24–25, Mark 13, Luke 21, and the body of the Book of the Revelation. If such scriptures were to clash, then our conclusions have failed the fundamental criterion and more examination is needed.

Harmony of Scripture

Who:

A basic rule is to always ask yourself to who is the author speaking, and who does the subject concern. Was, for example, the audience Jews still under the Law, or Messianic Jews? Was it to unsaved Gentiles, or new Christian coverts? Was the audience part of Jesus' inner circle of disciples? Were they Greeks, Romans, or Pharisees? Was it a combination of different people as Jesus often preached to on the Judean hillsides? Was it something Jesus was speaking prophetically to the Lost Sheep of Israel, or was it something that Paul was speaking prophetically of to the Church?

> **Verse by Verse Analysis: "Precept must be upon precept...line upon line"**
>
> "And Jesus went out, and departed from the temple: and his disciples came to him for to shew him the buildings of the temple. And Jesus said unto them, See ye not all these things? verily I say unto you, There shall not be left here one stone upon another, that shall not be thrown down." (Matthew 24:1-2)

As we begin Matthew 24, we read that Jesus was speaking of the Temple's destruction, however let us look closer at what actually initiated His statement and the discourse which was to follow.

In order to do that we need to look back several verses to Matthew 23:37–39. There we read that Jesus said to His disciples that they will not see Him "henceforth" (speaking of His death) until His return, when as is recorded in Hebrew Scripture, He will vanquish their enemies, be nationally recognized as the Messiah by the Jewish people and set up His earthly kingdom.[1314]

After leaving the Temple and making their way to the Mount of Olives, Jesus made the prediction concerning the fate of the Temple; "there shall not be left here one stone upon another that shall not be thrown down." His words gave rise to His disciple's asking questions which then prompted His lengthy "end time" prophecy.

> "And as he sat upon the mount of Olives, the disciples came unto him privately, saying, Tell us, when shall these things be? and what shall be the sign of thy coming, and of the end of the world?" (Matthew 24:3)

1314 Isaiah 63:1-8; Psalms 2; Job 2:18-21

The discourse begins when four Jewish disciples, Peter, James, John, and Andrew ask the Lord three pointed questions pertaining to Old Testament prophecies. "When shall these things be?" What shall be the sign of your coming and of the end of the world?" These questions were all relative to prophecies spoken of in the Hebrew Scriptures as they pertained to the Jewish Messiah and to the Jewish people in the latter days.

When:

It is remarkable that GOD has provided us with a timeline by using a sequence of events which will unfold in chronological order—beginning with the seven years prior to His return. We shall see that by using specific words and expressions, the chapter is divided into three progressive parts: a beginning, middle, and an end.

This becomes apparent when one recognizes time words and phrases which appeared in prophecies recorded in the Hebrew Holy Scriptures (Old Testament) and are then repeated in the New Testament.

There is for example, a "beginning of sorrows" (Matthew 24:8) which has a definitive end when we arrive at the mid-point (middle) of the seven years. The parallel scripture in association to the beginning of sorrows may be seen in Isaiah 66:7–9, Jeremiah 30:4–7, and then in Revelation 12:1.

The event in Matthew which identifies the midpoint of the seven years will occur when the Temple will be defiled by the "abomination of desolation."[1315] This same event "…and for the overspreading of abominations he shall make desolate" was first spoken of in Daniel 9:27. It is there we are told that this event will take place "in the midst (middle) of the Week." So it is that we have established a correlation between the testaments and a benchmark on the timeline.

The events which follow the abomination of desolation in Mathew 24:15 occur during the final half (the last three and a half years) of the seven years of "The Time of Jacob's Trouble." These forty-two months we are told are the "great tribulation"[1316] which was first presented in Deuteronomy 4:30 and later in Jeremiah 30:7, and then in Revelation 12:6.

The Great Tribulation concludes with "the coming of the Son of man."[1317] The word "coming" speaks of His physical appearance here on earth, not in a "meeting in the air."[1318] Upon His coming we read that He will judge men and nations and establish His kingdom here on earth for one thousand years—a.k.a. the Kingdom Age.[1319]

1315 Matthew 24:15
1316 Matthew 24:21
1317 Matthew 24:2, 29
1318 1 Thessalonians 4:17
1319 Ezekiel 43:2, 4, 7, 9; Matthew 25:31–46

The Signs and the Times

Throughout Matthew 24 we find statements which unmistakably refer to the Jewish people. It is the residents of "Judea" who are warned to flee from the region before their enemies are about to overwhelm them as prophesied by Isaiah[1320] and reiterated in Matthew 24:16. The sign by which they will know when they are to leave their land will be the time when the "abomination of desolation" is placed in the holy place—the Temple in Jerusalem.[1321]

It should now be obvious as whom this prophecy is directed to and to whom it pertains. It is clearly to, for, and about the Jewish people in Israel during Daniel's Seventieth Week. Once we recognize this, we are able to interpret the narrative of each verse more accurately.

> "And Jesus answered and said unto them, Take heed that no man deceive you. For many shall come in my name, saying, I am Christ (Messiah); and shall deceive many." (Matthew 24:4-5)

In Matthew 24:4–5 we have a warning which clearly speaks to a plurality of deceivers. "For many shall come in MY name (calling themselves Christians) and deceive many." The Matthew Henry commentary reads, "assuming to themselves the name particular to Him."[1322] This should be a red flag, for it speaks of a heretical group passing themselves off as Christians. This one remark (in My name) also eliminates Islam.

The Apostle Paul indicated that even then, when the Church was just taking shape, there arose individuals who claimed to be followers of Christ that were introducing false doctrine and drawing away disciples into a new brand of Christianity.

> "Take heed therefore unto yourselves, and to all the flock, over the which the Holy Ghost hath made you overseers, to feed the church of God, which he hath purchased with his own blood. For I know this, that after my departing shall grievous wolves enter in among you, not sparing the flock. Also of your own selves shall men arise, speaking perverse things, to draw away disciples after them. Therefore watch, and remember, that by the space of three years I ceased not to warn every one night and day with tears." (Acts 20:28-31)

As a teacher and having spent thousands of hours visiting the subject, I am convinced that this is a direct reference to an amalgamation of faiths that will come together under the auspices of the Church of Rome. It is clear from scripture that the False prophet (the Pontiff) will point to the Antichrist and claim him to be the worlds' savior and demand that all must worship him and his image.[1323] It well may be that the group which we are being warned about in Matthew 24:4–5 who will be pointing people to the false Christ, will, first and foremost be Roman clergy.

1320 Isaiah 16:1-4
1321 Matthew 24:15
1322 Matthew Henry Commentary, One Volume Edition, Zondervan Publishing House, p. 1326
1323 Revelation 13:15

> Note: As its name declares, the Church of Rome is now calling itself the Universal Church, which it has always aspired to be since its formation. The observant will see the collaboration forming between the Church of Rome and the New World Order. Students of theology have long referred to this end time empire as the Revised Roman Empire. The Roman Empire never completely dissolved even after it fell to Germanic invaders in 476 AD. After the fall of Rome and the dissolution of its political government and its military it continued to live on, morphing into and eventually becoming a religious government. Today, the words "religious government" are most appropriate as it has all the structure and infrastructure of a political government. The Prophet Daniel was shown a dreadful beast which was a representation of both the Ancient Roman Empire, and the Revised Roman Empire taking center stage in the last days.[1324]

The Deception

The warning about following false Christs (Messiahs) or this pseudo-Christianity is focused on the Jewish people at that time, as many Jews will be desperately looking for their Messiah to rescue them. Biblical Christians (Believers) have already found Him, so they are obviously not included in this warning. Students of the Bible, both Jew and Gentile who have read Zechariah or Revelation know that the Messiah will make His glorious return from the sky and defeat Israel's enemies at the battle of Armageddon.[1325] Consequently, it will be those who have not accepted Him at His first coming (the unsaved Jews) who will be deceived and drawn away; even the "very elect."[1326]

> Note: Isaiah made references to the Jews as His "elect" and even spoke of their disbelief as to who it is that is their Savior.

> "For Jacob my servant's sake, and Israel mine elect, I have even called thee by thy name: I have surnamed thee, though thou hast not known me." Verily thou art a God that hidest thyself, O God of Israel, the Saviour (Yahusha)." (Isaiah 45:4, 15)

During "The Time of Jacob's Trouble" there will be the opportunity for both Jews and Gentiles who receive the Good News to become "saved."[1327] These Messianic Jews (Jewish Christians) are among the remnant of Israel.[1328] Some will be translated in a second raptured during the first half of the tribulation,[1329] some will be martyred,[1330] while others will survive until His Coming at the end of the battle of Armageddon.[1331]

1324 Daniel 7:7
1325 Zechariah 14:4; Revelation 19:11-14
1326 Matthew 24:5, 24
1327 Joel 2:32
1328 Isaiah 11:10-11; Jeremiah 23:3; Joel 2:32; Amos 9:8-12
1329 Revelation 7:13-14
1330 Revelation 6:9
1331 1 Corinthians 15:23

> Note: The colloquial English word commonly used, though not found in the English Bible for "caught up,"[1332] is raptured. The word rapture was derived from the Latin translation where "caught up" is *rapturo*. The Koine Greek used the verb form ἁρπαγησόμεθα (*harpagēsometha*), which also means caught up or taken away. Both words imply a sudden event. Some translators supplied the word "suddenly" to make the idea clear. This corresponds with 1 Corinthians 15:52 which refers to "in the blink (twinkling) of an eye." The dictionary form of this Greek verb is *harpazō* (ἁρπάζω). This Greek verb for "caught up" is also used in Acts 8:39, 2 Corinthians 12:2-4, and Revelation 12:5.
>
> Note: In the Old Testament the Jewish people are referred to as GOD's "elect." During the present age (the New Testament dispensation) those who comprise the true Church (Jew and Gentile) and become "born again"[1333] are now GOD's elect.[1334] After the Church has been translated and during the Tribulation, all those (Jew and Gentile) who accept Yahusha-Jesus will also join the company of the "elect."
>
> Note: The tribulation (Hebrew, *tsar*) awaiting Israel in the last days is the theme of numerous prophecies. Moses was the first to present the prophecy thirty-five hundred years ago.

"When thou art in tribulation and all these things are come unto thee even in the latter days if thou turn to the Lord thou GOD and shall be obedient unto His voice; (For the Lord thy GOD is a merciful GOD;) HE will not forsake thee..." (Deuteronomy 4:30)

Moses' words will again be echoed by one hundred and forty-four thousand Messianic Jewish men and women[1335] who will become "believers" and attempt to awaken the Jewish people during those "latter days."

> Note: It is often assumed that the one hundred and forty-four thousand are virgin men which is incorrect. The one hundred and forty-four thousand in Revelation 7:4 are comprised of both men and women. If the statement were to be taken literally, it would prove they were all men, but if we were to take the second half of the statement literally, "that they were all virgins," it would mean that they are all women. The inference is one of spiritual purity. The one hundred and forty-four thousand are both men and women who have not polluted themselves in the religious system—the great whore.[1336]

1332 1 Thessalonians 4:17
1333 John 3:1-18
1334 Romans 8:28-33
1335 Revelation 7:4
1336 Revelation 17:1

"And ye shall hear of wars and rumours of wars: see that ye be not troubled: for all these things must come to pass, but the end is not yet. For nation shall rise against nation, and kingdom against kingdom: and there shall be famines, and pestilences, and earthquakes, in diverse places." (Matthew 24:6-7)

There are some who teach that this verse is describing the present age in which we now live. They point to wars, famine, and natural disasters and claim that earthquakes, hurricanes, and weather phenomena have been happening with greater and greater frequency. They maintain that "wars and the rumours of wars" are taking place throughout the world and that this too is proof we are in the "last days." They dismiss the fact that such occurrences and events have been happening in every age. "For we know the whole creation groaneth and travail in pain until now."[1337] But most significant is that this verse tells us that these catastrophic events are not signs of the end times!

The wars of which scripture does speak of and that will take place during that time (the end time) are presented in Joel chapter two. There we read that the, "day (return) of the Lord...is nigh at hand."[1338] These wars are outlined in Ezekiel 38 and 39,[1339] Daniel 11,[1340] and in Revelation 12.[1341] Finally, we are told of the ultimate battle to end all earthly wars in Revelation 19:19–21.

While the Jewish people will be in their own land[1342] as they are now, and while the land will be called Zion (Israel)[1343] which it is, there are still prophetic events which have not occurred. In order for the present time in which we now live to be included in the "latter days," the Temple must be built, and the sacrificial system reinstated.[1344]

During the Great Tribulation many Jewish people will still be in denial of who their savior is, but they will realize that without divine intervention their defeat is certain. Their enemies will mockingly exclaim, "Where is thy God?"[1345] The axis armies lead by the Antichrist will invade Israel and barrage the tiny nation with modern firepower. The question arises, "who can abide (survive) it?"[1346] Our Lord Jesus referred to this when He said, "And except those days be shortened, there shall be no flesh saved."[1347] It will then be in their greatest moment of despair that the Jewish people will cry out to Yahovah for their promised Messiah.[1348] Then, as all appears lost, their Savior, Yahusha Ha'Mashiach, the Lord Jesus Christ will suddenly come to their rescue and obliterate their enemies.[1349]

1337 Romans 8:22
1338 Joel 2:1
1339 Ezekiel 38:9, 16
1340 Daniel 11:40-44
1341 Revelation 12:4
1342 Revelation 2:23
1343 Revelation 2:27
1344 Daniel 9:27
1345 Joel 2:17
1346 Joel 2:11
1347 Matthew 24:22
1348 Joel 2:16
1349 Joel 2:17, 27; Revelation 16:16; Psalm 18:3

In summation: The final wars spoken of in Ezekiel, Daniel, Joel, Matthew,[1350] and the Revelation are not one battle but several. They will involve the nations of at least the three continents of Europe, Asia, and Africa as the scriptures speaks of armies from the North,[1351] the South[1352] (Africa), and the Far East.[1353] The final battle will be led by the Arab confederacy and take place in northern Israel, in the Jezreel Valley, under the shadow of Mount Megiddo.[1354] It should be evident that any wars currently taking place at the time of this writing (2018) have no correlation with this prophecy. Subsequently, we are not in the latter days or end times. These expressions refer to the final years just prior to Christ's return and the beginning of His millennial reign.[1355]

As we continue in our pursuit to attain a proper interpretation of the Olivet Discourse let us remember that at the time in which Jesus spoke the Discourse, the Church Age was an unknown. Even His disciples were not aware of GOD's plan for the Gentiles or that these non-Jews would become part of the Jewish Assembly (a.k.a. the Church). The closest hint given in the Hebrew Holy Scriptures which alludes to the development of the Church was a reference made by Isaiah.

> "I am sought of them that asked not for me; I am found of them that sought me not: I said, Behold me, behold me, unto a nation (Gentiles) that was not called by my name." (Isaiah 65:1)

(The above passage is also quoted in Romans 10:20–21 and referenced in Matthew 21:33; 22:9–10.) Had Jesus been describing the present age (the Church Age) instead of "The Time of Jacobs's Trouble," it would have certainly been an anachronism.

> Note: The definition of an anachronism is an error in chronology in which a person or event is assigned a date or period other than the correct one.

His Return

End time events had been a major theme presented by both Major and Minor Prophets in the Hebrew Scriptures. These prophecies concerned the Jewish people, Israel and the last days which culminate with the Coming of the Jewish Messiah and the establishment of His kingdom.

As Jesus had just told His disciples of His pending death,[1356] and knowing that their scriptures spoke of another coming, they wanted to know when or by what signs they could know of His imminent return. So it was that the focus of the Discourse is on the Lord's next "Coming" (Second Advent).[1357]

1350 Matthew 24:16-22
1351 Joel 2:20; Ezekiel 38, 39
1352 Daniel 11:40
1353 Revelation 16:12
1354 Revelation 16:16
1355 Joel 2:28-32; Daniel 8:19; John 6:39-40, 44, 54; 12:48
1356 John 14:1-3
1357 Matthew 23:39

Our Lord has been faithful to graciously forewarn His own as to what may be expected to overtake those who fail to heed His admonishments. Speaking of what was to happen to Sodom and the cities of the plain, He said in Genesis 18:12, "Shall I hide from Abraham the things which I do?" And in John 15:15; "...for all these things I have heard from My Father, I have made known to you." So, it was characteristic of GOD to share with His own what the future held. In this presentation He would give them signs as to how they might recognize the season of His return, and to do it in such a way as to not set a specific date.[1358]

> Note: Just as a pregnant woman knows when the time of delivery is approaching, she is still not certain of the day or the hour. So it is that those who have studied and believed the Scriptures will know the season, but not the day or the hour. Sudden destruction (the events described in the discourse and in the book of the Revelation) will overtake those who are not seeking or expecting Him and they will be trapped in the judgment (the Great Tribulation) which shall come upon the world.[1359]

It is important that we should see the remarkable similarities beginning with Matthew 24:6–7 and the opening of the seals in Revelation 6. Both introduce the tribulation with war (Matthew 24:6–7; Revelation 6:3–4), then famine (Matthew 24:7; Revelation 5:6), then pestilence and death (Matthew 24:7–9; Revelation 6:7–8), then martyrdom (Matthew 24:9–10, 16–22; Revelation 6:9–11).

Books in both testaments state the sun and moon shall be darkened, and the stars will appear to fall from the heavens (Matthew 24:29; Revelation 6:15–17), and both books point out that this will end in a time of judgement (Matthew 25:31–32; Revelation 6:15–17). These plagues and persecutions are presented in the book of the Revelation as the four horsemen of the Apocalypse (the White horse—the debut of the world leader (the Antichrist); the Red horse—War; the Black horse—Famine; the Pale horse—Death.

The Book of Revelation with all its imagery is thought by some to have so much symbolism that it must be speaking figuratively. This is not the case. The general rule of expository study is that prophesy, like other scripture, should first be approached as being literal. A second rule is that if a word or phrase appears abstract then one should look back to the Old Testament to see if it appears there and to what it applies. Most of the seemingly abstract images or Hebraic phrases used in the New Testament were first presented in the Old Testament. Therefore, they can best be understood if one refers to the Old Testament.

Because the Holy Scriptures were written so that men might understand—from bygone times to the present and on into the future, the Lord in His wisdom, spoke in such a way that the meaning would not be lost even as it was translated from Hebrew to Aramaic, to Greek, to English, etcetera. The Hebrew language is built on word pictures. Word pictures can describe things such as primal weapons (sword, bow, shield, weapons) without losing their Hebrew

---
1358 Matthew 24:36, 39, 42-51; 25:13; Mark 13:32
1359 Matthew 24:50

equivalent. A sword is a weapon carried by the individual solider. A bow is used to launch missiles, a shield is defensive armor, and weapons speak of diverse pieces of offensive military equipment. So it is that words and images in the book of the Revelation must be looked at through the prism of the Hebrew Holy Scriptures.

> "All these are the beginning of sorrows." (Matthew 24:8)

As the Discourse is presented in chronological order, we recognize that this verse is in the beginning of the first half of the seven-year Tribulation. Verse six had spoken of war, famine, pestilence and earthquakes. Here it is given a name, "the beginning of sorrows." The word "sorrows" is a Jewish idiom and literally translated "birth pangs."[1360] This expression comes from the Hebrew Scriptures where they refer to the horror and anguish which Israel will experience during this interval.[1361] If this portion of scripture were speaking of the Church Age then we are faced with an anomaly, as "birth pangs"—with wars, famines, and earthquakes would have begun and include all such events from the time the prophecy was given. This would then not qualify as a prophetic sign or indicator of the hour of His return.

The Talmud, Midrash, and the Gemara (Jewish commentaries of the first ten centuries) frequently speak of the "birth pangs" in relationship to the coming of the Messiah. The expression is found in Jewish Orthodox doctrine today. Like birthing, it will be a period of pain and suffering which precedes deliverance. After deliverance comes the joy of having birthed a child. Likewise, Israel will have its deliverance at the end of the Tribulation and at the Lords coming receive its promised Spiritual birth.[1362] Jeremiah uses still another Hebrew idiom, "travail" (Hebrew, *yalad*) to describe this painful ordeal which men will go through before their deliverance.[1363]

> "Ask ye now, and see whether a man doth travail with child? wherefore do I see every man with his hands on his loins, as a woman in travail, and all faces are turned into paleness? Alas! for that day is great (terrible), so that none is like it: it is even the time of Jacob's trouble; but he shall be saved out of it." (Jeremiah 30:6-7)

A reference to this birthing is seen in Revelation 12 where it speaks of the Sun-clad woman as national Israel, alluded to in Genesis 37:9–11. Here in Revelation 12, we see her with child, travailing in pain as she gives birth to her firstborn sons. Isaiah used an even more foreboding word—travailed, (Hebrew, *chuwl*), which means to writher in pain.[1364]

This Sun-clad woman is pictured in Revelation as having a crown upon her head having twelve stars. The stars refer to the twelve sons of Jacob; the twelve tribes.[1365] These tribes are

---

1360 Isaiah 21:3; Jeremiah 50:43
1361 Deuteronomy 4:30
1362 Ezekiel 36:16; 37:28
1363 Jeremiah 30:6; Revelation 16:9-11
1364 *Strong's Exhaustive Concordance*, Heb., #2342
1365 Revelation 7:4

also mentioned as the one hundred and forty-four thousand saved and sealed of Israel. It refers to Israel's first spiritual children (messianic believers) who have realized and received Yahusha-Jesus during that time.[1366]

> "Shall a nation be born at once? For as soon as Zion travailed, she brought forth her children." (Isaiah 66:8)

The word "travail" appears in the New Testament with a reference to the same period, "When they shall say, Peace and safety; then sudden destruction cometh upon them, as travail upon a woman with child; and they shall not escape."[1367]

> "Then shall they deliver you up to be afflicted, and shall kill you: and ye shall be hated of all nations for my name's sake." (Matthew 24:9)

Focusing on specific words validates who it is that the Scripture is referring to. For example, Matthew 24:9 reads, "Then shall they deliver you up to be afflicted, and shall kill you: and ye shall be hated of all nations for my name's sake."

In this passage, notice two words: "hated" and "nations." Though the Church has been persecuted, it has been Israel who has, as a nation, been hated by almost every nation on the planet; even from those who have had no direct contact with her. This hatred will intensify and crescendo during the Tribulation. More importantly it needs to be understood that the Church is not or ever has been a nation. Israel is a nation and became a nation under King David. Israel has once again become a nation in modern times.

In this same verse we read, "then shall they deliver you up to be afflicted, and shall kill you…" In keeping with the context of the verse (which refers to Israel), "you" then must refer to the Jews, not the Church.

In the final analysis, the Church is not mentioned as being on earth or referred to anywhere in this discourse, as most assuredly it would have been if it were present. The righteous Church will have been gathered up to heaven beforehand, while the wicked and the non-believer will experience the wrath of GOD during this time.[1368]

Insofar as the Church is concerned, its absence during the Tribulation is explained when Paul said, "For GOD hath not appointed us to wrath but to obtain salvation by our Lord Jesus Christ…Wherefore comfort yourselves together…"[1369]

One could hardly be expected to be "comforted" if they thought they might have to suffer the wrath of GOD in a Great Tribulation! There is no "refining fire"[1370] for HIS Church. Our past

---

1366 Revelation 14:4
1367 1 Thessalonians 5:3
1368 1 Thessalonians 4:16, 17; 2 Thessalonians 2:7-8; 1 Corinthians 15:51-52; Psalm 11:3-7
1369 1 Thessalonians 5:9, 11
1370 Malachi 3:2-3

sins which would otherwise have condemned us have been expunged the moment we accepted Christ.[1371] We have been justified, regenerated, and begun a walk of sanctification. Now we attempt to live a life holy and acceptable unto GOD, which is our reasonable service.[1372] All this is gifted to the believer because of what was achieved for us at the Cross at Calvary.

If one thinks logically about it, there is absolutely no reason why our Lord would take His righteous children through such an ordeal as the Tribulation. Scripture teaches that the purpose of it is to compel the Jewish people to return to YAHUAH (the father) and to accept Yahusha (the son) in order "to finish the (their) transgression and to make reconciliation for (their) iniquity…"[1373] This will only be accomplished at the conclusion of the Great Tribulation when they recognize their Messiah.[1374]

"I, even I, am the Lord; and beside me there is no Saviour." (Isaiah 43:11)

"Thus saith the Lord the King of Israel, and his redeemer the Lord of hosts; I am the first, and I am the last; and beside me there is no God." (Isaiah 44:6)

I want to point out that the Church is not seen or even mentioned in the Book of Revelation as being on earth after chapter three. Instead the Church reappears when it is seen returning with Yahusha-Jesus as He descends from the sky in Revelation 19:14.

There is seen in heaven "the numberless multitude."[1375] These are Tribulation saints, for they have "come out" of the great tribulation[1376] and join the "redeemed" (the Church) which is already in heaven even before the first seal is opened.[1377] The Tribulation saints in Revelation 7:14; many of which are martyred[1378] complete the "first resurrection" of believers depicted in 20:4–6. These saints are in heaven well before the final judgments (the last trumpet and vials) when the judgment and wrath of GOD reaches a climax.

The sealing and preserving of the tribulation saints on the earth at that time is in type comparable with GOD sealing and preserving Noah and his family. The Lord's closing the great door of the Ark is in type: the Lord removing HIS own before HE unleashed judgment on the earth.[1379]

After the Apostle John gives GOD's message to the churches of Asia Minor in Revelation chapters 2 and 3, the Church is no longer the subject of the book. Those seven churches were not only actual churches which existed during John's time but more importantly they are a

---

1371 Romans 8:1
1372 Romans 12:1
1373 Daniel 9:24
1374 Zechariah 12:10; 13:1
1375 Revelation 7:9-14
1376 Revelation 7:14
1377 Revelation 5:9-11
1378 Revelation 6:11
1379 Genesis 7:16; Matthew 24:39

representation of the nature and character of the different assemblies over the course of the Church Age. So it is that the Church age may be seen as having ended in chapter three, "I also will keep thee (the true Church) from the hour of temptation, which shall come upon all the world, that try them that dwell upon the earth."[1380]

It is afterward in Revelation chapter 4 that the prophecy pertaining to the Tribulation begins; for it is in the Greek language where the distinction is clearly made between the two dispensations.

As chapter four begins the prophecy, we read of a voice from heaven, "I will shew thee things which must be hereafter (after)" (Greek, *ha dei genesthai meta tauta*). It is understood as, "that which will be after these things." This is referring to the things which will follow the Church Age. It is "After this" (Greek, *meta tauta*)[1381] that the actual revelation begins. So what we have is a division between the things which "are" (were present in John's time), Revelation chapters 2 and 3, and the things which "must be hereafter," begin in Revelation 4:1.

To summarize: Some have impulsively and without evidence assumed that these last seven years are part of the Church Age when in reality they are a separate dispensation which will follow the Church Age. The seven years is a brief dispensation when the Lord will once again turn HIS full attention to Israel and the Jewish people.[1382] The prophet Jeremiah (30:3–11) spoke accordingly:

> 3. "For, lo, the days come, saith the Lord, that I will bring again the captivity of my people Israel and Judah, saith the Lord: and I will cause them to return to the land that I gave to their fathers, and they shall possess it.
>
> 4. And these are the words that the Lord spake concerning Israel and concerning Judah.
>
> 5. For thus saith the Lord; We have heard a voice of trembling, of fear, and not of peace.
>
> 6. Ask ye now, and see whether a man doth travail with child? wherefore do I see every man with his hands on his loins, as a woman in travail, and all faces are turned into paleness?
>
> 7. Alas! for that day is great, so that none is like it: it is even the time of Jacob's trouble, but he shall be saved out of it.
>
> 8. For it shall come to pass in that day, saith the Lord of hosts, that I will break his yoke from off thy (Jewish people's) neck, and will burst thy bonds, and strangers shall no more serve themselves of him:
>
> 9. But they shall serve the Lord their God, and David their king, whom I will raise up unto them.

1380 Revelation 3:10
1381 Revelation 4:1
1382 Daniel 12:1

10. Therefore fear thou not, O my servant Jacob, saith the Lord; neither be dismayed, O Israel: for, lo, I will save thee from afar, and thy seed from the land of their captivity; and Jacob shall return, and shall be in rest, and be quiet, and none shall make him afraid.

11. For I am with thee, saith the Lord, to save thee: though I make a full end of all nations whither I have scattered thee, yet I will not make a full end of thee: but I will correct thee in measure, and will not leave thee altogether unpunished."

Misapplication and Dislocation of Scripture

The Reverend Clarence Larkin (1850–1924) was a Baptist pastor, author, and draftsman, best known for his copious dispensational diagrams and charts that provide a visual reference for interpreting complex Biblical prophecies. In his work, *Dispensational Truth* and *Rightly Dividing the Word*, he made mention that there are two things which must be avoided in the handling of GOD's Word: misinterpretation, and misapplication, or what I like to call, "dislocation."

Misinterpretation is easily understood. One would think it could be easily avoided if one would simply compare Scripture with Scripture to see if it supports a premise or opposes it.

For example: Psalm 122:6 says, "Pray for the Peace of Jerusalem..." however the vast number of those who recite this part of the verse never complete it, for it continues, "...they that love thee (Israel) shall prosper." The word they choose to emphasize is the word "Peace" (Hebrew, *shalom*) which has numerous meanings; the primary of which is to convey a state of wellbeing, happiness, health, enjoying prosperity, and rest.[1383] However, the actual meaning of this verse is clarified by the second half of the verse, "they that love thee (Israel) shall prosper..." The completion of the verse supports the meaning of verse. When the verse is read in its entirety, the psalm is in essence saying, those who love and pray good things for GOD's people (the Jews and Israel) will prosper and receive GOD's blessings.

The word *shalom* in Hebrew does not mean the opposite of war, as it generally does in the English vernacular. The Hebrew word for peace from war is *shalam*.[1384] If Bible-believing Christians are praying for peace from war for Jerusalem, then their prayers are in conflict with Scripture, for Scripture tells us that horrendous war is coming, even Armageddon.[1385] Subsequently, by believing and conveying to others that we should be praying for peace from war, we are giving false hope to the naive and at the same time abetting the enemy who is setting up the Jewish people for deception and annihilation. So if a Scripture appears to conflicts with what other Scriptures teach, we undoubtedly have a misinterpretation or misapplication.

Dislocation could be described as man's propensity to take and relocate an event from its proper place or chronological order and assign it to where it does not belong. The result is a gross disfigurement of Scripture; hence a dislocation. Often an individual sees a word or phrase

---

[1383] *Strong's Exhaustive Concordance*, Heb., #7965
[1384] *Strong's Exhaustive Concordance*, Heb., #7999
[1385] 1 Thessalonians 5:3

which has a similarity to another prophecy. Then, without employing scholarly discipline, they coerce the Scripture to support their position. One example of this can be found in Matthew 24, where some make the mistake of believing that the separating of individuals spoken of in the passage refers to the rapture of the Church, when it clearly speaks of His Second "Coming"![1386]

It must be remembered that the "Church" did not come into existence until after Jesus' death. HIS disciples had no idea until they received the "Great Commission"[1387] just before His ascension that it would be part of GOD's divine plan to reach out to the Gentiles and create a people for Himself. The Lord's earthly ministry was to and for the Jewish people.

In the Olivet Discourse, Jesus begins by addressing three questions asked by His Jewish disciples about Messianic promises presented in the Hebrew Scriptures: "When shall these things be? What shall be the sign of thy coming……and of the end of the world?"[1388]

In the translation (rapture) of the Church, Believers will meet their Lord "in the air."[1389] He is not physically "Coming" to earth again until at the conclusion of the battle of Armageddon when He will set down on the Mount of Olives.[1390] By interpolating the Church into what is a Judgment scene,[1391] they perceive the rapture as taking place either in the middle (Mid-Tribulation) or at the end (Post-Tribulation) of this period.

One should also note that verse 24:41 begins with the word "Then." The same subject (The Judgment of Nations) is revisited in Matthew 25:31–46. Furthermore, it should be understood that this separating of individuals is that same separating which Joel spoke of, which will take place after the Messiah's return.[1392] There it is said that the heathen will be marshalled to the Valley of Jehoshaphat (Jehovah Judges) where HE will judge them. The "Catching up" was, at the time Jesus spoke, still a "mystery" which wasn't mentioned until nearly two decades later by Paul in 1 Thessalonians 4:16–17 and 1 Corinthians 15:51–52.

A summary of key points: This passage is about the Messiah's Second Coming, not the Rapture.

> Point 1. Mathew 24:39 refers to the "Coming of the Son" not a catching up of the Church. The Coming of the Son has a direct correlation with Revelation 19:11-14, where the Lord descends with His army from the sky and puts an end to the battle of Armageddon.
>
> Point 2. As previously noted, the first word and verb which begins verse 40 is "Then." It is used to give the chronological order to the events which will come after His second coming, presented in verse 39. It compares the unbelieving who were taken in the flood of Noah's day and destroyed, to those who will be destroyed at His second coming.

1386 Matthew 24:3, 27, 39, 42, 44
1387 Mark 16:14-18
1388 Matthew 24:3
1389 1 Thessalonians 4:17
1390 Zechariah 14:4
1391 Matthew 24:40-41
1392 Joel 3:11-13

> Point 3. The word "taken" used in the phrases "the one shall be taken" (verses 40, 41) is Greek, *paralambano*.[1393] It is one of twenty-two words for the word "taken" which might have otherwise been used. Vines Complete Expository Dictionary also defines the Greek word for "take:" *paralambano*. It is defined as "the removal of persons from earth in judgment when the Son of man is revealed."[1394]
>
> Point 4. Had the passage been a reference to the rapture, the word Greek *harpazo*, "to snatch or catch away" as used in 1 Thessalonians 4:17 would have been used in Matthew as well; which it is not. The Church cannot be introduced here without violating the entire context of the scripture.
>
> Point 5. The Bible was written to three classes of people; Jews, Gentiles, and the Church and although it was written for learning and instruction to all, it was not addressed to all. Its gospels were not written about the Church. Four-fifths of the Bible—including most of the New Testament—was written to and about the Jewish people. Only one-fifth is given to the origin, doctrine, history, and destiny of the Church. The three Synoptic gospels (Matthew, Mark, and Luke) were written to the Jewish people.
>
> Point 6. The observant Bible student should have no difficulty seeing that there are a multitude of scriptures (parallel scriptures) in chapters 4 through 19 in the book of the Revelation which correspond with those in the Olivet Discourse.

One of the most interesting points we have been given in both Matthew and in the Revelation is the exact number of days that remain from an important benchmark event. This event will tell those who are alive at that time—precisely when the Lord will come. In Matthew it is the desolation of abomination (also mentioned in Daniel) as being the mid-point of the last seven years. In Revelation 12, we are given the middle of the seven years, or the middle of what would be 2,520 days. This means that the number of days which remain from the midpoint to the Messiah's return is 1,260 days! At the present time, no one knows the hour of His Coming and speculation is at best speculation. However, this will not be the case once the abomination of desolation is set up in the Temple. Those who witness this event may begin counting forward from that moment.

> "And the woman (national Israel) fled into the wilderness, where she hath a place prepared of God, that they should feed her there a thousand two hundred and threescore days (1,260 days or 3 ½ years)." (Revelation 12:5-6)

[1393] *Strong's Exhaustive Concordance*, Gk., #3880
[1394] Vine's Complete Expository Dictionary of Old and New Testament, Thomas Nelson, 1996, p. 616

Matthew 24:16 places the abomination of desolation at the same time when those that understand the prophecy are told to flee into the mountains for the next three-and-one-half years and take refuge there during what is referred to as the Great Tribulation.[1395]

If one is familiar with the entire body of Scripture (both Testaments) one can verify that the prophecy in Matthew and Revelation, and those of the prophecies given by Jeremiah, Amos, Zephaniah, Joel, and Daniel all pertain to the same dispensation. All refer to the Jewish people and Israel in the last days.

From this point forward we will do a verse by verse—line by line analysis.

> "And then shall many be offended, and shall betray one another, and shall hate one another." (Matthew 24:10)

In Matthew 24:10 we read about being offended, betrayed and hatred. However, if we look at the parallel scripture in Mark 13:12, we actually have a more complete explanation. There we read, "Now the brother shall betray the brother to death, and the father the son; and children shall rise up against their parents, and shall cause them to be put to death." This predicts that households will be divided between those who hold fast to their belief in Christ and those who pledge their allegiance to the False Prophet and the Antichrist. Because worshiping the Antichrist will be mandatory—under penalty of death, it will cause some to betray their own family members to what will be tantamount to a new breed of Gestapo.

> Note: As in the past when Rome and the Church of Rome sought out Jews and Christians who refused to recognize, pledge loyalty, or bow before the Pontiff, they were exposed by informers who were loyal to the Church of Rome. The "confessional" where Roman Catholics confess their sins and are queried by a priest was first employed in order to obtain the names of dissenters of the Church of Rome. Once these names were divulged the protestors were labeled heretics, abducted from their beds and brought before the inquisitors for sentencing. It is entirely possible that those loyal to the Universal Church will obey their Pontiff and again divulge the names of dissenters; even members of their own family.[1396]

> "And many false prophets shall rise, and shall deceive many." (Matthew 24:11)

A false prophet is one who professes to speak on behalf of GOD but instead speaks lies. This brief verse has great implications by the fact that it is reinforced in Matthew 24:24. The implications are huge for it indicates that there shall arise religious leaders who will persuade the masses to receive, revere and worship a counterfeit Messiah.

Revelation 13:11–15 expounds on the central figure (the False Prophet) but the above verse speaks of a plurality (prophets) which suggest that it will be his cadre of priests that will

---

[1395] Joel 2:11; Amos 5:18; Zephaniah 1:14; Daniel 12:1
[1396] Revelation 13:15

propagate the lie. These pseudo-Christians and the clergy will attempt to proselytize the Jewish people. Some will be drawn in while others will refuse. We see today how enamored Catholics are with their pope and prelates. They unquestionably accept what they are told as if it were biblical and have entrusted their eternal destiny to charlatans.

> "And because iniquity shall abound, the love of many shall wax cold." (Matthew 24:12)

The word "iniquity" (Greek, *anomia*) means to violate the law. The Word of GOD (the Bible) will become even more irrelevant to the unsaved than it is today.[1397] Men will become even more self-indulgent. The Ten Commandments and the law will have no bearing on the way people will live their lives. When the people no longer believe the Holy Scriptures and the fear of GOD no longer exists, the love for GOD diminishes, grows cold, and dies.[1398]

> "But he that shall endure unto the end, the same shall be saved." (Matthew 24:13)

In this verse the reference to being "saved" does not refer to being spiritually saved, as no one is saved by their endurance and fortitude. Rather it is speaking to those tribulation saints who were not raptured in the first half of the Tribulation but accept the Lord during the second half of the Tribulation—the Great Tribulation. It refers to those who manage to survive the horrific persecution and the catastrophic events until the Lord appears. They will have endured to the end and will enter into the Millennial Kingdom without experiencing death.[1399]

> "And this gospel of the kingdom shall be preached in all the world for a witness unto all nations; and then shall the end come." (Matthew 24:14)

Matthew 24:14 is another commonly misconstrued verse which has caused a good deal of confusion. The "gospel of the Kingdom" will be one of two gospels which will be presented during the Tribulation.

In Revelation 7:4 we read that one hundred forty-four thousand Jews become believers in Christ and are sealed. They will undoubtedly become His anointed harbingers and tell the Jewish people, and whoever else will listen to them, of the nearness of His Coming. The initial message, or the first gospel will be the, "gospel of the Kingdom." It was the same gospel which John the Baptist proclaimed when he said, "Repent for the kingdom of heaven is at hand."[1400] The words the "Kingdom of heaven is at hand" was another way of saying the Messiah was at hand or present on earth at that time. It was the gospel of the Kingdom which announced Yahusha-Jesus

---

1397 2 Timothy 3:1-9
1398 2 Timothy 4:3-4
1399 Zechariah 13:9
1400 Matthew 3:1

and would prepare the people for what would be the second gospel—the good news—the offer of salvation to the Jewish people. The gospel of the Kingdom will be heralded by those who recognize from scripture the nearness of His return. We are told in Matthew 24:14 that it will be "preached" (Greek, *kerusso*); meaning—to herald.[1401] In Revelation 7:4 we learn who will be these heralders (evangelists). It shall be the one hundred and forty-four thousand Jews who become saved during the first half of the Tribulation.[1402] Then shall the end (the second half) begin and the vials of judgment poured out upon the earth.[1403]

> Note: The Gospel of Mark, (13:10) uses the word "published" instead of the word "preached," as in Matthew 24:14. However the same Greek word *"kerusso,"* meaning to preach or proclaim is used in both gospel narratives. So the word "published" as used in Mark does not actually mean that the Bible needs to be translated into all common languages throughout the world before the Lord returns. The word "published" would be more accurately rendered "preached" in the modern English vernacular. The Word proclaiming Jesus Christ as Yahusha Messiah has already been preached throughout the world many times to many generations. So too will it continue to be preached (*kerusso*) during the Tribulation.

The second gospel is not alluded to in this passage; however, it will nevertheless be offered during the Tribulation as well. It is the gospel of Grace—the Good News,[1404] also called the Gospel of Christ.[1405] The message of this gospel is, "Believe on the Lord Jesus Christ and thou shall be saved…"[1406] It was offered at Christ's first coming and has continued to be offered ever since, and it will continue to be offered during the Tribulation. It explains that "Christ died for our sins according to the scriptures…"[1407] It was, is, and always will be the true Christian mandate—the Great Commission. It is the message of the Cross which makes Christ and what His sacrifice accomplished on that Cross the object of our faith, to the exclusion of all else!

The Apostle Paul said it so well: "But we preach Christ crucified, unto the Jews a stumbling block, and unto the Greeks foolishness; But unto them which are called (Greek *kletos*—invited), both Jews and Greeks, Christ (is) the power of GOD, and the Wisdom of GOD."[1408]

> "When ye therefore shall see the abomination of desolation, spoken of by Daniel the prophet, stand in the holy place, (whoso readeth, let him understand)." (Matthew 24:15)

1401 *Strong's Exhaustive Concordance*, Gk., #2784
1402 Matthew 4:17, 23, 10:7, 25:6
1403 Revelation chapter 16
1404 Revelation 20:24
1405 2 Corinthians 4:3-6
1406 Acts 16:31
1407 1 Corinthians 15:1-3
1408 1 Corinthians 1:23-24

We have already mentioned the "abomination of desolation," (possible a speaking image or *holograma*—hologram) which the Antichrist will place in the sanctuary of the Temple in Jerusalem, thereby desecrating it. According to Daniel it will happen in the "midst" (middle) of the "Seventieth Week" (the final seven years) of the earth age. It is this act where we are given a definitive sign and fixed time which allows us to see in chronologic order of which events precede the desolation/desecration, and which events follow it. Those events which precede Matthew 24:15 take place during the first three and a half years of the Tribulation and the events following the desecration take place during the second three and a half years—the "Great Tribulation" as presented in Matthew 24:21.[1409]

> "then let them which be in Judea flee into the mountains: let him which is on the housetop not come down to take any thing out of his house: neither let him which is in the field return back to take his clothes." (Matthew 24:16-18)

Matthew 24:16–18 is a warning to those Jews who have accepted Christ and take to heart this passage in concert with Revelation 12:6. When these Jews see the "abomination of desolation" placed in the Temple, they are to immediately flee Jerusalem. They must not even hesitate to gather their belongings for Jerusalem will immediately be overtaken by their enemies. Their only hope is to take refuge in the wilderness where GOD will sovereignly protect them.[1410]

> "And woe unto them that are with child, and to them that give suck in those days! But pray ye that your flight be not in the winter, neither on the Sabbath day…" (Matthew 24:19-20)

In Matthew 24:19–20 the remnant of Jewish believers are told to "pray that your flight be not in winter, neither on the Sabbath day." This would be a strange way of speaking to Gentile Christians as the Sabbath is a Jewish word referring to a period from Friday sundown to Saturday sundown when Jews celebrate their day of rest and worship. During Sabbath, private and public transportation is limited, and all markets, including food markets are closed. This would make it difficult, if not impossible for Jews to evacuate the city if they wanted to. Furthermore, traveling on the Sabbath is a violation of the law, particularly to the orthodox. The reference to winter also indicates that travel, and particularly survival in a cold wilderness environment would make this even more of a hardship.[1411] The absence of any warning to the "Church" to flee is yet another indication that the Church will not be present on earth in those days; neither would it be possible for the collective Church to all be in Judea and flee to a rocky fortress such as the Jordanian city of Petra.

The epicenter of the wars described in the book of Revelation will take place geographically in what was the former Roman Empire. This will encompass Europe, North Africa, and the

---

1409 Revelation 13:14-15
1410 Isaiah 16:1-4
1411 Revelation 12:6, 14

Middle East (the entire Revised Roman Empire), not the entire planet; although the effects will be far reaching.

There will be Gentile (nations and individuals) who survived the Great Tribulation and did not align themselves with the Antichrist against Jerusalem. They will somehow avoid taking the "mark,"[1412] and they will not have persecuted Christ's brethren the Jews.[1413] These nations are referred to as the sheep nations. They will advance into the Millennial Kingdom as natural men, living out their lives, marrying and raising families.[1414] They will seek out the Jewish people to learn more about King Yahusha-Jesus and become His followers.[1415] Free choice to accept or reject the Lord will remain in effect even until the end of the Millennial Age.[1416]

There are ministers today who fail to understand that Old Testament scriptures are, speaking to the Jewish people. Prophetic promises in the Old Testament likewise have a direct application to the Jewish. Still, some persist in putting the Church into these prophecies. We see such an example in Joel 2:23 as it applies to the "latter rain" (the endowing of the Holy Spirit). "Be glad then, ye children of Zion, and rejoice in the Lord your God: for he hath given you the former rain moderately, and he will cause to come down for you the rain, the former rain, and the latter rain in the first month." And in Zechariah 10:1, "Ask ye of the Lord rain in the time of the latter rain; so the Lord shall make bright clouds, and give them showers of rain, to every one grass in the field."

The latter rain is for the children of Zion during the latter days. The latter days pertain to the Tribulation and to the millennium.[1417] So the latter rain does not refer to a promised revival for the Church at the end of the Church age. While we earnestly need to be seeking and travailing in prayer for a heaven-sent Awakening, there is no definitive promise in the Scriptures that we will have one before the Church is removed. "He reserveth to us the appointed weeks of the harvest…"[1418] therefore, any national Great Awakening is solely at HIS discretion. Having said this, the Holy Spirit is vigorously moving over the planet, reaching and saving hundreds of thousands by television and satellite ministry[1419] with the only message that saves the message of the Cross! "But God commendeth his love toward us, in that, while we were yet sinners, Christ died for us."[1420]

> "…for then shall be great tribulation, such as was not since the beginning of the world to this time, no, nor ever shall be. And except those days should be shortened, there should no flesh be saved: but for the elect's (Jewish people's) sake those days shall be shortened." (Matthew 24:21-22)

1412 Revelation 14:9-11
1413 Matthew 25:31-46
1414 Matthew 25:34-40
1415 Zechariah 8:23; Isaiah 11:9-10
1416 Zechariah 14:17-19
1417 Ezekiel 36:24-28
1418 Jeremiah 5:24
1419 SonLife Broadcasting Network, www.sonlifetv.com
1420 Romans 5:8

Matthew 24:21–22 clearly indicate that this scripture is speaking about the "Great" Tribulation (the last half of the seven-year tribulation). Here the Lord gives us an inkling of just how horrendous a time it will be. Man will be on the verge of extinction. War, plagues, famine, catastrophic atmospheric and geological events as portrayed in the escalating trumpets and bowls of Revelation spell planetary destruction. The fallout from the modern weapons will pollute and poison the atmosphere to the point that were it not for Yahusha-Jesus' intervention no one would survive.[1421]

> Note: The phrase "those days should be shortened" Matthew 24:22, is a Jewish idiom and one that has precedence in the Old Testament. It relates directly to Israel in the last days.[1422]

The Lord had made it clear to Jeremiah and Daniel why the Great Tribulation was required.

> "For I am with thee, saith the Lord, to save thee: though I make a full end of all nations whither I have scattered thee, yet I will not make a full end of thee: but I will correct thee in measure, and will not leave thee altogether unpunished." (Jeremiah 30:11)

> "Seventy weeks are determined upon thy people (the Jews) and upon thy holy city (Jerusalem), to finish the transgression, and to make an end of sins, and to make reconciliation for iniquity, and to bring in everlasting righteousness, and to seal up the vision and prophecy, and to anoint the most Holy." (Daniel 9:24)

(See Appendix C—Daniel's Vision of Seventy Weeks)

> "Then if any man shall say unto you, Lo, here is Christ, or there; believe it not. For there shall arise false Christs, and false prophets, and shall shew great signs and wonders; insomuch that, if it were possible, they shall deceive the very elect. Behold, I have told you before. Wherefore if they shall say unto you, Behold, he is in the desert; go not forth: behold, he is in the secret chambers; believe it not." (Matthew 24:23-26)

Mathew 24:23–26 speaks of both false Christs (better interpreted as false Christians) and false prophets (better interpreted as false Christian leaders) who will encourage their followers to believe in a false Messiah (the Antichrist). Empowered by Satan, these collaborators "shall show great signs and wonders," thereby deceiving the masses. The wonders they will perform will be of such magnitude as to persuade the biblically untaught that they are GOD's divine representatives. The genuine Messiah will not walk the earth as a man again; either in the desert or anywhere else. He will come from the sky with His army ending the battle of Armageddon and the age of human government.[1423]

1421 Matthew 24:22
1422 Joel 3:15-16; Amos 8:9; Isaiah 13:9-11
1423 Revelation 19:11-21

> Note: It is the false prophet who is most insidious. He is a leader of an existing religious organization[1424] complete with a worldwide government infrastructure. He has world recognition, autonomy, wields authority and has sway over a billion of his devotees who deify him. In blind submission and without having an understanding of GOD's Word they are lambs being led to the slaughter. Early on in the Tribulation the False Prophet will effortlessly persuade his followers to revere the Antichrist as the Christ. He will prescribe allegiance, obedience and worship to the counterfeit[1425] and the patrons will follow like lemmings.

The false prophet we are told in Revelation 13:11, has two horns like a male lamb and while he appears to be the epitome of a gentle lamb, he will in actuality be speaking as (for) a dragon (Satan). His fierceness is only exceeded by his cunning as he projects peace, acceptance and love to all mankind.[1426]

The persecuting power and the deeds of the religious empire, "the great whore"[1427] described in the Book of Revelation has been under the control of a succession of appointed religious emperors alleging to be GOD's earthly representatives. The masquerade has worked amazingly well for seventeen centuries.

History testifies of the Whore's cruel nature, which has been applied to those unwilling to recognize, convert and submit to her authority.[1428] This religious system over which the False Prophet will have control is spoken of in the female gender, for she has fornicated with kings and emperors throughout the world[1429] and claimed herself to be the queen of the King of Kings.[1430] Only one religious enterprise has ever made that claim.

Over time she has grown powerful, enlarging her presence and domain in every country in the world. We are told this mystery woman disguises herself in robes, and ornaments;[1431] that she has ridden on the backs of empires[1432] and who calls herself a queen, while GOD calls her a harlot.[1433] It is Roman Christianity who was conceived in pagan Babel of old and afterward took her seat in Rome. It is Romanism which will have great influence in the formulation of the Revised Roman Empire. It is the Roman Pontiff and his cadre who claims to speak for GOD; who have donned disguises and mesmerized their followers. And it is their leader (the False Prophet himself) who we are told will assume spiritual supremacy in the last days. (See Appendix D—Mystery Babylon)

> "For as the lightning cometh out of the east, and shineth even unto the west; so shall also the coming of the Son of man be." (Matthew 24:27)

1424 Revelation 17:2
1425 Revelation 13:8
1426 Revelation 13:11-14
1427 Revelation 17:1
1428 Revelation 17:6
1429 Revelation 17:4, 18:3
1430 Revelation 18:7
1431 Revelation 17:4
1432 Revelation 17:7
1433 Revelation 18:7

Beginning in Matthew 24:27, the Second Coming of Christ is described in length. He will not be found wandering in some desert, nor will He emerge on the world scene as a Gandhi or a Mandela. He will not be born an infant and grow up to manhood again, nor will he be a statesman, rising to world prominence through the political process. He will come quickly and in an hour which will catch most off guard.[1434] Those who have read the Bible will know that He will make His debut from the sky just as Israel is on the verge of being defeated.[1435]

The Jewish believers are the "the wise virgins,"[1436] who will know the season of His coming by the progression of events (signs) leading up to His arrival.[1437] They will even be able to accurately calculate the day of His coming by the number of days following the desecration of the Temple.[1438]

The Olivet Discourse encompasses two major divisions of time. The first division speaks of the signs leading up to His Coming. The second division speaks to the events that will take place at and after His Coming. Matthew 24:27–29 begins the second of these two divisions and clearly identifies that the scripture is speaking of His Coming itself. We read that the heavens will be shaken and the people will see "the Son of man coming in the clouds of heaven with power and great glory."[1439] He will descend from the sky and from the East with His army. "For as the lightning cometh out of the east, and shineth even unto the west; so shall also the coming of the Son of man be."

This Scripture has as its parallel in Revelation 19:11, 14–15, where we read, "And I saw heaven opened, and behold a white horse; and he that sat upon him was called Faithful and True, and in righteousness he doth judge and make war. And the armies which were in heaven followed him upon white horses, clothed in fine linen, white and clean. And out of his mouth goeth a sharp sword, that with it he should smite the nations: and he shall rule them with a rod of iron: and he treadeth the winepress of the fierceness and wrath of Almighty God."

Isaiah had earlier describe the event in Isaiah 11:4, where we read, "…and He shall smite the earth with the rod of His mouth, and with the breath of His lips shall He slay the wicked."

> "For wheresoever the carcass is, there will the eagles be gathered together." (Matthew 24:28)

The verse implies that when the Messiah comes and vanquishes the enemies of Israel the battlefields in and around Megiddo will be strewn with corpses. This Scripture is supported in Revelation 19:17–18 where we read,

> "And I saw an angel standing in the sun; and he cried with a loud voice, saying to all the fowls that fly in the midst of heaven, Come and gather yourselves together unto the supper

---

[1434] Matthew 24:44
[1435] Revelation 19:11-16
[1436] Matthew 25:1-13
[1437] Luke 21:28
[1438] Matthew 25:15; Revelation 12:6; Daniel 9:27
[1439] Luke 21:27

of the great God; that ye may eat the flesh of kings, and the flesh of captains, and the flesh of mighty men, and the flesh of horses, and of them that sit on them, and the flesh of all men, both free and bond, both small and great. (Revelation 19:17-18)

We read "there will the eagles be gathered together." Eagles (Greek, *aetos*) is better translated vultures, or birds known for eating carrion. These scavengers are depicted feasting on the dead who are destroyed at His coming.[1440] One may see this same judgment scene presented in Ezekiel 39:11–19.

"Immediately after the Tribulation of those days shall the sun be darkened, and the moon shall not give her light." (Matthew 24:29)

Matthew 24:29 informs us that in the aftermath of the Great Tribulation, the atmosphere above the earth will have been dramatically changed as the vials of GOD's wrath will have been poured out upon the earth and its inhabitants.[1441] Both the books of Matthew and Joel refer to the way the heavens (atmosphere) will appear at that time. It will have been (in part) a result of bombings, missile strikes and artillery barrages and very likely nuclear exchanges. Other phenomena of the natural variety (atmospheric, geologic—earthquakes and volcanic eruptions) will cause ash to encircle the globe.

Whether this contamination is a result of the fumes or war, or of so-called nature, we need to remember that it is GOD who will bring these events to bear, as it is HIS wrath which will be poured out upon the earth and its inhabitants.[1442]

We would do well to recognize that virtually all the end time events described in the New Testament were previously foretold by Old Testament prophets. The corresponding scripture of what is presented in Matthew concerning the end times, was given first to Moses (Deuteronomy 4:30) in 1410 BC; to the prophet Joel (2:28–32) about 800 BC; to Ezekiel (chapters 38 and 39) in 536 BC; and to Zechariah (chapter 14) in 487 BC. These are just several of the major and minor prophets that spoke to the last days and of the coming of the Lord.

It is also characteristic of the Lord to add more details and enlarge our understanding as the time of a prophetic event draws closer. Such is the case when here in the Olivet Discourse we recognize the events described in Joel have been expanded upon.

The Book of Daniel, like the Book of Joel, is another example of how the prophetic books of the Hebrew Scriptures dovetail with the prophetic passages in the New Testament. Daniel's messianic revelation in chapter nine, provides chronology to the prophetic.

Consequently, those who teach New Testament prophecies (as Matthew chapters 24, 25 or the Revelation) who are not studied in the Old Testament are fundamentally unqualified to defend some of the positions they put forth.

1440 Revelation 19:21
1441 Revelation 16:1-21
1442 Revelation 16:1

> "But there is a GOD in heaven that reveleath secrets, and maketh known...what shall be in the later days." (Daniel 2:28)

> "...and then shall appear the sign of the Son of man in heaven: and then shall all the tribes of the earth mourn, and they shall see the Son of man coming in the clouds of heaven with power and great glory." (Matthew 24:30)

We read in Matthew 24:30 that upon seeing their Messiah come down through the clouds, sweep over the Jezreel valley, destroys the enemy and set down on the Mount of Olives,[1443] that the Jewish people will have a spiritual awakening.

The "tribes that mourn" are the Jews who have survived the Great Tribulation. The vast majority will immediately recognize Jesus as their long-awaited Messiah when they see His nail scarred hands and feet. They will "mourn" for Him as the lost (having been missed) son (Messiah) of Israel.[1444] They will experience, remorse for having rejected Him and at the same time joy at His appearing.

> Note: Tribes refer to the twelve "lost" tribes of Israel. The term tribe has never been applied to Gentiles or to the Church. Though the Jewish people may have lost their tribal identity following the scattering and the diaspora, our Lord knows exactly who belongs to each and every tribe.[1445]

> "And he shall send his angels with a great sound of a trumpet, and they shall gather together His elect from the four winds, from one end of heaven to the other." (Matthew 24:31)

The restoration of the Jewish people to Palestine is one of the most momentous prophecies of Scripture; given even greater emphasis than their dispersion. The Lord repeatedly said He will bring them back to what is appropriately called their Promised Land. Here, in Matthew 24:31 the Lord is depicted dispatching His angels to the "four winds,"[1446] recovering His elect and planting them in the land He promised Abraham.[1447] This also satisfies the promise given to Moses that the Lord "will return and gather thee from the nations, wither the Lord thy God has scattered thee."[1448]

In this passage the elect (elected) Jews are "the remnant" who have been preserved and are now summoned to their ancient homeland. Their divinely imposed blindness[1449] will end at His appearing. In the course of the Great Tribulation the pride and arrogance which has been a char-

---

1443 Zechariah 14:4
1444 Zechariah 12:10; Revelation 1:7
1445 James 1:1
1446 Zechariah 2:6
1447 Isaiah 27:12, 60:8-9; Jerimiah 3:14, 16:16, 31:8-9; Ezekiel 39:28; Amos 9:15
1448 Deuteronomy 30:3
1449 Isaiah 6:10, 29:10

acteristic of the people[1450] since the time Moses lead them into the wilderness will at last have been tamed by hardship; they will have "pass(ed) under the rod" of correction[1451] for the last time.

> "The sacrifices of God are a broken spirit: a broken and a contrite heart, O God, thou wilt not despise." (Psalm 51:17)

The company of the righteous (as it pertains to the Jewish people) will include five companies of saints:

1. The faithful Old Testament Jews who like Abraham were saved by their faith in GOD their Savior.[1452]

2. The righteous Jews (messianics) of the New Testament who previously died (the dead in Christ).[1453]

3. Those who became saved during the Tribulation and may have been translated to heaven (as the one hundred and forty-four thousand) during the Tribulation.[1454]

4. The tribulation saints who were martyred for their faith in Yahusha-Jesus and would not bow a knee to Baal.[1455]

5. Those tribulation saints who against all odds managed to survive the Tribulation and become spiritually born again before the Lord returned.[1456]

> Note: The whole (Hebrew, *kowl*) house of Israel does not mean that all Jews—from time immemorial, are automatically saved or exonerated from having to accept Christ as their personal Savior. Rather it refers to those who have been restored. Those who, when the scales are removed from their eyes, see themselves as they truly are, and "shall loathe" themselves for "all the evil" they have committed.[1457] GOD will extend HIS mercy and grace to the penitent[1458] and they shall be saved and join Him on His holy mountain.[1459]

1450 Isaiah 65:2; Romans 10:21
1451 Ezekiel 20:34-40
1452 Hebrews 11:8, 13
1453 1 Thessalonians 4:16
1454 Revelation 7:4
1455 1 Kings 19:18
1456 Zechariah 13:8
1457 Ezekiel 20:43-44
1458 Ezekiel 39:25
1459 Revelation 21:10, 24, 22:14

> Note: The trumpet which will sound, mentioned in this[1460] scripture is not the "trump" (trumpet or shofar) mentioned in 1 Thessalonians 4:16 and subsequently has nothing to do with the "catching away" of the Church. That trump which sounds at the catching away of the Church comes before "The Time of Jacob's Trouble." In this passage the trumpet blast will be used as it was in ancient times when it called the nation of Israel to assemble.[1461]

Up to this point, the Discourse has given us an outline of future events based on Old Testament Scriptures and prophecies. From this point forward we are given deeper insight into the prophetic in a series of seven parables—all of which refer to the Jews and Israel. Once again, this is a continuum of the initial questions asked by Jewish disciples to their Jewish Messiah about the signs leading up to His actual second coming (physical return). It does not in any way refer to or include the Church.

> "Now learn a parable of the fig tree; When his branch is yet tender, and putteth forth leaves, ye know that summer is nigh: so likewise ye, when ye shall see all these things, know that it is near, even at the doors." (Matthew 24:32-33)

In speaking to His inquiring disciples about His return, Jesus tells them to learn the parable of the fig tree. The sign of the "fig tree" is generally understood to be a reference to the Jews and Israel and specifically to their nationhood. Other similar terms were used in other scriptures with specific inferences. The word "vine" for example, was used in referring to Israel's spiritual relationship,[1462] and the words "olive tree" were used when referring to Israel's religious practices.[1463]

To better understand the parable, one needs to know that the fig tree is unique from other trees. Often in spring, un-ripened fruit from the previous autumn blossoms and the first fruit appears early in the spring. Later the leaves appear on new branches and bring a second crop of figs in late summer or early fall. In an earlier chapter,[1464] as Jesus was nearing Jerusalem, He saw a fig tree with leaves on it. Having retained its leaves over the winter it should have had fruit. As the story goes, Jesus cursed the fig tree because—like Israel, it had not brought forth fruit and led the Gentile nations to the saving knowledge of their GOD and their Messiah when they were first expected to.

In Luke 13:6 we are given another example about a barren fig tree. The owner of the vineyard (GOD) said to his husbandman (Jesus), this tree has failed to bring forth fruit—cut it down. The husbandman tried for three years (the years of Christ's active ministry), digging about and fertilizing it, with only limited success. In Luke 3:9 we learn the fig tree was hewn down, as it was by

---

1460 Matthew 24:31
1461 Numbers 10:2-3
1462 Jeremiah 6:10; John 15:1-4
1463 Jeremiah 11:16-17; Romans 11:17-27
1464 Matthew 21:19

Titus in 70 AD. The root, however, was never removed and laid dormant beneath the soil. Typical of a root—it will one day send forth shoot which will grow into a tree once more and be fruitful.[1465]

So it is in Matthew 24:32–33 that when the tree, Israel, is bringing forth leaves (showing sign of life) as in the spring, it will soon be given a second opportunity to bring forth its fruit. Subsequently, Israel's national birth (bearing leaves) is a precursor and another indicator (a sign) of the nearness of the Lord's return—"even at the doors."

> "Verily I say unto you, This generation shall not pass, till all these things be fulfilled." (Matthew 24:34)

"This generation shall not pass away, till all these things be fulfilled" needs to be taken just as it is presented. The generation which is alive and sees the signs spoken of in this discourse shall be the same generation that will witness the Messiah coming; for the Tribulation is, from beginning to end, only a mere seven years.

> "Heaven and earth shall pass away, but my words shall not pass away. But of that day and hour knoweth no man, no, not the angels of heaven, but my Father only. (Matthew 24:35-36)

GOD is being emphatic! He is telling us that what is presented in this discourse will most assuredly come to pass. As to when the Tribulation will begin, this will remain GOD's secret.[1466]

However, once the Tribulation has begun, those who know the prophetic scriptures will be able to determine, by the unfolding sequence of events just how near the "Day of the Lord" is.

> "But as the days of Noah were, so shall also the coming of the Son of man be." (Matthew 24:37)

Following the parable of the fig tree, we are given seven more parables: Noah and the flood; the Two workers in the field; the Two women grinding at the mill; the Householder that was unprepared for the thief; the Wise servant who was prepared and the evil servant who was not; the Ten virgins; and the Talents entrusted to the servants.

> "For as in the days that were before the flood they were eating and drinking, marrying and giving in marriage, until the day that Noah entered into the ark, and knew not until the flood came, and took them all away; so shall also the coming of the Son of man be." (Matthew 24:38-39)

Matthew 24:37–39 makes a comparison between the people of Noah's day who were ambivalent to the warnings of HIS servant Noah and to that future generation who will be alive just prior to Christ's return. Just as people today are preoccupied with themselves and with everyday

---
1465 Zechariah 8:13, 23
1466 Matthew 24:44

affairs, so too will that future generation be. And, like those of Noah's day, they too will disregard the message and the messengers who bring the prophetic warnings.

Notice that Matthew 24:39 speaks of the "coming of the Son of man." We see the reference to His second coming repeated four times in just the span of eight verses of scripture.[1467]

To review: There are indeed two comings (one in a meeting in the air, the other a physical presence on the earth). The Rapture is not His coming to earth mentioned in the discourse when He will defeat Israel's enemies, reveal Himself to the Jewish people, judge the nations and set up His Kingdom on earth. In the rapture He comes in the air, meets His Church in the sky and then returns to heaven with them.[1468] Later He and His army of believers return to earth for the battle of Armageddon.[1469] The rapture will precede His second coming by no less than seven years.

In the Scriptures which follow, we understand that certain individuals are to be taken, while others are left behind. Once again, this has absolutely nothing to do with the rapture as is often taught by mid and post tribulation theorists to substantiate their supposition. All of these illustrations—Noah, the two workers in the field, the householder, the two servants, the ten virgins and the talents—all emphasize that when the Lord returns, He will find some aware and prepared and some totally unaware and unprepared. "Taking away and leaving behind" is a metaphor for universal judgment; a blessing (salvation) for some—a curse (damnation) for others.[1470]

Before examining the parables, themselves, allow me to remind the reader that a basic principle of expository hermeneutics is to apply scripture to that, or to those to which it applies. In this case we are referring to the Jewish people at the end of "The Time of Jacob's Trouble." The Church cannot be introduced here nor can one apply this to the present age without destroying the unity of scripture.

As we look at each of the parables, we can see that they all emphasize the separating of the righteous from the unrighteous and the need to be prepared for the Lord's return.

The Great Flood is given as a prime example of the contrast between these two types of people. In Genesis 6:5–11 we read that GOD saw the wickedness, corruption and violence which man had wrought. The people were unaware and unconcerned as to what was about to happen. Universal judgment was enacted. The righteous, Noah and his family, had been deeply invested in GOD; they remained safe within the Ark (in type, Jesus) and were both saved and kept. They survived to begin life anew on a new earth, and in a new dispensation. In type, the Believers will, like Noah and family, also begin life anew when the final purge has been completed.[1471] As we move from verse to verse looking at these parables, it should become evident that we are seeing a continuum of the theme, "as the days of Noah were, so shall also shall the coming of the Son of man be."[1472]

1467 Matthew 24:37, 39, 42, 44
1468 1 Thessalonians 4:17
1469 Revelation 19:14
1470 Matthew 25:34, 41
1471 2 Peter 2:4-5, 3:12
1472 Matthew 24:37

> "Then shall two be in the field; the one shall be taken, and the other left. Two women shall be grinding at the mill; the one shall be taken, and the other left." (Matthew 24:40-41)

In Matthew 24:40–41, we read about "two in the field," and "two women" who are "grinding at the mill;" "one shall be taken and the other left." These verses are sometimes quoted in connection with the rapture of the church, but it is incorrect to do so. The Lord is once again, as HE did with Noah and the flood, describing a judgment scene. We are told in numerous scriptures, as in Matthew 13:30–43, that at the end of the Earth Age HE will have HIS angels harvest souls and separate the wheat from the tares and the sheep from the goats.

> "The field is the world; the good seed are the children of the kingdom; but the tares are the children of the wicked one; The enemy that sowed them is the devil; the harvest is the end of the world; and the reapers are the angels. As therefore the tares are gathered and burned in the fire; so shall it be in the end of this world. The Son of man shall send forth his angels, and they shall gather out of his kingdom all things that offend, and them which do iniquity; And shall cast them into a furnace of fire: there shall be wailing and gnashing of teeth. Then shall the righteous shine forth as the sun in the kingdom of their Father. Who hath ears to hear, let him hear." (Matthew 13:38-43)

> "But know this that if the goodman of the house had known in what watch the thief would come, he would have watched, and would not have suffered his house to be broken up. Therefore be ye also ready: for in such an hour as ye think not the Son of man cometh. Who then is a faithful and wise servant, whom his lord hath made ruler over his household, to give them meat in due season? Blessed is that servant, whom his lord when he cometh shall find so doing. Verily I say unto you, That he shall make him ruler over all his goods. But and if that evil servant shall say in his heart, My lord delayeth his coming; and shall begin to smite his fellow servants, and to eat and drink with the drunken; the lord of that servant shall come in a day when he looketh not for him, and in an hour that he is not aware of, and shall cut him asunder, and appoint him his portion with the hypocrites: there shall be weeping and gnashing of teeth." (Matthew 24:43-51)

In Matthew 24:43–51, we see examples of what can best be described as passive indifference to the Lord's Coming and to the things that have a direct bearing on where one will spend eternity. It is perhaps, more than anything else, our cares, concerns and appetite for the temporal things of this earthly life that will bring us to that place of "weeping and gnashing of teeth."[1473] What a contrast indeed to, "thou shalt love the Lord thy God with all thine heart, and with all thy soul, and with all thy might."[1474]

1473 Matthew 25:30
1474 Deuteronomy 6:5

We see that if the "householder" knew when the thief was coming, he would have been watchful. However, he thought that the Messiah's coming was still well into the future and that he had plenty of time to prepare. The faithful "servant" represents those who, although they don't know the hour of His coming have prepared themselves. The faithful are rewarded while the unfaithful shall have their part in the lake of fire.

> "Then shall the kingdom of heaven be likened unto ten virgins, which took their lamps, and went forth to meet the bridegroom. And five of them were wise, and five were foolish. They that were foolish took their lamps, and took no oil with them: but the wise took oil in their vessels with their lamps. While the bridegroom tarried, they all slumbered and slept. And at midnight there was a cry made, Behold, the bridegroom cometh; go ye out to meet him. Then all those virgins arose, and trimmed their lamps. And the foolish said unto the wise, Give us of your oil; for our lamps are gone out. But the wise answered, saying, Not so; lest there be not enough for us and you: but go ye rather to them that sell, and buy for yourselves. And while they went to buy, the bridegroom came; and they that were ready went in with him to the marriage: and the door was shut. Afterward came also the other virgins, saying, Lord, Lord, open to us. But he answered and said, Verily I say unto you, I know you not. Watch therefore, for ye know neither the day nor the hour wherein the Son of man cometh." (Matthew 25:1-13)

The parable, a metaphor of ten virgins, is famous for being misinterpreted. Many teachers cannot resist imposing the Church into a Jewish parable. In retaining the fact that the Lord was speaking to His Jewish disciples about the Jewish people in the end times, we can recognize that it is the Jewish people who are unprepared to meet their Messiah. While the Jewish people have been expecting their bridegroom to come for ages, He has been anything but their focus. During the tribulation and their pending annihilation all that will change.

In this parable, preparedness is the oil. It is not something that can be distributed when a crisis occurs, nor can it be purchased. It must be cultured in a courtship relationship beforehand. Though oil is one of the symbols used to depict the Holy Spirit it is not representing Him in this passage, for He can neither be bought or sold.

The wise are those who will awake from their slumber before the bridegroom appears. Their lamps will be filled with love for Him and trimmed with expectation. The wise virgins are the Jewish people who will have come to realize Jesus is their Messiah. They will have turned to the Scriptures and recognized that the midnight hour, has by all accounts arrived. The foolish virgins are the Jewish people who will have resisted until it is too late and the "door was shut."[1475] As stated in another passage of the gospel of Matthew, the Lord will say, "I never knew you."[1476]

1475 Matthew 25:10
1476 Matthew 7:23

"For the kingdom of heaven is as a man travelling into a far country, who called his own servants, and delivered unto them his goods. And unto one he gave five talents, to another two, and to another one; to every man according to his several ability; and straightway took his journey. Then he that had received the five talents went and traded with the same, and made them other five talents. And likewise he that had received two, he also gained other two. But he that had received one went and digged in the earth, and hid his lord's money. After a long time the lord of those servants cometh, and reckoneth with them. And so he that had received five talents came and brought other five talents, saying, Lord, thou deliveredst unto me five talents: behold, I have gained beside them five talents more. His lord said unto him, Well done, thou good and faithful servant: thou hast been faithful over a few things, I will make thee ruler over many things: enter thou into the joy of thy lord. He also that had received two talents came and said, Lord, thou deliveredst unto me two talents: behold, I have gained two other talents beside them. His lord said unto him, Well done, good and faithful servant; thou hast been faithful over a few things, I will make thee ruler over many things: enter thou into the joy of thy lord. Then he which had received the one talent came and said, Lord, I knew thee that thou art an hard man, reaping where thou hast not sown, and gathering where thou hast not strawed: and I was afraid, and went and hid thy talent in the earth: lo, there thou hast that is thine. His lord answered and said unto him, Thou wicked and slothful servant, thou knewest that I reap where I sowed not, and gather where I have not strawed: thou oughtest therefore to have put my money to the exchangers, and then at my coming I should have received mine own with usury. Take therefore the talent from him, and give it unto him which hath ten talents. For unto every one that hath shall be given, and he shall have abundance: but from him that hath not shall be taken away even that which he hath. And cast ye the unprofitable servant into outer darkness: there shall be weeping and gnashing of teeth." (Matthew 25:14-30)

The parable of the talents is not about what we do with our GOD-given abilities and our natural talents, as is often taught today. Rather, it speaks of the eternal principal that it is through our faithfulness to HIM and to that which has been so graciously given us that we have been expected to invest and multiply. It is the truth (talents of truth) invested into the kingdom of GOD for the procuring of souls to which the faithful invest.[1477] The talents represent the Gospel of Grace which the Lord has given to us to invest by sharing the Good News with others.

This responsibility and commission of bringing Elohim to the world was initially given to the Jewish people. Patriarchs and prophets and those who truly believed in HIM invested their knowledge of HIM and passed it to others. Wherever they went, and under whatever circumstances they found themselves, they boldly proclaimed YAHUAH (Yahovah) and Yahusha (Yeshua) making believers of some and adding souls to the Kingdom.

1477 Luke 12:43-48

Moses confronted Pharaoh with the truth.[1478] Samuel reproved Saul with the truth.[1479] David defied Goliath with the truth,[1480] Elijah challenged and destroyed the priest of Baal with the truth,[1481] and Elisha took on the entire Syrian army[1482] and made them his prisoners as he believed and depended on truth. Each of these giants of the faith confronted their adversaries with total conviction. Each believer who receives talents of truth is responsible with what portion he has been given to invest it. Believers are not to retain this understanding for themselves, burying it under a bushel.[1483] The Lord expects His own to multiply the knowledge of Him to a lost and dying world.[1484]

The first believers in Yahusha-Jesus were Jews and during the first centuries they spread the Gospel message over three continents. It has been said that perhaps as many as a million Jews became believers and went forth missionizing; speaking the Word with all boldness.[1485] Over time however this diminished and the Jewish people withdrew to a religious form of Judaism; burying the talents of truth. So it was that the commission of investing these talents and ultimately the rewards associated with the saving of souls[1486] went to believing Gentiles. It would become their assignment to pick-up the message of the Cross[1487] and begin carrying out the Great Commission.[1488] True wealth is the Word of GOD and the Way of Salvation.[1489] These are the precious talents which are expected to be invested and from where rewards are obtained.

> "...but we preach Christ crucified, unto the Jews a stumbling block, and unto the Greeks foolishness..." (1 Corinthians 1:23)

> "For I determined not to know any thing among you, save Jesus Christ, and him crucified." (1 Corinthians 2:2)

> "When the Son of man shall come in his glory, and all the holy angels with him, then shall he sit upon the throne of his glory: And before him shall be gathered all nations: and he shall separate them one from another, as a shepherd divideth his sheep from the goats: And he shall set the sheep on his right hand, but the goats on the left. Then shall the King say unto them on his right hand, Come, ye blessed of my Father, inherit the kingdom prepared for you from the foundation of the world: For I was an hungred, and ye gave me

---

1478 Exodus 5:1
1479 1 Samuel 15:23
1480 1 Samuel 17:45-47
1481 1 Kings 22-40
1482 2 Kings 6:13-23
1483 Matthew 5:15
1484 Mark 16:15
1485 1 Thessalonians 2:2-4; Philippians 1:14; Acts 4:28-29
1486 2 Timothy 4:7-8
1487 1 Corinthians 1:23, 2:2
1488 Mark 16:15
1489 Matthew 13:46

meat: I was thirsty, and ye gave me drink: I was a stranger, and ye took me in: naked, and ye clothed me: I was sick, and ye visited me: I was in prison, and ye came unto me. Then shall the righteous answer him, saying, Lord, when saw we thee a hungred, and fed thee? or thirsty, and gave thee drink? When saw we thee a stranger, and took thee in? or naked, and clothed thee? Or when saw we thee sick, or in prison, and came unto thee? And the King shall answer and say unto them, Verily I say unto you, In as much as ye have done it unto one of the least of these my brethren (the Jew), ye have done it unto me. Then shall he say also unto them on the left hand, Depart from me, ye cursed, into everlasting fire, prepared for the devil and his angels: for I was ahungred, and ye gave me no meat: I was thirsty, and ye gave me no drink: I was a stranger, and ye took me not in: naked, and ye clothed me not: sick, and in prison, and ye visited me not. Then shall they also answer him, saying, Lord, when saw we thee ahungred, or athirst, or a stranger, or naked, or sick, or in prison, and did not minister unto thee? Then shall he answer them, saying, Verily I say unto you, In as much as ye did it not to one of the least of these, ye did it not to me. And these shall go away into everlasting punishment: but the righteous into life eternal." (Matthew 25:31-46)

Matthew 25:31–46 is the culmination of GOD's judgments upon those "nations" (also rendered Gentiles) who were still alive at the end of the Tribulation. So it is that this section of the discourse has appropriately been referred to as the "Judgment of Nations."

At that time Yahusha-Jesus will gather those who have survived the Great Tribulation before His earthly throne. This is not to be confused with the final Great White Throne Judgment of Revelation 20:11. The judgment described here is the dividing of the sheep nations from the goat nations. The sheep represent those who have stood with Israel and enter into His millennial kingdom without seeing death. The goat nations are those who opposed Israel in the final days.[1490]

We read that GOD will judge the Gentiles on the basis of how they treated Christ's "brethren." The word brethren refers to Jesus' brethren according to the flesh. As Jesus was a Jew in the flesh when He appeared on earth, these "brethren" refer to the Jewish people.[1491] We find the Old Testament parallel scripture in the book of Joel where the judgment is based on the "way the nations treated MY people…and MY heritage Israel."[1492] Joel 3:2, and following, definitively identifies "the brethren" as Israel, not the Church.

"I will also gather all nations, and will bring them down into the valley of Jehoshaphat, and will plead with them there for my people and for my heritage Israel, whom they have scattered among the nations, and parted my land. And they have cast lots for my people; and have given a boy for a harlot, and sold a girl for wine, that they might drink"…"The children also of Judah and the children of Jerusalem have ye sold unto the Grecians, that

---

1490 Isaiah 11:4
1491 Matthew 25:40
1492 Joel 3:2

ye might remove them far from their border."..."Egypt shall be a desolation, and Edom shall be a desolate wilderness, for the violence against the children of Judah, because they have shed innocent blood in their land. But Judah shall dwell forever, and Jerusalem from generation to generation." (Joel 3:2-3, 6, 19-20)

May America return to YAHUAH, make Yahusha-Jesus her Sovereign, and take Psalm 32 and Psalm 2 to heart while there is still time.

"Blessed is the nation whose GOD is the Lord; and the people whom HE hath chosen for His own inheritance...Behold the eye of the Lord is upon them that fear (reverence) HIM, upon them that hope in HIS mercy." (Psalm 33:12, 18)

"Be wise now therefore, O ye kings: be instructed, ye judges of the earth. Serve the Lord with fear, and rejoice with trembling. Kiss the Son (an expression of love), lest he be angry, and ye perish from the way, when his wrath is kindled but a little. Blessed are all they that put their trust in him." (Psalm 2:10-12)

APPENDIX C

DANIEL'S VISION OF SEVENTY WEEKS

A Messianic Prophecy (Daniel 9:20–27)

Prophecy is the signature of the omniscient Creator. No other sacred book: not Islam's Qur'an (Koran), the Hindu Vedas, its Baghavad Gita, or its Ramayana—or the Book of Mormon, can authenticate its authorship as divine by predicted events coming to pass. Only the Bible has this distinction.

While prophecy is the chronicle of what was predicted in the future for Israel and for the world at large, its greater purpose was to reveal and testify of the Israel's future King and Savior. We shall explore the most indisputable evidence provided in the Hebrew Scripture to identity and authenticate Him.

> "And I fell at his feet to worship him. And he said unto me, See thou do it not: I am thy fellow servant, and of thy brethren that have the testimony (or testify) of Jesus: worship God: for the testimony of Jesus is the spirit of prophecy." (Revelation 19:10)

(Image Source: GOODSALT)

Two-thirds of this Book of Books (the Bible) is prophetic revelation (futuristic.) It was conveyed to the prophets, "Then the Lord put forth His hand, and touched my mouth. And the Lord said unto me, Behold I have put My words in thy mouth,"[1493] and it was shown to some like Isaiah, Ezekiel, Daniel, Paul, and John in visions.

GOD knew that men would need evidence such as predictions coming to pass on which to anchor their

---

1493 Jeremiah 1:9

faith. And while ancient writings and archeological finds are supportive, there is no greater witness than seeing the foretold, become the fulfilled.

Dr. George Elden Ladd, a professor of New Testament exegesis and theology at Fuller Theological Seminary, in his book, I believe in the Resurrection of Jesus, wrote, "Faith does not mean a leap in the dark, an irrational credulity, a believing against evidence and against reason. It is believing in the light of historical evidence, on the basis of witness."[1494]

The Apostle Peter said it well, when he said,

> "We have also a more sure word of prophecy; whereunto ye do well that ye take heed, as unto a light that shineth in a dark place, until the day dawn, and the day star arise in your hearts..." (2 Peter 1:19)

Daniel 9:24–27

There are, as one may well appreciate, numerous interpretations of this prophetic passage. The contributions of others; some of whom have spent half a lifetime exploring this one prophecy have been graciously taken into account.

Scripture reassures us that we do well to build on the foundation which Christ alone has laid.[1495] As He is the author of all knowledge and revelation, and the giver of talents, and gifts, should He gracious share these with an individual, it is inappropriate for that individual to take credit for the unearthing. Likewise, it is unfitting for that individual to extract wealth for what the Lord graciously communicated to them—they have no legitimate copyright. It does not belong to them and it was intended to be shared.[1496] Freely ye have received, freely give.[1497]

Those of us who search the Scriptures and teach are but yokefellows in His harvest field,[1498] serving at His good pleasure,[1499] "for the perfecting of the saints, for the work of the ministry, for the edifying of the body of Christ."[1500]

The Purpose of this Study

The focus and abstract of this study is to provide scriptural evidence by correlating dates and events and then counting the number of days supplied in the scriptures which confirm that Yahusha-Jesus was and is the promised Messiah. No other Old Testament prophecy is as conclusive to this end as Daniel 9:24–27.

1494 George Eldon Ladd, *I believe in the Resurrection*, William B. Eerdmans Publishing Company, 1987
1495 1 Corinthians 3:10
1496 Ephesians 4:12
1497 Mathew 10:8
1498 Philippians 4:3; 1 Corinthians 3:6; John 4:34-38
1499 1 Corinthians 12:18
1500 Ephesians 4:12

Interpreting the Scriptures

In the interest of accuracy and to appreciate the magnitude of this prophecy, we will begin by introducing a number of the fundamentals of proper Bible exegesis. We will also present some history and background which provide continuity and undergird the prophecy itself.

We are told, "All scripture is profitable…"[1501] We are instructed not merely to read the scriptures but to "study to show ourselves approved unto GOD."[1502] We are told to "prove all things,"[1503] thereby safeguarding ourselves from error. We are also told that, "no prophecy of the scripture is of (for) private interpretation."[1504] So, in obedience we must allow scripture to speak for itself and bridle any preconceptions and prejudices we might have. Finally, we are told to "know the truth,"[1505] which indicates that the truth can be known.

In the quest to discover truth, all views must be scripturally supported and must, without coercion, unite with other scripture. Many Old Testament prophecies are concealed and may only be understood and verified when compared with corresponding scriptures in the New Testament. Much that was concealed in the Old Testament is revealed in the New.

The prophecy we are about to explore is such a passage. It can be an enigma to those who balk at seeing its development in the New Testament as with the book of the Revelation, or in the "Olivet Discourse" found in the gospels of Matthew,[1506] Mark,[1507] and Luke.[1508]

As we proceed, we will need to be on the lookout for Hebraic expressions which reappear in the New Testament, thereby associating the two. One such idiom used in Daniel 9:27 is also found in the Olivet Discourse. It is in Matthew 24:15 that Jesus spoke of the "abomination of desolation," referring to the "abomination" made "desolate" in Daniel 9:27. So it is that GOD has not only given us a correlation between the two testaments but HE has also given us this one event as a benchmark in time by which we can establish where we are on HIS prophetic timeline.

The book of Daniel was written in exile; that period in which the Jews of the Judean kingdom were displaced from their country after the destruction of the Temple by Nebuchadnezzar in 587 BC. It was during Daniel's captivity that while in prayer he was visited by the angel Gabriel who would reveal to him by the dates associated with certain events—when in the future the messiah would come. By correlating the dates and events both His first and second appearance could be affirmed. One crucial prophetic benchmark that was foretold would occur in the end times would be the defilement of the Temple.[1509]

In the book of Daniel, we read that this desolation (Hebrew, *shamem*—to lay waste) includes the mandate to cease the sacrifices and oblation (grain offering) and that this

---

[1501] 2 Timothy 3:16
[1502] 2 Timothy 2:15
[1503] 1 Thessalonians 5:21
[1504] 2 Peter 1:20
[1505] John 8:32
[1506] Matthew chapters 24 and 25
[1507] Mark 13:3-37
[1508] Luke 21:5-33
[1509] Daniel 9:27

will occur "in the midst (middle) of the Week." Therefore, when we read of the abomination of desolation in Matthew 24:15 we know that it is referring to the same event; that being the middle of the seven year Tribulation, which signals the beginning of the Great Tribulation.[1510] The word "Week" or "Weeks", (Hebrew, *shabua*) is the plural of the word seven and a Hebrew expression referring to divisions of time. Each Week has a numerical value of seven years.

Failing to see or acknowledge the correlation between scriptures in the Old Testament like Joel and Daniel, and the New Testament like Matthew and Revelation has caused certain teachers to err. Two common errors when interpreting Scripture are misapplication and dislocation. Some teachers have hastily and without scriptural evidence assumed that these last seven years are a part of the Church Age instead of being a separate dispensation which follows the Church Age. The Hebrew Holy scriptures are clear and emphatic that these series of "Weeks" (seventy in all) presented in Daniel 9:24 are all about Israel and the Jewish people.[1511] Subsequently, the corresponding passage referred to as the Olivet Discourse in Matthew chapters 24 and 25 are also all about the Jewish people and Israel during the last of those Weeks—the Seventieth Week.

It is important that we assign scriptures and promises which are specific to the Jewish people to them. Daniel 9:24 makes the subject of this prophecy obvious, for in the opening declaration we read, "Seventy weeks have been determined upon thy (Daniel's) people (the Jews) and upon thy holy city (Jerusalem)." Once this is understood, one can then recognize that this prophecy finds its completion in the Olivet Discourse and in Revelation chapters 4–19. If this is not understood, then the believing Church is apt to see itself in the dispensation of the Tribulation. This one misapplication has led to mid and post tribulation theories.

Daniel chapter 9 actually spans three dispensations. It originated under the Age of Law; pauses with the arrival and death of the Messiah, vaults over the entire Church Age (situated between the sixty-ninth and seventieth Week) and resumes with the seventieth Week—"The Time of Jacob's Trouble." The Church Age is not mentioned or even alluded to in the prophecy for the simple reason it has nothing to do with the Gentiles or the Church but is exclusive to the Jewish people.

A significant point often overlooked is the way in which the Weeks are presented. Instead of the angel Gabriel simply saying Seventy Weeks, he divides the Weeks into a segmented chronological progression. First is seven (7) Weeks, then sixty and two (62) Weeks, for a subtotal of 69 Weeks (Daniel 9:25). We are then left with one (1) final Week—the Seventieth Week, which was deliberately excluded from verse 25. This one Week is presented two verses later in verse 27 after a sequence of events is described. In presenting the Weeks in this way it places the Messiah's initial earthly arrival squarely at the end of the 69th Week and His reappearance at the end of the Seventieth Week, illustrating two comings.

1510 Matthew 24:21
1511 Daniel 9:24

Other Hebrew phrases used in the Old Testament which are synonymous with Seventieth Week include "the Time of Jacobs Trouble;"[1512] "The time of Trouble;"[1513] "The refiner's fire;"[1514] "the Day of the Lord;"[1515] and "the great and dreadful day of the Lord."[1516]

Some teachers have mistakenly included the Church into a Jewish prophecy based on seeing a single word commonly used of Believers in the New Testament Church. The word "saints" (Chaldean "*qadash*"),[1517] is used six times in the book of Daniel. It is not referring to the Believing Church. It simply means the consecrated, dedicated, sanctified, faithful and prepared.

When the word saints appears in the Old Testament it is referring to godly Jews who from time immemorial remained faithful to GOD. When the word saints appears in the book of the Revelation it speaks of the saints already in heaven; those Jews and Gentiles who become saved during those seven fateful years.[1518]

During the first half of the Tribulation this will include one hundred forty-four thousand providentially sealed (saved and divinely protected) Jews who become Believers.[1519] They will testify and present Yahusha Jesus, the Messiah to others. Many of these others will, over the course of the last three-and-one-half years, become Tribulation saints.[1520]

> "...and there shall be a time of trouble, such as never was since there was a nation...And they that be wise shall shine as the brightness of the firmament; and they that turn many to righteousness as the stars for ever and ever." (Daniel 12:1, 3)

While all branches of Christianity tend to agree and teach the same basic truths and tenets of faith concerning the death, burial and resurrection of Jesus Christ, they soon diverge simply because they fail to apply proper hermeneutical disciplines.

> Note: Bible hermeneutics may be described as the application of various disciplines used in deriving the intended meaning of scripture. It goes beyond Inductive Bible Study which is barely governed by standard rules and so allows each person to arrive at their own conclusion as to what they believe scripture is saying. While induction study may give the reader a general understanding, it is nevertheless still speculative. In contrast, hermeneutics uses grammatical rules, entomology (the origin of words), the historical setting, and the intent of the message the authors are trying to convey.

1512 Jeremiah 30:7
1513 Daniel 12:1
1514 Malachi 3:1-3
1515 Joel 2:11; Amos 5:18; Zephaniah 1:14
1516 Malachi 4:5
1517 *Strong's Exhaustive Concordance*, Heb., #6944
1518 Revelation 5:9, 15:3, 16:6, 17:6, 18:24, 19:8, 20:9
1519 Revelation 7:3-8
1520 Revelation 7:14

> It also asks who it was the speaker was addressing at that moment; e.g. Jews, Gentiles, Romans, Pharisees, or Believers? Hermeneutics asks, was there a covenant involved and was it presented to Israel in the O.T.; to individuals like David or Abram, or as in the New Covenant—to the believing born-again Church? It maintains all literary premises must complement and coincide with the message of the whole text (the entire chapter), or with the whole epistle (letter); or in the context of several letters, such as First and Second Thessalonians or First and Second Corinthians.

A scripture or passage must not become a stand-alone scripture. Basing a passage on a single scripture has caused divisions within the Church and birthed whole sects. For example, Mark 11:12–24 taken out of context has birthed the hyper-faith, a.k.a. the Word of Faith movement. Misinterpreting the word "published" in Matthew 24:14 became a basis for "Kingdom Theology," which believes that only when the Church has translated the Bible into every language, and everything is made right on earth will the Lord return. And, taking Galatians 3:29 out of context gave rise to "Restoration Theology" where the Church sees itself as Spiritual Israel.

All interpretation must all be held to the highest standards of exegetical principals; for we who claim to know enough to teach are the custodians of the most valuable treasure on earth and will be held all the more accountable if we are careless with it.

> "My brethren, be not many masters (teachers), knowing that we shall receive the greater condemnation." (James 3:1)

Schools of Thought

Having investigated the main schools of thought with regard to Daniel 9, including the Dispensational, the Premillennial, the A-millennial, the Historical-messianic, and the Hebraic Interpretation, I have found only one that meets the criteria mentioned. This is the Dispensational—pre-tribulation pre-millennial interpretation.

Non-Christological interpretations which do not recognize a Gentile dispensation (i.e. the Hebraic interpretation) are left mostly wanting. The rabbinic defenders cannot satisfactorily explain what GOD has been doing for the last nearly two thousand years since the Temple's destruction, and why this protracted time? They have failed to see that GOD's impartiality compels HIM to provide a season whereby all—even the Gentiles would be given the same opportunity as had been afforded the Jewish people; that being to accept HIS offer of salvation.[1521] One Jewish disciple of Yahusha-Jesus named Simon Peter, explained this opportunity presented to the Gentiles when he said, "Of a truth I perceive that GOD is no respecter of persons."[1522]

1521 Romans 3:29-30, 10:13
1522 Acts 10:34

> Note: Dispensationalists recognize that the Bible identifies seven primary ages (Greek, *aions*), bound on each side by eternity past and eternity future. The first dispensation may be called the Creative Age, when in Genesis, GOD renovated a chaotic planet and afterward created a man and woman and said to them, "...replenish the earth, and subdue it and have dominion over...every living thing..."[1523]
>
> Note: Science (true science) does not conflict with Creationism. Our prehistoric/pre-Adamic planet was, prior to Adam and Eve, undoubtably a beautiful earth—covered with vegetation and inhabited with all types of animal life (including dinosaurs), and with a human life form.[1524] (Take note of the referral to pre-Adamic cities in Jeremiah 4:26.) At some point in time GOD allowed a catastrophic event and the earth became a dead planet, formless and void.[1525] Its prehistoric (pre-recorded history) fossil record became submerged beneath the waters of the deep which covered the earth. The glacial period followed as the earth lay dormant for millenniums before GOD would again make it habitable. This was not the beginning of the first day as described in Genesis 1:3-5 and the other six days. Those six days refer to the restoration of the earth, not the original earth (Genesis 1:1). The pre-Adamic/prehistoric earth, Genesis 1:1 was an entirely different age, not discussed in scripture as it had no relevance to us or to our salvation. Note the words, "replenish the earth..." (Genesis 1:28)

The second dispensation may be called the Age of Innocence or the Age of Conscience when Adam, Eve, Cain, and Abel set the course for the human race and learned firsthand the difference between good and evil.[1526]

The third dispensation came after the great flood and may be called the Age of Human Government or the Age of Law when GOD first chose a people for HIMSELF and handed Moses HIS decrees.[1527]

The fourth dispensation, and the one not alluded to in the prophecy (Daniel 9) is referred to as the Age of the Church when GOD came to earth, died on a Roman Cross, and then at Pentecost (Hebrew, *Shavuot*) afforded the Gentiles adoption into the family of GOD.[1528]

The fifth dispensation is infinitely small in comparison to the others. It is a dispensation of only seven years; "The Time of Jacob's Trouble." The last three and a half of these seven are referred to as the Great Tribulation.[1529] These seven years compose the seventieth Week of the prophecy.[1530]

1523 Genesis 1:28
1524 Isaiah 45:18; Jeremiah 4:23-26
1525 Isaiah 1:2
1526 Isaiah 3:22
1527 Exodus 19:5-8
1528 Acts 1:8; John 6:40
1529 Jeremiah 30:7; Deuteronomy 4:30; Daniel 12:1
1530 Daniel 9:24-27

The sixth dispensation is called the Kingdom Age. It refers to that time when the Lord Jesus will return to earth, set up His kingdom and rule for one thousand years.[1531]

The seventh and last dispensation is the New Heaven and New Earth or the Perfect Age when GOD's heaven is relocated to the earth, and the GODhead—Elohim, presides forever with HIS own.[1532]

> "Thy Kingdom is an everlasting kingdom" (Hebrew, *Malchutcha Malchut Kol Olmim*). (Psalm 145:13)

The Prophetic Dates

Within the dispensational school there are variations between respected scholars regarding dates. In particular, and one of the two most important dates, is the date which began the prophecy and permits us to identify the Messiah. This is quintessential, as it gives us the starting point from which we can then calculate the exact number of days when Scripture tells us the Messiah was to make His initial public appearance. It would be this date which began the Prophetic clock of "Weeks" ticking. We are told in Daniel 9:25 it began with a command to rebuild the city Jerusalem after the emancipation of the Israelites from Babylon.

> "Knowing therefore and understand that from the going forth of the commandment to restore and to rebuild Jerusalem..." (Daniel 9:25)

The other important date needed to verify this Messianic prophecy is the date which marks the end of the 69th Week. This date would also temporarily pause the prophetic clock. According to the Hebrew Scriptures, this—the terminal date, was prophesied to occur when the Messiah would make His Triumphal entrance in Jerusalem and be publicly acknowledged for the first time as the Jewish Messiah.[1533] This event took place when many Jewish people acknowledged Yahusha-Jesus. He entered Jerusalem just days before He was crucified. It was there and then, just as foretold in Scripture, that the people collectively exclaimed, *"Baruch Haba B'shem Adonai;"* "Blessed is He that cometh in the name of the Lord...", "Hosanna in the Highest."[1534] It would be the number of days between these two dates, that according to the prophesy would authenticate the Messiah at His first coming.

It was at that moment of public acknowledgement that the 69th Week ended. It would be just weeks afterward, at the Feast of Pentecost (Hebrew, *Shavuot*) that GOD would officially interpolate another dispensation (not mentioned and not relevant to this prophecy in Daniel). We have come to call this protracted period the Church Age.

1531 Revelation 20:6
1532 Revelation 21:1-3
1533 Zechariah 9:9
1534 Matthew 21:11, 23:39; Psalm 118:26; Isaiah 62:11

The Church Age has been GOD's outreach to the Gentiles and would continue for an undisclosed period of time. It has, at the time of this writing, been going on for nearly two thousand years. Soon, at a time of HIS choosing, when HE has given the Gentiles ample time in which to find and accept their Savior, GOD will supernaturally remove the Church and once again turn HIS attention to the Jewish people and Israel.[1535] Thereafter and with a declaration by a world leader permitting the rebuilding of the next Temple, the prophetic clock will again begin ticking and commence the Seventieth Week (the final seven years)—"The Time of Jacob's Trouble."[1536]

According to Scripture, the Seventieth Week will occur sometime after the Jewish people have returned to their homeland and Israel has become a nation; as obviously the third Temple cannot be built until the Jewish people are back in their land. So the Seventieth Week could not have possibly begun before 1948, and because the Temple Mount is still in the hands of the Muslims, and there is no Jewish Temple, the Seventieth Week has not begun.

These final seven years will begin sometime (not necessarily immediately) after the genuine Church has been "caught up."[1537] At some point thereafter, an agreement between the Palestinian Muslims and Israeli Jews permitting the rebuilding the Temple will be ratified.[1538] This may become Oslo Accord 3 or 4. The same scripture tells us that this "covenant"—agreement (which commences the rebuilding) begins the prophetic clock ticking again and launches the final and (Seventieth) Week, when the Antichrist actual confirms it. It is at the very end of that seven years that the Messiah will return (His second coming), vanquish Israel's enemies and establish His government. Scripture also tells us that midway (three and one-half years) into this Week, the Temple will be desecrated when the Antichrist shall, "cause the sacrifice and oblation to cease, and for the overspreading of abominations he shall make it desolate..."[1539]

The *terminus ad quo,* and *terminus ad quem*

I have analyzed the works of Sir Isaac Newton, Sir Robert Anderson, Dr. Harold W. Hoehner, Dr. Thomas Ice, Rev. Clarence Larkin, and others and have found some disparity between them with regard to the *terminus ad quo* (beginning) and the *terminus ad quem* (end) dates as they apply to the 69 Weeks. But I have also found refinements in the work of Professor Samuel A. Smith whose research and conclusions I have determined to be accurate. His investigation established the beginning of the 69 Weeks as Nisan 1 444 BCE, as presented in Nehemiah 2:1. This was the Hebrew calendar year 3317 or our April 2, 444 BC. Professor Smith's findings fix the end of the 69th Week with Messiah's entering Jerusalem as Sunday, Nisan 9; the Hebrew calendar year 3793, or our March 29, 33 AD. These dates are central to our calculations for it will confirm not only the day, but the exact moment when the Messiah would make His Triumphal entrance into the Holy City, thereby authenticating Him.[1540]

1535 Isaiah 54:7
1536 Jeremiah 30:7
1537 1 Thessalonians 4:16-17; 2 Thessalonians 2:7-8
1538 Daniel 9:27
1539 Daniel 9:27
1540 Zechariah 9:9

Dates, Times, and Events

From at least the second century AD there has been controversy over what date the crucifixion of Jesus actually occurred. Much of the confusion stems from vagueness of the biblical account. All the gospels state that Jesus rose from the grave on the first day of the week (so named Sunday by sun worshiping pagans) three days after His crucifixion. They also refer to the "Last Supper" in relation to the annual Passover, which begins on Nisan 15 of the Jewish calendar, as specified in Exodus 12:6. The three Synoptic gospels allude to it as a Passover meal, but the Gospel of John clarifies it by indicating it was on the day before Passover—Nisan 14 (Hebrew, *Ereb Shabbat*). This confirms that the "Last Supper" was not the Passover meal (*Seder*). The Passover lamb was not served at the Last Supper. The sacrificial lamb would not be slaughtered until the next day just prior to the beginning of Passover at sundown. The Pascal lamb would be offered on that same day when Jesus was offered and died—Friday at 3 pm. Jesus was the anti-type, typifying the Passover lamb and the first fruits presented to GOD. He was sacrificed on the same day and even at the same hour when all the Passover lambs were killed.

> Note: The Passover lambs were to be chosen on Nisan 10 and killed on Nisan 14 around 3-4 pm. The lamb was then cooked and eaten after sundown on Nisan 15. If the "last supper" was the Passover, then the lamb was killed exactly 24 hours early than stated in the Bible and according to Jewish custom. Look carefully at the narrative in Matthew 26:17; "prepare the Passover." It refers specifically to preparing for the entire eight-day feast of unleavened bread. The choosing of the lamb was just one part of the preparations. Preparations would also include arranging for the use of the upper room and the meal itself in advance of the entire eight-day festival (Passover plus seven days of unleavened bread.) This misunderstanding is an impediment to the fact that the last supper was not the Passover meal. A timeline of the Passion Week is provided at the conclusion of this study.

Events Leading Up to Prophecy

Before looking at the prophecy itself, it is important to understand what led up to this historic moment and why GOD would dispatch an angel to give Daniel and his people such a vital and essential message.

The once great kingdom of David had long since disintegrated. The twelve tribes of Israel had split into two opposing nations; the Northern Kingdom—Israel, and the Southern Kingdom—Judah. Over time YAHUAH had become less than preeminent in the hearts and lives of the people in both kingdoms. We find the frequent use of the term "godless people" in the book of Proverbs, and in Job, and by the prophets Isaiah and Jeremiah who warned the people where complacency and self-interest would lead them. The term "godless" is most appropriate, for godless simply means, less GOD and more of self.

YAHUAH had stood by the Israelites, performing miracles and turning the tide against their enemies only to have them return to their pernicious ways. They transgressed the Mosaic laws and ordnances and gave assent to imaginary deities. They had become absorbed with the things of the world; sin had become a social norm. Pleasure, comfort, wealth and security had become their preoccupation. They chose to believe false prophets who told them what they wanted to hear rather than the prophets of GOD who told them what they needed to hear.[1541] In a phrase borrowed from a scripture found in the book of the Revelation as it applied to the Church, they had "left thy first love."[1542]

For their passive indifference and "transgressions" GOD would, as HE promised, make them subjects of the very heathens they despised.[1543] The Northern kingdom was first to fall when in 722 BC, Assyria's King Shalmaneser V laid siege and took its capital city Samaria, absorbing Israel into the Assyrian Empire. Over the next one hundred years the Babylonian Empire grew into a formidable kingdom, challenging the Assyrians for supremacy. In 625 BC the Babylonians (Chaldeans) drove the Assyrians out of Babylon. In 612 BC, the Assyrian capital of Nineveh fell just as it had been foretold by the prophets Nahum[1544] and Zephaniah.[1545] Then, in 609 BC, the Chaldeans seized the city of Harran which had been the last stronghold of the Assyrians. With its conquest the once great Assyrian empire ceased to exist. The Babylonian Empire then controlled the majority of the Middle East, but the human propensity feeds an insatiable appetite for more; more land, more power and more wealth.

In the expansion of the empire, the Babylonian King Nebuchadnezzar continued to move south and west intent on annexing, among other lands Judah and the city of Jerusalem. Jerusalem was the sought-after prize for it laid at the intersection of the principal trade routes from Africa, Asia and Europe. After numerous sieges, the city of Jerusalem final surrendered on March 16, 597 BC.

Once conquered, the Judean kingdom was reduced to a vassal state. Still, it would require some cultural (Jewish) management. To this end Nebuchadnezzar appointed King Zedekiah who would be the last king over the province of Judah. However, afterward when Zedekiah lead a revolt against the Chaldeans, Nebuchadnezzar's fury was unleashed, and he responded by destroying the city and the Temple in 586 BC.

What remained of Judah in the aftermath of the pilferage and destruction was but a shabby province of the Babylonian Empire. Those inhabitants of Judea who were not killed were taken prisoners and exiled to Babylon. Some of the lower-class were allowed to remain in the land and became serfs; their only purpose was to farm the land and support their Babylonian abductors. Among those abducted and taken hostage in the first of three waves of Nebuchadnezzar's campaign against Judah was a well-educated young Hebrew named Danielis, לְאִיָּנֵד—Daniel.

1541 Micah 3:1-12
1542 Revelation 2:4
1543 Deuteronomy 28:15-68
1544 Nahum 3:7
1545 Zephaniah 2:13

In 605 BCE, some eight years before Jerusalem surrendered, the prisoner Daniel was deported from Judah to Babylon along with other upper-class Jews. In the decades to follow, Daniel would serve five Babylonian kings: Nebuchadnezzar II who reigned from 605–562 BC, his son-in law, Neriglisser, who reigned 560–556 BC, his grandson, Labashi Marduk (murdered in 556 BC), Nabonidus who reigned 556–539 BC and his son, (possibly the grandson of Nebuchadnezzar II) co-regent Belshazzar.

As the ninth chapter of the book of Daniel begins in the year 538 BC, Daniel was still in Babylon, a subject of King Belshazzar. GOD had sent prophet after prophet to warn Judah of her declension. Among them were Isaiah, Zephaniah, Obadiah, Micah, Habakkuk, Jeremiah and Ezekiel. Each implored the people to return to Yahovah but to almost no avail. It had been Moses himself, who some 875 years earlier warned the Hebrews what their neglect, disregard and disobedience would result in. GOD would keep HIS word. The two nations (Israel and Judah) would be defeated and its people taken into captivity.

> "But if ye will not hearken unto me, and will not do all these commandments; And if ye shall despise my statutes, or if your soul abhor my judgments, so that ye will not do all my commandments, but that ye break my covenant: I also will do this unto you; I will even appoint over you terror, consumption, and the burning ague, that shall consume the eyes, and cause sorrow of heart: and ye shall sow your seed in vain, for your enemies shall eat it. And I will set my face against you, and ye shall be slain before your enemies: they that hate you shall reign over you; and ye shall flee when none pursueth you. And if ye will not yet for all this hearken unto me, then I will punish you seven times more for your sins. And I will break the pride of your power; and I will make your heaven as iron, and your earth as brass: And your strength shall be spent in vain: for your land shall not yield her increase, neither shall the trees of the land yield their fruits. And if ye walk contrary unto me, and will not hearken unto me; I will bring seven times more plagues upon you according to your sins. I will also send wild beasts among you, which shall rob you of your children, and destroy your cattle, and make you few in number; and your high ways shall be desolate. And if ye will not be reformed by me by these things, but will walk contrary unto me; Then will I also walk contrary unto you, and will punish you yet seven times for your sins." (Leviticus 26:14-24)

> "I will scatter you among the heathen, and will draw out a sword after you: and your land shall be desolate, and your cities waste." (Leviticus 26:33)

> "And ye shall perish among the heathen and the land of your enemies shall eat you up. And they that are left of you shall pine away in their iniquity in your enemies land..." (Leviticus 26:38-39)

Seventy Years

Just a few years before Nebuchadnezzar had sacked Jerusalem the prophet Jeremiah had been given a word from the Lord that the Judeans would be captives for seventy years.[1546] Afterward the Lord would permit them to return to their land and begin rebuilding the wall, the city and afterward the Temple.

> "For thus saith the Lord, That after seventy years be accomplished at Babylon I will visit you, and perform my good word toward you, in causing you to return to this place. For I know the thoughts that I think toward you, saith the Lord, thoughts of peace, and not of evil, to give you an expected end. Then shall ye call upon me, and ye shall go and pray unto me, and I will hearken unto you. And ye shall seek me, and find me, when ye shall search for me with all your heart. And I will be found of you, saith the Lord: and I will turn away your captivity, and I will gather you from all the nations, and from all the places whither I have driven you, saith the Lord; and I will bring you again into the place whence I caused you to be carried away captive." (Jeremiah 29:10-14)

> Note: The seventy years began with the first deportation of Judahites to Babylon in 606-605 BC and ended in 536 BC with a proclamation by King Cyrus of Persia. This restoration, "I will bring you again" spoke not only of the Jews returning to their homeland (in the time of Nehemiah); it would also have a dual application. It would also speak to the great and final restoration which will take place at the Lord's Second Coming, depicted in Zechariah as the remnant.[1547]

When Daniel was given the prophecy by the angel Gabriel it had been sixty-seven years since he had been apprehended and exiled to Babylon. He knew that according to the word given to Jeremiah; the captivity of the people was at an end. So he began praying for forgiveness for the sins of the nation, for the promised re-gathering of the people, and for the restoration of Jerusalem. Here in Daniel chapter nine, he receives an answer.

The Greatest Old Testament Prophecy

In the Book of Daniel, in a mere eight verses we are made privy to what is perhaps the most comprehensive series of prophecies in the briefest amount of words found in Scripture. I believe Daniel 9:20–27 to be the most profound prophetic passage in the Bible, for in it are references to events which will occur in measured spans of time (Weeks) which allowed the students of prophecy to calculate to the day, even to the hour, even to the exact moment when the Messiah

---

[1546] Jeremiah 29:10
[1547] Jeremiah 29:14; Zechariah 8:6, 8, 12

would make His first public appearance. In this way, the Jewish people could and can identify with certainty just who their Messiah was and is![1548]

The Great Sanhedrin was an assembly of Jewish judges who constituted the legislative body—the Supreme Court of Israel in Jesus' day. These scholars of scripture and prophecy could have; had they chose to, calculated the time of Messiah's coming and subsequently would have known that Jesus was indeed the "Promised One." However, as they watched the people flock to hear and be healed by this commoner their resentment grew. Consumed with their own self-importance and feeling their authority threatened, they ignored their own scriptures.

Certainly one would think that the next generation of priests and rabbinic who would see the destruction of the Temple would have even more conclusive evidence that Yahusha-Jesus was indeed the Messiah, for scripture indicated that the Messiah would be "cut off" before "the sanctuary" was destroyed![1549] To this day most rabbinic scholars evade this authenticating scripture while throughout the world they acknowledge the destruction of the Temple as having occurred in 70 AD, commemorating it at Tisha B'Av.

While the Christological interpretation clearly points to the Messiah coming before the destruction of the Temple, some Jewish scholars maintain that the prophetic passage ended with the destruction of the Temple by the Romans.* However, this view is untenable for it disregards the last verse (9:27) which clearly addresses the events which will take place during the final "One Week" (seven years). This (verse 27) clearly identifies itself as taking place at the conclusion of the latter days—with the phrase "even until the consummation." It also expounds on the rise of the "prince that shall come" (the Antichrist) whose brief reign completes the "Seventieth Week," thereby satisfying the prophecy.

> *Note: Daniel 9:24-27 was interpreted by Shlomo Yitzchaki (Rashi), 1040-1105 AD as foretelling events that happened during the Babylonian captivity until the rebuilding of the Second Temple and on to the Roman invasion. Rashi explained the phrase "Seventy weeks" refers to seventy times seven years, or 490 years. This he said refers to the seventy years of exile from the destruction of the First Temple until this vision, and the entire 420-year period of the Second Temple ending with Titus' invasion. Once again, Rashi completely evades explaining the initial coming of "Messiah the Prince,"[1550] as well as His physical execution—being "cut off;"[1551] as well as the "confirming of a covenant for One Week;" "the consummation" of the Age," and "the prince that shall come"—the Antichrist.

1548 Luke 19:44
1549 Daniel 9:28
1550 Daniel 9:25
1551 Daniel 9:26

The Prophecy

While I concede this prophecy is challenging, it may be understood by the earnest seeker whose heart is open. Our Lord is predisposed to cloak Himself from those whose heads are swollen with knowledge while their hearts are swollen with pride. In contrast, He reveals His mysteries to the humble and the tenderhearted who seek Him for understanding.[1552] Daniel was such a man.

> 20. "And while I was speaking, and praying, and confessing my sin and the sin of my people Israel, and presenting my supplication before the Lord my God for the holy mountain of my God;
>
> 21. yea, whiles I was speaking in prayer, even the man (messenger angel) Gabriel, whom I had seen in the vision at the beginning, being caused to fly swiftly, touched me about the time of the evening oblation.
>
> 22. And he informed me, and talked with me, and said, O Daniel, I am now come forth to give thee skill and understanding.
>
> 23. At the beginning of thy supplications the commandment came forth, and I am come to shew thee; for thou art greatly beloved: therefore understand the matter, and consider the vision.
>
> 24. Seventy weeks are determined upon thy people and upon thy holy city, to finish the transgression, and to make an end of sins, and to make reconciliation for iniquity, and to bring in everlasting righteousness, and to seal up the vision and prophecy, and to anoint the most Holy.
>
> 25. Know therefore and understand, that from the going forth of the commandment to restore and to build Jerusalem unto (until) the Messiah the Prince shall be seven weeks, and threescore and two weeks: the street shall be built again, and the wall, even in troublous times.
>
> 26. And after threescore and two weeks shall Messiah be cut off (killed), but not for himself: and the people of the prince that shall come shall destroy the city and the sanctuary; and the end thereof shall be with a flood, and unto the end of the war desolations are determined.
>
> 27. And he (the Anti-Christ) shall confirm the covenant with many for one week: and in the midst of the week he shall cause the sacrifice and the oblation to cease, and for the overspreading of abominations he shall make it desolate, even until the consummation, and that determined shall be poured upon the desolate." (Daniel 9:20-27)

1552 Matthew 11:25

Meant to Be Understood

Upon appearing to Daniel, the angel Gabriel told him, "thou art greatly beloved (of GOD); therefore" HE has sent me to give "skill and understanding" to the matter.[1553] To this point Daniel and those who would afterward study these scriptures would be able to know what was in the future for Israel; even the distant future.

> Note: Gabriel is GOD's foremost messenger when vital communications need to be hand delivered. It was Gabriel who GOD sent to bring this important revelation to a Jew named Daniel and later to a Jewess named Mariam (Mary). It was Gabriel who said to each of them, they were "greatly beloved" or "highly favored" by GOD.[1554] And, it was Gabriel who gave each of them a prophetic word relative to the Messiah's coming. Mary was told of His birth,[1555] and Daniel of His death.[1556]

The Story Begins

The story of the "Seventy Weeks" began when the angel Gabriel appeared to Daniel while he was in prayer for his own sins and for the sins of his people (the Jews).[1557] The people had transgressed (Hebrew, *pasha*)—broken away from GOD's just authority. They had integrated into the heathen Chaldean culture. They had adopted the attitudes and appetites so common to man.

In a most beautiful prayer of repentance[1558] Daniel poured himself out as a drink offering. His supplication touched GOD's heart in such a way that GOD dispatched Gabriel and told him to "fly swiftly" and deliver a revelation which went far beyond what Daniel had been pondering.[1559]

We are told in Daniel 9:2, that Daniel had "understood by books the number of the years, whereof the word of the Lord came to Jeremiah the prophet that HE would accomplish seventy years in the desolation of Jerusalem."[1560] These seventy years were also recorded in the book of Chronicles.

> "And them that had escaped from the sword carried he away to Babylon; where they were servants to him and his sons until the reign of the kingdom of Persia: to fulfil the word of the Lord by the mouth of Jeremiah, until the land had enjoyed (paid for) her sabbaths: for as long as she lay desolate she kept sabbath, to fulfil threescore and ten years." (2 Chronicles 36:20-21)

1553 Daniel 9:22
1554 Luke 1:26, 28, 31
1555 Luke 1:31
1556 Daniel 9:27
1557 Daniel 9:20
1558 Daniel 9:3-19
1559 Daniel 9:21
1560 Jeremiah 29:10

GOD had imposed a punishment on the Jewish people which HE said would be implemented if the people transgress.[1561] It would be realized in their being taken captive and in the desolation (ruin) of Jerusalem.[1562] With only three years (of the prescribed seventy years) of captivity remaining, Daniel would beseech the Lord for mercy and forgiveness, even if it were for GOD's own namesake.[1563]

The Five-fold Promise

> "Seventy weeks are determined upon thy people and upon thy holy city, to finish the transgression, and to make an end of sins, and to make reconciliation for iniquity, and to bring in everlasting righteousness, and to seal up the vision and prophecy, and to anoint the most Holy." (Daniel 9:24)

This all-important message would emphasize what GOD had long before spoken to Moses; HIS unwavering promise to punish disobedience and afterward, when the wrongdoer sees their wrongdoings and repents—to forgive them.

> Note: This is the Biblical model which parents are to use in correcting children. The child must recognize their wrongdoings, admit their guilt, ask for forgiveness, take their punishment, and vow to amend their ways. If the child is truly sorry and serves his punishment, the parent is to forgive and reconcile with the child.

As the prophecy unfolds, we are told in verse 24 what this portion of scripture is about. First, it is "to finish the transgressions and make an end of (their) sins." Second, it is to make "reconciliation for (their) iniquity" (by their accepting Him as their atonement). And third, it is "to bring in everlasting righteousness" (the return of the Savior; their being forgiven and found righteous, and the establishment of His everlasting Kingdom).

In order for this to take place the offender would need to first acknowledge their transgressions. Second, repent and reverse their behavior, and third, offer (actually accept) a suitable recompense (an atonement) for their transgression. Only then can reconciliation and restoration with GOD be had. Only then can one reach a state wherein it may be said they have attained everlasting righteousness.

This formula leading to everlasting righteousness was accomplished at the Cross of Calvary. Not only would this apply retroactively to Daniel's people (the Jewish people), but it would also apply to as many as would call upon their Savior and receive Him into their hearts.[1564]

> "For whosoever shall call upon the name of the Lord shall be saved." (Romans 10:13)

1561 Daniel 9:11; Leviticus 26:11-39
1562 Daniel 9:18; Jeremiah 25:11
1563 Daniel 9:19
1564 John 3:36

> "For thus saith the Lord God, the Holy One of Israel; In returning and rest shall ye be saved; in quietness and in confidence shall be your strength: and ye would not." (Isaiah 30:15)

It was at this point that Gabriel began to introduce who it is that will become the recompense and by whom reconciliation would be made. It would be the "Messiah,"[1565] the Savior, who would "finish their transgressions," "make an end to sin," and "bring in everlasting righteousness."

> Note: Isaiah 59:14-21 is a parallel Scripture using the same vernacular. It speaks of GOD's judgment being "turned back" and justice delayed until the people acknowledge their "transgressions" and turn from their sin. This will only come about when judgment (reconciliation for their iniquity) is dispensed in "The Time of Jacob's Trouble" (the Seventieth Week). Then will the "arm" of GOD—Yahusha-Jesus go forth, vanquish their enemies, and offer "salvation" and everlasting "righteousness".

In His foreknowledge the Lord knew that when He would first come, mainstream Judaism would, as a nation, reject Him.[1566] Sadly, one last horrendous Week (the Seventieth Week) will be required to break their haughty spirit[1567] and compel the Jewish people to see that it has been their own disobedience, disregard and denial of Him which has brought them to the verge of extinction. Only then will they call upon Him and plead for forgiveness. Only then will their Deliverer deliver them![1568]

> "How shall we escape, if we neglect so great salvation; which at the first began to be spoken by the Lord, and was confirmed unto us by them that heard him..." (Hebrews 2:3)

> "Oh that the salvation (Yahusha) of Israel were come out of Zion! when the Lord bringeth back the captivity of his people, Jacob shall rejoice, and Israel shall be glad." (Psalm 14:7)

> "Because he hath set his love upon me, therefore will I deliver him: I will set him on high, because he hath known my name. He shall call upon me, and I will answer him: I will be with him in trouble; I will deliver him, and honour him. With long life will I satisfy him, and shew him my salvation (Yahusha)." (Psalm 91:14-16)

As previously stated, Daniel believed that the people would soon be emancipated and permitted to return to rebuild the Holy City...But how would this occur, and after that, then what?

It would come to pass that in 539 BC Babylon would, in one night, fall to Darius the Mede and the Persians.[1569] Later, in 536 BC, King Cyrus of Persia realizing, (as had King Darius) that

---

1565 Daniel 9:25
1566 Isaiah 53:3
1567 Isaiah 10:33
1568 Psalm 18:2, 40:17, 70:5, 144:2; Romans 11:26
1569 Daniel 5:31

the god of the Israelites was indeed GOD.[1570] So it was that he would issue a proclamation which allowed 42,360 exiles to return to Jerusalem to rebuild GOD's House.[1571]

Work began and the foundation was laid, but construction was interrupted several times by opposing factions. Eventually the builders became discouraged and all progress ceased. The Temple would lay untouched for fourteen years as the people returned to rebuilding their own homes and to their day-to-day affairs.[1572]

Then Zerubbabel was appointed governor of Judah. He himself was a descendent of David and was successful in reinvigorating the Israelites to continue to build with the expectation that the son of David (the Messiah) would soon come. Two contemporary prophets, Haggi and Zechariah (called prophets of Messianic hope) believed that the Messiah would delay His coming until individual repentance became national repentance. They were indeed correct, for it will require the Great Tribulation[1573] before the nation of Israel will acknowledge Yahusha-Jesus and have its spiritual birth.[1574]

The prophets understood the need for the Temple. Before their captivity it had been part of Israel's identity. In its absence and over the course of their time in exile in Babylon the people had become indifferent to GOD and to a large extent unconcerned about what HIS Word had to say. Some Israelite men intermarried and took to themselves pagan wives, and with pagan wives they accepted pagan practices. The priest offered polluted bread to GOD and the hearts and minds of many became bent after the things of the Gentiles. The time in which the Israelites had spent in the sea of affliction in Babylon had to a large degree failed to bring the people back into an intimate relationship with YAHUAH. So it was that GOD appointed Zechariah and Haggi prophets in order to awake the people from their lethargy. At the same time Governor Zerubbabel and the high priest of that day Joshua would compel the people to resume construction of the Temple which was completed in 516 BC.

It has been GOD's plan to have a Temple that could serve as the center of the spiritual life of the nation. First and foremost, it would keep HIM in the forefront of their lives and serve as a reminder to HIS faithfulness and covenant promises. The sacrificial system would force the people to face their sins and the need for atonement. All of this was part of GOD's plan in order to reserve a people for HIMSELF.[1575]

Still, this edifice, built with the hands of man was itself a type and when the building was given too much adoration and became an idol and its priests assumed the role of aristocrats rather than ministers of GOD, HE would providentially have it leveled. The Temple was, after all, only a figure of where GOD actually wanted to dwell. The human heart of the Believer is the abiding place and temple of the Holy Spirit.

1570 Daniel 6:26
1571 Ezra 1:2-3, 2:64
1572 Ezra 4:21-24
1573 Jeremiah 30:6-9
1574 Ezekiel 36:24-27
1575 Deuteronomy 7:6-8

"Know ye not that ye are the temple of God, and that the Spirit of God dwelleth in you?" (1 Corinthians 3:16)

The Question

The Judahites had already served nearly seventy years in Babylonian captivity, but GOD "determined"[1576] that a total of Seventy Weeks (490 years) would be needed "to finish the transgression, and to make an end of sins, and to make reconciliation for iniquity, and to bring in everlasting righteousness."[1577]

It is in the Gospel of Luke that the answer is provided as to why a protracted span of hundreds of years would be required. There we read that as Jesus entered Jerusalem for the last time, He looked upon the city "and wept over it."[1578] However, it was not the city, or even the Temple which He knew would be destroyed in just a few decades which caused Him to weep. He wept for His people Israel; for they had missed the time of His "visitation."[1579] In just a matter of days many would not only reject Him but be swept up in mob mentality and call for His execution.[1580]

So it was that He said, "If thou hadst known, even thou, at least in this day, the things which belong unto thy peace! (the blessings you might have had, but forfeited) But now they are (will be) hid from thy eyes (for an extended period)."[1581] In essence the Lord was saying, had you received Me as your atonement, your transgressions would have been paid for, your sufferings would have ended; your blessings would have been innumerable[1582] and you would have been restored and become the glory of nations.[1583] Instead it will require the full measure of 490 years before as a nation, you realized this.

It was told in Leviticus 25:8 and here in 26:18—"And if you will not hearken unto Me, then I will punish you seven times more for your sins." Seven times the 70 (then near completion) is a total of 490 years.

Seventy Weeks

The expression "Seventy Weeks" (v. 24) is explained as the total number of years in which GOD would deal solely with the Jewish people for their transgressions. The word "Week" or "Weeks," (Hebrew, *shabua*) is the plural of the word seven and a Hebrew expression referring to divisions of time. Each Week has a numerical value of seven years, therefore Seventy Weeks is another way of saying seventy sevens, or 70 x 7, for a total of 490 years.

If one considers that a Week is seven years, then we understand that a day is equal to one year.

We can see an example of the way GOD metes out punishment in Numbers 13:1–33. It is there we read that GOD punished the Israelites for their disbelief and mistrust after HE told

---

1576 Daniel 9:24
1577 Daniel 9:24
1578 Luke 19:41
1579 Luke 19:44
1580 Acts 3:14-15
1581 Luke 19:42
1582 Deuteronomy 30:9
1583 Zechariah 8:23; Isaiah 45:14, 25, 60:14

Moses to send spies and search out the land of Canaan which HE would give to the children of Israel. The spies went as ordered and returned after forty days with a report. All but two of the spies doubted that they were able to possess the land as it was inhabited by giants who they believed were undefeatable. This was an insult to GOD for it showed distrust in HIS promise that HE would give them the land. For their distrust GOD would punish that generation and have them spend the next forty years wandering in the wilderness before they could appropriate the promise. That indicates that HE designated one year for each of the forty days as a recompense, (to make reconciliation for iniquity—v. 24).

While punishment may be a useful tool to an objective, it is not in itself regenerative. Transformation requires recognition and omission of one's miscarriages. Spiritual regeneration requires not only recognition and omission but that one turn to GOD for forgiveness and restoration. Israel's long and painful journey will end, not when their sentence is served, but when they recognize their culpability, seek forgiveness and above all, seek relationship with Him.

> "So teach us to number our days, that we may apply our hearts unto wisdom. Return, O Lord, how long? and let it repent thee concerning thy servants. O satisfy us early with thy mercy; that we may rejoice and be glad all our days. Make us glad according to the days wherein thou hast afflicted us, and the years wherein we have seen evil. Let thy work appear unto thy servants, and thy glory unto their children. And let the beauty of the Lord our God be upon us: and establish thou the work of our hands upon us; yea, the work of our hands establish thou it." (Psalm 90:12-17)

Before proceeding, it is important to reiterate that the Seventy Weeks encompasses only the time when GOD was, is, or will (the Tribulation) be dealing directly with the Jewish people as they are still under the rod of correction.[1584] This 490 years excludes the many centuries since Christ's death and particularly from the day of Pentecost forward, when GOD would turn His attention to the Gentiles; as stated, "all that are afar off."[1585] During the Gentile dispensation the Jewish people would, as foretold,[1586] be scattered among the heathen nations.[1587]

Included in what is referred to as the Time of the Gentiles[1588] is the entire Church Age which has been going on now for nearly two thousand years and will continue until such time as the Church is divinely removed. Only at some unrevealed time after the Church is "caught up"[1589] will the final One Week, the "Seventieth Week"—the last seven years—Jacob's Trouble, begin.

The way in which GOD had Gabriel express these Seventy Weeks is very significant. Gabriel did not simply say seventy weeks. To reiterate and expand on what was said earlier, Gabriel presented the Weeks in segments. The first segment would encompass a period of 7 Weeks (49

1584 Ezekiel 20:34-37
1585 Acts 2:39
1586 Leviticus 26:33; Ezekiel 12:15, 20:23, 22:15
1587 Leviticus 26:33
1588 Romans 11:25
1589 Acts 4:14

years) beginning with the command to rebuild Jerusalem following their captivity. Afterward the second period of 62 Weeks (434 years) would occur from Jerusalem (the city) having been built up until the Messiah was recognized and crucified. A third period of 1 Week (7 years—"The Time of Jacob's Trouble") would eventually come after the Church Age, "finishing the transgression and bringing in everlasting rightness" with the return of the Messiah. Hence, 7 Weeks = (49 years), plus 62 Weeks (434 years) = 69 Weeks (483 years) plus 1 Week (7 years) = 490 years.

> Note: Why the first segment of 7 Weeks (49 years) is differentiated from the second segment of 62 Weeks is a matter of conjecture among scholars. The best explanation appears to relate to Nehemiah's return to Jerusalem to repair the breaches in the walls and gates. The city had laid in ruin since Nebuchadnezzar's siege and was dilapidated. Those Judeans who returned with Nehemiah to rebuild the city—"streets"—had to, out of necessity, clear the rubble and build themselves dwellings to live in while construction went forward on the wall. "the streets shall be built again, and the wall, even in troublesome times."[1590]

Time in Captivity – Church Age – Jacob's Trouble

Timeline of Daniel's 70 Weeks

Messiah's 1st Advent - Church Age - Jacobs Trouble – Messiah's 2nd Advent

| 7 Weeks / 62 Weeks   †   undisclosed time   / Antichrists reign & defeat

69 Wks. - 483 yrs.   /   Church Age   /   70th Week - 7 years
  Messiah's 1st advent & death /   Messiah's 2nd advent /

        (Daniel 9:25-26)   (Isa. 26:21; 27:1; Zech.14:2-3; Rev. 19:11-16)

> Note: The seventy years spoken by Jeremiah is the equivalent of ten Sabbatical years or ten jubilees. However, we see in Leviticus 26:17-18, 21, 28 that GOD would chastise the people seven fold for their transgressions; ten jubilees (70 years) x 7 fold = 490 years.
>
> Note: Both the Book of Jeremiah and the Book of Daniel take into account the year of Jubilee which occurs every seventh year. Described in the Mosaic Law[1591] is the stipulation that seven Sabbaths (Weeks)—49 years is the maximum period that the Land of Israel could remain outside the possession of its original owner or their heirs. GOD would keep HIS own Word and permit the people to return according to HIS own law.

1590 Daniel 9:25
1591 Leviticus chapter 25

The Scriptures tell of the Israelites being removed, plucked up, and led captive for their failing to remain faithful to their GOD. However, unlike Israel, GOD would be faithful to His Word concerning the jubilee restoration. He would restore to the heirs of Israel (His remnant) that which He had promised Abram.[1592]

Beginning with their Egyptian bondage to their Exodus; from their Babylonian captivity to their emancipation and return to Jerusalem. From the destruction of the Temple and the diaspora, to their repatriation to Palestine in the twentieth century, the Israelites have been in a continual state of strife and unrest. After repeated opportunities to reform, their sins drew the curtain closed; with light excluded—darkness prevails.

But Israel's education is not over. While HIS people retained their identity and continued their religious practices and traditions, HE became a vague impersonal entity. Accepted and acknowledged as the Creator, yes…but marginalized; more a concept than a reality. In contrast, what HE wants is a deep personal relationship with each of us as evidenced in the Song of Songs. The litmus test is, who can say with conviction, "I am my beloved's, and my beloved is mine?"[1593]

GOD had spoken through the Prophet Hosea and speaking both for that time and prophetically, HE would tell the people that because they would not acknowledge their offense and seek their king (Messiah) when He would come, He would "return" to His throne in heaven.[1594]

> "I will go and return to My place (heaven), till they acknowledge their offence, and seek My face: in their affliction they will seek Me early." (Hosea 5:15)

When this occurs, He will once again leave His heavenly throne,[1595] in the "latter days" bringing the "latter rain" (Revival) and complete the harvest of the remnant.

> "For the children of Israel shall abide many days without a king, and without a prince, and without a sacrifice, and without an image, and without an ephod, and without teraphim: afterward shall the children of Israel return, and seek the Lord their God, and David their king (Messianic King—Yahusha); and shall fear the Lord and his goodness in the latter days." (Hosea 3:4-5)

> "Then shall we know (if) we follow on (desire) to know the Lord: His going forth is prepared as the morning; and He shall come unto us as the rain, as the latter and former rain upon the earth." (Hosea 6:3)

The question then might be asked, when will this occur? While Scripture does not tell us precisely, we are given some insight. If we consider 2 Peter 3:8; "But, beloved, be not ignorant of this one thing, that one day is with the Lord as a thousand years, and a thousand years as one

---

1592 2 Chronicles 30:9
1593 Hebrews 6:3
1594 Psalm 110:1
1595 Psalm 3:4-5

day." Then looking back to Hosea 5:2 we read, "After two days He will revive us: in the third day He will raise us up, and we shall live in His sight." From these scriptures we may appreciate that the Jewish people are on the brink of their deliverance. We are now approaching two days or two thousand years since the Lord made His first appearance and was recognized as the Messiah.[1596]

While the Jewish people have returned to the land and have even been granted statehood, they have not yet earnestly sought Him and exclaimed, "Come let us return to the Lord: for He hath torn, and He will heal us; He hath smitten (us) and will bind us up."[1597] Sadly, He has yet to become the centerpiece of their lives.

> "Then shall they know that I am the Lord their GOD which caused them to be lead into captivity among the heathen; but I have gathered them unto their own land, and have left none of them anymore. Neither will I hide my face any more from them: for I have poured out my spirit upon the house of Israel, saith the Lord God." (Ezekiel 39:28-29)

Today the Jewish people have returned to Palestine; however, they only possess a pittance of the divine land grant promised to Abraham. Even now what real estate they currently occupy is being subdivided by the New World Order and given to usurpers. Currently Israel's safety is in great peril as she nearly lost a former ally (the United States) who under its former president (Obama) pandered to her enemies.

The Bible speaks in many scriptures, as it does here in Daniel 9:27 that in the latter days, there will come great deceptions; notably the pretense of peace and the rise of a world leader who will charm the Jewish people.

The near annihilation of Judah and Jerusalem is also in Israel's future.[1598] Catastrophic events; a series of wars to be followed by the greatest of all wars will take place in that last "One Week" (the Seventieth Week) of the prophecy. The Battle of Armageddon will be the culmination of the Seventieth Week at which time Messiah the Prince will descend from the heavens and will defeat the Antichrist and all who oppose Israel.[1599] Then Yahusha-Jesus shall—for the last time—re-gather the surviving Jewish people from all over the world to what was the expanse of land promised Abraham.[1600] There and then, He will establish His kingdom on earth for a thousand years.[1601]

> "Behold, the Lord hath proclaimed unto the end of the world, Say ye to the daughter of Zion, Behold, thy salvation (Yahsha) cometh; behold, his reward (salvation) is with him, and his work before him." (Isaiah 62:11)

1596 Zechariah 9:9; Luke 19:33-38
1597 Hosea 5:1
1598 Joel 3:1
1599 Isaiah 59:16-20, 63:4
1600 Deuteronomy 30:3; Matthew 24:31
1601 Jeremiah 31:8-9; Deuteronomy 30:3; Matthew 24:31

The Partition of the Weeks

For the purpose of clarity, let us take a closer look at these four timeframes presented in the prophecy and what transpires during each.

We are told that Seventy Weeks would be the total amount of time required to make an end of their transgressions. Until that time the Jewish people would and will go through many ordeals. In times past they have relied largely upon their own skill, wit, and military might to deal with their enemies without earnestly seeking the Lord or petitioning HIM for divine intervention. Joel 2:17 tells us that HE actually wants them to rely on HIM and that "the priests and ministers of the Lord (are to come and) weep between the porch (the people) and the altar (HIMSELF), and let them say (to HIM) spare thy people…"

At the end of the first division of time (v. 25), a period of (7) Weeks (49 years) the Jewish people would begin returning from their seventy-year exile in Babylon to Judah. Although they would return, they were not entirely free, nor did they have their own nation. They were still subjects of the Persians who had replaced the Babylonians.[1602] The Judeans would afterward continue for many centuries under the oppressive heel of Gentile rulers because they still failed to recognize their transgression; neither had they comprehended what it means to turn one's heart completely over to GOD. "Love thy GOD with all thine heart…"[1603]

Nothing less than "all" of one's heart is acceptable! Simply acknowledging HIM as many do or following a religious practice does not meet GOD's criteria. The Israelites still had not grasped what Moses was so emphatic about.[1604]

> "That thou mayest love the Lord thy God, and that thou mayest obey his voice, and that thou mayest cleave unto him: for he is thy life, and the length of thy days: that thou mayest dwell in the land which the Lord sware unto thy fathers, to Abraham, to Isaac, and to Jacob, to give them." (Deuteronomy 30:20)

The second division of time is (62) sevens—(434 years). It would extend from the time that Jerusalem was built up (at the end of the 49 years), until the time when the Messiah would be revealed and be "cut off"—die (v. 26).

Recapping: The first division was Seven (7) Weeks, and the second division was Sixty-two (62) Weeks. We have therefore accounted for Sixty-Nine (69) Weeks (483 years). This leaves only One (1) Week (7 years) remaining in order for the prophecy to be fulfilled.

This last Week (the Seventieth) is not the third division as one might expect, but rather the fourth; for interpolated between the second division and the fourth is an unmentioned division/dispensation which was not told to either Daniel or to any of the Jewish prophets. It is what the Apostle Paul would later refer to as a "mystery."[1605] Furthermore, there aren't any numbers

---
1602 Daniel 5:30-31
1603 Deuteronomy 6:5
1604 Deuteronomy 30:15-20
1605 Ephesian 3:3-6, 9

of Weeks assigned to this division. It is simply a protracted period of time between the 69th and 70th Week.; the dispensation of the Church.

The reason it is omitted from the prophecy is really quite logical. It has nothing to do with the time in which Jewish people will be in their homeland as an autonomous nation. They will be serving out, as it were, their sentence in the great diaspora and scattered among the nations.

> "And the Lord shall scatter you among the nations, and ye shall be left few in number among the heathen, whither the Lord shall lead you…But if from thence thou shalt seek the Lord thy God, thou shalt find him, if thou seek him with all thy heart and with all thy soul. When thou art in tribulation, and all these things are come upon thee, even in the latter days, if thou turn to the Lord thy God, and shalt be obedient unto his voice; (For the Lord thy GOD is a merciful GOD;) HE will not forsake thee, neither destroy thee, nor forget the covenant with thy fathers which HE sware unto them."
> (Deuteronomy 4:27, 29-31)

This great gulf of time (the third division) would be necessary before the Jewish people would earnestly seek Him, find Him, and "cleave" to Him.[1606] It is this deep relationship of acknowledgement, dependency, and gratitude which the Lord Yahusha-Jesus would latter call the "Born-Again" experience; the spiritual birth.[1607]

Regardless of whether one is a Jew or a Gentile, it is this same imperative which is necessary if one is to be saved and accepted into the family of GOD.[1608] It is this very same imperative which eludes most of "religious" Christendom and differentiates those who think they are saved from those who according to Scripture actually are.[1609]

The Apostle Paul spoke of the third division as a "mystery;" an unknown. It would be offered when, through the New Covenant the Gentiles would be afforded a similar opportunity as had the Jewish people. They too could only find Him if they searched for Him with all of their hearts.[1610] This third dispensation is commonly referred to as the Church Age.

> "…how that by revelation he made known unto me the mystery; (as I wrote afore in few words, whereby, when ye read, ye may understand my knowledge in the mystery of Christ—Crucified) which in other ages was not made known unto the sons of men, as it is now revealed unto his holy apostles and prophets by the Spirit; that the Gentiles should be fellow heirs, and of the same body, and partakers of his promise in Christ by the gospel:…to make all men see what is the fellowship of the mystery, which from the beginning of the world hath been hid in God, who created all things by Jesus Christ…"
> (Ephesians 3:3-6, 9)

1606 Deuteronomy 30:20
1607 John 3:3
1608 Acts 4:12
1609 John 14:6
1610 Jeremiah 29:13

During the hiatus (the third division of time) the prophetic clock has been temporarily halted. The clock will begin ticking once again and begin counting down the final Week at the precise moment that an agreement is ratified by the Antichrist permitting the rebuilding of the Temple in Jerusalem. He will "confirm the covenant" (v.27), (Hebrew, *gabar*—a strong binding agreement) for one final Week. This final Week (7 years) is the fourth division which will end when, as spoken in Zechariah,[1611] the Lord shall touch down on the Mount of Olives fulfilling His promised Second Coming.[1612]

The elusive interval (the third division—the Church age) is why Gabriel spoke of the fourth division as "One Week," leaving a gap and separating it from the other 69 Weeks.

The fourth and last division is by all accounts almost upon us, for the Jewish people have once again returned and occupied their homeland and become an autonomous nation. Soon the True Church (to be distinguished from the false World Ecumenical Church) will, according to Scripture, disappear and be taken skyward in what is referred to as the Pre-tribulation snatching away (rapture), (Latin *rapturo*, Greek, *harpazo*).

> "Then we (Believers) which are alive and remain shall be caught up together with them in the clouds, to meet the Lord in the air: and so shall we ever be with the Lord." (1 Thessalonians 4:17)

With the Church gone, the third dispensation will have ended and GOD will once again turn HIS full attention to Israel.[1613] In the last half three and one half years of the of the seven years Tribulation GOD will authorize unimaginable sorrow.[1614] The world will convulse with war and natural disasters as the last of the "Four horsemen of Apocalypse"[1615] gallops into the arena. And yet in this final recompense for their transgression will arise the motivation for the nation of Israel to seek their Savior!

> "I will go and return to My place, till they acknowledge their offence, and seek My face: in their affliction they will seek Me early." (Hosea 5:15)

The Tribulation will begin with the possibility of peace and the rise of a charismatic leader who will give the illusion that peace in the Middle East has finally become a reality. Daniel spoke of him in Daniel chapter eight.

> "And in the latter time of their kingdom, when the transgressors are come to the full, a king of fierce countenance (Antichrist), and understanding dark sentences, shall stand

---

1611 Zechariah 14:4
1612 Joel 3:16-21
1613 Isaiah 54:7
1614 Zephaniah 1:14; Joel 2:2, 31; Isaiah 22:5; Amos 5:18-20
1615 Revelation 4:6-8

up (come to the forefront of world politics). And his power shall be mighty, but not by his own power (but by Satan's power): and he shall destroy wonderfully, and shall prosper (by pretense), and practice, and shall destroy the mighty and the holy people (the Jewish people). And through his policy also he shall cause craft to prosper (by deceit) in his hand; and he shall magnify himself in his heart, and by peace (the guise of peace) shall destroy many: he shall also stand up against the Prince of princes (Messiah); but he shall be broken (defeated) without hand (in the end)." (Daniel 8:23-25)

Only at the end of the 70th Week will GOD judge those who have managed to survive that last Week.[1616] Each survivor will then be judged in the "valley of Jehoshaphat" (Jehovah has Judged).[1617] It is then that the wheat will be separated from the chaff, and the sheep nations from the goat nations.[1618] Only then will HE reconcile to Himself the remaining remnant of the Jewish people, along with those Gentiles who have accepted Yahusha-Jesus as their Savior.

"For I will cleanse their blood that I have not cleansed: for the Lord dwelleth in Zion." (Joel 3:21)

Establishing the Actual Dates

As mentioned in the beginning of this study, in order to prove the prophecy, we first need to establish the date the prophecy was to begin. We are told it would be inaugurated with the issuance of a "commandment" to permit the rebuilding of the city in Jerusalem.

"Know therefore and understand, that from the going forth of the commandment to restore and to build Jerusalem..." (Daniel 9:25)

While there was a proclamation issued in writing by King Cyrus of Persia in 538 BCE,[1619] it was not the decree which started the prophetic clock and began the countdown of the "sixty-nine Weeks." Cyrus' proclamation spoke of the rebuilding of GOD's house (the Temple). However, Daniel's prophecy speaks of the rebuilding of the city itself.

Well before Ezra's time, King Jeconiah's grandson Zerubbabel led the return of tens of thousands of Jews back to Jerusalem in 537 BC. It was not until 457 BC that Ezra actually went to Jerusalem bringing gold, silver, and Temple vessels[1620] to an already existing Temple. He was not joined by Nehemiah until 444 BCE when Nehemiah arrived from the Persian court to complete the repair of the walls of the city.

1616 Zechariah 13:8
1617 Joel 3:12
1618 Mathew 25:32-33
1619 2 Chronicles 36:22, 23
1620 Ezra 7:11-26; 8:31

Looking again at Daniel 9:25 we see that it speaks of someone who would give a "commandment to restore and build Jerusalem" (the city). We see the fulfillment in Nehemiah 2:1–8 where we read that permission was given "in the month of Nisan, in the twentieth year of King Artaxerxes *(Longimanus)*." The year was 3317 in the Hebrew Calendar. That particular year happened to be a year with an intercalary month (II Adar) and that additional month was inserted into the calendar just before Nisan. In 3317, Nisan 1 fell on April 2, 444 BCE.

It is this proclamation which would begin the prophetic clock counting off the 69 weeks until the Messiah would be publicly revealed and acknowledged as the Messiah.

> Note: Hebrew months were based on visual observations of the moon. If the moon was obscured, corrections were made in subsequent months, which is why the intercalary month was inserted. Therefore, the dates above should be accurate to within one day at most.

To determine the end date of the 69 Weeks we again look at the scripture where we read, "unto the Messiah the Prince shall be seven weeks (7 years x 7 = 49 years), and threescore and two weeks (62 years x 7 = 434 years): the street shall be built again, and the wall, even in troublous times" (Daniel 9:25). Simple arithmetic determines that 49 years + 434 years = 483 years.

Scripture tells us the Sixty-Nine Weeks would conclude on the day the Messiah would be recognized by a great throng of Jews as He entered Jerusalem on a donkey. That was fulfilled on (Palm Sunday) March 29, 33 AD. This was just five days before Yahusha-Jesus's execution which took place on Friday, April 3, 33 AD.[1621] This was prophesied by the Prophet Zechariah more than five hundred years earlier (circa 487 BC).

> "Rejoice greatly, O daughter of Zion; shout, O daughter of Jerusalem: behold, thy King cometh unto thee: he is just, and having salvation; lowly, and riding upon an ass, and upon a colt the foal of an ass." (Zechariah 9:9)

Calculating the Time

Before we can prove the prophecy there remains yet one more measurement of time which must be qualified. That is how many days are in a prophetic year?

A Lunar year is 354 days. A Solar year is 365 days. A Julian calendar year is 365 ¼ days which is achieved by incorporating a leap year every fourth year. In Judaism it was customary to have a 12-month, 360-day year, inserting a thirteenth month (the intercalary month) to correct the calendar when necessary.

A Prophetic Year is a Biblical calendar year of 360 days. It supersedes all of man's calendars and disregards his various adjustments. We can verify that GOD's prophetic year is 360 days

---

[1621] Mark 11:7–10; Psalm 118:26

as we are told that exactly 1,260 days (42 months)[1622] marks the midpoint[1623] of the seven-year Tribulation and the beginning of the last three and a half years (the Great Tribulation).[1624]

Having scripturally established the dates of the 69 weeks as having begun on Nisan 1, 444 BCE (April 2, 444 BC), and have ended on Nisan 9, 33 AD (March 29, 33 AD), we can now verify the prophecy by doing the math.

In Daniel 9:27 we see that the last half of the "Week" is 1,260 days, therefore a "Week" is 2,520 days. If we then multiply the number of days (2,520) times the number of Weeks (69) we arrive at 173,880 days; the total number of days, between King Artaxerxes proclamation and Yahusha-Jesus's entry into Jerusalem.

We then need to adapt this number to the Julian calendar used today.

If we convert 173,880 to solar years (the time required for the earth to make one complete revolution around the sun) we arrive at 365 days, 5 hours, 48 minutes, 45.51 seconds or 365.24219. To complete this calculation, we divide 173,880; by 365.24219. This gives us the quotient 476.067443815. When rounded to its nearest integer (whole number) we have 476 solar years, or 173,855 days.

If we look to the Julian calendar, we see Nisan 1, 444 BCE (April 2, 444 BCE) is Julian day 1,559,344. If we add 173,855 days, we arrive on Julian day 1,733,199—Nisan 9, 33 AD (Sunday, March 29th 33 AD); the date Jesus made His triumphal entry into Jerusalem!

If we were to apply the 365 days, 5 hours, 48 minutes, 45.51 seconds or 365.24219 to the timeline from the beginning—to the end we have not only arrived at the day; not only the hour, but from what we can ascertain, we may have arrive at the very minute when the first shouts of acclamation as the Messiah sounded as He entered Jerusalem.

The Messiah to Die

In the next verse[1625] we are told that the Messiah would be "cut off," (referring to His crucifixion.) He would die, "but not for Himself,"[1626] but for those who accept Him as their Savior.

> "And after threescore and two weeks shall Messiah be cut off, but not for himself: and the people (army) of the prince (the Antichrist) that shall come shall destroy the city (Jerusalem) and the sanctuary (Temple); and the end thereof shall be with a flood (an army), and unto the end of the war desolations are determined." (Daniel 9:26)

It is halfway through Daniel 9:26 that the focus and the subject of the verse suddenly shifts from "Messiah the Prince" to another prince; "the people of the prince that shall come and

---

1622 Revelation 11:2, 12:6, 13:5
1623 Daniel 9:27; Matthew 24:15-16
1624 Matthew 24:21; Jeremiah 30:7; Daniel 12:1
1625 Daniel 9:26
1626 Daniel 9:26

destroy the city and sanctuary." This prince of the people is none other than the Antichrist—the prince who the people have revered; who works for the prince of darkness (Satan).[1627] He will, during the first three and one half years of the Tribulation, deceive many Jews into believing he is their long awaited Messiah.[1628] But then he exposes himself, for we read that in the "midst" (middle) of the week he will desecrate the sanctuary in the new Temple and begin to carry out his objective of annihilating the Jewish race.[1629] He will bring "a flood" (his army) against Israel, nearly destroying Jerusalem.[1630]

> "And he (Anti-Christ) shall confirm the covenant with many for one week (7 years): and in the midst (middle) of the week he shall cause the sacrifice and the oblation to cease, and for the overspreading of abominations he shall make it desolate, even until the consummation, and that determined shall be poured upon the desolate." (Daniel 9:27)

Jeremiah, as other prophets, made it abundantly clear that this will be a far worse time for the Jewish people and for Israel than anything they have ever experienced.[1631]

> "Alas for the day is so great, so that none is like it; it is even the time of Jacob's Trouble…" (Jeremiah 30:7)

This horrific time is depicted in great detail in the New Testament book of the Revelation where sixteen chapters (chapters 4–19) are devoted to the Jews and Israel during the last days.

> Note: Elsewhere in the book of Daniel, Daniel referred to this dark prince that shall come by other names: "the Little Horn,"[1632] "the King of Fierce Continence,"[1633] and the "Willful King."[1634] This false Messiah will arrive on the world stage a minimum of seven years before our actual Messiah, Yahusha-Jesus returns.

1627 2 Thessalonians 2:8-9
1628 Mark 13:5-6
1629 Revelation 12:13-17
1630 Daniel 9:26; Joel chapter 2; Ezekiel chapters 38, 39
1631 Daniel 12:1; Joel 2:11; Zephaniah 1:14-18
1632 Daniel 7:8, 8:9
1633 Daniel 8:23
1634 Daniel 11:36

Timeline of Daniel's Seventieth Week

| Resurrection (Rapture) of Believers. | Middle East Peace Accord. Israel's deceived. Permission for and the building of the 3rd Temple. | Peace Accord broken. Abomination of desolation desecrates the Temple. Antichrist attacks Israel. | Christ returns

Antichrists defeated |
|---|---|---|---|
| Church Age Ends. | Tribulation begins. | The Great Tribulation The time of Jacob's trouble. | Kingdom age begins |

|———|———— 3 ½ years ————|———— 3 ½ years of GOD's Judgement ————|

	Antichrist rises to power	Antichrist rules as world dictator	
	Time of tranquility World Government Established.	War looms	Israel persecuted. Divine Judgement escalates.	Armageddon

Israel recognizes Jesus |

Timeline of the Passion Week.

Saturday - Nisan 8 – March 28, 33 AD

- Jesus came to Bethany to visit Lazarus, Mary, and Martha. A dinner was served in His honor (John 12:1). This was the first of three suppers with them. Mary anointed Jesus's feet with spikenard (John 12:3).
- Out of envy, the Chief Priests think to kill Jesus.

Sunday - Nisan 9 – March 29 The end date of the 69th Week

- Messiah's Triumphal entrance into Jerusalem (Palm Sunday) (John 12:1–13).
- Jesus weeps over Jerusalem, curses moneychangers in the Temple, and returns to Bethany. Chief priests plot to kill Him.

Monday - Nisan 10 – March 30

- Jesus again comes from Bethany and curses the fig tree (Mark 11:12).
- Jesus cleanses the temple a second time (Matthew 21:12–13; Luke 19:46).

> Note: Mark records the actual sequence whereas Matthew's account combines the whole story into one factual account and is not chronological.

- Passover lambs are selected on Nisan 10 (Ref. Exodus 12:3). Jesus entered and cleansed the Temple of the money changers at which time the scribes and chief priest marked Him for death (Mark 11:18).

> Note: Presenting Himself in this manner was perhaps anti-typical of Exodus 12:3 where symbolically He was selected as the Lamb to be slain four days later.

- Jesus returns to Bethany (Mark 11:19).

Tuesday - Nisan 11 – March 31

- Jesus returns to Jerusalem. "And in the morning, as they passed by, they saw the fig tree dried up from the roots" (Mark 11:20).
- Jesus's authority is questioned (Mark 11:27).
- The Olivet Discourse – The destruction of Jerusalem in 70 AD is foretold (Matthew 24:1).

Wednesday - Nisan 12 – April 1

- This was "two days before Passover." Chief priests plot to take Jesus (Matthew 26:2–5; Mark 14:1–2; Luke 22:1–2).
- Judas conspires with chief priests to betray Jesus.
- Jesus retires to the Mount of Olives.

Thursday - Nisan 13 – April 2

- Disciples are sent to prepare the upper room for the eight-day Passover feast. Jesus celebrates a pre-Passover meal (His last supper) with His disciples. "…on the first day of unleavened bread" (Mark 14:12–16; Matthew 26:17–19; Luke 22:7–13). Judas betrays Jesus, and Jesus is seized, arrested, and given a nighttime trial.

Friday - Nisan 14 – April 3

- Friday, the 14th of Nisan, is the actual the day before the Passover. Passover was not celebrated for the Jewish people until sundown—about 6 pm that Friday. One minute after sundown on that Friday, Nissan 15 began (Ref. Leviticus 23:5).

> Note: Some confuse the actual Passover with the expression "day of preparation for the Passover" as recorded in John 19:14; Matthew 27:62.

Summary:

- Judas is identified as the betrayer (Matthew 26:21–25; Mark 14:18–21; Luke 22:21–23; John 13:21–30).
- Jesus did not eat the Passover meal but had a common meal—the Lord's Supper (Matthew 26:26–29; Mark 14:22–25; Luke 22:14–16). The Passover meal was not eaten until sundown after He was crucified, twenty-four hours after the Lord's Supper.
- Around midnight, Jesus retired to Gethsemane and was arrested (Matthew 26:30–56, Mark 14:26–52; Luke 22:39–53; John 18:1–12).
- Sometime between midnight and 6:00 am (but still Nisan 14), the trial before the high council took place while it was still dark.
- At the "sixth hour" (John 19:14–15) (Roman time: six hours after sunrise=noon) Jesus is brought before Pilate, sentenced to die, and is led away directly to be crucified.
- The Crucifixion began on the 14th of Nissan. Jesus dies three hours later at the ninth hour (Mark 15:34) (Roman time=Friday 3:00 pm). This was at the very moment the Passover lamb was to be slain at the Temple. From noon to 3:00 pm (the sixth to the ninth hours), the sky was dark. This may have been a literal fulfillment of Exodus 12:6 where the Passover lamb was to be killed at evening. In the Hebrew, evening actually reads "between the evenings," as the Jews had two evenings: three o'clock and six o'clock or sundown.
- It was between 3:00–4:00 pm that thousands of lambs are being slain for Passover and it was at the same time that Jesus died. Passover (Nissan 15) officially begins Friday at sundown. From the moment Jesus was laid in the tomb until sunset, the Jews reckoned it to be the first day in the grave, even though it was only a few hours.

Saturday - Nissan 15 – April 4

- Jesus is in the grave.

Sunday - Nissan 16 – April 5

- Jesus is Resurrected. "…when the Sabbath was past…And very early in the morning, the first day of the week, they came unto the sepulcher…". And a young man said to the women, "Ye seek Jesus of Nazareth, which was crucified…He is risen!" (Mark 16:1–2, 6)

APPENDIX D

MYSTERY BABYLON—REVELATION CHAPTER 17

"...I will tell thee the mystery of the women, and of the beast that carrieth her, which hath the seven heads and ten horns..." (Revelation 17:7)

Introduction

At the moment of our conception GOD implants a spirit in each of us. In that spirit HE embeds a germ of faith which not only testifies of a HIM but prompts us to want to know and please HIM.[1635]

Satan has capitalized on this wonderful inclination by inventing a man-made alternative to a personal relationship. We have come to call this substitute… religion.

Using his genius and talent of persuasion—as he once did in a pre-Adamic time when he convinced a third of heavens angels to follow him,[1636] he finds vulnerable men and women and enlists them into his service as his ministers.

(Image Source: GOODSALT)

> "Be sober, be vigilant; because your adversary the devil, as a roaring lion, walketh about, seeking who he may devour…" (1 Peter 5:8)

> "For such are false apostles, deceitful workers, transforming themselves into the apostles of Christ. And no marvel; for Satan himself is transformed into an angel of light. Therefore it is no great thing if his ministers also be transformed as the ministers of righteousness; whose end shall be according to their works." (2 Corinthians 11:13-15)

1635 Job 1:1
1636 Revelation 12:4

Most of these worker inductees truly love and fear GOD and have entered into clerical vocations or monastic life for admirable reasons. They are nevertheless pawns of Satan; indoctrinated to the point that they actually believe, and so perpetuate the lies which they have bought into.

> "He (the Lord Jesus) answered and said unto them (the religious Pharisees), Well hath Esaias (Isaiah) prophesied of you hypocrites, as it is written, This people honoureth Me with their lips, but their heart is far from me. Howbeit in vain do they worship me, teaching for doctrines the commandments of men." (Mark 7:6-7)

> "Ye are of your father the devil, and the lusts of your father ye will do. He was a murderer from the beginning, and abode not in the truth, because there is no truth in him. When he speaketh a lie, he speaketh of his own: for he is a liar, and the father of it." (John 8:44)

One religion claiming to be Christ's authentic church and earthly representative is nothing more than a political machine with an addiction for power and all that comes with it. Domination is at the pinnacle of human aspiration, even trumping wealth. So it is that by wearing the right garb, claiming divine authority, indoctrinating followers from childhood, and developing their own commandments and sacraments, these charlatans have managed to override mans' natural defenses to question the nonsensical and reject the absurd.[1637]

Using the five senses, particularly sight, sound, and smell, religion anesthetize their victims. Visually, it stimulates with imagery. Great cathedrals with Gothic spires rise above the landscape. Bellowing organs vibrate the theater with imposing authority. Strange incense rises from a thurible (censer) which is swung from a chain; its mysterious fragrance permeating the atmosphere adding to the mystic. Opulence of gold, statues of human gods and goddesses called saints and flickering candles all add to the aura. Rich bright vestments of silks and satins embroidered with gold cryptograms are worn by its priests while they perform a pagan ceremony called the mass.

In the grandeur of St. Peter's Basilica in Rome sits an aged, often feeble man on a pedestal while his priests lay prostrate on the marble floor before him. The parishioners, with the senses mesmerized by the drama of seeing the homage paid this human deity surrender their minds and become part of the great throng. The illusion is complete; the ruse has worked. Unless one can, in a moment of reason, manage to rouse from the hypnotic stupor and break free, they are in jeopardy of losing their very soul.[1638] However and sadly, without having heard the truth or studied the Word of GOD for themselves most are resigned to be but hostages.[1639]

Not unlike the Jewish people who have been persuaded by their clergy to reject Jesus as their Messiah, so have Gentiles been persuaded by their clergy to accept their propaganda that these humans hold the keys to heaven.

1637 2 Peter 2:1-3
1638 2 Peter 3:16-17
1639 Romans 10:17

In his treatise, *Religion: an "Opiate of the People,"* Dr. David Livingston quotes Marxist theorist Vladimir Lenin, who although being the father of modern communism, of political repression and of mass murder was quite correct when he said, "Religion is one of the forms of spiritual oppression that everywhere weighs on the masses of the people, who are crushed by perpetual toil… Religion is the opium of the people. Religion is a kind of spiritual gin in which the slaves of capital drown their human shape and their claims to any decent human life." Lenin, *Selected Works, XI: 658*

Dr. Livingston comments, "Religion as an 'opiate' is an extremely important concept to understand. What is meant by 'opiate'? An opiate is something that dulls, blinds, desensitizes, but gives a sense of well-being." What then is religion but mans' assumption of what he believes to be true about GOD and the universe. When religion has congealed into a cannon of beliefs it becomes a binding blinding system by which to manipulate its followers and capture more quarry."

Religion is the practical and rather impersonal alternative which Satan has devised to what would otherwise be a deep, personal, one on one relationship with GOD through the Savior.[1640]

In earlier studies we established that in the "latter days," Scripture indicates that a great hoax would be perpetrated on the Jewish people and the world at large. I now pose the question to you. Would GOD who made us for HIS good pleasure neglect to tell us who the perpetrator is so that we might recognize who it is and avoid being deceived?

As this enigmatic figure had not, at the time of Christ or the Apostle John materialized, it would be necessary for our Lord to describe "her" futuristically—that is, by giving us descriptions and details that would conclusively identity her. The Lord would give a fitting name to this mysterious figure: Mystery Woman, "the Great Mother of Harlots, and the Abomination of the Earth."[1641]

Mystery Babylon, the Great Mother of Harlots

The seventeenth chapter of the book of "the Revelation" is about a woman of ill repute; an adulterous, a harlot, a "whore." The word whore is a strong slang word indeed, but one used appropriately, for it is meant to grab our attention, stress her abominable acts, and compel us to want to identify who she is.

> "…Come hither; I will show unto thee the judgment of the great whore that setteth upon many waters…" (Revelation 17:1)

> "And upon her forehead was a name written Mystery Babylon The Great Mother of Harlots and Abomination of the Earth." (Revelation 17:5)

Before delving into this mysterious figure, we need to consider the book in which it is revealed. The abbreviated title of the last book of the Bible, "the Revelation," is derived from the Greek

---
1640 John 14:6
1641 Revelation 17:5

word "*apokalypsis,*" meaning to disclose or to unveil. The book it primarily about the Seventieth Week of Daniel—the last seven years of the earth age, which we are told has a threefold purpose. To "finish the transgression" of the Jewish people, "to make an end of sins," and "to bring in everlasting righteousness…"[1642]

The Prophet Jeremiah referred to this, the shortest of all dispensations, as "The Time of Jacob's Trouble."[1643] Like many Old Testament books, this New Testament book, commonly referred to as Revelation, addresses the future of Israel and the revelation and personage of the Jewish Mashiach. The identity of the Messiah is presented in the very first verse of the book, "The Revelation of Jesus Christ, which God gave unto him (John the Apostle) to shew unto his servants things which must shortly come to pass…"[1644] So we need to be clear that it is GOD's intent to show (reveal) to HIS own and to those who search HIS Word and seek its meaning, just what the many mystical metaphors in the book refer to.

It is unfortunate that many ministers today believe the book is too eclectic and too full of symbolism to be understood and sadly choose to avoid it. Consider how foolish indeed it would be for GOD to have taken the trouble to author a book within the Bible—much less a book of twenty-two chapters, whose very title means to reveal, if HE didn't want us to understand it. This is especially true when HE says in HIS opening statement, "Blessed is he that readeth, and they that hear the words of this prophecy…for the time is at hand."[1645]

Before beginning this study let me quantify who and what the Women on the Beast is and is not. The harlot is not a living figure, a demonic entity or an organization, but a representation of imaginary gods and goddesses of pagan cultures, false and mystery religions of every kind, and of idolatry in every form. In each case she has accompanied prominent empires from the ancient to the present day, dating back to the time of Babel where the false divines, Nimrod, Semiramis and Tammuz were first concocted; hence the name Mystery Babylon.

Conceived by Satan after the fall, she is portrayed as a harlot (more correctly—spiritual harlotry) that flourishes with despotic rule. She is the mechanism of deception which predates the Egyptian, Assyrian, Babylonian, Medo-Persian, Grecian and Roman empires. This shadowy figure is now operating largely through the apostate Universal Church of Rome which will attempt to bring all false religions together under its monarchy during the formation of the Revised Roman Empire. So, Papal Rome is not itself the harlot, but the vehicle Satan has used and is using during the Church dispensation in his final attempt to bring the world under his domination.

Because of the integration between the figure of spiritual adultery and Romanism (that has been in existence for the last seventeen hundred years) the two will be perceived historically and futuristically (as John was shown)—as one and the same.

The Bible is emphatic that apostate Christianity will flourish after the Church has been raptured which is why the Lord felt it important for an angel to describe to John and to His Church who this woman and the beast are. "He that hath an ear, let him hear what the Spirit saith to the Church."

1642 Daniel 9:24
1643 Jeremiah 30:7
1644 Revelation 1:1
1645 Revelation 1:3

All Things in Their Appointed Time

> "Blessed is he that readeth, and they that hear the words of this prophecy, and keep those things which are written therein: for the time is at hand." (Revelation 1:3)

Besides the obvious blessing imparted to the seeker in Revelation 1:3, take special note of the words "for the time is at hand." Apocalyptic books and prophecy in general, whether Old Testament (e.g., Joel, Ezekiel, Daniel, Zechariah), or New Testament (Matthew 24, 25; Mark 13; Luke 21; Revelation) were intended to be understood by the believers on a "need to know" basis or at a specific time. In Daniel's day he was shown several prophetic visions of future events, yet it was told to him that they were not all to be revealed or understood by that generation. Rather, these prophecies would be more significant and needful for latter generations and particularly for the last generation.

> "But thou O Daniel, shut up the words, and seal the book, even to the time of the end..." (Daniel 12:4)

The Lord reveals things to HIS people which are relative to them and important to their assigned mission at a given point in time. For example, the Early Church had no need to become eschatologists (students of end time prophecies). They didn't need to know of the development of the Church of Rome, the Crusades, the Reformation, or of the details of Seals, Trumpets, and Vials mentioned in the Revelation. It was for this reason that the last Apostle (John) would not be given the revelation until 96 AD. The Early Church would instead need to learn foundational truths and receive the Holy Spirit so they could focus on spreading the gospel and missionizing the world.

Now however, the Church of today—the true Church of today—has a somewhat different mission; a dual mission. That is because it now finds itself on the brink of the greatest prophecy in the Bible being fulfilled: the return of Jesus Christ. As such, it is needful for this generation to understand what is about to unfold, that they may prepare themselves and others and make a decision to accept Christ or be duped and be among the left behind.

The Book of Revelation describes seven years of turmoil. I use the word turmoil as opposed to the word catastrophe only because the first forty-two months of this dispensation are somewhat promising—as concessions and peace in the Middle East will appear to have become a reality. According to Scripture, the Temple in Jerusalem will finally be constructed, and sacrifices begun. However, this time of tranquility[1646] is a deception and will abruptly end three and a half years after it has begun; after which[1647] the Jewish people will find themselves under siege.

The Prophet Jeremiah said, "Alas! for that day is great (terrible), so that none is like it..."[1648]

[1646] Ezekiel 38:11
[1647] Daniel 9:27
[1648] Jeremiah 30:7

The Prophet Daniel said, "…and there shall be a time of trouble, such as never was since there was a nation even to that same time…"[1649]

The Prophet Joel referred to it as "…the great and terrible day of the LORD."[1650]

Jesus would afterward phrase it this way:

> "For then shall be great tribulation, such as was not since the beginning of the world to this time, no, nor ever shall be." (Matthew 24:21)

After recording the horrors of this period to the Apostle John in Revelation, the Lord gives one last plea to those who had become entwined in the web of the Mystery woman.

> "And I heard another voice from heaven, saying, Come out of her (Babylon), my people, that ye be not partakers of her sins, and that ye receive not of her plagues." (Revelation 18:4)

> Note: Babylon (literal Babylon) represents the world system.[1651] Because the harlot is called Mystery Babylon there is a connection. Literal Babylon is always associated with demonic religions and idolatry in Scripture.

So it is at the juncture that we find ourselves faced with a decision. Do we believe the Bible is HIS Word? Do we believe HE is warning us? Do we believe HE is now going to reveal what is essential for this generation to understand? We will now begin looking at what it is that we are told to "come out of" by examining Scripture.

The Mystery

The word "Mystery" and the word "Babylon" need to be looked at in their Biblical application. In the New Testament a "mystery" is a fresh revelation of truth, even a truth concealed in the Old Testament. Therefore, Mystery Babylon is a new revelation about "Babylon." Upon examination we find that Babylon is mentioned nearly three hundred times in the Bible, so let us see how an ancient city or empire has relevance to futuristic Babylon presented in "the Revelation."

First, let us clear up a misnomer. Some teach that Babylon in the Book of Revelation (chapters 18 and 19) refers to the ancient city and therefore a new Babylon must be built before Christ's return. This was a view advanced by the historical school of interpretation for many years. This prospect is unsustainable, for according to the Scriptures the ancient city of Babylon would after its defeat (539 AD)[1652] and later its destruction remain perpetually desolate.[1653] Today what was

---

1649 Daniel 12:1
1650 Joel 2:31
1651 Revelation 14:8
1652 Daniel 5:31
1653 Isaiah 13:19-22; Jeremiah 50:13, 39

once the greatest city of the ancient world is little more than a mound of broken mud bricks and debris. Therefore, it must be conceded that the Babylon spoken of in the Book of Revelation is unrelated and altogether different from ancient Babylon.

Babel of Genesis and Babylon of Revelation

It is no coincidence that we find the first city of human government in Genesis called "Babel," and the last (figurative) city—an empire of human government in Revelation—called "Babylon."

It was in Genesis where Babylon had its origin, deriving its name from the ancient city (Hebrew: *Bab-el,* "gate of god"). Babel came into existence shortly after the Great Flood of Noah's day when Noah begat Ham, who begat Cush. Cush and his family migrated southeast from the mountains of Ararat and established the first kingdom "Kish" in the land of Shinar (Mesopotamia). Cush, we are told, begat a son, Nimrod.[1654] Nimrod is derived from the Hebrew verb *marad,* meaning "we will revolt" and is presumed to be more a title than an actual name. By adding an "n" before the "m" *marad* it becomes an infinitive construct, translated "Nimrod." According to the Jewish Encyclopedia, even the way Nimrod's name is presented implies rebellion.[1655] According to the Jewish historian Josephus, Nimrod fostered contempt for GOD among the people.[1656] So the name Nimrod is appropriate in describing those who would follow a leader to revolt against GOD.

Nimrod inherited or established a kingdom which included the cities of Babel, Erech, Akkad, and Calneh. We read he was "a mighty one" and "a mighty hunter"[1657] and as such, he assumed power, eventually becoming a demigod; transforming his kingdom into a religio-political state (a religion coupled with a government).

Before the city of Babel, tribal communities existed where the strong ruled the weak by force. But under Nimrod a new and more efficient paradigm had been discovered. Not only was he the strongest, but he came to the realization that by assuming godlikeness he could command with impunity, bending all who lived in his kingdom to his will without the sword.

Lucifer (Satan) had used this tactic once before when in a pre-Adamic age he assumed god-likeness and said, "…I will be like the most High."[1658] So persuasive was he at that time that he was able to convince one-third of heaven's angels to revere him and oppose their Creator. Though Lucifer's rebellion failed, he would employ this same strategy again in the human model Nimrod. The plan was rather simple; elevate a man to godhood (which degrades GOD), replace relationship with a facsimile (religion) and subjugate the subjects by use of lies. So it was that Nimrod would be the first of many who would afterward claim to be a demigod (being partially divine and partially human).

1654 Genesis 10:6-10
1655 Jewish Encyclopedia, vol. 9, p.309
1656 Josephus, *Antiquities of the Jews*, Bk. 1, 4:2, 3
1657 Josephus, *Antiquities of the Jews*, Bk. 10:8, 9
1658 Isaiah 14:14

Caesars and Roman emperors would do the same. After the Roman Empire disintegrated, leaving the Church of Rome as its legacy, it was a small matter for the empirical head of the Church of Rome—the Pontif Maxim (chief priest) to emulate his predecessors, assume a level of divinity, and become partially divine and partially human.

Religion had been born! Babel had been its fountainhead. The dye had been cast and this religio-political form of government became a template for the cultures and societies which would follow. For 4,000 years, men claiming divine right have followed the Sumerian system. Akkad, Assyria, Babylon, Persia, Greece, and eventually Rome were all ruled by men who claimed some measure of divine status. Today it remains the same, be they pontiffs, lamas, or shamans. They each maintain control over their followers by proclaiming their connection, and subsequently their authority comes from GOD.

> Note: In 2 Thessalonians 2:7, the Apostle Paul tells us that the "mystery of iniquity" (mystery of evil), the workings of Satan, not only existed but were thriving in the Roman Empire. These pagan beliefs systems, of which there were at least eighty, included beliefs and gods from Egypt to the Orient. All these belief systems shared the same origin: they had all been born in Babel and left with the various tribes to different lands when GOD confused their common language.

When man persists and resists the truth, GOD eventually gives them over to their delusion.

> "...they received not the love of the truth, that they might be saved...sending them strong delusion (error), that they should believe a lie: That they all might be damned who believe not the truth..." (2 Thessalonians 2:10-12)

> "Because that, when they knew God, they glorified him not as God, neither were thankful; but became vain in their imaginations...Who changed the truth of God into a lie, and worshipped and served the creature (themselves) more than the Creator..." (Romans 1:21, 25)

As it was then, it remains today; GOD gives the stubborn who continue to resist Him and HIS truth to believe their imaginations and the contrivances of men.[1659] HE has given this a name and calls it mystery religion.

> Note: The Akkadian Empire was an ancient Semitic empire centered in the lost city of Akkad in ancient Mesopotamia. There the indigenous Akkadian-speaking Semites and the Sumerians came together under one rule within a multilingual empire. The ancient Hebraic would be one of many Semitic dialects which evolved from the region.

1659 2 Thessalonians 2:4, 11; Matthew 15:9

Babel to Nebuchadnezzar's Babylon

Midway between Genesis' Babel and Revelations' Babylon, in the book of Daniel is an extensive amount of scripture about both the Babylon of Daniel's day and a futuristic Babylon that would form in the latter days.[1660]

In a series of dreams given to King Nebuchadnezzar, the Lord gave the prophet Daniel the interpretation of what the king saw. In one of these dreams, the king saw a Colossus; an imposing statue composed of various metals.[1661] The prophet was shown the succession of empires beginning with then-King Nebuchadnezzar's Babylon and ending with the last human government on earth—futuristic Babylon.[1662]

At the top of the statue was a head of gold which then changed to less valued metals and finally to iron and clay.

> "But there is a God in heaven that revealeth secrets (mysteries), and maketh known to the king Nebuchadnezzar what shall be in the latter days." (Daniel 2:28)

Colossus
(Image Source: GOODSALT)

Gold: Babylonian Empire

Silver: Medo-Persian Empire

Brass: Grecian Empire

Iron: Roman Empire

Holy Roman Empire (East and West):

Iron (The Holy Roman Empire [East and West]) and Clay (The Islamic Empire) are mingled to form the future government Babylon.

The head of gold represented Nebuchadnezzar's then-Babylon Empire.

The two arms of silver and the torso represented the Medo and the Persian Empire.

The waist of brass would represent the next empire: the Grecian Empire.

The two legs of iron would represent the Roman Empire, which would after it dissolved, mutate into two branches, the Western Church of Rome and its cousin, the Eastern Orthodox Church.

(These two branches (legs) are shown to continue to the end of the earth age.)

1660 Revelation chapters 18 and 19
1661 Daniel 2:39-43
1662 Revelation 14:8

The feet begin with iron and then mingle with clay and depict the last human empire (government) on earth: Babylon the Great.[1663]

The Eastern Roman Empire (Byzantine Empire) split from her Roman cousin in 364 AD. Like her Roman counterpart, she too has remained alive as a religious entity to this day. The image depicts the iron legs continuing from the thigh—Ancient Roman Empire (for the last seventeen hundred years) all the way down to its feet where it then mixes with clay and become ten toes (ten regional governments).

> "And whereas thou sawest the feet and toes, part of potters' clay, and part of iron, the kingdom shall be divided; but there shall be in it of the strength of the iron, forasmuch as thou sawest the iron mixed with miry clay. And as the toes of the feet were part of iron, and part of clay, so the kingdom shall be partly strong, and partly broken. And whereas thou sawest iron mixed with miry clay, they shall mingle themselves with the seed of men: but they shall not cleave one to another, even as iron is not mixed with clay." (Daniel 2:41-43)

Significant in Daniel 2:43 is that we are told that the iron becomes "mixed with the miry clay" and that "they shall mingle." Obviously, iron and clay cannot be mixed as their physical properties don't allow that. In the spiritual application we see that two spiritual ideologies won't allow them to mix either, but they can and will mingle.

The clay represents the Islamic Empire as well as various other religions that will mingle with the iron (The Holy (Revised) Roman Empire). The clay—the Islamic empire—will (under the Antichrist) at first interact with Romanism but afterward break with her and eventually eliminate her.[1664]

The "seed of men [that] shall not cleave"[1665] refers to those in the various belief systems who though mingle together in the one world religion, they will never cleave together either.

Traditional conservative scholars believe this is the only tenable position which correlates with Daniel 2:43. It is in verse 44 that we also learn that in the end, GOD will destroy all demonic kingdoms and establish His Messianic kingdom.

It would be 690 years after Daniel was given the above interpretation that on the small Greek island of Patmos in the Aegean Sea that GOD would reveal much more about these "secrets" to another prophet: the Apostle John. John was told that in the latter days a great empire, not unlike the Babylonian Empire of Daniel's day, will arise. The characteristics of this new empire or empirical government will be eerily similar to that of King Nebuchadnezzar's.

Just as Nebuchadnezzar was an extraordinarily powerful world ruler, "Thou, O king, art a king of kings:"[1666]—so shall come another world ruler in the latter days with extraordinary power become a king over all kings.[1667]

1663 Revelation 14:8
1664 Revelation 17:16
1665 Daniel 2:43
1666 Daniel 2:37
1667 Revelation 13:12

Just as Nebuchadnezzar established what was then a world government, so too shall another world ruler establish a new world government.

Just as Nebuchadnezzar instituted mandatory edicts; so too will another despot initiate edicts throughout his empire.

Just as Nebuchadnezzar had an image constructed before which the people had to bow and worship under penalty of death as with Shadrach, Meshach, and Abednego,[1668] so will the new world dictator create an image and sentence to death any who refuse to reverence the abomination of desolation[1669] and deify him.[1670]

The similarities between Daniel 3:1–7 and those presented in Revelation 13:14–18 are unmistakable; therefore, we can appreciate that our Lord enlarges our understanding by presenting parallels in the Old and New Testaments.

Our GOD is indeed the "…GOD in heaven that revealeth secrets…(of) what shall be in the latter days."[1671]

To recap: the term "Babylon" is synonymous with an empire in rebellion to GOD; to a world in subjugation to a man who demands worship, and to an image and leader which must be revered under penalty of death. These characteristics shared by the Babylon of Genesis under Nimrod and by the Babylon of Daniel's day under Nebuchadnezzar will likewise be shared by the Babylon of the Revelation, under the Antichrist. All three Babylons had or will have paganism at the root, false doctrine as authority and the elevation of a man to godlikeness.

> Note: I would be remiss if I didn't draw attention to the fact that the same geographical area of Nebuchadnezzar's Ancient Babylon is the same area which the last Babylon Empire in Revelation[1672] will occupy (the Mid-East). It is from this very same region which is now becoming an Islamic Caliphate that the Antichrist will emerge, set up his capital, and preside as dictator of the world government. According to Revelation 19:10-21, it will become the epicenter of the new common market and of world commerce. Today we see the emergence of an old pagan empire which was destined to return, and which shares its name with its successor. The book of the Revelation calls it by its identifiable name—Babylon.

It is in the human DNA for man to want to be revered as a god, or at least god-like.[1673] Having a connection with divinity is the trademark of those who claim headship and governance over their respective religion. In fact, the greater the religion, the more its monarch is revered as divine.

1668 Daniel 3:6
1669 Mark 24:15; Mark 13:14
1670 Daniel 13:14-15
1671 Daniel 2:28
1672 Revelation chapters 18-19
1673 Genesis 3:5

Existing as far back as Egyptian pharaohs, man may be seen crowning himself with a pagan fish-head mitre headpiece, holding a scepter of power, and cloaking himself in royal robes. I daresay history can attest to what Scripture warns.

> "Beware of false prophets (religious leaders), which come to you in sheep's clothing, but inwardly they are ravening wolves." (Matthew 7:15)

So it is that in Revelation, chapters 13 and 17 we are told of a religious accomplice to the Antichrist referred to as the False Prophet who will hold the reins of global religion. From his lofty throne, he will exalt the New World leader and require that this leader be worshiped and obeyed.[1674] Together these two collaborators will deceive the world under the guise of piety, peace, and tolerance. It will be this False Prophet, this vendor of lies, this shepherd of the deceived, who will bring to a climax the great apostasy which began in Babel and which the Apostle Paul warned of.

> "Let no man deceive you by any means: for that day shall not come, except there come a falling away (from truth) first, and that man of sin be revealed, the son of perdition (Antichrist); Who opposeth and exalteth himself above all that is called God, or that is worshipped; so that he as God sitteth in the temple of God, shewing himself that he is God. Remember ye not, that, when I was yet with you, I told you these things? And now ye know what withholdeth that he might be revealed in his time." (2 Thessalonians 2:3-6)

Because The Universal Church of Rome had not yet come into existence when the Lord gave the Apostle John the vision in the revelation, and because she would be affiliated with Babylon, the Lord would give her the name Mystery Babylon, the Great Whore, who today sits on many waters (lands) throughout the world.[1675]

After the Universal Church has succeeded in its goal to become the World Church, her reign will end; for after having served her purpose of deceiving the masses and bringing them into subjugation to the Antichrist she will no longer be needed or wanted. She will be abruptly abolished by the Antichrist and by the "ten horns" (governors) of the global cabal—Babylon.[1676] In the end Babylon, which held control over all world finance and commerce, will suddenly be divinely destroyed.[1677] The "kings of the earth" will "bewail and lament" when the Lord ends the age of human government and establishes His theocracy on earth.[1678]

1674 Revelation 13:8, 15-16
1675 Revelation 17:1
1676 Revelation 17:16
1677 Revelation 17:11; Daniel 2:30-45
1678 Revelation 18:8, 19

> Note: The word whore, Greek *"pórni,"*[1679] from where the words pornographic and pornography are derived, is a prostitute, a woman who sells herself sexually. She is one who is not legally and legitimately married to a man but who takes the most intimate role of a wife. We know that Jesus is alluded to metaphorically as the bridegroom in Matthew 25:1-6, and in Revelation 18:23, so it is apparent this harlot is not the bride of Christ which she claims herself to be (Revelation 18:7) but rather a pretender (Revelation 19:2). I should like to point out that there is no other religion on earth (Islam, Hinduism, Buddhism, etcetera) which makes the claim to be the bride of Christ except for Romanism!
>
> Note: Scripture makes a distinction between the spiritual wife and the bride. Scripture also applies the term wife differently in the two Testaments. In the Old Testament, Israel is presented as a wife. For example, in the book of Hosea, Israel is symbolic of the unfaithful wife of Jahovah. In the New Testament, Revelation 19:7, the phrase "his wife has made herself ready" refers to every true Christian (Jew and Gentile)—praising GOD as the marriage supper is prepared.

The term "bride" or "bride to be" refers specifically to those in Christ (Believers) whether they are Jews (Messianic Believers) or Gentiles Believers. The five wise virgins in Matthew 25:2, for example, refers to Messianic Jews who were anxiously awaiting the arrival of the bridegroom. The marriage symbolism is beautifully fulfilled in the relationship of Christ to His Church.[1680] Spiritually speaking, the wedding contract is consummated the moment one accepts Christ. The marriage supper takes place after the vows of fidelity are pledged.

It is afterward that the husband and wife proceed to the banquet celebration. This (the marriage feast) will, from all accounts, occur after every last Believer (tribulation saints included) have been retrieved. This places the feast after the Second Advent.[1681] Were the marriage feast during the Tribulation, it surely would be mentioned in the Book of Revelation as taking place in heaven at that time.

The Origin and Evolution of Paganism and Romanism

Before we dissect Revelation, chapter 17 verse by verse, allow me to set the stage by looking back in recorded history and follow the evolution of paganism, and the contrast between the primitive (first century) Church, and the modern Church of today.

It was Babel where a combination of humanism and paganism had its origin, after which GOD scattered the people.[1682] Those speaking the same tongue formed tribes and developed their own beliefs and deities which would evolve into numerous polytheistic cults (hence the mother of harlots). Each group appointed their own high priest and priesthood who would

---
1679 *Strong's Exhaustive Concordance*, Gk., #4204
1680 Ephesians 5:22-25
1681 Revelation 19:9
1682 Genesis 11:8-9

claim mystical powers just as priests are known to do today (e.g., transubstantiation). Many of their gods, high places, and temples are mentioned throughout the Hebrew Holy Scriptures and the New Testament, and GOD abhors all of them.

> Note: Some prominent pagan gods presented in the Holy Scriptures include: Adrammelech (sun-god), 2 Kings 17:31; Amon (sun-god), Jeremiah 46:25; Anammelech (moon-god), 2 Kings 17:31; Asherah/Asherim/Ashtoreth (fertility/love goddess), 1 Kings 11:5, 11:33, 2 Kings 23:13; Ashima, 2 Kings 17:30; Baal and Bel (supreme god), 2 Kings 10:18-28; Isaiah 41; Jeremiah 52:2; Castor and Pollux (twin brothers, protectors of sailors), Acts 28:11; Chemosh (destroyer of enemies), 1 Kings 11:7, 33; Dagon (god of grain), 1 Samuel 5:2-7; Diana/Artemis (moon goddess, virginity, and hunting), Acts 19:24-35; Jupiter/Zeus (supreme god, ruler of heaven), Acts 14:12; Molech/Moloch, (destroyer of enemies), Leviticus 20:2-5; Rimmon (god of weather), 2 Kings 5:18; Tammuz (god of vegetation), Ezekiel 8:14; Tartak (prince of darkness), 2 Kings 17:31.

The various groups (tribes) of common tongues migrated from Babel; some journeying to Africa and Egypt, some traveled to the Arabian wilderness. Some remained in Asia Minor and Mesopotamia, and some settled in what became Italia. However, it would be many centuries (circa 753 BC—traditional date) before a city named Roma would emerge along the Tiber River in what is today Italy. Italic tribes such as the Latins, the Sabines, and the Etruscans from Lydia (Pergamos) settled on the Italian peninsula bringing their polytheism with them. It was not coincidental that the Bible tells us that Italy's Pergamos was the center of paganism and is referred to as "Satan's seat."[1683]

The fertile land of Italy was ideal for herdsman and for farming. Centrally located and extending into the Mediterranean, it was ideal for shipping and commerce. So it was that the tribal settlements eventually grew to a province which would become a city. One city, Roma (Rome), was to become the megalopolis of the ancient world and the melting pot of the world's religions. It is no coincidence that a city (Vatican City) within the city of Roma would become a sacerdotal and monarchical state.

It wouldn't be until the fourth century (323 AD) under Roman Emperor Constantine that the various pagan religions of the Roman empire would, for the sake of solidarity and to give greater control to the emperor, become homogenized into a state religion under the guise of Christianity. Prelates from the various belief systems and sects in the domain were summoned to come together and draw up tenets they could agree upon. These views were then put before the emperor to ratify or reject. Their various gods of pagan religions, and especially goddesses, were then integrated into one belief system and given new names under a universal state religion: The Universal (Catholic) Church of Rome.

It took several decades for an actual institution to evolve and solidify, but finally in 378 AD, Emperor Flavius Gratianus Augustus relinquished his title over the religious sphere of the empire

---

[1683] Revelation 2:13

and appointed its first official non-emperor to its head. It would be a Portuguese elder named "Damasus" who assumed the title Pontiff Maximus. In 380 AD, the Edict of Thessalonica made it official, ordering all subjects of the Roman Empire to profess their faith and allegiance to the bishops of Rome and Alexandria.

The formation and evolution of an ecclesiastical empire (the papal church) was a "mystery" in the Apostle John's day, hence the name Mystery Babylon. But it would be the Apostle Paul who by divine revelation would recognize and tell us that the "Mystery of Iniquity" was already at work.[1684] The mystery religion, although it had not coalesced into an organization at that time, was still apparent to the apostles, for Babylonian cults, and Roman-Greek philosophies were thriving during the first century. Pagan practices,[1685] fallacious doctrines, and damnable heresies[1686] from Babel's origin had even managed to infiltrate the apostolic Church.[1687]

> "Beloved, when I gave all diligence to write unto you of the common salvation, it was needful for me to write unto you, and exhort you that ye should earnestly contend for the faith which was once delivered unto the saints. For there are certain men crept in unawares, who were before of old ordained to this condemnation, ungodly men, turning the grace of our God into lasciviousness, and denying (that salvation comes exclusively through) the only GOD, and our Lord Jesus Christ." (Jude 3, 4)

Some twenty-four years after this admonishment was written to the Church, the Apostle John was directed by GOD to write letters to each of seven churches in Asia Minor.[1688] Five of the seven were given dire warnings and are recorded in chapters 2 and 3 of the Book of the Revelation. It speaks of the various intrusions, heretical doctrines and general passivity which had infiltrated their respective assemblies.

From the time the Bible first became a bound book, renowned scholars studied the Apocalypse and recognized Mystery Babylon as the Church of Rome. Gradually, with the Renaissance came a resurgence of Gnosticism wherein man's opinions and higher criticisms began to eclipse the simplicity of the Word. Where once laureates of Scripture devoted their entire lives in the pursuit of truth, their counterparts became cavalier. With the Industrial Revolution came the modern era and with it came Evolution, Rationalism, Darwinism, Nihilism, Existentialism, and a host of other "-isms." Variant translations of the Bible were published ad nauseam. Unwitting ministers disregarded the admonitions of scripture; left the Textus Receptus (Received Text) based on manuscript evidence as used in the King James Bible and supplemented dynamic equivalents (a process where the writer attempts to express their thoughts using what they believe to be an equivalent expression from a contemporary language).

1684 2 Thessalonians 2:7
1685 1 Corinthians 10:14-22
1686 1 Peter 2:1
1687 Revelation 2:14-15, 20
1688 Revelation 1:14

In the last century, less and less emphasis has been placed on exacting the meaning of Scripture. Over the past seventy years, expository study among ministers has gone the way of the dinosaur. Today, I daresay the modern minister has less understanding of the Bible than had the layman of the 1800s.

Belief in, and acceptance of the Full Gospel (the entire Bible) with its convicting and life changing scriptures, and not having certain portions of scripture dismissed or amputated is a rarity. The rejection of the overwhelming of the Holy Spirit (the Baptism of the Holy Spirit) evidenced by of ecstatic manifestations and impartations (tongues) is denied by the sanctimonious and is just one example of man's disregard for the Full Gospel. Unwelcome in His own house the Holy Spirit has moved on, leaving an epitaph over the church's doors—*"Ichabod"*—The glory is departed.[1689]

Perhaps as much as half of what is being taught in churches today is being misinterpreted or misapplied. What scripture tells us to do and what is quintessential—"Rightly dividing the Word of truth,"[1690] has become a cliché not a practice. Much of what is taught today is "milk, not meat;"[1691] which seems to be all that the spoon-fed congregation wants. Teaching has been replaced with allegorical sermons. Super spiritualizing the Word, (taking a scripture out of context and giving it some new exaggerated or unscriptural meaning) has become commonplace as ministers struggle to come up a new revelation for next week's sermon. Counterfeit ecstatic experiences such as the "laughter movement" mock the Holy Spirit who beckons men to see themselves undone and afterward cry out for forgiveness. Ministers in silk suits are lauded as apostles and prophets but bear no resemblance to the authentic that wore sackcloth and ashes and wept and fasted that they might hear a mere word from GOD.

> "For such are false apostles, deceitful workers, transforming themselves into the apostles of Christ." (2 Corinthians 11:13)

> "...they which say they are apostles and who are not." (Revelation 2:2)

The sacred platform has become a theatrical stage with all the glitter and glamor of its secular cousin Hollywood. A million dollars or several million may be spent on lighting, sound systems and staging; all of which is intended to build a mega-church. These narcissists justify themselves by saying, this is how we will reach the unchurched; and though they may fill their stadiums with souls, the entertainment never stops, and the enlightenment never begins.

A Seeker-sensitive tactic using friendly approaches makes one feel good rather than have to confront their sin and repent. A corporate business model with an intensive marketing strategy targets the affluent young professional. Feel good sermons by motivational speakers, their faces

---

[1689] 1 Samuel 4:19-22
[1690] 2 Timothy 2:15
[1691] 1 Corinthians 3:2

carved with a permanent smile like the Howdy Doody puppet (circa 1950) address anything except sin or what is required to attain heaven.[1692]

Today a man or woman can stand behind the sacred desk with a smattering of knowledge and less understanding, so long as they have charisma. They should only remember what the Apostle James told us, "My brethren, be not many masters (teachers), knowing that we (teachers) shall receive the greater condemnation."[1693]

All of us, but especially those who claim to be ministers of the Word will one day have to give an account of what they taught to those over which they assumed oversight.

"Whom shall He teach knowledge? And whom shall He make to understand doctrine? Them that are weaned from the milk and are drawn from the breast." (Isaiah 28:9)

Today, politically correct pastors have swallowed the ecumenical bait. Mainline denominations and evangelicals alike believe that to incriminate the Church of Rome for her past "indiscretions" is too divisive a subject to be recalled or discussed. They now see Romanism as having mended her ways. Moreover, she is now seen as the ambassador of peace, welcoming all faiths to come together in the spirit of reconciliation and unity.

The ministers who still refer to themselves as Protestants—"protest-ants" have forgotten why they were called such and are now overturning the Reformation. The hangings and dissections; the saints who were dangled on poles and became human torches for their testimonies have been forgotten. The likes of Stephen, Andrew, Peter, Polycarp, John Wycliffe, Jan Hus, Zwingli, William Tyndale, and the rolls of the nameless who would not bow their knee to Baal have become a distant memory. Sadly, but prophetically the Church is no longer set for the defense of the gospel and has shirked its responsibility as guardians of the Word and sentinels on the wall. And where, I might ask, are those rabbinic who have enough understanding of the scriptures to know by all prophetic indications that the time is at hand to, "Blow the Trumpet in Zion, and sound the alarm in my (GOD's) holy mountain...for the day of the Lord is at hand."[1694]

When the Word is no longer taught, and the truth no longer known, and the watchmen are no longer awake on the tower, the purveyors of heresy and religion go unhindered; free to capture a quarry of souls which is exactly what Satan is counting on if only to break the heart of GOD.

Tricked

For Catholics salvation does not come through one receiving Christ as their personal Savior. Rather it is a decision made by the parents for their newborn infant which begins with the unbiblical practice of infant baptism. From that point on the child is consigned to be a Catholic for the rest of his or her life. This ritual uses fear based on a lie that a child will not go to

---
1692 Luke 13:3; John 3:3
1693 James 3:1
1694 Joel 2:1

heaven proper but be relegated to another place for unbaptized children should the child die before being baptized. This led to the invention of a place, for lack of a better name called Limbo (Latin, *limbus inlfantium*). The Vatican's position and that put forth in the Catholic Catechism has tried to walk back what it historically taught from Medieval times. Its current position is ambiguous at best, saying that based on what they know from the scriptures there are grounds for prayerful hope that unbaptized infants are saved, though this is not a "sure knowledge."[1695]

As soon as the child is old enough to enter elementary school their indoctrination begins in earnest as they are enrolled into religious instruction. A catechism (a summary of religious doctrine in the form of questions) is used to solicit what is deemed as the appropriate answer. Prayers are taught venerating Mary and professing allegiance to the one Catholic (Universal) and apostolic church. This programing of the child begins at the age six or seven and is used to prepare them for another fabrication—their first Holy Communion. This theatrical production, with little boys and girls dressed in white suits and dresses is designed to further bind the child to the institution as they first partake of a wafer they are taught is GOD.

> Note: Biblically, a communion is simply a coming together of the saints, at which time they are to pause and "remember" what the Lord said to His disciples when He last supped with them.[1696] This coming together was then, and is now, only for those who have reached the age of accountability and are mature enough to understand the weight of sin and make a decision to follow Christ. The age of accountability is recognized in the Jewish faith (and correctly so) as the Bar and Bat Mitzvah—generally at age thirteen. At the Bar or Bat (female) Mitzvah, the male youngster, would publicly make the declaration, "O my GOD and GOD of my fathers! On this solemn and sacred day, which marks my passage from boyhood to manhood, I humbly raise my eyes unto thee, and declare with sincerity and truth, that henceforth I will keep thy commandments, and undertake and bear the responsibly of my actions toward thee."

Participation in Christian communion is only for those who have apprehended and internalized the wages of sin and the cost of their redemption. This is referred to as the message of the Cross and is as simple as it is profound.

> "But God commendeth his love toward us, in that, while we were yet sinners, Christ died for us." (Romans 5:8)

So it is to this day, that communion should only be shared by those who are truly Born Again and who trust in Him alone for their salvation. It is not for those who believe that their salvation is also dependent upon being a faithful and compliant Catholic.

1695 www.Catholic Encyclopedia.com/limbo
1696 1 Corinthians 11:24-25

> "For there must be also heresies among you, that they which are approved (as being truly Born Again) may be manifest (known) among you...But let each man examine himself (that he or she is a genuine Christian) and so let him eat and drink that cup (partaking of the benefits and promises earned by Christ's death). For he that eateth and drinketh unworthly, (for the sake of merely eating) eatheth and drinketh damnation to himself not discerning (understanding) the Lord's body (His sacrifice on the Cross)." (1 Corinthians 11:19, 28-29)

As the religious instruction continues and the youngster approaches adolescence, they are prepared for another fabrication called Confirmation. According to Catholic doctrine, Confirmation is a sacrament where the participant is sealed with the gifts of the Holy Spirit and strengthened in his or her Christian life. This so-called sacrament is one of seven alleged by Romanism which was codified in the documents of the Council of Trent (1545–1563).

Biblically, there are only two sacred rituals (ordinances) which Christ not only gave us but participated in. They are, the Baptism of Repentance (a.k.a. Water Baptism), and the Lord's Supper (a.k.a. Communion). Both ordinances are a profession of one's faith in what Christ accomplish by His death, burial and resurrection for them. Although our Lord had no sin, He wanted us to recognize that we do; so water baptism is not for the infant but for those who have reached the age of accountability; which is why it is referred to as the Baptism of Repentance. In Judaism[1697] and genuine Christianity, which takes its guidance from the Bible, the infant is "dedicated" to the Lord by his or her parents, not baptized.

The Baptism of Repentance is an outward expression of an inward change that has taken place. The individual is not only admitting that they acknowledge their sins, but that they are willing to die to sin and have become born again. This immersion ritual expresses just that. He or she is momentarily submerged under water, which is symbolic of the individual dying to his or her former self and being buried beneath the surface. Resurfacing from the water is symbolic of being "born anew" and beginning a new life, lived in and for Christ.

> "Therefore if any man be in Christ, he is a new creature: old things are passed away; behold, all things are become new." (2 Corinthians 5:17)

> "Therefore we are buried with him by baptism into death: that like as Christ was raised up from the dead by the glory of the Father, even so we also should walk in newness of life. Knowing this, that our old man is crucified with him, that the body of sin might be destroyed, that henceforth we should not serve sin." (Romans 6:4-6)

The second Scriptural (Biblical) sacrament (sacred ordinance) is the Lord's Supper which is also an outward profession of the Believer's faith and trust in what was accomplished at the Cross. This act of "remembrance", "this do in remembrance of me"[1698] is a memorial and com-

---

[1697] 1 Samuel 1:11
[1698] 1 Corinthians 11:24

memoration, and like a memorial it is a time in which to reflect on what He did for Believers by sacrificing Himself for them. Like the Baptism of Repentance, it is only for those who have fully appropriated the meaning of the Cross and understood the magnitude of the New Covenant—bought and paid for in His blood.[1699] At the same time, this coming together of saints testifies of the Believer's desire to have an ongoing spiritual communion with both the Trinity and with the human family of GOD.

Communion can be celebrated any time Believers come together and break bread together. They are to simply pause, give thanks, and remember why the Lord needed to die for them. We need to always remind ourselves what it cost to inaugurate the new and everlasting covenant.

> "He that believeth (complete faith) on the Son hath everlasting life: and he that believeth not the Son shall not see life; but the wrath of GOD abideth on him." (John 3:36)

Each participant is to examine himself to see that he is in the faith—a true Christian and has put aside all heretical beliefs[1700] before partaking, lest he partake unworthily and bring sickness and death upon himself. Like water baptism it is only for the individual who has entered into what is a "one-on-one" covenant with Christ and made an unwavering commitment to follow Him forevermore. Neither water baptism nor communion has any saving power in themselves. Believers are baptized and partake in communion not in order to be saved, but because they are saved.

The climax of the Catholic "Mass" is the unscriptural Catholic Communion consecration. There, the "Eucharist" (a wafer and wine) is alleged to undergo a transformation. This they call the "transubstantiation," which is defined as a conversion of substance. They teach that these emblems actually become the incarnate body and blood of Christ. The priest holds up the Eucharistic wafer and says, "This is the Lamb of God, happy are those that are called to His supper." The priest's proclamation maintains that the wafer is literally the Lamb of GOD Yahusha-Jesus! Unable to offer any reasonable explanation as to how or why GOD becomes a cracker, they evade the question by calling it a mystery.

Catholic doctrine and tradition supplant the Bible. Catechism and religious instruction program the mind. Vows taken at Holy Communion and Confirmation seal the pact. Thereafter the youngster has unwittingly become an indentured servant to Holy Mother Church for life.

In Romanism, salvation comes through participation in the sacraments, penance, good works, suffering for one's sins here and now, or afterward in a factious place called Purgatory.[1701] They have invented indulgences which are purchased in order to exact money from their devotees, telling them it will reduce the purgatorial sentences of deceased love ones. There are endless masses, novenas, and rosaries—most of which are repetitious prayers[1702] to a

---

[1699] 1 Corinthians 11:24-25
[1700] 1 Corinthians 11:19, 27-39
[1701] Hebrews 9:27
[1702] Matthew 6:7

deceased creation claimed to be GOD's mother, or the Queen of heaven.[1703] Add to that the audacious claim that Roman priests have the power to forgive sin and grant absolution, or the preposterous assertion that the pontiff has the power to excommunicate a person and exile a soul to hell for eternity. Catholics even adhere to the belief that their pontiffs have infallibility and speak, Latin, *Ex cathedra* in matters of Sacred Magisterium. All of this is the antithesis of the Gospel of the Grace of GOD through Jesus Christ Crucified.[1704] All of this destroys the ability and sufficiency ascribed to the blood of Christ.[1705] All of this is heresy and blasphemy. But all of this serves the intended purpose which is uncontested obedience. It worked well on the biblical naïve during the Dark Ages, and it works equally well on the biblically naive today.

> "But if our gospel (the truth) be hid, it is hid to them that are lost: In whom the god of this world (Satan) hath blinded the minds of them which believe not, lest the light of the glorious gospel of Christ, who is the image of GOD, should shine upon them (be revealed)." (2 Corinthians 4:3-4)

> Note: The word image (*Gk. eikon,*) as applied in the above scripture means a representation or manifestation. *Thayer Greek-English Lexicon of the New Testament*; #1504.

"There are none so blind as those who will not see" is not a direct quote from the Bible but rather a saying which likely has its roots in Jeremiah 5:12[1706] and Isaiah 6:9–10. Still, this phrase conveys a great truth. The most deluded people are those who choose to ignore what is so apparent and what they already know to be true.

> Note: The staunch position long held by the Catholic Church that one must be a Catholic in order to attain heaven has recently been repealed. According to the Huffington Post, May 2013, Pope Francis is quoted as saying, "The Lord has redeemed all of us, all of us, with the Blood of Christ: all of us, not just Catholics. Everyone!" A question was raised to the pontiff, "'Father, the atheists?" The pope answered, "Even the atheists. Everyone! We must meet one another doing good." The questioner then said, "But I don't believe, Father, I am an atheist!" The pope replied, "But do good: we will meet one another there."

Now it appears (according to the Pope's statement) that Jesus went through the scourging and the crucifixion for nothing. Simply doing good apparently gets everyone into Catholic heaven!

1703 Jeremiah 44:17
1704 Acts 20:24; 1 Corinthians 1:23
1705 1 Peter 1:18-19
1706 *Random House Dictionary of Popular Proverbs and Sayings* by Gregory Y. Titelman (Random House, NY, 1996

The False Prophet

The False Prophet of Revelation will be the Pontiff Maximus and be lauded above all former pontiffs at the beginning of the Tribulation. Seen as the great unifier, he will be able to not only hypnotize his own devotees but those of other faiths. He will acknowledge all religions and adapt Catholicism to accommodate all beliefs just as Emperor Constantine did seventeen hundred years earlier.

The Unification of World Religions (Image Source: GETTY)

Assisi, Francis, October 27, 2011. Interfaith Gathering—The Day of Reflection, Dialogue, Prayer. Pope Benedict XVI (4th L), Rabbi David Rosen (5th L), Archbishop of Canterbury Rowan Williams (2nd L) and Patriarch Bartholomew (3rd L) gather together with approximately three hundred religious' leaders. Photo by 2430/Gamma-Rapho.

A universal world government must have a universal religion without which the differing ideologies will, as they have always been, at war with one another. So it will be that a universal church will become a reality and will require one imperial leader.

Even today, the pope is the most admired man on earth as even kings and presidents bow in respect when given an audience, and a billion plus devotees' fawn over him as if, like his roman emperor predecessors, he was in some measure a divine.

The final pope's stature, influence and power will exceed anything his predecessors might have imagined, and when he is able to call fire down from heaven it will appear that he has indisputable endorsement from on high.[1707]

In one sweeping declaration, he will bring an end to sectarian violence and unify the religions of the world by asserting that a New World Leader is the long awaited One! This world

---

1707 Revelation 13:13-14

leader will be the acclaimed Christ to the Catholic, the Messiah to the Jew,[1708] the Mahdi to the Muslim, the Maitreya to the Buddhist, the Kalki to the Hindu, and the Li Hong to the Taoist.[1709]

Sometime after this acclaimed savior has ascended to world prominence, the Pontiff will require everyone to worship him. Just as in bygone eras when the Roman religion mandated either convert or die, those who hold fast to the GOD of Scripture and refuse to surrender will be sought out and put to death.[1710]

Revelation 13:11–18 describes this second beast (the False Prophet) who occupies a supporting role to the first beast (the Antichrist). He is pictured as having two horns "like (Greek, *homolos*) a lamb". The word, *homolos*, is given to mean "in appearance and character."[1711] The description of the lamb suggests he has a religious character; "a wolf in sheep's clothing."[1712] The scriptures are clear that this prophet is the antithesis of a prophet who speaks for GOD; hence the name "false prophet."

He will use his office as high priest, undergirded with satanic power to deliver miracles with which to deceive the masses.[1713] It is quite probable that these miracles (like healing the multitudes of sick with the raising of his hand) will be seen as coming from GOD, when in fact it will be Satan ordering his minion spirits of infirmities to release their victims.

Later in Scripture we read, that even after the religious empire that he oversaw has been dissolved by the Antichrist, the false prophet will live on.[1714] In the end, and at Christ's return, both he and the Antichrist will be cast into the eternal lake of fire prepared for the devil and his angels.[1715]

It should be evident to the student of the Bible that Romanism is the counterfeit and culmination of apostate Christianity, which the Apostle Paul spoke is apex of the great "falling away" (apostasy).[1716] The falling away refers to those, who even at the time of the apostles had been part of the Biblical Church but who were cajoled into accepting heretical doctrine.[1717] This we are told will intensify in the "latter times."

> "Now the Spirit speaketh expressly, that in the latter times some shall depart from the faith, giving heed to seducing spirits, and doctrines of devils..." (1 Timothy 4:1)

This begs the question: just how many ministers today teach their congregants that the Church of Rome is the whore of Revelation? Are they themselves among the deceived who like the Pharisees of Jesus's day led the people into a ditch?[1718]

1708 John 5:43
1709 Revelation 13:8
1710 Revelation 13:7, 15
1711 *Strong's Exhaustive Concordance*, #3664
1712 Matthew 7:15
1713 Revelation 13:14
1714 Revelation 17:16
1715 Revelation 19:20; Matthew 25:41
1716 2 Thessalonians 2:3
1717 Acts 20:29-30; Galatians 3:1
1718 Matthew 15:14

Ecclesiastes 12:3 says of the genuine teacher, "And moreover, because the preacher was wise, he still taught the people knowledge; yea, he gave good heed, and sought out, and set in order many proverbs."

Shame on those who are ignorant of the Word they claim to know, interpret, and teach. Or worse; who are among those which know the truth and will not speak it. Such are not only derelict, but conspirators. It is they who will, as Jude pointed out, be the instruments of deception in the end times and who will undoubtedly aid and abet the rise of the Antichrist.[1719]

I am reminded of an ex-Catholic Canadian priest who was martyred for his beliefs. His name was Charles Chiniquy. Here is an excerpt from his final Will written to fellow priests.

> "I renounce more than ever the errors of the church of Rome. Believing more than ever that the 'church' and its pope are in error, but being more than ever convinced that the church of Rome and its popes, that its priest, its religious orders and its monks are the greatest enemies which Jesus Christ has had and still has on earth. I pray my dear compatriots more than ever to abandon that false religion of the popes of Rome, which deceives them, seduces them and ruins them both for time and eternity." January 10, 1899[1720]

It is a sad commentary on contemporary Christendom which even now can be seen as having an overwhelming desire to return to Rome. According to the book of Revelation, it is not atheism which will be Satan's last and principal playing card—but religion. The Church of Roman will sit astride the Beast, believing she has finally attained her destiny to preside over the World Church. Totalitarianism has always been her objective, and though it would wax and wane depending on what kings ruled what countries at any given time, her Latin maxim, *"semper eadem"*—"always the same," has never changed.

Apostate Protestantism will adopt its new harlot mother as will other world religions. Scripture tells us that the Papal Church will accept, absorb and govern the New World Order with impunity.[1721] She is the only institution on the planet that has in place today a worldwide ecclesiastic government and an infrastructure capable of managing spiritual affairs on a global scale.

> Note: The Scriptures indicates that after the Jewish people have been allowed to rebuild their brick and mortar Temple they will be temporarily pacified.[1722] Placated in the belief that after thousands of years of persecution that peace has finally come to Jerusalem and that this could only have come about by the promised "Prince of Peace".[1723] Were they to know and believe their prophets of old and the apostles who followed, they would see the baited trap before them—for both Testaments spoke of the one and same future World Leader and imposter.

1719 Jude 4
1720 Clark Butterfield, *Night Journey from Rome*, p.8
1721 Revelation 13:12
1722 Daniel 9:27
1723 Isaiah 9:6

The "King of Babylon,"[1724] "The Little Horn,"[1725] "A King of Fierce Countenance,"[1726] "The Prince that Shall Come,"[1727] "The Willful King,"[1728] "The Assyrian,"[1729] "The Man of Sin," "The Son of Perdition," and "That Wicked,"[1730] "Antichrist,"[1731] "The Beast,"[1732] and "Gog."[1733]

Precept Upon Precept, Line Upon Line

Let us now examine each verse of Revelation 17 and permit Scripture to reveal what it will.

Like an artist sketching a portrait, each line drawn makes the identity of the subject more certain; so too does each line of Scripture. From this point forward, by a process of application we can determine just who this mystery woman is. It will become more and more apparent that only one religion flawlessly matches the description in the narrative of Revelation Chapters 17 and 18.

> 1. "And there came one of the seven angels which had the seven vials, and talked with me, saying unto me, Come hither; I will shew unto thee the judgment of the great whore that sitteth upon many waters:
>
> 2. With whom the kings of the earth have committed fornication, and the inhabitants of the earth have been made drunk with the wine of her fornication.
>
> 3. So he carried me away in the spirit into the wilderness: and I saw a woman sit upon a scarlet coloured beast, full of names of blasphemy, having seven heads and ten horns.
>
> 4. And the woman was arrayed in purple and scarlet colour, and decked with gold and precious stones and pearls, having a golden cup in her hand full of abominations and filthiness of her fornication:
>
> 5. And upon her forehead was a name written, Mystery, Babylon The Great, The Mother Of Harlots And Abominations Of The Earth." (Revelation 17:1-5)

The opening verse tells us not only of a woman who enriches herself by fornication, but that she has been "the mother"—(the birther) of other prostitutes, all of which are an abomination to GOD. So whoever this mystery woman is, she has been around for centuries and has birthed many offshoots.

1724 Isaiah 14:4
1725 Daniel 7:8, 8:9
1726 Daniel 8:23
1727 Daniel 9:26
1728 Daniel 11:36
1729 Micah 5:6
1730 2 Thessalonians 2:3-8
1731 1 John. 2:18
1732 Revelation 13:1
1733 Revelation 20:8

We are also told here in verse 2, and also in Revelation 8:3 that she has collaborated with the kings, governments and merchants of the earth, and they have grown rich together by her delicacies (Greek, *strenos*)—"strength which longs to break forth"— interpreted as her quest for power."[1734]

She is depicted riding a beast with seven heads (seven ancient empires overseen by seven demonic princes) which she has colluded with for centuries.

> "And there came one of the seven angels which had the seven vials, and talked with me, saying unto me, Come hither; I will shew unto thee the judgment of the great whore that sitteth upon many waters: with whom the kings of the earth have committed fornication, and the inhabitants of the earth have been made drunk with the wine of her fornication." (Revelation 17:1-2)

Verse 1. The whore sitting on "many waters" refers to the fact that this mystery woman has become an established religion throughout the world and is found in virtually every country and on every continent. This is later confirmed in Revelation 17:15 where we read, "The waters which thou sawest, where the whore setteth are, peoples, and multitudes, and nations and tongues."

Verse 2. "The kings of the earth have committed fornication with her" refers to the fact that over the centuries she has conspired with virtually every government, and every government with her. She and been in league with ruthless despots and dictators in her insatiable appetite for world domination.

Before the Caesars of Rome and after the Hitlers', Mussolinis', Francos', and Palelics' (the Ustashi barbarian), she has caused multitudes to believe she has divine right and authority. Today she presides over an alleged billion devotees managing to convince them that she is the epitome of holiness and goodness. She has made her subjects—as it were "drunk" (stupefied, dumbed down, convinced) that she is GOD's representative and the bride of Christ on earth.

In his book *Fifty Years in the Church of Rome*, ex-Catholic priest Charles Chiniquy, after giving an account of the numerous attempts on his life before he was eventually martyred wrote,

"I do not mention these facts here, to create bad feelings against the poor blind slaves of the pope. It is only to show the world that the Church of Rome of today is absolutely the same as when she reddened Europe with the blood of millions of martyrs."[1735]

> "So he carried me away in the spirit into the wilderness: and I saw a woman sit upon a scarlet coloured beast, full of names of blasphemy, having seven heads and ten horns. And the woman was arrayed in purple and scarlet colour, and decked with gold and precious stones and pearls, having a golden cup in her hand full of abominations and filthiness of her fornication..." (Revelation 17:3-4)

1734 Thayer, Greek-English Lexicon, #4764

1735 Father Charles Chiniquy, *Fifty Years in the Church of Rome*, Fleming Revell Co., NY, Chicago, Toronto, OLLC 343196, Archived from original June 2008

Verse 3. This woman is seen riding on a "scarlet colored beast." Scarlet (red) is the color of war and of blood; to which it may be said, steadily streamed from the Roman coliseums to the Crusades, from the Inquisitions to the Holocaust and beyond. In addition, it is fitting to point out that no other religious body, but Romanism and its offshoots adorn themselves in the finery described.

The Church of Rome has been riding on the backs of empires since her conception, and while the world was engaged in two World Wars she remained unscathed and became a profiteer from the looted treasures of Europe. Her ability to continue, grow and flourish over the centuries has given her standing and status and made her into a powerful nation-state. Her prestigious place in the global community is made possible in part by the wealth she wields in the world financial markets; it has given her a platform equal to that of great governments. She has always been involved in world politics but never more than she does today. Under the guise of peace and unity she pursues what she believes is her destiny.

The seven-headed beast refers to a succession of the seven world empires with whom the Harlot has had sway from the time of Babel. Each of these empires had a bearing on Israel. Each of these empires was under a demonic prince, so named for the empires they controlled. The Prince of Persia and the Prince of Grecia were two so aptly named princes.[1736]

So it is that we are to understand that "seven heads" refers to both empires and their different demonic princes.[1737] The seventh head on this beast refers to the second to the last of eight empires, the Roman Empire. The name of this demonic prince, though unnamed, could for example, very well be called the Prince of Roma. In any case, this particular prince has been in control from the time of the Old Roman Empire until now, as the Revised Roman Empire is evolving.

Since the fall of the Old Roman Empire, and without having a political king by which to do his bidding, this demonic Prince of the Roman has continued his control through the Holy Roman Empire (The Church of Rome) by using pontiff kings.

In Daniel chapter seven, we are given yet another example wherein the prophet himself had a vision and saw a "fourth beast" which had iron teeth and depicted both the Old Roman and the Revised Roman Empire. This is made clear by the fact that both Daniel and John saw the beast with ten horns (governors of regions). Furthermore, both Daniel and John saw in their respective visions a little horn (the Antichrist) come out of one of these horns. The little horn then terminates three of these horns, after which the remaining seven submit and give the little horn their allegiance and absolute authority. After conceding their authority, the Government of Seven (G7) will support him in his assault against Israel.[1738]

1736 Daniel 10:13, 20
1737 Ephesians 6:12
1738 Zechariah 14:2

The Seven Headed Beast

In the Apostle John's vison, he saw a seven headed beast. Each head represented a demonic prince. Each of the seven princes has, during their appointed term, fed their egocentric appetites for power. As is the nature of demonic entities, they fought and still fight among themselves for supremacy. Soon however, under Satan's mandate they will be forced to put aside their individual quests for control and unify in one last concerted effort to change their shared destiny.[1739] It is one of these seven "heads" (princes)—not a man, of who it is written, appeared to have been wounded unto death, but who surprisingly recovered, which scripture is referring to in Revelation 13:3. It is this demonic prince who was formally one of the seven who Satan will again give control to and who will be prince over the final eighth kingdom.[1740]

> Note: The True Church will be "caught up," (Gk. *harpazo*) snatched from this world before the Tribulation begins. The Papal Church and her followers will be left here on earth where she will then lead the masses to worship the Antichrist. Her devotees will, just as they do now, profess they are Christians; "having a form (a religious form) of godliness."[1741] During the tribulation some will awaken to having been deceived and become part of the tribulation sainthood; others will be drawn into the Papal Church, take a "mark" (Greek, *charagma*—scratched or etched, stamp or badge of servitude) and be eternally lost.[1742]
>
> Note: The "ten horns" represent ten kings who will be in control of ten kingdoms (e.g., the Americas), and form a political, economic and military alliance before the Antichrist assumes complete power. This union is often referred to by theologians as the Revised Roman Empire as it will encompass at least as much of the same geography as did the ancient Roman Empire at its zenith. It also bears the name Roman Empire, as it has remained under the governorship of the Prince of Rome even before the time of Christ.

Verse 4. The woman is herself "arrayed in purple and scarlet." These are the official royal colors of the Church of Rome as seen in the vestments worn by her hierarchy of cardinals and archbishops. Precious stones, jewels and pearls adorn the vestige of the pontiff when in full regalia, after which in the modern era he quickly changes into the unpretentious white frock, portraying simplicity, humility and purity.

For seventeen hundred years the Harlot absconded with the treasures of European nations just before their collapse. Her colossal wealth in gold, art and treasures remains largely hidden in vaults beneath Vatican City, as well as in depositories in Rome, England, New York, and possibly Switzerland. Today she retains by either primeval grant, deceit or conquest much of

---

1739 Revelation 17:17
1740 Revelation 17:11
1741 2 Timothy 3:5
1742 Revelation 7:14

the real estate of Europe. Her tangible wealth, which includes her enormous land holdings, is matched by her investments in giant corporations, trusts, and mega-banks.

She often holds sway over commodity markets, pulling brokers and investors behind her in a vacuum when her investment managers make huge trades on her behalf. Often after running the market in one direction her brokers will abruptly reverse position, thereby making a massive profit as other investors panic and attempt to reverse their positions. These trades net her millions of new dollars on Wall Street virtually every day. Money is power and power is her addiction.

> Note: Perhaps the most famous forgery in European history was in the middle of the eighth century by Pope Stephen II. Stephen had sought Frankish King Pepin to drive out the Lombards and restore the papal real estate, "the domain of St. Peter." So it was that Stephen presented to Pepin what he alleged to be an ancient document, the *"Donation of Constantine"* dated March 30, 315 AD. It was proclaimed that as Constantine left Rome to establish his new headquarters in Constantinople, he bequeathed to Peter, the first Vicar of the Son of God and his successors the following gift.[1743] "Lo, we give and grant, not only our palace as aforesaid, but also the city of Rome, and all the palaces and city of Italy and of the western regions, to our aforementioned most blessed Pontiff and Universal Pope."[1744] Rome used this forgery for centuries afterward, claiming primal grant. Only in 1789 did Pope Pius VI admit the decretal was a fraud. This only came after Latin scholar Laurentius Valla's work, *De Falso Credita et Ementita Constantini Donatione Declamatio* was published. Valla proved the document false and deceitful by comparing it philologically to surviving documents from the time of Constantine. It should be recognized that according to when the forgery ("The Donation") was supposed to have been written (315 AD), it would mean that when Constantine (Pontiff Maximus) left for Constantinople, that he bequeathed Rome to himself, for there was no appointed "pontifex" until 380 AD.

As we continue to read on in Verse 4 it says, "…having a golden cup in her hand full of abominations and filthiness of her fornication…"

The most striking article presented in this verse is that she is depicted holding a "golden cup" in her hand of which it is said to be "full of abominations and filthiness of her fornications." Yes it is utter contempt to suppose her mortal priests can lift up a chalice of factory-made "melt in your mouth" wafers, say what amounts to Hocus pocus, (Latin *"hoe est corpus meum"*—"This is my body") and transform a commercial cracker into the body of the Savior of the World. Then, as if that wasn't enough, they eat Him and serve Him up to others from a brass goblet. This is the epitome of sacrilege and makes a mockery of how one is to receive the Savior.[1745] Hebrews

---
1743 Ronald C. Thompson, *Champions of Christianity, In Search of Truth*, Vol. 1, Teach Services, Inc., NY, p.41
1744 Earnest F. Henderson, translated and edited, *Select and Historic Documents of the Middle Ages*, George Bell & Son Publisher, London, 1903, pp. 319-329
1745 Romans 10:9-13

10:10 says, that we have been "sanctified through the offering of the body of Jesus Christ" on the Cross "once (and) for all." No priest can offer Him; much less offer Him again, and again and again and again at each mass any more than a mere sinful man is capable of absolving another man of his sins. Romanism has made this moment of remembrance, a sacrament; changing it from a sacrament to a sacrilege.

Apart from what I mentioned about the Catholic Eucharist and the brass chalice, the "golden cup in her hand" actually has a different meaning, for it speaks of her being "full of abominations." These abominations she holds over her devotees speaks of the heresy, the spurious doctrine, the claim as having GOD's authority and being shepherd over Christ's flock.

She is full and she is filthy with abominations too numerous to count, if only measured in the souls she has sent to hell by having her devotees trust her for their salvation.

Gospel singer-composer Kristian Stanfill in the lyrics of the song "Jesus Paid It All," said it perfectly when he wrote, "Jesus paid it all / All to Him I owe / Sin had left a crimson stain / He washed it white as snow."

Dr. Henry Alford's in, *The Greek New Testament*, IV, p. 705, put it well when referring to the golden cup wrote,

> "The most striking aspect of her presentation is that she has a golden cup in her hand described as 'full of abominations and filthiness of her fornication.' The Word of GOD does not spare words in describing the utter filthiness of this adulterous relationship in the sight of GOD. Few crimes in Scripture are spoken of in more unsparing terms than the crime of spiritual adultery of which this woman is the epitome. As alliance with the world and showy pomp increase, so spiritual truth and purity decline."

> "...and upon her forehead was a name written, MYSTERY, BABYLON THE GREAT, THE MOTHER OF HARLOTS AND ABOMINATIONS OF THE EARTH. And I saw the woman drunken with the blood of the saints, and with the blood of the martyrs of Jesus: and when I saw her, I wondered with great admiration." (Revelation 17:5-6)

Verse 5. The first thing we should notice is the reference to "Mystery Babylon the Great Mother of Harlots..." Her name is paired to her Babel/Babylonian origin.

The Babylonian cult had plagued Israel throughout the Old Testament and it has followed her into the New. It assailed the Jews and Gentile believers during the early years of the Church. It gathered and sentenced those who refused to recognize the deity of her Roman Emperor—Pontifex Maximus to death in the Coliseum. She labeled those unwilling to convert to Romanism heretics and burned them at the stake. She called for Holy Wars—Crusades and stalked Christians and Jews throughout the Dark and High Middle Ages across Europe and Africa. And she set up Inquisitions making martyrs of tens of millions. Her intolerance and persecution caused many to flee for their lives and seek asylum in the New World.

Her defenders say that the Church of Rome wasn't in existence when this Mystery religion was revealed to the Apostle John and therefore could not be one and the same. They conveniently neglect to acknowledge that this was a prophecy—which speaks to the future; therefore, describing her before she had taken her pious shape and come to power.

Our Lord does not hold back HIS contempt in calling this Mystery religion the "Mother of Harlots and the Abomination of the Earth." Her false doctrines, pagan rites, idolatry and practices crept into the early church just as the Apostle Paul had warned they would. Furthermore, Paul said these corruptions would not all originate from outside the true Church, but from a transformation that would develop from within.

> "Take heed therefore unto yourselves, and to all the flock, over the which the Holy Ghost hath made you overseers, to feed the church of God, which he hath purchased with his own blood. For I know this, that after my departing shall grievous wolves enter in among you, not sparing the flock. Also of your own selves shall men arise, speaking perverse things, to draw away disciples after them. Therefore watch, and remember, that by the space of three years I ceased not to warn every one night and day with tears." (Acts 20:28-31)

History has proved the prophecy to be genuine for it was not long after Paul was martyred that the winds of change began to blow. As the Church increased, men thought it needed their guiding hand and so began the transition from eldership to authoritarianism. Author, John W. Kennedy of India wrote, "When the Lordship of Christ ceases to be the sole impetus of the Church, and self-sufficient man takes over, there are bound to be changes in the spiritual pattern which suggests themselves in the name of efficiency, for the spiritual pattern just does not work when man and not GOD is in control."[1746]

With Christianity under constant threat of heathen influence, well-meaning bishops like Ignatius, Bishop of Antioch (115 AD) believed that a monarchal system would best protect the church from heresies. His intention may have been noble, but it would become the very mechanism which would birth a special class of pharisee as the notion spread from assembly to assembly. Alas, the ecclesiastical class was born. Thereafter, they dubbed themselves with special powers and authority and built an aura of mystery around themselves. Leaven had been introduced, and apart from grounded believers the loaf would thereafter be corrupted.[1747] Like mold spores on bread, they quickly multiplied.

With forgery, fabrication, and falsehoods Satan has managed to draw part of the once biblical Church into his snare. The Church, which had before put its entire dependency, trust, and salvation in Christ and Christ alone had found a substitute; a form of godliness.[1748] The biblical unschooled were and are soon persuaded to believe whatever their priest told or tells them; entrusting their very salvation to men and membership in a monarchial institution.

[1746] John W. Kennedy of India, *The Torch and the Testimony*, Christian Book Pub. House, Auburn, ME, 1965, p.50
[1747] 1 Corinthians 5:6
[1748] 2 Timothy 3:5

> Note: The word for Abomination (*Strong's Exhaustive Concordance* #946) used here is the Greek word "*bdelugma*" which means something that disgusts. GOD does not use this word "abomination" indiscriminately or often, but only in regard to what HE most vehemently hates. It means, as found in Leviticus 18:22, (Hebrew, *towebah*,[1749]— gross sin); as with homosexuality.

"And I saw the woman drunken with the blood of the saints, and with the blood of the martyrs of Jesus: and when I saw her, I wondered with great admiration." (Revelation 17:6)

Verse 6. It would be hard for anyone to deny just who this verse is describing other than to Rome, Romanism, and futuristically—to the Revised Roman Empire. It was Rome and Romanism in an unholy alliance of church and state who for centuries choreographed the torture and death of Believers, Jews, and Muslims alike; anyone who refused to convert. But what is worse is that to this day, having associated the name Christianity with Catholicism and Catholicism with the atrocities perpetrated on the Jewish people; the Jewish people have rejected their own Messiah! In this way Satan has succeeded in carrying out the greatest ruse ever.

"And fear not them which kill the body, but are not able to kill the soul: but rather fear him which is able to destroy both soul and body in hell." (Matthew 10:28)

> Note: The following statement and the statistics are not to suggest that the Church of Rome was responsible for the deaths reported, nor does it exempt them. Having said that, according to the Center for Study of Global Christianity, David B. Barrett's organization, and publisher of the *World Christian Encyclopedia* and of the *Atlas of Global Christianity*, *World Christian Trends*, researchers' Barrett and Johnson made the following assessment: "Up to the year 2000 there had been some 70 million Christian martyrs, of which 45 million were concentrated in the twentieth century."
>
> Note: These statistics were presented before in the twenty-first century, Muslim ISIS or the genocide in Syria ever materialized. They regarded Christian martyrs as those killed because of their status as Christian believers ascribed by those who killed them, irrespective of whether they were at the time of their killing actively proclaiming the faith. The count excluded those killed for national, ethnic or political reasons who just happened to be Christian.

A significant word association is made in Verse 6 that needs to be emphasized. Notice the word "martyrs of Jesus." The word does not apply to genocide, holocaust, or ethnic cleansing. The word martyrs is used in reference to Jesus; as such it relates specifically to those saints—who for their unwavering belief in Him refused to accept another gospel and were put to death. There

---

[1749] *Strong's Exhaustive Concordance*, Heb., #8441

is only one group, one orchestrator, one facilitator, one actuator which fits this description of judge, jury, and executioner in the martyring of true Believers.

> Note: The Greek word for martyrs as used in the New Testament is translated "witness." Therefore, when Jesus said, as recorded in Acts 1:8, "ye shall be witnesses unto me" it had great significance to the Church. He was in essence saying to His own that they may be martyred for their faith and fidelity to Him, and for the preaching of the gospel of grace.

Insofar as the future is concerned, the blood already shed will only be eclipsed by that which is forecast for the tribulation saints. "I saw the souls of them that were beheaded for the witness of Jesus, and for the word of GOD…"[1750] As for the Jews, we are told in the book of Zechariah that only one third of the Jewish population which are alive when the Tribulation begins will survive to the end.[1751] We have no way of knowing how many of these survivors will be practicing Jews and how many will be Messianic Jews at the time of the Lord's coming. Scripturally speaking there will be both.

> Note: Today, under Sharia law, Muslim jihadists execute in the manner described in this verse—by "beheading." The Antichrist (the great Assyrian)[1752] will be a Muslim, so it will be his followers, the Arab-Muslims that will execute those not willing to take the mark of the beast. The Scriptures also tell us it will not be the Antichrist who will order the saints of GOD to their death, but the False Prophet who will assume the role of the Grand Inquisitor.[1753]

The historical record of the Church of Rome; a record of torture, death and tyranny may have faded from view; disguised by her aura of peace and plea for tolerance. However, she has never varied from her quest to dominate; only her method to achieve that end has changed. Her greatest enemy and the one she will have to silence when the Tribulation begins is truth. It is the truth of the gospel of grace which exposes her as a fraud. It is the Good News made complete in Jesus Christ and which requires nothing else which she fears the most.

"And ye shall know the truth, and the truth shall make you free." (John 8:32)

"For by grace are ye saved through faith; and not of yourselves: it is the gift of GOD…" (Ephesians 2:8)

1750 Revelation 20:4
1751 Zechariah 13:8
1752 Micah 5:6
1753 Revelation 13:15

It is in the conclusion of Verse 6 where we find one of the most revealing clues of who it is that Scripture is referring to, for it says, "I (John) wondered with great admiration" (Greek, *thauma*)[1754] meaning, a "wonderful thing."[1755]

In the vision given John, he saw something which boggled his mind, for there before him was what appeared to be this amazing world church.

(Image Source: GETTY)

From the standpoint of one seeing this for the first time, it must have appeared as if the early Church had evolved into a magnificent empire for Jesus. John was apparently so astonished that he wondered with great "admiration" at the possibility that the Church could have come so far. I dare say only the grandeur of the Church of Rome and the splendor of its Basilica in Vatican City could have solicited such a response.

But just as quickly as the vision appeared to John, the angel of GOD suddenly interrupted the vision, jolting him from his admiration to reveal its evil.

"And the angel said unto me, Wherefore didst thou marvel? I will tell thee the mystery of the woman, and of the beast that carrieth her, which hath the seven heads and ten horns." (Revelation 17:7)

Verse 7. Verse seven tells of an angel sent to John to reveal to him, and subsequently to us, the "mystery of the woman." The angel did not give her a name, but better still, he would identify her through her affiliations with past, present and future empires and the demonic princes (beasts) which governed them.

Visions of the Beast of the Eighth Kingdom Expounded

"The beast (demonic prince) that thou sawest was (once ruled over an earthly kingdom), and is not (not in authority when John was alive); and shall ascend out of the bottomless pit, and go into perdition: and they that dwell on the earth shall wonder (Revelation 13:3—as it was thought, he was permanently defeated—his reign being over), whose names were not written in the book of life from the foundation of the world, when they behold the beast that was (a former demonic prince), and is not (not in power during John's day), and yet is (still exists and will come to power again during the Great Tribulation)." (Revelation 17:8)

1754 *Strong's Exhaustive Concordance*, Gk., #2295
1755 Thayer, Greek- English Lexicon of the NT, Baker Book House, Grand Rapids, MI

Verse 8. The central figure of verses 8–13 is about one of the heads (princes) formally of the seven headed beast (empires) on which the woman sat. Notice that the beast John was given to see was released from a subterranean chamber (the bottomless pit) where it had been incarcerated, so it was a demonic prince which is being referred to. These inference to "beasts" and "heads" (Revelations 13:1) do not refer to a man, or to men, as is often taught, but to demonic princes and the empires they controlled.

> "And here is the mind which hath wisdom. The seven heads are seven mountains (demonic dominions), on which the woman setteth (has existed from ancient pagan times). And there are seven kings (demonic princes): five are fallen (are no longer in power), and one is (existing in John's day—the Prince over the Roman Empire), and the other (the seventh—the Revised Roman Empire) is not yet come; and when he (this prince of Rome) cometh, he must continue a short space (the first half 3 ½ years of the Tribulation). And the beast (demonic prince) that was (before John's day), and is not (not in power in John's day), even he is the eighth and is one of the seven, (a former demonic princes) and goeth into perdition." (He was the Prince of Grecia, and he will rise again to take control of the eighth and final kingdom.) (Revelation 17:9-11)

> Note: Six empires (Seven, when including the prince over the Revised Roman Empire) and their satanic princes will form a confederation, but this one prince, the Prince of Grecia, (whose name is mentioned more often than any other demonic prince in scripture) will arise from the bottomless pit at that time and be appointed theater commander over the other six. Exactly why Satan chooses the Prince of Grecia over the other princes we are not told. What has been given us is enough.

To authenticate the identity of the seventh head, we look to the Old Testament, to the seventh chapter of Daniel, where in a vision Daniel was shown a succession of four (actually five) beastly empires. It is there in Daniel 7:19–23 (in the interpretation of the vision) that we see that Daniel's fourth beast is the same as John's sixth and seventh beast (the Prince of Rome). Both apply to the Old Roman Empire as well as the futuristic Revised Roman Empire. This prince of the Revised Rome will continue for a "short space" (the first three and a half years of the Tribulation, Rev.12:12, 14) before an eighth and final kingdom the Prince of Grecia replaces him. The Prince of Grecia will then control the eighth empire and support the Antichrist during the last three and a half years (v.25).

Once we have recognized that Satan has appointed demon princes over empire after empire, we can better understand why the various human kings and tyrants have had such contempt for Israel. Even today a demonic prince is trying his best to destroy Israel while one of GOD's own princes, the "great prince Michael" fights on her behalf.[1756]

At the time of this writing the Prince of Rome is gaining power and building the seventh empire—the political New World Order; theologically referred to as the Revised Roman Empire.

1756 Daniel 12:1

Verse 9 also continues to illustrate the dual meaning of heads as it pertains to both princes and empires for it tells us that "seven heads are seven mountains on which the woman sits." Mountains in this scripture refer to temporal dominions or empires. If we keep the revelation in context, we can see this could not be referring to physical mountains. The word "mountains" (Greek, *oros*) is defined as something that rises from the plain (essentially from nothing). As a general rule, princes control kingdoms or empires and empires rise up from obscurity, so mountains refer to empires. The interpretation reinforces the fact that each of these demonic princes has in the past presided over a physical empire. The Prince of Rome or Roma is now in power. The prince of Grecia will in the end usurp him during the Great Tribulation.

To recap: Seven heads refer to seven demonic princes that dominated seven ancient empires. The mystery woman (spiritual harlotry) we are told has ridden on the backs of each of these empires; meaning, she has been involved with each of the demonic princes and their respective empires. It has been, and will continue to be the goal of these princes to destroy the Jewish people and the nation of Israel.

The Apostle John was permitted to see the succession of these seven empires, beginning with the Egyptian Empire and continuing through the course of human history which will end with an eighth and final empire.[1757]

Six hundred forty-one years before John had received his vision, Daniel had also been given a vision of a beast; however, his vision was limited. Daniel was shown but four beastly empires described and identified by characteristics of carnivorous animals. John on the other hand was not shown various animal-beasts, but a single beast with seven heads.[1758]

There was one distinguishing physical feature which both Daniel and John's beast shared. Daniel's fourth and John's seventh beast each had ten horns.[1759] The ten horns we are told represent ten kings.[1760] The ten kings represent ten human governors ruling over ten regions, which today would be comparable to the Government of Ten (G10).

These ten kings will afterward come under the headship of an end time dictator; an imperial world president. He was seen by Daniel as a little horn which would grow out of one of the G10.[1761] He is revealed in John's revelation as the notorious Antichrist who will himself serve under a demonic prince who previously controlled an earlier empire. So it was a former prince and one of the seven heads which John saw that Satan will again appoint over what will be the eighth and final kingdom during the last three and one half years of the Tribulation (a.k.a. the Great Tribulation).[1762]

We are first told of this eighth prince and eight empires in Revelation 17:10–11 where we read; "…and the other is not yet come, and when he cometh, he must continue for a short space,. And the beast that was and is not, he is even the eighth and is of the seven."

1757 Revelation 17:11
1758 Revelation 17:7
1759 Daniel 7:7; Revelation 13:1, 17:7, 12
1760 Revelation 17:12
1761 Daniel 7:20
1762 Revelation 17:11

From what we have learned thus far we see that it is not a man who received what appeared to be a deadly wound[1763] (which was spoken of metaphorically) but a demonic prince and the empire he presided over who was perceived to have been eliminated by the succeeding demonic prince in line (the Prince of Roma). It is this once wounded prince who will be healed—(restored) as the prince over the eighth and final kingdom.

> Note: The word used in Revelation 13:3 is heads (plural) and refers to one of the empires, not someone's head. That word head and heads used in describing the beast refers to being high in authority and rank, such as the head of the family. In Numbers 1:16, the "princes" were called "heads" (cf. Judges 10:18). The word pertains to those who represent or lead. In this application if a head receives a deadly wound unto death, it suggests that the spiritual being (prince) has lost his leadership position. If he makes a recovery, it can be said that he was healed.
>
> Note: John F. Walvoord in his commentary, *The Revelation of Jesus Christ*, Moody Press, 1966, qualifies this on pages 199 and 200; "The person is often a symbol of the government and what is said of the government can be said about him….The beast is both personal and the empire itself; so also, is the head."
>
> Note: Worthy of mention is that Daniel and John were not the only ones who were made privy to the Antichrist. The Apostle Paul, though not spoken of as having had a vision was nevertheless given insight into the little horn (Daniel 7:20), as he too spoke of the rise of "that man of sin—the Son of Perdition," who would appear on the scene in the last days.[1764]

The Different Beasts

It would have been unnecessary and even bewildering had Daniel been shown the entire beast which John was later to see. GOD gives more revelation when it is needed and particularly after history begins to unfold—as more can then be understood.

The New Testament, wherein John's vision is recorded, would prepare future generations for the end times. The Whore herself would not be recognizable as she is now, as she only materialized centuries after John was given his vision. Likewise, neither could her historic record of torture and collaboration with earthly kings be verified. Today her description provided in Revelations chapters 13 and 17 is discernable and will be indispensable to those who will be alive during "The Time of Jacob's Trouble."

1763 Revelation 13:3
1764 2 Thessalonians 2:3

Identifying the Beasts

The multi-headed beast which John saw included not only the four world empires which Daniel saw but all seven which had in the past or would in the future plague Israel.

Daniel was given to see four beasts. Two empires were empires which existed during his lifetime: First, the Babylonian Empire and second, the Medo-Persian Empire. He was also shown two empires which would form afterward: Third, the Grecian Empire and fourth, the Roman Empire, which also included by extension the Revised Roman Empire.[1765]

John's vision would be more extensive as he was shown all the empires. He saw the two empires which had existed even prior to Daniel's time; the Egyptian Empire and the Assyrian Empire. He also saw what Daniel was given to see, the Babylonian, the Medo-Persian, the Grecian and the Roman. John would also be shown Daniel's fourth beast, the dreadful beast, but for John and because he was shown seven, he would see this as the seventh head (empire) of the beast; the Revised Roman Empire.

After the Revised Roman Empire has achieved what Satan needs it to achieve (a World Government), it too will be superseded by what John was told would be an "eighth empire."[1766] This empire is the former Grecian empire, under the Prince of Grecia[1767] who will lend his power along with Satan himself to the Antichrist at the onset of the Great Tribulation.[1768] It is in Daniel 8:23 where we read, "And in the latter times of their (the old Grecian Empire) kingdom, when the transgressors are come to the full, a king of fierce countenance (Antichrist), and understanding dark sentence, shall stand up (come to power)."

> Note: The O.T. parallel scripture to Revelation 17:11 which identifies this final empire (the eighth) and to the prince which will be in control at that time is revealed in context in Daniel 8:17-25.
>
> Note: The Church Age ends with the rapture of the true invisible Church—the body of Christ, which is composed of genuine believers who have divorced themselves from religiosity and institutionalism and who have received Christ as their personal Savior. Those who place their faith in the Church of Roman will be among the left behind and likely enter into the brief dispensation of the Tribulation when the Church of Rome reaches its zenith.

Three of the beasts Daniel was shown would be depicted by familiar animals, each having characteristics of the ruler or the empire itself. Babylon was likened to a lion.[1769] Medo-Persia

---

1765 Daniel 7:4-7
1766 Revelation 17:11
1767 Daniel 8:20, 23, 24
1768 Revelation 13:4
1769 Daniel 7:4

was likened to a bear.[1770] Afterward would come the Grecian Empire under Alexander the Great, which was likened to a swift leopard;[1771] characteristic of Alexander's tactical assaults against his enemies.

Still later would come a fourth empire (beast) said to be a "dreadful and terrible and exceedingly strong" and having ten horns.[1772] This is a reference to the Roman Empire which officially came into existence in 27 BC.

The satanically empowered (demonic) Prince of Rome has been in power continuously for a protracted period of some two thousand years. He will continue to reign until the onset of the Great Tribulation when he will surrender leadership to the Prince of Grecia whose presence—however obscure, is still apparent in five chapters of the book of Daniel (Chapters 7, 8, 9, 10, 11). These chapters have a good deal to say about the latter days.[1773]

> Note: Daniel's fourth beast with its ten horns would provide the prophet with only a scant view of what has been a continuum—that being the Old Roman empire morphing into the "Revised" Roman Empire. John would see these horns on the seventh beast (the Revised Roman Empire).
>
> Note: In the latter days a facsimile of the Old Roman political system encompassing the territories of the Old Roman Empire which fell to Germanic invaders; traditionally accepted as occurring on September 4, 476 AD will reemerge as the Revised Roman Empire. Despite the destruction of the government of Western Rome, her religious arm lived on as the un-Holy Roman Church. A continuous succession of popes replaced the emperors and took the imperial reins, steering her into a vast religious empire.
>
> Note: It is not uncommon in scripture for the Lord to use a single verse or passage to make a reference to the similarities between two prophetic empires (e.g., Ancient Babylon in Daniel's day and the Future Babylon in Revelation). This is called the "Law of double reference." In describing the fourth beast,[1774] the Lord is using a dualism (a double reference), making the association to both the Old Roman Empire and to the future Revised Roman Empire.

1770 Daniel 7:5
1771 Daniel 7:6
1772 Daniel 7:7
1773 Daniel 8:22
1774 Daniel 7:7–8

Daniel and John's Beastly Visions and the Succession of Empires They Represented

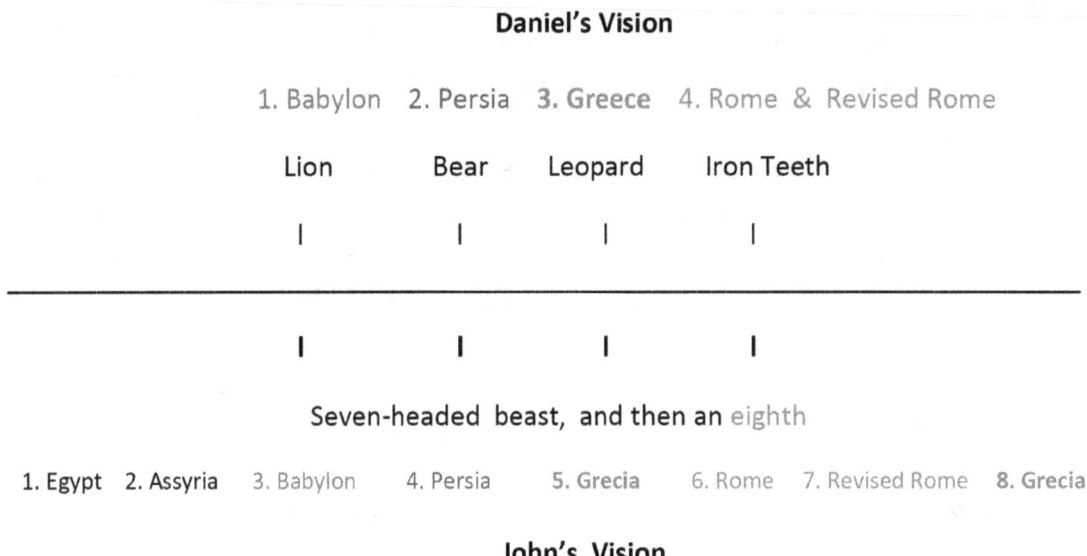

So let us recap. Daniel only saw four empirical empires, whereas 645 years later John would be shown seven and even an eighth. Daniel saw a beast relative to the time in which he lived under the domination of two empires (Babylon and Medo-Persia). He was also shown two future empires, a third (the Grecian Empire), and a fourth in a duality: the Roman and Revised Roman Empire. It was as if Daniel was only permitted to look "downstream" from the time in which he lived, whereas John in Revelation was permitted to look both "upstream" and see the Egyptian and the Assyrian empires as well as "downstream," seeing the future empires as well.

The Ten Horns, the New World Order, and the Little Horn

> "And the ten horns which thou sawest are ten kings, which have received no kingdom as yet; but receive power as kings (governors) one hour (a brief time) with the beast. These have one mind (objective) and shall give their power and strength unto the beast (Antichrist)." (Revelation 17:12-13)

Verses 12 and 13 have a direct correlation with Daniel 7:7–8. Here we learn that "ten horns" represent ten kings or "heads of state" over ten regions. By all indications this Government of Ten will soon take their respective places on the world stage as, the New World Order—the Global Government—the Revised Roman Empire solidifies. We are told however that their authority as world governors is very brief, "one hour." Midway through the Tribulation this G10 will be reduced to the G7, after which they will yield all authority to the Antichrist and become mere figureheads. At that point (midway through the seven-years) the totalitarian-eighth kingdom will be established.

"These (the New World Order, the seven demonic princes and the Antichrist) shall make war with the Lamb (Yahusha-Jesus), and the Lamb shall overcome them (defeat them at Armageddon): for He is Lord of lords, and King of kings: and they (the Believers)[1775] that are with him are called, and chosen, and faithful." (Revelation 17:14-15)

As inconceivable as it may seem, the world will soon begin to hate the Lamb. Even now we are seeing much more opposition than in years past. Even speaking the name Jesus Christ is seen by some as socially unacceptable and even as hate speech. The anti-Judeo/Christian movement has taken a foothold in society. Prayer at public events or schools is an affront to some. Crosses are being removed from public places, government institutions and even cemeteries. Christ has been removed from Christmas, replaced with Happy Holidays. Even the U.S. military establishment has compromised as its chaplains are all but forbidden to mention the Savior's name as it suggests proselytizing. A Navy chaplain, Gordon Klingenschmitt, was court-martialed and dismissed from the service for ending his public prayers "in Jesus' name." This is but a harbinger of what is to come.

"And he saith unto me, The waters (nations) which thou sawest, where the whore sitteth (has established herself), are peoples, and multitudes, and nations, and tongues. And the ten horns which thou sawest upon the beast, these shall (afterward) hate the whore, and shall make her desolate and naked, and shall eat her flesh, and burn her with fire. For God hath put in their hearts to fulfil his will, and to agree, and give their kingdom unto the beast (Antichrist), until the words of God shall be fulfilled." (Revelation 17:15-17)

When the eighth kingdom is formed, and the Antichrist assumes totalitarian power it will be determined that Mystery Babylon has served her usefulness as the world's religious unifier. She is then seen as a hindrance. The new regime will strip her of her wealth, confiscate her real estate and disband her. The Antichrist will blaspheme GOD and demand all worship be to him and to Satan.[1776] He will in fact be the embodiment of Satan. The last part of this verse tells us that all of what has taken place has been a part of GOD's plan.

> Note: The pursuits and claims of the Papal Church actually blaspheme GOD. The hierarchy has actually become so deluded as to actually believe they have divine rights and authority. The authority they assume, according to Scripture belongs only to GOD and to His Church of Believers[1777] which is overseen only by the Holy Spirit. GOD in HIS providence will use this Satan empowered man (Antichrist) just as HE has used the pagan emperors of the past to accomplish HIS ultimate goal of birthing spiritual Israel.[1778]

1775 Revelation 19:14
1776 Revelation 13:4-8
1777 Mark 16:18; Luke 10:17-19
1778 Ezekiel 36:27, chapter 37

> "And the woman which thou sawest is that great city, which reigneth over the kings of the earth." (Revelation 17:18)

It is in this final verse where the woman's identity becomes irrefutable. The mystery woman who has cohabited with kings and governments, who has been drunk with the blood of the saints, who adorns herself in royal apparel and holds a golden cup full of abominable doctrines—is the only religious body inseparable from a great city. It is a city so directly associated with her as to be synonymous with her Vatican City in Rome.

Before Rome existed, before the cornerstones of Egypt's pyramids were laid, Mystery Babylon was there. She was a contrivance born in the mind of Lucifer who waited upon the mountains of an antediluvian age after his angelic rebellion had failed.[1779] He would use the natural inclinations of man who inwardly wants to worship his creator and redirect them.

What began in Babel with paganism and idolatry became a contagion which would be passed to each successive empire. Then the day came when various fictitious gods and goddesses, along with their idols and practices were integrated into a universal state religion masquerading as Christianity. Spurious manuscripts were then produced to indemnify an ecclesiastical hierarchy.

There can be no question that Mystery Babylon has been an evolution of evil, torture, persecution, heresy, and power. She is the great city which reigneth over the kings of the earth.[1780] She is the mother of all false religions which has cajoled the masses and managed to overturn the Reformation using apostate ministers who wantonly left the Cross for self-interest.[1781] Today, under the guise of peace, tolerance and unity—masquerading as a lamb she carries out the pernicious will of the dragon, swooning the gullible to return to her bosom.[1782]

The Creator has gone to great lengths to warn us so that man is without excuse.

Twenty-one of the twenty-seven books of the New Testament have Scriptures warning us of "false teachers," "false doctrines," "ministers of Satan," "false prophets," "wolves in sheep's clothing," "another gospel," and "the great falling away." The truth be known, next to HIS plan of salvation, no other theme is spoken about or given more emphasis in the New Testament than the warning of counterfeits.

> "For I am jealous over you with godly jealousy: for I have exposed you to one husband that I might present you as a chaste virgin to Christ.
>
> But I fear, lest by any means, as the serpent beguiled Eve through his subtilty, so your minds shall be corrupted from the simplicity which is in Christ Jesus...
>
> For such are false apostles, deceitful workers, transforming themselves into apostles of Christ. And no marvel; for Satan himself is transformed into an angel of light.

1779 Isaiah 14:12; Ezekiel 28:1-19; Revelation 12:4
1780 Isaiah 17:18
1781 Matthew 16:24
1782 Matthew 13:11

Therefore it is no great thing if his ministers also be transformed as the ministers of righteousness..." (2 Corinthians 11:2-3, 13-15)

The day will soon come when GOD will look down upon this perishing world and sweep away all of its evils. With it will go the priest of the wafer god, their pretense of celibacy, their soul damning auricular confession which has no purpose but to degrade and disgrace woman and make men slaves to their confessors under the threat that they will otherwise burn in hell.

The great Babylon Empire will at last crumble, and the saints and angels will cheer from their balcony in heaven. Nations will no longer satisfy themselves at the table of abominations, for they and their ambassadors will have perished in the very fires their confessors promised they were be able to keep others from. Those who escape the Whore's clutches, who have been set free by His living Word and washed their robes in the blood of the Lamb will enter into a new world. A world that Paul described as being so magnificent and unfathomable that "Eye hath not seen, nor ear heard, neither hath (it) entered into the heart of man, the things which GOD hath prepared for them that love Him."[1783]

1783 1 Corinthians 2:9

EPILOGUE

Our study of Mystery Babylon will end here; however, the fate of Babylon, the "political-economic empire" does not end here. The saga continues as the entire eighteenth chapter of the Revelation describes the whore and the system in their death throes.

"Babylon the empire" will be brought down in "one hour" just as certainly as when the hand of GOD wrote on the wall foretelling the imminent fall of Babylon in Belshazzar's day—"Thou art weighed in the balances, and art found wanting." Before the sun rose the next morning, the king was dead and the Great Empire of Babylon had been taken over by the Medes.[1784]

In Noah's day, the inhabitants of the region must have snickered as he labored to build the Ark on a a dry bed of earth; for the prospect of an impending flood of such magnitude as to end civilization and require a new beginning was beyond all reason. "…As in the days of Noah were, so shall also the Coming of the Son of man be."[1785] Had the spectators who mused over Noah's project sought GOD themselves they would have left their temporal riches, abundances, and delicacies and entered into the Ark while the great door was still open. But the day came when GOD, not Noah, closed the great portal.[1786] The portal to heaven will likewise be closed when GOD so determines.

As I began this study I spoke of the difference between religion and relationship, between loyalty to a system and loyalty to Christ. In the final analysis religion is a substitute, a deterrent, a deception. The sinner is saved only when he sees himself as a sinner destined for an eternal hell. Each of us must look to the Savior who spent hours nailed, bleeding and suffocating on a Roman Cross. Each of us must recognize that it was for them that He came, died, and rose from the dead. Only to the one who internalizes His love for them and surrenders, will the fountain of His grace be poured out; bathing, cleansing, and drenching them in His love.

As the songwriter wrote, "Jesus paid it all / All to Him I owe / Sin had left a crimson stain / He washed it white as snow."[1787] So did Isaiah say, "…though your sins be as scarlet, they shall be as white as snow; though they be red like crimson, they shall be as wool."[1788]

1784 Daniel 5:25
1785 Matthew 24:37
1786 Genesis 7:16
1787 "Jesus Paid It All," lyricist Kristian Stanfill; music, John Grape
1788 Isaiah 1:18

In the final analysis there is but One who saves and restores us to the Father, and HIS message could not be any clearer,

"I AM the Way, the Truth, and the LIFE: no man cometh unto the Father, but by ME." (John 14:6)

He is the Way, the only Way. His Word is Truth, the only Truth, and He is Life—Life eternal to those who receive Him.

If you have been blessed, please consider gifting a copy of this book to someone GOD has put on your heart that they may find the treasure hid in a field and the pearl of great price.[1789]

1789 Matthew 13:44-46

www.ingramcontent.com/pod-product-compliance
Lightning Source LLC
Chambersburg PA
CBHW080847020526
44118CB00037B/2244